From Ornament to Object

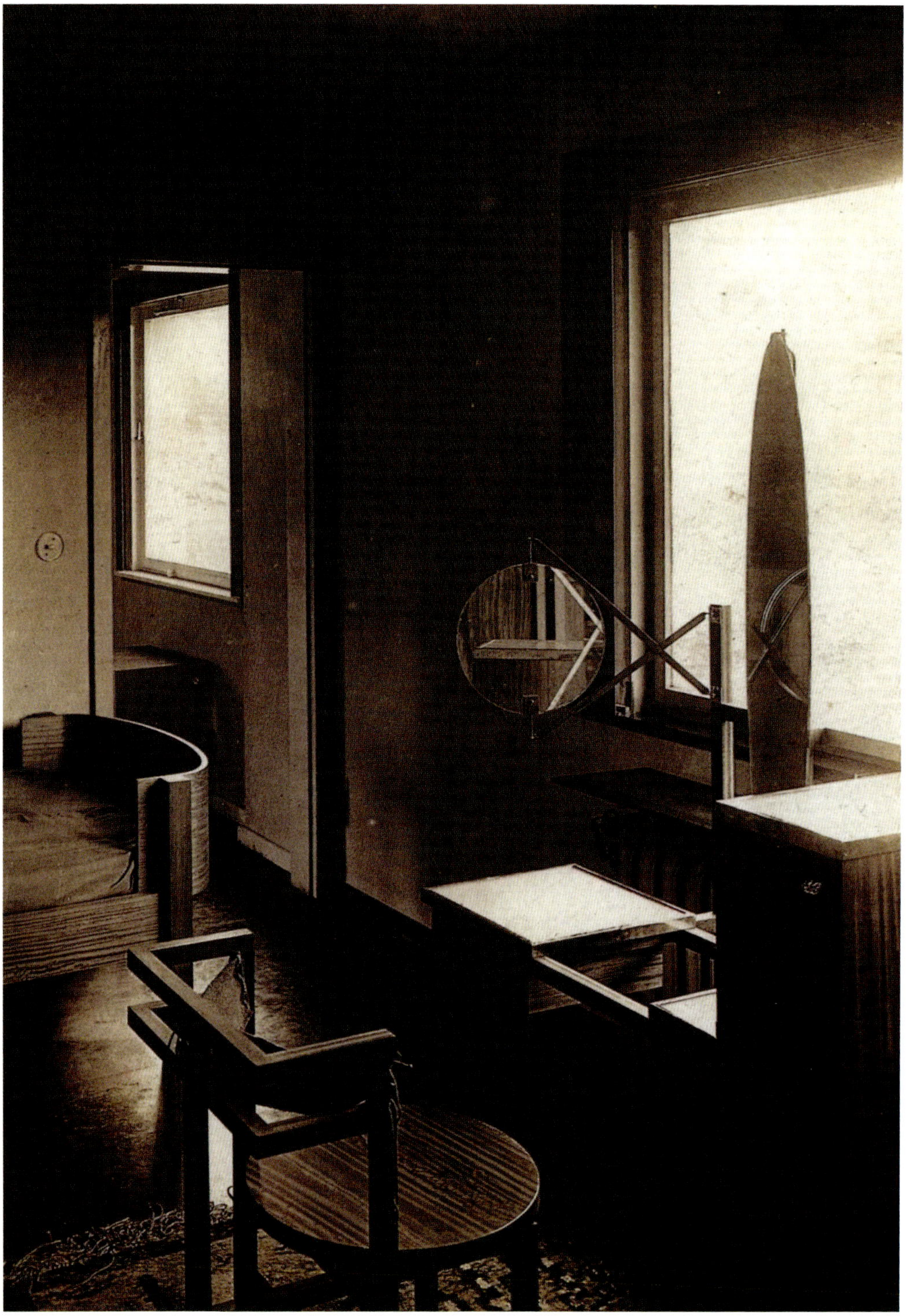

Alina Payne

FROM ORNAMENT TO OBJECT

GENEALOGIES OF ARCHITECTURAL MODERNISM

YALE UNIVERSITY PRESS NEW HAVEN AND LONDON

yalebooks.com

Designed by Leslie Fitch
Set in ScalaPro and CronosPro type by Leslie Fitch
Printed in China by Regent Publishing Services Limited

LIBRARY OF CONGRESS CATALOGING-IN-PUBLICATION DATA

Payne, Alina Alexandra.
From ornament to object : genealogies of architectural modernism / Alina Payne.
pages cm
Includes bibliographical references and index.
ISBN 978-0-300-17533-2 (hardback)
1. Architecture, Modern—19th century—Themes, motives. 2. Architecture, Modern—20th century—Themes, motives. 3. Decorative arts—History—19th century—Themes, motives. 4. Decorative arts—History—20th century—Themes, motives. 5. Modernism (Aesthetics) I. Title.
NA645.5.M63P39 2012
724'.6—dc23 2012002910

A catalogue record for this book is available from the British Library.

This paper meets therequirements of ANSI/NISO Z 39.48–1992 (Permanence of Paper).
10 9 8 7 6 5 4 3 2 1

Frontispiece: Marcel Breuer, *Room for a Woman, Haus-am-Horn,* 1923. (Fig. 166.)

P. x: Typewriter in Walter Gropius's House, Dessau, 1926. (Fig. 147.)

Jacket illustrations: (front) Louis-Émile Durandelle, *Le Nouvel Opéra de Paris: Sculpture Ornamentale,* 1865–72. (Detail of Fig. 12.); (back) Hannes Meyer, Coop Zimmer, 1926. (Fig. 8.)

For Peter, always

Publication of this book is
made possible by a grant from
Figure Foundation.

CONTENTS

ACKNOWLEDGMENTS

This book has been long in the making. Although the questions that I raise here began to occupy me in the mid-1990s, when I was teaching at the University of Toronto, and were the subject of conferences and panels I organized starting with the College Art Association meeting in 1998, of talks I gave and courses I taught, the written trace of this work spanned a good decade. Indeed, the very first course I taught at Harvard in 1999 was on architecture and the discourse on ornament.

Naturally a project that has extended over a long period of time has incurred many debts. I wish to thank the institutions that gave me the resources, space, and time to pursue this work: the University of Toronto, Harvard University, the Max Planck Institute Florence and Max Planck Institute Rome, I Tatti (Florence), and the Institute of Advanced Study, Bucharest. I am grateful to the libraries and librarians at these institutions, as well as to the Fondation Le Corbusier, and the Bernard Berenson Archive. To the Max Planck and Alexander von Humboldt Foundations, the Social Sciences and Humanities Research Council of Canada, and Harvard University I am especially grateful for financial support. However, more than anything I owe a debt of gratitude to friends, colleagues, students, and family, who all helped in essential ways along the way—discussing, reading, responding, inviting me to speak or conduct research at their institutions, or just keeping me going when the task seemed too demanding and the climb too steep. To Neil Levine I owe heartfelt thanks for reading the manuscript with much sympathy and enthusiasm, diligently and attentively, with a sharp and critical eye, and for gently nudging me to confront issues I might otherwise have not addressed. Equally important were the two anonymous readers for Yale University Press, who attended to the manuscript with much care and whose wise and perceptive comments have made this a better book. David Kim was a lively, immensely stimulating, and generous partner in discussions, and a reader whose own early modern perspective reminded me of issues that traversed historical periods. I am grateful to Danny Abramson, Yve-Alain Bois, Scott Cohen,

Joseph Connors, Daniela Del Pesco, Magdalena Droste, Aliki Economides, Sabine Frommel, Maurizio Ghelardi, Colleen Humer, Elizabeth Kassler-Taub, Elizabeth Kieven, Erika Kim, Phyllis Lambert, Cammie MacAttee, Harry Mallgrave, Marzia Marandola, Gulru Necipoglu, Elysse Newman, Morgan Ng, Jason Nguyen, Anca Oroveanu, David Pullins, Cara Rachele, Louise Rice, Myra Rosenfeld, Michelangelo Sabatino, Anne-Marie Sankovitch, Robin Schuldenfrei, Brigitte Shim, Matthew Sohm, Howard Sutcliffe, Nicola Suthor, Rachel Taylor, Marvin Trachtenberg, Nancy Troy, Wendy Walgate, Gerhard Wolf, Ana-Maria Zahariade, and Ion Zahariade for the many ways in which they helped me move the project along. Teaching students at the University of Toronto and at Harvard made the work less solitary and more fun; with their enthusiasm, challenges, and probing questions they helped me think twice about many an argument. Finally, the Yale University Press team—Michelle Komie, Heidi Downey, Katherine Boller, and Mary Mayer—was an ideal partner to see this project to completion, with its infectious enthusiasm and commitment to making this the best book possible.

Always last to be mentioned but never least, my deepest gratitude goes to my family—to my parents and Julia, who were a constant source of love and support; and to Peter, the great absence at the end of this project, who taught me by example.

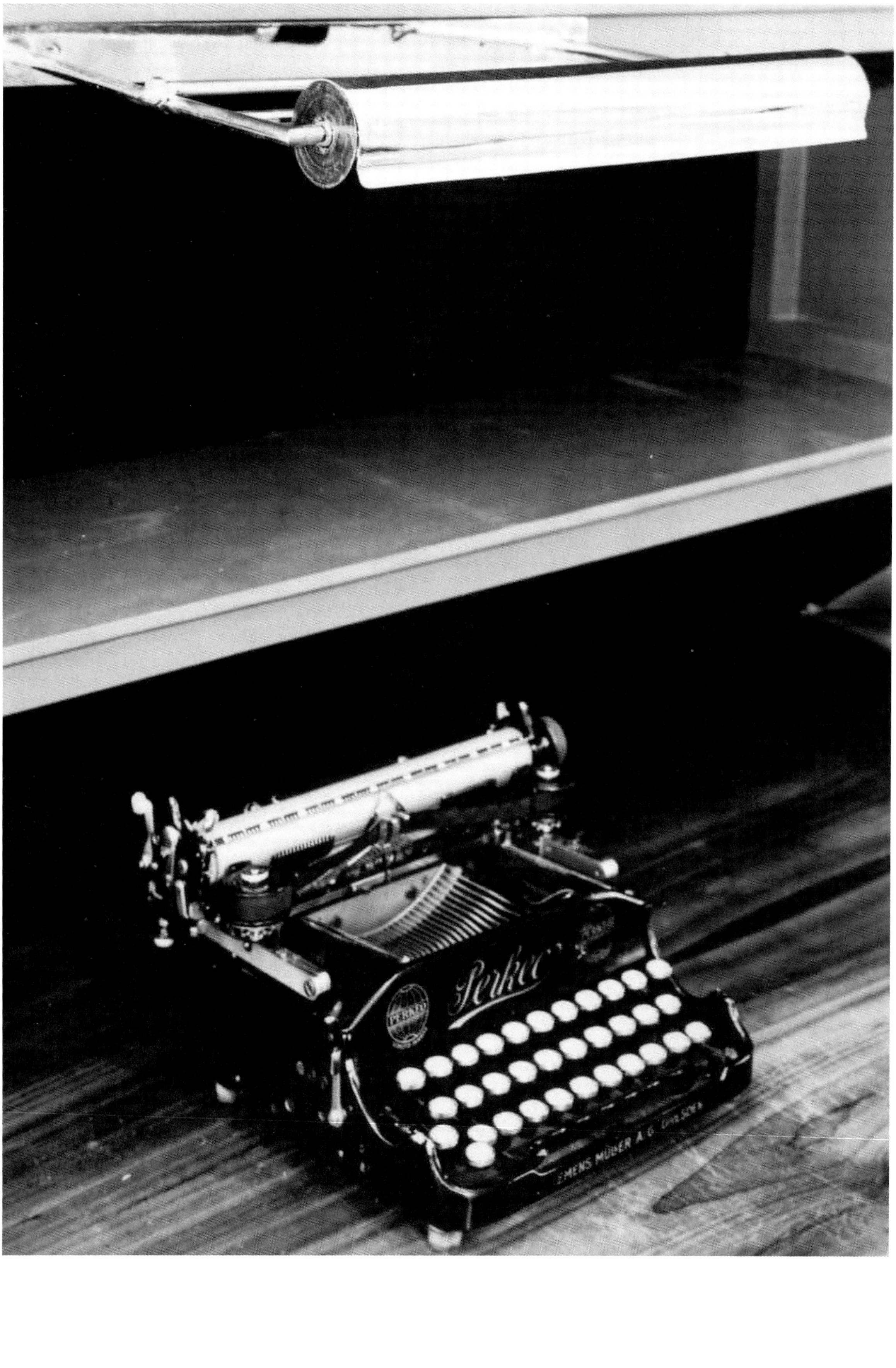
Perkeo

Introduction

> The most significant event of our times is the rise in importance of the object.
> —FERNAND LÉGER

In 1908, Adolf Loos wrote his essay "Ornament and Crime."[1] Whatever reaction it sparked at the time, this was far less than posterity would accord it. Translated and widely read over the next decades, eventually it acquired the power of an icon or a sign—modernism's self-proclamation in its most lucid and concise form. Manifestoes and books followed in quick succession—longer, more comprehensive, some more practical, others more theoretical—but for architecture this text remained its inaugural battle cry, its true awakening, its Lacanian moment: it looked in the mirror but did not like what it saw. To be sure, dissatisfaction and debate had been fomenting for some time, but nothing as crisp, pithy, and uncompromising had yet come out in any of the milieus located at the eye of the modernist storm. Coming as it did out of Vienna, such a critique was additionally shocking, for among the centers vying for intellectual and artistic leadership, here the pulse of modernism seemed to beat fastest. The lone voice that dared condemn everything it saw in the city of Otto Wagner, Josef Hoffmann, and the Secession, and dramatically turn to *food* and *clothes* as referents for contemporary architecture, had to give pause.[2]

What followed is well known: the vocabulary of architecture discarded ornament, and buildings became more and more abstract, shedding surface embellishment—representational or geometric, incised or sculptural, applied or integral to the structure. As modernism's vocabulary grew increasingly consistent in this respect over the next two decades, if we are to take the 1927 German Werkbund exhibition in Stuttgart as a moment of coming of age, it became clear that something fundamental had been abolished (fig. 1). Profoundly a part of architecture's rhetorical apparatus since time immemorial, ornament had apparently ceased to exist.

In 1925, some twenty years after Loos's opening salvo and at about the time that planning was beginning for the Weissenhof Siedlung, Le Corbusier published one of his four manifestoes on the arts, *The Decorative Art of Today.*

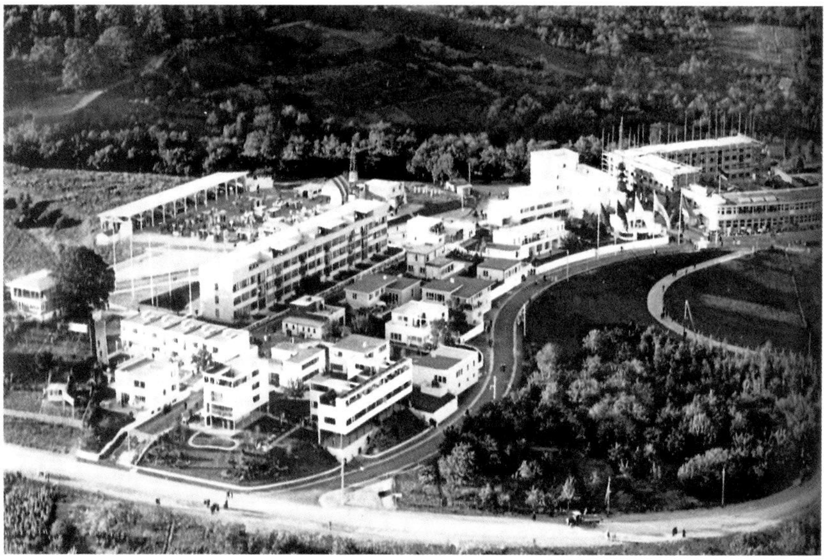

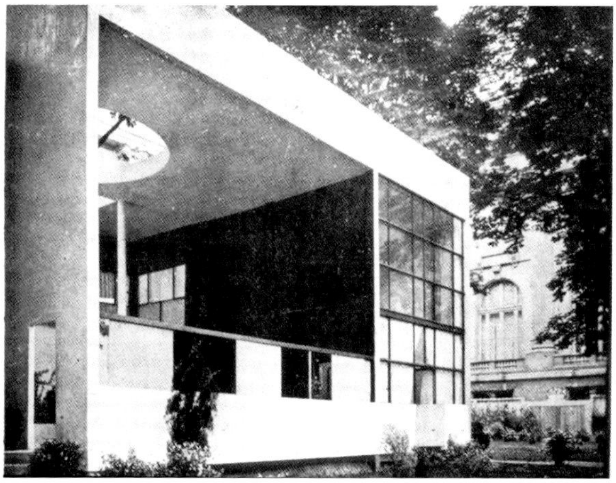

FIGURE 1
Ludwig Mies van der Rohe, Weissenhof, Stuttgart, Werkbundsiedlung, 1927. *100 Jahre Deutscher Werkbund 1907/2007* (exh. cat.) [Ausstellungskatalog: München, Architekturmuseum TU, Pinakothek der Moderne, 19.4.-26.8.2007] (Bonn: VG Bild-Kunst, 2007), S. 166.

FIGURE 2
Le Corbusier and Pierre Jeanneret, *Pavillon de l'Esprit Nouveau*, 1925. From Le Corbusier, *Almanach d'architecture moderne* (Paris, 1925).

The topic had preoccupied critics, architects, educators, decorators, industrialists, economists, and politicians for the better part of a century. His bottom line, equally emphatic though delivered over much more space than Loos's pithy essay, was that "modern decorative art is not decorated."[3] Echoing as he often did a position already taken in Germany—in this case the catalogue "Die Form ohne Ornament" by Wolfgang Pfleiderer, which accompanied the Werkbund exhibition "Die Form" of 1924 in Stuttgart—he delivered the message with greater power and precision.[4]

What gave his book more punch and a potential *succès de scandale* was the fact that it was accompanied by his and Amédée Ozenfant's entry in the Paris Exposition of the Decorative Arts of the same year: the Pavillon de l'Esprit Nouveau. This unit of architecture, seemingly parachuted behind the Grand

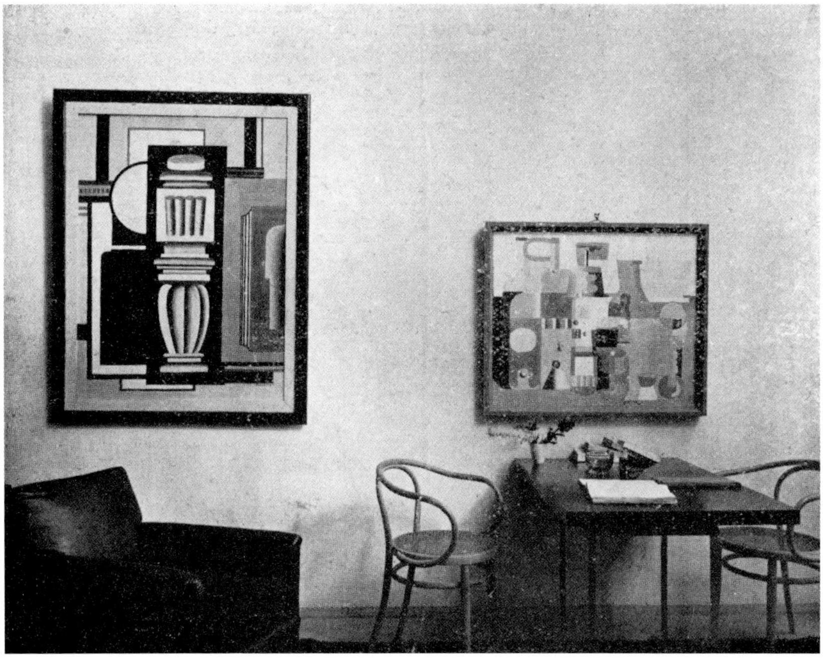

Palais from a larger urban conglomerate of which it was just one cell, offered an instructive glimpse into the pair's definition of modernity (fig. 2). Architecturally speaking, the combination of volume and light was its primary message. Indeed, for those familiar with the hundreds of Paris apartments built in the nineteenth century—slices of deep blocks of flats with few windows where light and air penetrated with difficulty into their recesses—this could come as a revelation. The materials were simple and modest, the products mostly prefabricated, and the aims were ease of assembly and reduction of construction trades.[5] The whole was a statement about simplification, about economy and mass production, about the standardization of the "machine à habiter"—in short, about modern life and style. Needless to say, there was no adornment, no ornament, no decoration.

But what *was* equally if not more remarkable were the pavilion's furnishings. Few and apparently simple objects inhabited the space: a few bentwood Thonet chairs, a plain table, a couple of simple leather armchairs, a patterned oriental carpet, a bank of drawers (fig. 3). Beyond an appearance that clearly resisted luxury status, what was particularly striking was that these objects existed in a dialogue with the paintings on the walls, a haunting gallery of similar objects. These paintings by Ozenfant, Le Corbusier, and Fernand Léger represented a collection of still lifes of ordinary objects: cups and saucers, bottles and carafes, tables and pipes confronting the three-dimensional "still lifes" of the interiors, which were also made up of cups and saucers, bottles and carafes, chairs and tables. Purist paintings confronted purist interiors. The most important painting

FIGURE 3
Interior of Pavillon de l'Esprit Nouveau, 1925. From *Almanach d'architecture moderne.*

among them, and the largest, was Léger's *Le Balustre* (fig. 4). Although all the paintings represented a selection of objects scattered across the pavilion, Léger's was the most emphatic: it monumentalized a single, banal object, the stair baluster, giving it a presence and importance in the interior that overshadowed anything else. Dramatic and assertive alongside the quiet and reflective works of Le Corbusier and Ozenfant, it acted like a general in this army of objects, delivering the battle cry. The paintings pointed the finger back at the objects and identified them as the principal actors on this stage. Clearly, the Pavillon de l'Esprit Nouveau was about objects.

A powerful yet layered image, *Le Balustre* calls up memories of stone- and wood-turning in the modest stair or balcony baluster, and combines them with references to the human body (as totem or fetish) on the one hand and to quasi-industrial precision, evoked by tangential visual references to the scale and operation of large machines—pistons, pumps, gears, and augers—on the other. It is ironic and serious at the same time. As scale is erased, the viewer whose "besoin type" and "émotion type" Le Corbusier targeted, is literally asked to comprehend the "city machine" and "house machine" through this slippage from machine to art and back by way of the handheld object and its image, which draws all the other scattered objects into its net. The objects and the *maison outil* ("house instrument") blend into one enhanced experience.[6] As in Le Corbusier's purist canvases (alongside which it is hung), where the pile of plates can be read simultaneously as a column and as a compressor and the bottle as an extruded form, in the universe of the machine the painting functions as its icon. And what it signals is the object. In short, with characteristic artistic economy the painting delivers the point of the Esprit Nouveau pavilion-as-manifesto.

To be sure, the theme of the exposition required such an emphasis on objects, for, after all, it was an exposition celebrating the decorative arts. Maverick-like, Le Corbusier undercut it, and instead of offering examples of furnishings he offered architecture. Yet his architecture was one with its objects. This alien-looking habitation unit, which seemed to have landed on the lawn surrounding the Grand Palais as if from the moon, was itself a discrete "object" on display, seemingly as portable or mobile as any of the objects it contained. In Le Corbusier's narrative about the city and the "vie contemporaine" of few and mobile possessions, focused and essential, objects and living cell conveyed the same message—a position he would radicalize further in the 1930s (fig. 5). This was not because the furnishings were built-in or somehow physically continuous with the architecture, as was the case in every other pavilion, but because they were not. Indeed, without the objects in it the pavilion's message would have been unclear. It was the objects—the chair, the table, the mortar and beaker, the glasses, and the vase, all so deliberately anodyne, so understated, and so obviously

FIGURE 4
Fernand Léger, *The Baluster*, 1925. Oil on canvas, 51 × 38¼ in. (129.5 × 97.2 cm). Museum of Modern Art, New York/Scala/Art Resource, NY.

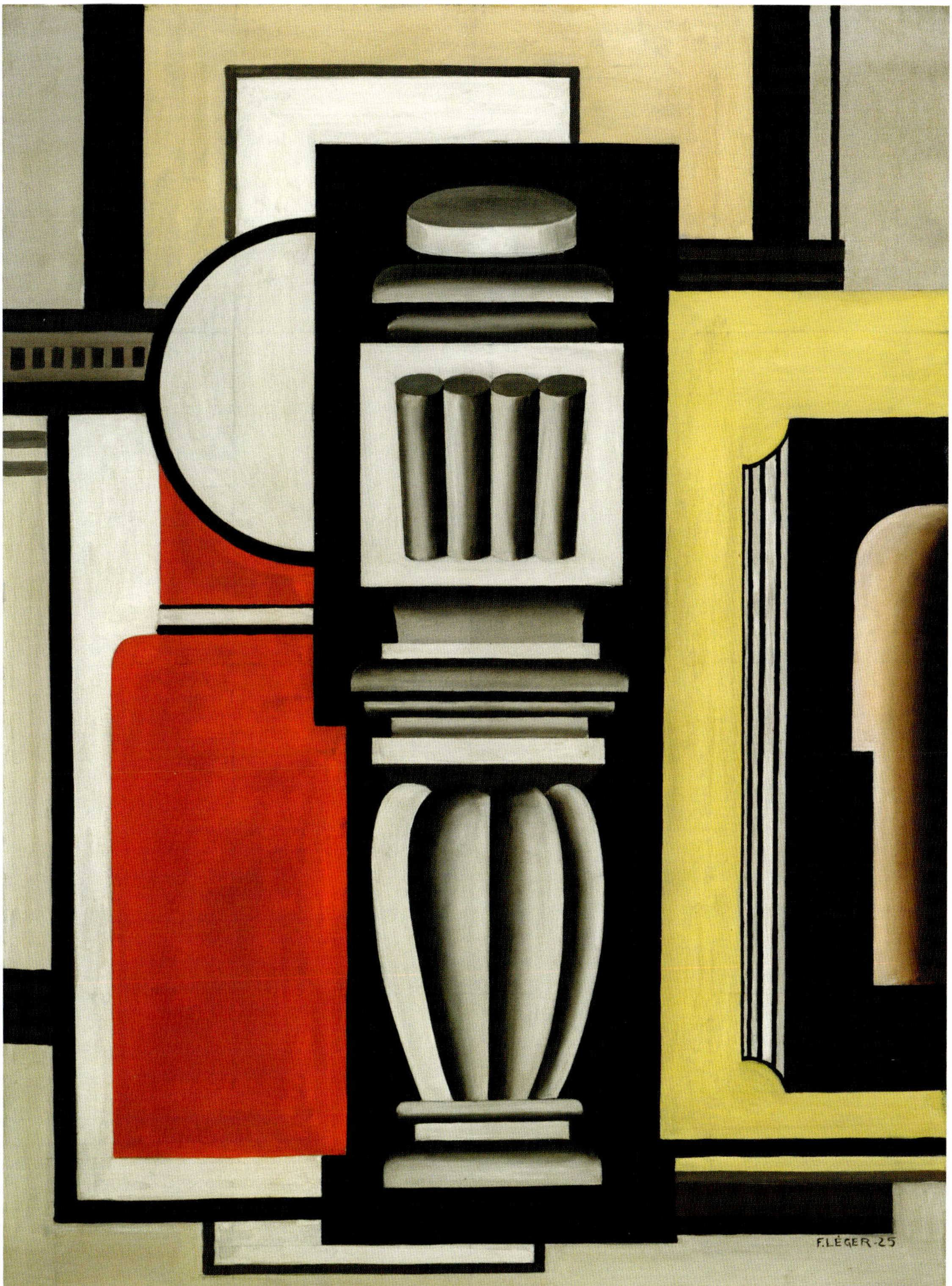
F.LÉGER-25

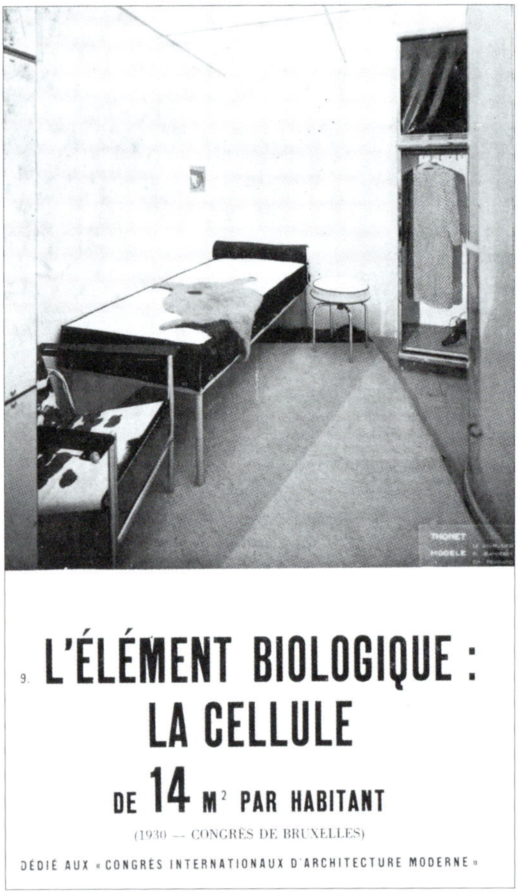

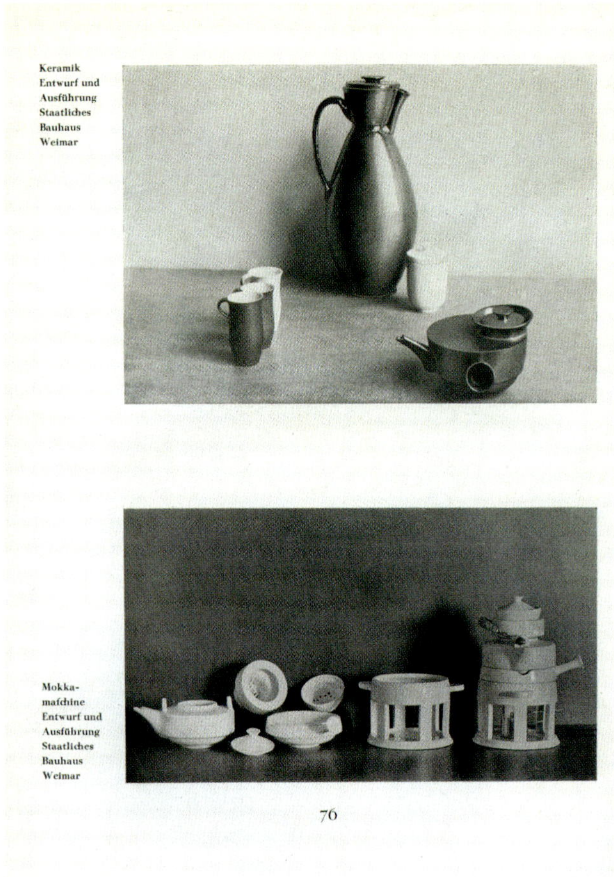

Left **FIGURE 5**
Charlotte Perriand and Le Corbusier, "L'Elément Biologique: la celulle de 14 m² par habitant." From *La ville radieuse, éléments d'une doctrine d'urbanisme pour l'équipement de la civilisation machiniste* (Paris, 1935).

Right **FIGURE 6**
Ceramics and porcelain vessels, design and execution Bauhaus, Weimar. From W. Riezler, ed., *Die Form ohne Ornament* (1924).

mass-produced (even if they were not)—that provided the eloquence of the whole.[7] Each object was a sign about uncluttered living, body habits, and basic gestures, describing a way of sitting, of lounging, of occupying space, of leaving few traces. Most importantly, they entered into a dialogue with the architecture across the body that used them. The objects "explained" the architecture; they were its most tangible rhetorical dimension.

Undoubtedly the Pavillon de l'Esprit Nouveau was a powerful statement about the relevance of objects for architecture. But it was not the only one at the time. The Bauhaus, with its programmatic focus on the house and the full range of objects of daily use, was active in the same arena (fig. 6). Indeed, rising out of the ashes of the Weimar School of Arts and Crafts after World War I, it had kept the interest in recrafting everyday life that moved the original founders to such a degree that the teaching of architecture had been a much later addition to the curriculum. Perhaps an even more extreme case of collapsing architecture and objects was Gerrit Rietveld's Schroeder House in Utrecht (1925), another icon of modernist architecture (fig. 7). A modernist box intersected by a colored grid, it functioned like a giant Rubik's cube in which stairs, doors, walls, and balustrades moved, collapsed, expanded, and contracted, as if it were an articulated piece of furniture, an armoire or an extendable table. After all, it was designed by a furniture maker, and indeed it drew on a tradition in Dutch interiors that went back to the early modern period and beyond: wooden cubes within wooden cubes, such as beds-as-rooms and beds-as-armoires collapsing the distinction between furniture and architecture. But no such precedent could explain Hannes Meyer's radical Coop Zimmer of 1926 that abandoned architecture altogether: in a tentlike interior, all the pieces displayed—bed, bookshelves, chair, table—were collapsible and light, portable and transient, fit for modern man's nomadic condition. A dramatic statement about impermanence, mobility, and portability, it was made more dramatic still by the fact that it came from an architect, the very head of the architecture department when it was finally introduced at the Bauhaus in 1927. Coming from him then, such a statement spelled out a new regime for architecture in which essential objects of daily life performed *as* architecture, replacing it. To be sure, his was a Marxist and *Existenzminimum* manifesto, but a signal nonetheless of the architectural significance and power of objects (fig. 8). Some ten years later, at a moment of stock-taking for modernism, J. M. Richards zeroes in on the message in a major article for *Architectural Review:* airplanes and T-squares, typewriters and cooling towers, travel gear and plumbing are seemingly interchangeable, and he delights in playing games with their presentation as if they were at the same scale, communicating with each other (fig. 9).[8] It seems as if the objects had *become* architecture.

These are only a few examples, but, central as they are to the discourse on modernism—indeed, they are some of its most sacred cows— they signal a prominence for objects that was unprecedented. This is not to say that architecture and objects had not "conversed" before. In every historical period objects

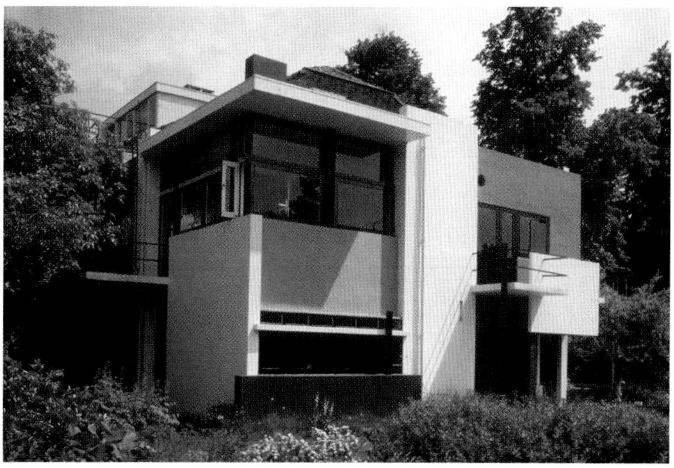

FIGURE 7
Gerrit Rietveld, Schroeder House, Utrecht, 1924. Hay Kranen, Wikipedia Commons.

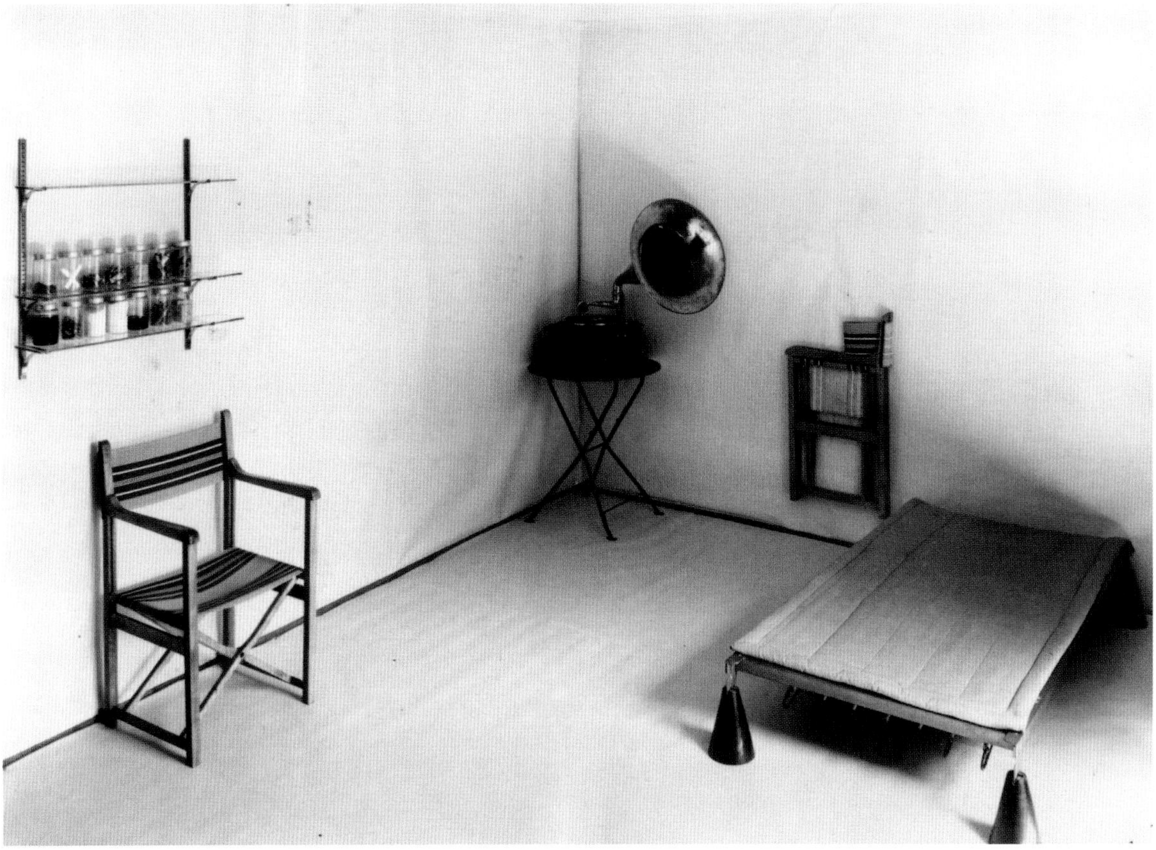

FIGURE 8
Hannes Meyer, Coop Zimmer, 1926. Bauhaus Archiv.

and architecture had existed in profound synchronicity. But what seemed new here was the self-consciousness of their deployment, the subtle because nondiscursive theoretical attention they received, a form of coming of age as subjects of reflection in and of themselves. They were not just functional and mass produced; they were not just made to "go" with the architecture as an effort toward aesthetic coherence, nor were they embedded in it. One has the sense that architecture *needed* them. A theoretical space had opened up just as another, the millennial one of ornament, had imploded.

Was this a coincidence or a causal relationship? Traditionally, architectural ornament had functioned as the vehicle to "explain" architecture, to domesticate its abstraction in terms accessible to a viewer—figural, three-dimensional, more representational and animated, scaled to communicate with the bodies that inhabited it. Elliptically discursive, it was an attached layer of the same material and achieved with the same tools as architecture. Had that space of discursiveness, of reflection *upon* and *about* architecture, disappeared altogether with the demise of ornament? Or—and this is my contention—had it been cut from its moorings and relocated in the objects that populated architecture's spaces?

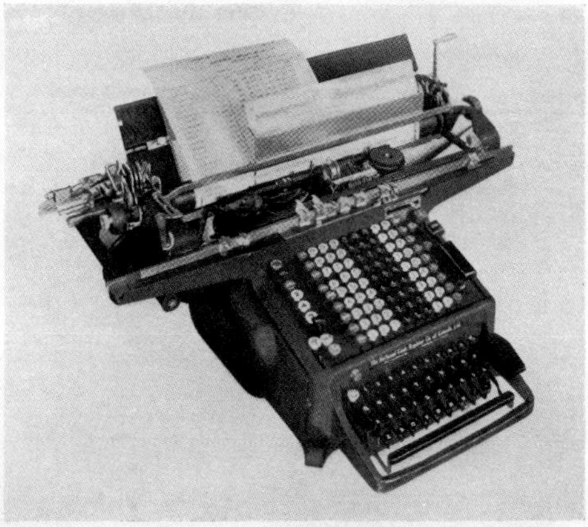

15

The typical modern virtue of regimentation, the æsthetic value of the serial repetition of identical forms, is displayed in 16, an air-view of a battery of cooling towers (from "The New Vision," by L. Moholy-Nagy). The photograph also suggests the extent to which the development of air-photography has assisted the appreciation of this quality. 15 shows the same quality to a smaller scale, apparent in the pattern value of the keys of an accounting machine, by the National Cash Register Company.

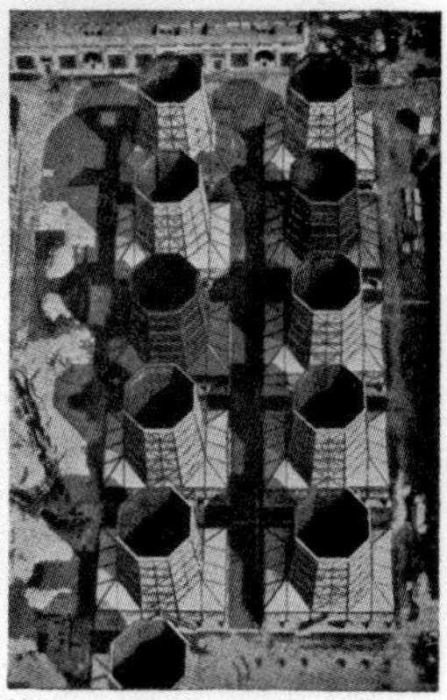

16

Had that attached layer become *detached,* impinging even more upon the viewers and pushing even closer into their proximity, descending among them as objects familiar to the hand, as that inconspicuous layer of "limb-objects," as Le Corbusier called them, which had now taken over this rhetorical function (fig. 10)? And is this why the issue of applied ornament becomes such a raw nerve at the turn of the century? A projection of the anxiety attending this transition, of the baring of the surface of architecture and its translation into myriad objects seemingly outside of architecture's control?

This scenario is precisely what this book proposes. And in so doing it raises a host of other questions. Was this move from ornament to objects a move from optic to haptic, to paraphrase (and invert) Alois Riegl—that is, a move away from reading a building from a distance by way of the ornament attached to its parapets and cornices, balconies and window frames to literally feeling its nerve endings in the objects that populated its interiors like so many accessible small sculptures? Were the objects surrounding the body and in the most intimate contact with it—from clothes to domestic tools to furniture—seen to create an in-between layer that permitted it to interact more knowledgeably and more

FIGURE 9
J. M. Richards, "Towards a Rational Aesthetic," *Architectural Review* 78 (December 1935).

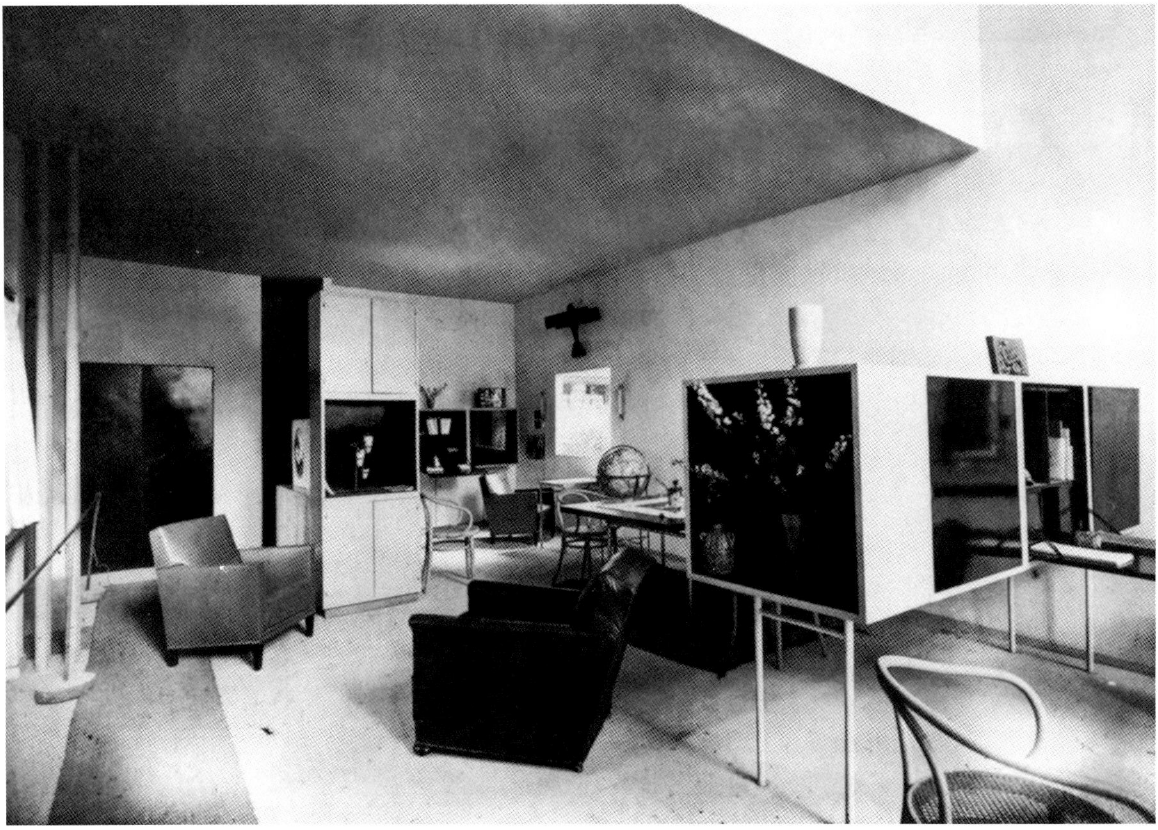

FIGURE 10
Interior of Pavillon de l'Esprit Nouveau, 1925. From Le Corbusier, *Almanach d'architecture moderne.*

insightfully with the outermost layer, architecture? Was the mobile world of objects the other "subconscious" of architecture, to use Sigfried Giedion's famous simile, alongside and in dialogue with structure and assemblage?[9] Were Walter Benjamin's *Etuimensch* and man-as-mollusk more than negative metaphors of the bourgeoisie and perhaps acknowledged intuitively the relationship between the body as the soft core of architecture and its environment?[10] It has been argued that Bertolt Brecht spelled out the crisis of the modern dwelling when he claimed that "Scheerbart with his glass, and the Bauhaus, with its steel, have now created spaces in which it is difficult to leave traces."[11] But what if in fact this was not a crisis but a *shift,* and the object-as-ornament *was* the underbelly of modernism, the "other" coordinate for its discourse that connected it to the history of architecture in the *longue durée* and that was erased in the critics' overenthusiastic eagerness to promote a way of building that offered *absolutely* no connection to the past? And who were the agents of this shift, of this change? What allowed it to happen so covertly, below the radar of attention such that it has not been addressed until now?

Of course the term "object" is a capacious holdall that contains many categories of things, not all of which entered—or were seen to enter—into dialogue with architecture. However, to narrow its meaning too much at this point would be premature, for unexpected categories of objects may well turn out to have participated in this exchange. What concerns me in this book—and I cast my net deliberately wide—is the object as that class of man-made products that are (potentially) mobile, even portable, hence of a scale and physical integrity that permits circulation and removal from a specific site. Such is, for example, the equipment of the domestic space—from cups and saucers to luggage, furniture, and paintings on the wall—as is, indeed, the equipment of any environment (church, office, laboratory, and so forth). Belonging to a collectivity aptly called in German *Sachkultur* and embracing everything from luxury goods to everyday items, objects are collected and consumed, are detached and detachable, discrete and unrooted, transient, short-lived, both close to the body and discardable at the same time. Indeed, they represent an antithesis of architecture. So unlike architecture is the behavior of objects that when the Pergamon altar was bodily lifted from its Anatolian hilltop and reassembled in a museum in Berlin—therefore, when it behaved as an object—the sheer unexpectedness of the event caused such a severe shock that it reconfigured the aesthetic outlook of an entire generation and opened the door to the reevaluation of the baroque.[12]

Objects have drawn increasing attention of late. As the trend away from theory's abstraction has moved the tectonic plates of research more and more toward materiality, so has its manifestation in "things" attracted greater interest. The move has made itself felt across disciplines from social studies to anthropology (admittedly always object-focused) and philosophy, as well as in a renewed interest in the museum and the object "collected" and displayed.[13] Inasmuch as this book inquires after the relationships between architecture and objects—as material things that enter into physical contact with users rather than behave as vehicles or paradigms of design—and shines a light on them as unsung catalysts and integral components of modern architecture, it participates in this trend. Yet it takes it in another direction. Objects invite agency. And discussions of objects in general terms can go only so far. The presence of objects as a rising concern for architects starting in the later nineteenth century, however, suggests a very specific context for such agency and offers the opportunity to explore it historically. Theory and manufacture of objects coincided and caused a high-density point for thinking about them. This was a historically grounded, specific phenomenon, and it caused significant changes. The rise of a theory of objects in a particular cultural context and its impact upon the most basic environmental container—architecture—that shapes everyday life should thus provide not only additional information on how objects function but also what the mechanism and consequences of such agency might be. As Peter Stallybrass has argued, "Things were the materials from which one constructed a life; they were the supplements the undoing of which was the annihilation of the self."[14] Commodities, but also the ingredients of existence itself, objects were and are important carriers of a hermeneutical charge. And the realization of this importance was historically contingent.

This book then is a *history* of the theory that developed around objects and drew them together with architecture. It is my contention that the interest in objects that we experience today was conditioned by specific historical circumstances whose genealogy needs to be recovered, and that the academic disciplines—sociology, anthropology, archaeology, art history, and so on—that today engage this topic emerged precisely at the moment when objects began to claim theoretical weight. And it is also my contention that, as a seismograph of cultural swings, architecture records this moment and allows us to study it; that in a manner of speaking, like in a chemical reaction, architecture *is* the precipitate or residue of the objects/culture interaction.

If one pole of this investigation is the object, ornament is the other. Like the object, ornament has also attracted increasing attention, both in the scholarly literature—from art history to literary and gender studies—and in architectural practice itself.[15] And within the field of architecture more specifically there has been no lack of work on either ornament or objects (as the applied arts).[16] Yet the question of agency has not been posed. If Marxist scholarship has examined the causal relationship between objects and architecture, it has been from the perspective of the effects of a new capitalist production mentality that absorbed architecture and made it both its instrument and its resistance.[17] But what of the connection with ornament, and the relationship of both to their container, architecture? Indeed, at first blush architectural ornament and objects may seem strange bedfellows in a book devoted to modern architecture. One was associated with regimes of viewing of "old" art, from antiquity to the threshold of modernism, when it was categorically rejected, the other profoundly important to, if not invented by, modern culture since the Industrial Revolution. It is certainly not difficult to continue the list of differences between them. Ornament was always an important component of architecture (though not exclusively), while objects were not; one was securely and permanently anchored to buildings, the other portable, detached, a mobile layer of forms. One was attributed to known architects and as such was ennobled by this participation in the œuvre of the artist-as-genius, the other was either mass-produced or created by makers/artisans less famous for being less attended by history. Finally, one came with a large body of theory going back to antiquity and was further enhanced by the tradition of classical rhetoric treatises in which the *ornatus* of the speech received substantial attention, while the other moved below the radar of theoretization. In short, in an aesthetic regime divided between high arts and minor arts, ornament and objects did not belong to the same category.[18]

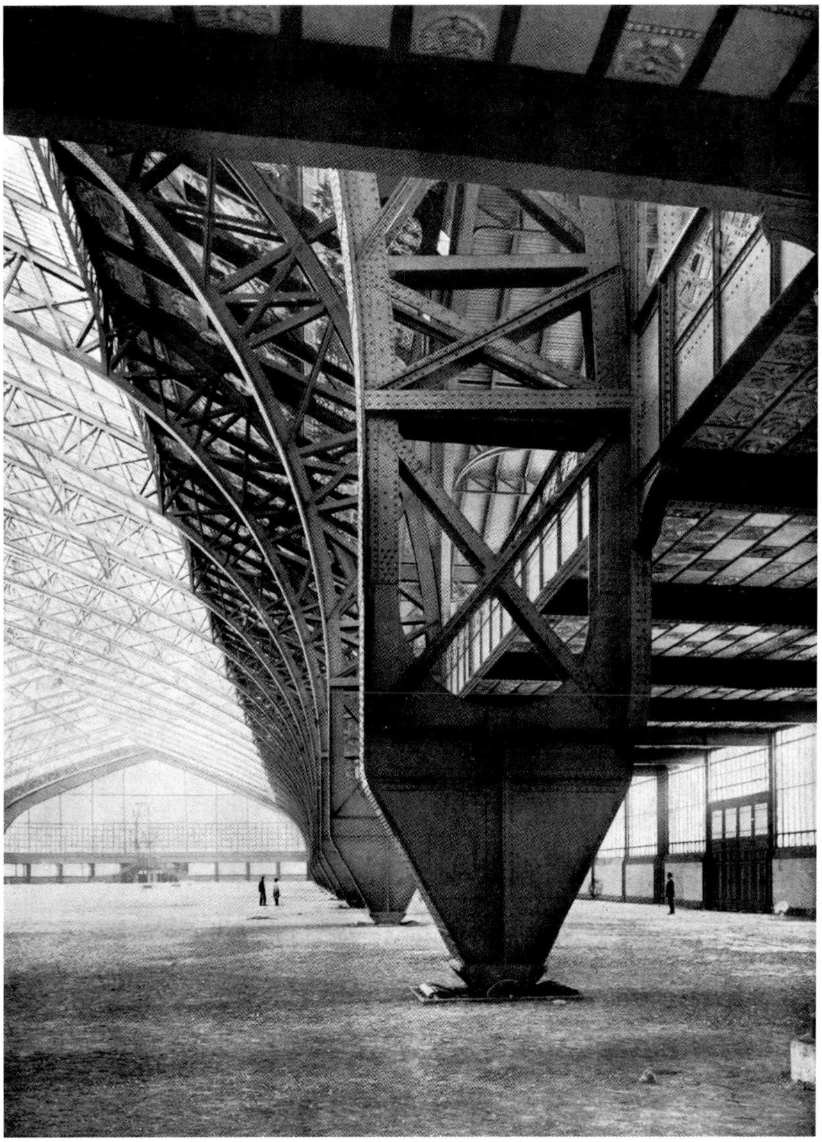

FIGURE 11
Charles-Louis Ferdinand Dutert, Gallerie des Machines at the Exposition Universelle in Paris, 1889. From Sigfried Gideon, *Bauen in Frankreich, Eisen, Eisenbeton* (1928), photograph Chevojon.

But one could also argue that they share as many features as separate them. Both are small scale relative to architecture; both are (mostly) three-dimensional, whether carved or cast, assembled or poured; and both elicit the sense of touch, projecting "graspability," the potential of being held in the hand. Yet these may be precisely the reasons why that scholarship has not brought them into a triangular proximity with modern architecture. In architecture scholarship, the small scale, the crafted and intricate have been long marginalized. As far as significance goes, Louis Sullivan's ornament in his late small buildings could never quite trump the Hall of the Machines at the 1889 Paris Exhibition (fig. 11). Associated with the feminine (on grounds of delicacy), with the artisan and the pre-industrial world, the small gesture and its site—whether ornament, miniature architecture, or object—has thus led a separate life, frequently in the shadow of mainstream scholarship on architecture.[19] Interest in the detail in modern buildings has attracted significant attention, to be sure, especially in relation to the work of architects such as Frank Lloyd Wright, Mies van der Rohe, and Carlo Scarpa.[20] But the prevailing line of inquiry has focused on tectonics and its formulation in industrially produced forms, not the aesthetic significance of the small scale as such.

This is not only a prejudice affecting modern architectural scholarship; it has been telescoped onto the past as well. For example, Rudolf Wittkower's Renaissance, first formulated in the 1930s and 1940s, had been a modernist one that set the stage for much that followed. Proportion, geometry, abstract forms and grids, mathematics, and science were its main coordinates.[21] One body of scholarship reinforced another, and though focused on different time periods they presented a consensus as to what architecture was and what pertained to it. Even though in the 1930s some voices had signaled that a collapse of scale between architecture and objects had been a productive way of thinking for modernist architects—Herbert Read, Nikolaus Pevsner, and J. M. Richards among them—this proposal remained essentially unheeded.[22] Subsequent work on modernism, though attending to the objects created in various milieus and acknowledging that the experience with the mass production of objects had a salutary effect on cleansing the architects' "palette" of historical references, did not push the question of a relationship much deeper. The broader discourse was much more indebted to Giedion's work of the 1920s and 1930s and his emphasis on monumental engineering in books such as *Bauen in Frankreich, Bauen in Eisen, Bauen in Eisenbeton* than on Pevsner and the English attention to objects.[23] Perhaps the continuous presence of an Arts and Crafts sensibility, never quite extinguished in Britain, had converted Pevsner, whose early work had been much more marked by the Turbine Factory aesthetic of the Werkbund, by Behrens and Gropius, than by the origins of the Bauhaus in a turn of the century school of applied arts.[24] In the end he embraced both, but he remained essentially isolated in this emphasis among the early historians of the Modern Movement.[25] This is not to say that scholarship on the impact of organizations such as the Werkbund and the AEG on architecture has not continued to attract scholars and produce significant work, as has scholarship on the industrial production of objects of daily use, such as those produced by the Bauhaus or the Deutsche Werkstätte.[26] But ornament was of course not part of this argument.

If scale was an obstacle in the acceptance of ornament and objects as principal actors in the advent of modernism in architecture, their association with

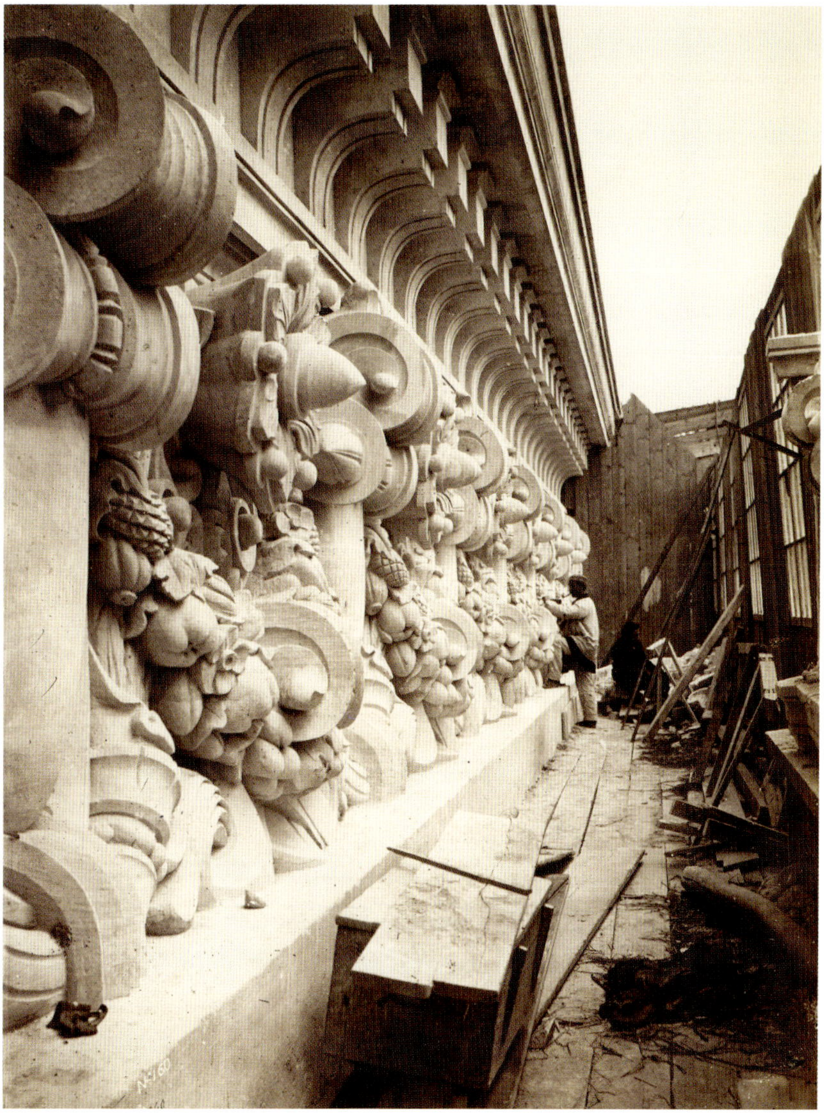

FIGURE 12
Louis-Émile Durandelle, *Le Nouvel Opéra de Paris: Sculpture Ornamentale*, 1865–72. Albumen print, 15⅛ × 11 in. (38.3 × 27.9 cm). Yale University Art Gallery.

sculpture posed another problem. Designated a sculptural "add-on," ornament signaled wastefulness and anachronism and was profoundly suspect in an industrial economy. True, architecture had been seen as overscaled abstract sculpture both in criticism at the time and in scholarship later, and sympathy in this respect might have been expected.[27] But the function of the sculptural matter *on* architecture rather than its overall *Gestalt*—the shells and garlands, masks and urns, reliefs and figures attached to walls of premodernist work—tended to be left out of discussions and remain on the periphery of scholarship to this day (fig. 12). The exception was the columnar orders, which, albeit classified as ornament, connected of old to the idea of structure and thus survived the modernist turn in historical scholarship.[28] Since ornamental sculpture essentially meant representation and representation was eliminated from the toolbox of the modern architect, so did it disappear from critical attention.[29] In truth this disappearance amounted to a kind of collective *damnatio memoriae* across many stripes of historical scholarship. That ornamental forms could be and were in fact mass produced in the nineteenth century gave them no reprieve from this condemnation, for their visual referents were not industry and the machine but historical and/or mimetic styles—references to classical or Gothic forms, or floral/vegetal (Art Nouveau).[30] Indeed, it is probably this organic animation that caused most of the resistance since the more abstract forms—the geometrically derived ones, be they surface lines, as in the work of the Viennese Secessionists or of Behrens, or those associated with the orders in earlier work—were compatible with the technology-driven aesthetic and as such were drawn into discussions about architecture. Adolf Behne makes precisely this point when he accuses modern classicists of preaching "Technizismus" in disguise—that is, he sees them fundamentally allied to the rationalism of the machine aesthetic, unlike the Expressionists (with their Gothic roots) whom he champions.[31] As a result, within such a scholarly atmosphere, the fact that ornament cut across scales and mediated between architecture and sculpture placed it even further outside the mainstream. Any connection to the objects of daily use that inhabited architectural space and were in effect miniature sculptures—a connection readily made by many modernist architects now forgotten—was not even considered.[32] Ornament and architecture was a topic, albeit a negative one, and objects and architecture was another; but no questions connected the three.

Lastly, the *tertium comparationis* that connects scale and sculpture (small or large, architectural or object-based) is the human body, which engages directly, physically and haptically, the three-dimensional world that surrounds it. Yet much as the human body had offered a matrix for architecture since time immemorial, scholars agreed that with the advent of the Industrial Revolution it had been displaced from the center by the machine. The rejection of empathy theory—much in vogue at the turn of the century, riding on the coattails of the new science of psychology—from the methodologies of art history is only one of the consequences of this position. Likewise, in architectural scholarship questions related to the human body receded into the background. This has been somewhat corrected as the all too engaged positions of the early proselytizers have given way to more balanced approaches that recognize the multiplicity of voices in the early phases of modernism.[33] Yet the body remains one of the less addressed topics of modern architecture, and inquiries into how and where the interaction between body and architecture was understood to occur have remained essentially outside the problematic of research.[34]

Recent scholarship across historical periods has turned the tables on some of these prejudices, and more and more reevaluations of ornament, as well as objects and their collecting, their making, and their influence, are being produced both inside and outside the area of modern scholarship. On the one hand, as we have seen, this trend emerges from a reaction to theory and a desire to refocus on the concrete; on the other, it was caused by a reappraisal of the small scale. Starting in philosophy and literary criticism, as well as gender studies, where these issues were first aired, the wave extended into art history—medieval and Islamic, in particular, with a ricochet to the *Wunderkammer,* the site of the minute and precious par excellence—before finding a home in studies on the museum.[35] The beneficiaries have been studies of ornament and objects, sometimes more broadly denominated "things."[36] Perhaps inevitably museums are now leading this charge, the Victoria & Albert Museum in particular.[37] Granted, its collection of objects that cut across media—reaching from architecture at one end to sculpture at the other, across models and fragments, gems, clothes, ivories, reliquaries, and other smaller-scale items—invites such efforts. But it also stems from a current reassessment of objects as cultural disseminators, portable and therefore accessible, viewed and handled more readily than large works of art rooted to their places of origin.[38] The presentation of architectural ornament as miniature sculpture in dialogue with furniture has also been most evocatively suggested if not stated outright by most recent museum installations of Rococo works.[39] But the question of how this layer of mobile works might have communicated or interacted with architecture nevertheless remains in abeyance.[40]

Of course these are broad generalizations, and it is the job of this book to unpack them; but generalizations have their uses, and for now it seems important to identify a departure point for a discussion that brings them, architecture, ornament, and objects—however eccentrically—together. As I started working on these questions I realized that to see how and why ornament and objects seemed to move on inverse curves in modernism—one rising abruptly while the other fell—and how it all related to architecture, I needed to go back to the sources of the phenomenon to learn what had really been at stake. In short I realized that I was looking at the end of a process, not the beginning. And so a journey that I assumed would be a twentieth-century one became predominantly a nineteenth-century undertaking. Clearly the move towards object-hood had swept across all the arts and at about the same time. The fiction of the painting (or the sculpture, for that matter) that invited the viewer to look beyond its materiality through a window in the wall at another reality, as per Leon Battista Alberti's famous simile, had been under severe attack. Starting with the Impressionists—that is, in the later nineteenth century and moving through Cubist collage, Dada, and Constructivism to assemblage and ready-mades—artists had deliberately sought the domain of the physical object that interacted with the subject beyond its narrative or subject matter. Art had stopped being a window and had also become a *thing*.[41]

Architecture moved along a similar trajectory, but other phenomena had also been at work. Clearly the object was propelled into the foreground of Western collective consciousness with the Industrial Revolution and the emergence of a first, real global economy. In Chapter 1, I chart this coming of age for industry, trade, and global economy manifested in a spectacular display of objects at the Great Exhibitions that succeeded each other almost yearly in the great capitals of the world. These were paradigmatic sites for nineteenth-century thought. Showcasing the rise of the machine but also the breakdown of distances, they brought together cultures at various stages of development, collapsing geography and history at one and the same time. The resulting juxtapositions, both compelling and stark, precipitated radical reassessments and struck many, in many walks of the academy, but none perhaps as powerfully as those engaged with the arts. Gottfried Semper responded to the challenge as an architect, but also as an educator and art historian (as he claimed to be), and he is the figure around which this chapter teases out the complex and reciprocal relationship between architecture, ornament, and objects that he laid out in his revolutionary treatise *Der Stil*. Making sense of the object world through aesthetics was the default setting of his generation. As Winfried Menninghaus has shown, even Darwin turned to aesthetics in his attempt to understand the natural world.[42] It is not surprising then that the terrain on which the proliferation of objects—found, excavated, mass produced, crafted, traded, and consumed—should be dealt with was aesthetics and that the arts (more than philosophy proper) should emerge as its host.

An inaugural œuvre in its directness and impact, it was nevertheless not without its context. As Bruno Latour has argued in his seminal work on Louis Pasteur, discoveries are never the beginning of a process but the end; they are received and acknowledged as such, but only because the public is already prepared to accept them.[43] In Chapter 2, I examine this context that "produced" Semper and that responded to him, the many strands of an exuberant and wide-ranging scholarship that radiated from the fascination with the object—excavated, exhibited, evaluated, bought, and sold—and found ways to develop various types of histories of culture at whose center it lay. Anthropology, ethnography, art history, history, museum studies, and education, as well as archaeology, rubbed shoulders using the same type of material evidence and developed models of understanding cultural evolution that revolved overwhelmingly around the concept of style. Ornament and objects were their primary sites of investigation, whether they worked on Maori people, German folk art, Etruscan ruins, and histories of costume, or attempted to preserve national memory in the museum. Works that preceded Semper and that followed in his wake made ornament and the objects upon which it was deployed into the center of discourse, thus giving their assessment both urgency and prominence. They also presented them as interchangeable. Thus was created a condition of exchange between art objects and objects *tout-court,* in which the aura of art was extended to absorb every walk of life to the point of its disappearance. As Hans Heinz Holz has observed, there was no art left, only artists. Such a collapse of the two categories offered theoretical and practical opportunities that the next generations seized upon.[44]

In keeping with the alliance between objects and aesthetics in contemporary discourse, in Chapter 3, I turn to art historians from Wölfflin to Warburg across Riegl and Schmarsow, Geymüller and Wilhelm von Bode. Profoundly indebted to the generation of Semper, they were the group who developed the theoretical base for style and therefore the principal tool for understanding culture. The early alliance of art history with aesthetics had encouraged such a turn toward large system-building, and the expansive scholarship on objects and ornament they inherited allowed them to absorb it into a theory of culture. They did not all produce the same theory, of course, but they created a corpus of approaches to style and culture, to the roots of art and its evolution, that had much in common. Moreover, as most of them were working on the Italian Renaissance and Baroque—an art deeply engaged both with ornament and bodies as vehicles of communication between viewers and art object (be it painting, sculpture, or architecture)—they also developed a theory of art-making and culture in keeping with that interest, with the problems their art posed and the forms in which those problems were couched. Most importantly, they raised the object of everyday use to the level of diagnostic site for a culture. Absorbed into the mainstream—however distorted by such hugely successful authors as Julius Langbehn or Oswald Spengler—as well as in the architectural academy, their proposals channeled a host of ideas from a wide array of disciplines into architectural theory.[45] As a discipline in its infancy and thus open to infiltrations from neighboring fields, art history functioned as a transitional site for architecture, providing it with the tools to engage its own predicaments: the threefold crises of fabrication, ornament, and the human body as referent that the Industrial Revolution had wrought.

In Chapter 4, I look to the dissemination of this discourse among architects and the avenues and sites where it took place: the lecture hall, the professional journal, the critical essay, and the public debate (or review). Having risen to the level of signs of artistic DNA in the work of cultural and art historians, the objects of daily use become additionally significant because they are seen by these authors to enter the collective subconscious and inform it. Because they belong to no narrative, are not representational, and are handled daily—so these authors argue—they domesticate the modern and allow new materials and types of habitation to be comprehensible and ultimately acceptable. The objects are architecture's rhetorical devices, just as ornament once was. Interestingly enough, theirs is a logocentric discourse, not a visual one, as almost none of the authors illustrated their writings. Not Streiter or Gurlitt, and very few of the journal article authors. When images occurred it was by implication and verbal description. Beyond the text, the diffusion was mostly oral, and its sites the classroom and the public lecture hall. Indeed, most of the authors I follow in this and earlier chapters—Gurlitt, Streiter, Wölfflin, Lipps—taught either architects or future academics. Even Le Corbusier's 1910/11 interaction with his German hosts that was to leave such a profound imprint on his work, was oral—the obsessive notebooks he fills are records of conversations, of visits, of people who tell him things, of him listening.

Finally, in Chapters 5 and 6, I look for the reception of this buildup of ideas in the texts and work of those traditionally identified as watershed figures of the modernist Pantheon: Muthesius and Loos, the Bauhaus and Le Corbusier. They are connected in a singular triangulation: Muthesius is the brain of the Werkbund and as such the godfather of what would become the Bauhaus under Gropius. His words speak to that future. Loos offers a different perspective, more nihilist, a near-Dada point of view; Le Corbusier provides a synthesis. As two sets of doubles of different generations, their paths intersected. Together they represent the various directions in which the dialogue between objects and architecture would go, erasing its traces and origins in the nineteenth-century discourse that crisscrossed so many fields of study. The artistic context also comes into focus here. Architecture's dialogue with the object had a longer trajectory, but the insight offered by artists in the first decades of the twentieth century played a role, and both sharpened the response to the object and made it subtler.

Le Corbusier may seem an unexpected figure to bring this book to a close: an outsider as disseminator and prophet of a German and a nineteenth-century tradition. Yet as an itinerant through Europe he befriends Muthesius and Behrens and has access to Loos in Vienna and later in Paris, as he has to the artists gathering there in the aftermath of the war. The very fact that he is an interloper in this story demonstrates that the ideas on objects had "arrived," that they had permeated a culture of architectural thinking so thoroughly that an outsider could make use of them and disseminate them as if self-understood truths. What was incubating for the better part of a century finally comes to a head.

While Chapter 5 circles around the year 1900, Chapter 6 looks toward 1925. Both were moments of significance in the history of architecture and objects.

In scholarly literature, 1900 has been taken as a threshold—the climax of Art Nouveau and the end of revivalism, a chasm if not necessarily a new beginning. The year 1925 was ostensibly the coming of age of the domestic interior conceived as "style" in and of itself. Yet styles of architecture do not figure in my story. Instead, the thread I follow here is that of accretive theory-building, of a development in thinking about detached, mobile, virtually inconspicuous objects aimed at extending human gestures and movements, not at illustrating them. And at how, perhaps surprisingly, they interacted with architecture.

Ultimately this book is about the agents that operated this sleight of hand. And they turn out not to be the usual suspects: not philosophy or science, or theories of mass culture, but anthropology and ethnography; art history and the museum; archaeology and psychology. What emerges is a profound continuity between nineteenth-century theory and modernism that existed precisely at the point where the break was most decisive and obvious: in the realm of ornament. Paradoxically, through its demise and necessary replacement ornament emerges as a significant nerve ending of modern culture, and ties the theory of architectural modernism back into a historical continuum.

A few caveats. Although objects figure large in this book, it is not a book about industrial design. It is about architecture and *Kleinarchitektur,* about furniture ("die Kleinwelt der Möbel," as Wölfflin calls it) and small portable objects. It is also about armor and joinery and everyday objects of household use, about tools, the *poiesis* of mechanical fastening, and clothes. They are all linked in my story. Yet although all of them are either close to the body or instruments used by the body, this is not a book about empathy theory, even if it charts a discourse that has the body at the center. Instead, this book lies at the intersection of several fields of inquiry that are not normally connected: ornament, objects and the decorative arts, art historiography, museum history, modernist architecture, art, and industry. As such it may seem to be mixing types of historical inquiry that have discrete contours of their own. But this is precisely the point. I follow a discourse until it peaks in one field and moves to another, transposed into a discipline-specific language but nevertheless imported from elsewhere; a discourse that reaches a critical mass at different times and in different places: in the 1850s–70s in the museums and exhibition world, focused on ornament and the decorative arts; c. 1880–1900 in art history; from 1900 onward in architecture. Such a meandering path means that objects and words about objects become laden with baggage by the time they engage architects in a serious way. What happens in the Bauhaus, Werkbund, or the Esprit Nouveau pavilion is about that baggage, and it is my contention that unless one understands that baggage—or that genealogy—these critical moments in the history of modernity will also remain opaque. As it turns out, style is one shared category that allows discourse to travel across disciplinary boundaries; the body is another.

As its title suggests, this book is about the theoretization of the object of everyday use; it is a history of theory and theoretical thought, not of buildings as such, though eventually buildings do pick up the thread of the narrative. The focus is on episodes that were critical. This is neither a continuous nor a comprehensive story. It does not deal with all the usual suspects, though quite a few do turn up on these pages. It is not about fashion, consumption, politics, or economics—though these are all stories that are relevant and have been admirably told.[46] Instead, the book follows the public discourse associated with the object—that is, the printed word, the exhibitions, the buildings, and the images that originated from various and often heterogeneous environments and entered the public domain, that were available for architects, historians, and critics in developing their definitions and evaluations of what it meant to be modern. My aim is not to reconstruct individual œuvres, for this is neither a monograph nor a collection of monographs; rather, my aim is to follow what was available and when, and note impact. The many unpublished versions of Semper's treatise for example—like the manuscript papers of Riegl, Wölfflin, or Burckhardt—are important in reconstructing their own thought processes but were not part of the corpus that reached and affected those who were building buildings and commenting on them and leading the modernist charge.

With a subject this vast I had to make choices. Thus I am looking at those who wrote consistently—not the occasional piece, but as a major and public engagement of their professional activity. Not Behrens, Hoffmann, or Mies, but Le Corbusier and Loos, though they are all a part of my story. I also do not look at all the writers to the same degree—less at Karl Scheffler, August Lux, Otto Wagner, or Henry van de Velde and more at Richard Streiter, Hermann Muthesius, Cornelius Gurlitt, and Alois Riegl. By not attempting to be exhaustive I am offering a different cut through the literature: I look at texts both rarely considered in the context of the architecture theory of modernism and well known ones to see how they interacted, how they appear if placed against a different backdrop, how the history of modern architecture emerges if one adjusts the Hitchcock-Giedion-Pevsner glasses (which more recent narratives have continued to reinforce all the while refining) to include a different class of historical material.

Most important, this is a case study focused on the German-speaking world—Swiss, Austrian, and German. The choice was not random. Through the privilege of a shared language and publication venues, art historians, architects, critics, museum administrators, and patrons enjoyed access to and participated in a rapidly evolving discussion. A shared sense of urgency to respond to the industrial challenge posed by France and Britain also gave this group a common purpose that decisively affected the discourse that emerged. But this context is also an ideal case study of the relationship between object/modernist architecture because in the German-speaking countries the connection between them was made, was significant, and was promoted in its most radical form. In France and Britain the discourse moved in other directions: toward *patrimoine* in France and social issues in Britain. In the German-speaking countries, however, the longstanding connection between art history and philosophy/aesthetics and their reverberations in the architectural discourse created a particularly fertile terrain for the development of theoretical thinking among all those concerned with architecture. And it is this thinking and its consequences that I have set out to reconstruct.

As a towering mid-century theoretician—perhaps the last in an age-old tradition of architect/authors—Semper may seem to hover over this story. But the fact is that in German-language scholarship of many stripes he cast a long shadow; his theories were developed over several decades and his name continued to be invoked. And even when his voice was no longer heard and his argument had moved location and had been both complicated and transformed, the initial impetus is still worth noting. For a book concerned with genealogy tracing the *longue durée* of ideas is essential.

A final word on disciplinary boundaries. My parallel work on the architecture of the Renaissance played a role in this book as well. Working on an architecture profoundly engaged with ornament—both in theoretical terms and in unspoken though equally compelling practical ways at the level of building—I became increasingly convinced that architecture has always needed, and always will need, a site which is *about* itself, a finger pointing back at its meaning, at its self-definition. Books were and are not enough, for architecture's own language is not the language of words but that of forms. To be sure, architects have always engaged with words more consistently than have any other artists, both as a way to explain to themselves what they were doing and why, that is, how design decisions would be consistent rather than random, and to convey to others what was at stake in their work. But written views do not make architectural forms, and a verbal discourse need not accompany formal innovation—indeed, it precedes it more often than not—and even when it is simultaneous it is certainly not its carbon copy. Thus the other significant and non-discursive site for architecture's self-reflection has always been made of its own materials, in its own language of forms. And for a long time the principal site of nonverbal discursiveness was ornament. As that "superfluous" and additional element enhancing beauty—so Alberti—it was a rhetorical flourish, a poetic gesture, a sign *about* architecture, unpacking its monolithic geometry and mass to render it accessible to viewers. Whether attached or not to the structural frame—an issue that scholars and architects addressed with gusto at various historical junctures—whether sculpted, incised, or painted, is immaterial in this case. The fact of ornament's presence rather than its fastening is what counts for this rhetorical function, for its significance as self-referential sign—unless, of course, fastening itself becomes a rhetorical gesture and then crosses over into the domain of discursiveness and, hence, ornament.

Indeed, this is not to say that, like fastenings, color (not just polychromy, but even white), surface finish, the materials themselves, cannot be construed as ornament.[47] And that its definition cannot be expanded to include any artistic gesture provided that it was conceived with the object of adding aesthetic punch to a form already self-sufficient; simplicity itself could be construed as ornamental. Even in the Renaissance Leon Battista Alberti referred to gates, palaces, and churches as ornaments—of the city, in this case. However, in this book I look at *actors' categories*. When Wolfgang Pfleiderer wrote the introduction to the Werkbund exhibition *Die Form ohne Ornament* (1924), or when Adolf Loos associated ornament to crime and Le Corbusier proclaimed that "the decorative arts are not decorated," they fully understood what the other meant, and they were *not* thinking of color, surface, or material richness. Instead, what they understood and what was understood in common parlance by the term "ornament" at the time was sculptural forms extrinsic to architecture (or to objects), pattern, inlays. Polished marble did not figure among the sins of ornamentation they tabulated. To be sure, once traditional ornament is eliminated anything can be invested with significance, and even the most subtle or commonplace of gestures can acquire rhetorical power. But objects are different. They are more radical (more unexpected, and therefore more powerful) as sites of architectural discursiveness precisely because they are not tied to architecture and are not part of it in any obvious way. I do not argue that objects become ornament (nor yet that they have anything to do with architectural beauty), only that they pick up its function of mediation.

And so, given the significance of this function for architecture I found it hard to believe that this space would remain empty once vacated by ornament when it was denounced as irrelevant in the early years of the twentieth century.

The result of this disbelief and the subsequent quest to find what filled this void is the book before you.

1 | Semper's Heritage

Even what we call ornament (paregra), i.e., what does not belong to the whole presentation of the object as an intrinsic constituent, but is only an extrinsic addition, does indeed increase our taste's liking, yet it too does so only by its form, as in the case of picture frames, or drapery on statues, or colonnades around magnificent buildings.—IMMANUEL KANT, *Critique of Judgement*

The whole analytic of aesthetic judgement forever assumes that one can distinguish rigorously between the intrinsic and the extrinsic.—JACQUES DERRIDA, *Parergon: The Truth in Painting*

ORNAMENT AND THE GLOBAL MARKETPLACE

It would be no exaggeration to say that the nineteenth century marked a climax in preoccupations with the object of daily use. Everything from luxury to everyday items—from furniture, pottery, silverware, textiles, and wall coverings to hardware and dress—came under sustained scrutiny. Whereas such concerns, if voiced at all, formerly had been the province of artists, artisans, and decorator/architects—from Cochin to Robert Adam—the discussion now drew into its orbit historians, politicians, museum administrators, and education officials. The rise of mechanical processes to obtain both utilitarian and artistic objects of household use, and the invention of new materials and alloys that industry made possible, all precipitated what amounted to a crisis of fabrication both with respect to quantity (which was high) and quality (which was low). Turning to pen and paper to make sense of this situation was a natural reaction of an overwhelmed body of makers and critics faced with a phenomenon of runaway material expansion that conjured up the image of the rising waters in *The Sorcerer's Apprentice*.

Ostensibly, the wakeup call to the unsuspected though immense economic potential of mass-produced household wares and their role in society came with the Great London Exhibition of 1851 (fig. 13). It has become something of a scholarly commonplace, fueled early by historian/critics like Nikolaus Pevsner and Sigfried Giedion, to give this event a watershed status, particularly in the history of architecture.[1] Not only the monumental glass container by Paxton heralded

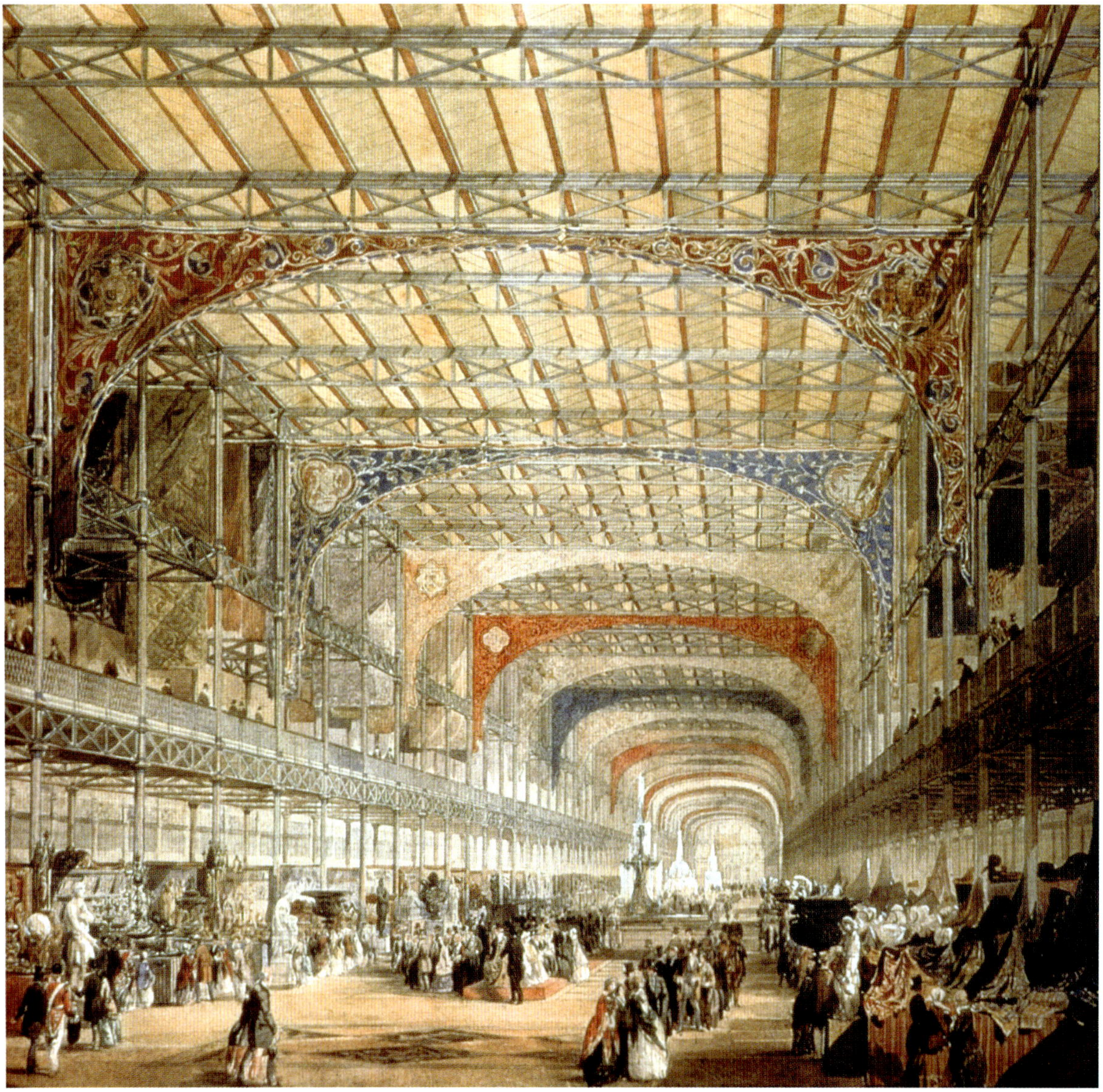

FIGURE 13
Interior perspective of the Crystal Palace at London's Great Exhibition, 1851. From *Dickinson's Comprehensive Pictures of the Great Exhibition* (London, 1851). Color lithograph, 16½ × 22⅞ in. (42 × 58 cm).

the union of architecture, technology, and new materials, but also the spirit of confidence in the new industrial future so visibly celebrated there has been linked to the trends and goals in twentieth-century architecture (of which Walter Gropius, Mies van der Rohe, and Le Corbusier were a sort of inevitable epiphany). But these were not the only issues at stake at the time, nor were they the most hotly debated. The economic and cultural role of the objects of daily consumption exhibited so profusely in London upstaged the architecture-based discussion. Both competitiveness between nations and the sense of an emerging global market—or at the very least a growing international market—gripped organizers and exhibitors alike. The reaction of the Austrian cultural administrators to this event is a case in point. Their alarm at the poor figure their country cut in this international forum prompted remedial action.[2] The same pattern was evident in Britain and Germany. Indeed, Britain subsequently moved faster than its neighbors in responding to this situation, pioneering a comprehensive cultural program focused on enhancing the design quality of household objects. The founding of the South Kensington Museum (now Victoria and Albert Museum), complete with its educational arm, the Department of Practical Art (later Department of Science and Art), was a direct response to the politicians' and educators' concern with the poor quality of British wares and their lack of export success.[3]

As a leading industrial power at the time, Britain had provided some of the earliest responses to the challenges—both opportunities and dangers—that the industrial production of objects posed. Rather than originating these concerns, the first of the Great Exhibitions was in fact their outcome. The recently formed Society of the Arts and the Schools of Design (set up by an 1837 Act of Parliament), like the yearly exhibitions of manufactured objects, which were copiously reviewed in newly minted decorative arts journals, had raised the issues into the consciousness of educators, artists, and the public alike. Henry Cole, the influential public servant who engineered many of the reforms affecting the arts in the 1840s and 1850s, together with a group of like-minded artists and architects—Owen Jones, Richard Redgrave, and Matthew Digby Wyatt—who surrounded and supported him, was among those most enthusiastically and effectively involved in this early phase. His own writings, like those of his friends, did much to promote the study of the phenomenon and to develop strategies for the government to intervene in arts education; in the process he also raised the bar of criticism quite high.[4]

But alongside the many reports and reviews of events that spoke mainly to the governing elite, the flurry of books that accompanied the 1851 Exhibition was aimed at the mass market and was a far cry from the exquisite and expensive folios prepared by architects in the eighteenth century for an exclusive audience of rich would-be patrons, dilettantes, and colleagues (fig. 14).[5] Not only those involved in the production process—industrialists, artists, teachers, and craftsmen—were targeted, but also the ubiquitous man in the street (or at least bourgeois in the street)—that is, the potential consumer of these mass-produced wares. This period saw the rapid rise of more popularly conceived textbooks and of arts and craft journals with titles ranging from *Kunst und Handwerk* (started 1849/50) to *Kunst für Alle* (started 1886) and *Innen-Dekoration* (started 1889/90) that addressed both the artisan and the larger buying public (fig. 15).[6] In keeping with the social concerns of English reformers, the short-lived *Journal of Design and Manufacturers* (1849–52), founded by Henry Cole, advocated the cultivation

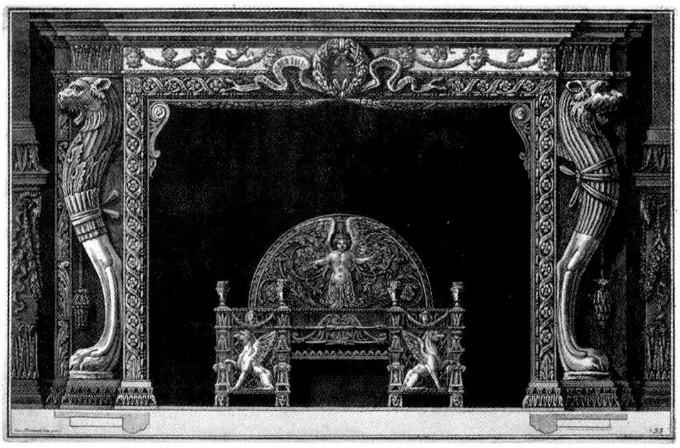

FIGURE 14
Giovanni Battista Piranesi, *Chimney-piece*. From *Diverse Maniere d'Adornare I Cammini* (Rome, 1769). Harvard University, Fogg Museum.

of taste through education for the working classes as well.[7] The polemical edge in A. N. W. Pugin's architectural writings from the 1830s and 1840s, with titles like *True Principles of Pointed or Christian Architecture* (1841), had already signaled the change from patron-seeking, self-promoting publications to those concerned with the larger issues confronting the young industrial society.[8] As we will see presently, one can certainly draw a distinction between the pre-1851 publications and those that followed, when the phenomenon came into its real flowering and the momentum increased. But a concern with artistic quality and economic gain were linked from the beginning in most of these early writings. So were concerns with the social, moral, and religious welfare of both producers and consumers, particularly in the British literature on the subject.[9] However different from each other, the publications of Pugin, John Ruskin, and William Morris and his circle are only the best-known examples of a larger trend (fig. 16).[10] Yet despite such intense activity, the connection between the so-called "minor," or decorative, and "high" arts remained an open and often uneasy, if acknowledged, question.[11]

This is not to say that eminent scholars did not turn their attention to these poorer relations of the art world. But the domain was neither theorized nor harmonized with that of the traditional academic arts. The great bulk of publications tended to retain a model-book flavor and a light tone compatible with the audience targeted. As women—the traditional keepers of the household flame—were often directly addressed in these tomes and speeches, such a tone was perhaps condescendingly understood to be appropriate to their "limited" understanding.[12] But this was also true of more practically and didactically conceived manuals for craftsmen and architects. Such were, for example, the books of Jakob von Falke (director of the Museum für Kunst und Industrie in Vienna), *Die Kunst im Hause* (1871) in Austria, Charles Blanc's *Grammaire des arts décoratifs: Décoration intérieure de la maison* (1882) in France, and Lewis F. Day's *Every-Day Art* (1882) in England.[13] At best these publications were attempts to promote a particular historical style,

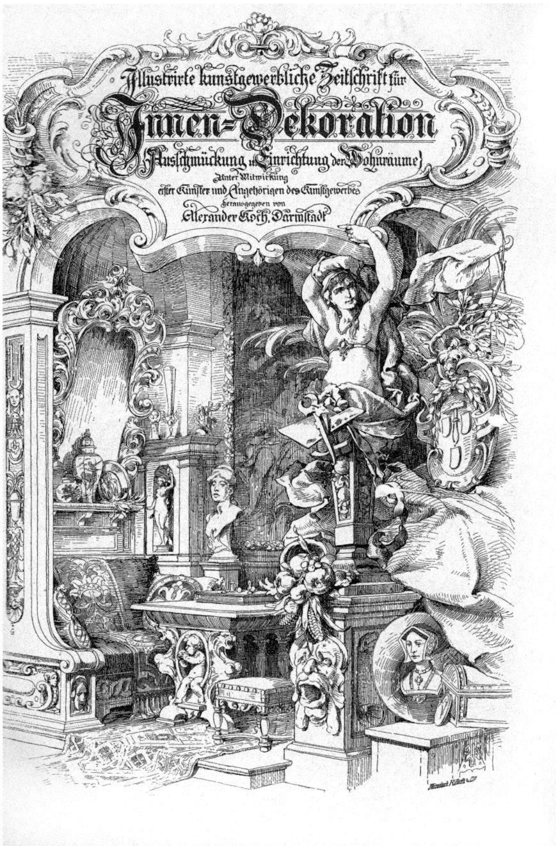

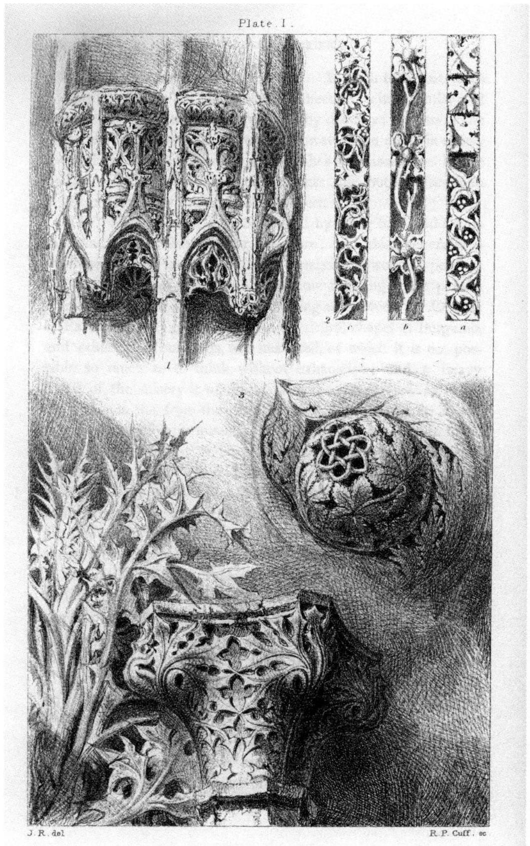

as had been the case when Pugin championed the Gothic, or an educational curriculum, as was the case for William Dyce and Richard Redgrave, the champions of the Schools of Design and later of the South Kensington Museum and its education arm. But their theoretical fiber remained weak.[14]

Naturally there were national differences in how these issues were dealt with. In Britain for example, economic imperatives, social reform, and religious controversies set the tone for many publications. In France the long established system of state support for manufacturers and organizations aimed at exhibiting and encouraging their work provided an authority lacking elsewhere and a site for discussions. Moreover, the country's acknowledged excellent craftsmen were a coveted commodity throughout Europe of old.[15] National agendas also led to much envy among continental competitors that colored the rhetorical garb of these publications and gave them a flavor all their own. This was the case in Germany and Austria, where there was no established centralized context for the development of the decorative arts, industrial or otherwise, and where there was a great sense of urgency to compete on the world market in the first global economy, or, as it came to be known in German, in the "Wettlauf der Nationen."[16]

Left **FIGURE 15**
From *Illustrierte Kunstgewerbliche Zeitschrift für Innen-Dekoration*, 1892.

Right **FIGURE 16**
John Ruskin, "Ornaments from Rouen, St. Lo, and Venice." From Ruskin, *The Seven Lamps of Architecture* (London, 1849).

Viewed from the point of subject matter, these pre- and post-1851 publications fall naturally into some broader categories: social/economic investigations of the arts and crafts,[17] books and manuals on ornament and its history,[18] on *Kunstgewerbe* (decorative arts) and exhibitions,[19] on histories of taste,[20] on "art and life,"[21] on costume,[22] as well as on house decorating or the arts in the home.[23] But in fact, neither the genres nor the topics were ultimately that distinct from each other, and a manner of productive confusion marked the field and signaled its almost unbridled growth energy, which was not unlike that propelling the economic world markets it was trying to affect. It was productive because it allowed arguments to flow easily from one medium and scholarly domain to another, resulting in unexpected avenues for discourse. But confusing it nevertheless remained, and one looks in vain for any definitions of terms or clear boundaries between topics in this exuberant free for all.

Such was the case, in particular, with the term "ornament," which cropped up in at least half the titles. Not only did ornament and decoration function as equivalents for each other, but no distinction was made between its manifestation in architecture, decorative arts, and apparel. Perhaps the connection between architectural ornament and rich clothing, jewelery, even makeup was so established—as far back as the texts of classical antiquity and the Renaissance, to Cicero, Lucian, Alberti, Serlio, and so on—and so embedded in the discourse that it did not seem necessary to draw lines between them to define each domain more closely.[24] Yet this broadly and vaguely circumscribed category "ornament," which had come to lead a semi-autonomous existence, came increasingly under pressure, and some urgency to clarify the issues was beginning to be felt.

In architecture, ornament had been traditionally a significant condensation point for theory, and its presence in so many nineteenth-century publications was a natural consequence of this long-standing theoretical weight. Buttressed by a copious literature from rhetoric and poetics available from antiquity that filled in significant gaps in the literature on the visual arts and provided a formidable critical and theoretical apparatus, ornament had slowly become a nearly distinct category in architecture as well.[25] More important still, it had absorbed theory to become the prime locus for discussions of architectural aesthetics—of architectural beauty, decorum, and imitation, of representations of civic, monarchical, and individual power and magnificence, and so on.[26] The treatise on the orders—that is, not only on the column as isolated vertical support but as one member of a complex grid of geometric and naturalistic, horizontal and vertical, abstract and figural elements—had been the staple location for such theoretical discussions ever since Leon Battista Alberti defined the column as the "most noble ornament without any doubt" in his monumental *De re aedificatoria* (1486). Although city planning, building materials, and building design occupied a sizeable part of architectural treatises, the domain of ornament captured most theory. As tersely stated by Vincenzo Borghini—a prominent Italian historian and art theorist of the later sixteenth century—architecture's place among the visual arts was tenuous, and it was really only through its ornament that it could claim sisterly status. For Borghini, ornament represented something that transcended utility and was essentially superfluous, and it was precisely this superfluity that allowed architecture to participate in a discourse on beauty and pleasure.[27] As the exceptionally rich architectural literature of the Renaissance and its offshoots in the seventeenth century set up the space within which architectural theory subsequently evolved, it should come as no surprise that the new domain that opened up around the time of the Great Exhibition should slide easily into this apparently related and well-established discourse. Since architectural ornament had been essentially isolated from the building and had claimed an increasingly separate aesthetic identity, ornament on objects could be seen to belong to the same discourse and was drawn into dialogue with it.

To be sure, the definition of "ornament" had attracted attention among philosophers, not least of all from Kant in his *Kritik der Urteilskraft* (1790).[28] But there were few if any bridges between the abstractions of philosophical propositions on aesthetics (such as the distinction between "free" and "dependent" beauty) and the physical objects of the visual and decorative arts. Even Karl Philip Moritz, who, in his ambitiously titled *Vorbegriffe zu einer Theorie der Ornamente* (Berlin, 1793) sought to bring some coherence to the subject, did not ultimately carry it off. A collection of previously published letters and newspaper articles that covered subjects from grotesques and arabesques to frames, interior decoration, and architectural criticism, his volume did not ultimately amount to a synthetic view, and the subject remained as fragmented as ever.[29]

As architect, professor at the Berliner Akademie der Künste, friend of Goethe (whose essays of 1788 and 1795 on architecture find an echo in his writings), and follower of Schinkel, Moritz presents that mixture of philosophical aesthetics and a new turn toward a conception of the applied arts as an economic asset that would later grip the nineteenth century. At the aesthetic level we can still hear echoes of Borghini, as Moritz argues for the autonomy of ornament, and he defines it in terms very similar to Alberti's classic statement formulated at the dawn of the Renaissance.[30] However, despite belonging to this tradition, he also includes objects of the decorative arts in his theory on ornament—vases, buttons, shoe buckles, clothes, and household objects—and he discusses them as symbols/representations of fundamental conditions of being such as lightness, delicacy, fragility, or containment.[31] One senses that he wishes to elevate the objects of Kunstgewerbe to the same level as the ornaments of architecture, and this is probably a direct result of his teaching mandate at the Berlin academy (where he had started in 1789), which also embraced manufacture since the reforms of 1786. Indeed, like Britain, Germany had also confronted early on the issues arising from the industrialization of manufacture. And thus when Moritz promotes Kunstgewerbe as an economic asset that would allow Germany to compete with France and England, he does so in much the same language as his nineteenth-century counterparts would argue several decades later.[32]

The fact that the terminological rigor of ancient rhetoric had long since been lost and that "ornament" was interchangeably used with "decoration" and "adornment" (*Ornament, Schmuck, Zierat, Verzierung* in German) also allowed an expanded field of objects to find shelter under its capacious umbrella.[33] To be sure, this easy movement from architectural ornament to object of everyday use and back again also owed to contemporary philosophical positions. For Kant, and later for F. W. Schelling, architecture was a branch of sculpture (*Plastik*) that also included household objects (the work of the carpenter) for being an art of "truth to the senses" (*Sinneswahrheit*) rather than appearance (*Schein*) like painting, wallpaper, makeup, clothes, and wall painting. By the mid-nineteenth century, when Schelling taught at Berlin, he was even more specific and included Kunstgewerbe—sarcophagi, urns, candelabra, vases, goblets, drapery, and clothes (*Bekleidung*)—under the rubric of architecture.[34] The issue of function gave him pause, however, as it had given Borghini nearly three hundred years before when he argued that only the truly superfluous belonged to art. But the fact remains that in this aesthetics and philosophy of perception, as it had been laid out by Kant and his followers, monumental and small objects were bracketed together. The power of this tradition cannot be underestimated, and it remained operative throughout the nineteenth century.

And yet, although Moritz's book was one of the first to bring this range of media explicitly under the umbrella of ornament as it became commonplace later in the nineteenth century, like his successors he failed to consider the implications of this near-universal application of the term. As we will see, the threads embedded in publications such as his and those of the following century, which isolated and detached parts of the architectural ensemble and treated them as discrete objects, fed a host of object-focused subdisciplines that came into being around this time. Monument preservation, the museum movement, art history, and industrial design all contributed to the objectification of architecture that could now be assessed, viewed, exhibited, and evaluated as any other object of mass consumption or artistic production. But as regards developing a theoretical field that addressed the mutual relationship between the "minor" and "higher" arts, not to mention the place of ornament as their point of intersection, the leadership eventually came from architecture.

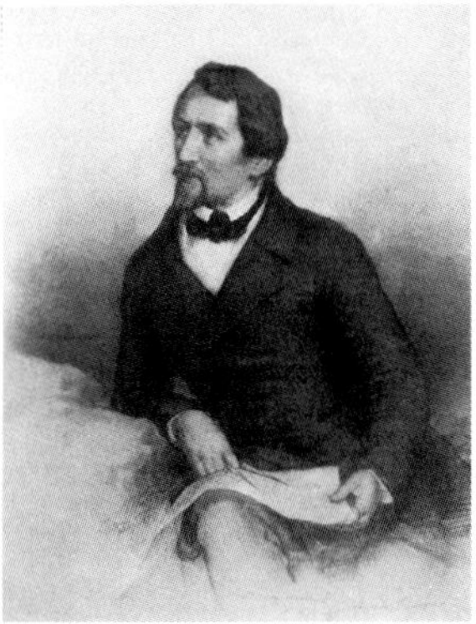

FIGURE 17
Julius Ernst Benedikt Kietz, *Gottfried Semper in Paris*, 1850. ETH Zürich, Institut für Geschichte und Theorie der Architektur, Semper Archiv.

ARCHITECTURE AS *KUNSTINDUSTRIE*

It is to this lively yet inchoate theoretical context that the work of Gottfried Semper made a groundbreaking contribution (fig. 17). His firsthand involvement with the London exhibition, his work as an architect and teacher in Germany, England, Switzerland, and Austria over a career spanning some forty years (from the 1830s to 1879), and the substantial built corpus he left behind indicate his wide exposure to a variety of milieus, as well as the impact he had on them. A prolific and committed writer and thinker, Semper also produced a literary œuvre of impressive scope. Indeed, a case can be made for Semper as the fountainhead of the discourse on objects and ornament in architecture even if he was not the first or the only influential author to turn to this topic: his writings survived longer, touched more people, spoke more directly to more disciplines from aesthetics to anthropology, and he affected architectural theory as well as the thinking about its materiality more profoundly. From the point of view of our inquiry, his most important achievement was that he gave prominence and status to two questions: What is the role of consumer objects in the culture of a society? And what is the place of the decorative arts in the pantheon of the fine arts? As we shall see, the lucid and synthetic picture he drew of these enmeshed issues, and the answers he proposed, would leave a deep imprint on architectural and art historical discussions for the next fifty years.[35]

Unlike his British contemporaries Richard Redgrave or Henry Cole, or even John Ruskin, Semper's object was not primarily education, politics, economics, or a desire to provide a thesaurus of forms for use in the many branches of the decorative arts, although he had attended to all of these issues in his earlier polemical writings and these affected the course of events both in England and on the Continent. Entering an already fomenting environment when he moved to London in September 1850—one need only think of Owen Jones's and Henry Cole's work, even if it was not to see the light of print till well after the exhibition, like Count Leon de Laborde's voluminous report on the exhibition of 1851 and its consequences for France—and profoundly aware that he was witnessing a crisis situation, he identified the issues and moved fast.[36] Essentially shipwrecked in England after his exile from Germany, Semper embraced the environment in which he had to find a livelihood, ready to absorb and to participate in whatever London threw at him. Of course, he did not come empty-handed. As professor and head of the department of architecture at the Dresden Academy of Fine Arts (1834–49) he had lectured and published on the very topics being debated in London at the time, and he was preparing a book that synthesized his thinking.[37] A year in Paris—involving meetings with Charles Blanc and Ignaz Hittorff and long sessions in the antiquities department of the Louvre—before finding

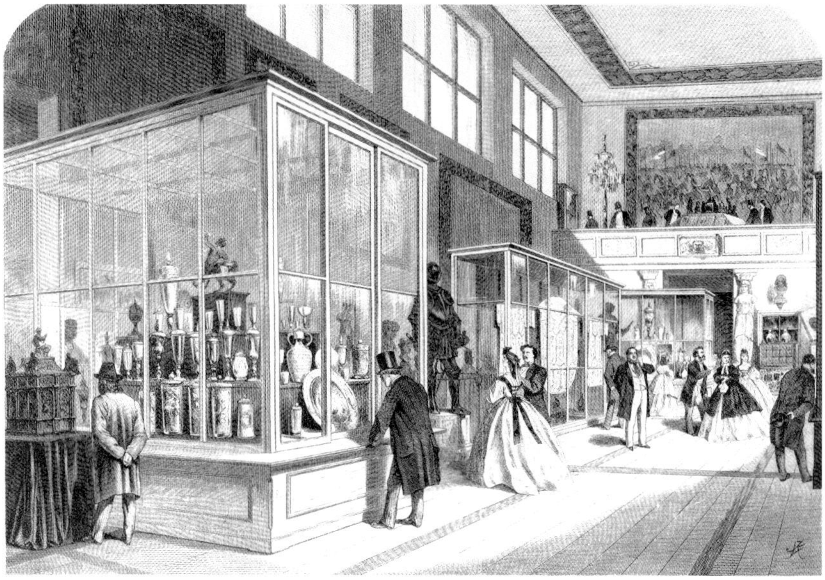

his way to London had also left a mark. However, it was the Great Exhibition, where he was active on the periphery as architect-decorator for the Canadian, Turkish, Norwegian, and Danish sections, and where he was exposed to the vast number of exhibits and to the lively discourse surrounding them, that sharpened his questions and heightened his desire to make his voice also heard. By 1852 he had published the highly influential essay "Wissenschaft, Industrie und Kunst" (Science, Industry, and Art) and had succeeded in making himself known in English-German political circles gravitating around Prince Albert.[38] The foundation of the South Kensington Museum in which Semper played a part as advisor, designer, and teacher was the immediate sequel and an example eagerly taken up on the Continent.[39] The Museum für Kunst und Industrie in Vienna, founded in 1867, where Alois Riegl was to spend an important part of his working life, was only one of its most famous progeny that can be closely tied to Semper (fig. 18).

That Semper was an architect was particularly important for the direction he gave the raging debate on objects, for he not only brought the authority of an established art upon a burgeoning discourse but he framed the questions from the vantage point of architecture. His most important and often quoted work—then and now—is without a doubt his voluminous yet unfinished treatise *Der Stil,* first published in 1860–63 and reissued in 1878 (with some modifications) by his art historian son Hans Semper. Other writings, most notably *Die vier Elemente der Baukunst* (1851) and the two short essays that achieved cult status in their time, "Wissenschaft, Industrie und Kunst" (1852) and "Practical Art in Metal and Hard Materials and Its Technology and History" (written 1852 and available only in manuscript form until 1903, when it was published as "Ideales Museum

FIGURE 18
Vinzenz Katzler, interior view of Das Museum für Kunst und Industrie in Vienna, 1864. Österreichische Nationalbibliothek, Bildarchiv/ONB, Wien, Inv. Nr. 13909.

für Metallotechnik"), were also known, as were a few of his speeches and articles contained in *Kleine Schriften von Gottfried Semper* (1884).[40] This collection included a series of lectures given in London in the 1850s that became the basis of *Der Stil,* as well as his 1856 opening address at the Politechnikum in Zurich, "Über die formelle Gesetzmässigkeit des Schmuckes und dessen Bedeutung als Kunstsymbol," which contained much material later developed in his magnum opus, though, as was often the case with him, in a more direct and hence more accessible form.[41] However, despite their availability, these texts could not compete with *Der Stil* in its continued impact on several generations of scholars, from architects and art historians to anthropologists and museum administrators.[42]

Indeed, when Gottfried Semper's *Der Stil* finally came out in 1860 it marked the beginning of a new era in the writing of architectural treatises. As a treatise written by an architect, everything about it was somewhat unusual, starting with the title: *Der Stil in den technischen und tektonischen Künsten oder Praktische Aesthetik: Handbuch für Techniker, Künstler und Kunstfreunde* (Style in the Technical and Tectonic Arts or, Practical Aesthetics: A Handbook for Technicians, Artists and Art Lovers). Most surprising about this otherwise copious title was the absence of the term architecture. Absorbed into the technical and tectonic arts, architecture was deliberately denied any independent status. Nor were architects given prominence, as they, like their art, were subsumed under the rubric technicians (Techniker). Perhaps even more striking was the additional title of volume 1, the only one to be published at that time: *Textile Art,* and in much smaller print *Considered in Itself and in Relation to the Art of Building.* Having titled the treatise *Der Stil* and qualified it as a "practical aesthetics," Semper thus proceeded to devote it to textiles, particularly as they related to architecture. This was certainly the bottom rung of the arts—a decorative, small-scale, manual, and mostly female art—ever since Leon Battista Alberti had suggested a ranking of media and genres in the fifteenth century.[43] Such qualitative evaluations had stuck, and it had been no more than thirty years since Hegel had designated architecture, sculpture, painting, music, and poetry (in ascending order) as the arts "proceeding from the absolute Idea" and whose role it was to offer the "sensuous representation of the absolute itself."[44] Any connection between idea and the crafts was noticeably absent. In one single move Semper had apparently denied centuries of efforts on the artists' part to align their work with that of poets and philosophers and allow it entry into the rarefied Olympian world of the mind.

That Semper should connect architecture to the crafts was central to his provocative thesis. But the challenge he set his contemporaries did not lie in his bringing together architecture and the decorative arts into one discussion, for as we have seen, such an angle was no longer a novelty at this time. What *was* revolutionary was Semper's decided view that a monumental art such as architecture had evolved its formal vocabulary and meaning from the objects of daily use, or *Kunstindustrie,* which "had reached a high level before architecture as an independent art had even been thought of."[45] As he described it, his purpose in writing this treatise was straightforward: convinced that the present had lost its artistic drive and was witnessing a decline, he wished to intervene and identify the fundamental laws of art so as to offer some guidance for the development of an art of the future.[46] His contribution, he claimed, lay in the fact that, unlike his peers, he was not interested in art as a product but as a process, that he sought the "how" not the "what" of artistic endeavour. It is for this reason, Semper concluded, that he could open up a new avenue for inquiry and offer something useful for the present dilemma.

In its way this ambition was not new. Ever since architects had put pen to paper, from Vitruvius through Filarete to Palladio and beyond, they had all held a melancholy view of the present and offered their efforts as a potential remedy. Yet it is from here that Semper's unique thesis really took off. In his view—and he expresses this forcefully in the Prolegomena to the work—it was in the objects of daily use, in what he called the technical arts (jewelry, arms, pots, textiles, and other household wares) that the instinct for art first manifested itself; it was in this modest domain of small-scale objects that the elemental forms-as-symbols were conceived; and it was therefore here that the foundational laws of art were most clearly revealed, and, consequently, should be sought.[47] Like nature, he argued, art draws on very few form types ("root forms," or *Normalformen,* embedded in these small artifacts); even if these forms suffer endless variation and subsequent enrichment, they remain present at the symbolic, formal, and technical level in all subsequently developed (high or monumental) arts.[48] And, he continued, if the contemporary situation is to be bettered, then the level of the artistic sensibility of the people (*Volk*) must be raised, for it is the *Kunstindustrie* that it produces and consumes that lies at the root of a healthy monumental art.

The idea to associate the crafts with architecture into one meta-art had been already mooted in Germany as elsewhere. And the term *Kunstindustrie*—what was to become the rallying cry for the Central European version of the Arts and Crafts movement—was already in use in the eighteenth century.[49] As we have seen, the issue was present and developed in Philip Moritz's work, which owed both to the philosophical environment in Berlin and to the architectural discourse developing around Schinkel. Another Schinkel student, Carl Bötticher—more widely published than Moritz and far better known—had picked up this thread several decades later and included it in a work that became a principal reference point for classical-minded architects.[50] His *Tektonik der Hellenen* (1846–52) also presented strong similarities to Semper's ideas and was contemporary with his early writings. Whether and how much Bötticher had influenced Semper (despite

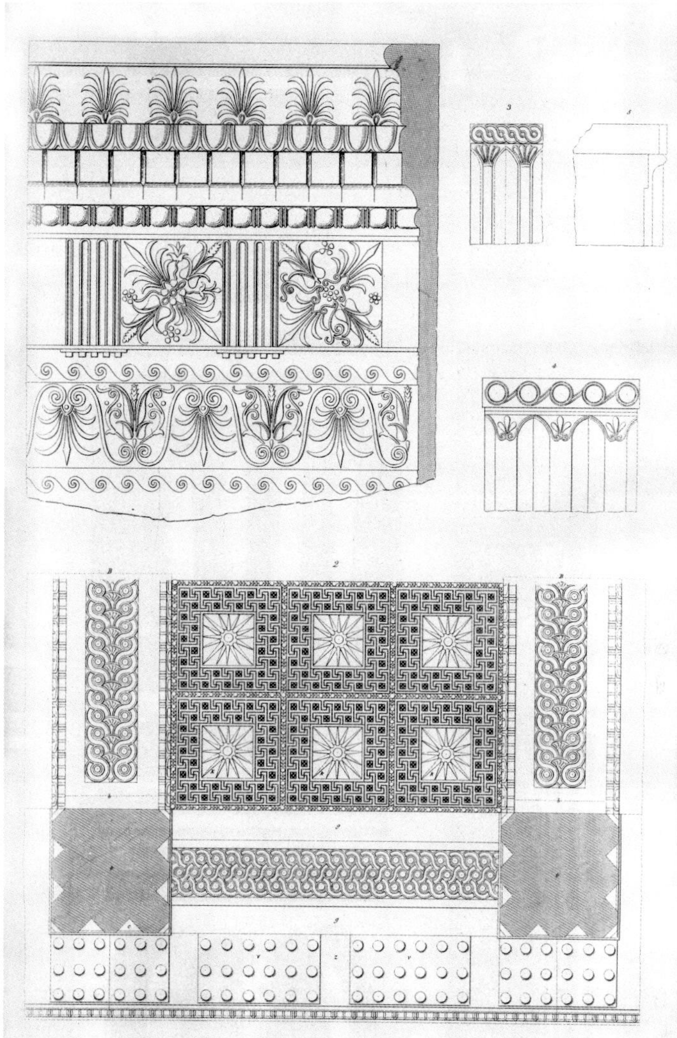

FIGURE 19
Karl Gottlieb Wilhelm Bötticher. Architectural details. From *Die Tektonik der Hellenen*, vol. 3 (1852 ed.).

much antagonism on the latter's part) is not important in this context.[51] What is important is that Bötticher's celebrated work represented a sympathetic "chorus" to Semper's more revolutionary peal. Like Moritz, Bötticher was also involved with the education of craftsmen before he turned to architecture. His publications of the 1830s and 1840s had been on model books of ornament "for fabricators and artists" and accompanied his teaching first at the Royal Prozellan-Manufaktur and then at the Berlin Gewerbe Institut.[52] Moreover, his earliest published work had been on textile ornament. Not surprisingly perhaps, in his principal and most influential work, *Tektonik,* he also looked to carpets as sources for wall and ceiling treatments (fig. 19). Likewise, his tectonic analyses extended to objects and instruments to which he applied the same analogies ("bildliche Formensprache") as he did to architecture: a core form (*Kernform*) that was materially conditioned

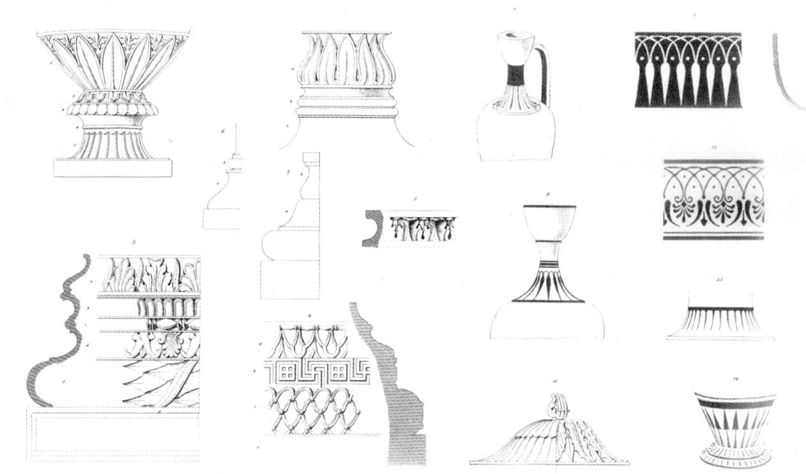

(as well as functionally) and an artistic form (*Kunstform*) that enveloped it (fig. 20). For Bötticher *Kunstform* was synonymous with ornament.[53] Yet despite numerous similarities to Semper's ideas—their focus on materials (stone in Bötticher's case) as the determinant to form, on the eloquence of assemblages and especially joints (*Junktur*), their phenomenological reading of form, and their concentration on ornament—Bötticher's work remained tied to the Greek ideal and the Schinkel school and less to that new and heterogeneous world that had been the eye-opening moment of the great exhibitions. Less expansive, Bötticher did not venture outside his discipline to import ideas and methods from neighboring fields. And despite his influence on contemporary archaeologists, he did not go out to dig or see for himself, and it was many years after the publication of his work that he first set foot in Greece.[54] Yet, even if less radical than Semper, Bötticher provided readers with a context (vocabulary and ideas) within which Semper's more radical positions could be understood.

SYMBOLS, ORNAMENT, AND OBJECTS

How does Semper set out to convince his readers of his contentious thesis? His entire theoretical edifice rests on the critical link he makes between *Kunstindustrie,* ornament, and architecture. Indeed, he had already gone as far as to equate them in his opening address at Zurich (published in 1856): "The Greek word for building means also adorning, a similar double meaning as that of the previously noted term cosmos. The wall-hanging, the crown, and that nameless ornament that marks direction, are the most important symbols that Greek architecture uses so as to attain the suggestive. These do not have their immediate origins in nature, but almost exclusively in the ornaments that adorn the human body."[55]

FIGURE 20
Karl Gottlieb Wilhelm Bötticher. Column base and vase details. From *Die Tektonik der Hellenen.*

The objects of daily use were heavily adorned, he argues: "Luxury dwelt in huts, tents, and crude mounds; the arts were far advanced in their application to adornment, weapons, implements, and vessels many thousands of years before the monuments were built." And this adornment, which was at one and the same time "in harmony with the law of nature" and heavily dependent on the materials and fabrication techniques used, became formal archetypes (*Urmotifs*), a collective memory of forms and the source of architectural ornament.[56]

Consistent with his statement in the Prolegomena that process is more revealing than the finished product, Semper attributes great significance to the technical aspect of the early *Kunstindustrie*—the materials, their manipulation, the tools involved in their fabrication—and to the functional needs it responded to. Indeed, he titles this section of his introduction "Every Technical Product a Result of Its Function and Material." Yet he is careful to deny (quite vehemently) that he is proposing a purely materialistic reading of art. Material and function are key criteria for him, but he sees them as inextricably intertwined with symbol.[57] For example, the swelling belly of a clay pot is functional inasmuch as it is meant to hold liquids; yet, Semper argues, this predominant form to which spout, handle, and so forth are subordinated and reinforce, also symbolically signifies or represents its function.[58] According to him, then, an inquiry into the function/symbol relationship in objects is necessarily ahistorical because it refers to basic human needs and gestures that do not change over time, and it lies therefore in the domain of formal/aesthetic investigation. The materials and instruments, however, change over time and therefore belong to the history of style.[59] This, he notes, is the accompanying historical thread of his argument.

From this starting point Semper proceeds to follow both threads. But materials remain the backbone of this prehistory of architecture. And he divides them according to their physical properties into four categories from "flexible, viscous" through "brittle" to "solid," which translates into the sections of his treatise: textile arts, ceramics, carpentry, metalwork, and stereotomy, thus moving from woven fabrics across clay pots and furniture to architecture.[60] There is an important historical sequence at work here as well, since Semper presents a progression from the first material, used in response to the basic primitive needs of shelter, body-covering, fire/hearth, and so forth, to more complex ones. As elemental human needs do not change (this is the ahistorical thread of his argument) even though materials do, later generations, he argues, necessarily adapt a received formal language to new materials. This theory of translation from one material to another is fundamental to his argument.[61] According to his thesis, the properties and handling of each material generate specific forms just as much as the function of the objects and leave indelible traces on the form of objects. More specifically, it is the ornament that retains these traces, carrying them from one

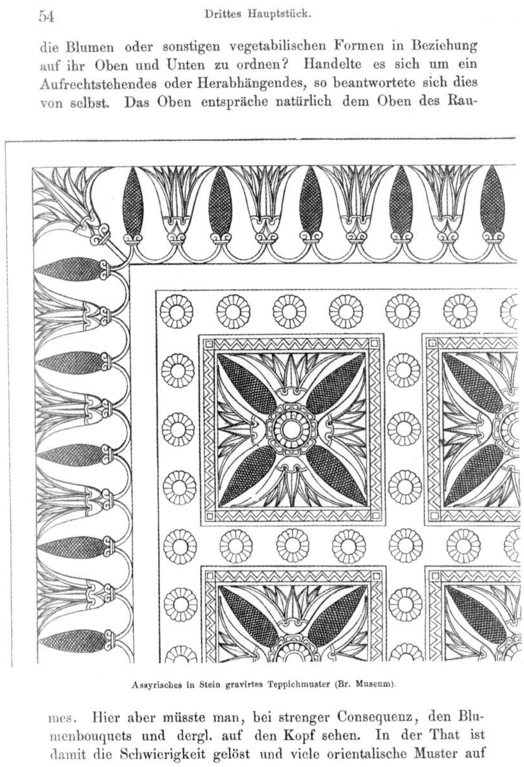

54 Drittes Hauptstück.

die Blumen oder sonstigen vegetabilischen Formen in Beziehung auf ihr Oben und Unten zu ordnen? Handelte es sich um ein Aufrechtstehendes oder Herabhängendes, so beantwortete sich dies von selbst. Das Oben entspräche natürlich dem Oben des Rau-

Assyrisches in Stein gravirtes Teppichmuster (Br. Museum).

mes. Hier aber müsste man, bei strenger Consequenz, den Blumenbouquets und dergl. auf den Kopf sehen. In der That ist damit die Schwierigkeit gelöst und viele orientalische Muster auf

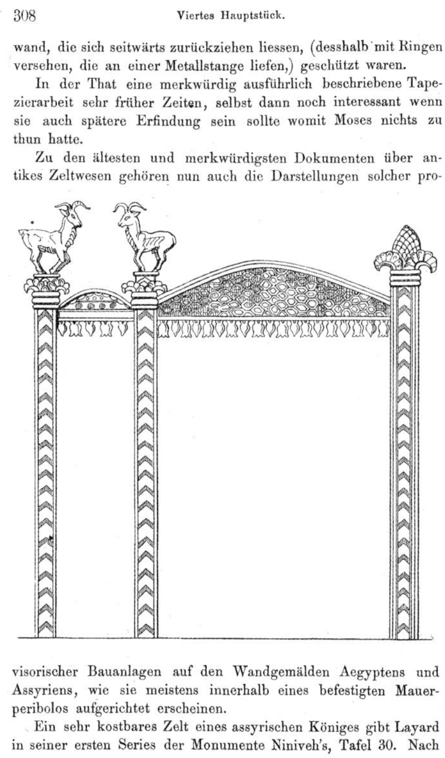

308 Viertes Hauptstück.

wand, die sich seitwärts zurückziehen liessen, (desshalb mit Ringen versehen, die an einer Metallstange liefen,) geschützt waren.

In der That eine merkwürdig ausführlich beschriebene Tapezierarbeit sehr früher Zeiten, selbst dann noch interessant wenn sie auch spätere Erfindung sein sollte womit Moses nichts zu thun hatte.

Zu den ältesten und merkwürdigsten Dokumenten über antikes Zeltwesen gehören nun auch die Darstellungen solcher provisorischer Bauanlagen auf den Wandgemälden Aegyptens und Assyriens, wie sie meistens innerhalb eines befestigten Mauerperibolos aufgerichtet erscheinen.

Ein sehr kostbares Zelt eines assyrischen Königes gibt Layard in seiner ersten Series der Monumente Niniveh's, Tafel 30. Nach

Left **FIGURE 21**
Gottfried Semper, "Stone-Engraved Assyrian Carpet Pattern." From Semper, *Der Stil in den technischen und tektonischen Künsten* (1878 ed.).

Right **FIGURE 22**
Gottfried Semper, "Royal Assyrian Tent." From *Der Stil.*

material to another, laden with layers of memory in the manner of a palimpsest. And it is these layers that Semper proceeds to recover.

How does this theory of metamorphosis across materials affect Semper's reading of architecture? Setting himself up against a formidable text chain that went back to Vitruvius and that had argued more or less consistently that architecture had arisen from the translation of the primitive hut's wooden structural system of columns and beams into marble, he argues that textiles had in fact lain at the origin of building.[62] This was also a deliberate attack on another current, positivist theory on the origins of architectural forms that sought them in the nature of stone itself. Probably with a deliberate swipe at Bötticher, who championed the latter (and whose *Tektonik der Hellenen* he had read in 1852 with much benefit if not always with approval) and at Viollet-le-Duc, who vehemently supported the former in his *Entretiens* of 1863, Semper labeled this theory a "crass materialist conception."[63] Instead, he proposes that the wall enclosure (arising from the basic need to shelter the body) was the baseline from which architecture and its language of signs had evolved, not the structural system of columns and beams, and that the archetypal "wall" had been textile.[64] For him the unmediated transposition of a utilitarian building into stone columnar architecture, which had been the cornerstone of the Vitruvian theory, was an impossibility (fig. 21).[65]

In Semper's view, the fundamental meaning or symbol embedded in the vocabulary of architecture was shelter and covering—or, his new term, dressing (*Bekleidung*)—not support (that is, not the columns).[66] In truth, this behavioral and proto-anthropological reading owed to Vitruvius as well, though to another passage (2: 1–4). Here Vitruvius had described the origin of building as the result of a need for shelter and the sociable nature of man. Even the reference to textiles was embedded in this vignette: "imitating the nests of swallows" men "wove their walls" (*parietas texerunt*), he had stated. The story had not passed unnoticed, but it was Vitruvius's description of the origin of columnar architecture that had had the longest half-life. Semper not only rejected this cherished theory but in so doing also set himself squarely against the tradition that privileged the column and saw the wall as infill.[67] The original temple had been an enclosure, a room, not a colonnade, he argued.[68] And to definitively set Vitruvius on his head he offered a different version of the paradigmatic primitive hut. For him the hut had in fact been a tent: Moses' *Stiftshütte* ("the oldest and most famous magnificent tent"), which demonstrated a "new application of the dressing principle in the architecture of the earliest times, namely the dressing of the constructive parts of a building."[69] Columns and epistyles, he continued, were and still are covered with fabric for major feasts, and architectural ornament itself represented an "ancient petrifaction of veiling."[70] Indeed, the root forms employed in wood construction or tectonics predated architecture itself and had reached full expression in the pre-monumental period in the mobile objects of household use.[71] And to nail down the relationship between textiles and architecture he drew attention to the etymological link between the German words *Wand* (wall) and *Gewand* (fabric).[72]

A variety of dressing materials (*Bekleidungstoffe)* and their historical succession that Semper reviewed in parts 4 and 5—such as terra-cotta ornament on ancient temples,[73] stucco veneers,[74] upholstery, poured bronze, even clothing ("the art of vestments"),[75] all gathered under the rubric of architectural equipment[76]—confirmed that this desire to dress the structure survived across time and cultures (fig. 22).[77] The "Textrin," the primary art that had originally supplied draperies, carpets, and wall hangings as spatial dividers, informed later "carpet-like" treatments of the wall.[78] Thus painted wall hangings came to cover the walls of stoas and temple cellas inside and out. Semper drew on Richard Redgrave for this argument (whom he quoted at length), and on a newly invented material, wallpaper, to buttress his assertions. Redgrave's defense and explication of the meaning of wallpaper confirmed Semper's notion of the persistence of the principle of *Bekleidung* across the ages.[79]

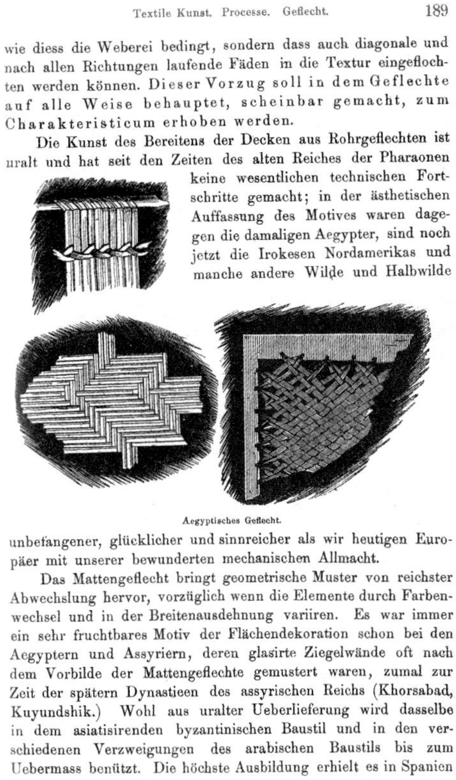
Textile Kunst. Processe. Geflecht. 189

wie diess die Weberei bedingt, sondern dass auch diagonale und nach allen Richtungen laufende Fäden in die Textur eingeflochten werden können. Dieser Vorzug soll in dem Geflechte auf alle Weise behauptet, scheinbar gemacht, zum Charakteristicum erhoben werden.

Die Kunst des Bereitens der Decken aus Rohrgeflechten ist uralt und hat seit den Zeiten des alten Reiches der Pharaonen keine wesentlichen technischen Fortschritte gemacht; in der ästhetischen Auffassung des Motives waren dagegen die damaligen Aegypter, sind noch jetzt die Irokesen Nordamerikas und manche andere Wilde und Halbwilde

Aegyptisches Geflecht.

unbefangener, glücklicher und sinnreicher als wir heutigen Europäer mit unserer bewunderten mechanischen Allmacht.

Das Mattengeflecht bringt geometrische Muster von reichster Abwechslung hervor, vorzüglich wenn die Elemente durch Farbenwechsel und in der Breitenausdehnung variiren. Es war immer ein sehr fruchtbares Motiv der Flächendekoration schon bei den Aegyptern und Assyriern, deren glasirte Ziegelwände oft nach dem Vorbilde der Mattengeflechte gemustert waren, zumal zur Zeit der spätern Dynastieen des assyrischen Reichs (Khorsabad, Kuyundshik.) Wohl aus uralter Ueberlieferung wird dasselbe in dem asiatisirenden byzantinischen Baustil und in den verschiedenen Verzweigungen des arabischen Baustils bis zum Uebermass benützt. Die höchste Ausbildung erhielt es in Spanien

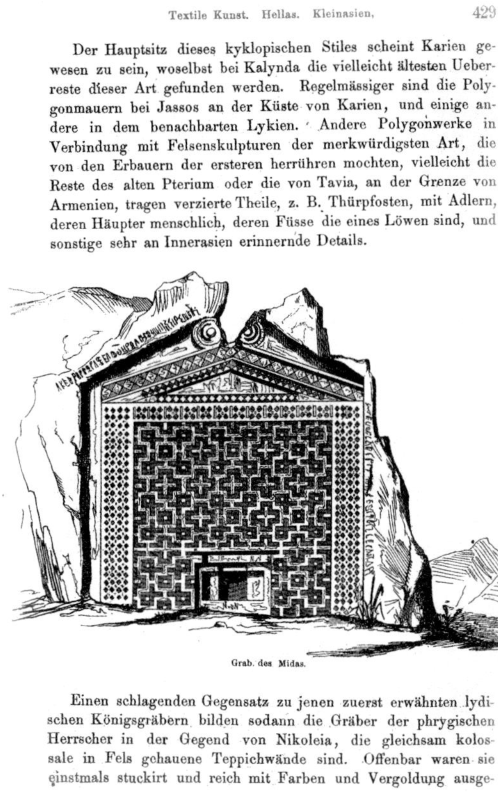
Textile Kunst. Hellas. Kleinasien. 429

Der Hauptsitz dieses kyklopischen Stiles scheint Karien gewesen zu sein, woselbst bei Kalynda die vielleicht ältesten Ueberreste dieser Art gefunden werden. Regelmässiger sind die Polygonmauern bei Jassos an der Küste von Karien, und einige andere in dem benachbarten Lykien. Andere Polygonwerke in Verbindung mit Felsenskulpturen der merkwürdigsten Art, die von den Erbauern der ersteren herrühren mochten, vielleicht die Reste des alten Pterium oder die von Tavia, an der Grenze von Armenien, tragen verzierte Theile, z. B. Thürpfosten, mit Adlern, deren Häupter menschlich, deren Füsse die eines Löwen sind, und sonstige sehr an Innerasien erinnernde Details.

Grab. des Midas.

Einen schlagenden Gegensatz zu jenen zuerst erwähnten lydischen Königsgräbern bilden sodann die Gräber der phrygischen Herrscher in der Gegend von Nikoleia, die gleichsam kolossale in Fels gehauene Teppichwände sind. Offenbar waren sie einstmals stuckirt und reich mit Farben und Vergoldung ausge-

Left **FIGURE 23**
Gottfried Semper, "Egyptian Wickerwork." From *Der Stil.*

Right **FIGURE 24**
Gottfried Semper, "The Tomb of Midas." From *Der Stil.*

However, according to Semper, not only the symbolic function but also the symbolism associated with the materials and their manipulation survived in the formal vocabulary of architecture. Consistent with his thesis on the transpositions of materials, he argued that the fabrication techniques of the original textile wall enclosures—thatching, weaving, knotting, and so forth—remained embedded in the collective memory of building as "dressing the walls" ("Bekleiden der Wände") and informed the later stone progeny, which ranged from mosaics, incrustations, and stucco to actual relief carving (fig. 23).[80] For example, he showed that textile reminiscences could be found in sculpted and carved details. And, to justify his overarching argument about the origin of forms in the textile art, he claimed that the more plastic ornamented Doric was the older, archaic form of the order, not the simpler, painted Doric, as many scholars (whom he ridicules) claimed.[81]

Dressing and dressing materials inevitably raised the issues of a core (*Kern*) and a surface (which Semper terms *Kunstform,* or artistic form), and of their respective relevance for the architectural vocabulary.[82] This was delicate terrain to tread for Semper, as it could have easily upset his thesis that privileged materials and fabrication in the development of form. Yet he offered a sophisticated, though somewhat forced, aesthetics-informed answer. Thus he admits that in antiquity the core materials remained hidden (such as wood covered by stucco veneer) and were not acknowledged as such on the surface, nor were they used as decoration. Yet he notes that, paradoxically, ancient authors like Pliny or Pausanias passed over the surface materials in their descriptions of architecture, noting only the core/*Kern*. This was so precisely because the core was essential for the development of an artistic outer form (*Kunstform*) that elevated it above materiality and at the same time denied it.[83] Ornament (the outer layer) was thus fundamentally and positively representational.

As he had planned, Semper did not stop at textiles. Perhaps the greatest strength of his argument lay in its systematic quality. As he presented it, materials, fabrication, and symbolism translated across centuries, nations, and habits, from simple to complex and from utilitarian to monumental, in a smooth and almost linear sequence leading from ancient Mycenae and Assyria through Egypt to Paestum and to the Renaissance and beyond (fig. 24). Each material, he claimed, caused a particular archetypal form to come into being. Thus in volume 2 (1863), in which he looked at increasingly "dense" or "hard" materials (clay, wood, metal, stone), Semper identified a surprising chain reaction that led from textiles to clay pots to carved capitals and that enabled him to account for the development and invention of all architectural forms. Whereas volume 1 laid out the basic premises of his work and developed the concept of dressing that underpinned it, this volume (though often traversing the same ground) moved faster through the materials and contained the historical *demonstranda*.

As he had done for textiles, Semper showed not only that the fabrication and physical properties of clay, metal, wood, and stone carried through historically from necessity to ornament, he also identified formal archetypes specific to each material. For example, in volume 1 he identified the principle of binding to be textile related, and the band, ribbon, and belt its characteristic forms (fig. 25).[84] And he argued that these forms, complete with their meaning, survived as ornament in the ancient stone column bases. Similarly, he identified the origins of the Corinthian capital in the "clay pot style."[85] And to remain consistent with his theory of a historical succession of materials and production methods, he argued—again *contra* tradition—that the Corinthian order was as old as, if not older than, the Doric and Ionic.[86] In volume 2 he went even further in identifying the *Kunstindustrie* as the embryo of monumental art when he observed that the "fundamental laws of all Egyptian architecture seem to be contained in embryonic form in the Nile pitcher; no less striking is the kinship between

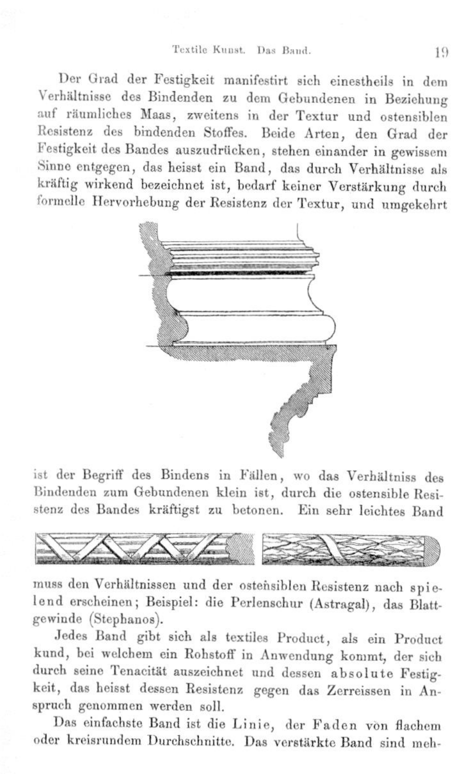

Der Grad der Festigkeit manifestirt sich einestheils in dem Verhältnisse des Bindenden zu dem Gebundenen in Beziehung auf räumliches Maas, zweitens in der Textur und ostensiblen Resistenz des bindenden Stoffes. Beide Arten, den Grad der Festigkeit des Bandes auszudrücken, stehen einander in gewissem Sinne entgegen, das heisst ein Band, das durch Verhältnisse als kräftig wirkend bezeichnet ist, bedarf keiner Verstärkung durch formelle Hervorhebung der Resistenz der Textur, und umgekehrt ist der Begriff des Bindens in Fällen, wo das Verhältniss des Bindenden zum Gebundenen klein ist, durch die ostensible Resistenz des Bandes kräftigst zu betonen. Ein sehr leichtes Band muss den Verhältnissen und der ostensiblen Resistenz nach spielend erscheinen; Beispiel: die Perlenschur (Astragal), das Blattgewinde (Stephanos).

Jedes Band gibt sich als textiles Product, als ein Product kund, bei welchem ein Rohstoff in Anwendung kommt, der sich durch seine Tenacität auszeichnet und dessen absolute Festigkeit, das heisst dessen Resistenz gegen das Zerreissen in Anspruch genommen werden soll.

Das einfachste Band ist die Linie, der Faden von flachem oder kreisrundem Durchschnitte. Das verstärkte Band sind meh-

FIGURE 25
Gottfried Semper, "Fixed Band Ornament." From *Der Stil.*

the hydria and certain form-types of the Doric style. Both forms are prophetic of what architecture invented as it sought to express the natures of both people in monumental form."[87]

In subsequently analyzing the pot and its parts in detail, Semper identified innate principles of assemblage and form-making that remained present in subsequent architectural connections and that went beyond the specific function and symbolism of the objects themselves.[88] For example, he argued, the relationship between the belly of the pot and the spout, base, and handle codified principles of assemblage that would be taken up in architecture. Thus he not only identified a common thesaurus of forms that tied pottery to architecture but he argued that the basic laws governing form-making and the relationship between parts were identical for the two arts.[89] The same was true of spoons, candelabra, armoires, and chairs, all of which revealed and bequeathed formal and symbolic features to architecture, he concluded.

In short, for Semper the decorative arts, or *Kunstindustrie,* lay at the root of all architectural forms and even explained the polychromy of ancient temples, a recent but painful thorn in the side of most archaeologists and architectural historians.[90] In fact, for him polychromy added more useful grist to the mill since in his view paint application on architecture was a form of "dressing." What had

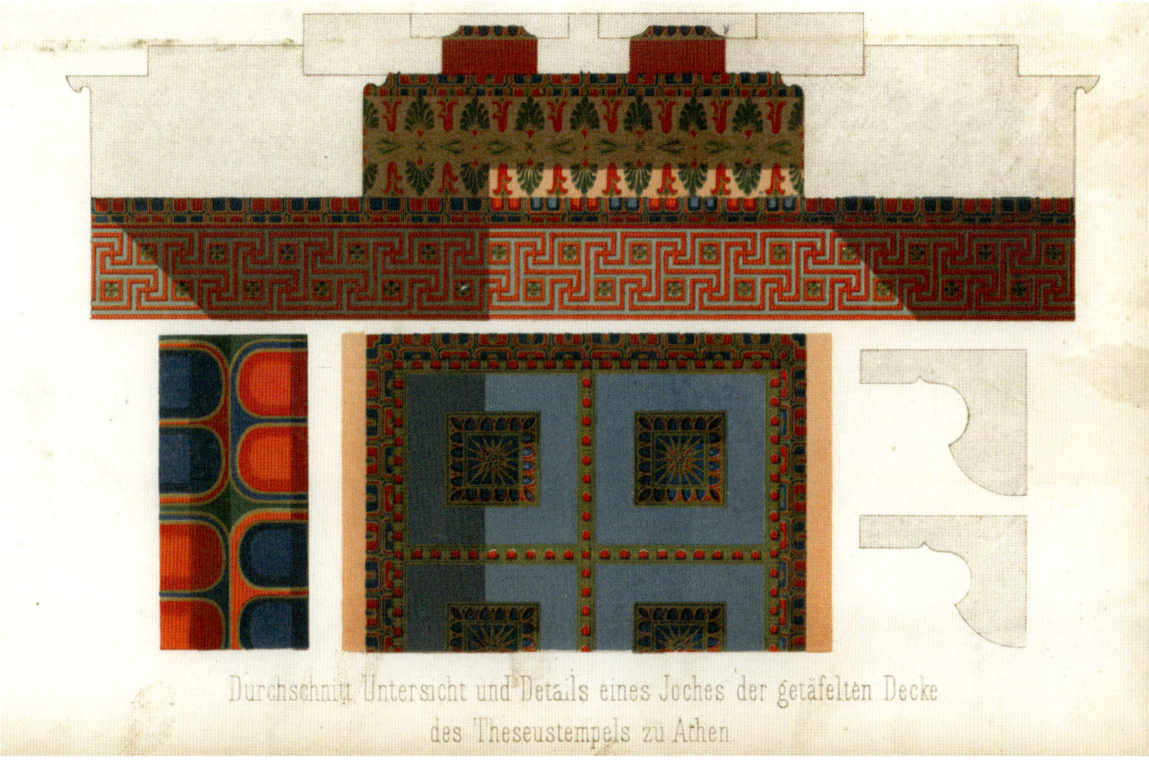

seemed an aberration to those upholding the neoclassical view of a white and pristine ancient architecture had actually been Semper's starting point. Studying in Paris in 1826–30 in the studio of the German Franz Christian Gau he had become acquainted with the new discoveries on polychrome ancient architecture published both by Gau in 1822 and more famously by Jakob Ignaz Hittorff beginning in 1830, a literature to which he also contributed thereafter.[91] Inexplicable from a Winckelmannian perspective, polychromy allowed Semper—who had examined the ruins and discovered more traces of color during his extended archaeological trip through Italy, Sicily, and Greece in 1830–33—to begin developing his theory of layers. Thus in the chapter on carpentry (tectonics) he could argue that wood required *Bekleidung* through painting because it could otherwise not withstand the elements, and he drew on ancient Greek through old Germanic and even Tartar examples to illustrate the universal application of this principle (fig. 26).[92] He used the same argument for all revetments from stucco, through mosaic and gilding. Such was the importance of polychromy for him that he had intended to title his *Four Elements of Architecture* (1851) "On Polychromy and Its Origin." Such a synthetic explanation was no mean achievement since those upholding the traditional model of the structural origin of architecture could not explain polychromy, and this is why the contention that the marble architecture of the

FIGURE 26
Gottfried Semper, details of polychrome Greek architecture. From *Der Stil.*

Greeks had in fact been heavily painted caused something of a scholarly scandal when it was first mooted. Conversely, for Semper, architectural polychromy was the linchpin of his argument and the very starting point of his inquiry, its presence the very question he had set out to answer.[93]

STYLE AND MATERIALS

If the importance of *Kunstindustrie* for the arts was one red thread of Semper's treatise, the other was certainly his concentration on the concept of style, as the title—*Der Stil*—already clearly proclaimed. Indeed, what was particularly interesting was that the two themes were tightly interwoven, and their handling equally unorthodox. That Semper should title his treatise *Der Stil* was not altogether surprising. The issue of style for architecture was a hotly debated one at the time, and had been for a good half century. Public exchanges such as the one initiated by Heinrich Hübsch in 1825 and provocatively titled *In What Style Should We Build?* had set the stage for an interest in architectural style as topic.[94] As framed both by Hübsch and in the debates that proliferated subsequently (notorious among them being Pugin's campaign for Gothic in British ecclesiastical architecture and later the Battle of Styles), the issue was historical style—that is, not so much the origins of style and its definitions as a critical category for architecture, but the choice of appropriate garb for the many new building types emerging and the new materials in which they were being built.[95]

Semper's take was rather different. He sought neither to offer guidance in selecting the correct style from the collective historical closet nor to identify and discuss personal style or even a modern period style, as art historians would.[96] In fact, he was rather dismissive about the latter method.[97] Consistent with his project to identify first principles, he sought the archetype (or *Urmotif*) where the "basic idea that pervades the composition like a theme" was first perceivable.[98] For him this was the fountainhead of style. And, not surprisingly, in his view these begetters of style were to be found in the *Kunstindustrie*.[99] Already in 1852 he had stated as much in "Wissenschaft, Industrie und Kunst." If, he had argued, style "means giving emphasis and artistic significance to the basic idea and to all intrinsic and extrinsic coefficients that modify the embodiment of the theme in a work of art," and "in the same way the technical arts are also based on certain archetypal forms as the simplest expression of the idea," then logically it follows that the "basic form" is to be found in these objects of daily use.[100]

As we have seen, Semper saw two principal aspects to the theory of style: a historical thread (which he allowed to be the province of the art historian) and a technical one.[101] It is this latter aspect of style that lay closest to his heart, for it was intimately connected with materials and fabrication techniques. For him these were fundamental for the forms of the *Kunstindustrie*, and hence necessarily determinant components of style. The Great Exhibition and the deployment of new materials and processes displayed there had drawn his attention to the theory of materials and fabrication as originators of style. Its sheer scale and the heterogeneous variety of exhibits raised the issue into the consciousness of architects and designers in a way that no event had done before. To be sure, Semper's revolutionary approach was in keeping with his politics and life history, full of twists and turns, exiles and returns, caused by his combative nature if not always by his revolutionary leanings.[102] But if his character was one of the causes behind his maverick position, the other—as he proclaimed from the very first pages of *Der Stil*—was the 1851 London Great Exhibition, which carried deeper methodological seeds.[103] As early as 1852, Semper had argued that "basic form, as the simplest expression of the idea, is modified in particular by the materials that are used in developing the form as well as by the tools that fashion it."[104] In the more developed argument in *Der Stil,* statements on the impact of materials on style are frequent, turning up almost by the way, so imbued of its self-evidence is the whole demonstration.[105]

However, despite this excess of means showcased in London (or perhaps because of it), the technical theory of style still presented difficulties for Semper at this point. If historically he could posit a connection between, say, cloth and enclosure, the relationship between materials, means of production (crafting), and artifact in the present could only be posed since no clear directions could be discerned as yet. Indeed, this concern with the present conditions fueled much of Semper's work. Since, he observed, the mechanical fabrication of objects was geared toward mimicking the work of the hand, it produced shams; form and ornament did not record the passage of tools, and their encounter with the nature of the material (hard, soft, rigid, malleable, and so forth), but had lost all meaning. Not surprising therefore, he argued, that modern art was in such a sorry state, unable to evolve a genuine style of its own. To drive home his point he turned to a traditional material and asked: "How should we treat granite now?" His concern was clear: when all manner of modern machinery can be employed to cut, carve, and turn, even to perforate it into forms unthinkable to the stonecutter, it could lose its material significance (durability, massiveness), in which "resides its magic."[106] Semper leveled a similar criticism at the Thonet bentwood products (vol. 2) and berated modern industry for using machines to make materials behave in unnatural ways, thus sacrificing their "intrinsic meaning."[107] Even more interesting, Semper also looked at very new materials, wondering what that "intrinsic meaning" might be; in fact, they had been the ones that forced him to pose the question at all. Thus in a long aside, he turned to rubber, which fascinated him and to which he devoted three sections of chapter 1, in which he prophetically anticipated its use as roofing membrane.[108]

Of course Semper did not ignore what he called "influences extrinsic to the work of art," that is, the local, temporal, and personal features operative in its making. This is his third component of style. Climate, available materials, tradition, local culture, and the patron are such external variables. In a throwback to his youthful political leanings, he was also concerned with their manifestation as market forces, speculation, and abundance of means. A capitalist market system and fashion, he observed, played against the artist's initiative and essentially paralyzed the unfolding of the "internal" aspects of style.[109] And with acute foresight that anticipated Adolf Loos's *Ornament and Crime* he asked: "When does the depreciation of materials brought about by the machine, by their surrogates, and by so many new inventions lead us? What effect will the depreciation of labor... have on the painted, sculpted and other kinds of decorative work?"[110]

ANTHROPOLOGY AND THE PRIMITIVE

Semper had claimed to leave the history of style in the care of art historians, yet much of his argument was nevertheless concerned with it, and in truth hinged on it, as Alois Riegl was to observe (and mercilessly criticize) three decades later in his *Problems of Style* (1893).[111] To demonstrate that woven or molded forms survived in the ornament of monumental art was after all dependent on a historical analysis. The Great Exhibition had offered him the means to make that analysis. Semper was quick to express his enthusiasm in his 1852 essay: "What rich material for its (history of style) comparison and reflection offered the London Exhibition by the works already noted by people still living in the earlier stages of cultural development."[112] And in this endeavor the new science of anthropology offered much help.

As has been often noted in the scholarly literature, anthropology was a significant dimension for Semper in two complementary ways: in focusing attention on the manipulation of materials (as diagnostic artistic behavior) and on the primitive as origin of "deep" patterns.[113] Indeed, what was most striking in Semper's theory of style was that, despite this socioeconomic dimension in his agenda, it was the hand of the maker that remained the "most powerful external agent" for him as the mediator between material and fabrication.[114] This was not the same hand of the artist that had been associated with style at least since Giorgio Vasari by art critics eager to identify the idiosyncrasies of a particular artistic personality.[115] Instead, Semper's interest was consistent with his opening statement in the introduction where he had announced that, unlike art historians, he was seeking to analyze artistic process, not the end product. In order to offer a workable solution to the distressing deterioration of the arts, he argued, the very root of artistic *behavior* and its role in the development of form had to

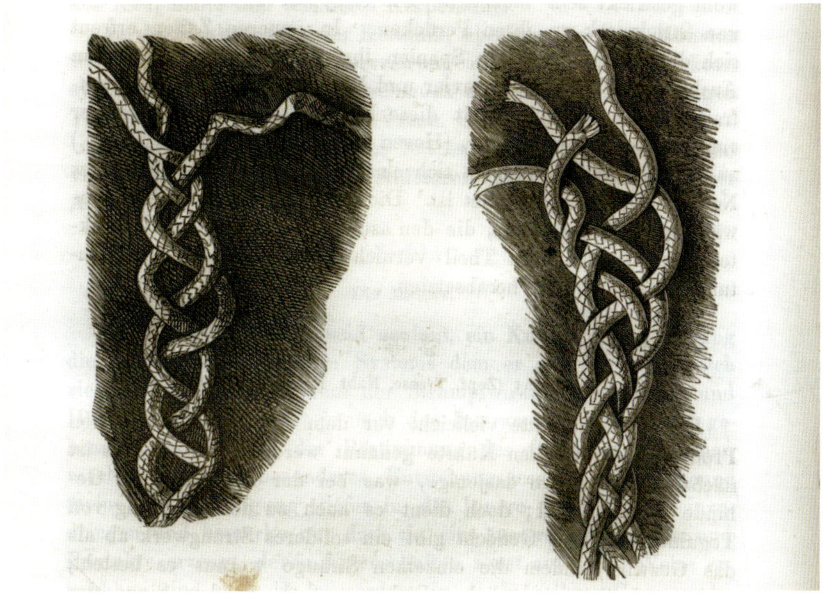

be explored—hence his emphasis on making and its agent, the artisan's hand. His project was essentially anthropological in its ambition, and as such offered a new direction for art and architectural history.[116]

This is not to say that Semper did not pay heed to the current notion, available to him from art historians like Rumohr and others, of a fundamental artistic "idea."[117] But even this was transformed by an anthropological slant: in his view the "idea" issued from a deep-seated human urge to ornament, and it was reified through manipulation of specific materials. And he developed an entire system of classification of the "technical arts" based on the physical properties of the materials they employ. As one type of human manual dexterity led to another, so grew the obstacles posed by the increasingly demanding materials used. From the flexible thread of the weaver (category 1), through the soft and malleable clay of the potter (category 2) to the elastic and stick-shaped lumber of the carpenter (category 3) and the solid and dense stone of the mason (category 4), the primitive artisan developed forms and ornament in keeping with the nature of these materials and the manner of their manufacture.[118] Pressing, tying, stretching, bending are some of the elemental manipulations that corresponded to these materials and generated characteristic forms.[119] The knot and the veneer that resulted were just as significant in achieving the *Urformen* Semper was seeking as was the function-cum-symbol of containing (liquids, for a vessel) or sheltering (for fabrics and enclosures) (fig. 27).[120]

FIGURE 27
Gottfried Semper, "Plaits." From *Der Stil.*

Semper's early interest in the natural sciences, prehistoric archaeology and biology, that is, in the founding sciences of the new field of anthropology, lay at the root of this conception.[121] As is well-known, plant morphology and taxonomy as formulated by Georges Cuvier and evolutionary theories such as Darwin's had marked his thinking as well.[122] In this sense he participated in a larger trend, to which belonged Owen Jones, Richard Redgrave, and Christopher Dresser in England and Viollet-le-Duc in France, and that looked at the natural sciences (botany and anatomy in their case) in rethinking the relationship between architecture, ornament, and natural form.[123] Yet it was characteristic of Semper that the human dimension in this relationship should attract him more. Identifying the interaction between maker, raw materials, society, and object was after all his ultimate goal. Once again, Cuvier may have acted as a catalyst in the anthropological direction Semper took. In his work on the animal kingdom Cuvier had offered an analysis of the human hand that may have suggested to Semper how important the evolution of its functional ability would be for his own project.[124] Linguistics, another participating field in the creation of anthropology as a discipline, also attracted Semper's attention. Parallels between the etymological root of words and archetypes in the technical arts are among his favorite *comparanda*.[125] But it was archaeology and the recent excavation results from Nineveh and Nimrud (Assyria), Egypt and Persia by Paul-Émile Botta, Henry Layard, Pascal Coste, and Christian Lassen that filled in the gaps of prehistoric knowledge and provided Semper with the key insights for his work.[126] Indeed, archaeology was an important bridge between disciplines. Its early alliance with anthropology, on the one hand, and its traditional relationship to architecture, on the other, allowed a circulation of ideas across disciplinary boundaries. Semper's own experience with archaeology early in his career had opened the door for a real understanding of field work and of the significance of "things" dug up and assembled to make a vanished culture emerge from its ashes.[127] And as he was not seeking the epistemological underpinnings of art, and as anthropology was neither strictly archaeological, nor philosophical, it offered an appealing middle ground between positivism and speculation.

Semper's emphasis on the human hand was anthropologically conceived, and so was his choice of exempla (material culture, and especially objects related to household use and funerary rituals). Yet characteristically, his expansive approach to other fields of learning made him reach beyond evidence typically used in anthropological research, and also draw on palaeontology. For instance, he quotes Alexandre Brongniart's *Tableau des genres de végétaux fossiles* (1849) in arguing that clay objects offer evidence for the history of mankind similar to what fossils reveal about the history of the natural world (fig. 28).[128] Such a connection seemed self-evident to him, since he perceived art and architecture to be an extension of nature, obeying similar laws.

But beyond the focus on materials and their manipulation, Semper's concept of ornamentation as a basic human urge was also anthropologically conceived;

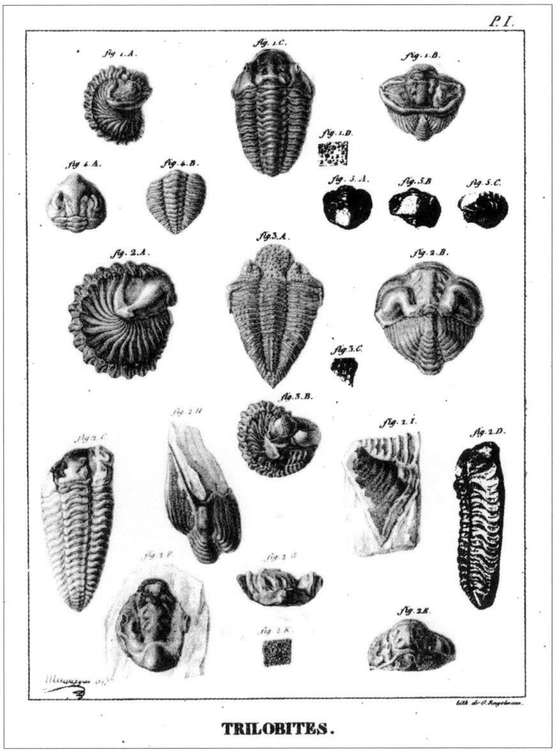

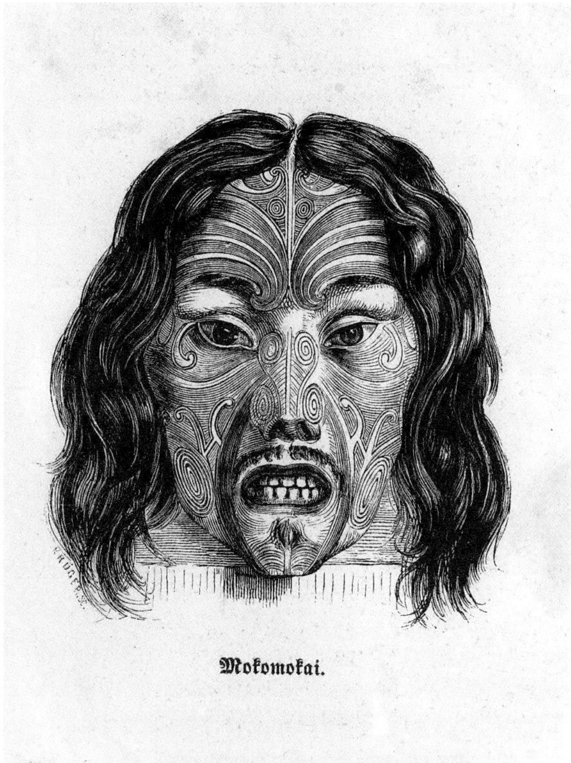

indeed, "taking pleasure in ornament," he argued, is so deeply seated in the human psyche that it extends beyond objects and includes the practice of tattooing, that is, the body itself. Once again Semper put on the theoretical map a concept that Adolf Loos would dramatically propel to attention in his classic *Ornament and Crime* nearly half a century later and that would lie at the root of Alois Riegl's *Kunstwollen*.[129] The tattoo was very present in contemporary texts as a sign of human nature's instinct to adorn what it prized—the body and those instruments with which it came into contact. In addition to the Great Exhibition, where Maori ornamentation came to prominence, Semper could have come across dramatic illustrations of the Maoris' exquisite tattoos in Gustav Klemm's multi-volume *Kulturgeschichte der Menschheit* (1843–52) even before coming to England (fig. 29).[130] Painting or coating buildings with veneers arises from the same instinct as body painting, Semper argued. And, in an effort to show the general validity of the pattern, he documented this basic human behavior among the peoples of New Guinea and New Zealand, as well as among the ancient Egyptians, even the Romans and the Greeks.[131] The same (proto-) anthropological approach is evident in the categories Semper establishes to classify the origins of shelter patterns evident in architecture. *Bekleidung* responds to the basic need to shelter the body; and the hearth, at the core of the shelter, both responds to and symbolizes this need.[132]

Left **FIGURE 28**
Alexandre Brongniart, "Trilobites." From *Histoire naturelle des crustacés fossiles, sous les rapports zoologiques et géologiques* (Paris, 1822). Harvard University, Museum of Comparative Zoology Special Collections.

Right **FIGURE 29**
Gustav Friedrich Klemm, "Mokomokai." From *Allgemeine Cultur-Geschichte der Menschheit* (Leipzig, 1843).

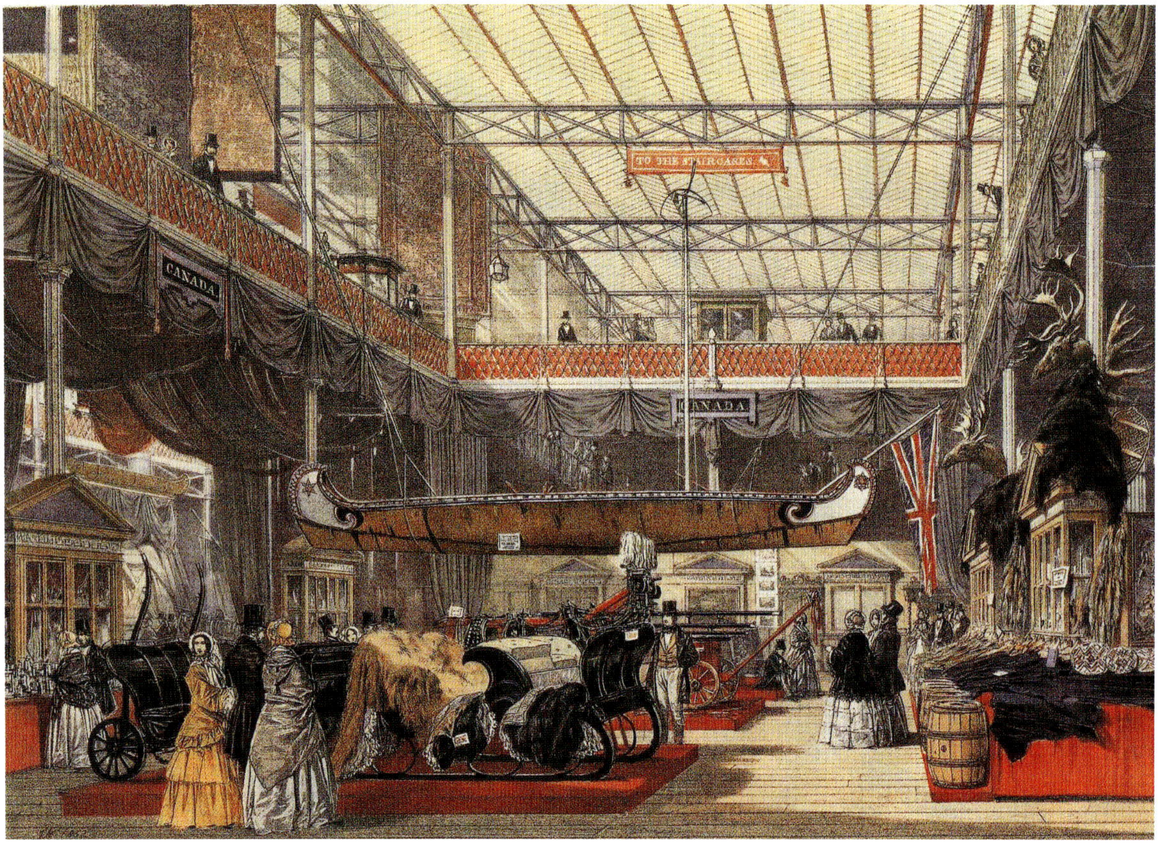

FIGURE 30
Canadian Exhibition in the Crystal Palace at London's Great Exhibition, 1851. From *Dickinson's Comprehensive Pictures of the Great Exhibition* (London, 1851). Color lithograph, 16½ × 22⅞ in. (42 × 58 cm).

Another strand that Semper followed in his rethinking of architecture along anthropological lines was the diagnostic value of primitive cultures. Not only had the Great Exhibition played a catalyst role in confronting Semper with the importance of the objects of daily consumption, it had also provided him with related clues about the history of artistic production. And these were offered by the so-called "primitive" peoples prominently displayed on this occasion. Clearly this was a watershed moment. Confrontation with the marvelous and alien of primitive cultures, which had been accessible before only through dangerous travel, was now available virtually as an armchair experience. The issue of the origins of culture was dramatically posed.

And for Semper, despite his interest in both anthropology and ethnology (as forms of archaeology) before his move to London, it was this encounter with living primitive forms that had opened genuinely new horizons. In charge of laying out several countries' displays, among which was Canada's, he had come into direct contact with "unspoilt" cultures that would subsequently become the "specimens" of classical anthropological research. His design for the Canadian exhibit, which privileged Indian-made artifacts such as the highly

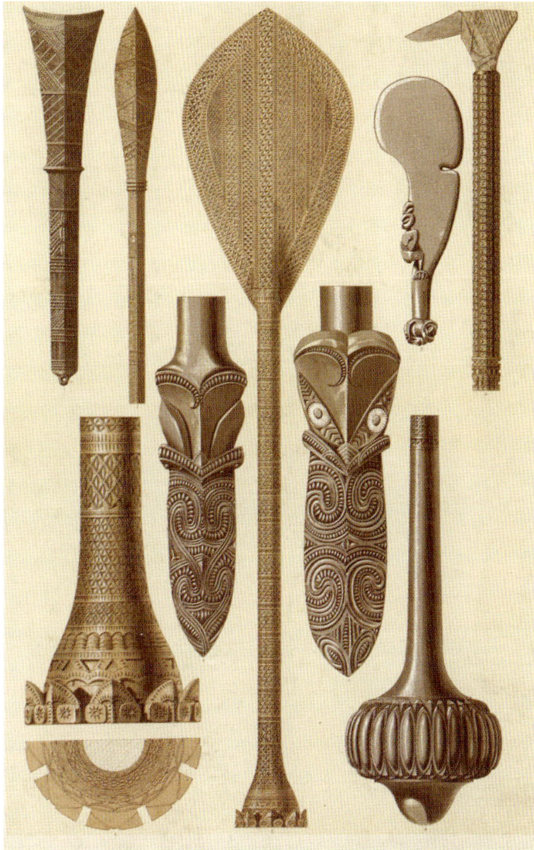

FIGURE 31
Owen Jones, "Ornament of Savage Tribes." From Jones, *The Grammar of Ornament* (1856).

ornamented canoes dramatically hung from the rafters, clearly showed his response to this intellectual challenge (fig. 30). The impact of this experience survived in *Der Stil*.[133] The mats, the carpets, and the tepees he had seen and on which he dwells at length in his book confirmed his theory of the primacy of the textile arts, just as the Maori tattoos confirmed the basic human urge to ornament.[134] For him, "barbaric" peoples ("people still living in the earlier stages of cultural development") and ancient archaic cultures counted as the same and illuminated one another. The arts of New Zealand were among Semper's favorite examples, as they showed in its "purest form" how weaving and braiding motifs metamorphosed into monumental art.[135] Observing the Maori and the North American Indian allowed him to "see that in ancient times, from the Assyrians to the Romans and later in the Middle Ages, the division and ornamentation of the wall, the principles of coloring, even the historical painting and floor decorations—in short, all related arts—remained dependent on the primordial motif, either consciously or unconsciously in a traditional way."[136] Similarly, they confirmed the importance and origins of polychromy (fig. 31).[137]

Ironically, although this confrontation of archaic and modern cultures at the Great Exhibition revealed the historical paths that styles had traveled, it also had a powerful ahistorical effect. Thus for Semper, contemporary "primitive" examples and ancient Ninevite, Assyrian, and Chinese ornamental forms spoke to the same truth documenting fundamental human drives that existed outside time.[138] They also laid the foundation of another powerful argument. If, as he argued, primitive cultures were the begetters of the archetypal forms that produced style, and if the modest object of everyday life contained the seeds of later monumental forms—that is, if style and its ignition mechanism were not to be sought in the work of the leading artists nor the high arts—the door was opened to an appreciation of the value of anonymous production and of popular art, or *Volkskunst*. Although Semper did not state this in so many words, his definition of style and his proselytizing for the education of the people, the *Volk,* as the true taproot of artistic energy in any culture could not be missed.

The connection between the primitive contemporary societies and folk art was itself embedded in the relationship between anthropology and another burgeoning science, ethnography (*Völkerkunde*). Whereas one was concerned with human practices in general terms, the other narrowed it down to those of specific cultures and sought their identities or cultural physiognomies. Semper drew on both and referred more than once to his experiences and to the insights he had gained in the ethnographic museums of London. Thus, when he introduced the spoon as example of an elemental crafted form he advanced an anthropological argument, but the evidence he drew on was ethnographic—that is, specific to a particular culture (Inuit and ancient inhabitants of Alaska, in this case).[139]

The subtle reference to a national identity residing in the objects of daily use could not have come up at a better time, and it led to a blossoming of national art museums throughout Europe. A moment of victory and assurance, the Great Exhibition had nevertheless precipitated a triple crisis: a crisis of history, a crisis of materials, and a crisis of fabrication. The effects of erasing history between ancient and contemporary primitive cultures, introducing new materials that made traditional ones obsolete, and triumphantly showcasing the potential of the machine vis-à-vis human labor touched architecture in its most sensitive spots. Out of them Semper crafted his unique theory of style in which, as we have seen, the making and the hand of the maker were central. The issue of style was a topical one, though certainly not new. For art historians it had been a basic periodization vehicle, at least since Giorgio Vasari's *Lives of the Artists* of 1550.[140] Personal style, regional style, and period style were categories that he first connected with the idea of progress in the arts. Yet in architecture the concept of style had a more complex history even than this, for Vasari himself had found the topic thorny. In the Renaissance, the columnar orders Doric, Ionic, Corinthian, and Tuscan were known by the same term: *maniere* (styles). By referring to Greek and Italic tribes they were implicitly associated with an ethnic and an ethnic-based rhetorical tradition rather than with personal artistic expression.[141] It can be argued that the principle was the same. Personal style was to the individual what the ethnic style embedded in the nomenclature of the orders was to the nation: an unself-conscious expression of its profoundest nature, an expression of its emotional and psychological stirrings. Yet if for Vasari's Tuscan compatriots there was an obvious gratification in following this route, there were only so many orders to go around, and other national definitions had been slow to emerge.

Moreover, the conception of an ethnic style in architecture opened up a Pandora's box of applications: if personal style could distinguish an artist from his contemporaries, and period style a historical moment from another, architectural style with its ethnic overtones could distinguish among nations. In the early modern period, attempts had been made, most notably by Philibert de l'Orme, to introduce a native order into sixteenth-century French architecture. Conversely, the use of the classical vocabulary in its Palladian or Vignolesque forms across Western Europe and the New World signaled participation in an elite classical internationalism. At a historical juncture such as the mid-nineteenth century, when nationalism and nation building (rebuilding and even inventing) were pan-European concerns, and would grow till the conflagration of the two world wars, this conception of style naturally developed apace and became absorbed into larger cultural histories and philosophies of history. Half a century later Oswald Spengler's *Untergang des Abendlandes* (1918, written over the previous ten years) was only the most extreme example of an effort to exploit the notion at the level of *Geistesgeschichte*. He identified the arts as the "symbol of the higher order, the visible manifestation of the style of a Culture" that encompassed art, religion, thought, and the "style of life itself." For him the task of art history was "to write the comparative biographies of the great styles"; it was also "something inaccessible to art-reason, a revelation of the metaphysical order, a mysterious 'must,' a Destiny."[142] Deeply indebted as Spengler was to the contemporary exaltation of the symbol, his concept of style nevertheless offered a snapshot of the threads that had gradually collected under this term/notion.[143]

But if the tendency in post-Hegelian German historical scholarship—of which Spengler is an exaggerated illustration—was to connect style to the increasingly rarefied worlds of the spirit and its emanations, for Semper style and its roots were to be found elsewhere. Granted, national spirit played a determining role for both. Yet for Semper style had a tangible and concrete origin in folk art. The term *Volkskunst* has been (wrongly) attributed to Riegl, yet the notion of its symptomatic nature and its distillation of a national artistic sensibility were already apparent in most of Semper's texts.[144] Indeed, he collected into one argument the Vitruvian wooden hut, the Caribbean primitive cabin, and the Bavarian Tyrolese farmhouse (which he illustrated exhaustively) (figs. 32, 33).[145] The frequency with which a nation was referred to as an individual by Semper and others ("the German," "the Englishman," and so on) is indicative of a larger trend to transfer the category of personal style onto the nation as a whole. *Kunstindustrie,* primitive cultures and folk art with their profound reliance on manual production, were thus prophetically tied by Semper into a single conception of style in which primitive became equated not so much with a lower position on the developmental totem pole but with the archetypes (*Urformen*) at the foundation of a vigorous monumental art.

ORNAMENT, DETAIL, AND THE HUMAN BODY

If connecting architecture with *Kunstindustrie* and style with the primitive were two significant contributions that Semper made to the architectural discourse at mid-century, an equally important third was his blending of ornament with the detail. While ornament could be construed as a detail, conversely, a detail did not necessarily have to be ornament. Modern architecture has amply demonstrated this. In a culture programmatically opposed to ornament, the detail flourished and garnered much attention in buildings and texts.[146] The enthusiastic reception in architectural circles of Warburg's quip that "Gott ist im Detail," to the point of obscuring its origin, is a testament to this fact. Whether a detail by Mies van der Rohe was indeed functioning as ornament remains a question to which we will return at the end of this book. But at the time, architects perceived the two as distinct. Yet the distinction was not always a sine qua non. In this, as in so many other issues, Semper constituted a turning point.

That the detail should rise in importance in Semper's œuvre was inevitable. His argument about the translation of fundamental craft-based forms across materials and their survival in the collective memory of building as decorative motifs long after the material necessity they responded to had disappeared, invited looking *in detail* and *at details.* As he tried to establish textile as the Ur-art, embedded in all subsequent art forms, he needed to look at details that connected walling and framing with binding and sewing, weaving and braiding, and with the band, seam, hem, and edging. If textiles, and later wickerwork and clay vessels, had set such patterns, their persistence had to be sought in wall treatments, joinery, and connections between parts, and not in plans, volumes, or building silhouettes.[147] In fact, it is a peculiarity of Semper's treatise that these latter issues never come up at all. Scale was critical for this argument. Since ornament was the place that recorded the imperceptible passage of forms from *Kunstindustrie* to architecture, Semper could not but pay attention to the small scale, that is,

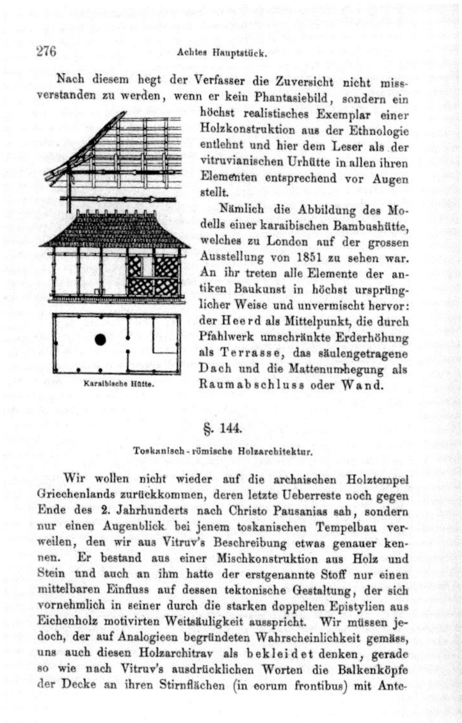

276 Achtes Hauptstück.

Nach diesem hegt der Verfasser die Zuversicht nicht missverstanden zu werden, wenn er kein Phantasiebild, sondern ein höchst realistisches Exemplar einer Holzkonstruktion aus der Ethnologie entlehnt und hier dem Leser als der vitruvianischen Urhütte in allen ihren Elementen entsprechend vor Augen stellt.

Karaibische Hütte.

Nämlich die Abbildung des Modells einer karaibischen Bambushütte, welches zu London auf der grossen Ausstellung von 1851 zu sehen war. An ihr treten alle Elemente der antiken Baukunst in höchst ursprünglicher Weise und unvermischt hervor: der Heerd als Mittelpunkt, die durch Pfahlwerk umschränkte Erderhöhung als Terrasse, das säulengetragene Dach und die Mattenumhegung als Raumabschluss oder Wand.

§. 144.

Toskanisch-römische Holzarchitektur.

Wir wollen nicht wieder auf die archaischen Holztempel Griechenlands zurückkommen, deren letzte Ueberreste noch gegen Ende des 2. Jahrhunderts nach Christo Pausanias sah, sondern nur einen Augenblick bei jenem toskanischen Tempelbau verweilen, den wir aus Vitruv's Beschreibung etwas genauer kennen. Er bestand aus einer Mischkonstruktion aus Holz und Stein und auch an ihm hatte der erstgenannte Stoff nur einen mittelbaren Einfluss auf dessen tektonische Gestaltung, der sich vornehmlich in seiner durch die starken doppelten Epistylien aus Eichenholz motivirten Weitsäuligkeit ausspricht. Wir müssen jedoch, der auf Analogieen begründeten Wahrscheinlichkeit gemäss, uns auch diesen Holzarchitrav als bekleidet denken, gerade so wie nach Vitruv's ausdrücklichen Worten die Balkenköpfe der Decke an ihren Stirnflächen (in eorum frontibus) mit Ante-

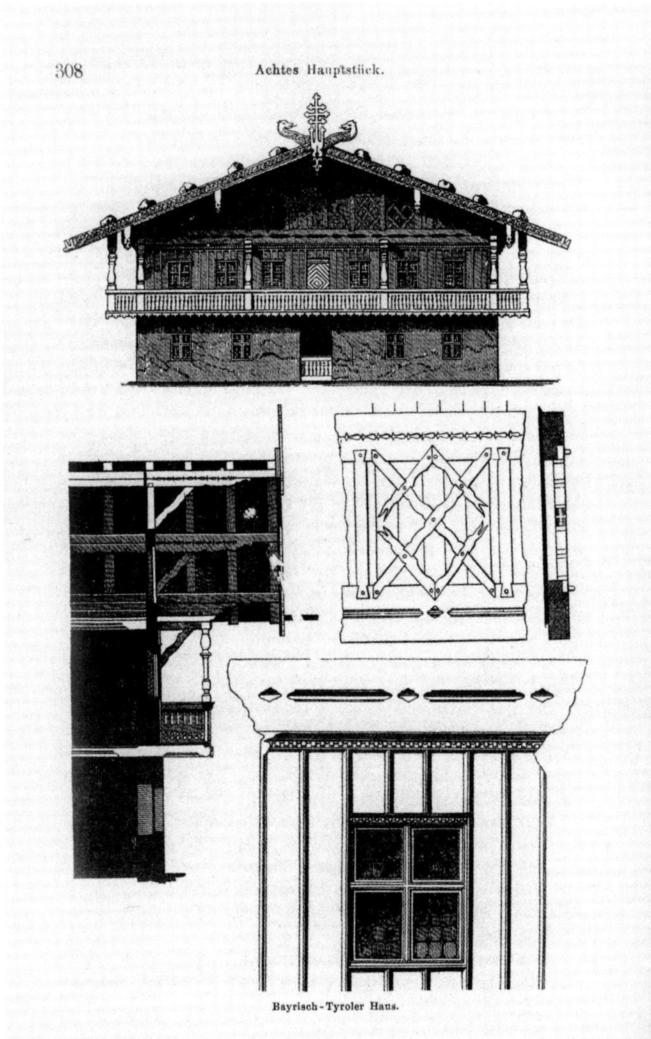

Left **FIGURE 32**
Gottfried Semper, "Caribbean Hut." From *Der Stil.*

Right **FIGURE 33**
Gottfried Semper, "Bavarian-Tyrolean House." From *Der Stil.*

the detail: only at this scale could he relate architecture to the small-scale objects (textile and ceramics) that had determined its forms.

Clearly the ancient references to weaving and plaiting surviving in ornament lay in the domain of representation. But by analyzing the "work"—that is, the constructive roots discernable behind these references (for example, the knot and braid behind textiles and thatching)—Semper had opened a door: architectural details emerged as deeply revealing moments for the building as a whole.[148] Long before Sherlock Holmes, Freud, and Morelli, as Carlo Ginzburg argues, the searchlight had been trained on the insignificant and the easily overlooked as key sites for understanding style.[149] Of course it was the principle that was new, and it was a "movable" one. The joint between column and podium did not have to be a stone Attic column base; it could be any material connecting any vertical support with the foundation. What Semper had done was to focus attention on these locations; he lifted them to the level of signifiers and offered a broad theoretical framework for their discussion. In short, he had invested them with the value of clues: clues to crafting techniques, to the culture that produced them, and, beyond this, to human nature itself.[150] The minute had risen to gigantic importance.

The joining of elements in an architectural assemblage was a particularly important site for Semper. In his view it is at junctions that much of the symbolism of both decorative and monumental art resided. Indeed he defined architecture as the "joining of materials into an organized form."[151] For example, the connections between column and podium (the base) like that of the handle to the cup were laden with meaning.[152] For him, the belly of the pot was its principal feature (functional and symbolic), while the others, such as the base and the handle, reinforced it formally and symbolically. These relationships between parts remained embedded in the architectural elements that derived from it. Earlier in the text he had argued that the column originates in the stele, which in turn derives from the vase, hence the parts of the vase—belly, base, and so forth—will be recalled in the column.[153] Connections between fabric and seams in the "art of vestments" (*vestiarische Kunst*) signaled similar moments in the composition of an assemblage. The fact that junction points were deeply significant is revealed to Semper by their similarity to the joints in the human body. In art as in nature these are the places that attracted attention and where ornament—or jewelry, that is, body decoration (bracelets, anklets, belts)—was traditionally applied (fig. 34).[154]

Beyond flagging junction points, much of Semper's interest lay in the principles of assemblage governing them. For example, he identifies the transference from textile to architecture through the survival of another assemblage principle, that of tying. The band on the column base recalls the belt; the free fluttering of flags finds parallels in acroteria; and so forth.[155] In all cases he strives to identify what he calls "natural" (*naturwüchsig*) principles.

In keeping with his concern for a natural conception of objects, another crucial proposal Semper made was to connect the detail to the body, to which in any event it was closer in scale—not only to the body as maker, to the hand of the artist, but also to the body as repository of basic human instincts translated into form by a process both mimetic and symbolic. Thus for him the forces of gravity, growth, resistance, and inertia lie at the root of a deep-seated desire for equilibrium, symmetry, and verticality that makes itself felt in all human products.[156] As a result, motifs such as the belt tying parts together, the hem of the dress delineating the intersection between vertical and horizontal, the dialectic between load and support evident in framing elements and infill, and so on are

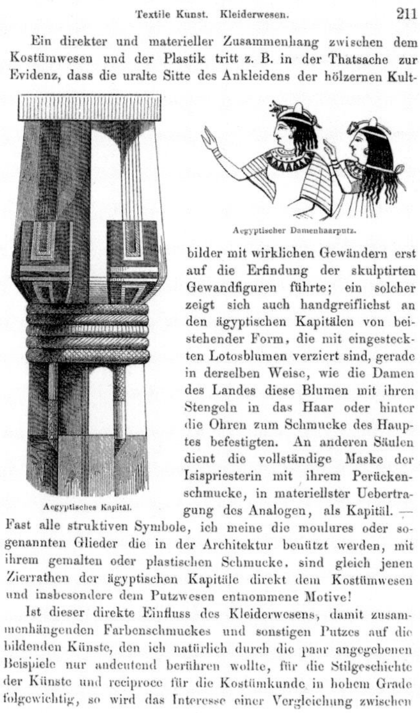
Textile Kunst. Kleiderwesen. 211

Ein direkter und materieller Zusammenhang zwischen dem Kostümwesen und der Plastik tritt z. B. in der Thatsache zur Evidenz, dass die uralte Sitte des Ankleidens der hölzernen Kult-

Aegyptischer Damenhaarputz.

bilder mit wirklichen Gewändern erst auf die Erfindung der skulptirten Gewandfiguren führte; ein solcher zeigt sich auch handgreiflichst an den ägyptischen Kapitälen von beistehender Form, die mit eingesteckten Lotosblumen verziert sind, gerade in derselben Weise, wie die Damen des Landes diese Blumen mit ihren Stengeln in das Haar oder hinter die Ohren zum Schmucke des Hauptes befestigten. An anderen Säulen dient die vollständige Maske der Isispriesterin mit ihrem Perückenschmucke, in materiellster Uebertragung des Analogen, als Kapitäl. — Fast alle struktiven Symbole, ich meine die moulures oder sogenannten Glieder die in der Architektur benützt werden, mit ihrem gemalten oder plastischen Schmucke, sind gleich jenen Zierrathen der ägyptischen Kapitäle direkt dem Kostümwesen und insbesondere dem Putzwesen entnommene Motive!

Aegyptisches Kapitäl.

Ist dieser direkte Einfluss des Kleiderwesens, damit zusammenhängenden Farbenschmuckes und sonstigen Putzes auf die bildenden Künste, den ich natürlich durch die paar angegebenen Beispiele nur andeutend berühren wollte, für die Stilgeschichte der Künste und reciproce für die Kostümkunde in hohem Grade folgewichtig, so wird das Interesse einer Vergleichung zwischen

so many recognizable moments in objects and buildings that speak directly to the body and are immediately understood.[157] Their translation into architectural ornamental motifs, argues Semper, is a natural and inevitable consequence.[158]

But Semper makes even clearer references to the body and adds further analogies to the long-standing Vitruvian vignette of the *homo bene figuratus,* the origin of architectural anthropomorphism theory. Tattooing is one of them. As the patterns used by the Maoris teach him, these tattoos testify not only to an inborn need to ornament, but also to a deeper connection with the body: tattoo patterns follow the lines of the principal muscles and hence facial motion, and convey a message about strength and tension.[159] Moreover, in his view the practice of body painting and architectural polychromy were indissolubly connected and lay at the very origins of art.[160] Likewise, embedded in his *Bekleidung* metaphor lies another body connection. Like a human body, the building was "clothed" or "dressed," not just painted (*polychromiert*).[161] Carpets, wickerwork, mosaics, and stucco covered and protected the building core just as textiles enveloped and veiled the body. The initial sheltering instinct that distinguished man from beast was not to replicate the cave but to replicate clothing/body covering, he concluded.

But perhaps even more important, Semper's definition of the origins of the architectural detail invited a further connection to the body. His emphasis

FIGURE 34
Gottfried Semper, "Egyptian Capital and Adornment for Women's Hair." From *Der Stil.*

on fabrication, on the manipulation by the hand that translates into ornament the memory of manufacture, of what it feels like to mold the material, heightened the significance of the link between body and detail. And his symbol-based anthropomorphic tectonics reinforced it further. In his "Über die formelle Gesetzmässigkeit des Schmuckes" (his inaugural address at Zurich, published in 1856, unlike many of his other lectures which remained in manuscript form) he identified three main classes of ornament: those associated with hanging, with ring formations, and with directional ornament. In his view, these forms, used in architecture to convey ideas of weight and support, of linking, of movement, and so forth, "do not find their analogies directly in nature, but strictly in the ornaments that decorate the body."[162] The maker's and viewer's bodies were drawn into this elliptical architectural narrative that signaled the power of the detail in both making and viewing.

Clearly such a body-conscious theory of architecture is related to the rise of the empathy (*Einfühlung*) theory, developed in the 1860s and 1870s in aesthetics and psychology by scholars like Hermann Lotze, Robert Vischer, and Johannes Volkelt, and appropriated into art and architectural history decisively by Heinrich Wölfflin in 1886 with his "Prolegomena zu einer Psychologie der Architektur."[163] The origins of Semper's ideas, however, are harder to pinpoint. It is a fact that organicism was a topic in Berlin during Schinkel's lifetime, and under the influence of Goethe he had espoused it himself.[164] This is of course not the same as the psychology-based empathy theory, but it has points of contact with Semper's views, and it supplied the neo-Renaissance school with a working theory for the meaning of forms. A blend of a phenomenology and empathy reading of form is already evident in Bötticher—who emerges from the same Schinkel milieu—as well as in Moritz, himself under the influence of both Goethe and Schinkel.[165] Another source may have been Fr. Th. Vischer, author of *Ästhetik* (1846–47) and an early empathy theory proponent, whom Semper befriended at Zurich.[166] Yet it is possible that the influence worked both ways, as Semper had formulated the core of his theories by the time he reached Zurich and met Vischer.[167]

ARCHITECTURE IN THE MUSEUM

If one direction Semper offered later theorists was to connect the detail with the human body, by isolating ornament and treating it as detail (or joint) he also came close to discussing it as a manufactured object. Indeed, aside from the phenomenological aspect of his arguments, the essence of his theory is about putting materials and pieces together, about assembling parts and manipulating instruments. This was not the current reading of ornament, which had veered of late more toward pattern as lines on surfaces and existed in a disembodied realm in which its materiality had been virtually erased. Instead, by focusing on materials and fabrication, Semper had opened a door to the objectification of architecture and in this sense had touched another nerve of nineteenth-century culture: the museum movement.

In this as in so many other things, the Great Exhibition had proved a turning point.[168] If it precipitated an awareness of alternative sources and methods to be drawn into discussions on the arts, its very existence as exhibition also affected these discussions. Exhibiting the industrial and artistic products of the world, it also exhibited their container, architecture, and brought it—as icon, fetish, even item of mass consumption—within the display and museum culture focused on the object. Semper's reaction to the Great Exhibition as if it were an exhibition *of* architecture or *about* architecture was immediately manifest in his 1852 essay in which he identified the museum as a means to cognition and raised the associated question of how to organize a truly educational display. His primary concern was the classification categories used by the Royal Commission (raw materials, machinery, manufactures, fine art) that did not correspond to the categories of "objects leading to monumental arts" that he had identified himself.[169] For Semper, this system, based on appearances rather than the evolution of making, turned the natural order of things upside down. And to correct it he proposed a model museum drawn from his (evolving) theory of architecture:

> In an industrial exhibition the products of the applied arts, because they come from the need for nourishment, shelter, protection, the measurement of space and time, and so forth, should serve as the first and most essential items of consideration. Each category must consist of subdivisions, following the peculiarities of objects, the materials, and the means used in their fabrication. As a further supplement, a place must be found as well for the raw materials, tools, machines—in short, for all the factors of production.[170]

Semper's interest was in the "intrinsic bonds and thematic relationships of objects," and for him this unity could be provided only by architecture. The plan of his museum was based on four categories of exhibits, all of which related to components of architecture: to the hearth, the wall, the terrace, and the roof. High art (where the four would intersect and therefore would be working together) would reveal the "derivation of objects and forms from their primordial motifs/patterns (*Urmotiven*) and style changes conditioned by circumstances."[171] Needless to say, the four areas were organized according to materials (as he would later do in his treatise), and the resultant high art was architecture. As a result, architecture was also implicitly on display in this model: the exhibits not only exposed their own roots and constituting elements, but their installation into a spiral-like sequence also showed how they led up to architecture as climax.

Even more important for Semper, this organization was a means to an end, literally turning the museum into a "sanatorium" for the ailing masses that were no longer able to produce monumental arts of significance. By walking through the exhibits organized along the path from object to architecture, they would enact and appreciate what this path of transformation had once produced and could do again in the future. Indeed, in his plea for the education of the *Volk* through the development of collections he articulated his concept of the museum once again and stressed the function of the movable object as the ground level from which art slowly rises up:

> Objects of art that were created for no particular place are far better suited to such collections. The public's taste must be restored to health on these because they were the earliest objects on which the artistic sense of man was active. Among these objects, there are two very distinct classes that dominate a wide field of art, and under which are grouped many species and families. I am thinking of the ceramic and textile arts.[172]

Semper had already given this topic concentrated attention. Although "Wissenschaft, Industrie und Kunst" has been a privileged text among architectural historians for leading in an almost straight line to *Der Stil,* there was a second and arguably as significant text by Semper that followed it closely in 1852 and constituted its genuine other half. Its title (added in 1867) was "Ideales Museum für Metalltechnik," and it was originally intended for the South Kensington Museum as "Practical Art in Metals and Hard Materials: Its Technology, History and Styles." Though known in manuscript form, it was not published until 1903 in Julius Leisching's essay "Gottfried Semper und die Museen" in *Mitteilungen des Mährischen Gewerbemuseums.*[173] The dates of the original text, of the added title, and the essay's eventual publication are all significant, as they mark three important historical junctures in the rise of a theory of the object. Semper's text, written in English, followed close on the heels of the Great London Exhibition; it was dedicated later by Semper to Rudolf von Eitelberger, the first director of the Vienna Museum für Kunst und Industrie, and sent as a gift on the occasion of its opening in 1867; and its publication, fifty years after it was written, testifies to the continued relevance of Semper up to the turn of the century. Julius Leisching translated the essay into German in 1889 at a point in time when the *Kunstindustrie* debates—fueled in Vienna by Riegl, Eitelberger's student, and the rise in art and crafts museums and exhibitions in both Austria and Germany—were reaching their zenith (fig. 35).[174] In his introduction Leisching makes a strong case for Semper's significance not only to the *Kunstindustrie* movement, but also to that of the museum, describing him as the "creator of our decorative art

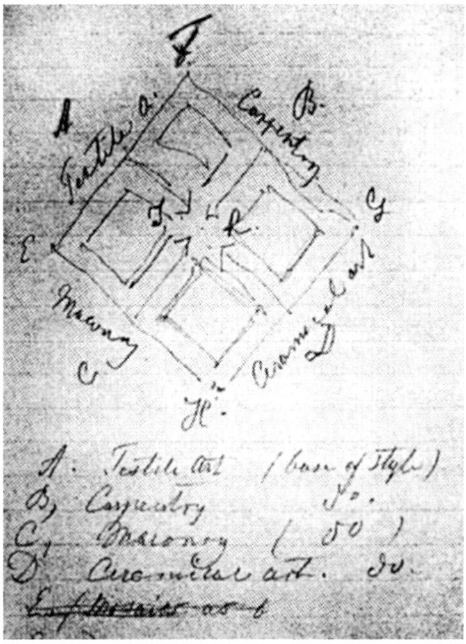

FIGURE 35
Gottfried Semper, "Plan for an Ideal Cultural History Museum," 1852. Sketch in manuscript "Practical Art in Metal and Hard Metals."

museums."[175] As we have seen, in his model of a museum, architecture is not on display as such. However, the intersection of the four areas/materials "produces" architecture which, as a result, symbolically occupies the void at the center.

As the publication history shows, "Ideales Museum" became a text of some significance for the museum world in one of those bifurcations that characterize many fields as they come of age. For a moment, architectural history, art history, anthropology, archaeology, and the museum had cohabited, if not under one roof, at least under one publication title. As Semper himself had said, the charge of every collection must be to offer the "history of ethnography and philosophy of culture." His interaction with the Zurich of Burckhardt and Wölfflin, and with the Vienna of Riegl and Otto Wagner, where he taught and built, meant that he had been influential in two milieus that were key for the future of both art history and architecture. Henceforth the two disciplines would move on separate courses, yet their common roots in his work would—still—occasionally draw them together.

Even such a synoptic review of Semper's work reveals a host of new and unusual features. Not only did Semper revolutionize the field with his new interpretation of the development of the arts, but he also drew attention to a number of new sources relevant to such discussions (archaeology, anthropology, ethnography, folklore studies, and so forth). For all his enthusiasm for the new sciences and the reality of manufacturing, and true to his German intellectual heritage, Semper also steered the discussion toward aesthetics and phenomenology. This perspective continued to inform German-language architectural theory and gave it its particular flavor. For the most part unavailable in English or French, his written work was addressed mainly by theorists in German—in Switzerland, Austria, and Germany—who followed in his footsteps.

But identifying *Kunstindustrie* as an index of culture was perhaps Semper's most radical move. In so doing he not only contributed to the discourse on the applied arts, but he imported what was essentially a discrete body of literature associated with them into architecture and art history at one and the same time. To be sure, the discourse on objects existed before he came along, and the concept that style depended on the manipulation of materials had been proposed by Karl Friedrich Rumohr long ago.[176] But Semper united, channeled, and lifted these discussions onto a larger plane. In connecting objects of daily use by way of materials with the ornament of monumental architecture he implicitly offered a way for the theory of architectural ornament to slide seamlessly into that on the object. Dressing/*Bekleidung* (the body wrap idea transposed to the house), the detail/ornament connection and its association with the human body, the new definition of style and its sources, not to mention the museum and the classificatory ambition behind Semper's work that fueled a conception of architecture as objects—all were so many time bombs, ready to explode under the right circumstances. That they did just that will be explored in the next chapters.

2 | The Ubiquity of Objects

> It will suffice to say that the concept of costume and architecture originate in the preparation for the protection of the body, that is, in its covering and housing, and that, therefore, "portable dwelling" is a most appropriate way to designate this, their most primitive quality. —ERNST KAPP, *Grundlinien einer Philosophie der Technik*

THE PUBLICATION EXPLOSION

If Semper was revolutionary inasmuch as he had singlehandedly broken the tradition of architectural treatise writing and reconfigured problems, questions, and relationships between maker and object, materials and maker, society and culture, and so on, he was nevertheless himself the product of a whole cultural context. His work is in fact the tip of a vast iceberg of related publications on which he drew and to which he responded. Historical work in particular—of many sorts and in many fields—had fed his inquiry.[1] And it continued to be produced on an exponential curve after him. Indeed, *Der Stil* was perhaps the last time a broad synthesis of methods and information coming from many different directions was possible. Toward the turn of the century each discipline, each field, each subject expanded by leaps and bounds, developed and refined its own methods, and produced a learned literature that prohibited synthetic assimilation ever again. Archaeology, anthropology, ethnology, conservation, art history, art education, and architecture went their own ways. The sheer quantity of work and the multiple sources feeding the interest in objects meant a lively if somewhat opportunistic interaction between discourses. This unruly environment, in which rigid academic lines had not yet been drawn, created many opportunities for intersection and cross-fertilization. Given the infectious energy and hybridity of this intellectual free-for-all, the context in which Semper's contribution was embedded also determined how he reached his readers. After Semper the various discourses absorbed his work, and channeled it in different directions. How the discourse was transformed, how it was reconfigured, and how it was returned to architecture, as well as what mechanisms allowed this conversation between disciplines to take place, deserves to be addressed in greater detail.

The prominence that Semper gave the object of daily use in his pantheon of architecture was not entirely unexpected. As we have seen, the definition of *Tektonik* (understood to be the essence of architecture) proposed by philosophers—among them Kant, Schelling, Schopenhauer—that placed the tangible object, albeit small, in the same category as architecture, certainly prepared the way for such a reading. Other publications that predated Semper had also shown a swing in interest toward both the decorative arts and the household objects, which received increasingly direct and individual attention. To be sure, there was little theory or philosophical speculation to be found in these earlier works, focused as they were on providing compendia of forms mainly for the use of the craftsman and patron, nor was there much reflection on their relationship with architecture. This was particularly the case in Britain, where both the enthusiasm for recovering its Gothic vernacular and the concern for the poor performance of the country's wares on the international market, even before 1851, had encouraged both architects and educators to put pen to paper.[2] Henry Shaw suggested as much in his introduction to his *Encyclopedia of Ornament* (1842) when he stated: "The Author trusts that the present Collection will be highly conducive to the enlargement of correct taste in all branches of decorative art."[3] Indeed, this was the heyday of British publications on ornament and the decorative arts that ranged from Pugin's *Floriated Ornament* (1849) to Ralph Wornum's more ponderously titled *Analysis of Ornament: The Characteristics of Styles. An Introduction to the Study of the History of Ornamental Art* of 1852 (based on lectures given in 1848–50 at governmental schools of design throughout Britain) and Owen Jones's classic *Grammar of Ornament* (1856) (fig. 36).[4]

Of course, each country produced a body of literature coherent with its own political-economic and cultural agendas. In France, for example, the interest had been driven more by a concern with recuperation and preservation in the wake of the destruction perpetrated at the time of the 1789 revolution than by a concern with objects in and of themselves. For this reason the discourse had a particular cast, and the kinds of questions, issues, and theory developed elsewhere in connection with design only rarely reached the surface here. Thus whereas Charles-Antoine Jombert's *Repertoire d'artistes, ou recueil de compositions d'architecture et d'ornement antiques et modernes, de toutes espèce* (1764) provided a thesaurus of forms in the tradition of eighteenth-century publications not unlike, if more exhaustive than, Robert Adam's, it was Alexandre Du Sommerard's *Les Arts au Moyen Âge et de la Renaissance* of 1838–46 that breathed a different, more robust historical air in which the objects were less exempla to be followed than historical clues that could help reconstruct a culture in danger of disappearing.[5] As American journalist Jules Janin described Du Sommerard's collection (from which his publication arose), material culture rather than art

FIGURE 36
Owen Jones, "Egyptian Ornament." From Jones, *The Grammar of Ornament* (1856).

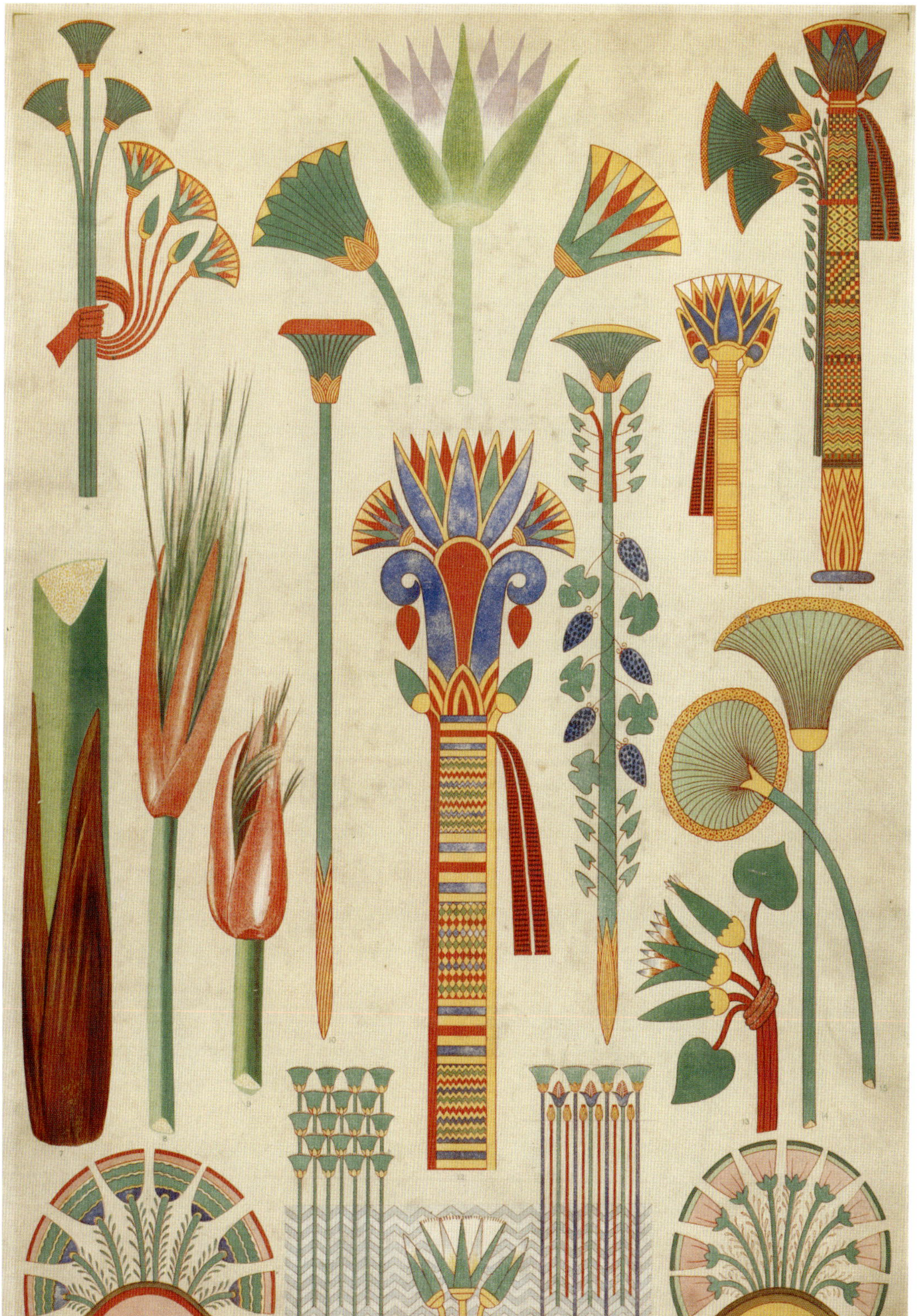

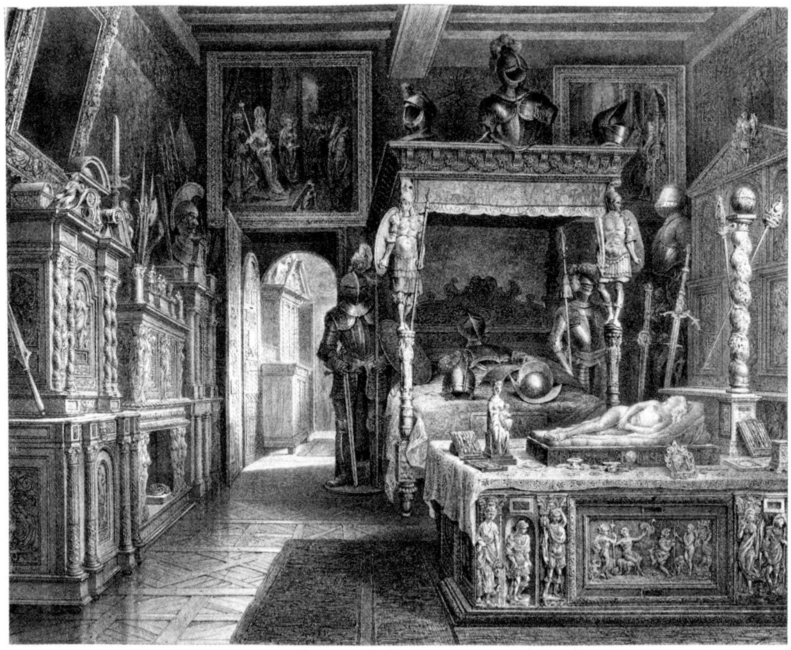

FIGURE 37
"Chambre de François Ier." From Alexandre Du Sommerard, *Les Arts au Moyen Âge et de la Renaissance* (1838–46).

offered the positive indices or clues necessary to effect his exegesis: "He reduced the whole history to a thousand little details of the greatest amusement; carpets, ribands, garments, windows, halberds, laces, dresses for the ladies, armor for the heroes, books for the learned; he knew the condition of the people under Charlemagne by their cabinets; he knew the position of the court at the time of Francis I by their dishes and plates" (fig. 37).[6] The contemporary collection of historical bric-a-brac of Charles Sauvageot and the "dépôt d'objets" of Alexandre Lenoir (which was to form the basis of his Musée des monuments français, the catalogue of which he published between 1800 and 1821) sprang from a similar concern with recuperation.[7] The value and makeup of such collections did not escape English travelers to Paris and left their mark on the likes of John Charles Robinson and Richard Redgrave, who were instrumental in the subsequent creation of the South Kensington Museum and who applied their experiences in Paris to develop a discourse all their own.[8]

However, after the 1851 Great Exhibition, the publications concerned with the objects of household use subsumed under the heading of decorative arts grew exponentially, as they were driven by different imperatives. Identified with marketable goods that not only represented the national achievements but, more importantly, assured economic prominence on the global market, the decorative arts had risen to national significance.[9] France and America—generally acknowledged to be leading the pack—were less concerned with their economic prospects and entered the publication craze with somewhat less enthusiasm.[10] Germany,

Austria, and Britain, on the other hand, felt an urgent need to stem the tide of imports and promote a shift in outlook and education that would eventually pay off in the world marketplace.[11] Thus in France, publications followed in the footsteps of Du Sommerard's and tended to service more the historical disciplines focused on the *patrimoine* than to advocate a radical renewal of the education system, which, in any event, had been much praised. Léon de Laborde's *De l'union des arts et de l'industrie* of 1856, an account of his experience with the 1851 Exhibition, where he had masterminded the French exhibit, was a somewhat isolated event. Moreover, it was neither illustrated nor written in such a manner as to be accessible to the larger circles at which English- and German-language publications were aimed. Laborde was aware that France had to fight to retain its advantage, and his purpose was didactic to be sure, but his most didactic chapter—on "maintenance of public taste," in the second volume, titled "The Future"—had been cut for reasons of space, he claimed, and so he had relegated it, in reduced form, to an appendix. Sensing that the other nations were breathing down France's neck, he asked: "How can we fight to maintain our still uncontested supremacy on all these fronts?"[12] The education of the public, the regeneration of arts education, and government financial commitment were his answers. Like Semper, he too looked to the works of artists; the museums, libraries, and public courses of instruction; affordable publications; and good architecture and urban design to educate the public, though his list was even more comprehensive and included physical education, the enjoyment of nature, and the removal of anything that offended good taste. Still, Laborde did not offer a theory for the arts, nor did he claim to do so. If he felt an urgency to preserve France's leadership, others did not, and nothing like the German, British, and Austrian reactions materialized there. In 1901, in a volume on the *Krisis im Kunstgewerbe* edited by Richard Graul and intended to take stock of the situation at the turn of the century, Léonce Benedite outlined a more positive history of the movement in France, in which both the Musée des Arts Décoratifs (founded in 1905) and the Union des Arts Décoratifs loomed large.[13] Yet for a country whose leadership had been enviously acknowledged in 1851, the various institutions created to promote the decorative arts in the following boom years were comparatively late and were centered primarily on Paris (and to some degree in Lyon), and their mandates were not nearly as radical as elsewhere in Europe. Similarly, although authors like Jules Bourgoin, Auguste Racinet, Charles Blanc, and especially Viollet-le-Duc published copiously, they did not bring about a shift in discourse or generate a body of literature to feed it, as was the case elsewhere in Europe. In 1876, Rudolf von Eitelberger, the first director of the Museum für Kunst und Industrie in Vienna, praised these works for being the only ones that offered designs of superior quality for craftsmen and deplored the absence of their equivalents in German-language publications.[14] But precisely because the infrastructure to build up the decorative arts was not in place in the German-speaking nations, it led to more sustained reflection and action.

The aim of the publications that flooded the market after 1851 was principally to educate the makers but also to educate the masses and a parvenu prosperous middle class that reveled in excessive ornament, gaudy details, and cheap luxury sadly churned out by the machine in huge numbers. This was a widespread phenomenon that elicited even more strictures and concern in London, Berlin, and Vienna than in Paris (though it was a concern there too). Interested in larger issues of civilization and aesthetics, Semper had not addressed this problem in so many words, but others did. What united them all across the better part of fifty years and national borders—Jakob von Falke and Viollet-le-Duc with Muthesius and Adolf Loos—was the sense that current taste veered toward self-aggrandizement and excessive display without concern for quality, and that these were the symptoms of a culture in decline. It was sentiments like these that moved Viollet-le-Duc to write his *Dictionnaire raisonné du mobilier français de l'époque carlovingienne à la renaissance* (1858–75) and thus enter the domain of domestic aesthetics: "Today everyone wants to furnish their houses with the luxury that belongs to the financier; . . . the fabricators strive to give the appearance of luxury and richness to the most vulgar objects, both in form and materials."[15] And, calling for the end of sham, he endorsed simplicity and concern with the nature of materials in words that would have warmed both Semper's and Loos's hearts: "Among these cheap splendors, this false taste and false luxury, we are delighted when we can find a well-made bench, a good oak table firm on its legs, woolen curtains which look like wool, a comfortable and solid chair, an armoire that opens and closes properly."[16] Though less negative in his evaluation of contemporary taste, in his *Grammaire des arts décoratifs* (1882) subtitled "Décoration intérieure de la maison," Charles Blanc sought, like Laborde, to maintain the acknowledged good taste of his compatriots: "I believe more than anyone in the virtue of principles; even if they don't lead to beautiful things, at least they prevent the production of bad ones; that's already a lot."[17]

Although in France such views remained a matter of statements rather than a comprehensive effort toward change, in Austria and Germany a program very much along the lines of what Semper had outlined was put in place. As Jakob von Falke, the second director of the Vienna Museum für Kunst und Industrie and director of the Vienna Exhibition of 1873 testifies, by the 1870s France's leadership had been seriously challenged.[18] Much had been modeled on Britain. As Falke noted, the English had been quickest off the mark to remedy what was a potential economic disaster with a sustained program of museums and schools, and their success was already clearly visible at the second World's

Fair in London (1862).[19] Ruskin, Morris, and Walter Crane had added significant theoretical muscle to the movement, and their works, translated into German, had also traveled.[20] Indeed, by 1897 Fritz Schumacher could hail Ruskin as the "Apostle of the modern English arts movement," as did Hermann Muthesius in the epistles he was sending home from London.[21] The English reformers, however, were becoming more and more concerned with the social situation of the working class, and were less interested in the theory of form or cultural aesthetics, or even history, than were their German and Austrian counterparts.[22] This split in direction had complex origins, but it may have been, at least in part, the direct result of the backgrounds of those who spearheaded the decorative arts movements in their respective countries. While in Britain the reformers were architects, artisans, philosophers, and even politicians, in the German-speaking countries the early leadership was principally in the hands of art historians and museums. Rudolf von Eitelberger, Jakob von Falke, Arthur von Scala—the three directors of the museum in Vienna who saw it from its foundation to the dawn of the twentieth century—were all art historians. Indeed, Eitelberger, the first chair of art history at Vienna University, retained the position when he took up the museum directorship in 1864. It should come as no surprise then that their approach to the problems of the present was colored by their discipline's epistemic makeup, which favored questions of aesthetics and cultural history. Falke even adds *Zeitgeist* into the equation and unambiguously argues that, like the high arts, the decorative arts are its characteristic manifestations.[23] Moreover, some of the British reformers' anti-capitalist stance was accompanied by a pronounced antipathy toward the machine, although Morris may have softened his view on this issue near the end of his life and embraced the concept of industrial manufacture.[24] Paradoxically, perhaps, aesthetics and economics worked hand in glove in Austria and Germany. The national economic interests were seen to be well served by the institutions developed around the decorative arts and were mirrored in the publications of their art historian directors and curators. In Falke's words, the object in the later nineteenth century was a "question of culture . . . a question of state as well as of the house."[25]

In German-speaking countries, publications about household objects fell into two broad categories: on the one hand, histories (of ornament, of the house, of costume, of art and life, of taste), which in Falke's words were essential as "models for the renewal of a good and correct taste," and, on the other, evaluations of contemporary needs and situations (whether in the economic field, domestic architecture, or the decorative arts movement, to which also belonged house-decorating manuals and a host of new journals).[26] The entire spectrum of portable objects and their architectural contexts came under scrutiny as new genres of publications emerged that spanned the full range from scholarly to popular taste and culture. Indeed, not only was there a significant rise in scholarly publications, but the larger public was also targeted as more popular genres were broached. In Britain, for example, a whole segment of literature arose (frequently by women and for women) to deal with "art in the home."[27] Perhaps none were more representative of this new demand for publications than the birth of the decorating magazine, with titles like *Kunst für Alle* or *Innendekoration, Deutsche Kunst und Dekoration, Kunst und Handwerk,* and a host of new museum journals like *Blätter für Kunstgewerbe, Kunst und Gewerbe, Kunstgewerbeblatt.*[28] In Germany and Austria much of this publication explosion happened against the background of the Semper reception, and it is not surprising to see his work quoted in the most diverse contexts.[29] Even if not directly quoted, *Der Stil,* the best known of his published works, had become a self-understood foundation for most treatments of its many subjects. Thus, the fact that thirty years after the publication of *Der Stil,* Alois Riegl, then curator of textiles at the Vienna Museum für Kunst und Industrie, was moved to write his *Stilfragen* (1893) in response to Semper (whom he mostly approved of) and the Semperians (whom he did not) testifies to its staying power. Thus, in his encomium commemorating Semper's hundredth birthday (1903) Julius Leisching declared him the "begetter of our decorative arts museums" ("Schöpfer unserer Kunstgewerbemuseen") and noted those who had celebrated this event: architects, scholars (of art), and the museum world, that is, the large range of audiences to whom Semper had spoken and who still drew on his work. As art historian and critic Cornelius Gurlitt noted in 1887 in the *Deutsche Bauzeitung,* the book had been a resounding success even though the "aesthetes" (by which he meant a particular type of art historian wedded to the concept of high art as pinnacle of artistic achievement) had tried to obliterate it by passing it over in silence (*todschweigen*).[30]

OBJECTS, HOUSE, AND CULTURE

Many publications were compendia and model books. But a significant number of them shared a concern with culture—whether historical or modern—and its visual manifestation in the domestic sphere. In fact, culture had become synonymous with the domestic environment. By a logical process the objects of household use, ennobled by Semper as the repository of the kernels of high art in any civilization, had propelled the house, that is, the environment in which they were to be found, to the epicenter of discourse. As a result, a continuous discursive thread connected costume, textiles, objects, ornament, and architecture, what was portable and what was fixed. And in these works the most representative formulations of "art and life" were not deemed to be either churches or palaces but the full range of habitations and therefore of lifestyles, and their respective instruments, from princely to modest. In short, the arena where art and life met

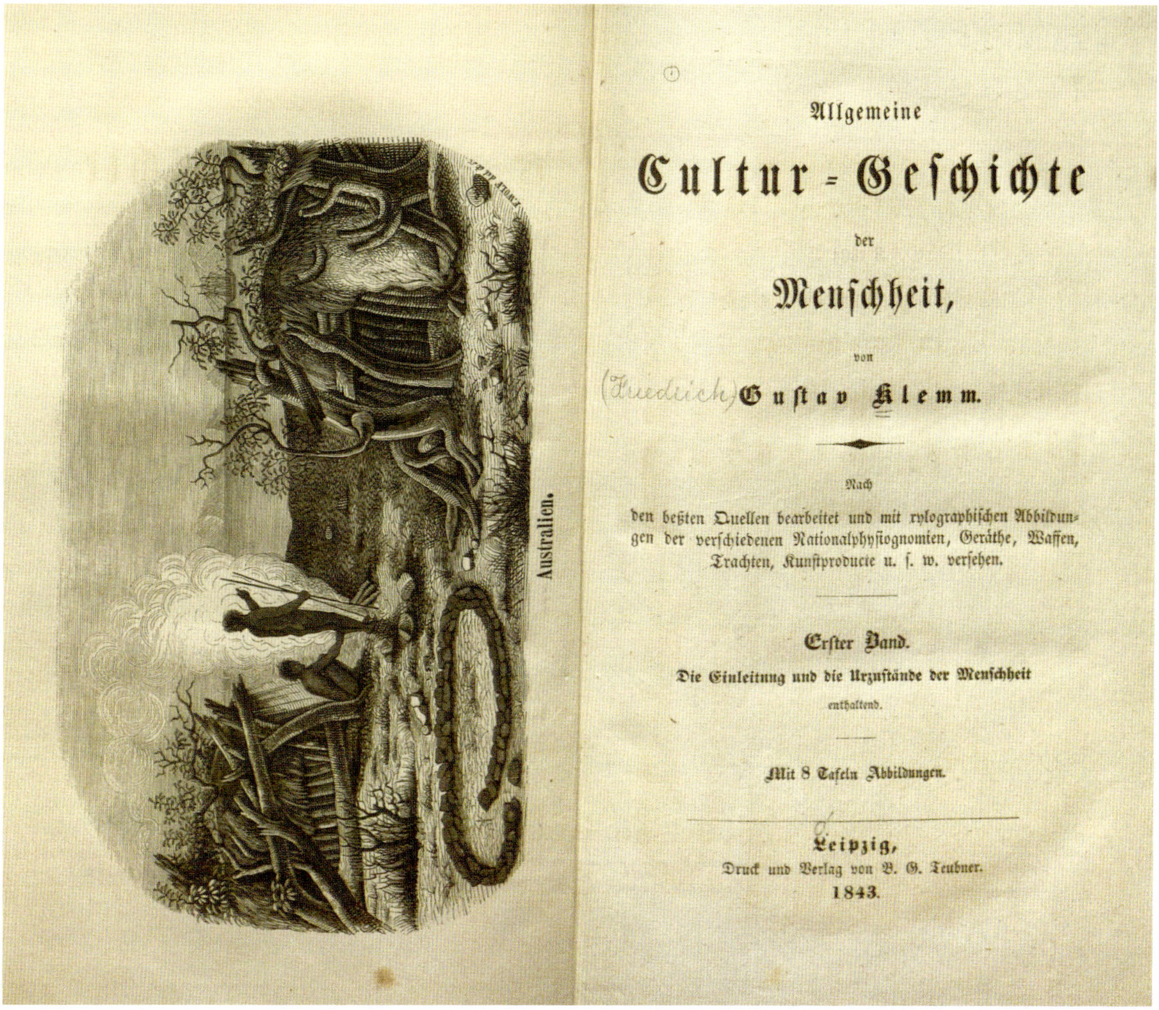

Australien.

Allgemeine
Cultur-Geschichte
der
Menschheit,
von
(Friedrich) Gustav Klemm.

Nach
den besten Quellen bearbeitet und mit xylographischen Abbildungen der verschiedenen Nationalphysiognomien, Geräthe, Waffen, Trachten, Kunstproducte u. s. w. versehen.

Erster Band.
Die Einleitung und die Urzustände der Menschheit
enthaltend.

Mit 8 Tafeln Abbildungen.

Leipzig,
Druck und Verlag von B. G. Teubner.
1843.

FIGURE 38
Gustav Friedrich Klemm, *Allgemeine Cultur-Geschichte der Menschheit*, vol. 1 (1843).

was the house. Such was the power of this trend that Charles Garnier's "Histoire de l'habitation humaine" (in collaboration with the historian A. Ammann), an impressive and much noticed exhibit at the Paris Fair of 1889, focused on the houses of the "people or the middle classes" so as to "give an idea of the general civilization which the masses of that nation had reached," as was immediately reported in the *Deutsche Bauzeitung*.[31] Yet the success of this exhibit was only partial precisely because Garnier and Ammann had not fully responded to the interest of their public, so the German architect reported. Despite his enthusiasm, it is precisely the historical interiors that would have brought these houses to life that he expected and, when faced with their absence, deplored.[32] What he was looking for was the "intimate life in the house, the coming and going, the interior arrangement, the dwellers' costumes, their way of walking, of standing, of working and resting."[33] One consequence of this trend was that the professional

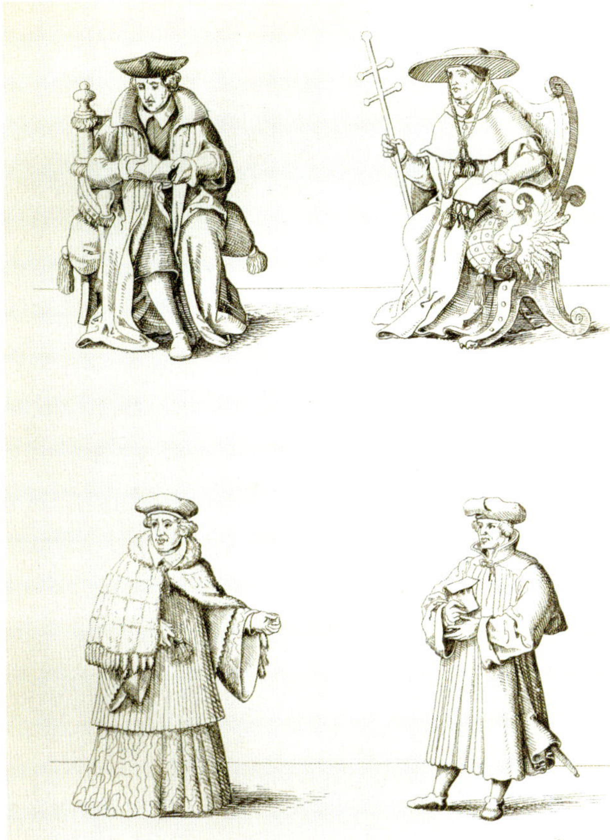

searchlight was trained on the domestic sphere and its architecture, and it became one of the principal areas of research for a host of academic disciplines. The substantial publications by the art historian Falke are but one example of a robust trend. Among architects, Viollet-le-Duc, for example, made this quite clear: drawn by the subject he not only offered historical exempla of interior decoration and domestic life but also proposed modern designs in his *Habitations modernes* of 1875–77.[34] Years later, with the perceptiveness of hindsight, Hermann Muthesius, one the founders of the German Werkbund, identified the profound connection between the development of the house and of the decorative arts movement in England that remained at the core of developments elsewhere on the Continent.[35]

Such an anecdotal interest in the domestic world of historical periods was perhaps to be expected of the romantic popular taste intent on fictionalizing the past, but it also testified to a concern with "Kultur" in the scholarly disciplines, of which Burckhardt's *Kultur der Renaissance in Italien* of 1860 was only its most famous symptom and manifestation. Indeed, in Austria and Germany, far more than in France, the term "Kultur" became associated with a genre of publications that covered taste, costume, and daily life of more or less remote times and that

FIGURE 39
Auguste von Eye and Jakob von Falke, Ecclesiastical costumes of the fifteenth century. From von Eye and Falke, *Kunst und Leben der Vorzeit* (1868–69).

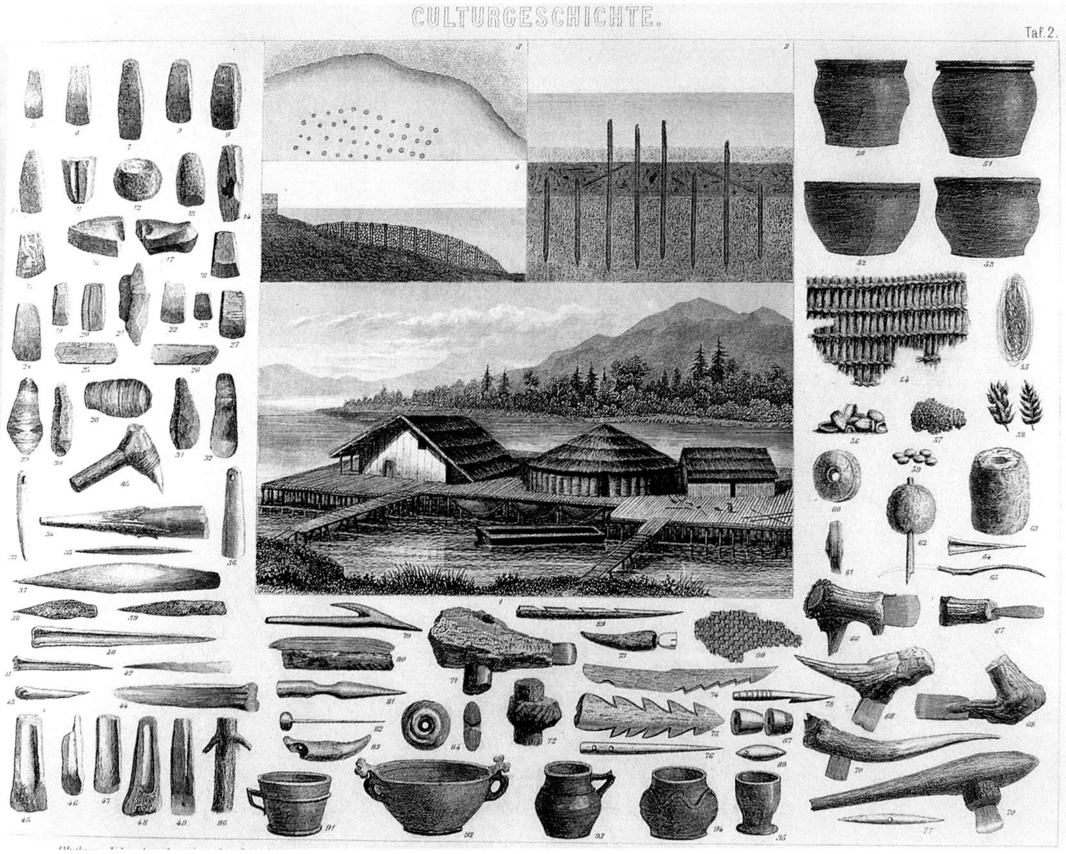

were written by leading scholars. The trend was already present in the earlier nineteenth century in the work of Gustav Klemm, whose work coincided with and influenced that of Semper, as we have seen.[36] However, what was something of an eccentric undertaking of cultural anthropology when Klemm started his twenty-three-volume *Allgemeine Cultur-Geschichte der Menschheit* from prehistory to the present had moved to the center of discourse in the intervening years (fig. 38). Jakob von Falke was particularly active in this arena: witness his books on costume and taste that invariably used the term "culture" in their titles and where the term occurs like a mantra (fig. 39).[37] But he was certainly not alone, and German scholars such as August von Eye, who taught art history at the applied arts school in Dresden and who wrote the *Atlas der Culturgeschichte* (1875), were equally gripped by this theme (fig. 40). Even when the term did not appear the implication was there and lay also behind such books as Falke's and von Eye's joint publication *Kunst und Leben der Vorzeit* (1868–69), as it did behind the new journals and magazines.[38] Prehistory and contemporary life had come together.

FIGURE 40
August von Eye, "Speculative Reconstruction of Ancient Stilt-houses." From von Eye, *Atlas der Culturgeschichte* (1875).

To be sure, Alexandre Lenoir had implied such an underlying thread for his collection and catalogue as early as the first decades of the 1800s, when he connected in his title his ambition to serve the history of art and the history of France with his descriptions of sculpture, tombs, and historical dress.[39] However, his compatriots had not developed his insight, and their books, such as Charles Blanc's *L'art de la parure* and Auguste Racinet's *Le costume historique* (1876–88) were more in the nature of exquisite catalogues than cultural histories.[40] Viollet-le-Duc's pointed remarks in his *Dictionnaire raisonnée du mobilier français* (1873–74) specifically addressing the shortcomings of his contemporaries were therefore more of an isolated event: "It seems ridiculous today to see a woman in a hoop dress seated in an armchair in the Greek style ... or to see men dressed as we are in a Louis XV style armchair."[41] The harmonious formal vocabulary evident in the internal universe of the rich and the poor in the Middle Ages and the Renaissance that he described—in furniture and dress, headgear and shoes, tapestries and ironwork, utensils and armor, corsets and jewelry—was exemplary, and for him it stood in stark contrast to the prevailing approach to contemporary *Wohnungskultur,* as Muthesius would name it several decades later. "What we would like to find in our dwellings is a perfect harmony between architecture, furniture, clothes and customs."[42] And he continues to make his point quite clear: "The most certain sign of an advanced civilization is the harmony between its customs, the various expressions of the arts and the products of industry. Show me your furniture and I will tell you who you are."[43] The concept of harmonious culture and what constitutes civilization so polemically laid out by Loos and Muthesius at the turn of the century was here already fully expressed, if associated with a historical investigation of the Gothic (fig. 41).

In Austria, Jakob von Falke had posited the concept of harmony that connected life and the domestic sphere even earlier in 1871 in his *Kunst im Hause* (a successful book that went through several editions and was already translated into English for the American market by 1879). Less pedantic than Viollet-le-Duc in that he recommended eclecticism and spoke against the tyranny of the interior-as-complete-work-of-art, he nonetheless did so from a shared conviction that every historical environment is stylistically homogeneous and is as much in evidence in furniture as it is in costume.[44] In 1902, Wilhelm von Bode, Renaissance scholar and the director of all Berlin art museums, known as the "Bismarck of museums," went even further when he justified his work on Italian furniture (*Hausrat*) of the Renaissance, speaking as if from general consensus: "It is a valuable help in the study of high art, of architecture as of painting. From a cultural history perspective it provides a glimpse into the daily life of peoples; one has called furniture 'the soul of the house' with some right. It is of extreme importance for the knowledge of style and its development at different times and for different peoples."[45] The humble object by an unknown maker had become the agent of stylistic ordering. And Bode went further still, as he organized the

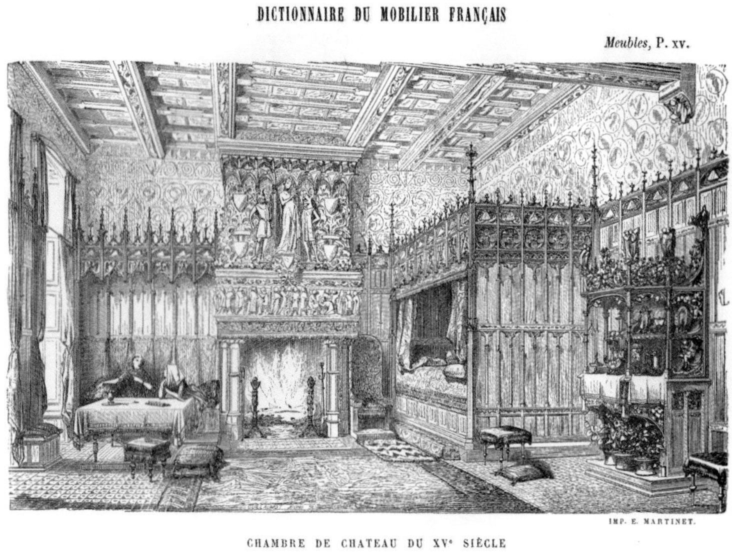

FIGURE 41
Eugène-Emmanuel Viollet-le-Duc, "Room of fifteenth-century castle." From Viollet-le-Duc, *Dictionnaire raisonné du mobilier français* (1858–75).

paintings in the Berlin collection to be shown in historical interiors, that is, in the environments in which they had hung originally. He even attempted to encourage patronage for applied arts through exhibitions of historical material.[46] By 1908 the connection between culture and the applied arts was so established that it could show up in the title of a work on political economy such as Werner Sombart's *Kunstgewerbe und Kultur.*[47]

Perhaps this orientation toward the idea of harmonious culture is not surprising in German-language scholarship, given that art historians were responsible for many of the publications (both scholarly and popular) and the concept of *Zeitgeist* had become a basic tenet for the discipline. As we have seen, already in 1866 Falke had invoked it in this context precisely to stress the "simultaneity of culture" that embraced both "high" and "low" art.[48] One reason that art historians had been drawn into the nascent field of cultural studies was that, given the historicizing orientation evident in nineteenth-century discourse across the board, the focus lay with the historical evaluation of cultures, and such work was naturally sympathetic to a historical discipline. The other was that the principal remedy used to improve the quality of the decorative arts and its consumable goods by way of education and example was the museum. Although the focus of these collections was new inasmuch as they did not revolve around high art, their historical slant and aesthetic ambition made art historians a natural choice for curators and directors. Rudolf von Eitelberger, Jakob von Falke, and Arthur von Scala were only the most prominent such figures at the Museum für Kunst und Industrie in Vienna.[49] Prolific authors of books on everything from contemporary decorative arts to historical costume and histories of taste, they were also holders of art history chairs at the University of Vienna. Indeed, the members of the famous Vienna school of art history were also the staff of the museum, a trend that continued well into the next century: Alois Riegl was curator of textiles and later held an art history chair, while Julius von Schlosser, who was director of the sculpture and applied arts section of the Vienna museum, also started his scholarly activity writing on the decorative arts and objects. Indeed, his then forthcoming (and now famous) essay on curiosity cabinets was advertised in "Monographien des Kunstgewerbes" published by Dr. Jean Louis Sponsel for Hermann Seemann Verlag in Leipzig in 1901, as was his *Höfische Wohnungskunst im Mittelalter,* though the latter seems never to have been completed. Interestingly, the term *Wohnungskunst* (household art) in his title was current in the vocabulary developed around the objects of everyday use and prominent in the title of the journal *Innen-Dekoration: Die gesamte Wohnungskunst in Bild und Wort,* which had made its debut in the previous year (1890). Moreover, Schlosser's works were advertised alongside books intended to serve the "massive swell in the decorative arts," which had seen an "unprecedented development" in the last decades and which included works by Walter Crane, William Morris, and Henry van de Velde.[50] Also listed as forthcoming was *Die Wohnung in den Niederlanden und Frankreich im 15. Jahrhundert* by Franz Wickhoff (another leading member of the Vienna school). Such publications allied somewhat surprisingly the art historians with other participants on this vast project: museum directors like Heinrich Angst (the founder of the Schweizer Landesmuseum in Zurich, famous for its historical interiors), Justus Brinckmann (director of the Museum für Kunst und Handwerk in Hamburg), Alfred Lichtwark (director of the Hamburg Kunsthalle), and Friedrich Deneken (director of the Kaiser Wilhelm Museum in Krefeld).

Vienna was not alone in bringing together art historians and the applied arts. In Germany, Wilhelm von Bode was also the author of a book on carpets, published as volume 1 in the same Seemann series of monographs on the decorative arts.[51] This was a topic that Semper had famously put on the map and that Riegl had dealt with at length in his *Altorientalische Teppiche* of 1891 (which Bode seemed to ignore, much to Riegl's chagrin). In addition, Bode not only published on furniture but also planned volumes on picture frames and majolica (fig. 42).[52] But his collection of writings from the 1890s that included articles on the exhibition in Chicago and on the aims of the decorative arts museums was perhaps his most direct statement on modern culture.[53] Like his Austrian colleagues, Bode also noted the vertiginous rise in consumption of *Kunstgewerbe* and the concomitant decline in its quality, though he was even more outspoken in arguing against the imitation of past styles, and he looked to America as a source of a fresh approach.[54] As all these examples suggest, the leading lights among art

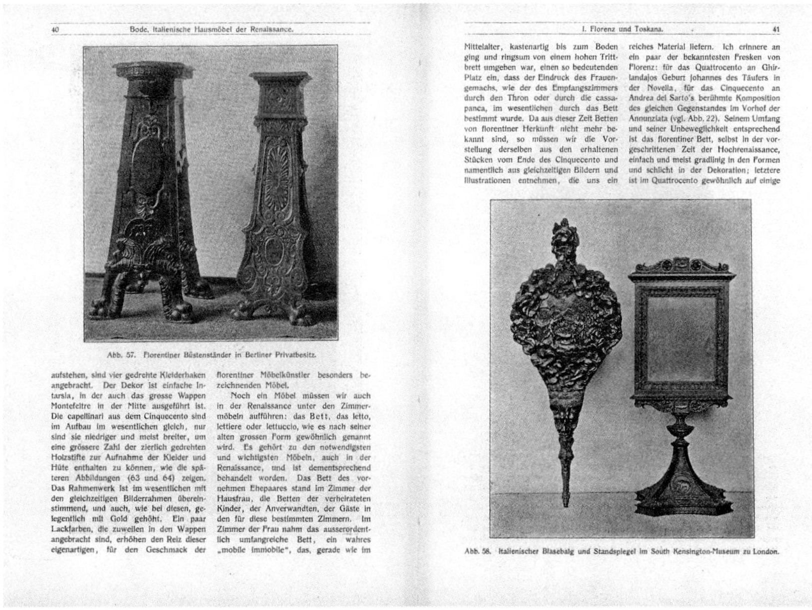

40 Bode, Italienische Hausmöbel der Renaissance.

Abb. 57. Florentiner Büstenständer in Berliner Privatbesitz.

aufstehen, sind vier gedrehte Kleiderhaken angebracht. Der Dekor ist einfache Intarsia, in der auch das grosse Wappen Montefeltre in der Mitte ausgeführt ist. Die capellinari aus dem Cinquecento sind im Aufbau im wesentlichen gleich, nur sind sie niedriger und meist breiter, um eine grössere Zahl der zierlich gedrehten Holzstifte zur Aufnahme der Kleider und Hüte enthalten zu können, wie die späteren Abbildungen (63 und 64) zeigen. Das Rahmenwerk ist im wesentlichen mit den gleichzeitigen Bilderrahmen übereinstimmend, und auch, wie bei diesen, gelegentlich mit Gold gehöht. Ein paar Lackfarben, die zuweilen in den Wappen angebracht sind, erhöhen den Reiz dieser eigenartigen, für den Geschmack der florentiner Möbelkünstler besonders bezeichnenden Möbel.

Noch ein Möbel müssen wir auch in der Renaissance unter den Zimmermöbeln aufführen: das Bett, das letto, lettiere oder lettuccio, wie es nach seiner alten grossen Form gewöhnlich genannt wird. Es gehört zu den notwendigsten und wichtigsten Möbeln, auch in der Renaissance, und ist dementsprechend behandelt worden. Das Bett des vornehmen Ehepaares stand im Zimmer der Hausfrau, die Betten der verheirateten Kinder, der Anverwandten, der Gäste in den für diese bestimmten Zimmern. Im Zimmer der Frau nahm das ausserordentlich umfangreiche Bett, ein wahres „mobile immobile", das, gerade wie im

I. Florenz und Toskana. 41

Mittelalter, kastenartig bis zum Boden ging und ringsum von einem hohen Trittbrett umgeben war, einen so bedeutenden Platz ein, dass der Eindruck des Frauengemachs, wie der des Empfangszimmers durch den Thron oder durch die cassapanca, im wesentlichen durch das Bett bestimmt wurde. Da aus dieser Zeit Betten von florentiner Herkunft nicht mehr bekannt sind, so müssen wir die Vorstellung derselben aus den erhaltenen Stücken vom Ende des Cinquecento und namentlich aus gleichzeitigen Bildern und Illustrationen entnehmen, die uns ein reiches Material liefern. Ich erinnere an ein paar der bekanntesten Fresken von Florenz: für das Quattrocento an Ghirlandajos Geburt Johannes des Täufers in der Novella, für das Cinquecento an Andrea del Sarto's berühmte Komposition des gleichen Gegenstandes im Vorhof der Annunziata (vgl. Abb. 22). Seinem Umfang und seiner Unbeweglichkeit entsprechend ist das florentiner Bett, selbst in der vorgeschrittenen Zeit der Hochrenaissance, einfach und meist gradlinig in den Formen und schlicht in der Dekoration; letztere ist im Quattrocento gewöhnlich auf einige

Abb. 58. Italienischer Blasebalg und Standspiegel im South Kensington-Museum zu London.

historians were aware and drawn into the discourse on modern applied arts, which they engaged enthusiastically and to which they added a significant and systematic historical component.

ERNST KAPP AND THE MACHINE AS BODY

One interesting feature in this publication frenzy was the absorption of costume and other apparel into the domain of the decorative arts and its history and, by extension, into that of the "culture of the house" (*Wohnungskultur*).[55] Clearly the house as epicenter of culture also included the body inhabiting it. Semper had certainly opened the doors to this line of thinking, as he saw a continuous thread that united tattoos, jewelry, vestments, textiles, carpets, upholstery, and architecture across a variety of other household objects at the levels of both manipulation of materials and their symbolism. That he owed such readings to authors like Bötticher and Moritz and to philosophers like Fr. Th. Vischer, who was articulating the basis of the empathy theory at the time of their interaction in Zurich, is clear. But although this theory, arising as it did from the nascent field of psychology, would soon galvanize much of the art world (artists, architects, critics, and historians) in the plethora of publications on objects after Semper, the relationship between household objects, apparel, and the domestic interior did not elicit much discussion or theoretization as such.

One notable exception, however, was the work of Ernst Kapp, whose book on the philosophy of technology of 1877 (which he subtitled *Zur Entstehungsgeschichte der Cultur aus neuen Gesichtspunkten,* and thus connects with the contemporary

FIGURE 42
Wilhelm von Bode, from his *Die italienischen Hausmöbel der Renaissance* (1902).

concern with culture) pioneered a branch of philosophy intimately connected with the rise of the machine.[56] Basing his central argument on a definition of the machine that he took from physicist and physiologist Hermann von Helmholtz—who had argued that the work of the machine is derived from a comparison with the work of the hand—he proposes that if the machine is to replace man's work, then logically it has to correspond to the organism it is going to replace.[57] Unlike instruments, the machine as a whole imitates the body less, but nonetheless there are parts of the machine that resemble various organs.[58] Many fields served Kapp in developing this concept, and his references to Franz Reuleaux, Wilhelm Wundt, Adolf Zeising, and Theodor Fechner testify to their variety, which ranged from psychology and empathy theory, from medicine to engineering, from physics to aesthetics.

However, although he paid homage to Reuleux, the established authority on machine theory, Kapp's main argument was completely original, indeed revolutionary. He did not propose direct imitation; instead, in his view all objects made by man became extensions of his body, unself-consciously conceptualized as such through "organ projection" (*Organprojektion),* a term he introduces here for the first time.[59] In this almost instinctual process, he argues, low mechanization and high technology meet: the hammer meets the telegraph as they both carry memories of human bodies that conceive them, of the arm and the nervous system, respectively (fig. 43).[60] Such a view was fundamentally different from the imitation of human limbs, which, according to him was a superficial means of obtaining functional mechanical contraptions. And he illustrated his concept by distinguishing between the metal glove of Götz von Berlichingen's armor (which followed the contours of his hand) and instruments that *extended* the ability of the hand, such as the hammer (figs. 44, 45).[61] Likewise he compared the architecture [*sic*] of bones with the architecture of iron bridges: both contained a network of trussed matter.[62] He admitted that unlike tools the machine as a whole reflects the body less, but he insisted nonetheless that there are parts of the machine that resemble various organs.[63] Like Semper, but at an even more physical than symbolic level, Kapp proposed a continuity between the body and "containers, tools, furniture, arms, clothes, carpets, jewelry and so on up to . . . architecture and finally to ornament" (fig. 46).[64] In his view all are ultimately organism-dependent and enjoy a reciprocal relationship as a result. Even the movement of machines is an unconscious translation of human/organic movement, he continued.[65] Finally he turned to instruments that man cannot part from: clothes and architecture. This was not a haphazard connection, as he defined *Bekleidung* as "a portable habitation" ("eine portative Wohnung") and argued for the etymological connection between *Gewand* (dress) and *Wand* (wall)—a connection that Semper had already made though apparently unknown to Kapp.[66] And he extended the

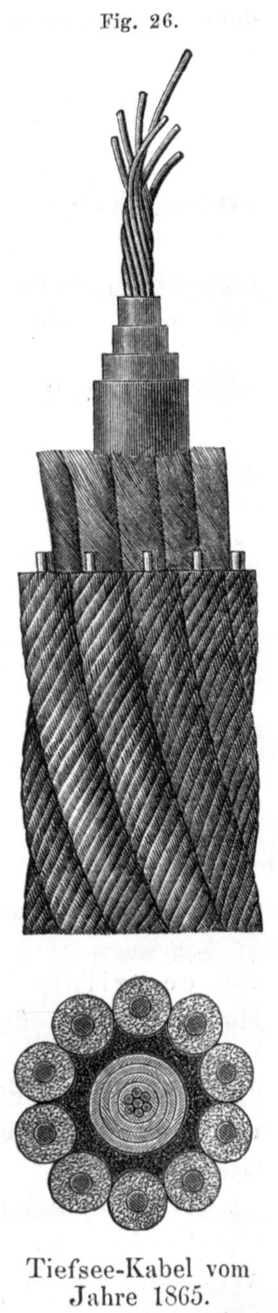

FIGURE 43
Ernst Kapp. "Deep-sea cable from 1865." From *Grundlinien einer Philosophie der Technik* (1877).

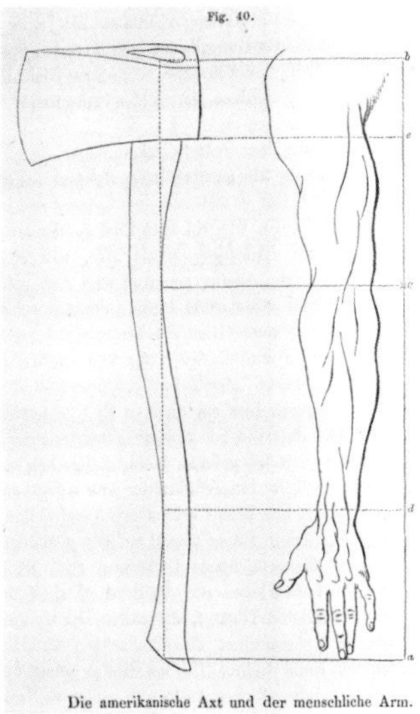

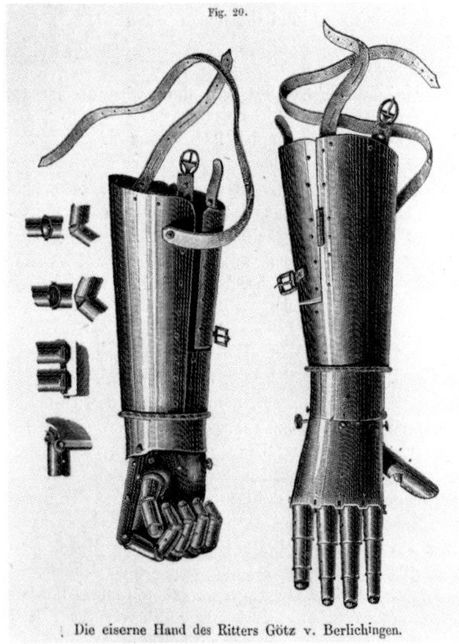

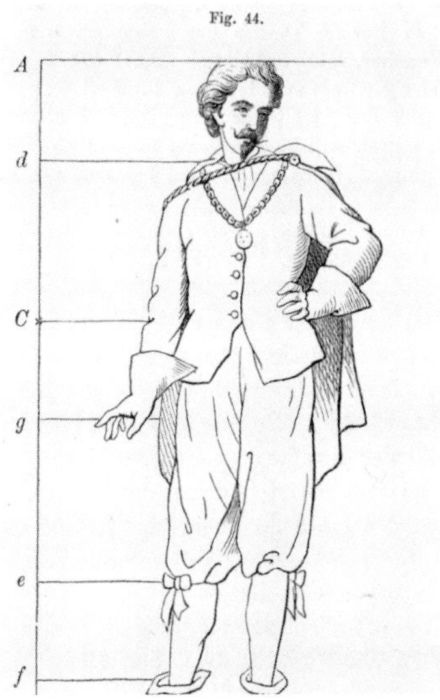

Left **FIGURE 44**
Ernst Kapp, "The American ax and the human arm." From *Grundlinien einer Philosophie der Technik.*

Center **FIGURE 45**
Ernst Kapp, "The iron hand of the knight Götz von Berlichingen." From *Grundlinien einer Philosophie der Technik.* Original: "Die eiserne Hand des Ritters Götz v. Berlichingen."

Right **FIGURE 46**
Ernst Kapp, "Male costume." From *Grundlinien einer Philosophie der Technik.*

term *Costüm* in the representational arts from clothes to "everything the body wears, including the furnishing of the living space done by the hand and from there the surrounding that it borders on,"[67] referring to the work of Wittstein, from whom he borrowed illustrations, and to Hermann Klencke who had demonstrated the presence of the Golden Section in clothes in his *Kosmetik* (1869).[68] More importantly, he quoted art historian August von Eye's lecture of 1876 on "Das Kunstgewerbe der Neutzeit" in which he argued that "room, space, house and garden are an extension, an expansion of our clothes," thus connecting dressing (*Bekleidung*), housing (*Behausung*), and organ projection.[69] As von Eye was a notable presence at the Dresden school of decorative arts and museum, such a link clearly illustrates lively communication between academic fields.

The concept of continuity between clothes, furniture, interiors, and exteriors (that is, architecture) was certainly "in the air" and lay implicit in so many statements and publications at the time. When Viollet-le-Duc illustrated clothes and armor and the manner in which they envelop the body among his images of Gothic furniture, this continuity was implicit even if he does not state it outright (fig. 47). Others had made similar connections. Still, it was a very far cry from Viollet to Kapp—a totally different problematic, not implied but clearly stated. Much of it was subsumed under the broader concept of "culture," but once the newly minted empathy theory was added to a rising fascination with machines, the continuity body/instrument (soft or hard, clothes or machine) becomes inevitable. Indeed, it is not coincidental that armor—that example of body-hugging medieval "machinery"—should come up in examples time and again, as it does in Kapp's argument (fig. 48). The fascination with the automaton—the mechanical human body—is almost as old as Western civilization itself.

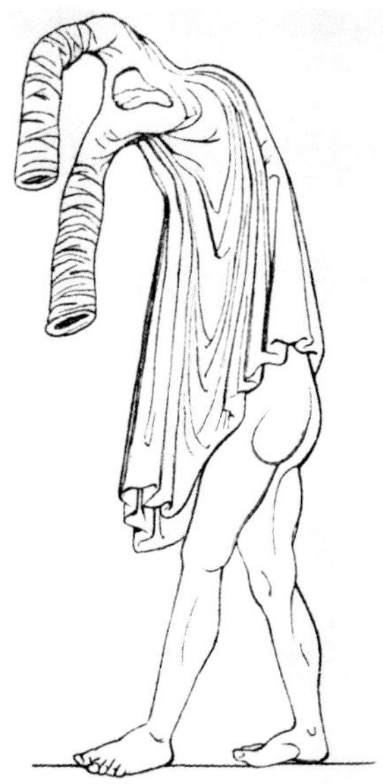

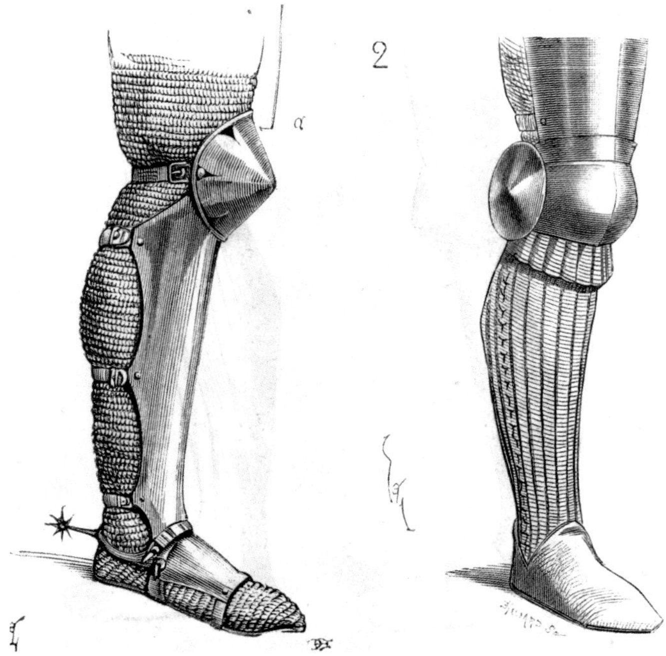

Above **FIGURE 47**
Man dressing. From Eugène-Emmanuel Viollet-le-Duc, *Dictionnaire raisonné du mobilier français de l'époque carlovingienne à la renaissance* (Paris, 1872–75).

Right **FIGURE 48**
Grèves. From Viollet-le-Duc, *Dictionnaire raisonné du mobilier français de l'époque carlovingienne à la renaissance.*

But the wrapping of the body in metal, the "machine" inhabited by a real body, takes on a resonance all its own at the dawn of the Industrial Revolution. At a moment when the machine is taking over so many human activities (of cutting, joining, turning, pushing, and so on), this relationship, however remote, ties into a long history of anthropomorphism that it revamps in a modern key. The idea is not to explain forces by adducing the human body as analogue or understand it as an abstraction of forces that would be equivalent in any inanimate object or building, as had done the begetters of iatromechanics (medical application of physics) such as Giovanni Borelli in the seventeenth century (fig. 49). Kapp's organ projection presents the body continuous with its tools—be they hammers, clothes, or architecture, as they all project outwards from the soft core of the body itself. In this model architecture becomes a tool and an extension of the body just as surely as any jewelry or ribbon in Semper's derivation of ornament. With this proposal Kapp opened a new way of thinking about the relationship between the body and its container, architecture, in which clothes and objects took significant roles as mediators. Nor was he a voice in the wilderness: as we shall see his work was read and absorbed within architectural publications.

ARCHITECTURAL ORNAMENT

One consequence of theories such as Kapp's was that the traditional site of body/architecture interface—architectural ornament—plunged into crisis. Until now, architectural ornament had been the acknowledged site of an intersection

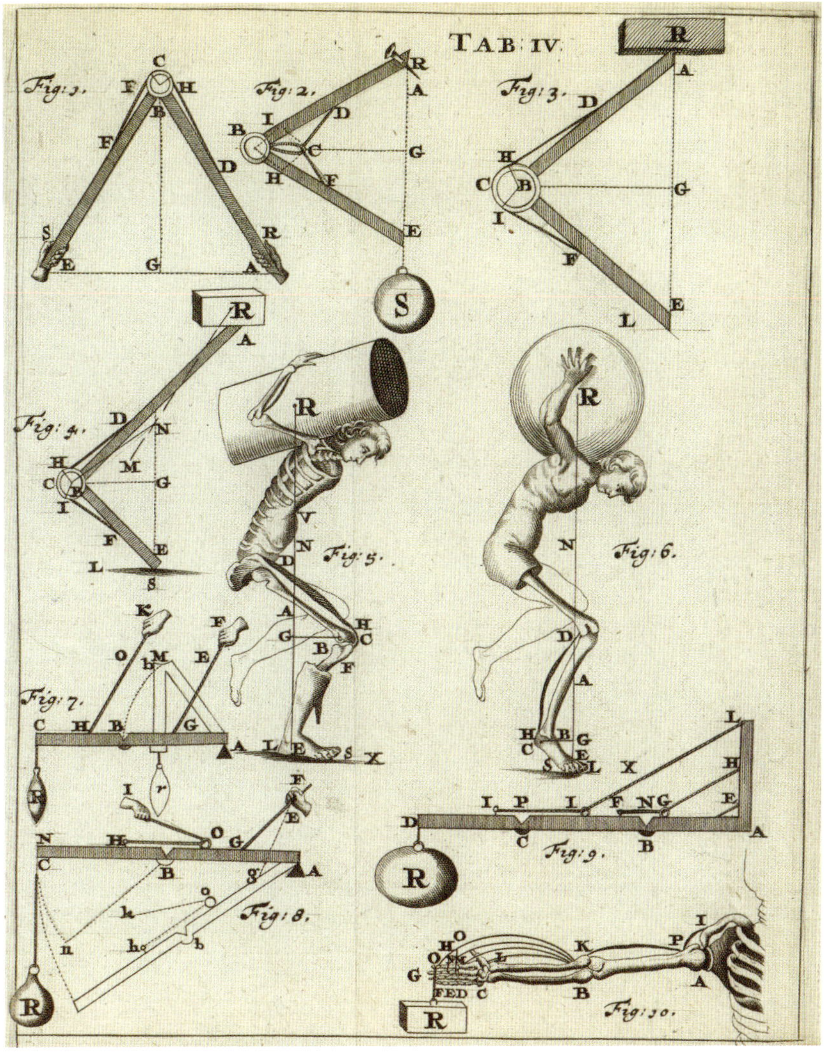

FIGURE 49
Giovanni Borelli, *Levers, Tab. IV.* From Borelli, *De motu animalium* (1685).

between architecture and the organic world, animal and vegetal. Following this tradition Ruskin had long since turned the spotlight on these forms with his lyrical illustrations of the smallest creatures buried among carved foliage on Italian Gothic buildings (fig. 50). Kapp, too, had drawn ornament into his demonstration of organ projection. However, in his perspective the body/architecture connection that had lain in ornament for so long was expanded to include other realms of more moment for contemporary discourse, such as the machine and the products of technology. Although Kapp may have been something of an extreme example at the time he wrote, the shift of gravity in discourse from architectural ornament to the objects of household use remains a fact: embraced by industry in a way in which architectural ornament could never be—mobile, consumable, and therefore widely accessible and economically significant—the

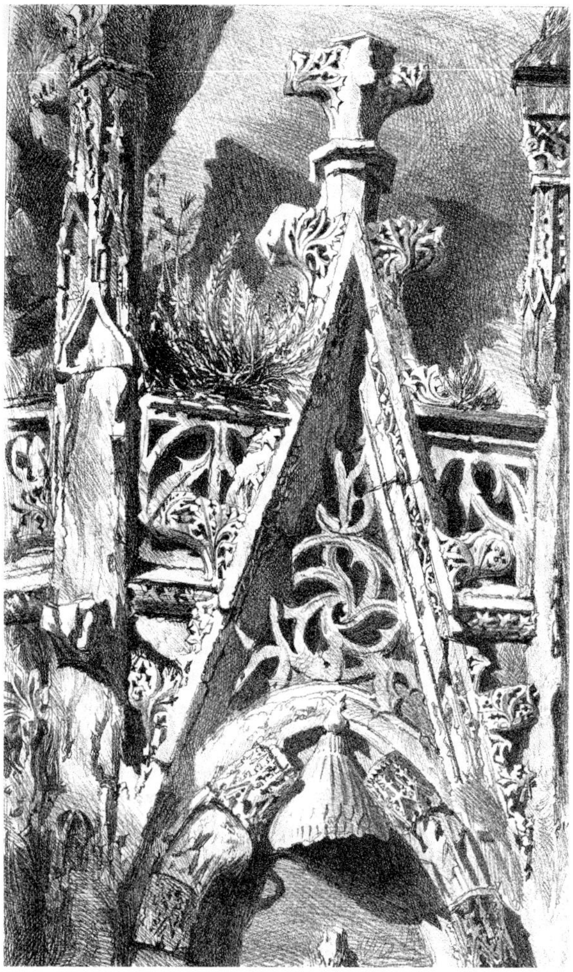

FIGURE 50
John Ruskin, "Part of the Cathedral of St. Lo, Normandy." From Ruskin, *The Seven Lamps of Architecture* (1849).

object increasingly claimed the lion's share of attention both in and of itself and as interface with the architecture of the house. To be sure, terra-cotta and zinc stamped ornament was machine-made, as were iron details, but they tended to be building specific not "off the rack" items; and when included in catalogues of manufacturers, their sheer variety belied the advantages of standardization.[70] Machine-produced but not standardized across the industry, they realized the true potential of the machine only halfway.

Moreover, the objects of daily use entered into "active" rather than "passive" relationships with their users: not confined to a single and fixed location, they entered into direct contact with the hand and the body. Transferable, insidious, pervasive, and endlessly multiplying, the object engaged the viewer in more intimate ways and was more ubiquitously present than architectural ornament could ever be. It is no wonder then that in the ever-expanding discourse on the manufacture and cultural significance of the household goods variously denominated in German as *Gewerbe, Kunstgewerbe, Kleingerät, Kleinkünste, Hausrat, Kunstindustrie, Dekorative Kunst,* and *Allgemeingewerbe* (a terminological density that signals its importance), architectural ornament as an intrinsic component of a vocabulary about building faded into the background. However, it did not disappear altogether but was modified to serve the new interest in objects. In this new democracy of the arts, architectural ornament descended from buildings and, emancipated from its erstwhile location, became "decorative design" that could just as easily turn up on coffeepots, tiles, and textiles as on cornices. Its traditional link with architecture severed, ornament became a "movable feast" and rubbed shoulders with other portable objects.

In architecture the term ornament referred at least since Vitruvius to those elements of the temple that replicated in stone (or, in his words, were the *imago* of) the working members of the original timber structure. Thus mutules, triglyphs, dentils, and the like were representations and as such termed *ornamenta.*[71] Other types of ornament not associated with the structural frame—such as garlands, foliage, inlays, incrustation, figural sculpture, and reliefs—did not elicit a body of theory and lived a kind of half-life, both in antiquity and later.[72] Initially, the column did not explicitly belong to the *ornamenta* group as defined by Vitruvius, and it was not until the fifteenth century that Alberti proclaimed it "the most beautiful ornament without any doubt," thus implying that it too functioned as *imago.* Whether this was indeed Alberti's meaning is another matter; what is important is the fact that it is this definition of the *ornamenta as image,* complete with its implication of superficial application, that retained theoretical weight in the centuries to come. And it is as such that architectural ornament could be easily absorbed into discussions of decorative forms applied to *any* object.

Such a background and open breach into the walls of architecture therefore meant that once *Kunstgewerbe* captured the imagination of artists and scholars, discussions about ornament could shift location and become detached from architecture. Since the Renaissance period at the very least, architectural ornament had been associated with the fragments and pieces detached from the architectural ensemble. This was a natural consequence of architects' encounter with the classical vocabulary in the form of ruins, as broken pediments, haphazardly preserved columns, capitals and friezes, and thinking of them as "mobile objects" was not that much of a stretch.[73] The collections of antiquities were displays of architectural fragments, embedded, literally mortared, into the walls of palaces, villas, and courtyards. In these "museums" architects did not seek to preserve the historical integrity of pieces in the manner of the nineteenth-century historical scholarship but instead reconnected them into new and original combinations and assemblages. As a result, the practice of thinking

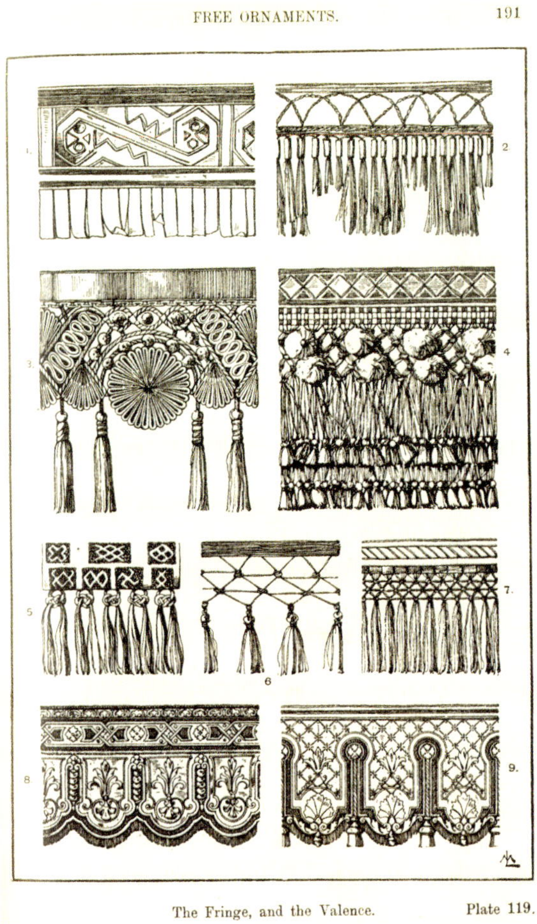

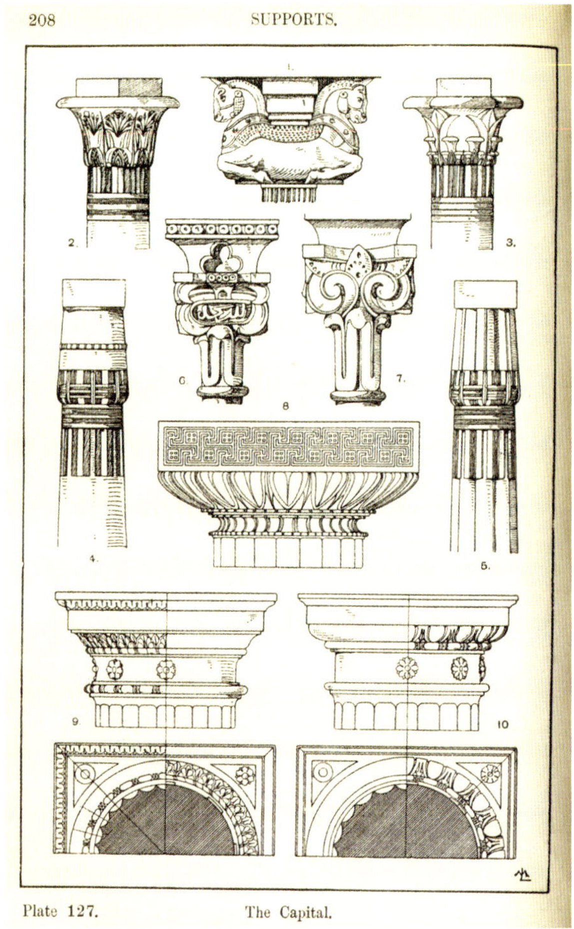

about ornamental components in isolation (independently) from their context grew apace even then, and many architectural treatises tended to focus on this aspect alone.[74] This trend, reinforced as it was by the archaeological work of most architects—from the sketchbooks of Bramante and Raphael to the publications of Desgodetz and Piranesi—experienced a slight though important shift in the nineteenth century: as the decorative arts became a magnet for interest and discourse, they absorbed architectural ornament as well. Relinquishing its original architectural association, ornament was increasingly conceived of and presented in isolation and, indeed, as interchangeable with the objects of *Kunstindustrie*. The fact that the terminological distinction between ornament and decoration also disappeared for all intents and purposes clearly signaled this shift. Franz Sales Meyer's *Ornamentale Formenlehre* (as a portfolio of three hundred plates in 1886, reissued several times as *Handbook of Ornament* through the 1890s), including, as it does, equally attentive evaluations and drawings of balusters,

Left **FIGURE 51**
Franz Sales Meyer, "The Fringe, and the Valence." From Meyer, *Ornamentale Formenlehre* (Leipzig, 1886).

Right **FIGURE 52**
Franz Sales Meyer, "The Capital." From Meyer, *Ornamentale Formenlehre*.

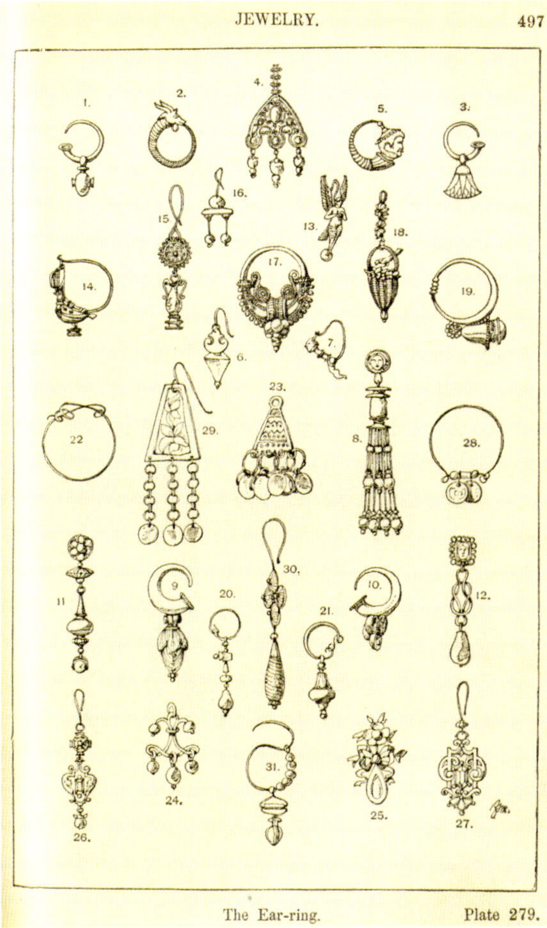

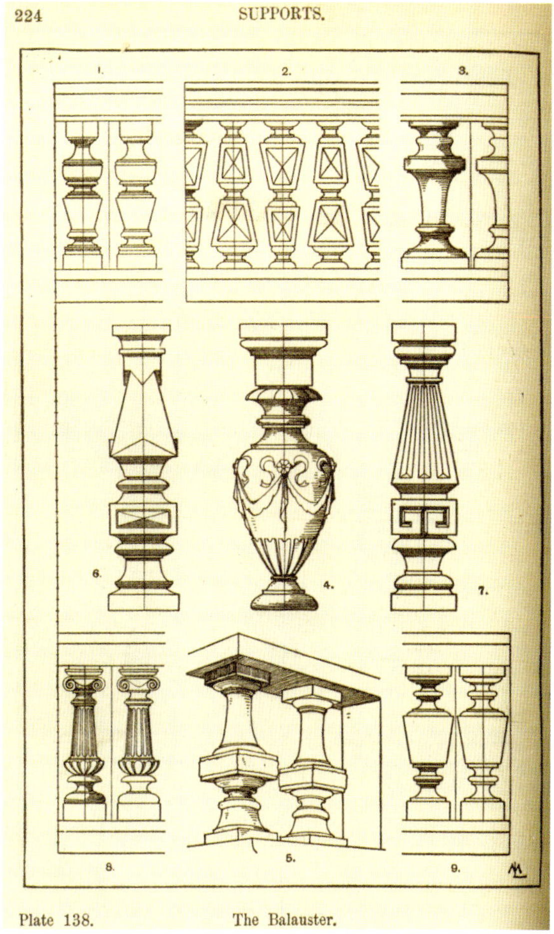

Left **FIGURE 53**
Franz Sales Meyer, "The Earring." From Meyer, *Ornamentale Formenlehre.*

Right **FIGURE 54**
Franz Sales Meyer, "The Balauster." From Meyer, *Ornamentale Formenlehre.*

earrings, column capitals, and embroidery, illustrates a trend that was at work for the better part of half a century (1906) (figs. 51–54).

This slippage from architectural ornament to a much broader range of applications can be observed in publications across the board and across Europe. Thus, in England it is already at work in Henry Shaw's *Encyclopaedia of Ornament* (1842), the "doyen" of most ornament books of the nineteenth century. Covering architectural details, tiles, embroidery, textile, metalwork, jewelry, stained glass, and wood carving, it juxtaposes and presents the most unexpected combinations. The Certosa di Pavia and a plate design by Israel van Meeken, ancient lacework and keystone ornaments from Normandy, or stained glass, needlework, and metal stair railings placed on the same or facing pages suggest deep affinities (figs. 55, 56). At the level of pattern, of linear complexity, rhythm, and density, the juxtapositions are insightful, coherent, and visually subtle. Moreover, the strategy is so consistent, and the shock of comparison so much belied by similarity, that

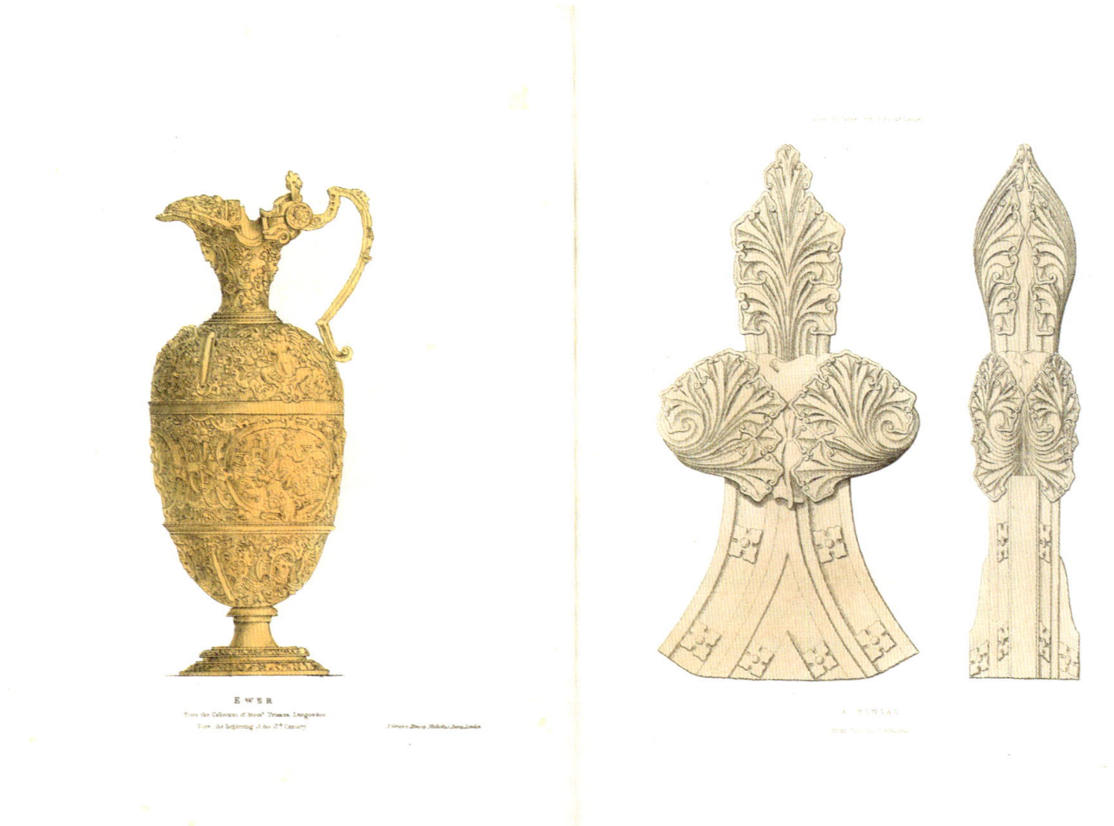

FIGURE 55
Henry Shaw, "Ewer, Finial." From *Encyclopaedia of Ornament* (1842).

a message about the mobility of ornamental form is unmistakable. The same approach is still at work much later in manuals like Richard Glazier's (1899), and even as late as in A. Hamlin's *History of Ornament* (1916), when he makes a point of noting transference across materials.[75]

This trend was true not only of English publications. Much work on the Continent followed the same pattern: Alfredo Melani in Italy (who includes architecture, too), Auguste Racinet, E. Collinot and A. de Beaumont, Franz Sales Meyer, Heinrich Dolmetsch, and others (fig. 57).[76] The thirst for the wider category of ornament as a self-contained domain touched even the architectural/art history domain and led to such publications as Cornelius Gurlitt's *Das Barock-und Rococo-Ornament Deutschlands* (1883–89) in a series that brought together architecture and the decorative arts.[77] In addition, ornament, disembodied and detached from a stable home, began to be treated as the foundation for the art of forms and was used to evolve theories of composition. This is certainly the case in the English model books and treatises that run from Richard Wornum's *Analysis of Ornament* (1855, based on his lectures of 1848–50 and now considered to be the earliest standard history of ornament) to the more popularly conceived *Lessons on Decorative Design* (1913) by Andrew Jackson.[78]

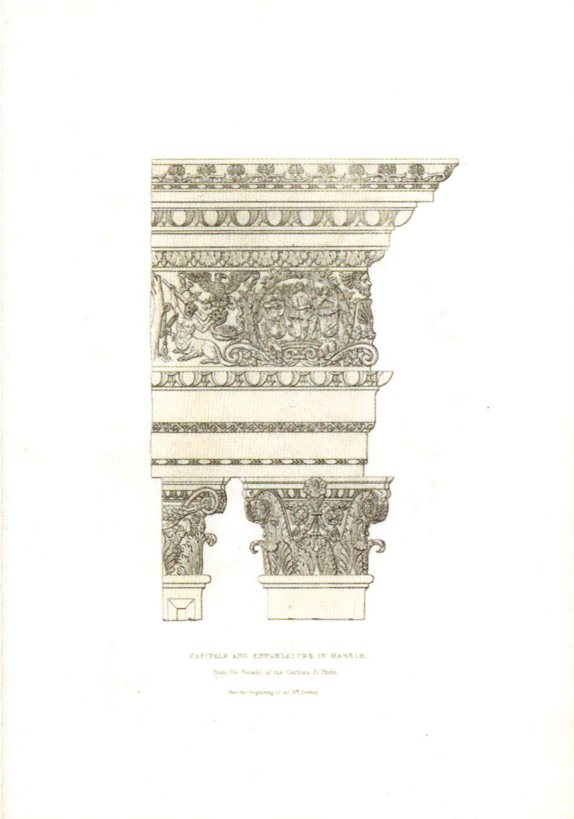

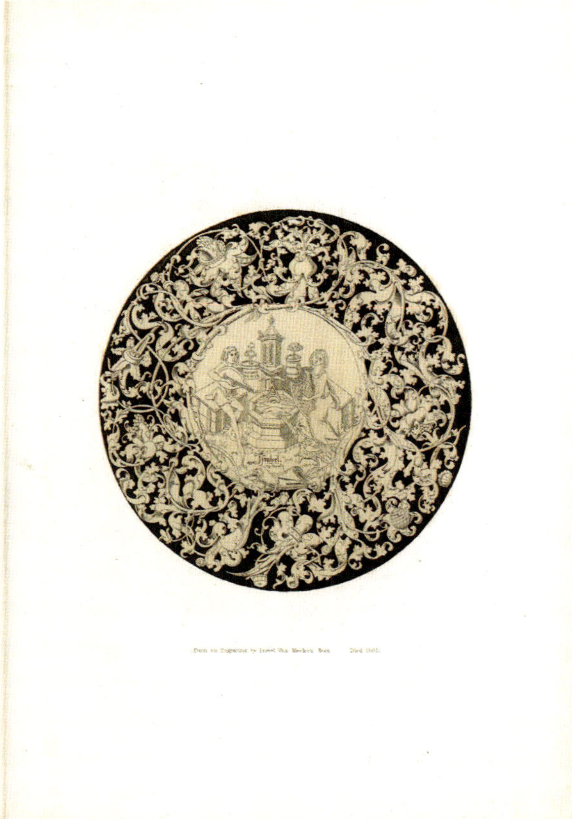

FIGURE 56
Henry Shaw, "Capitals and Entablature in Marble, Plate Design." From *Encyclopaedia of Ornament.*

The same was true of later European publications, such as Eugène Grasset and G. de Recy's *L'evolution ornamentale* (1913), which drew on the whole line of books on ornament, from Owen Jones to anthropological works, and was read to the Geographical Society.

There was one other feature new to the nineteenth century that drew the objects of daily use and architectural ornament into one discourse. For Ruskin and Morris architectural ornament was the location of artistic expression for the craftsman. With this move they associated ornament with its anonymous artisan-maker and in so doing operated a similar dislocation that we find in Semper: artistic content moved from the monument and its genius artist to the humble object. In both cases the anonymous maker is the artist and the ornament the repository of the anonymous *Volk*'s spirit and spiritual salvation. Since the architect does not directly handle the materials of his art, this also meant driving a wedge between architecture and ornament. The creative independence that Ruskin attributed to the artisan allowed architectural ornament to float away from architecture and be included in the domain of crafted things.[79] This tendency and its association to medieval work in particular was so strong that it reverberated into scholarly historical publications, and it took some time for the field to acknowledge that superbly crafted marble intarsia work, such as the altar rails and pulpits of late medieval Tuscany, were actually signed by the artists.[80]

This centripetal diffusion of ornament away from its architectural core and its marriage to forms of decoration associated with other materials led to a peculiar paradox: although its territory expanded, its specificity was reduced, and in publications and education ornament was conceived of separately, as a layer transferable from one material to another, from architecture to embroidery to porcelain. Indeed, this was observed at the time, and German architect Fritz Schumacher, for example, criticized this approach later.[81] An advertisement by a drawing firm to produce ornamental designs for carpets, glass, porcelain, wallpaper, metal decorations, lace, and fabrics in *Kunst und Gewerbe* (1868) reveals how quickly professions and the marketplace adapted to this new fluidity between artistic domains.[82]

Thus, the vast majority of books on ornament addressed broadly the entire subject and remained curiously neutral or devoid of much theoretical consequence or ramifications. With the exception of Ruskin and the connection he made between carved ornament, ethics, and labor, no connection with *Kultur* was attempted in most books. The intensity of debate had shifted to the decorative arts—and closer to the user. *Kunstgewerbe* and *Gewerbe* (whose definitions essentially overlapped) were the subject of news, not ornament.[83] Exhibiting a high index of "contemporaneity" since they were made by the machine, these objects seemed far more tied to the present than to traditional architectural ornament. Reports from the great exhibitions, evaluations of contemporary trends, and historical accounts flourished, and museum directors, historians, and art historians (especially in Germany and Austria), from Eitelberger through Bruno Bucher to Wilhelm von Bode, entered the fray.[84] Nor was their interest a passing or modish whim; they turned to the topic with much energy and with a conviction that showed up in the numerous titles they published. This intellectual excitement for objects extended to economics, arguably the engine of the whole phenomenon, and included the work of theorists of capitalism such as Werner Sombart and Heinrich Waentig, who brought together the critical topics of the century: technology, labor, *Kunstgewerbe*, and culture.[85]

VISUAL DISPLAY AND THE CULTURE OF MUSEUMS

Although publications propelled the object of daily use into the foreground of public attention and aesthetic concern, its visibility was assured by the museum display. The two phenomena—the rise of the object as focus for discourse and the museum movement—were intertwined since there was a tight connection between publication campaigns and museums.[86] However, the visual epicenter remained the physical display of objects in exhibitions: be they temporary venues, such as the great exhibitions that functioned as a pageant of objects to the millions

FIGURE 57
Auguste Racinet, "Egyptian Ornament." From *L'ornement polychrome* (1885–87).

EGYPTIAN. # EGYPTIEN. AEGYPTISCH

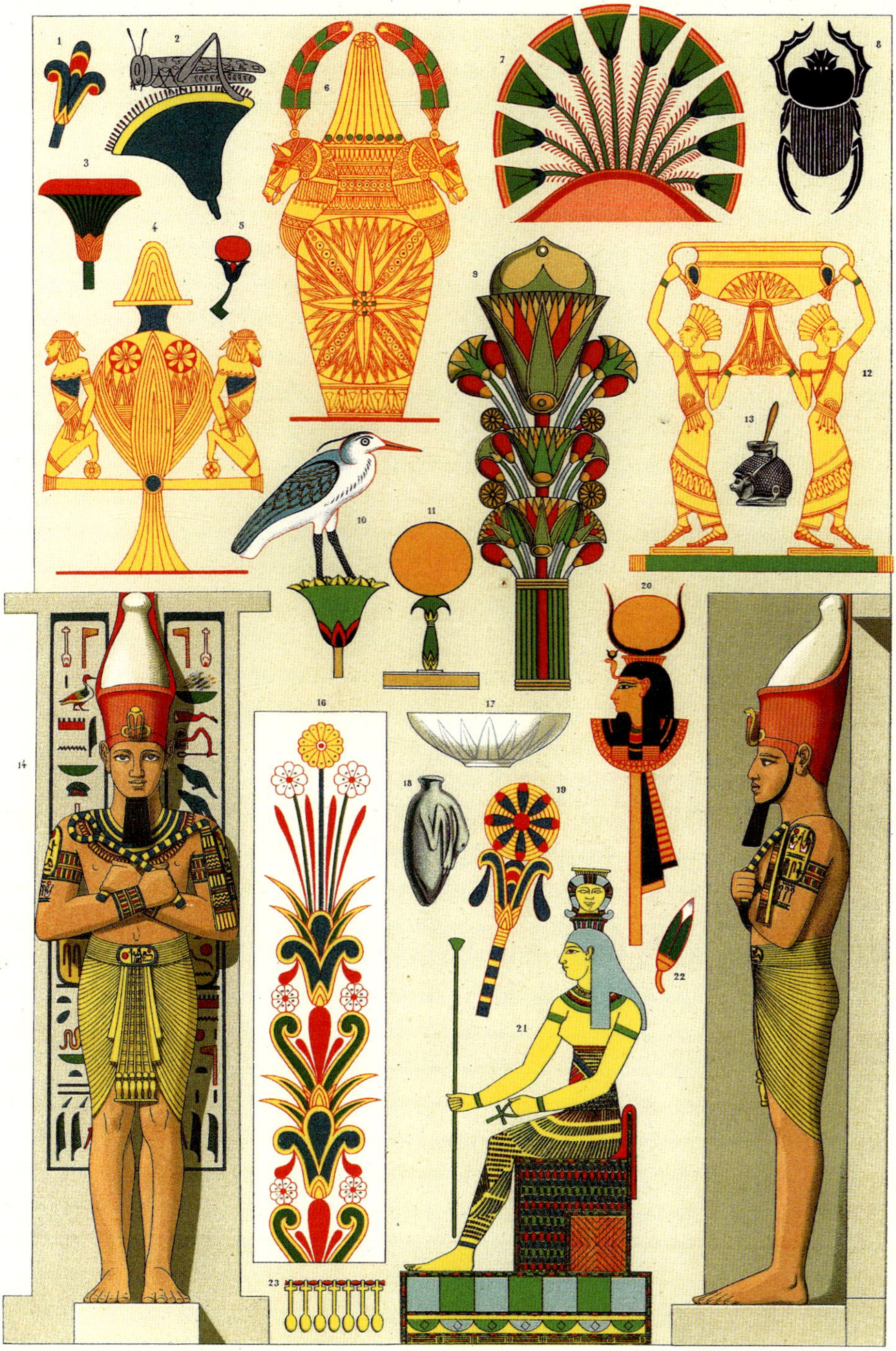

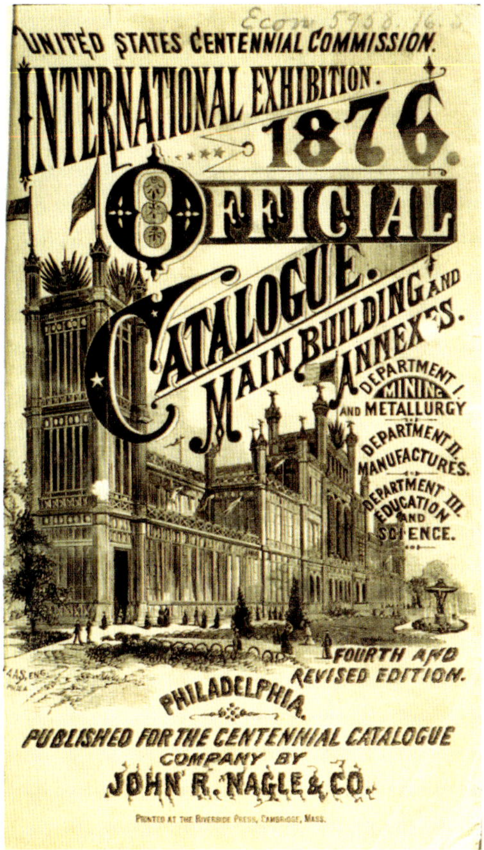

FIGURE 58
Title Page of United States Centennial Commission International Exhibition, Official Catalogue, 1876.

of visitors who flocked to these almost yearly events, or permanent ones—the museums of industry, art, ethnology, antiquities, folk art—that burst on the scene as national institutions and identified the material, organized it into various areas of knowledge, and classified it. The first World Exhibitions were perhaps the most important ones, as they set the trends and parameters for the discourse on objects. The highlights were certainly London 1851, Paris 1855, Vienna 1873, Paris 1889, Chicago 1893, and Paris 1900 (fig. 58). However, smaller venues also emerged in their fulsome wake, focused either thematically or regionally. Such were, for example, the 1886 Colonial and Indian Exhibition in London, the 1884 Esposizione Industriale in Turin, or the 1896 Berlin Gewerbeausstellung.[87] In these exhibitions objects intimately connected with domestic architecture as historical, folkloric, or ethnographic display were singled out in an even more direct way than was possible in the Great Exhibitions. Henry Cole had identified this development with great insight when, in his "Paris Exhibition of 1855," he prophesized: "The tendency of future Exhibitions (after 1851), in their foreign departments, will be to exhibit not rare and costly production, required by very few purchasers, but manufactures; and especially those manufactures the use of which is universal, and not merely national or peculiar."[88] In fact, an entirely new type of museum arose as result of the Great Exhibitions: the museum of decorative and industrial arts.

An overt economic agenda lay behind the educational mission of these museums, as the subtitle of Semper's essay "Wissenschaft, Industrie und Kunst" of 1852—"Proposals for the development of a national art at the closing of the London industrial exhibition"—had suggested long ago. Political imperatives also lay behind the enthusiasm to acquire and display objects in ever-greater numbers and dictated some of the moves. Both nationalism and a keen eye trained on the global markets were behind the creation of the Museum für Kunst und Industrie in Vienna, as well as the many applied arts museums in all the German *Länder*. This was not a factor across the board. The development of a national economy, the policy of spreading employment in depressed areas and of allowing for local identities were far more central to a newly reconstituted state like Germany or of a brittle conglomerate of cultures such as the Austrian empire than to Britain or France. In Austria, the connection between exhibits, teaching, publications, and development of economies within the empire was at the root of the museum's function and was steadily reinforced and developed.[89]

In the push to further the national economic agenda, museums became associated with the practical educational arm of the movement, some maintaining close ties with the craft schools or *Gewerbeschulen* (sharing professorial staff, tying exhibitions and collecting strategies to the needs of the students), others embracing the school within its own institutional mandate on the model of the South Kensington Museum. Such was the case of the Vienna museum and the many new decorative arts museums in Germany, like those in Dresden, Krefeld, Hamburg, Düsseldorf, Cologne, or Hagen. On the whole, this was the prevailing model, but gradually nuances arose.[90] Many museums were not only concerned with the industrial economy but also developed programs to revive the production of folk art.[91] For example, under its first director, Rudolf von Eitelberger, the Vienna museum sought to promote folk industries, such as woodworking, as a way of improving the economy in the poor mountain areas, such as in the Tyrol. And the encouragement of carpet-weaving in such territories as Bukovina had just as much to do with the desire to keep the nationalities pacified as to promote some economic improvement in areas that were lagging behind.[92] Eitelberger's successor, Jakob von Falke, reinforced this agenda and used the 1873 Vienna Great Exhibition to introduce the new category "The International Village," which promoted the folk arts even more (fig. 59). The decorative arts focus was also shared with museums of ethnography and even (high) art, as was the case of the Folkwang Museum in Hagen, which housed Karl Osthaus's Asian and African ethnographic collection of *Gewerbe*, or the Hamburg Kunsthalle, where Alfred Lichtwark was later director.[93] Other museums, even more in tune with the

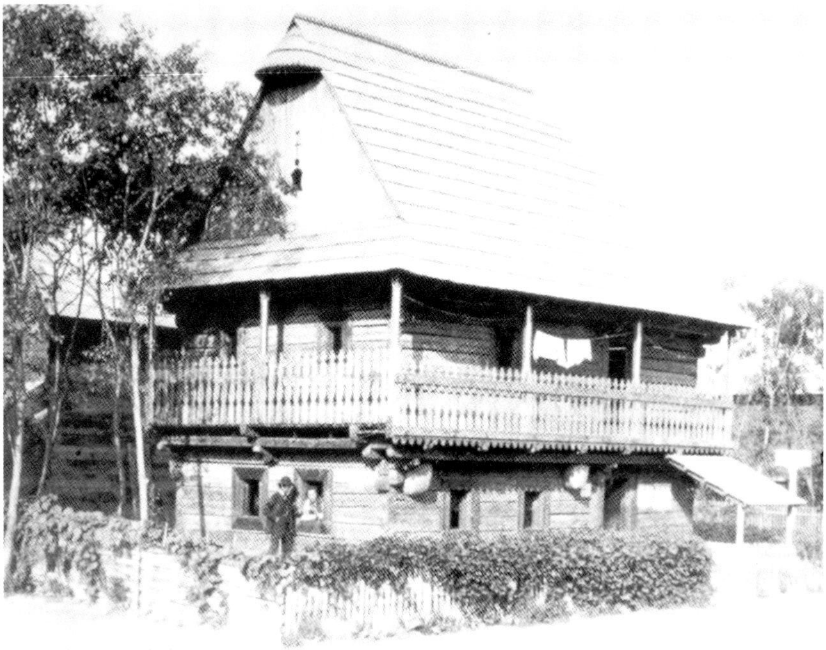

FIGURE 59
Das Internationale Dorf, Vienna Great Exhibition, 1873.

nationalist agenda that propelled the whole museum movement, blended artifacts and history and claimed regional or national museum status. Such was the case of the Germanisches Nationalmuseum in Nuremberg (founded by Hans von Aufsess in 1852), the Schweizer Landesmuseum in Zurich (founded by Heinrich Angst in 1898), or the Bayerisches Nationalmuseum in Munich, all of which focused on decorative arts and historical interiors (rather than paintings and sculpture, the prerogative of art history museums) and provided yet another context for the cultural relevance of objects of domestic use (fig. 60). Perhaps Georg Fuchs, a state administrator in Darmstadt, conveyed the ramifications of the decorative arts phenomenon within state politics most succinctly: "The time will come when it will be seen that the promotion of artistic culture is synonymous with enhancing the creative forces of a nation."[94] The place for debate, promotion, and news was assured by a host of journals created in conjunction with these museums. This meant that a criticism literature and vocabulary associated with objects developed alongside the collections themselves. As they drew on art historians, museum curators, historians, and artists/architects, it also meant that they provided a forum for overlap and cross-fertilization between fields.[95]

If the lion's share of attention in publications and exhibitions went to the portable object, the fast developing museum culture also affected the definition and conception of architecture. Exhibited in the same venues as the object of the decorative arts and industrial manufacture, that is, the Great Exhibition and the *Kunstgewerbe* museum, architecture came to be thought of as an "object" too.

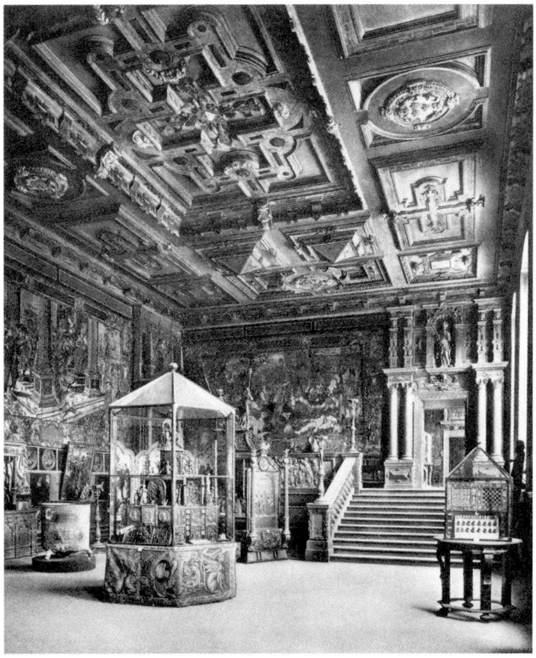

Once on display, architecture became subject to the same rules and aesthetics as its smaller-scale siblings, available for consumption to the same degree, detached from its surroundings and on view, and implicitly inviting comparison. In the Great Exhibitions architecture was on display and objectified not only as pavilions (thus starting an important tradition for architecture that led to the Pavillon de l'Esprit Nouveau and the Barcelona Pavilion in the twentieth century, among others), but also in other forms (fig. 61). Particularly important were the peasant and primitive dwellings reinforcing the emphasis on the house for being easier to transport and re-erect, but also for more aptly illustrating a nation in an international context.[96] As "history of habitation" it satisfied the historical curiosity of the public while the technological achievements of other structures (such as the Gallerie des Machines or the Eiffel Tower in 1889) illustrated feats of science and engineering.

However, the connection between the applied arts museum and architecture was even more important, as it struck at the very core of its definition. Ever since Semper there was a tacit understanding that the objects of the decorative arts, whether handmade or mass produced, pertained to and somehow involved architecture. And as we have seen, Semper had made the connection between architecture and the objects of household use the core of his essay "Ideales Museum für Metallotechnik," published by Julius Leisching. In this piece Semper recommended a path through the exhibits and hence an installation strategy that focused on materials rather than on the geographic origin of the objects:

FIGURE 60
Dachau Hall in Bayerisches Nationalmuseum, Munich. From *Der Neubau des Bayerischen Nationalmuseums in München* (Munich, 1902).

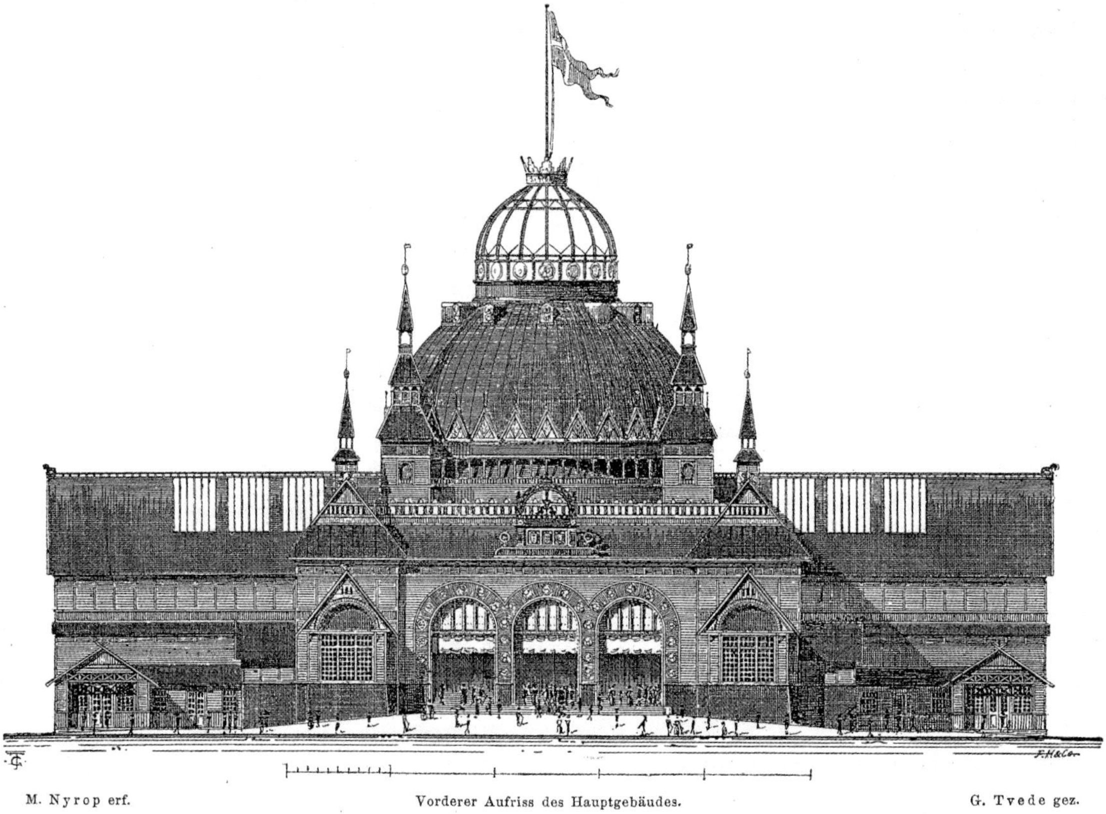

FIGURE 61
Pavilions from the 1888 Nordic Exhibition in Copenhagen. *Deutsche Bauzeitung*, February 9, 1889.

moving from textiles through clay and wood to metal and stone, as he had done in *Der Stil*, the spiral movement inside the museum he described would have brought the viewer finally to architecture, the center and climax of the circuit. As Leisching summarized it: "A collection of industrial and artistic objects would be best achieved if it were divided in five classes, one for each fundamental motif and a fifth class for the connection of the four elements: for the high art of architecture."[97]

NEW DISCIPLINES: ANTHROPOLOGY, ARCHAEOLOGY, AND FOLK STUDIES

Not all debates took place among arts-based disciplines. As scientific interest caught up to the initial economic impetus behind the Great Fairs, a host of learned disciplines arose to process the objects that were flooding the market and populating the museums and exhibition grounds: produced by industry, excavated by historians of various stripes, obtained as result of colonial expansion and domination, they posed new questions that needed new tools in order to be answered. Their contribution to the discourse on objects and ornament in architecture constituted an important if amorphous background rumbling.

Indeed, if a discourse about the everyday visual environment and its components was propelled to the attention of the book-reading public from the scholar to the *Hausfrau* by publications that flooded the market, and if the museum was its most public and visible corollary, what drove the whole engine were the newly minted scholarly organizations that heralded the maturity of a host of disciplines. Truly new they were not, as much of anthropology, archaeology, art history, aesthetics, folk studies, and cultural history had been present in one form or another for centuries. But delimiting their objects, disengaging them from each other and articulating the uniqueness of their respective purposes into fully fledged academic disciplines happened in the later decades of the nineteenth century, when they found their identity and founded their professional organizations.[98]

Anthropology, linguistics, culture theories, ethnology, and especially history—particularly with reference to national character, *Völkerpsychologie/Volksgeist* and its material culture—all had interacted and been amorphously constituted in the eighteenth to the mid-nineteenth century. In Germany, Wilhelm and Alexander von Humboldt, Fichte, Schiller, Herder, Kant, Ranke, Lazarus, Herbart, and Dilthey, all "spoke" to each other and affected the course of these disciplines.[99] It is precisely this ambiguity of borders inherited from previous generations that allowed much exchange and conversation, even as each discipline was moving toward its own methodologies and problematics. As the vicissitudes of the museums indicated, their material was so interchangeable that sometimes it was not clear where certain collections belonged or which discipline should curate it. Thus, for example, the Japanese ethnographic collection from the Vienna Exhibition of 1873 was split between several museums, with some works going to the Museum für Kunst und Industrie and others being kept in limbo by Arthur von Scala in his own Oriental Museum until the Natural History Museum finally opened an ethnography subsection and gave them a permanent home.[100] What is interesting here is not so much how collection-driven each of these disciplines was, but that their intersection point was the world of *Kunstgewerbe*, whether their interest lay in modernity, history, or prehistory. Material culture, that is, portable objects, often of humble, unsigned pieces by anonymous makers, was used as a means to reconstruct ancient monuments and sites by the archaeologist, to understand foreign (so-called primitive) cultures by the anthropologist, to preserve and exhibit the natural artistic genius of the nation by way of folk art by the ethnologist, to place "high" art in a cultural context by art historians, and to draw attention to the achievement of the machine and the artisan's workshop by the founders of what would later become "industrial design."

What these disciplines shared was thus perhaps more important than what divided them: an orientation toward history; a fascination with psychology and

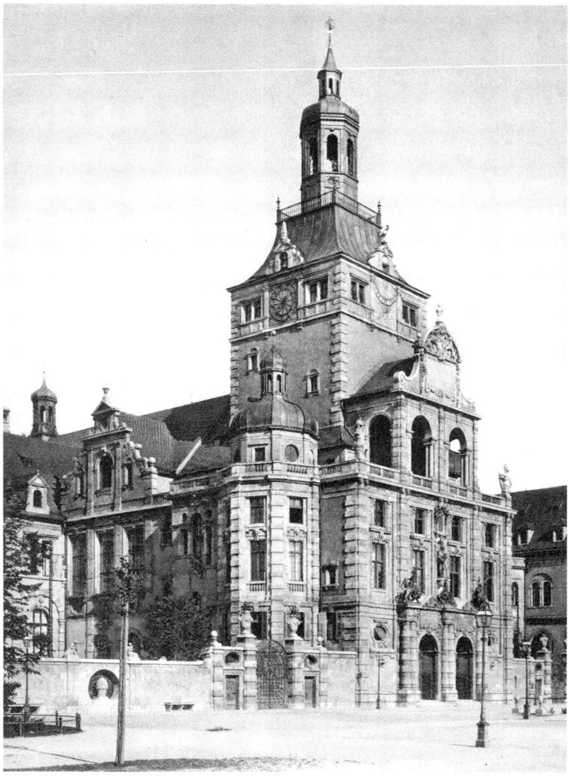

FIGURE 62
Tower façade of Bayerisches National-museum, Munich. From *Der Neubau des Bayerischen Nationalmuseums in München* (Munich, 1902).

ornament (which were linked); and a methodology based on stylistic classification. Their main energy was channeled toward organizing the treasure chest of the world, and style became the classification tool they all embraced. Moreover, these disciplines also shared the fact that none was innocent of political and economic undercurrents, as the museums associated with them showed only too plainly. The search for a national cultural identity was deeply enmeshed with the museum movement, and while this led to collecting (for example, the museum movement in Germany was part of its self-conception as *Kulturnation*), it also caused the rise of ethnology and folk studies, as well as the commodification of the nation. This phenomenon was due to different reasons in different countries.[101] In France, preservation claimed the greatest attention, and much historical work was associated with the *Monuments historiques*. In Germany, the creation of institutions such as the National Museum in Bavaria revealed the dual face of the identity problem after unification: preservation of regional identity on the one hand, and efforts to forge the larger German identity on the other (fig. 62). In Austria it was the need to keep together a multicultural state, against the pressures of local nationalisms, that sustained a variety of anthropology and ethnology discourses.[102]

The competition among nations for markets and economic gain also lay behind—and sometimes quite openly—the scholarly work and cultural policies that supported the development of educational institutions, museums, and the like. As long as histories and museums dealt with marketable goods that were produced on a mass scale such connections into the mercantile world and its political corollaries were inevitable. But not all connections were as obvious as the state-sponsored program to educate craftsmen attached to the South Kensington Museum or the Vienna Museum für Kunst und Industrie. Some discourses moved into the disinterested scientific domain—no matter how they were used by others or upon what crest of wave they rode, while studies on ethnic identity as revealed in folk art were an (almost) overt corollary of the nationalism debates. However, the work on definitions of culture, though equally pertinent to this political issue, appeared to maintain a proper scientific distance from the parliamentary fray and the street brawl. Archaeology and anthropology, as well as the related discipline of art history, dwelled in this realm.

The rise of anthropology was connected to the discoveries in prehistoric archaeology and the heated debates they led to at the time on the origin of man and origin of peoples, which had been at the center of discourse in any event since Darwin's revolutionary publications. Such concerns touched on many fields, from anatomy and psychology to geography and linguistics. Indeed, in Austria the anthropological association was founded in 1870 under an anatomist, Carl Rokitansky, who saw anatomy as the basis of anthropology and the first permanent anthropological exhibit, in 1876, was in the Natural History Museum, where anthropology was defined as the natural history of man.[103] However, much anthropological work was psychology-based, as it involved the personalization of the *Volk*. This was potentially delicate ground to tread, as much of nineteenth-century politics revolved around nation formation. Such a delicate balance was nowhere more true than in Austria, whose multicultural makeup, its survival even, depended on definitions of national identities and races.[104] The major Austrian enterprise *Die österreichisch-ungarische Monarchie in Wort und Bild* (1886–1902), also known as *Kronprinzwerk,* was such an effort at acknowledging and dealing with the ethnic cultures and geography of the empire from varied points of view: geo-scientific, bio-zoological, anthro-ethnological, and historical.[105] Here as elsewhere the concept of *Volk* became a key reference point in scholarly discourse as well as in popular literature across the board.[106]

However, the vehicle by which anthropologists arrived at their conclusions was even more important in fostering conversation between disciplines than were the various conclusions that were drawn. Ornament was the point of intersection. In their eagerness to classify objects they focused on ornament, and in so doing they borrowed from art history and archaeology, while in turn they pushed into the spotlight the anonymous objects of daily use as primary evidence for understanding culture. This reciprocal insemination, indeed these fields' very ability to "speak" to each other, should not seem unexpected, since they shared a reading of Semper. He himself had drawn from a variety of heterogeneous sources, and the issues and vocabulary he developed could be easily reappropriated into these cognate disciplines. Among the first to make and publish systematic studies of ornament in the 1890s were Swedish anthropologist Hjalmar Stolpe and his English colleague H. Colley March. For Stolpe the comparative study of ornament ("vergleichende Studium der Ornamentik") was the most valuable aid in developing a classification system for both museum display and research purposes.[107] Writing in 1893, Henry Balfour, curator of the ethnographic museum at Oxford (which was essentially the collection of General Pitt Rivers), located the interest in the "absolute origins" of the various arts of mankind in the stimulus generated by the work and collection of Pitt Rivers in the 1870s and 1880s: "The illustration of the gradual growth of Decorative Art from simple beginnings was a part of his scheme for establishing series of objects with a view to tracing the stages in the evolution of all the material arts of mankind."[108] Indeed, in many ways Pitt Rivers's method and findings were of a piece with Semper's: his series, intended to show the origin and growth, "step by step," and variations of certain patterns, identified "degradation" of designs, successive copying, and derivations such as on gourds and pottery "from the strings by which once vessels were carried."[109] And in a prophetic conclusion that seems intended to set the stage for Riegl's exactly contemporary *Stilfragen* focused on the arabesque and palmette, Balfour added that "whole chapters might easily be written upon the history and variations of single designs or patterns."[110]

Most of the early anthropologists had read Semper and had taken his theories to heart. Indeed, it became the norm for anthropologists like Hjalmar Stolpe (who inaugurated the practice within his discipline) to use ornament to identify style and hence to establish the provenance of objects.[111] H. Colley March also sounded very Semperian: "As soon as man began to make things, to fasten a handle to a stone implement, to construct a wattle roof, to weave a mat, skeuomorphs (structure-form) became an inseparable part of his brain, and ultimately occasioned a mental craving or expectancy."[112] German anthropologist Franz Boas went even further and used decorative typology to examine body painting among North American Indians.[113] These writings, processing Semper's ideas, were read in turn by art historians like Riegl and Aby Warburg. Thus, in a strange concatenation of influences, Semper's theories converged with theirs across anthropology.

In anthropology, especially as it evolved in the German-speaking world, a principal issue was culture—as in art history—but its location was sought in humble objects of daily use rather than in high art. This was no longer Semper's model, although in other respects his approach and focus owed much to the excavation site and to anthropological practices. This shift from materials and making as ordering principles to cultural specificity is nowhere more apparent than in an 1877 debate at the U.S. National Museum in New York. Recently arrived in America and involved in curating the museum's collection, Boas moved to place culture at the center when he fought against the Semperian classification and display strategy of ordering objects according to physical resemblance irrespective of the cultures that had produced them. Instead he pioneered the "vitrines" as display strategy—the reenactment of a moment in time—and fought for the placement of objects in the setting of their own culture as a means to illustrate and understand their real meaning. This approach was perceived as radical at the time and caused a well-publicized debate between Boas and Otis T. Mason, curator at the museum.[114] Perhaps it is not surprising that Boas, educated in the German environment where the history of culture was a prominent concern across disciplines, should have pioneered this strategy for anthropology.[115] His vitrines, so illustrative and visually appealing, spoke equally to the scientific concerns of the field and to the exhibition-as-show (or as panoramas) mentality that was generated by the universal exhibitions and pervaded the scholarly museums world.[116] Indeed, Boas conceived his vitrines like panoramas in which sculpture and painting blended into each other to create realistic likenesses, with figures and objects emerging from a chiaroscuro background that facilitated and enhanced the illusion of life.

Active in the 1890s and crossing disciplinary boundaries even more than his colleagues, Alfred C. Haddon, a biologist and professor of zoology at Dublin and equally at home in the fields of archaeology and anthropology, developed an original theory for the derivation of decorative forms.[117] Although in his *Evolution in Art: As Illustrated by the Life-Histories of Design* (1902) he drew on and acknowledged ideas first broached by Colley March, Stolpe, and especially Semper, he brought those ideas together into a comprehensive system.[118] "Professor G. Semper was the first to show that the basket-maker, the weaver, and the potter originated those combinations of line and colour which the ornamentalist turned to his own use when he had to decorate walls, cornices and ceilings." Typically he illustrated his argument with images of tattoos and ornaments derived from basic implements such as fishhooks (fig. 63). But he went even further. Colley March had argued that structure conditioned ornament; Semper that technique had done so. Instead, Haddon argued that fauna and flora also did. Although Haddon was interested in classification and hence in style, he was also (and mainly) interested in meaning. And with his skeuomorphs (decorative transformations of artificial objects such as fastenings, textiles, pottery, and stone and their transference onto

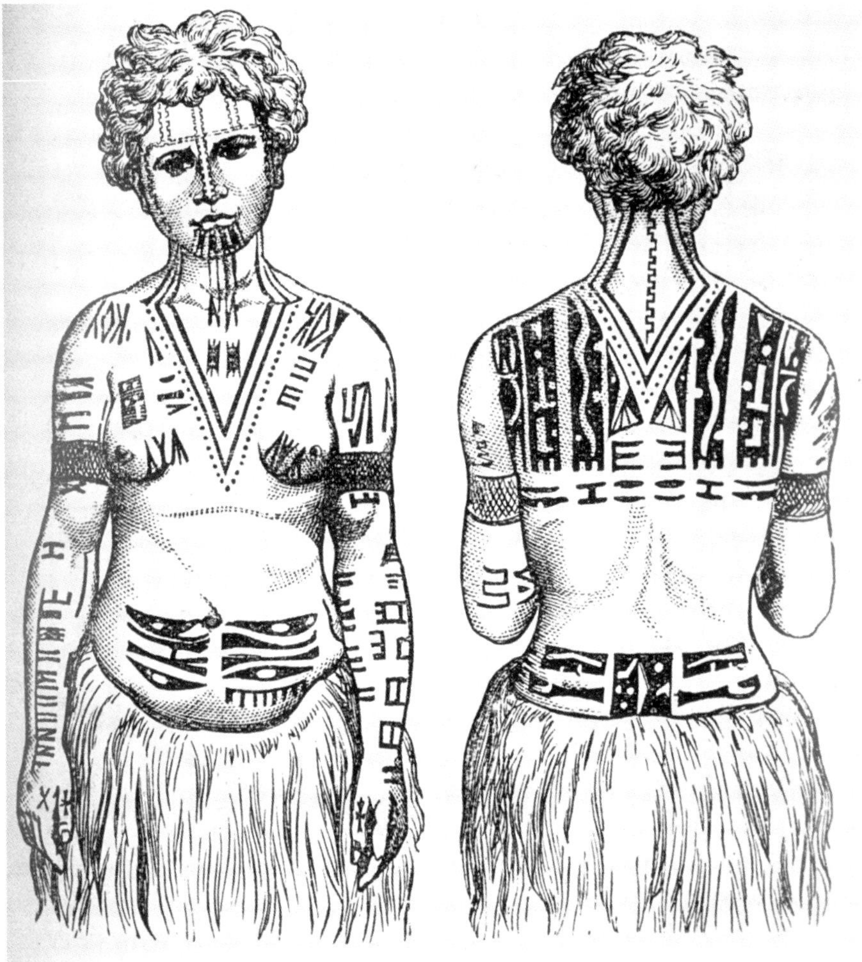

FIGURE 63
Alfred Haddon, Motu tattoos. From *Evolution in Art* (1902).

wooden buildings), biomorphs (decorative transformations of natural objects) as well as zoomorphs, phyllomorphs, and anthropomorphs he developed a detailed theory of material transformations (figs. 64–66). Like Semper he too reached across media from lace to pottery to architecture, arguing that "what was no longer wanted as a necessity was kept up as ornament."[119] His ultimate conclusions belong to anthropology but they turn the spotlight on ornament with additional brightness: "It will often be found that the more pure and homogeneous a people are, the more uniformity will be found in their art work, and that florescence of decorative art is a frequent result of race mixture."[120]

In the later nineteenth century the rise of archaeology as *Grosswissenschaft* (large-scale science) paralleling the phenomena of the *Grossindustrie* (large-scale industry) and *Grossstadt* (metropolis) meant that large excavations produced a vast number of recovered objects that needed to be processed—that is, needed to be classified and displayed.[121] As in today's archaeological digs, the sheer quantity

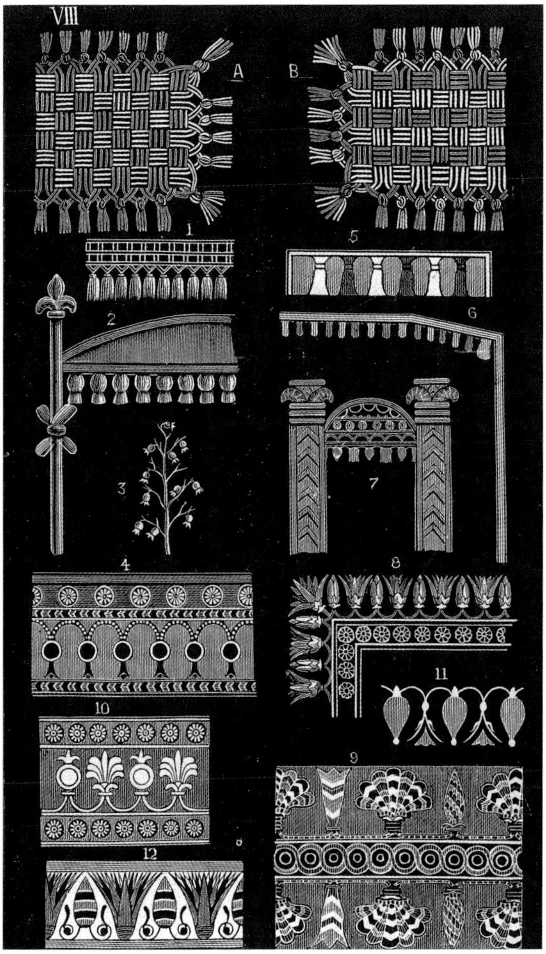

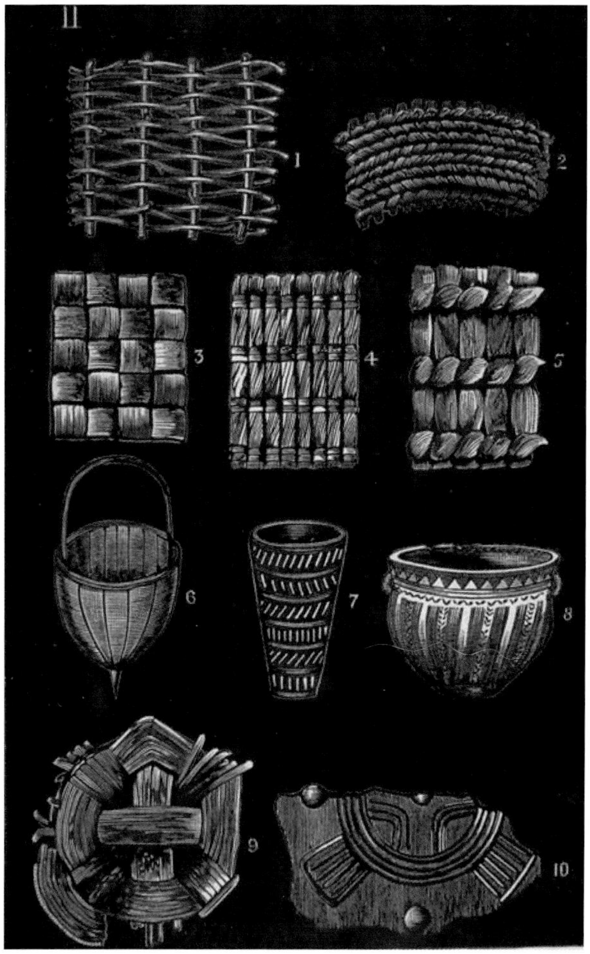

Left **FIGURE 64**
Alfred Haddon, phyllomorphs. From *Evolution in Art.*

Right **FIGURE 65**
Alfred Haddon, skeuomorphs of wattlework. From *Evolution in Art.*

of fragments excavated was formidable, as hundreds of crates were shipped from ports like Smyrna to the museums of Western Europe. Since scientific archaeologists, like the members of the Deutsches Archaeologisches Institut, regarded all objects recovered as equal, they were all kept and needed to be processed, stored, and displayed. Stylistic analysis was an efficient way to sort them and the museum was the prime vehicle to display them. Thus the ever-expanding quantity of artifacts that archaeologists dug up also led to the exponential growth of the museum as a place where these items could be collected. In Germany in particular, where enthusiasm for archaeology reached a climax in the nineteenth century, the phenomenon was associated with the desire to put the country on the international map as a *Kulturnation*. The state-sponsored excavations were thus underpinned by political interests that facilitated negotiations to export the artifacts. Such was the case of the major finds at Pergamon that put the other major German excavation site—Olympia—almost in the shade.[122]

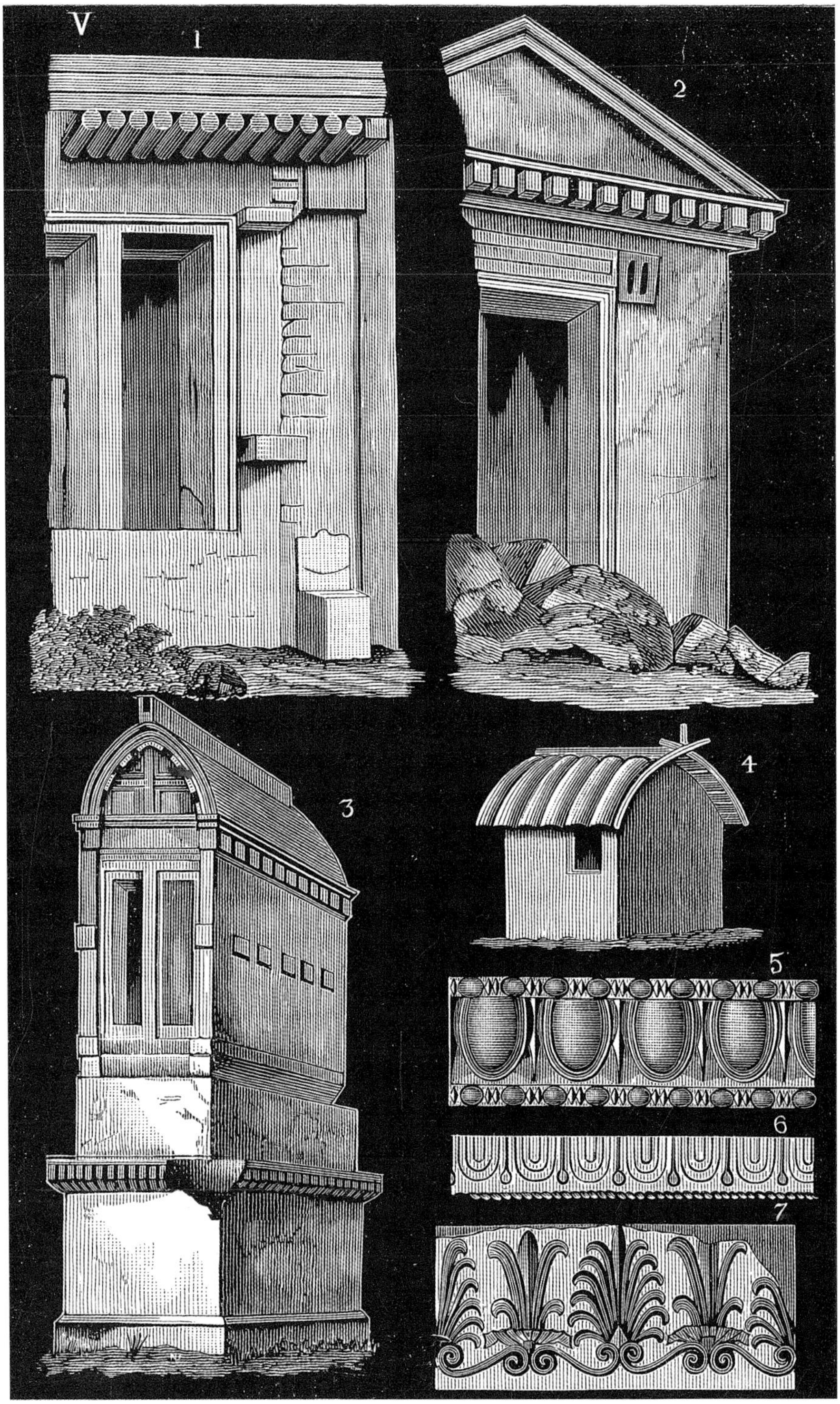

FIGURE 66

Alfred Haddon, skeuomorphs of timbering. From *Evolution in Art*.

Forced to make sense of the artifacts that these sites yielded, particularly as they reached beyond the historical periods and touched on prehistory or on geographically remote cultures, meant that archaeology interacted with anthropology. Moreover, as the findings that could most easily be exported and more frequently found were household wares—pots, jewelry, arms, and so forth—rather than the monumental ensembles such as the Pergamon altar, the objects that archaeology was primarily dealing with belonged to *Kunstgewerbe,* that is, to the same species as those of anthropology and the rising decorative arts movement. Increasingly after 1870 pottery and the minor arts began to play an important role in archaeological treatises. As Suzanne Marchand has noted, regional pottery typologies were elaborated as humble objects lent themselves more easily to positivistic sequencing and national typologies than did monumental sculpture.[123] Classification works best with quantity and consistent "quality" rather than with unique objects of great genius. As a result, museums became "archives" rather than display institutions, and the focus on minute details and the most modest finds was accompanied by an increasing attention on measurable objects and chronology.

Moreover, archaeologists borrowed from philology as they did from palaeontology and anthropology. This environment of hybrid methods affected art history and, as we will see, gave rise to the Morellian connoisseurship method, and was in turn affected by it.[124] Works like Alexander Conze's *Melische Thongefässe* (1862) or his *Frammenti di vaso di bronzo* (1874) belong to this trend, and, as Alois Riegl's later exploitation of these works for his *Stilfragen* (1893) indicate, they were easily absorbed into the art historical discourse with a decorative arts slant. Indeed, in this period sculpture experienced a diminution in status that went hand in hand with the rise of interest in these ancient objects of everyday use (fig. 67).[125] Arguably miniature sculptures, they had the added appeal of providing a cultural coefficient, whereas the great works of sculpture could not. Often archaeological and anthropological *Kunstgewerbe* concerns also merged, as did their publications. W. G. Goodyear's *The Grammar of the Lotus* (London, 1891), much used by Riegl, was one such example. Cross-publications also helped to pollinate disciplines: anthropologist Haddon published in *Illustrated Archaeologist,* vol. 1 (1893), as did Riegl at about the same time in anthropology journals.

In his melting pot of methodologies and philosophical threads, Semper had looked to style as a fundamental category of objects. Archaeology also turned to style, borrowing and enriching this art historical instrument at the same time. Indeed, the rise of archaeology as *Grosswissenschaft* buttressed the development of stylistic analysis as classification instrument. The large quantity of objects quarried and excavated in foreign lands, then crated and shipped, needed to be sorted quickly once they reached their distant museum destinations.[126] It is not surprising, therefore, to see this moment marking a climax in the development of stylistic

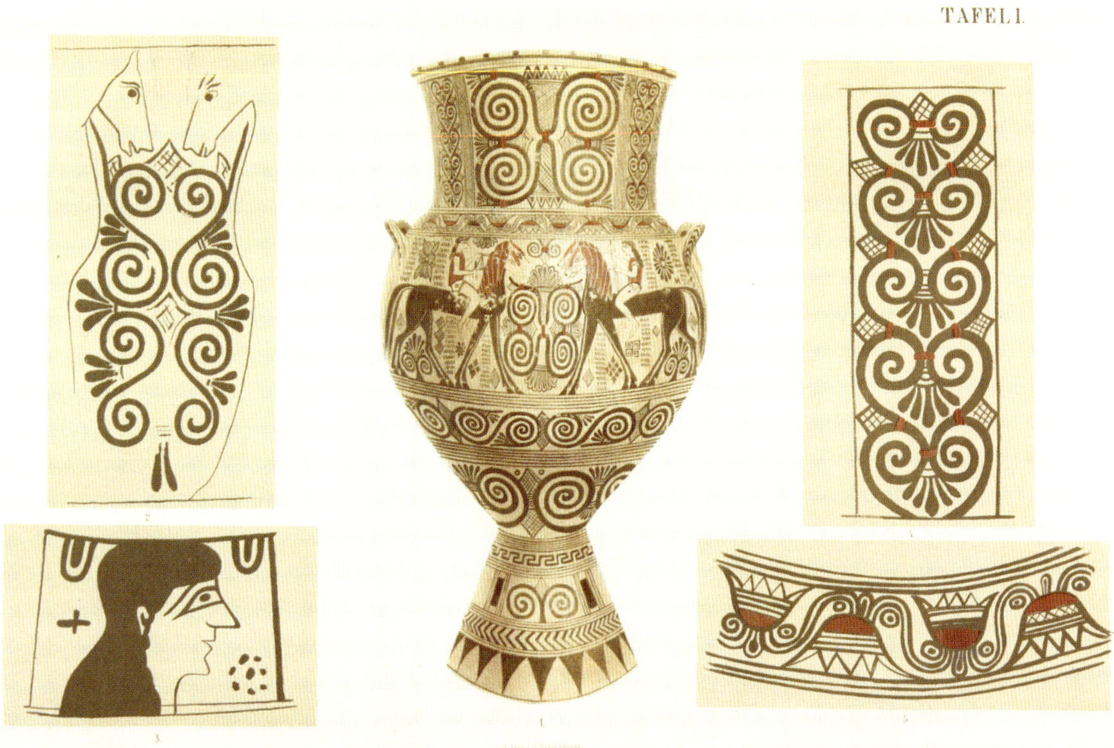

FIGURE 67
Alexander Conze, Plate I. From *Melische Thongefässe* (Leipzig, 1862).

analysis and its methodologies. And it is also not surprising to see the father of art connoisseurship—Giovanni Morelli—developing his own method of close analysis of details from a positivistic foundation in palaeography and studies of palaeontology—that is, sciences whose materials were the faint traces of long disappeared cultures or life forms, or the minute evidence of variations in script (fig. 68).[127]

The connection between architecture and archaeology was simultaneous and equally marked. Traditionally, and still today, architects populate archaeological sites, and indeed, this had been Semper's starting point after all. As Ernst Curtius described in his "Nekrolog" for Adolf Michaelis, the excavator of Olympia, who was influenced by Bötticher and Schinkel and remained faithful to the idea of a fundamental Greek correspondence between form and content, he used architects on many sites: Friedrich Adler, Wilhelm Dörpfeld, Alois Hauser, Carl Humann, Furtwängler.[128] Moreover, archaeologists also allowed their discipline to spill over into popular culture by participating in exhibitions and delivering lectures at memorable events and to large audiences. Curtius, for example, gave famous anniversary speeches at Göttingen for the birthday of the king of Hannover and for the annual Schinkelfest, which were also published.[129]

In addition, the interest in primitive cultures that grew in the wake of the first universal exhibitions also expanded to include folk art, which was increasingly seen as its geographically more accessible European equivalent, with the added bonus that it supported a nationalist agenda. Here too Semper had pioneered the way with his interest in the art of the "primitive" non-European peoples and the importance he attached to instinct. Like anthropology and archaeology, and perhaps even more so, folk studies also rose on the crest of the nationalist wave. Given the exaltation of the *Volksgeist/Volksgemüt/Volkscharakter* in German lands in all culture-related issues in this period, the concern with *Volk* increased across all disciplines. Also like its disciplinary siblings, *Volkskunde* was connected to psychology, though in this case to the *Völkerpsychologie* of the anthropologists developed in the 1850s by Moritz Lazarus (who applied Herbartian psychology to larger units, such as the *Volk*) and Heymann Steinthal, who started the *Zeitschrift für Völkerpsychologie und Sprachwissenschaft* (1859). Inspired by Wilhelm von

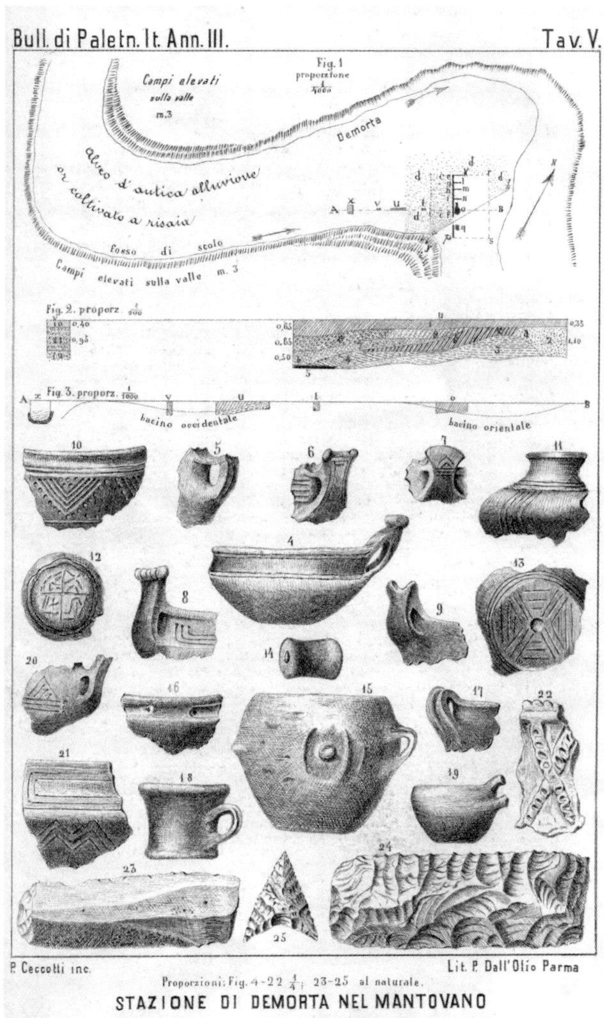

FIGURE 68
"Stazione di Demorta nel Mantovano." From *Bullettino di paletnologia italiana* 3, no. 5 (May 1877). Harvard University, Museum of Comparative Zoology.

Humboldt and Herder's concept of *Nationalcharakter,* they sought to identify the *Volksgeist* and found its purest expression in language, mythology, and customs.[130] In Germany it was tied to the rising peasant ideology in the 1890s, to which Julius Langbehn's wildly successful *Rembrandt als Erzieher* (thirty-nine editions in the first two years after publication in 1890) greatly contributed. Langbehn connected art, leadership, and nationalism with a personalized *Volk,* and equated *Volkstum* with *Bauerntum* (peasantry) and the *Volksseele* (people's soul) with *Bauernseele* (peasant's soul). Such an approach, notwithstanding the association with a Dutch rather than a German artist, touched the sensitive nerve of "Germanic euphoria" following the unification, which looked for its archetypal artistic and architectural patrimony.[131] Making the momentous connection between art (Rembrandt) and *Volk,* Langbehn permitted art and architectural history and criticism to breach the gap between disciplines.

In folk studies the prominence of the anonymous object and of ornament reigned supreme as the whole movement was primarily focused on the culture of objects, or *Sachkultur.* This was in part because the *Kunstgewerbe* movement had fed the interest in *Volkskultur* in the first place. Indeed, the two movements were almost synonymous, as the term *Hausindustrie* (a synonym for *Gewerbe*) was only replaced by *Volkskunst* after a couple of decades.[132] Interest in both folk costume and architecture started in c. 1800, and, in Germany, for example, it was fed by economic measures to improve agriculture (the interest in designing the most efficient farm led to interest in peasant houses), as well as by the landscape preservation movement (concerned with the beautification of the countryside).[133] Originally architects were not much involved, and it was the women's magazines such as *Illustrierte Frauen-Zeitung* that played a more important role in promoting the *Hausindustrie* in the 1880s.[134] Its main interest was in embroidery and lace making, subjects that increasingly attracted attention such that even an art historian like Riegl turned to these topics, treating them with as much seriousness as he had carpets or architecture.[135] Indeed, many art historians entered the folk studies arena—Falke, Eitelberg, even Warburg, who organized a *Volkskundekongress* in Hamburg in 1905, as well as *Kunstgewerbe* theorists like Bruno Bucher and Julius Lessing—that is, the very same personalities who were otherwise fully engaged in the decorative arts movement.[136]

Like so many other disciplines, folk studies also came to maturity as result of the Great Exhibitions, in this case the one in Vienna (1873) where, under Jakob von Falke's leadership, a section on *Hausindustrie,* as well as an exhibit titled "The International Village" (*Das Internationale Dorf*), were included for the first time.[137] The value of *Volkskunst* was that it had national characteristics as well as aesthetic merit, hence it was deemed a worthy, because authentic,

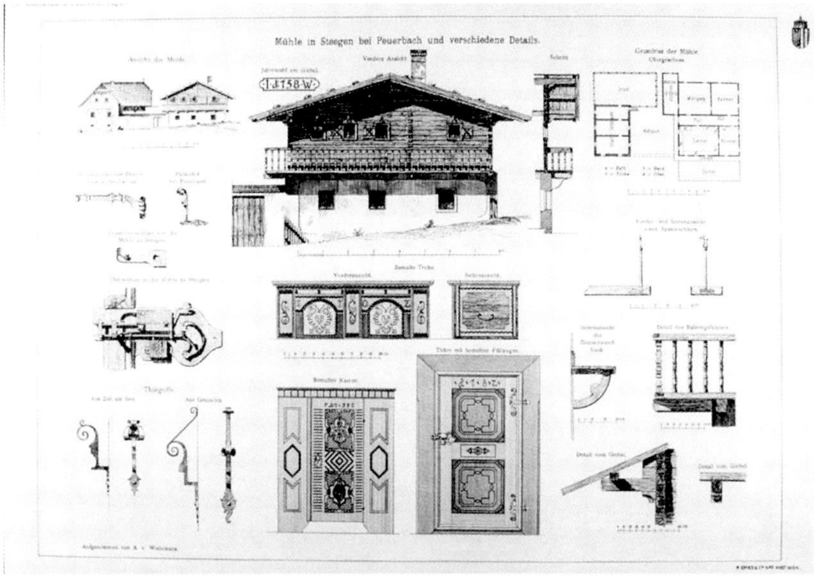

model for the *Kunstgewerbe*. Directly associated with industrial production, it also reinforced economic nationalism.[138] Not surprisingly, then, and once again like its siblings, *Volkskunde* also revolved around the public presentation of objects, that is, around the museum. In some cases the Museum für Volkskunde—in Vienna and Berlin—arose from anthropology museums, which lent it an anthropological/ethnographic direction.[139] However, elsewhere the overlap was with the *Kunstgewerbe* museums, as in the case of the Kaiser Wilhelm Museum in Kreefeld under the leadership of Friedrich Deneken. Preservation and reinvigoration of folk art and production through industry was a major concern of these institutions, and much literature was concerned with the passing of folk arts and their manufacturing techniques. Not only was Riegl one of the first to ring the alarm in his *Volkskunst, Haussfleiss und Hausindustrie* (1894), but such concerns were voiced at the very heart of the literature on *Kunstgewerbe* as late as Richard Graul's *Krisis im Kunstgewerbe* (1901) alongside essays by Muthesius and Fritz Schumacher.[140] The very fact of the association shows the multiple vectors along which Muthesius's (and the modernists') intellectual base informing their arguments needs to be evaluated.

At first, architectural publications like W. H. Riehl's "Kunstarchitektur und Volksbauart" were included in larger historical accounts focused on specific regions.[141] However, a sustained architectural activity started around 1900 with (among others) August Thiersch, professor at the Technische Hochschule in Munich, and the series on *Das Bauernhaus* spearheaded in 1894 by the German, Swiss, and Austrian engineers' and architects' association, respectively (fig. 69).[142]

FIGURE 69
Mill in Steegen near Peuerbach, with various details. From *Das Bauernhaus in Österreich-Ungarn und in seinen Grenzgebieten* (Vienna, 1901–6).

The arguments they used to justify the work made much of ornament and the freshness of motifs that could be used in contemporary work.[143] Michael Haberlandt, director of the Vienna Volkskunde museum, wrote the historical introduction and pressed the expected buttons of nationalist feeling by defining folk architecture as the "most meaningful embodiment of the folk spirit" and a "national document." In using a metaphor that Walter Benjamin would turn on its head several decades later for his concept of the *Etuimensch,* Haberlandt compared the *Bauernhaus* to a natural "house" (that of the snail, that grows around the body of the mollusk) unlike that of the "rootless, houseless city dweller," praising it for responding to the requirements of location and materials.[144] His reference apparatus is interesting in itself as it shows how effectively so many threads of discourse came together to generate another. Thus Haberlandt mentions Hellwald's anthropology oriented *Haus und Hof,* as well as the *Kronprinzwerk,* quotes Viollet-le-Duc's "house" entry in his *Dictionnaire,* and, most importantly, he includes a large section on ornament where he quotes Semper on the transference of textile motifs to walls.[145] Finally, in ways that announce Riegl's later work on *Hausindustrie,* he describes folk art as house-bound and taught, depending on a manual dexterity that transfers across all domains of life.[146]

Through the many strands of its discourse, folk studies invested the object with several important qualities: 1) the folkloric object, rising as it did out of ethnography and anthropology, was seen to be ahistorical (and so could later appeal to modernists once they chose to forsake history); 2) it stood for the value of anonymity just like the artifacts of archaeology and anthropology; 3) it was associated with and became almost synonymous with ornament (all objects are heavily ornamented); 4) for economic, political and aesthetic reasons it became a model for industry (to rebuild dying rural industries; to bolster nationalism) because its ornament was mostly abstract and hence appropriate for the machine to copy; 5) it showcased the relation between aesthetics and the fabrication and materials of objects (qualities first raised by Semper); 6) it added to the buzz about humble objects, about *Hausindustrie* and *Sachkultur* rather than artistic *Kunstgewerbe,* and could easily merge with the later enthusiasm for machine production by the equally anonymous machine; 7) it was entirely focused on the house, thus fundamentally reinforcing the interest in domestic culture; 8) and finally and most importantly, the folk object was construed as a DNA of culture (a view to which Semper had also contributed).

Most important of all, perhaps, in all three disciplines (folk studies, anthropology, and archaeology) the crucial issue was culture—and it was seen to reside in the objects of daily use rather than in high art. In folk studies the focus was a primitive *Sachkultur* albeit autochthonous, produced by a culture distant from that of the metropolis from which it seemed alien. The same was the case in anthropology (except that it looked to exotic cultures, distant in space) and in archaeology because humble objects were what was found in greatest quantity, and quite frequently they also belonged to primitive cultures distant in time. In the process each discipline contributed much to the discourse of the others. Together they had made the object synonymous with *Kultur*.

But thrusting the object of everyday use into the foreground was not all these disciplines achieved. They also contributed to the pendulum of theoretical density swinging in its direction. The object became a locus of debate and interest, as well as theory by sheer quantity of publications and events. As a group these publications propelled the object dramatically into the forefront as subject of inquiry. Some revolved around the direct consumption of art and its immediacy; others offered a context for the aestheticization of the domestic sphere; others still used them as access to history. In the process, ornament lost its status as theory site for architecture and relinquished it to the object of daily use—which absorbed it and gradually attracted the architects as well. In a world focused on display, architecture itself entered the world of objects. It may not be too much to say that the body of theory surrounding the object became more sophisticated and interesting than that surrounding ornament. Indeed, ornament retained an interest only inasmuch as it interacted with objects and its relationship to architecture faded into the background. As Stephen Bann has noted, once the past "could be aroused by the unmediated perception of objects" and gained an "experiential reality" through them, that is, as history moved from metonymy to synecdoche, objects became invested with significant theoretical power.[147] The road from here could only be upward.

3 | Art Historians, Objects, and Empathy

> Architecture is in fact like clothing, a projection of man and his body-sense outward. —HEINRICH WÖLFFLIN, *Klassische Kunst*

> It is evident that all instruments and objects man invents and makes, must be adapted to his body and members; they become one with the live organs they serve. —AUGUST SCHMARSOW, *Unser Verhältnis zu den bildenden Künsten*

> Where do all the questions come from regarding the enigmas of empathy in front of inanimate nature? It is because in fact for man there exists a state which can unite him to something—precisely in handling and holding things—with something that corresponds to him, but that does not flow through his veins. The tragedy of clothes and of the tool is the history of the human tragedy in the broadest sense. —ABY WARBURG, *Notes for Seminar, Kreuzlingen*

ART HISTORY AT THE TURN OF THE CENTURY

The discourse Semper initiated on objects, architecture, and ornament found an echo in many disciplines, but it gained most prominence in art history. Several themes he had tabulated were worked out in this neighboring academic field, far more closely connected to architecture than archaeology, anthropology, or the museums could ever be. As art history had been one of the disciplinary umbrellas under which Semper had written and that he had claimed, his call was not lost on its practitioners. Likewise, the art-historian museum directors who were principal actors in the *Kunstgewerbe* movement articulated the issues further and in more traditional historical terms. Although previously concerned with aesthetics, art historians had moved into a more positivist territory in the later nineteenth century, driven by an ambition to forge their own scientific approaches in keeping with those developed in the emerging man-based disciplines. Moreover, as a young discipline whose objects were as yet not internally limited, art history was in a "receiving" mode, developing its own identity while acting as a melting pot or funnel for the theories about culture and civilization that were circulating in the academic world.[1] Thus it drew on aesthetics, anthropology, archaeology, ethnography, folk studies, history, psychology, economics, and the museum, and could assimilate and rework this material and channel it back to architecture in a "digestible" form—that is, in a language that architects and critics could use.[2] Given art history's evaluative and analytical orientation—unlike architectural theory, which was normative by definition—it was also the site where specific problems of architecture (such as style, its history, its evolution, and so forth) were telescoped and worked out, only to be reabsorbed in due course by way of teaching and publications—that is, by way of the "strong" academic discourse of the profession. In addition, since contemporary architecture was historical, the work of art/architecture historians was naturally perceived to be profoundly relevant. History became a locus where theory verified itself.

But there was a second avenue open for art history to pollinate architecture. This was so because the more general theories about culture, nationalism, race, life (such as the domestic world of the interiors) that art history provided were also absorbed into popular culture and from there found their way once again into architecture. Thus both the high and the low end of art historical discourses operated upon architects and their theories. Most art historians were active in both arenas, lecturing broadly and publishing in the principal newspapers and non-specialist journals such that their views, debates, and proposals became available to a far larger audience than is the case today.[3] Schoolbooks and Great Exhibitions also disseminated art historical finds and consensus, and so operated upon the public at a more general level. The much-publicized discovery of the Pergamon altar in 1879, for example, received as much attention in the popular press as in academic venues.[4] In short, art history also fed a "soft" discourse that, among other things, accompanied the aestheticization of the domestic sphere. This predated Semper but intensified after him, as we have seen, and though it moved along its own independent channels it certainly existed in a situation of exchange with art history.

What art history processed and passed on had to do principally with definitions of culture. But it also had to do with definitions of the art-object/subject relationship, and with its own methodological tools. For example, the blend of aesthetics and psychology which produced the empathy (apperception) theory affected in various degrees art historians of many stripes. Architects tilled this field as well, but they did so in a sustained dialogue with art historians, a fact that is not noted often enough.[5] Another area of exchange was the attention that art history channeled onto the detail, which gained additional validity as the principal tool of connoisseurship. The detail had already been flagged as a site of intense interest because the unself-conscious revelation of artistic drive in archaeology, anthropology, psychology, and philology, but it was nevertheless a decisive moment for the arts when art history embraced this notion.[6] Once the detail became the critical working instrument for an academic discipline it moved into the foreground of consciousness for any number of issues and generated a whole new angle from which to evaluate and chart development, change, and innovation. While there is no direct route from this to architecture, the methodological turn that privileged the detail was broadly disseminated and hence available, and if Aby Warburg's quip that "Gott ist im Detail" (God is in the detail) came in time to be attributed to Mies van der Rohe, the confusion of authorship may not be without its measure of insight.

The contribution of art historians to the discourse on objects, and, in turn, the latter's impact on art history's methodological instruments, was facilitated by two facts: first, that art historians had participated in the decorative arts movement, as we have seen; and second, that on the crest of the wave of intense interest in *Sachkultur* in various disciplines, a new branch of art history had also developed: the art historical study of *Kunstindustrie*. Art historians like Alois Riegl may have been more interested in theory and system building, but they were of the same species as scholars like de Gheltof and Falke, that is, not concerned with teaching design but with identifying a history or evolution of ornamental forms.[7] In short, there was considerable traffic between art history and the study of objects in all their forms. Thus, alongside the objects that penetrated art history, all the disciplinary contributions attached to them also seeped in.

Perhaps one of the most critical contributions of art history to architecture and the discourse on objects was the intense scrutiny to which it subjected the concept of style. The issue was central in architecture of old—and as we have seen, Semper's title *Der Stil* acknowledged as much—but the theoretical interest in the second half of the nineteenth century turned not so much toward which style to choose for new buildings (though the debates carried on more or less acrimoniously in the press) but to *the definition of style* in art more broadly and to the causes behind changes in styles.[8] To be sure, the interest in artistic style was no newcomer to the slate of problems that art historians were considering. Indeed, it had been a central concern at least since the Renaissance and Vasari's days.[9] But in the nineteenth century this issue acquired far greater visibility in architecture, both with respect to its selection of styles from a historical range and the theoretical-cum-critical writings this precipitated. In the figural arts the situation was not nearly as dramatic or obvious. Given architecture's very public floundering for a style—or so it seemed from the vantage point of a *Zeitgeist* mentality—it was inevitable that it was here that a starting point for a renewed inquiry into its mechanics should surface. Faced with the conundrum of a multiplicity of styles coexisting in architecture, art historians turned to examine style even if their concern was not so much personal style or architectural styles as such, but larger units, styles of epochs and of countries, and their questions about why or how styles changed rather than what the characteristics of individual styles might have been.

Semper had contributed to this discussion, too. As we have seen, for him the convergence of materials, manufacturing, and meaning (or symbol) in small-scale objects produced style, and he had endeavored to trace the translation of these motifs into monumental ones over centuries, even millennia. But a contradiction remained buried deep at the very heart of his remedies for the problems of modernity: he wished to see an almost instant transition from an improved *Kunstindustrie* to architecture take place in his own time. This accelerated process was completely at odds with the slow transformation and metamorphosis of symbols and responses to materials into ornament that he had charted for Western culture. The entire education system he proposed to deal with this issue (museums, traveling exhibitions, and education for the masses, lectures, publications, and craft schools) revealed the paradox at the root of his philosophy—it was not a genuine bottom-up system but a top-down one that was fundamentally at odds with the evolutionary history he outlined so passionately. His recipe for the present collapsed the process in time. Yet the polemic on industry and objects arose precisely from the radical change in speed of production and evolution of forms from slow, hand manufacture to quick industrial production that had brought the concept of style into crisis. Both Semper and the literature that followed him amply testify to this fact. Faced with the anxiety arising from the simultaneous crisis of fabrication, evolution, and ornament that rampant industrialization caused, the concepts of beauty and style also demanded a critical assessment. And this is where art historians could step in.

Among those in whose work most of these threads came together at the close of the century, Heinrich Wölfflin, Alois Riegl, and August Schmarsow were arguably the three most important German-speaking art historians (Swiss, Austrian, and German).[10] Popular teachers and widely recognized scholars in their own time, their conception of form seeped into the criticism and theory of architecture and became a part of the ongoing debates on style and its origins. It is also interesting to note that these art historians worked primarily on Italian early modern art with its roots in Greco-Roman antiquity. Inevitably, their insights—which became paradigm-changing contributions—were colored by the objects of their study.[11] Even when they looked to other types of art—be it medieval or northern, even Asian, and Riegl worked on all three—it was from the perspective of the tools they had forged with respect to Italian material and that had swept the discipline. Thus both their work and the work of the next generation promoted ways of understanding form that were peculiar to Italian, and even more so to Renaissance and Baroque art—in short, to an art where the human body constituted both the content and its principal rhetorical devices. This inherent body-focus opened avenues for exchange with such man-based sciences as anthropology and psychology (especially empathy theory) that had risen recently and facilitated yet another dialogue across disciplines.

WÖLFFLIN, FORMGEFÜHL, AND CORPOREAL FORM

On the face of it, Heinrich Wölfflin (1864–1945) seems to have been less involved with the objects of daily use and their ornaments than were art historians associated with the museums or working on *Kunstindustrie,* and we have no works on *Gewerbe* from his pen in the manner of Falke, Bode, and others. Yet, despite this absence, his publications set in motion the scholarly apparatus that would ultimately assimilate, transform, and reapply the findings associated with objects within the discipline of art history. Today his name is synonymous with formalism and an art history without artists or context, and his best-known text remains *Principles of Art History* of 1915. However, the fact that this book is the outcome of an inquiry into the arts and the mechanisms driving them, which began from the perspective of architecture and its scholarship, tends to be forgotten: both his dissertation (*Prolegomena zu einer Psychologie der Architektur,* 1886) and his Habilitation (*Renaissance und Barock,* 1888) concerned architecture, and this is where Wölfflin formulated his basic concepts—his focus on empathy as mode of reception, his interest in style—that would lead to his later and now better known work. Thus, although about ten years younger than Riegl and Schmarsow, Wölfflin was the first to turn to architecture as a case study for understanding style, and the first to engage a dialogue with architect/scholars. As result, his findings were also the first to claim a position in their discourse.[12] To be sure, Wölfflin's general concepts from *Principles* and his emphasis on form owed much to the emerging aesthetic of abstraction in painting and to his personal interest in the work of Arnold Böcklin, Hans von Marees, Adolf von Hildebrand, Max Liebermann, and Ferdinand Hodler.[13] But his path into *Principles* had been shaped by architecture as much as by his friends Adolf von Hildebrand or Konrad Fiedler: the *Prolegomena,* perhaps his most lucid and powerful statement, dealt only with architecture; so did *Renaissance und Barock,* though here his interest veered from reception of form to style and the laws of its changes. *Classic Art* (1899) turned to painting and the High Renaissance, but as an effort to apply to the figural arts the concepts he had developed in his earlier books. His fundamental interaction with Hildebrand in this period, and the continued impact of his teacher Heinrich von Brunn, particularly his work on Raphael from 1867, 1885, and 1891, had much to do with it, but Wölfflin's concern with style remained constant.[14] Finally, *Principles* represents an effort to revisit the issue of style and its connection to ways of seeing applied systematically to all three arts, in other words, it amounts to a summa of his previous three books.

Wölfflin turned to architecture from the peculiar vantage point that his somewhat heterogeneous education afforded him. Oscillating among philosophy, psychology, and art history, and influenced by his philologist father on the one hand and his teachers in Basel, Munich, and Berlin on the other—the philosophers Volkelt and Dilthey, historians Burckhardt and Riehl, the psychologist Wilhelm Wundt, and art historian Heinrich von Brunn (to whom he dedicated *Renaissance und Barock*)—he was at the confluence of a number of significant developments in precisely those fields that affected the rising discourse on objects.[15] In addition, studying in Munich during the years of the Bavarian debates about *Volk,* the rise of Seidel's neo-vernacular-cum-German Renaissance architectural style, and the publication of von Riehl's monumental work on Bavarian folk art, architecture, and culture, he could hardly have been ignorant of the folklore/ethnology/nationalism discussions raging about him.[16] If nothing else, his exposure to Wundt's 1874 *Völkerpsychologie* would have made him particularly sensitive to these issues.

Most important, the new subfield of psychological aesthetics that looked at the reception of art rather than its production drew Wölfflin toward empathy and the role of the body as instrument of aesthetic experience. The *Einfühlung* theory had swept through German late nineteenth-century aesthetics like wildfire and touched many disciplines. Among its theoreticians—Johann Friedrich Herbart, Robert Zimmermann, G. Theodor Fechner, Fr. Th. Vischer, Robert Vischer, and Theodor Lipps—Wölfflin's direct interlocutor was Johannes Volkelt (who did much to popularize earlier theories such as R. Vischer's).[17] As his student and familiar with Semper's work by way of Dilthey and von Brunn, both of whom admired him, Wölfflin was able to absorb much of the current empathy aesthetic. In addition, through his friendship with Adolf von Hildebrand and his Florentine circle—which started in 1889—as well as his exposure to the debates surrounding the aesthetic/archaeological/stylistic readings of the Pergamon altar, which arrived in Berlin beginning in 1879 and caused something of an aesthetic revolution, he developed a reading of architecture that drew a number of threads together.[18] The baroque features of the Pergamon altar so spectacularly based on the body, von Brunn's concept of *malerisch* sculpture, and Hildebrand's concern with its purely optic reception (where space collapses and three-dimensional art becomes relief) in his *Das Problem der Form* (1893), all blended with the notion of empathy and determined Wölfflin's interests over the next decades.

In some ways it seems singular that unlike his mentor Burckhardt, who devoted a full half of his *Geschichte der Renaissance in Italien* to "Decoration," Wölfflin should ignore the objects—the altars, candelabra, screens, tombs, chancels, ciboria, and so forth—that existed in a tight material and ornamental exchange with architecture in the Renaissance.[19] Indeed, this omission would suggest that his interest lay with the principal three visual arts and that he did not engage the discourse of the century that had trained the spotlight of scholarship on the movable, small-scale objects of mass consumption and their historical precedents and models. Yet, if the objects as such had not attracted his attention, his training had nevertheless prepared him to examine with sensitivity and new insights the traditional architectural ornament that elsewhere had lost its identity and, at the hands of his contemporaries, had become abstract compositional devices applicable to fabrics and pottery, wallpaper and metalwork.[20] Indeed, he saw his interest in a psychology of aesthetic reception to be best examined with respect to architectural ornament. And the *Prolegomena* was the result of this blend of interests.

True to his goal of teasing out a psychology of architecture, here Wölfflin focuses on the effects of architecture upon the viewer and proposes the body as principal reference point for aesthetic experience. Blending an anthropomorphic reading of architecture with empathy theory, he argues that architecture—any architecture, but the classical vocabulary is his real model—represents the opposition between matter and "energy to form" (*Formkraft*)—that is, it represents a dynamic condition that finds a profound resonance in the viewer's (and maker's) body.[21] It is then in analogy to his sense of bodily self (breathing rhythm, heartbeat, muscular elasticity, weight-bearing), he argues, that the artist creates and the viewer receives the work.[22] Even space is not so much a void as the expression of a solid mass that offers resistance to an internal force that pushes outward against it. Such a corporeal conception of architecture clearly allied it to sculpture, and it led Wölfflin to focus on the modulation of the carved wall and on ornament which, as sculptural aggregate of forms, inevitably became the linchpin of his argument.[23] Capitals and bases, balusters and acroteria were so many small sculptures. For him, as for Semper (whom he quotes), they were eloquent signs of sometimes contained, sometimes exuberant energy to form key moments in the architectural narrative.[24] Indeed, Wölfflin's theory of reception owed much to Semper even if he did not refer to him as a principal source. Lotze, Volkelt, Vischer, and others had developed the empathy theory, but its application to architecture, and his categories—eurhythmy, symmetry, the attached ornaments such as "Behang, Ring und Band"—are evident throwbacks to *Der Stil*.

Perhaps most telling of this sculptural reading of architectural form is the fact that Wölfflin drew his clinching argument from the Pergamon altar gigantomachy (fig. 70). When he describes the acroteria figures on the ancient temple as the celebration of *Formkraft* (force to form) in ornament, it is to von Brunn's 1888 analysis of the relationship between architecture and sculpture in the altar that he refers with enthusiastic approval.[25] Von Brunn, himself leaning on Semper, proposed that the figural composition on the altar's base conveyed

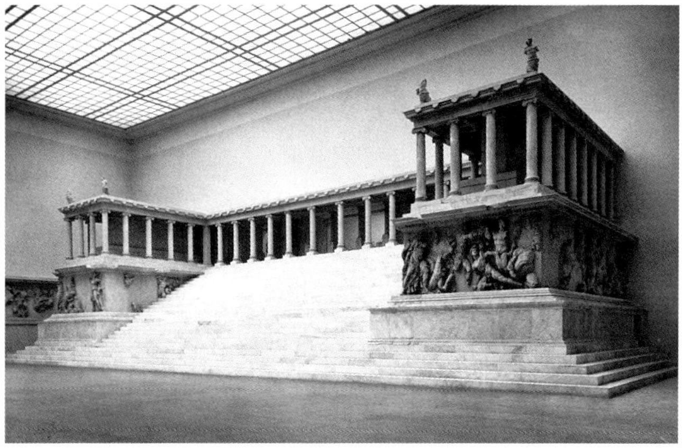

the stresses present within the architectural ensemble and evaluated the relief as "tectonic-decorative art," describing it as the "reciprocal interpenetration of architecture and representation."[26] The Pergamon altar—displayed as an object and contained within a museum—had thus led Wölfflin to develop a powerful argument for reading architecture as sculpture, that is, as object, significant in its solidity rather than its hollowness. Once a bridge between architecture and objects was established, a continuity between buildings and small, sculpture-like architecture (*Kleinarchitektur*), as well as ornament and other free-standing objects, could also be envisaged.[27] Heinrich von Geymüller, another of Burckhardt's intimates, did precisely that when in his *Die Architektur der Renaissance in Toscana* (written in the same years as Wölfflin's work) he included the architectural decorative work of sculptors such as Donatello (fig. 71). Governed by the same laws and appealing to the same faculty of apperception in the viewer, the scale difference between them became immaterial. Indeed, it is the continuity across scales that struck Wölfflin as significant, and it is precisely to this issue that he turned in his next book.

Renaissance und Barock builds upon this understanding of architecture as a body-centered art and develops further the haptic conception of ornament.[28] What is more noticeable here, however, is the fact that Wölfflin looks beyond ornament to even smaller details—to outlines, profiles, and the smaller component parts of ornaments. Whereas before he analyzed the column, the base, or the capital as a whole ornamental unit, now he takes his cue from the neck molds and astragals that make up these compound shapes and dissects them in ever smaller tranches. And it is in these details that he looks for the shifts from a Renaissance to a Baroque style:

> The Renaissance work looks fragile. Its brittle stuff terminates in sharp edges and hard angles, while the baroque forms are full, opulent, and

FIGURE 70
Great Altar of Pergamon, second quarter of second century B.C. Pergamonmuseum, Berlin. Preussisches Bildarchiv, Berlin/Art Resource.

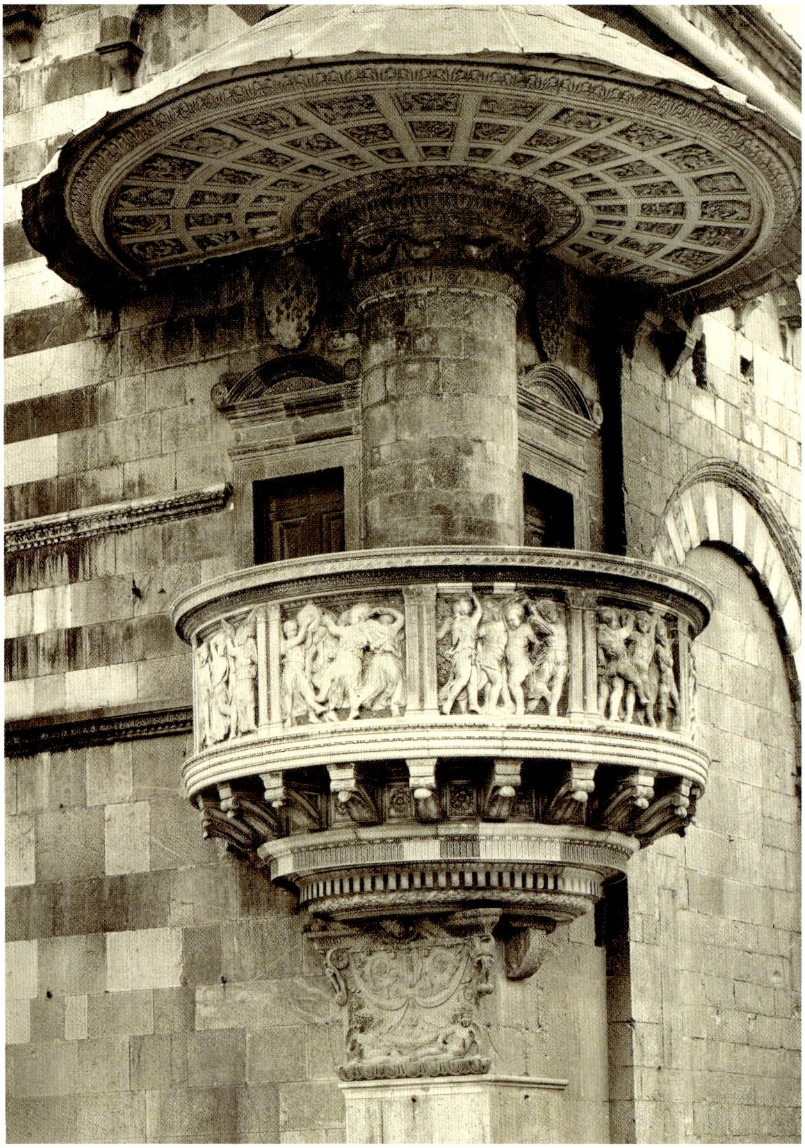

> curled over in round and generous whorls. . . . Particular care was taken to see that the profiles of moldings should be soft and fluid. Their component parts were merged into one continuous line; right angles were avoided altogether.[29]

FIGURE 71
Michelozzo and Donatello, Pulpit, Cathedral of S. Stefano, Prato, 1428–38. From Heinrich von Geymüller and Carl von Stegmann, *Die Architektur der Renaissance in Toscana* (Munich, 1885–1908).

For Wölfflin, if the detail reveals the characteristics of a new style, it is because of its links across scale and media to what man wears and holds, manipulates and surrounds his body with. It is these more intimate objects, these miniature "sculptures," that literally touch his body and condition his response to form and therefore to its making:

> The pulse of a people's temper must be sought elsewhere; not in the heavy and ponderous forms of architecture, but in the smaller decorative arts; it is in them that formal sensibility (*Formgefühl*) finds a direct and unconstrained outlet, and in them that the first traces of a renewal of style will be discovered.[30]

The path from the body to architecture passes through and, indeed, is mediated by, all the objects that lie between them. And Wölfflin can then argue that the origin of a new style lies in the "pre-architecture" stage of objects of daily use that herald, contain, and develop all at the same time the feeling for form (*Formgefühl*) that is in the process of crystallization. What caused stylistic change, therefore, he argued later in *Classic Art,* were changes in the perception of the self as body, which was then translated into mimetic as well as more abstract artistic/architectural devices.[31]

If corporeality (*Körperlichkeit*) was a red thread through Wölfflin's work, another was style. For him the two intersected in a significant way, and the connection became evident in his first real art historical investigation, *Renaissance und Barock*. It is in this book, with its historical focus and concern with two periods in architecture that were currently in sustained revival mode (from the neo-Renaissancism of a Semper to the neo-Baroque of a Garnier), that he entered the contemporary architecture discourse fully. Style change was his real concern and the transition from Renaissance to the Baroque his case study. The issue was a live one among architects. Adolf Göller, architect and professor at the Stuttgart Polytechnikum, had devoted two books to its investigation and had developed the concept of sensory fatigue or visual satiety (*Ermüdung des Formgefühls*) to explain a disenchantment with the excessive repetition of forms and a diminished response to their stimulation as origin of style changed.[32] The work had been enthusiastically taken up by the architectural community in reviews and articles in such leading journals as *Allgemeine Bauzeitung* and *Deutsche Bauzeitung,* and it is precisely this debate that Wölfflin set out to engage.[33]

Like so much else, Semper may be sensed behind Wölfflin's reading of style even if he is not interested in the physical production of art objects, but in their form alone. Across his work from 1886 through 1915 there is a constant swaying between terms that designate forms of seeing and forms of feeling (*Sehen, Formgefühl, Formgeschmack, Lebensgefühl, Grundstimmung der Zeit, Volksgemüt*) as the origin of forms. Ultimately, they are so many ways of defining the root of style, which, as their visible manifestation, remained the real object of his inquiry throughout.[34] Clearly Wölfflin's reading of style and his history of seeing plucked many chords and went through multiple changes.[35] What is important for our context, however, is what remained constant and what he carried over from his

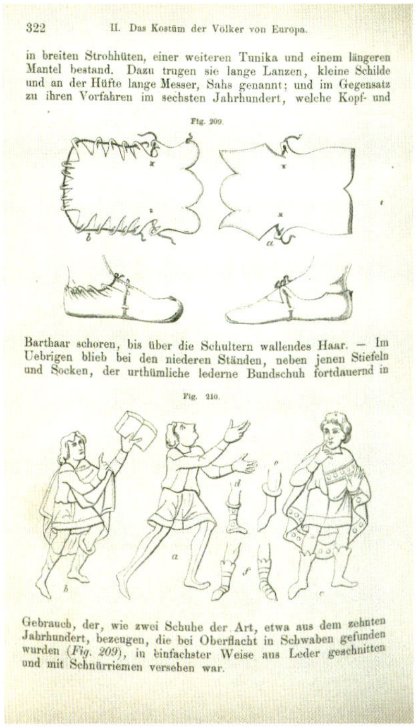

322 II. Das Kostüm der Völker von Europa.

in breiten Strohhüten, einer weiteren Tunika und einem längeren Mantel bestand. Dazu trugen sie lange Lanzen, kleine Schilde und an der Hüfte lange Messer, Sahs genannt; und im Gegensatz zu ihren Vorfahren im sechsten Jahrhundert, welche Kopf- und

Fig. 209.

Barthaar schoren, bis über die Schultern wallendes Haar. — Im Uebrigen blieb bei den niederen Ständen, neben jenen Stiefeln und Socken, der urthümliche lederne Bundschuh fortdauernd in

Fig. 210.

Gebrauch, der, wie zwei Schuhe der Art, etwa aus dem zehnten Jahrhundert, bezeugen, die bei Oberflacht in Schwaben gefunden wurden (*Fig. 209*), in einfachster Weise aus Leder geschnitten und mit Schnürriemen versehen war.

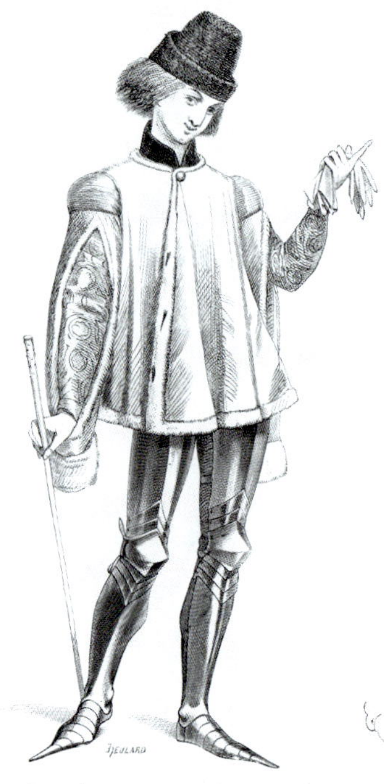

Left **FIGURE 72**
From Hermann Weiss, *Kostümkunde: Geschichte der Tracht und des Geräths*, vol. 2 (Stuttgart, 1881–83).

Right **FIGURE 73**
"Personnage en habit de voyage." From Eugène-Emmanuel Viollet-le-Duc, *Dictionnaire raisonné du mobilier français de l'époque carlovingienne à la renaissance* (Paris, 1868–75).

reading of architecture into the mainstream of art history: the importance of the detail and of the movable objects of daily use (large and small) in the development of a style and the relation of both to culture (by way of the body).

Already in his dissertation of 1886, Wölfflin had identified the origin of a style in the small-scale miscellanea of daily life—in the decorative objects and clothes, in script and decorative patterns. Costume in particular—even closer to the body than the tools and objects of daily use—allowed him to connect the forms of architecture with those of the body, and it is here that he offered the first formulation of his now famous Gothic shoe analogy:

> How people like to move and carry themselves is expressed above all in their costume, and it is not difficult to show that architecture corresponds to the architecture of the period. . . . The human foot points forward, but does that show in the blunt outline in which it terminates? No. The Gothic age was troubled by this lack of the precise expression of a will, and so it devised a shoe with a long pointed toe (the crakow appears in the twelfth century).[36]

Perhaps not unexpectedly, Wölfflin's reference was to Hermann Weiss's 1878 *Kostümkunde*, that is, to the literature on the history of costume of the type that had so often throughout the century proposed a continuity between architecture, interior, and dress (fig. 72).[37]

The connection between artistic style and costume that Wölfflin made was certainly not new. It was essential for Semper, who connected vestments (*vestiarische Kunst*), general apparel, and upholstery to architecture. Fechner had also proposed it in his *Vorschule der Ästhetik* (1876), and should Wölfflin have missed it there, Eduard von Hartmann, philosophy professor at Leipzig, had also drawn attention to it in his own essay on architecture "Gehört die Baukunst zu den freien Künsten?" published in *Gegenwart* in 1887.[38] As we have seen, the connection of architecture and clothes also went back to Schelling, who included architecture among the plastic arts (*Plastik*) alongside applied arts (sarcophagi, urns, vases, candelabra, goblets), drapery, and clothes (*Bekleidung*).[39] However, for Schelling and Fechner such indices of style as clothes or hairstyles represented a lower level of taste expression, and neither placed them at the center of an art historical inquiry, as Semper and Wölfflin did later. The connection lay both implicit and explicit, however, in so many period illustrations and books, from Viollet-le-Duc to Jakob Falke, and even if Wölfflin turned to Weiss for his material, he could have turned just as easily to any number of similar books (fig. 73).

Not much of this view had changed by the time Wölfflin wrote *Renaissance und Barock* in 1888 except that it was now associated with a specific group of historical forms. The connection of "feeling for form" (*Formgefühl*) to style and the origin of style in the decorative objects remained his core arguments, and he expressed them in almost identical terms.[40] The connection is even clearer in his diaries from the same period, where this statement is tied to an acute observation of modern life: in an entry of December 8, 1888, he notes that the feeling for form is revealed in architecture, furniture, books, cars, and objects (he specifies fork, knife, plates), as well as clothing.[41] The whole gamut of objects that had been absorbed into culture/*Kultur* makes its appearance here (fig. 74). This time, however, Wölfflin acknowledges Semper's due even if he disagrees with him on the origin of style: in his view the feeling for form precedes any impact of the material on the object made.[42]

Clothing, with its inevitable close connection to the body, remained a favorite reference. The Gothic shoe returns as the effective example, but the statement is couched in more definitive terms: "The most immediate formal expression of a chosen form of deportment and movement is by means of costume. We have only to compare a Gothic shoe with a Renaissance one to see that each conveys a completely different way of stepping."[43] And, scoring a point against Semper (who, he notes, had described the Gothic as scholasticism in stone), he adds ironically: "What, first of all, determines the artist's creative attitude to form? It has been said to be the character of the age he lives in; for the Gothic period, for instance, feudalism, scholasticism, the life of the spirit. But we still have to find the path that leads from the cell of the scholar to the mason's yard."[44] For him,

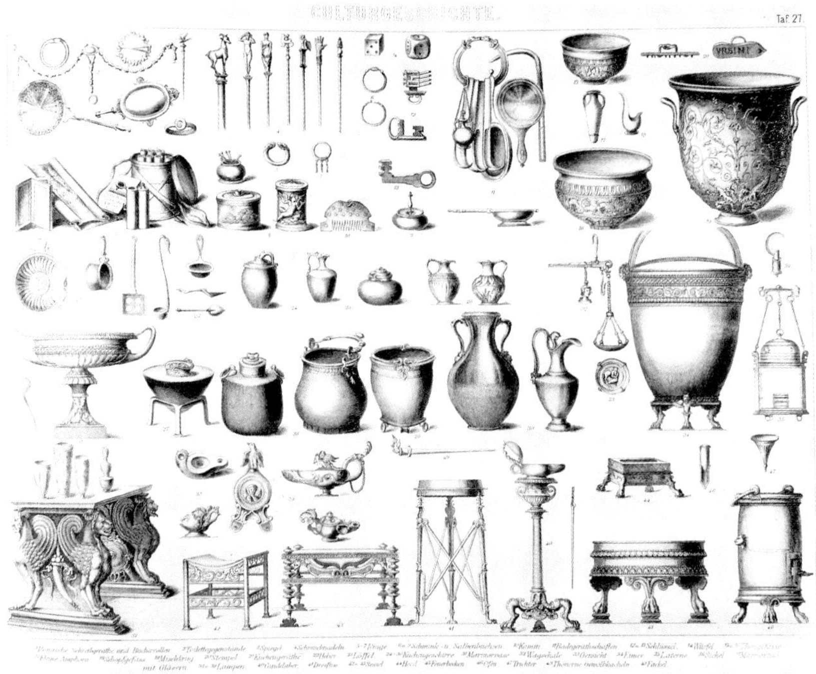

FIGURE 74
"Roman objects." From August von Eye, *Atlas der Culturgeschichte* (1875).

"the path" and the instrument of *Zeitgeist* is evidently the body. Whereas art historians like Bode simply saw a connection between furniture and style, Wölfflin looked deeper and connected both by means of the period body-sense—more instinctual, unreflective, and unself-conscious.[45]

The later writings retained and developed these insights. Even more important is that, having drawn a number of threads from various disciplines into a forceful synthesis, these writings—widely circulated and often reprinted—allowed it to reach an increasingly wider readership and to acquire general currency. Such a text was *Klassische Kunst* of 1899, in which Wölfflin formulated the connection between body, objects, and style with even greater precision. Although, he argued, a new style can be detected in what surrounds the body ("die Umgebung des Menschen")—architecture, small objects, clothes—styles change because the body's sense of self changes.[46] And he proceeded to define architecture as a projection of the *Körpergefühl* outwards, "like clothing."[47] Such a reading recalls with some force both August von Eye and Ernst Kapp, who saw the world of objects as an extension of the body, a part of the ripple effect that starts with the body, moves across clothing—as body-wrap and the closest layer to the body itself—to the objects manipulated by the hand, to those that served as support, container and beyond, to architecture and even gardens. That the detail was still very much on Wölfflin's mind in this period is made clear from his review of Theodor Lipps's *Raumästhetik* in 1898: in the very short space he had at his disposal he chose to focus on Lipps's critique of art history for neglecting precisely these small building blocks of form. And he quoted at length, with evident approval, when Lipps berated the discipline for not having produced sufficiently differentiated terms to describe the aesthetic effects of an astragal, neck mold, bead-and-reel, or egg-and-dart.[48]

Finally, in his *Grundbegriffe* of 1915 Wölfflin made famous a way of thinking about the arts that looked to the unself-conscious detail as the repository of style. The objects of daily use or decorative arts were no longer the critical symptoms of a new way of seeing; but, just as small and unself-consciously produced, and just as marginal, the details of the work itself moved into the foreground. Here Wölfflin shifts from the body's immediate surroundings (*Umgebung*) and posture (*Haltung*) as origin of style change to the eye. *Formgefühl* has become more precisely defined as "decorative feeling," the basis for some fundamental "decorative scheme" that underlies all art of a particular period, or *Zeitstil*.[49] Although the body retains its importance in his thinking, the center of gravity has now shifted from apperception and anthropomorphism to pure visibility (or *Sichtbarkeit*, in Fiedler's terms).[50] Wölfflin does not forsake either psychology or the importance of the small objects surrounding the body, but the question of why the ways of seeing change from one period to another is not broached any more in *Grundbegriffe*.[51] What remains is the understanding that he had derived long ago from architecture, that the details, the small objects surrounding the body, the unself-conscious, and the marginal reveal the essence of a style.

This insight into the place of small-scale in determining the roots and essence of an architectural style, which went back to Semper, had much in common with Giovanni Morelli's connoisseurship method. Whereas for Wölfflin clothes, shoes, and sundry objects of daily use were so many unself-conscious clues to the period style, for Morelli, fingernails, hands, ears, and such marginal elements in a painting were the most characteristic features of personal style and hence a tool for attribution (fig. 75).[52] Morelli's path to his system of evaluating what Freud called the "detritus or refuse of our observation" had gone from medicine and anatomy through Cuvier and natural science, as well as paleoethnology, and therefore traveled a similar (if not identical) path to Semper's.[53] Even if Wölfflin's immediate interest was more in human psychology than morphology, it is easy to see how having drawn from Semper, Morelli's approach would also strike a familiar chord. And that there would be a direct path from his interest in a nostril or drapery in a painting to his interest in architectural detail such that he could sum it all up: "The essential of form perception is already evident in the smallest fragment."[54]

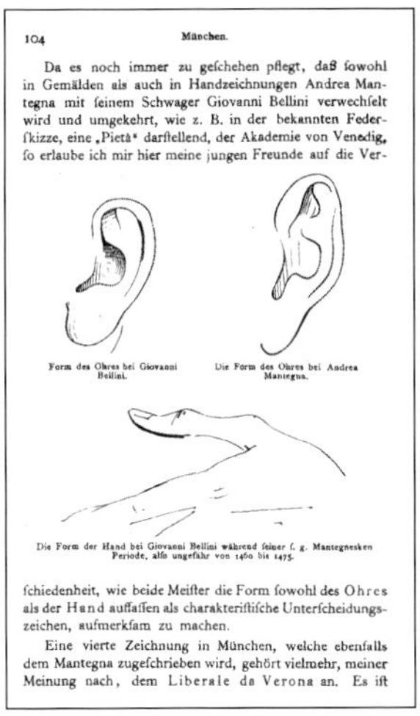
104 München.

Da es noch immer zu geſchehen pflegt, daß ſowohl in Gemälden als auch in Handzeichnungen Andrea Mantegna mit ſeinem Schwager Giovanni Bellini verwechſelt wird und umgekehrt, wie z. B. in der bekannten Federſkizze, eine „Pietà" darſtellend, der Akademie von Venedig, ſo erlaube ich mir hier meine jungen Freunde auf die Ver-

Form des Ohres bei Giovanni Bellini.

Die Form des Ohres bei Andrea Mantegna.

Die Form der Hand bei Giovanni Bellini während ſeiner ſ. g. Mantegnesken Periode, alſo ungefähr von 1460 bis 1475.

ſchiedenheit, wie beide Meiſter die Form ſowohl des Ohres als der Hand auffaſſen als charakteriſtiſche Unterſcheidungszeichen, aufmerkſam zu machen.

Eine vierte Zeichnung in München, welche ebenfalls dem Mantegna zugeſchrieben wird, gehört vielmehr, meiner Meinung nach, dem Liberale da Verona an. Es iſt

FIGURE 75
From Giovanni Morelli, *Die Werke italienischer Meister in den Galerien von München, Dresden und Berlin: Ein kritischer Versuch von Ivan Lermolieff* (Leipzig, 1880).

Repetition and the ubiquitous presence of physical incident also drew Wölfflin to reflect upon the typical. In *Grundbegriffe* the detail is "typisch" because it is repeated, and Wölfflin looks for "typical examples of linearity"; it is also

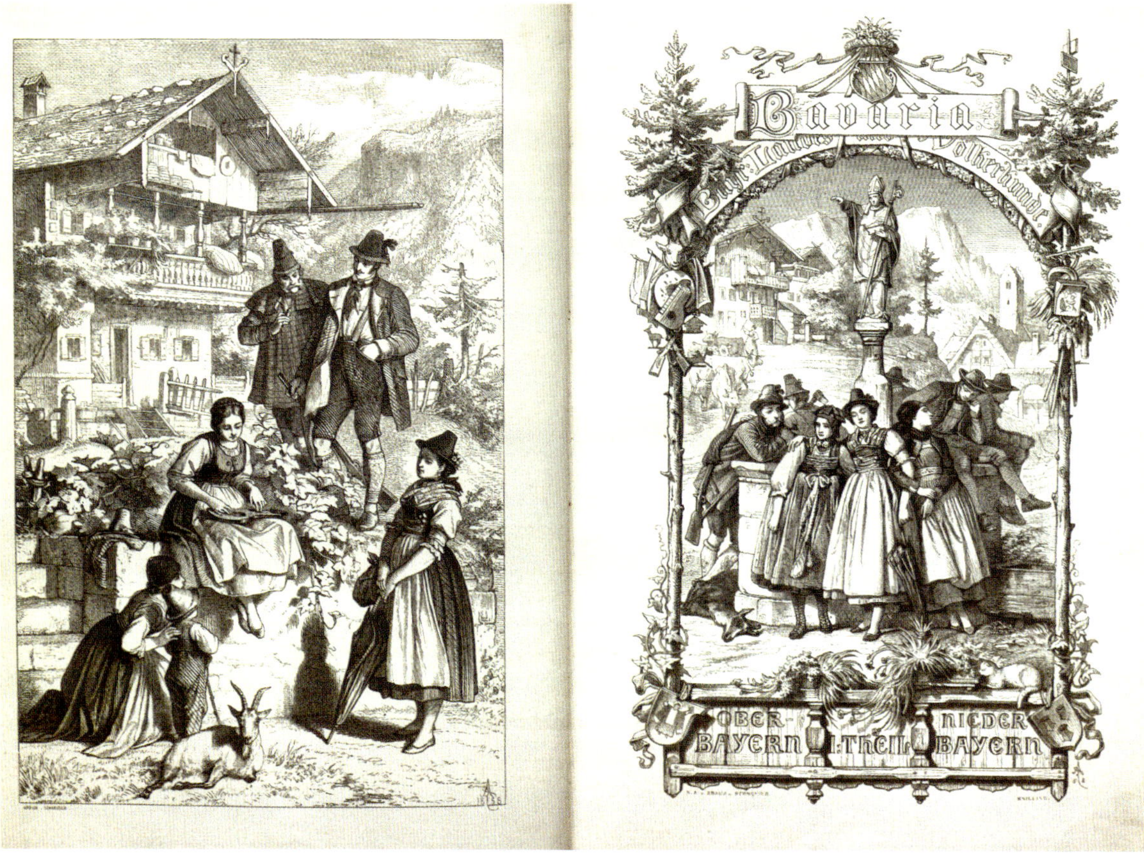

FIGURE 76
"Bavaria." From Wilhelm Heinrich Riehl, ed., *Landes-und Volkskunde des Königreichs Bayern* (Munich, 1860–68), vol. 1.

unself-conscious (*unwillkürlich*), and it is in this marginality and almost automatic quality that its value as index for style lies.[55] Indeed, this is how Morelli's technique was understood, and in 1890 the architect and historian Cornelius Gurlitt's review of his book in the newspaper *Die Gegenwart* presents it precisely in these terms, as an apology of the typical.[56] Typical form had become a major interest of Wölfflin's in the wake of his exposure to Hildebrand and Marees, and it is what had appealed to him in the latter's work: "to experience the typical in the individual."[57]

Wölfflin plucked one more chord that allowed his concept of style and its location to be additionally effective with a broad audience of readers. While he looked to the nature of artistic "seeing" he also drew the concept of national sensibility, that is, of the *Volk*, into the mix.[58] Should Wölfflin have needed further exposure to such commonly held views on *Volksgemüt* and *Volksgeschmack*, it was certainly offered by von Riehl, who in his "Kunstarchitektur und Volksbauart" of 1860 held that monumental art displays the *Volkscharakter* as surely as the folksong resonates in classical music (fig. 76).[59] Among the visual arts, it is particularly architecture and the *Gewerbe* that turned to folk art as a powerful paradigm, and therefore Wölfflin's inclusive approach opened one more avenue for this audience to engage and use his work.

If architecture's gradual slippage into objecthood needed a theoretical reference point in addition to Semper, Wölfflin certainly provided it. This was all the more so as his books, short, rhetorically consummate and beautifully written, were eminently accessible to a larger circle of readers than most of the ponderous and belabored tomes produced by the German academic community. In fact, the prose Wölfflin uses could just as easily have figured in one of his popular public lectures or in a newspaper or journal article such as the readers of *Allgemeine Bauzeitung* or *Deutsche Bauzeitung* (and to which he occasionally contributed) were used to.[60] As such his work was also more accessible to the artist/architect, since he did not seek to write as a historian for the historian but to uncover basic formal artistic and psychological denominators that went beyond content, authorship or patronage, that is, beyond historical contingencies. In addition, by relativizing stylistic changes—the Renaissance and Baroque were only test cases of a meta-historical phenomenon—that is, in making his theory of style applicable to the ancient past as much as to the present, his theory became transferable and could affect modernity.[61]

Wölfflin's students were not the least important of disseminators of his ideas, and Sigfried Giedion probably more so, and more effectively than most.[62] Even if not directly, Wölfflin's accessible, well-known, and debated theories, with their new insights and syntheses of scholarship from various disciplines, flowed into the larger stream of thinking about the arts and affected its course in decisive ways.[63] If the architect and Werkbund member Fritz Schumacher could review *Principles* in 1918 and argue that it is aimed "precisely to the architect," and if the architect Hans Willich could produce a new edition of *Renaissance und Barock* in 1906 which met with Wölfflin's full approval, and, furthermore, if the architect/engineer (and likewise member of the Werkbund) Julius Baum could still refer to it as a fundamental work in 1920—evidently the author and both books must have had a presence in the world of the architect.[64] Moreover, Wölfflin's books, for all the shifts and differences between them, retained a common core. Even if Fritz Schumacher had never read *Renaissance und Barock* or the *Prolegomena* he would have gotten the message about bodies, details, and culture from *Principles*.

Ironically, despite the fact that he made a determined and passionate appeal to look at artistic form beyond its cultural contexts of authorship, patronage, intellectual climate, and so forth, Wölfflin made a significant contribution to the development of a theory of culture. For him the body was both the fundamental departure point for a historical analysis of culture (through deportment, costume, instruments, crafts, etc.) and the origin of ways of seeing. By pushing the body into the foreground, as the site where the physical aspects of culture come together, he formulated what was implicit in the vast and often heterogeneous literature on objects of the nineteenth century. Culture—any culture, since Wölfflin is adamant about recurring phenomena—starts with the body and builds outward to its surroundings and finally to its art. Style makes this continuity visible, though it reveals itself best in details (of daily life or of the body, of art or of architecture) because they are its most unself-conscious products. From this view Wölfflin never strayed, wherever else his investigations led him. For him the decorative arts and ornament, as well as decorative schemas or the decorative feeling, were a form of *deep structure* that tied body and form together at a most basic level. Such a view could have provided another source for the idea of a "subconscious of architecture" for his student Giedion. After all, Wölfflin acknowledged that he built a psychological argument.

ALOIS RIEGL AND ANONYMOUS CULTURE

Unlike Wölfflin, who kept his eye steadily trained on the Renaissance and Baroque, Alois Riegl was more concerned with primitive, non-Western, and ancient cultures in developing his concept of *Kunstwollen*. Such an orientation resulted in the first place from the circumstance of his position as curator of textiles at the Museum für Kunst und Industrie in Vienna. It has often been noted with much sadness that Riegl had spent a good part of his career well away from the center of art history, locked away in a textile museum department. However, he took on this position with eagerness and engaged his objects with evident enthusiasm, and this perspective ultimately determined his results. Moreover, by Riegl's time and in Semper's wake, textiles had become a high density point for theory—cultural, anthropological, and artistic—such that Riegl's path was very much on the crest of a contemporary wave. Like Wölfflin's, his art history was also without artists, but this was not because he looked beyond them to the fundamental ways of seeing or feeling of their cultures (though he did that, too) but because the objects he dealt with from the beginning of his career were without known authors—they were genuinely anonymous.[65] Thus, although he produced a theory of culture and art that was general in its application, he did so from a diametrically opposed departure point than Wölfflin's. Directly involved with the *Kunstindustrie* movement, his work started from the detail and the object of daily use, and they remained at the core of his system.

Riegl's education prepared him to engage art with a different set of tools than Wölfflin's. Trained in Vienna by Rudolf von Eitelberger, the first director of the Museum für Kunst und Industrie and doyen of the Vienna School of art history, and by Theodor von Sickel and medievalist Moritz Thausing, and coming also under the influence of Jakob von Falke (Eitelberger's vice-director and successor), Riegl had been more decidedly focused on a rigorous study of history and art and less concerned with philosophy, psychology, or even art making in his writings.[66] Instead, closely connected with the museum, the museum exhibit, and the world of *Kunstindustrie* both as student and later as curator meant that his focus was on the object of everyday use (however much it may have been dignified by antiquity or distance) and that he was able to pull together a number of different disciplines and discourses to arrive at his definition of culture.

One important feature of Riegl's education was that his milieu had been greatly affected by Semper: not only in general terms as result of his presence in Vienna as architect, but also in connection with the foundation of the Museum für Kunst und Industrie. As we have seen, it is on the occasion of its inauguration that Semper had sent Eitelberger his famous essay "Museum der Metalltechnik" and dedicated it to him. Moreover, the interest in the detail and the small, unselfconscious gesture—in other words, the exposure to the detail paradigm—that was so central to Semper's theory of art fell on fertile soil. Reinforced by Riegl's law studies (which promoted a "clue mentality" that he shared with another jurist, Bode), by his teacher Moritz Thausing, a devoted friend and supporter of Morelli's and his connoisseurship technique, and by his training in paleography (the analysis of script), Riegl was already well on his way to recognizing the importance of the detail, the closeup, and the insignificant.[67] Even Robert Zimmermann, who was the leading figure in Austrian aesthetics and with whom he had studied philosophy originally, had fed this interest. With a twist that brought together Semper with current psychological aesthetics, Zimmermann had collapsed scale between artistic media and argued that objects of daily use slipped into architectural ornament and sculpture.[68]

Unlike Wölfflin, who started with the study of Renaissance architecture, Riegl worked on medieval art. As medievalists have always insisted, most medieval objects, although embellished, were not intended primarily as art but as cult objects or objects of use. Though this is true of most religious items in the Renaissance as well, the difference, though subtle, is nevertheless fundamental: aesthetic achievement in the Middle Ages was seen as a reflection of devotion, and the autonomy of the aesthetic did not become an issue until the early modern period.[69] The contemporary art literature, with Ruskin as its most vociferous representative, made much of this difference and fed the Gothic versus Classical revival debate. In part, this polarization also owed to the fact that most medieval production was anonymous. Even if known and respected at the time, most artists' names were lost, and the loss itself testified to a lack of concern with the identity of makers vis-à-vis the much more important fact of the cult object made. Such a view of an anonymous artistic production in the Middle Ages—which was even more exaggerated than it need have been—was particularly entrenched in the nineteenth century and was used by the apologists of the Gothic style (in

France, England, and Germany), for example, to promote it as a direct emanation of a national spirit and as indigenous as *Volkskunst*. As a result, there was a general understanding, successfully promoted by critics like Ruskin, that medieval makers of art objects were artisans not "authors" and therefore belonged to an undifferentiated mass of workers who left their personal imprint on the small items they painted or carved.[70]

Riegl's doctoral work and first publication on medieval calendars (1889) exposed him to this body of anonymous material and to the methods developed to deal with it: focusing on miniature ornament (*Miniaturschmuck*), he dealt with phenomena of copying and used script methodologies to place them in time and space.[71] His interest in related peasant wood calendars (on which he published in 1888) also brought him into the orbit of a type of refined and equally anonymous folk art—to which also belonged textiles, embroidery, and carpets—and to which he would devote his subsequent years of research.[72] His Habilitation on oriental carpets (*Altorientalische Teppiche,* 1891) as well as his interest in the Eastern European tradition of carpet weaving brought him within the orbit of ethnology and the rising new discipline of folk studies, which provided him with yet another set of disciplinary tools to engage anonymous artifacts. Moreover, these artifacts were still being produced, still anonymously and in much the same manner and form. And it is here that the Industrial Revolution touched Riegl's world most closely: it is precisely these crafts that were most vulnerable to the machine and state intervention. Indeed, in his long essay *Volkskunst, Hausfleiss und Hausindustrie* of 1894, Riegl summarizes his position on the issue of domestic economy and its traditional systems of exchange that he had often touched upon in his numerous articles in the specialized media and produced his own version of Levi-Strauss's *Tristes tropiques*. Fully aware of the destruction of this vulnerable and essentially manual mode of production by the well-meaning efforts of museums to encourage the crafts from the top down, he recognized (as had Eitelberger before him) and warned of the demise of primitive cultures under the axe of industrialization.[73]

Riegl took the index value of the object and of the ornament-as-detail, and the associated notion of anonymous production of folk objects (some distant in time, others not) straight on and developed a new system of art historical inquiry at whose core these issues lay. Although his two seminal texts are *Problems of Style (Stilfragen)* of 1893 and *Spätrömische Kunstindustrie* of 1901, most of his findings were published in a series of articles from the 1880s onward. A few recurring themes characterize his work: 1) the theoretical investment in ornament and the decorative arts (which he places at the core of his definition of aesthetic drive, or *Kunstwollen*); 2) the prominence of the anonymous objects of daily use (carpets, buckles, pots, clasps, weapons, jewelry); and 3) the spotlight he places on the term *Kunstindustrie,* denoting a small-scale domestic economy, in the context of an art historical œuvre that proposed a new system for evaluating the high arts and aesthetics. None of these issues were new in themselves—but their combination was, particularly its location at the heart of *Kunstwissenschaft*. Although Riegl himself moved on after 1901, what is most important is that he developed his larger *Kunstwollen* theory starting from his observations on anonymous and/or folk art (both ancient or contemporary). In so doing he raised it from the status of material culture in ethnological and anthropological investigations to *the* key ingredient in the making and understanding of high art. By absorbing perspectives from these disciplines he allowed them entry into art history: what had been evidence in one discipline became usable as evidence in another. Even if his successors and readers did not follow the same path, art history and its instruments retained the memory of the anonymous art object that Riegl had embedded in its methodology.

None of Riegl's numerous early publications on the crafts that appeared in anthropology, decorative arts, and art history journals—this threefold orientation is symptomatic of the domains he felt his work addressed—were much in the public eye.[74] However, thus equipped, Riegl finally stepped into the limelight of art historical debate with *Stilfragen: Grundlegungen zu einer Geschichte der Ornamentik* in 1893 (which emerged from his lectures at the University of Vienna from 1890/91).[75] The title was very topical and certainly pregnant with references—to the rising literature on style, to the half-century-old preoccupation with ornament, and to Semper's *Der Stil* in particular. Beyond Semper the most important contributions to the question of ornament had come from anthropology and archaeology. As we have seen, in the arts the interest had either been oriented toward the education of artists (so as to improve the quality of industrial products), or toward the analysis of principles underlying ornamental motifs. Although on the whole more attracted by the findings of the anthropologists, as an art historian, Riegl was less interested in the evolution of man than he was in the evolution of forms, and his ultimate project was to identify basic instincts ("immanenter künstlerischer Schaffungstrieb") that governed their production at any time and any place.[76] Like Wölfflin he also responded to the then fashionable materialist view of style—a view generally and erroneously attributed to Gottfried Semper.[77] He had already demolished Semper's claim that materials were the origin of form and of the primacy of textiles in his 1890 article on New Zealand (Maori) ornament. In a close historical analysis he had argued for an innate ability in man to produce certain elementary ornamental forms independent of outside agents.[78] His choice of the Maori example was also laden with meaning. On the one hand he entered into dialogue with the literature on ornament and tattoo that Owen Jones and Semper had initiated in the 1850s (fig. 77); on the

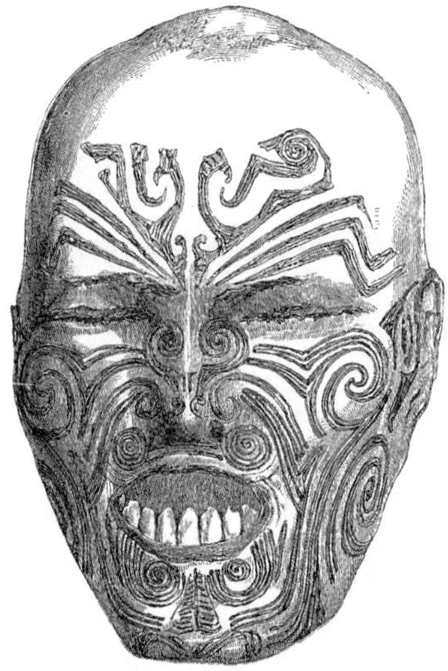

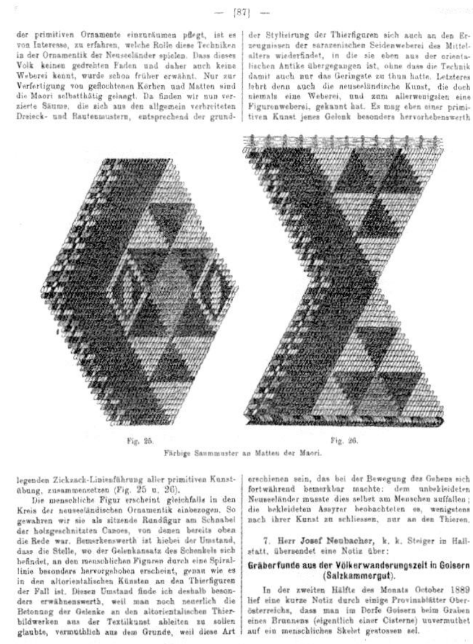

— [87] —

der primitiven Ornamente einzuräumen pflegt, ist es von Interesse, zu erfahren, welche Rolle diese Techniken in der Ornamentik der Neuseeländer spielen. Dass dieses Volk keinen gedrehten Faden und daher auch keine Weberei kennt, wurde schon früher erwähnt. Nur zur Verfertigung von geflochtenen Körben und Matten sind die Maori selbstthätig gelangt. Da finden wir nun verzierte Säume, die sich aus den allgemein verbreiteten Dreieck- und Rautenmustern, entsprechend der grundlegenden Zickzack-Linienführung aller primitiven Kunstübung, zusammensetzen (*Fig.* 25 u. 26).

Die menschliche Figur erscheint gleichfalls in den Kreis der neuseeländischen Ornamentik einbezogen. So gewahren wir sie als sitzende Randfigur am Schnabel der holzgeschnitzten Canoes, von denen bereits oben die Rede war. Bemerkenswerth ist hiebei der Umstand, dass die Stelle, wo der Gelenkansatz des Schenkels sich befindet, an den menschlichen Figuren durch eine Spirallinie besonders hervorgehoben erscheint, genau wie es in den altorientalischen Künsten an den Thierfiguren der Fall ist. Diesen Umstand finde ich deshalb besonders erwähnenswerth, weil man noch neuerlich die Betonung der Gelenke an den altorientalischen Thierbildwerken aus der Textilkunst ableiten zu sollen glaubte, vermuthlich aus dem Grunde, weil diese Art der Stylisirung der Thierfiguren sich auch an den Erzeugnissen der sarazenischen Seidenweberei des Mittelalters wiederfindet, in die sie eben aus der orientalischen Antike übergegangen ist, ohne dass die Technik damit auch nur das Geringste zu thun hatte. Letzteres lehrt denn auch die neuseeländische Kunst, die doch niemals eine Weberei, und zum allerwenigsten eine Figurenweberei, gekannt hat. Es mag eben einer primitiven Kunst jenes Gelenk besonders hervorhebenswerth erschienen sein, das bei der Bewegung des Gehens sich fortwährend bemerkbar machte: dem unbekleideten Neuseeländer musste dies selbst am Menschen auffallen; die bekleideten Assyrer beobachteten es, wenigstens nach ihrer Kunst zu schliessen, nur an den Thieren.

Fig. 25. Fig. 26.

Färbige Saummuster an Matten der Maori.

7. Herr **Josef Neubacher**, k. k. Steiger in Hallstatt, übersendet eine Notiz über:

Gräberfunde aus der Völkerwanderungszeit in Goisern (Salzkammergut).

In der zweiten Hälfte des Monats October 1889 lief eine kurze Notiz durch einige Provinzblätter Oberösterreichs, dass man im Dorfe Goisern beim Graben eines Brunnens (eigentlich einer Cisterne) unvermuthet auf ein menschliches Skelet gestossen sei.

other, his topic was on the leading edge of anthropological research and very close to that of pioneers in the field like Colley-March and Stolpe, whose work was of exactly the same date. Not unexpectedly Riegl's texts were published in the *Austrian Journal of Anthropology* (fig. 78).

However, it is in *Stilfragen* that Riegl nailed his colors to the mast and took on Semper, Bötticher, the "Kunstmaterialisten," and a misapplied Darwinism that was increasingly used to explain the evolution of the arts. This latter was a very topical issue in the specialist press.[79] Not coincidentally, Vienna's leading architecture journal, *Allgemeine Bauzeitung,* had published in 1891 a long article on the development of architectural styles, titled "Darwinistische Studien," a topic to which its author, G. Heuser, returned in 1894 ("Das Werden von Stylformen: Fortsetzung Darwinistischer Studien") and to which we will turn in the next chapter. In between these two dates lay Riegl's 1893 *Stilfragen.*

Riegl's opening gambit was nothing if not direct: "In the case of the Geometric Style, it is especially necessary to dispel once and for all the misconceptions surrounding its purely technical, material origin and the allegedly ahistorical nature of its development."[80] Instead, and following on his claims in the article on Maori ornament, he sought to show that certain patterns and forms appealed at a purely aesthetic level. In proving that the spiral motif, for example, appeared in a variety of media in the Maori culture (including the tattoo), none of which were connected with textiles, he not only countered Semper's emphasis on the materiality of art production and the primacy of textiles but also proved an instinctive aesthetic inclination toward certain forms.[81] Rather than being materially produced, he would argue later, this desire or will to form collides

Left **FIGURE 77**
"Female Head from New Zealand, in the Museum, Chester." From Owen Jones, *The Grammar of Ornament* (London, 1856).

Right **FIGURE 78**
"Maori Patterns." From Alois Riegl, "Neuseeländische Ornamentik," *Mittheilungen der anthropologischen Gesellschaft in Wien* 20 (1890).

with the material possibilities available, and it is from this very collision that art results.[82] To prove his point Riegl surveyed in minute detail the origins and development of geometric and naturalistic ornamental motifs in a *longue durée* study that started in ancient Egypt and ended in the Middle Ages. In the end this rigorous historical study allowed him to conclude:

> The theory now hopelessly outdated has never been able to explain the actual source of the pleasure (*Gefallen*) that human beings, according to the proposition, derived from rhythmic interweaving threads; nor does it explain what induced them to repeat the patterns in other materials even when it was no longer technically necessary.... Our counterargument has rested from the very outset on the assumption that whatever capacity allows human beings to take pleasure in formal beauty... also enables them to create combinations of geometric lines freely and independently without the intervention of material factors.[83]

Although in responding to Semper's elevation of textiles to the level of cultural symbols—and indeed Semper is quoted repeatedly and is the shadow behind the argument—Riegl rejected what he calls "the mechanistic conception of the art work," he too dwelled among the objects of daily use: pots, caskets, diadems, embroidery, mosaics, and carpets, as well as architectural ornament and tattoos (figs. 79, 80).[84] All these are objects without authors that he adduced beside architectural fragments (mostly late antique and medieval). Indeed, Riegl's material was closer to that of archaeologists and anthropologists than of art historians. His reading of ornament was also more anthropological, informed as it was by the latest archaeological findings, than was that of Wölfflin, who stayed closer to psychology and aesthetics. Perhaps the Austrian climate in which he found himself encouraged this particular direction in his work. As we have seen, the findings of anthropology, ethnology, and *Volkskunst* were critical to

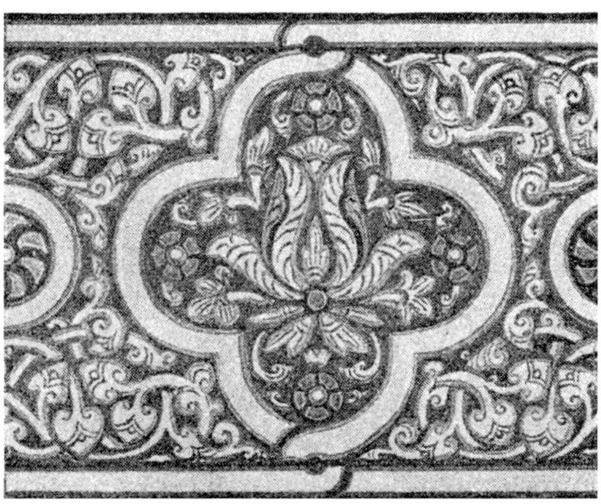

Below, left **FIGURE 79**
"Calyx-palmette and tendril decoration." From Alois Riegl, *Stilfragen: Grundlegungen zu einer Geschichte der Ornamentik* (Berlin, 1893).

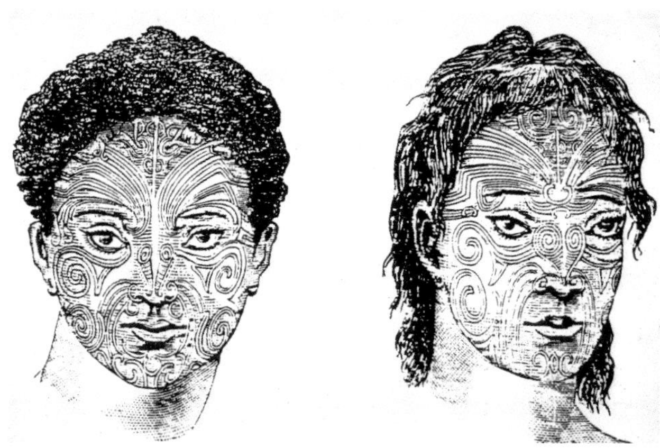

Below, right **FIGURE 80**
From "Maori Tattoos." Riegl, *Stilfragen*.

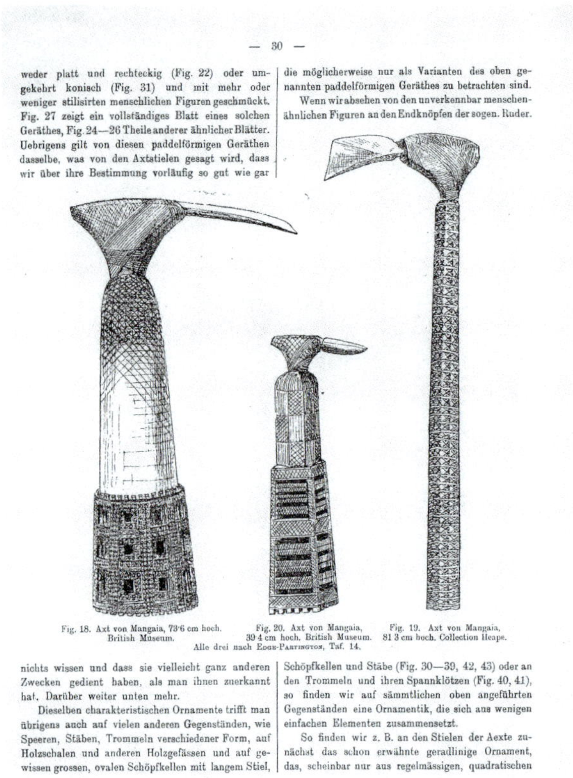

— 30 —

weder platt und rechteckig (Fig. 22) oder umgekehrt konisch (Fig. 31) und mit mehr oder weniger stilisirten menschlichen Figuren geschmückt. Fig. 27 zeigt ein vollständiges Blatt eines solchen Geräthes, Fig. 24—26 Theile anderer ähnlicher Blätter. Uebrigens gilt von diesen paddelförmigen Geräthen dasselbe, was von den Axtstielen gesagt wird, dass wir über ihre Bestimmung vorläufig so gut wie gar die möglicherweise nur als Varianten des oben genannten paddelförmigen Geräthes zu betrachten sind.

Wenn wir absehen von den unverkennbar menschenähnlichen Figuren an den Endknöpfen der sogen. Ruder.

Fig. 18. Axt von Mangaia, 73·6 cm hoch. British Museum. Fig. 20. Axt von Mangaia, 39·4 cm hoch. British Museum. Fig. 19. Axt von Mangaia, 81·3 cm hoch. Collection Heape.
Alle drei nach Edge-Partington, Taf. 14.

nichts wissen und dass sie vielleicht ganz anderen Zwecken gedient haben, als man ihnen zuerkannt hat. Darüber weiter unten mehr.

Dieselben charakteristischen Ornamente trifft man übrigens auch auf vielen anderen Gegenständen, wie Speeren, Stäben, Trommeln verschiedener Form, auf Holzschalen und anderen Holzgefässen und auf gewissen grossen, ovalen Schöpfkellen mit langem Stiel, Schöpfkellen und Stäbe (Fig. 30—39, 42, 43) oder an den Trommeln und ihren Spannklötzen (Fig. 40, 41), so finden wir auf sämmtlichen oben angeführten Gegenständen eine Ornamentik, die sich aus wenigen einfachen Elementen zusammensetzt.

So finden wir z. B. an den Stielen der Aexte zunächst das schon erwähnte geradlinige Ornament, das, scheinbar nur aus regelmässigen, quadratischen

Left **FIGURE 81**
Mangaian axes. From Hjalmar Stolpe, "Entwicklungerscheinungen in der Ornamentik der Naturvolker," *Mittheilungen der Anthropologischen Gesellschaft in Wien* 22 (1890).

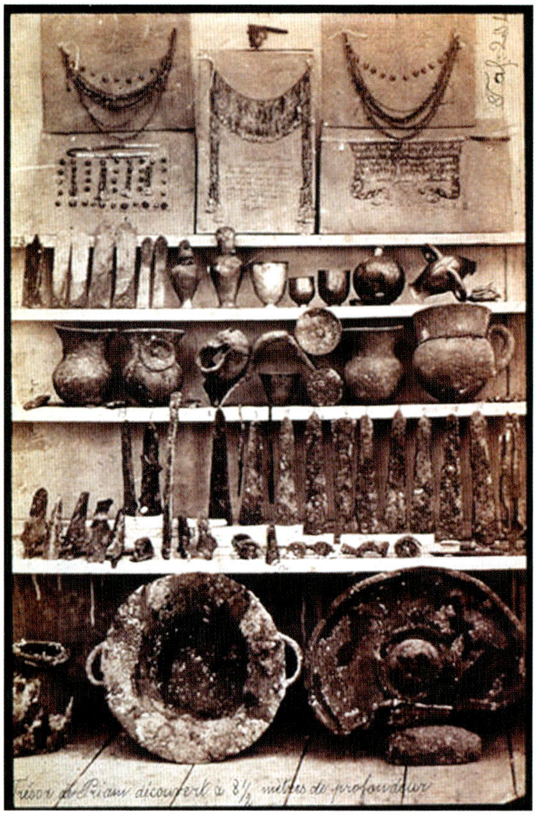

Right **FIGURE 82**
"Priam's Treasure." From Heinrich Schliemann, *Atlas Trojanische Alterthümer* (Leipzig, 1874).

Austria at this juncture in its history. As a multination state it was trying to keep its ethnically diverse provinces together in an effort to fight against Slav, Hungarian, Ruthenian, and other nationalistic identity-building efforts. A form of Habsburgian internationalism was one consequence; the interest in a universal, supra-national style or origin thereof in basic human instincts that surfaced in Riegl's work may well have been another.[85] Certainly his corpus of references almost entirely eschews art historians, placing anthropologists like Stolpe and Colley-March and archaeologists like Curtius, Perrot-Chipiez, Kekulé, Goodyear, Layard, Furtwangler, Conze, Puchstein, and Schliemann in the foreground (figs. 81, 82). His choices were well informed, as he used the cutting edge of the literature in both fields, both when he agreed with the conclusions and when he disagreed with them (as he does with Conze and Kekulé).

In *Stilfragen,* Riegl's aim was thus apparently modest: to correct the erroneous location of the origins of naturalistic ornament in Central Asia and its connection to the production of carpets. By knowing Riegl's later work, however, it is easy to see here the origins of many strands that he was to follow up as he developed his concept of *Kunstwollen,* particularly his focus on small, anonymously produced artifacts. Indeed, the connection that he posited between folk art, ornament, and industry in his works on oriental carpets, *Stilfragen* and *Volkskunst,* are also the context for *Spätrömische Kunstindustrie* (1901).

Of the many facets of this work—such as the desire to fight the notion of decline in late antique art and to wrench the discourse back from an excessive reliance on literary sources to the art itself—two are especially important for our discussion.[86] In this text Riegl continues to privilege anonymous artifacts; most importantly these are the objects that Riegl sees as the true and best indices of *Kunstwollen,* around which his work now fully revolves. In an attempt to recast the field's prevailing interest in style, Riegl seeks to look even deeper for the patterns that characterize the artistic production of specific historical periods. This is neither the body nor the eye, though they both play their role. Instead, according to him, a basic human drive toward art animates every period and can be identified across the arts. Architecture and the decorative arts, however, reflect its laws most accurately, "with near mathematical purity."[87] Riegl here comes very close to Wölfflin, whose concept of *Formgefühl* and its "purest" representation in the decorative arts offers a remarkable parallel to his *Kunstwollen.*[88] Ornament, in particular, functions as the revealing doodle or DNA of an entire culture, and the lowlier the object that displays it, the more unadulterated the representation of the instinct behind it.[89] By proposing in effect a form of *Strukturanalyse* Riegl moves the discussion—and the objects of daily use alongside ornament—to an even higher plane (figs. 83, 84).[90]

Riegl also sees this work as his opportunity to fight back against the prejudice that separates the so-called "minor arts" from their more noble sisters architecture, painting, and sculpture—the same prejudice that had left *Stilfragen* without much response within the art historical community, he argues.[91] The issue of *Kunstwollen* that he adumbrated earlier and was ignored, he now reintroduces by demonstrating how it applies to all the arts. However, in order to strengthen his argument, he continues, he will leave the decorative arts to the last chapter, although they constitute *Kunstwollen's* truest index. Indeed, the last chapter bears the title of the whole book: *Kunstindustrie.* By thus naming his work Riegl flamboyantly flagged the production objects (whether conceived as art or not) that had preoccupied historians, politicians, and scientists of many stripes ever since the Great London Exhibition. Such a title effectively placed his book at the core of contemporary discourse, far better than an alternative (and better suited) one such as "Spätrömische Kunst" might have done. The book, of a size and weight previously accorded only to such works as Stegmann and Geymüller's *Architektur der Toscana,* literally stood for the importance the subject had acquired at last. To be sure, the publication was caused by the desire to showcase archaeological finds of Roman artifacts on Austrian soil, and both scale and importance of the volume were meant to consecrate the (national)

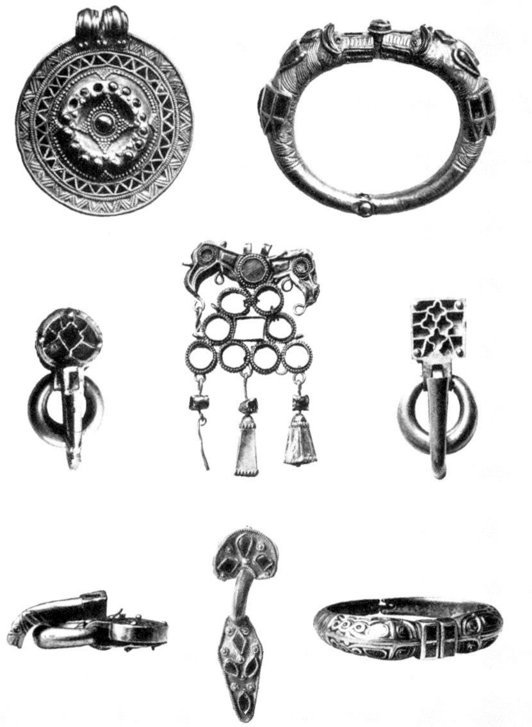

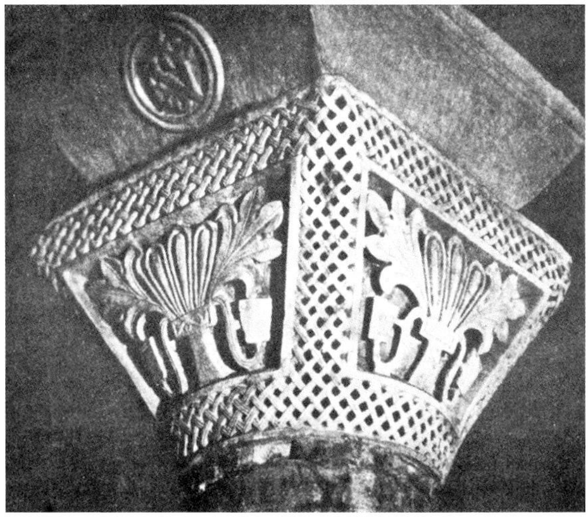

significance of the event.[92] But external forces can only explain intellectual work up to a certain point.

Although the book concerns all the arts of late antiquity, the center of gravity is divided between sculpture and small artifacts, which take up by far the most pages. This pairing (which Riegl acknowledges) recalls Wölfflin's concept of the decorative arts as miniature sculptures, arising from similar impulses. Riegl's category optic/haptic (*optisch/haptisch*) is also of one family with Wölfflin's painterly/plastic and his empathy-based reading of form.[93] Even if Riegl does not subscribe to the theory as such, his interest in materiality (*stoffliche Individualität*) and in the connection between sight and touch flagged the significance of the tactile dimension.[94] Such an emphasis in Riegl's work has been attributed to a museum curator's orientation toward the work of art as "object" displayed.[95] But the museum movement itself—the impulse to collect and display (if not to sell) to large audiences—was a consequence of the industrial society processing its products in the marketplace. The traffic in objects heightened the awareness of "object-qualities" across the board.

Yet what Riegl does in *Spätromische Kunstindustrie* that is perhaps even more significant is to split the unified argument from *Stilfragen* in the interest

Left **FIGURE 83**
Goldwork. From Alois Riegl, *Die spätrömische Kunst-Industrie, nach den Funden in Österreich-Ungarn* (Vienna, 1901).

Right **FIGURE 84**
Column Capital, S. Vitale, Ravenna. From Riegl, *Die spätrömische Kunst-Industrie, nach den Funden in Österreich-Ungarn.*

of convincing his readers. In *Stilfragen* he swept between architectural ornament—capitals, friezes, stone carvings—to objects of daily use without distinguishing between them. Ornament and the decorative arts were part of one discourse, and equals. However, in *Spätrömische Kunstindustrie* Riegl acknowledges the division by media. Although he still looks at ornament primarily when he looks at architecture, ornament and the decorative arts are dissociated. Yet, this very split ensured that Riegl's work retained its interest among architects and critics. His argument could survive precisely because he had divided the ability to reveal the innermost stirrings of the human aesthetic sensibility between architectural ornament and the decorative arts. Even if the former would disappear from aesthetic interest in contemporary architecture, the conduit to *Kunstwollen* was rescued by the latter. Consecrated as *Kunstindustrie* (rather than *Kunstgewerbe* or *technische Künste*), dignified as the true sign of *Kunstwollen* and as the deep structure of culture, elevated to rank alongside architecture as part of an art historical system, the object of daily use had at last entered the hallowed halls of the academy.

The last chapter of Riegl's involvement with architecture and objects would play itself out on the unlikely seeming terrain of preservation. It is here, in *Denkmalpflege*—literally the preservation of monuments—that Riegl acted on the "objectification" tendency that had brought together all aspects of culture into a "vitrine" mentality. Unlike Semper, who placed architecture at the center of his museum, Riegl promoted the isolation of a building as a monument away from its context and contamination with the urban layers that surrounded it and that were stylistically "impure." This was part of the same mentality that isolated objects or artworks and exhibited them in museums. Indeed, it is Riegl's commitment and formation in the museum that speaks through his *Denkmalpflege* essay of 1905: architecture cannot be detached and protected in the safe environment of a museum, therefore it must be provided with a halo or aura (in Benjamin's sense) *on site* so as to protect it but also to exhibit it for the education of posterity.[96]

Although Riegl's work was too specialized and detailed to make general reading, his theories did penetrate into the larger stream of discourse. As reviewer and author of articles, he published often in the principal newspapers in Austria and Germany. Thus in Sedlmayr's words he had offered an "incomparable, broad synopsis" of his *Kunstwollen* theory from *Kunstindustrie* in a debate with Strzygowski in two issues of the *Münchner Allgemeine Zeitung* (1903).[97] At least starting from 1896 he had written repeatedly for this newspaper, as well as for the *Neue Freie Presse*, *Wiener Abendpost*, and the *Wiener Zeitung*, all leading newspapers. He also lectured to various groups outside his own university classroom and often summarized his theories in more accessible form. One such example was his lecture "Uber antike und moderne Kunstfreunde," to the Gesellschaft der Wiener Kunstfreunde, in which he reviewed his concept of the tactile and optical stimuli that objects (*Dinge*) generate in the viewer.[98] But perhaps Riegl's most read (though admittedly coarse) popularizer for the next generation was Oswald Spengler, who borrowed much from him for his *Untergang des Abendlandes* of 1918.[99]

Riegl's object-related themes were important for the discourse of modernist architecture for three reasons that went beyond the larger application of *Kunstwollen*.[100] First, because they showcased the small object, its relevance for culture, its body closeness, and its fabrication origin on some instinctual level of the human psyche. As such, the object of domestic use acquired an aura of authenticity that was tied to its frequent and almost mechanical use. Riegl's emphasis on the haptic/optic response to aesthetic stimuli reinforced the relevance of objects as miniature sculptures in bodily contact with the viewer, able to signal in this unmediated way larger artistic impulses. Second, and connected with the first, folk *Hausindustrie/Hausfleiss* touched what would be later called domestic culture (or *Wohnkultur*). Part of a similar discourse, this association allowed ideas worked out with reference to *Hausindustrie* to enter discussions about the modern domestic realm. And it is in this domestic realm that the center of gravity of experimentation for modernist architecture would lie—in the villas, prefabricated houses, apartment buildings, and *Siedlungen*. Third, although the folk object was seen as a crystallization of national identity, for modernists—and here Riegl helped—it was relevant for its ahistorical qualities: it existed outside style and was a keeper of some permanent characteristic that was eternally valid rather than only culture specific. Riegl's smooth and almost self-evident transition from medieval art to folk art and back to small artifacts of historical periods showed the natural affinities between the study of these bodies of materials and a passage from one to the other that could occur again, such as in the early self-definition of the Bauhaus, whose origins were much colored by a fascination with German medievalism. Moreover, the folk object as reference point permitted modernists a way to bypass history. Finally, and perhaps most obviously, Riegl contributed to his own field, art history, and its way of defining culture with an emphasis on the object, and in so doing he propelled it into the foreground in a discipline closely tied to architecture.

SCHMARSOW AND ORNAMENT AS THE TYPICAL

August Schmarsow, the third member of this art historical trinity, did not propose a system of interpretation as significant or comprehensive as had Wölfflin and Riegl. However, though their approaches had little in common, as a group they nevertheless represented the most radical thinking in the field at the time, and in their own ways they responded to the proposals Semper had put on the table. As such, their work records the directions and spectrum of issues that art history explored and circulated at the turn of the century. All three spent most of their working lives looking at painting, and architecture, if present at all, was secondary. Yet each contributed in his own way to and interacted with the world of architecture. Moreover, they each illustrate the vectors along which the evaluations of style moved and the available ideas about the origins of style within the discipline.

A student of Anton Springer and Carl Justi, Schmarsow first taught at Göttingen and Breslau in the 1880s, only to take the chair at Leipzig in 1893, winning the appointment over Wölfflin. An admirer of Semper even as he criticized him, Schmarsow, like Wölfflin, also worked on Italian art and wrote on the Baroque.[101] Founder of the Kunsthistorisches Instiut in Florence in 1888, he taught there, counting the young Warburg among his students.[102] Much more has been made of Schmarsow and architecture than has been of Riegl and Wölfflin. On the face of it, Wölfflin's and (more laterally) Riegl's empathy orientation, while invoked with respect to architecture, did not lead to the mature theory of modernism in a direct line. Expressionism at best had been deemed to be its offspring—at the level of cultural osmosis and not much else, and primarily through the agency of Wilhelm Worringer's *Abstraction and Empathy* (1907). And as the apologists of modernism from Giedion onward endeavored to show, that had been a dead end.[103] The "strong" line had been that of mass-production and glass, of engineering and standardization—in other words, Giedion's poetic of mechanization, of time and space. And, having tabulated the notion of a moving body and the primacy of space for architecture, to this "strong" story Schmarsow belonged.[104]

One of his life's works was to examine and reclaim the separate identities of the arts. Not disputing overlaps between them, he nevertheless wished to reestablish a discourse that acknowledged their distinct identities, which alone in his view could illuminate their mutual relationship. In so doing Schmarsow also wanted to resist the trend to isolate ornament and the applied arts that had become such a prevailing approach. In the process he wished to embed them back into the larger framework of the three arts: surface bound (painting), plastic (sculpture), and spatial (architecture).[105] Early on—already in 1897—he had taken issue with Wölfflin and started a twenty-year-long attack on his corporeal (*körperlich*) conception of architecture. This was part and parcel of his effort to combat the development of categories that brought the arts together rather than focusing on their particularities. *Malerisch,* famously associated with Wölfflin, was his bugbear, and he wrote two books and several articles to challenge it.[106] Most important (or so he said), he wanted to resist the effects of the then current empathy theory that exalted anthropomorphism and apperception and that increasingly led critics and art historians to blur the boundaries between the arts.[107] Schmarsow put it down to the persistence of the "plastisches Ideal" associated with the equally persistent fascination with ancient art and pointed to the impact of the Pergamon altar that had popularized the concept of "pictorial relief." For Schmarsow the category *malerisch* seemed central to such a confusion of concepts and therefore in urgent need of reevaluation.[108] Although the term was made famous if not invented by Wölfflin, it is also to Riegl that this criticism was addressed.[109] The two sides fought it out with vigor: Schmarsow's attacks were tough, even mean-spirited; Franz Wickhoff, defending the Vienna point of view, attacked with even greater fury back, while Wölfflin remained aloof though dismissive.[110] Typically, perhaps, Riegl stayed politely out of the fray.[111] Not that Schmarsow did not himself turn to empathy theory to analyze the *Raumgefühl,* which he had put on the map. Still, his truculent endorsement of architecture as *Hohlraum* (void) and emphasis on *Raumgefühl* over *Körperlichkeit* would seem to place him outside the thread that runs from Semper across the myriad publications on objects, ornament, and *Kunstgewerbe* to Wölfflin and Riegl. And yet despite this advocacy, both ornament and objects find a central place in Schmarsow's aesthetic, and one that has been relatively neglected, so strong and appealing was his connection with the classic modernist line of space and time.[112]

Schmarsow's inaugural speech at the University of Leipzig in 1893 (published in 1894) was perhaps his most concise and accessible statement about architecture.[113] Having won his nomination over Wölfflin, he made the most of the differences between them, most notably on the particular nature of architecture as a space-molding art (*Raumgestalterin*). Even more important, perhaps, is that here he outlined his intellectual debts. Among the very few names he included (none belonging to art historians) were Semper, Hartmann, Lotze, Wundt, and Lipps, that is, names associated with the empathy theory and the phenomenological reading of form.[114] However, it was not until his *Unser Verhältnis zu den bildenden Künsten* of 1903 that he developed his own brand of empathy theory fully.

The work is far more aesthetics driven than art historical in the sense of Riegl or even Wölfflin—no specific artwork, period, or artist is named or analyzed. Schmarsow's main theme is the role of the body as primary instrument for aesthetic enjoyment, and origin of all products.[115] And this is particularly true of tectonics and architecture, he argues.[116] After covering bodily expression in mimic and pantomime, which leads him to sculpture as another form of gesture-based art, in his fourth lecture he turns to tectonics, decorative arts, the *Körpergefühl,* and mimetic and plastic values in sculpture and architecture. More important, he proposes a theory of objects, which hold an important place in his aesthetic. Like Semper he too starts with the tattoo, jewelry as decoration, costume and uniforms (armor)—all of which are "value signifiers of one's own body"—to move on to objects and finally architecture.[117] Having observed that the human hands are "living instruments," Schmarsow argues that "all instruments and artifacts man invents and makes must be adapted to his body and members; they become one with the live organs they serve."[118] As such they transcend their function as tools and become the owner's partners (*Genossen*).[119] The resemblance to Ernst Kapp and his *Organprojection* theory, discussed at length in the professional press (by Heuser in *Allgemeine Bauzeitung* in 1890), is remarkable, particularly his example of the saw as frozen movement ("in transitorischer Gebärde erstarrt") and as a near-human limb.[120] Although Schmarsow mentions all objects (including furniture) that surround the body, his key example is the perceptual link that ties the pitcher (a handheld object) with the vase, the baluster, and the column, that is, he moves fluidly from objects and instruments in a smooth line to architecture, from plastic form to architectural form. As semi-mimetic objects they all elicit responses from the body.

This conception of the classical column as tectonic-plastic construct ("a related construct to our bodies, from the head to the feet") comes close to Wölfflin's concept of corporeality. However, Schmarsow moves on from here to argue for a dynamic situation in which this solid bodily core literally expands outward and creates a tactile zone surrounding it and beyond that, a zone available only to the eye (*Sehraum*).[121] While the extension of the empathy concept into movement and the third dimension was an important addition in aesthetics and architecture that Schmarsow could claim as his own, connections with the body of high and low literature that linked objects and architecture is evident. His main contribution here is to argue that "every engagement between man and objects which he encounters... occurs from the perspective of his own body" and is based on almost instantenous "comparisons between our own bodily state and the objects that surround us."[122]

In his first public address, Schmarsow acknowledged Theodor Lipps as an influence. Indeed, shortly before 1903, Lipps had published on space perception, and by 1906 he had formulated the most systematic and extensive definition of ornament, in *Die ästhetische Betrachtung und die bildende Kunst,* in which he made much of both architecture and objects.[123] In his work the limits between them were fluid, even inconsequential. Like Wundt, who had inspired the work of a whole generation of art historians (Wölfflin, Schmarsow, Warburg, Gurlitt, even the philosopher of technology Ernst Kapp refer to him) and whose student he was, Lipps had a profound effect on turn-of-the-century aesthetics. One of the principal proponents of *Einfühlung,* he taught at Breslau and Munich, and through his lectures (as popular as Wölfflin's), his students—architect/critic Richard Streiter most notable among them—and his publications in the popular

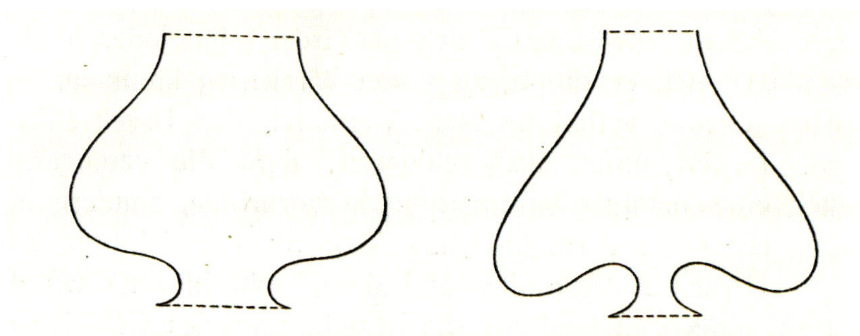

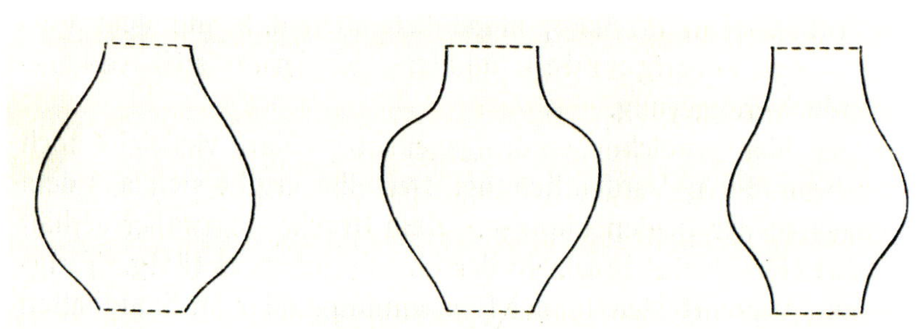

Top **FIGURE 85**
From Theodor Lipps, *Ästhetik: Psychologie des Schönen und der Kunst* (Leipzig, 1903–6).

Bottom **FIGURE 86**
Lipps, *Ästhetik: Psychologie des Schönen und der Kunst.*

press he reached far into the world of art, artists, architects, and aesthetics.[124] Like Schmarsow, Lipps used almost no footnotes, and so it is hard to pinpoint the works and scholars he chose as friends or foes. However, it is evident enough that both Semper and Bötticher had marked his reading of ornament deeply, as had the phenomenological line of philosophers and their followers.

Architecture accounts for a good two-thirds of Lipps's *Ästhetische Betrachtung* and is covered both under *Raumästhetik* (space aesthetics) and technical arts (indeed he makes much of the "technische Kunstwerk"). Like Semper, he includes architecture among the latter, alongside "applied and industrial arts or decorative arts . . . buildings, furniture, railings, containers, carpets."[125] Although they may be functional objects, in their case "the aim of the aesthetic observation is certainly not the capacities or the function of the material . . . but . . . the empathized life."[126] Under *Raumästhetik* he had dealt at length with the effects of one particular and, for him, paradigmatic form that arouses empathy and is shared by a number of small objects—vases, cups, vessels—and larger-scale sculptural pieces like balusters and column shafts and capitals. This form, which he calls "swelling" (*Wulst*), is present across the board and is associated with containment, weight/support, expansion/contraction/elasticity, and other experiences shared by organic bodies (figs. 85, 86). With such an analysis Lipps reduces the empathy-generating forms to abstractions that could be found anywhere, in architecture as in objects of daily use, and thus levels the field much as Semper and Riegl had done. Most important of all, Lipps does not prescribe any scale for objects that contain or derive from this form—they can be infinitely small or large, as the active principle remains the same.

In part 6 of his book, Lipps returns to *Wulst* and reviews it with reference to ornament specifically. In keeping with his focus on the empathy-generating power of three-dimensional objects he is more concerned with assessing them in terms of solid form or profile than surface.[127] Indeed, he disagrees with Semper's view that the *Kunstform* (ornament) veils the *Werkform* (work form) and represents it symbolically. Instead, he argues, in architecture and the technical arts all forms are *Kunstformen*.[128] In the end, these ornamental forms are for him neither imitations nor representations but function like metaphors.[129] However, he distinguishes between "thing" (*Sache*) and "image" (*Bild*). For example, for a column base these are the swelling of the torus on the one hand and the braiding that ornaments it on the other; one is sculptural, the other textile-based. By coming from two different realms, by being alien to each other, these forms emphasize with greater power the elastic pull that the swelling and the braiding share. For Lipps this contrast between *Sache* and *Bild* is fundamental, as therein lies their aesthetic importance. Were they to coincide, then it would be a case of painting architecture on architecture, and that, he concludes, would be a lie.[130] Thus for Lipps the object as a bodily (or sculptural) entity in itself, not just its surface ornamentation, is essential for the aesthetic effect upon the viewer.

Lipps was certainly influential in his own time and well known in the art history field. Among his apologists, Schmarsow was most outspoken and made much of his work. Certainly his conception of ornament and objects owes a great deal to him. Indeed, "Anfangsgründe jeder Ornamentik," Schmarsow's article of 1910, must count with *Verhältnis* as his most radical statement on this subject.[131] In it he draws once again on the entire spectrum of problems that had been associated with ornament to date: tattoo (or body ornament as evidence of the human's instinct to adorn itself), clothes, jewelry, objects of daily (and repeated) use, prehistoric and primitive art, which he illustrates (fig. 87).[132] Like Semper and contemporary anthropologists (whom he acknowledges, as he does ethnologists, psychologists, and historians of culture), he defines *Ornamentik* as the origin of all the arts,[133] and (stylistic) change as the result of sensory fatigue (following Göller).[134] His prose is here at its most complex and abstract, but what he is struggling to convey is clear nevertheless: in his view the critical features of ornament are its seriality and the typical. Earlier authors had said as much. Ralph Wornum, for example, had identified contrast, repetition, and seriality as the foundations of the grammar of ornament in his book of 1856; and Semper likewise had drawn attention to these characteristics. But neither had made them into the principal coordinates of their respective discussions. For Schmarsow, however, the function of ornament is "to convey, emphasize, and accompany" the

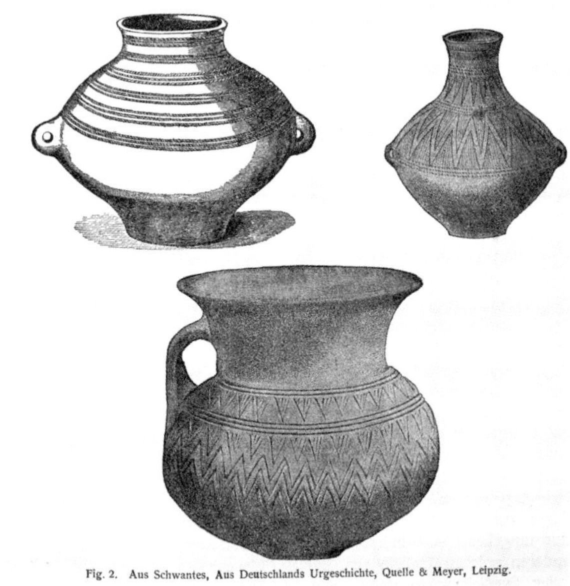

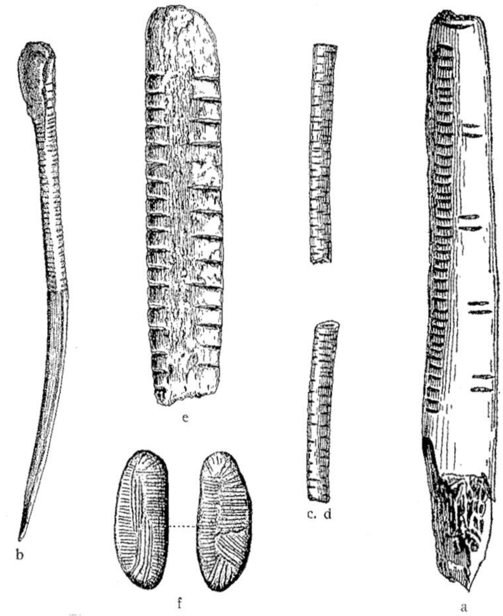

Left **FIGURE 87**
Prehistoric pots. From August Schmarsow, "Anfangsgründe jeder Ornamentik," *Zeitschrift für Ästhetik und allgemeine Kunstwissenschaft* 5 (1910).

Right **FIGURE 88**
Prehistoric tools. From August Schmarsow, "Anfangsgründe jeder Ornamentik."

higher artistic expression of the work through the steady repetition of a relative (or typical) value that stands in counterpoint to the individuality of the whole. The word "type," he concludes, means "essential form."[135] For him ornament does not function as symbol—it is a device that "points to," not one that "is"—it comments, invites us to slow down and pay attention, it designates value. In short, ornament must be typical so that the eye of the viewer does not dwell on it; it must not usurp the function of the artwork itself. If it symbolizes something, then it crosses the border into the other arts. And it is precisely because it is not independent that ornament is an essential component of art—it allows art to speak, otherwise it is mute.

The idea was not entirely new. Over three decades earlier (1876), at the height of the discussions on ornament, Gustavus George Zerffi had already argued for the "signaling" function of ornament in a passage strongly reminiscent of Karl Philip Moritz.

> Ornament takes its origin in the effort to express, to designate, or to mark out the controlling element. The ornamented object has only then a meaning, when it expresses visibly the hidden idea of the controlling element, say the idea of fastening or keeping together, as in clasps, brooches, buckles; or the idea of equilibrium in earrings.[136]

Far from calling for the elimination of ornament, in closing Schmarsow insists on its mediating function: ornament points, comments, invites one to slow down and pay attention as one examines the work of art, but it is nothing in and of itself; ornament merely designates value.[137] In short, ornament is a site of eloquence.

Moving along the evolutionary line from body ornament to the objects of domestic use, that is, of temporary but repeated use, as the next stage in the development of "art," Schmarsow argues against the idea of technical translation of motifs (against Semper) in favor of a "living empathy" from one object to another.[138] In his view the geometric forms (ornament) that adorn the prehistoric carved tools he examines are the result of regulated expressive movements made visible (like repeated punching) and are tied to the intimate traffic between *Kunstgewerbe* and the "warm human body" (fig. 88).[139] The more these objects move outside of man's direct touch, the more distant they are from his body, the more they display analogies with (but not imitation of) it, in both ornament and overall plasticity.[140] In his view this relationship confirms the basic empathy origin of their form and decoration. Schmarsow thus argues for an immediate and empathy-based origin to artistic form, and he makes a spirited effort to demolish both Hegel's and current anthropology's vision of the beginnings of all art in symbol. For him typical form must predate the symbolic one in order for it to acquire any kind of symbolic meaning.[141]

Despite the rather forbidding quality of his writings—dense, abstract, not illustrated—Schmarsow's ideas on ornament, like his concepts of space, were not without a following. And it is interesting to find the various strands that came together in the literature on this topic in the work of one of his doctoral students. Elizabeth Wilson's dissertation *Das Ornament auf ethnologischer und prähistorischer Grundlage,* submitted to the University of Leipzig in 1914, revisits and synthesizes many of the positions that anthropology and art history shared. Unlike her senior art historian colleagues, who included few notes and no bibliographies in their books, she displays her reference apparatus and so allows us to see with greater clarity what made up the contours of the discussion of ornament in her academic milieu, what was read and by whom. In her bibliography she lists the principal actors of the objects debates, as well as the champions of empathy theory, the anthropologists and art historians as well as the museum curators, thus confirming the tight links between them and the sustained interest that ornament enjoyed. Wundt, Worringer, Schmarsow, and Lipps turn up, as one might expect from a Schmarsow student. But she also lists Boas, Stolpe, Colley-March, and Haddon, and, as if to confirm that the conversation spanned the better part of a century, she also lists Philip Moritz and Riegl, as well as Owen Jones, August von Eye, and Falke, bringing them all together under the capacious umbrella of ornament.

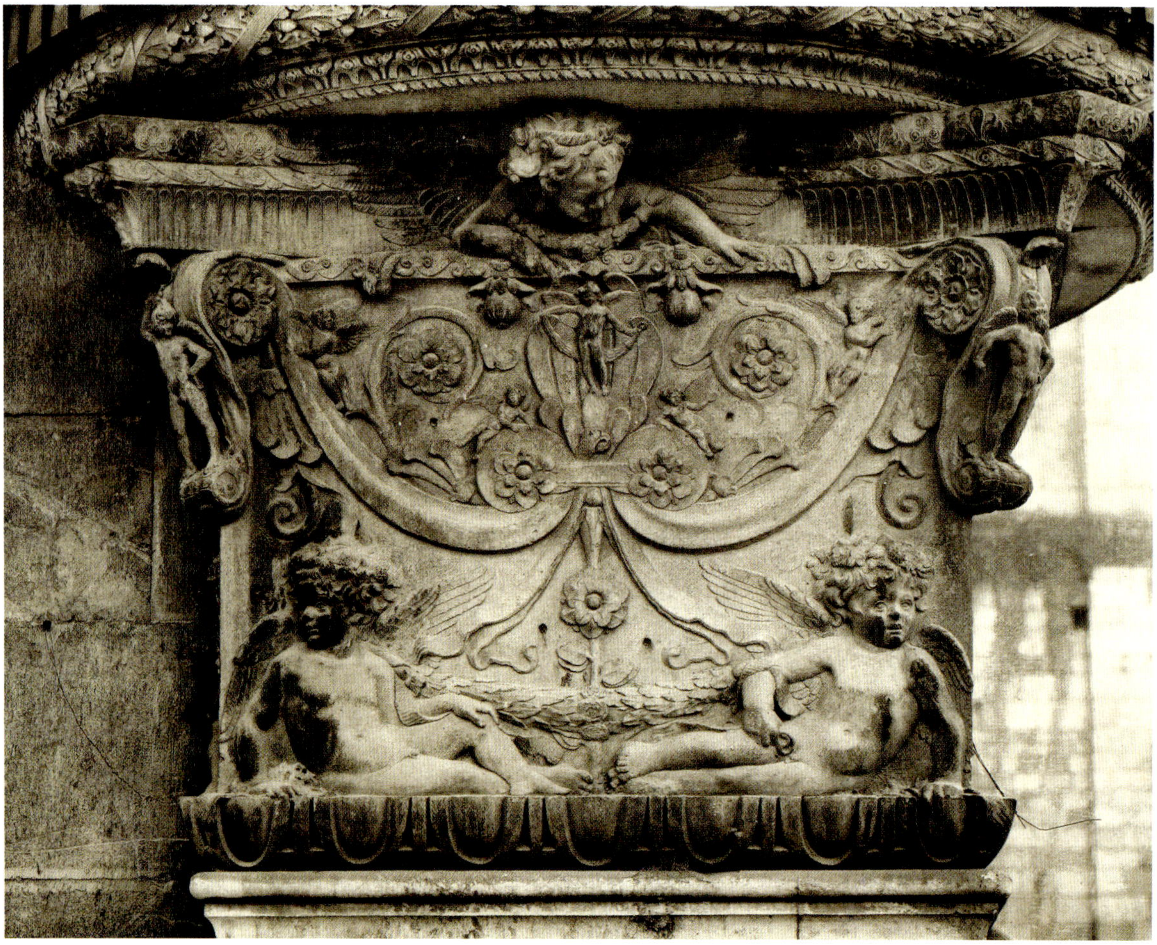

FIGURE 89
Donatello, bronze capital, Cathedral of S. Stefano, Prato. From Heinrich von Geymüller and Carl von Stegmann, *Die Architektur der Renaissance in Toscana* (Munich, 1885–1908).

KLEINARCHITEKTUR AND THE MOBILITY OF ART

The contemporary interest in objects of mass consumption and their artistic value also led to a shift in interest among art historians more broadly. While work on the masterpieces and geniuses of the Renaissance and antiquity continued apace, the literature on historical *Kunstindustrie* acquired a stable place in academic scholarship.[142] In addition, a newly minted category, *Kleinarchitektur,* surfaced in art historical work and established itself as a staple category. From Hermann Lotze to Georg Dehio, from Cornelius Gurlitt to Alois Riegl, from August Thiersch to Hermann Muthesius, the field of architecture and art history embraced it.[143] It also penetrated the education curriculum and turns up as a course topic in German polytechnics.[144] The term seemed so well suited to a larger application that it appeared also in discussions of folk art, preservation, and national patrimonies.[145] To a certain degree Burckhardt's section on "decoration" in his *Geschichte der Renaissance in Italien* (1867) for Franz Kugler's series may be at the origin of the enthusiasm for *Kleinarchitektur.* Although he does not use the term, his readers—as, for example, Fritz Hoeber in his *Orientierende Vorstudien zur Systematik der Architekturproportionen* (1906)—referred in these terms to his examples of wall tombs and sarcophagi, chancel screens, baptismal fonts, chimneypieces, gates, and rood screens.[146]

Kleinarchitektur, literally meaning small architecture, denominated a class of objects that straddled sculpture and crafted objects and looked like miniature architecture. Usually carved and assembled by the designer himself (rather than by proxy, as is normal practice in architecture), they populated churches and squares, interiors and outdoor spaces. Pulpits and ciboria, choir stalls and altars, fountains and chancels were perceived as so many extensions of architecture that brought both details and forms closer to the viewer and hence offered them for a more intimate enjoyment than the large forms of architecture itself.

What united them was a high degree of ornamentation and exquisite crafting that period photographs and the accompanying texts—like Geymüller's for his *Die Architektur der Renaissance in Toscana*—lovingly explored (fig. 89).[147] Geymüller, who was both an architect and historian and a close friend of Jacob Burckhardt's, responded to both trends in the field and imported them into Renaissance scholarship: to the alliance between the two disciplines but also to the profound turn toward ornament, crafting, and applied arts in nineteenth-century culture more generally. The description of these hybrid works—part sculpture, part architecture, part mobile objects—drew on architectural vocabulary, and, as such, analogies with monumental work were frequent. Thus Geymüller, for example, describes the lanterns on the Palazzo Strozzi, designed by Benedetto da Maiano and executed in bronze by Caparra, as containing miniature "tempietti" and insists that they were conceived architecturally.[148] The highly decorative aspect of such works was certainly among their most attractive features, thus connecting in one place the current fascination with ornament and objects (fig. 90). When Geymüller described the ciborium in Siena Cathedral as a "jewel of decorative art" and two lines further down as the work of an accomplished architect, comparing it with the cupola of Bramante's Tempietto in Rome, he acted on all these impulses latent in the field.[149]

Such an interest in the hybrid space of *Kleinarchitektur* had been at least in part prepared by those who noted a relationship between furniture, objects, and architecture. Viollet-le-Duc, for example, signaled the transference across these three domains when he insisted that their makers conceived pieces such as dressers and armoires as small architecture ("l'architecture en petit").[150] The fact itself was not a discovery: many medieval (and both earlier and later) objects such as staffs, altarpieces, armoires, door frames, chests, and so forth were exercises in diminutive architecture. What is important is that it should turn up in Viollet-le-Duc, that tireless author and teacher, much read both in France and

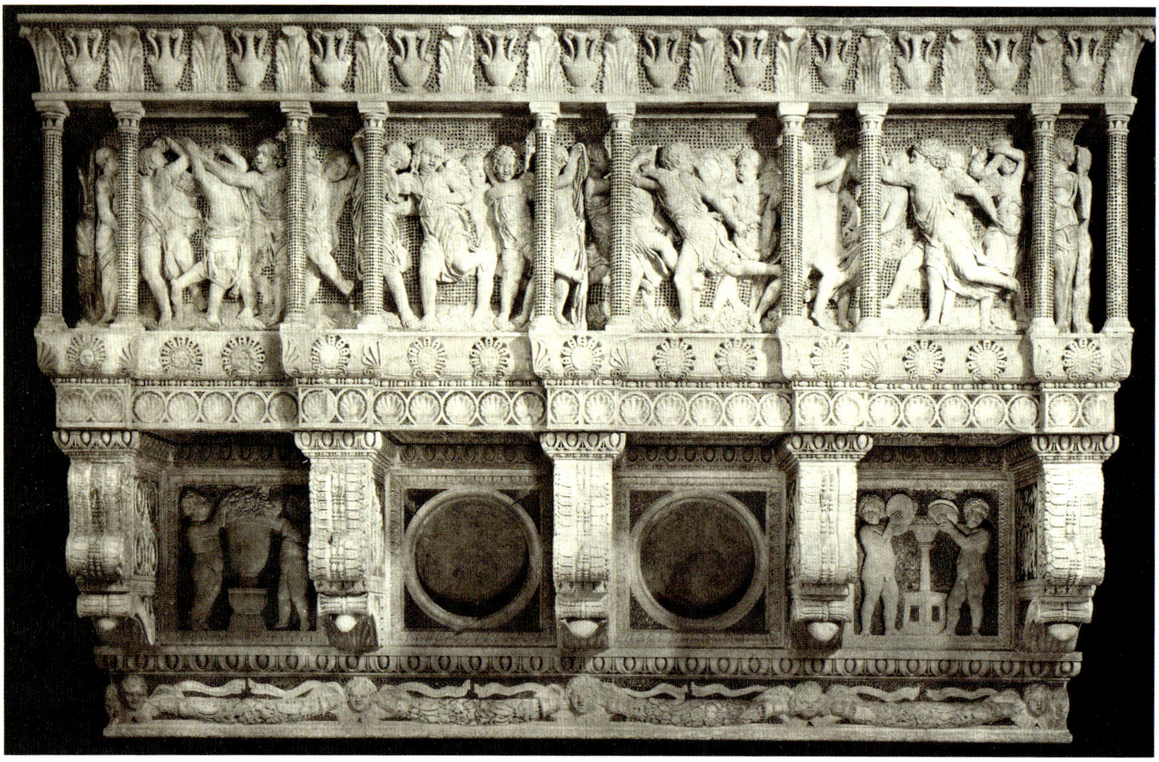

abroad. Moreover, he recognized in furniture an important model for architecture, allowing mobility to an otherwise firmly rooted art. Such a view suggests that Viollet-le-Duc understood furniture and architecture to involve similar principles. Indeed, when he discussed the influence of the Middle East on medieval Western architecture he noted the role of mobile pieces: "One does not transport buildings, but one transports easily a piece of furniture."[151]

The concept of mobile art (*bewegliche Kunst*) as co-extensive with architecture had also turned up earlier in Burckhardt's work, most prominently in his opening paragraph for Part 2 of his *Geschichte Baukunst,* "Decoration."[152] Several decades later it reappeared in the work of architect Paul Zucker, a follower of Wölfflin's, and confirmed that such a category had infiltrated thinking about architecture. Drawing equally on Schmarsow as on Wölfflin, Zucker worked on the spatial representations of the Renaissance, and he turned the spotlight on "*bewegliche* (and even *beweglichste*) *Kunst.*" Echoing Wölfflin, he saw this as a hybrid realm of the arts in which the differences between artistic genres were erased and which signaled the coming style characteristics.[153] For him this mobile art was composed of objects, and he insisted that every instrument and object of household use, every aspect of daily life, every insignificant and marginal detail was imprinted with the characteristics of style.[154] Semper and Wölfflin clearly ring in the background.

FIGURE 90
Donatello, Cantoria, 1439. From Geymüller and Stegmann, *Die Architektur der Renaissance in Toscana.*

In some ways this new attention paid to small architecture also went hand in hand with the rise of interest in tactility (as was the case for Riegl's now famous category *haptisch/taktisch*) and in empathy (its psychology-based collateral).[155] Even if not all art historians dealt explicitly with empathy issues or adhered to the theory "à la lettre," the concepts were widely available and affected the sensibility of an entire generation. For the field at large Wölfflin could have provided one entry point, but Riegl certainly provided another. They were not that far apart. Indeed, Wölfflin made the point himself in his unusually harsh criticism of *Entstehung der Barockkunst in Rom,* where he claimed that Riegl's now famous categories "haptic" and "optic" were his own "plastic" and "painterly" (*plastisch* and *malerisch*) renamed.[156]

In addition, the fascination with tactility and expressive ornament that empathy readings privileged also found an important consequence in the choice of art historical research. This was of course a two-way street. Many art historians of the generation of the turn of the century, such as Wölfflin, Riegl, Schmarsow, and Gurlitt, turned to the Baroque under the influence of a variety of external factors—late Hellenistic discoveries such as the Pergamon altar and large-scale contemporary architectural projects being only two factors, not to mention corresponding imperial politics—but the attention that empathy theory channeled to sculptural details also contributed to this shift in taste.[157] The interest in the sculptural dimension of art and its effects on the viewer is the common denominator that brings these historians together in their project—to reassess the Baroque and how to reassess it. As a result of this orientation toward an emphatically multimedia art, traditional definitions of boundaries between the arts, architecture, and objects were also increasingly dissolved. Thus in their own discipline-specific way art historians as a group additionally contributed to the slippage across media that allowed and signaled a shift of attention toward a space in between that connected mobile objects with monumental architecture.

WARBURG AND THE TRAGEDY OF OBJECTS

Between the concise and rhetorically consummate writings of Wölfflin, the deeply historical and slow-moving prose of Riegl, to the often abstract and demanding texts of Schmarsow and the extensive, overly elaborated aesthetics of Lipps, the theory of empathy as inflected by each one of them with respect to ornament and objects nevertheless penetrated deep into the discourse on the arts. And its reciprocal relationship with the discourse on objects remained a constant. Even when those who followed did not embrace it as such, the field of art history carried traces of this work and allowed it to spill beyond its own confines through teaching, public lectures, and publications into the nonspecialist press. Aby Warburg's scholarly activity, though essentially unrelated to architecture, whether

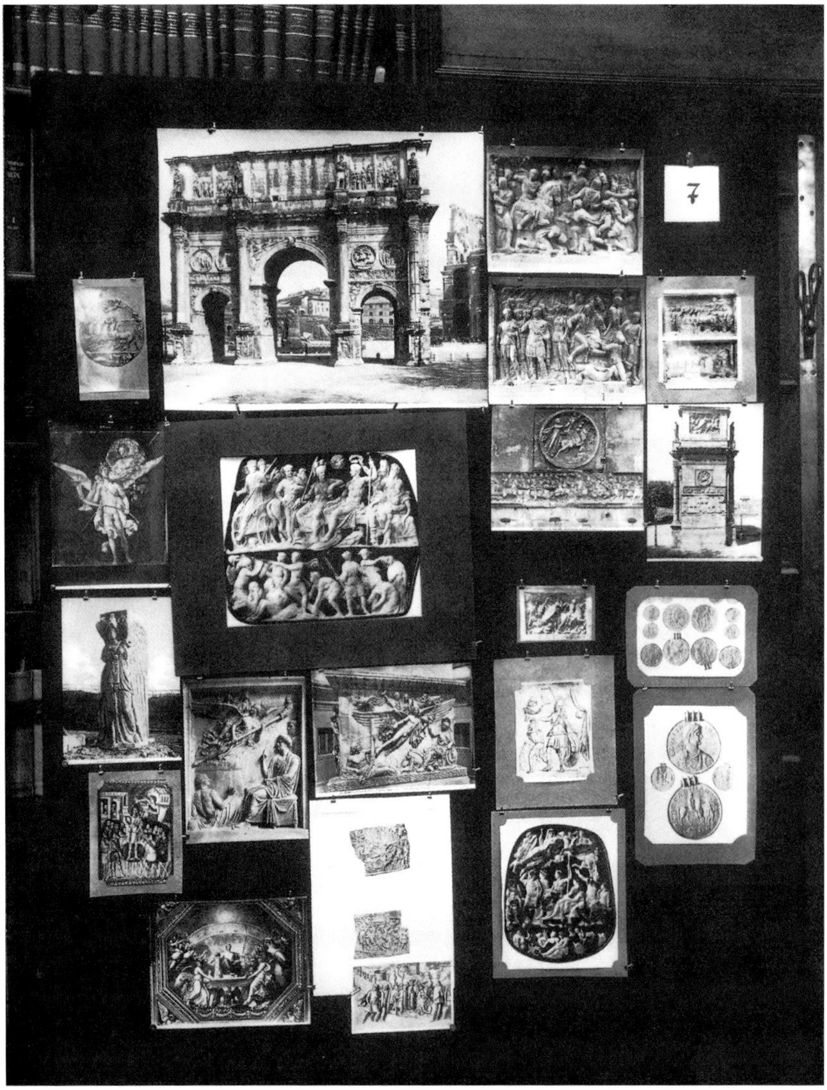

FIGURE 91
Aby Warburg, *Mnemosyne-Atlas*, 1924–29, no. 7. Warburg Institute, London.

modern or historical, nevertheless serves as an apt conclusion to this chapter. Like a seismograph, to use Didi-Huberman's evocative term, he responded to the ideas available in the world surrounding him—the deluge of objects, books, inventions, and anachronisms—and reveals what lay latent within this discourse, what was possible, what could be made from an exposure to the combination of scholarly and popular literature that engaged the culture of the nineteenth century as a culture in crisis.

A student of Schmarsow and Karl Lamprecht, and a reader of Wundt and Robert Vischer, Warburg came early under the influence of psychologically based aesthetics.[158] Like most art historians of his generation, he was certainly aware of the commotion the Pergamon altar had caused and the literature surrounding it, which was so closely connected with a rereading of the Baroque and empathy theory more generally.[159] In addition, medicine, Morelli (the champion of the significance of the insignificant), and Darwin (the champion of a body-based aesthetics in the animal kingdom) left their imprint on his thinking.[160] Influenced early on by anthropologists like Edward B. Tylor, Adolf Bastian, and Franz Boas (with whom he interacted during his American journey 1895/96) he sought historical insight in the detail and in anonymous works, in the detritus of history, which he viewed with as much interest as the classical monuments of art history.[161] Thus Warburg's work grew out of his interest in objects of daily use, in clothes, wax effigies and dance, in tapestries and folk objects, in the residue that was attached to them and that was passed on through their physical handling, in the importance of the body as core of all experience. His very concepts of survival or *Nachleben,* of *Nachfühlung,* and of images as embodiment (*Verleibung* and *Verkörperung*) are close cousins of *Einfühlung* applied to specific historical material.[162] Indeed, his own unfinished *Mnemosyne* project, where cameos and triumphal arches, thumbnail woodcuts and large fresco cycles claimed equal space on its panels, was a pictorial atlas not unlike those of another art historian/anthropologist, August von Eye, and of the whole *Culturatlas* tradition of the nineteenth century (figs. 91, 92).

Already Gertrude Bing had acknowledged Warburg's peculiar path and deep interest in both Semper ("a towering figure in the art theory of the late nineteenth century") and Adolf von Hildebrand.[163] Reacting against the broad strokes

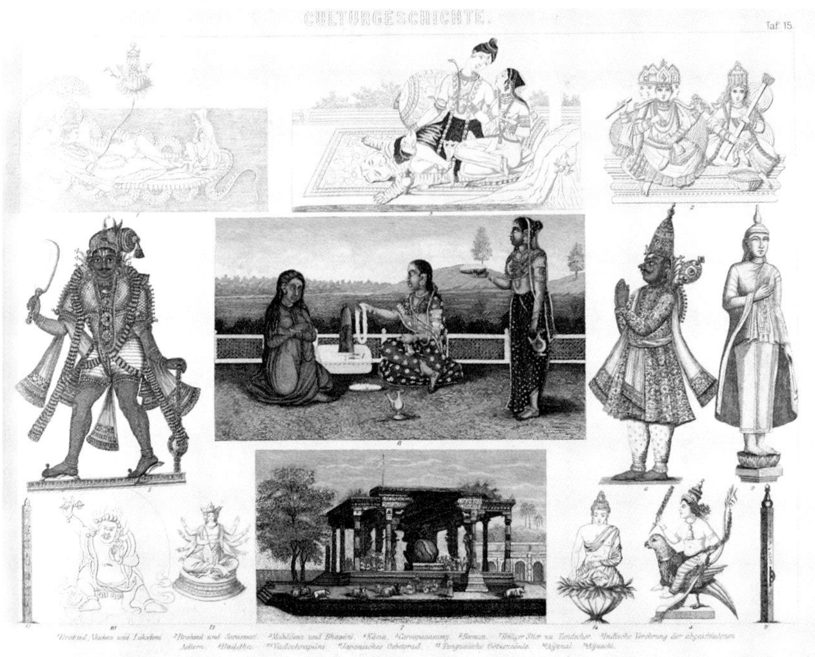

FIGURE 92
"Indian Culture." From August von Eye, *Atlas der Culturgeschichte* (1875).

of *Geistesgeschichte,* Warburg used antiquarian methods and looked at historical details, costumes, tools, and domestic equipment to understand the living habits of the Renaissance actors he was studying: "No sphere of existence must be considered too lowly, too obscure or too ephemeral to provide evidence."[164] According to Bing he

> dissociated himself from the formalistic distinction, widely made at his time, between monumental and applied arts. . . . Decorations were, for him, neither a means to convey an abstract significance nor the result of man's incorrigible urge to cover empty surfaces. The ornaments of tournament banners, tapestried bed hangings or marriage chests are inseparable from the functional character of such objects as tools of daily life and must therefore necessarily give some indication of the particular occasions and the personal intentions which they had served.[165]

Thus Warburg worked on German calendars, court festivals, quack medicines, chap prints (*feuilles volantes*), and dance (as body in movement), and as Didi-Huberman has argued, anticipated Walter Benjamin's likewise unfinished *Arkadenprojekt* in looking for the overlooked (the connection is not fortuitous, as Benjamin was much influenced by Riegl's reevaluation of the insignificant).[166] As Forster notes, there is a kinship between Warburg and Riegl, as well as Semper before them, in this turn to the marginal.[167]

While interested in the marginal, Warburg also looked to *Kunstgewerbe* and signaled its importance in the introduction of "Peasants at Work in Burgundian Tapestries" (1907):

> If we refuse to be distracted by the current tendency to regulate art-historical inquiry by posting border-guards, then it becomes evident that monumental pictorial forces are at work within this "inferior" region of Northern European applied art, and there is no difficulty in assigning all of this Burgundian genre art to its place within a general stylistic evolution.[168]

Although the literature has made little of this so far, Warburg was also involved with the world of objects beyond art history. In 1905 he organized a *Volkskundekongress* in Hamburg, and he was a listed member of the Werkbund in 1911, which later led him to entrust the commission for his house/library at 116 Heilwigstrasse in Hamburg in 1925 to Fritz Schumacher and Gerhard Langmaack (both members of the Werkbund).[169] Like Riegl, and in keeping with the affinities between discourses at the time, Warburg also interacted with the anthropological world directly: not only did he meet and correspond with Boas (whose earliest writings had been on tattoos and body art), but he collected Indian artifacts in Arizona and donated them to the Völkerkunde Museum in

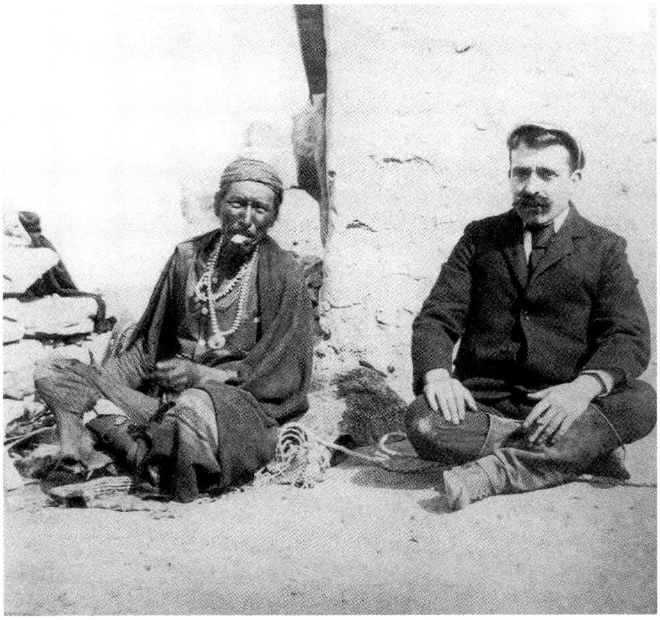

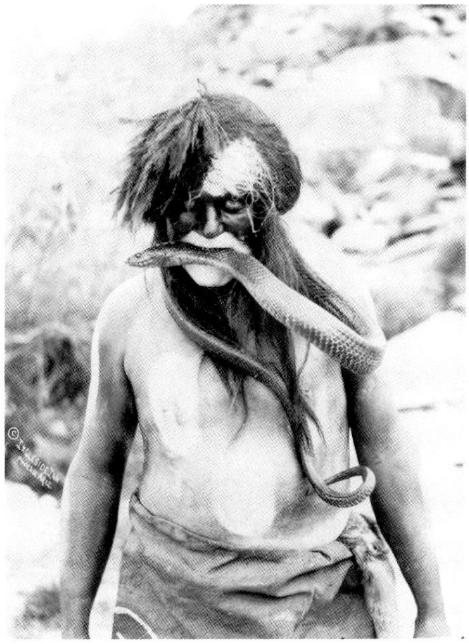

Hamburg (1905) where he also held conferences before the photographic (1897) and anthropological societies.[170]

But perhaps Warburg's most intense commentary on objects in the world of sensory perception occurred somewhat later, in his now famous 1923 Kreuzlingen seminar in which he drew on his encounter with the Hopi Indian culture in Arizona at the turn of the century (fig. 93). This was a contaminated culture—ancient Indian with Christian Mexican overlays. In this sense it was similar to the ancient and Renaissance cultures, likewise overlaid upon each other, one pagan and the other Christian. As is well known, this insight illuminated Warburg's Renaissance work, and his 1903 Ghirlandaio essay was vastly different from the 1893 Botticelli work.[171] But what constituted the real watershed was the experience of the snake ritual of the Pueblo Indians, which revealed to him, with a vividness that no theory-writing could achieve, the importance of the body as lightning rod of reception, the importance of touching and handling as epistemological moments, as moments of great intensity that throw the user into an abyss of time and allow vertiginous shortcuts to exist between cultures (fig. 94). For him, Bernardo Buontalenti's dancing figures from the *Intermezzi* (1589), the *nympha* with its *bewegtes Beiwerk,* and the Hopi Indians' bodily experience of the snake ritual spoke to the same truth (fig. 95).

The anthropological approach that had seeped into art history, the issue of rituals embedded in objects and transmitted by them that had come to fascinate Warburg, is blended with empathy theory into a harmonious if tragic definition of objects in his own tragic Kreuzlingen seminar. The passage is so rich, and so

Left **FIGURE 93**
Aby Warburg with a Hopi Indian, 1895–96. Photographic print. Warburg Institute, London.

Right **FIGURE 94**
Hopi Indian, 1924. Photographic print. Library of Congress, Washington, D.C.

powerful, and, indeed, brings together with such clarity threads that had been infiltrating art-historical discourse from so many sources for so long, that it deserves to be quoted at some length:

> The departure point is the following: I consider man to be an animal who handles things, whose activity consists in establishing connections and separations. This causes the loss of the organic sentiment of the "I" because the hand allows him to grasp concrete objects, which have no nervous system because they are inorganic, but which extend nevertheless the "I" through this inorganic agent. Here lies the tragedy of man who in handling things extends beyond his organic limits.... Where do all these questions come from regarding the enigmas of empathy in front of inanimate nature? Because in fact there exists for man a state which can unite him to something—precisely in handling and holding things—with something that corresponds to him, but that does not flow through his veins. The tragedy of clothes and of the tool is the history of the human tragedy in the broadest sense, and the most profound book written on this is the *Sartor Resartus* by Carlyle.[172]

Thomas Carlyle's book on the "philosophy of clothes" (1836), with its gently mocking tone and parable against materialism, may seem an odd reference, but it was nevertheless speaking a language Warburg knew well. Neither Semper nor Wölfflin seem far away when Carlyle argues that

> in all his Modes, and habilatory endeavors an Architectural Idea will be found lurking; his Body and the Cloth are the site and materials whereon and whereby his beautified edifice, of a Person, is to be built.... Whether he flow gracefully out in folded mantles, based on light sandals; tower-up in high headgear, from amid the peaks, spangles, and bell-girdles; swell out in starched ruffs... will depend on the nature of such Architectural Idea: whether Grecian, Gothic, later-Gothic, or altogether Modern.[173]

But Warburg goes further than the *Sartor,* and his early teacher Schmarsow, whose concept of objects as extensions of organs he shares, for he wants to reach beyond empathy theory and psychology as well, to understand how physical contact produces insight. In the end he intuits a "schizophrenic" relationship between man and object: although at the moment of touch the limits between them are blurred, they do not interpenetrate, and the "I" who has lost the sense of its own boundaries is thrown into crisis.[174] This is the issue of objects taken to its limit.

Warburg's is a tragic conception of body apparel and tools—an extreme insight into the accumulated thinking about clothes as shell, second skin, as

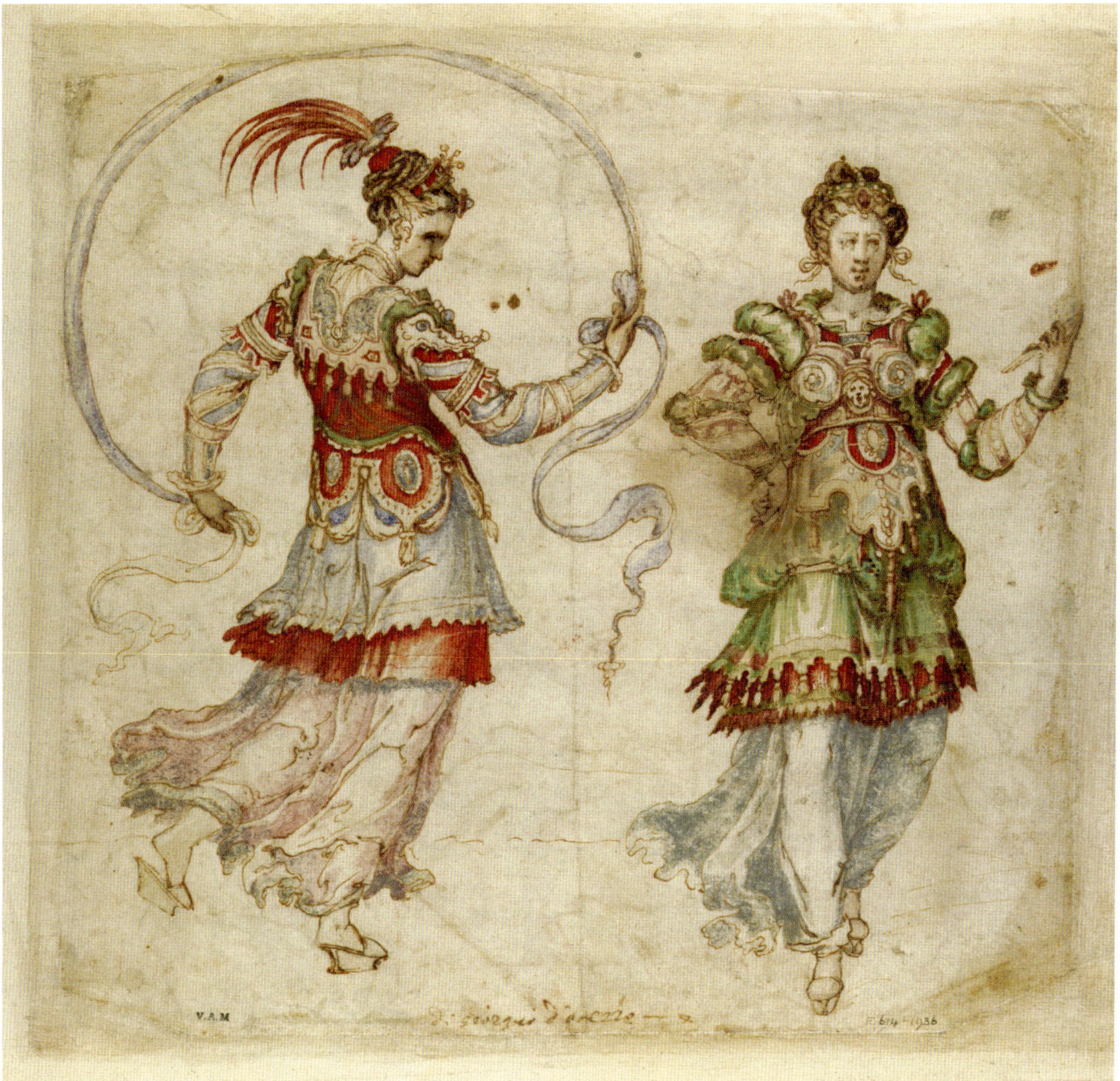

extension of the body and interface with culture. If this tragic reading is peculiar to himself, it nevertheless develops themes that were latent in many branches of nineteenth-century discourse and in so doing records them with extraordinary vividness.

Besides working through the category style, art historians had offered several significant openings that could be seized upon by architects. For one thing, they had drawn attention to the small scale. Whether attending to ornament, details, or mobile art that crossed the borders between architecture and sculpture, they

FIGURE 95
Bernardo Buontalenti, Design for the *Intermezzi of 1589*. Victoria and Albert Museum, London.

had signaled another category of objects and gave them significant theoretical intensity. This is not to say that the explosion in publications on the subject had not raised them to everybody's attention, but in art history they were dignified with the mantle of an academic discipline and systematically studied as they interacted with other domains of art. Even more important, they were embedded in theories of style and culture as part of larger, comprehensive systems. In addition, art historians had also absorbed the theory of empathy that had arisen in an amorphous space between psychology and aesthetics and likewise drawn it into a systematic evaluation of the arts. The importance that the small scale acquired in this process was one more reason for objects to become invested with theoretical weight, as well as novelty.

4 | The Architect's World Between Culture and Style

> Our eyes and our tactile sense have become accustomed more and more to the structure-technical *Sachlichkeit* through continued seeing and handling of the products of modern technology, and our tectonic form-sense has been influenced correspondingly. So has our body-sense become very sensitive to ponderous and obstructing ballast as result of the remarkable development of the means of transportation and our consequent expectation of much greater facility for movement. —RICHARD STREITER, *Ausgewählte Schriften*

Not unexpectedly, style was the lens through which the questions posed by objects and ornament were processed within the world of the architect—be it the professional press, the lecture halls, or the publications of its historians. Indeed, style had become a theoretical catchall that had saturated discourse and provided a convenient common denominator for the debates discussed here. The origin of style, the mechanisms at work in its transformation, the causes for its changes and shifts, its relationship to *Volk* and *Zeitgeist,* constituted a *locus classicus* for the field, and it is here that varied publications (almost overwhelming in their number) from various disciplines were brought into play. It is with reference to the problem of style that Wölfflin and Göller, Riegl and Semper, Schmarsow and Lipps, anthropologists, archaeologists, ethnologists, and defenders of *Kunstgewerbe* (in and out of museums) addressed the issue of architecture and objects. The topic was certainly not unknown in architecture, and much had been written on the subject throughout the nineteenth century.[1] But what could have become an autonomous discourse was profoundly affected by the broader attention that style received on the larger stage of cultural studies.

If style was thus one lens through which architecture's place within the world of objects was reconfigured, culture was another. The two were not unrelated, and one could argue that culture was the other side of the style coin. For nineteenth-century theorists and practitioners, style was the visible manifestation of culture, and cries for a harmonious culture were really cries for a harmonious style. Indeed, it is no coincidence that Semper's theory of modern culture developed in "Science, Industry and Art" should have become the foundation for his magnum opus on style. By the end of the century the crisis of style and culture that Semper had felt acutely when confronted with the world-in-a-glass-house of the Great Exhibition, and that had galvanized research in so many new disciplines, had finally reached a boiling point. The debates, experiments, and proposals it had generated in the intervening fifty years could now be recovered into architecture and brought into a form of synthesis.

Discontent with the status quo and the desire for change were recurrent themes in the architectural literature of the nineteenth century. Faced with a world of rapid, mechanized production, where the traditional connections between maker and objects had been transformed, Semper had suggested a way toward a healthy art: educate the public, educate the craftsmen, and recognize that any and all monumental art gains its strength, or has its origins, in the objects of daily use where basic approaches to fabrication and its meanings are first manifested. If these ideas were not entirely new, their theoretical underpinning was, and the long half-life of his treatise, which had affected so many disciplines, illustrates vividly how useful it was for those caught in the dilemma of modernity. As we have seen, the art historical literature after Semper—which drew on a host of emerging disciplines, such as psychology, anthropology, folk studies, and archaeology, and old ones, like philology—refined this view. In the work of the leading lights of the discipline, Wölfflin, Riegl, Schmarsow, and Warburg even, the reception of art took precedence over its making, and the role of the body (both the maker's and the viewer's), as well as the psychological devices that drew on the body, gained prominence. The body as seismograph as it emerges in Warburg's work offered perhaps the most powerful metaphor for this change in perspective.[2] In this view, the body and its sensory apparatus through which man knows the world united artist and viewer; it lay at the basis of style and drew together all the arts as their common denominator. Whether the body was static and dependent on the eye to mediate sensory stimuli, or in movement and physically interacting with the objects surrounding it, it remained the center of attention for the interpretation of historical art forms—from ancient through Gothic to Renaissance and Baroque. Not surprisingly, this tendency to understand the reception of art among art historians owed much to the theory of empathy that had also emerged in this period in the field of psychology. Crossing disciplinary boundaries from psychology to science to aesthetics, it affected art history in a way that went beyond the work of its direct apologists and shaped or, better still, added another significant category to the reading of art more generally.[3]

To be sure, this vantage point did not affect only the understanding of art, its making and reception, but left a significant if less empathy-focused imprint upon readings of culture broadly conceived. Like the focus on style, empathy theory was also a product of its time and responded to the rise in interest in the body in other domains. For all those who turned their attention to definitions of culture—from anthropologists to historians of costume or philosophers of technology—the body had gained an unprecedented visibility. It could be argued that this trend was an extension of the romantic subjectivist sensibility, and it may well be that it emerged from the same reaction to profound shifts in science and technology and the attending rise of positivism. Be that as it may, these readings of art and of culture found their way into the world of the architect, with some avenues for this traffic of ideas being direct, others less so. Public lectures—from the *Festreden* in Germany directed at the emperor or the anniversaries of major architects such as Schinkel to more intimate events for groups of collectors or museum patrons in Vienna—university courses, and publications in the popular press were opportunities for these ruminations to burst upon a larger public. The specialized journals and scholarly books offered another conduit for dissemination. Finally, events in the public eye, such as the building of a museum, an architectural competition, the mobilization of well-wishers toward the preservation of historical or folk heritage—that is, sections of culture especially destabilized by the Industrial Revolution—often generated debate and more forcefully pushed into the foreground both issues and personalities.

THE PROFESSIONAL PRESS

Perhaps the most accurate means to measure the wax and wane of ideas and their appropriation inside the architectural community is to look to the architectural press in the years when Wölfflin and Riegl worked out their great art historical syntheses. The articles published in these venues recorded the pulse of debates and the reception of the ideas that were fomenting more generally across the disciplines from which the far lesser-known authors of articles themselves had drawn. The principal professional journals in the German-speaking world were the *Deutsche Bauzeitung* (issued from Berlin) and *Allgemeine Bauzeitung* (issued from Vienna) (fig. 96). But their impact was not limited to these countries, as they knew a wide international circulation such that one contributor to the Viennese journal could note in 1891 that it reached "from Stockholm to Capetown, from Texas to Melbourne and Moscow, from Berlin to New York," and that this was precisely the reason he had chosen to publish there.[4] Indeed, Americans also occasionally published in these venues, and the journal was available in the libraries of American universities, thus illustrating their wide circulation and reach.[5]

A sample decade, between 1880 and 1890, reveals the topics and interests that drew readers. As could be expected, historical architecture still held a significant position. *Deutsche Bauzeitung*, for example, featured a series of "Briefe aus Florenz" (letters from Florence) that concerned mainly late medieval and Renaissance architecture from Florence and elsewhere in Tuscany (as far as Abruzzi). Likewise, in *Allgemeine Bauzeitung*, in the period 1883–1900, Rudolf

Redtenbacher published a series of articles on Renaissance Italian architecture, while others wrote on the German Renaissance (especially on Hanover) and on ancient architecture (a frequent topic). Reviews of architectural history books, as well as art history and aesthetics, were a constant in both journals: Cornelius Gurlitt, for example, not only reviewed Giovanni Morelli but also Adolf Göller, while Wölfflin reviewed August Thiersch—the father of dynamic symmetry and begetter of the so-called *lex thierschiana*, which both Wölfflin and Jay Hambidge would later develop into a new generation of Golden Section studies.[6] The golden ratios applied to architecture (in Thiersch's work) as well as ancient Greek pottery (in Hambidge's) drew together once again *Gewerbe* and monuments into one discourse and found significant dissemination in modern art and architecture (most famously the theory of the artists of the Section d'Or in Paris and Le Corbusier).

Equally prominent as a theme was the interest in *Kunstgewerbe*. Sometimes it took the form of extended essays on its role in contemporary culture, as in the case of R. Adamy's article "Decorative Arts and Architecture in the System of the Arts" (Kunsthandwerk und Architektur im System der Künste) of 1889 in *Deutsche Bauzeitung*, but more frequently it appeared as reviews and evaluations of exhibitions of decorative arts.[7] The whole market-cum-curiosity-fair that had replaced the collector's cabinet and opened the world to the masses of visitors, of industrialists and educators—that is, to both producers and consumers—had emerged as a leading topic. Indeed, the exhibition, be it of the Great Exhibition variety, or smaller and more theme-oriented, was handsomely illustrated and described in these journals. Most often the journals promoted not only the exhibition wares but also the pavilions as an architectural "type," examples of the "latest" in architectural development across the world thus reinforcing the fact that architecture itself was exhibited as an object of display alongside the objects of *Kunstgewerbe*.

Clearly much of the literature on *Kunstgewerbe*—new, old, in exhibitions, in industrial production—was to be found in the newly minted specialty journals, such as the various *Mittheilungen* of museums to which Alois Riegl so often contributed or those intended for both artists and collectors/consumers. But architecture journals embraced the topic, too. For example, the architect H. Schatteburg wrote several articles on the crafts and industry in the Vienna-based *Allgemeine Bauzeitung* in the early 1890s in terms that echo (or even anticipate) Riegl.[8] Not only does he argue against the copying of historical examples (as do Riegl and Arthur von Scala at the Museum für Kunst und Industrie in Vienna), but he turns to themes first noted by Semper: the supremacy of France, the cultural mission of the decorative art schools, the education of the *Volk* through free exhibitions and illustrated magazines. More economically sensitive perhaps than Semper, he notes that such measures would produce a knowledgeable

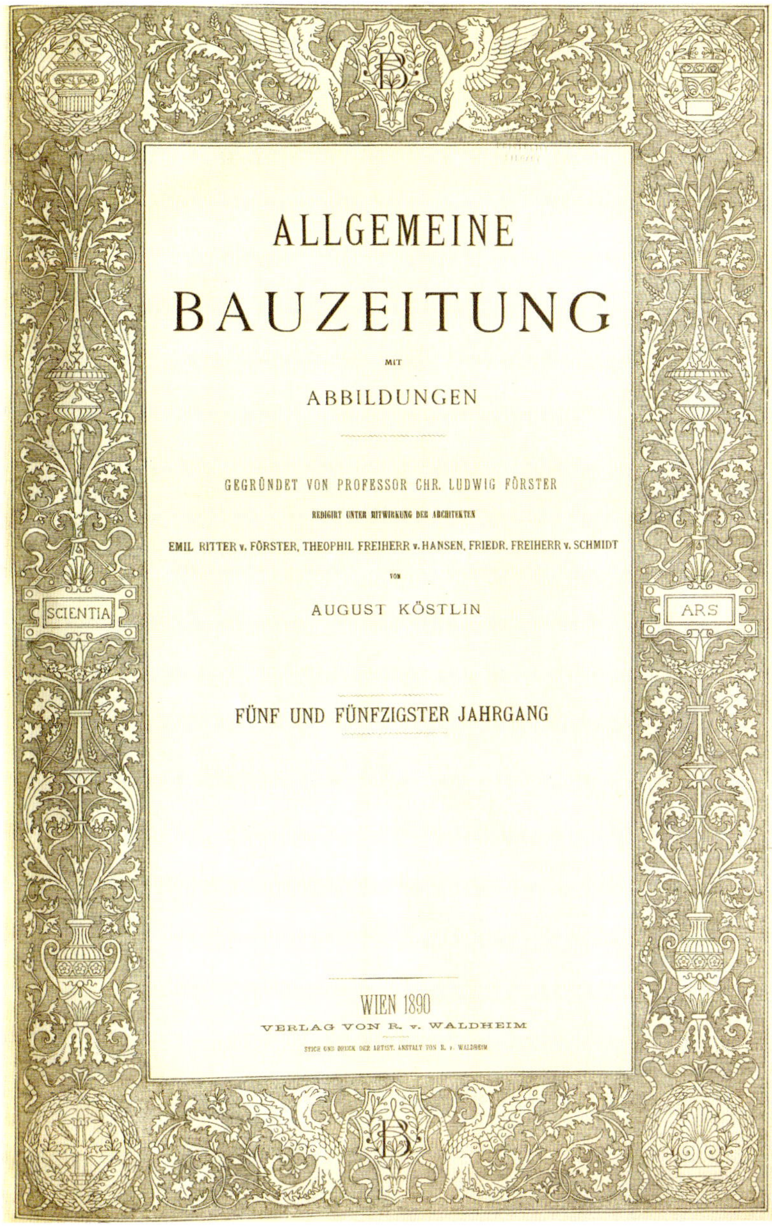
SCIENTIA

ARS

ALLGEMEINE

BAUZEITUNG

MIT

ABBILDUNGEN

GEGRÜNDET VON PROFESSOR CHR. LUDWIG FÖRSTER

REDIGIRT UNTER MITWIRKUNG DER ARCHITEKTEN

EMIL RITTER v. FÖRSTER, THEOPHIL FREIHERR v. HANSEN, FRIEDR. FREIHERR v. SCHMIDT

VON

AUGUST KÖSTLIN

FÜNF UND FÜNFZIGSTER JAHRGANG

WIEN 1890

VERLAG VON R. v. WALDHEIM

STICH UND DRUCK DER ARTIST. ANSTALT VON R. v. WALDHEIM

marketplace (*Publikum*) and he concludes: "Artistic sense gauges the cultural level a people has acquired."[9] The argument contains throwbacks to many of the *Kunstgewerbe* debates earlier in the century but is all the more interesting here because it is used without a reference, completely assimilated into an architectural context. The origin of Hermann Muthesius's c. 1900 articles for an aesthetic of the domestic sphere is clearly discernable here, as is the emphasis on culture, suggesting that radicalism is never without its genealogy, and its success never conceivable without a terrain well prepared to receive it.[10]

FIGURE 96
Allgemeine Bauzeitung (Vienna, 1890).

Particularly interesting is the fact that the issue of *Gewerbe* was only rarely isolated as a topic but came up, as a matter of course, in any number of discussions of style and culture. Indeed, the articles that predominated, and sometimes extended beyond one issue or even beyond one year and had several *Fortsätzungen* tended to revolve around issues of style. Ornament, culture, and the evolution of form were topics that came up together as if naturally intertwined, and it is here that both direct references to and echoes of Semper, Wölfflin, Riegl, and Bötticher, of anthropologists, philosophers, and cultural historians, can be found. This was the testimony of an important trickle-down effect that recorded the impact of specialized literature onto a neighboring discipline and profession. For example, it is such an imbrication of discourses that lies at the basis of Schatteburg's articles when he turns to the topic of style and color in architecture in his articles of 1894 and 1895.[11] But he was not alone. Two further examples of such an interweaving of discourses are the articles of Albert Hoffmann, a frequent contributor to *Allgemeine Bauzeitung* in the 1890s, and of Adamy. Indeed, Adamy's more philosophically constructed article of 1889 in *Deutsche Bauzeitung* was often quoted and found its way back into art historical texts, not least by way of Schmarsow, who cited it in his inaugural speech at Leipzig in 1893, making it one of the very few references he acknowledged.[12]

But Hoffmann's article deserves more than a passing comment. His critique of Garnier's *Histoire de l'habitation humaine* exhibition of 1889 illustrates the rapid spread of ideas recently put on the scholarly map by art historians such as Wölfflin. Thus Hoffmann regrets the absence of interior furnishings in the habitations because this is what reveals the most about culture: "the intimate life in the house, the daily activities, the furnishing and organization of the rooms, the costume of the inhabitants and *their deportment, their way of walking and standing, of working and resting*."[13] This anthropological and empathy-based reading—certainly not footnoted to Wölfflin, despite the clear reference to deportment and body sense as the underlying matrix of the domestic environment—testifies to the almost self-understood importance that the body and behavior had acquired among architects after the publication explosion in the man-based disciplines of the second half of the nineteenth century. Indeed, Hoffmann's 1890 article on style ("Im welchen Style sollen wir bauen?") poses the question at the level of culture and argues that style depends on society, materials, customs, and climate. His references are to cultural history as well as to art history, in the shapes of cultural historian Friedrich von Hellwald, art historians Wilhelm Lübke and Cornelius Gurlitt, and also Julius Langbehn, the author of *Rembrandt als Erzieher* and popularizer who crossed these two disciplines.[14] Langbehn's appeal for a German style that responds to the *Zeitgeist*, to a rebirth of the imperial age and the "grosse Volksidee," ultimately helps Hoffmann focus on the German

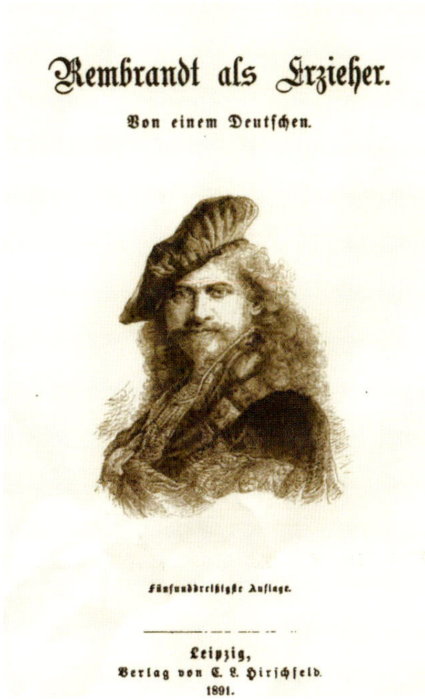
Rembrandt als Erzieher.

Von einem Deutschen.

Fünfunddreißigste Auflage.

Leipzig,
Verlag von C. L. Hirschfeld.
1891.

Renaissance. Taking a Semperian turn, he concludes that this is the appropriate national style not only because of its picturesque quality but also because it marked the climax for German *Kunstgewerbe* (fig. 97). The function of objects as infrastructure to architecture lies just beneath the surface of this argument.[15]

Also in 1890, an even more interestingly derived argument was put forward by the Cologne architect G. Heuser, also in *Allgemeine Bauzeitung*. His topic is a style of his own coining, if not invention—the *Gefachstyl* or *Gelenkstyl* (the articulation style). Taking a post-Semper materialist view and using Darwin's evolution theory as his justification, Heuser argues that architectural styles are not invented but evolve naturally from the materials employed.[16] What is particularly revealing is the breadth and apparent heterogeneity of his reference material: Semper and Darwin head the list, but it also includes Göller, Zeising (the begetter of the Golden Section theory), Virchow (on the nervous system), and Hermann Grimm (on Michelangelo). His terms—*Bekleidung, Zierform, Kunstform, Kernform*—are equally loaded as they declare their origin in the architectural literature of the nineteenth century from Bötticher onward as well as throwbacks to Lipps and Semper (fig. 98).

Perhaps the most remarkable aspect of this article is that Heuser offers an in-depth reading of Ernst Kapp's *Philosophie der Technik* (1877) in the architectural press. As we have seen, Kapp's concept of organ projection illustrated the increased interest and fascination with the culture of the machine and at the same time testified to a submerged anxiety about the body in this shifting world.[17] By

FIGURE 97
Julius Langbehn, *Rembrandt als Erzieher: Von einem Deutschen* (Leipzig, 1891).

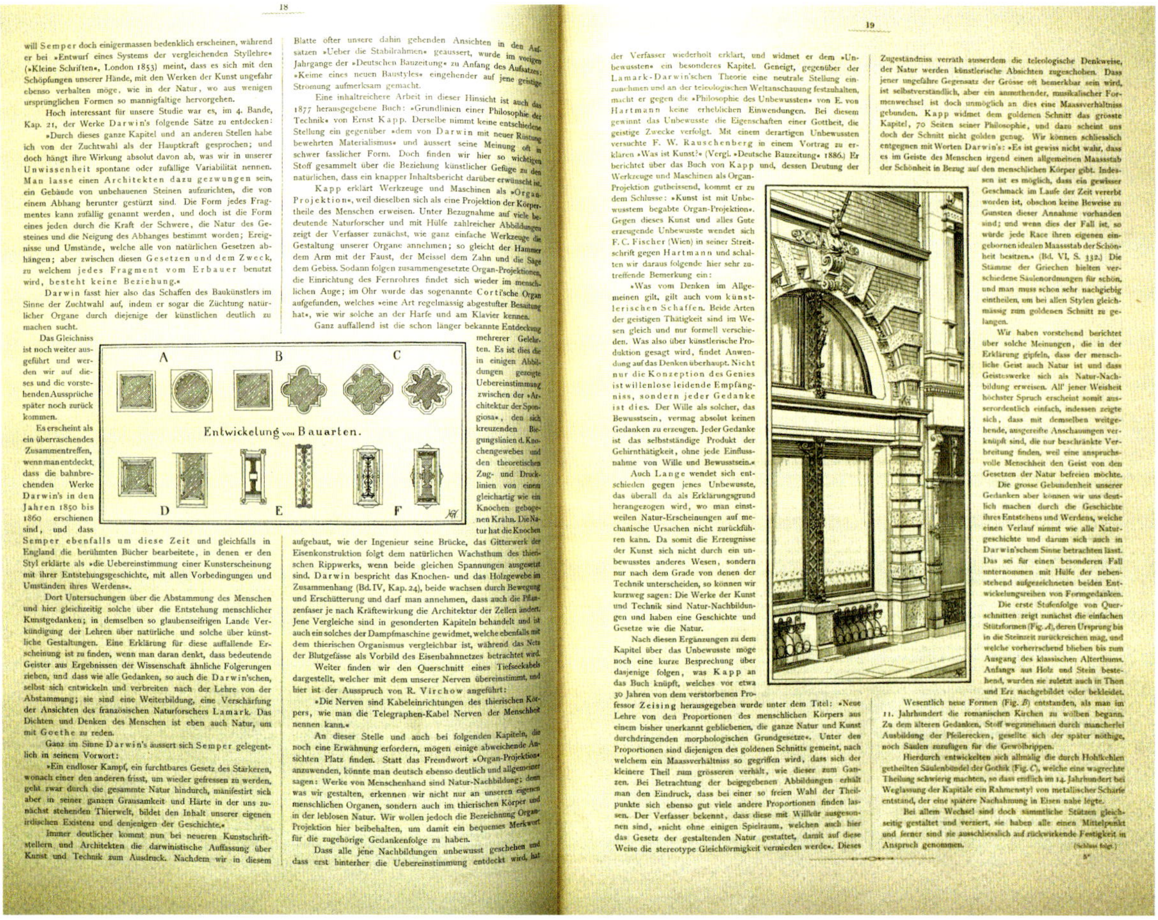

Fig. 21.

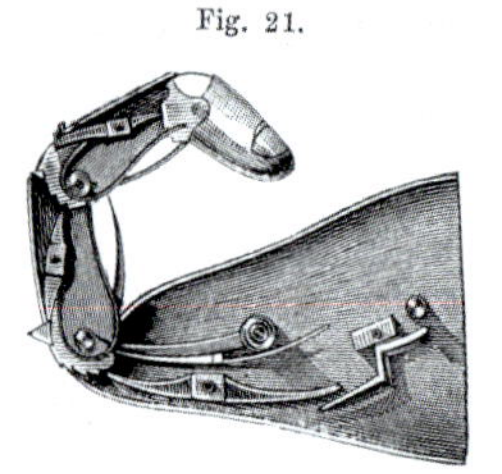

Ein Finger der eisernen Hand.

Top **FIGURE 98**
"Gelenkstyl." From G. Heuser, "Darwinistisches über Kunst und Technik," *Allgemeine Bauzeitung* 25 (1890).

Above **FIGURE 99**
Iron joint. From Ernst Kapp, *Grundlinien einer Philosophie der Technik* (Braunschweig, 1877).

foregrounding Kapp's book Heuser flagged a work that not only brought together anthropology, anatomy/medicine, and history of instruments, costume, and architecture, but more importantly presented technology as a universal biologically driven phenomenon.[18] Kapp connected instruments and the human body by way of subconscious transference, and it is precisely his concern with their shared inner principles of force, movement, and joints that attracted Heuser and presumably the architectural profession as well (fig. 99).[19]

It is with reference to Kapp, then, that Heuser derives the concept of "Natur-Nachbildung," which eschews traditional corporeal imitation and instead focuses on analogy: body articulations and machine connections are analogous in their operation, not in their form. The mechanical articulations he illustrates—the points of torsion (*Drehpunkte*) and the joints (*Gelenke*)—are the starting points for a style, he argues; that is, they are in harmony both with the body and the technology of contemporary industry, and, thus, an ideal representation of the *Zeitgeist*. *Gewerbe* as such is not Heuser's subject, but his reference point in instruments indicates his conception of a dialogue between architecture and objects. And

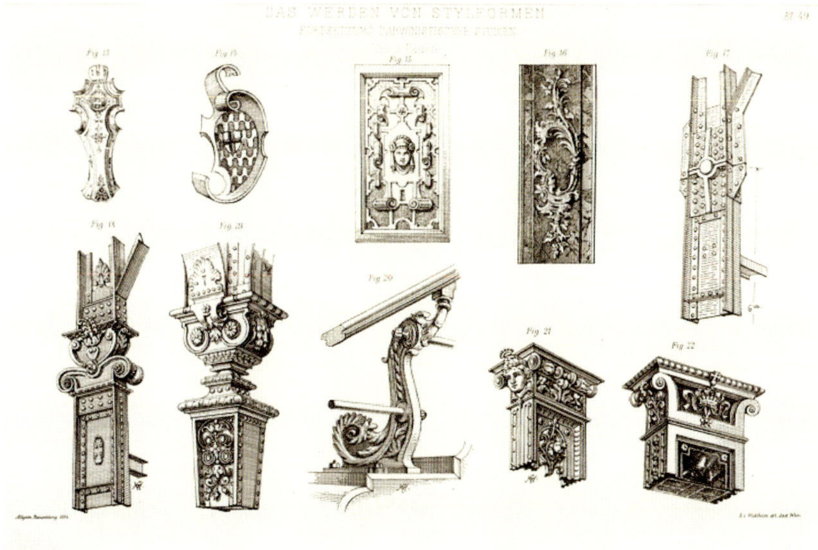

FIGURE 100
G. Heuser, "Das Werden von Stylformen: Fortsetzung Darwinistischer Studien." *Allgemeine Bauzeitung* (1894).

here Kapp was essential because he blended the object made by the hand with technology and the body, such that there was no gap between them. Based on this model then, Heuser looks to ball joints as characteristic of new iron construction and, as such, the *Kunstform* (artistic form) to be developed into his new style, the *Gefachstyl*. Zeroing in on the points of rotation in iron structures is perceptive of Heuser from an engineering point of view, as it is precisely these mobile joints that permitted the construction of large spans and trusses that characterized the most technologically advanced buildings of the age (fig. 100). But this focus also had points of contact with a form of anthropomorphism, or organ projection, in Kapp's terms. Hip, knee, and elbow are skeletal joints analogous to those of iron structures, Heuser argues, and ornamental members should arise out of functional ones such as these joints, and he points to the connectors that anchor the Frankfurt railway station trusses into their foundations as such "utilitarian organs" with aesthetic potential.[20]

Even more eloquently Heuser turned to armor to strengthen his argument. He drew on armor and the art of arms manufacturing (*Waffenschmiedekunst*)—a *locus classicus* by now, after Semper and Kapp, for the overlap between technology and the body—with his own Wölfflinian analysis in which he connected its sharp edges, raised seams, and fluting (*Riefen*) with the features of Gothic architecture.[21] Among historians and architects Viollet-le-Duc had paid most attention to armor in his own work on medieval furniture of the 1870s. His highly detailed illustrations, with multiple closeups of the fastenings, suggest visually the fascination with technology that connected his enthusiasm for iron construction with that for the metal sheaths enveloping the body (fig. 101). Yet, despite the almost excessive attention he paid these metal body sheaths, his interest stopped there with

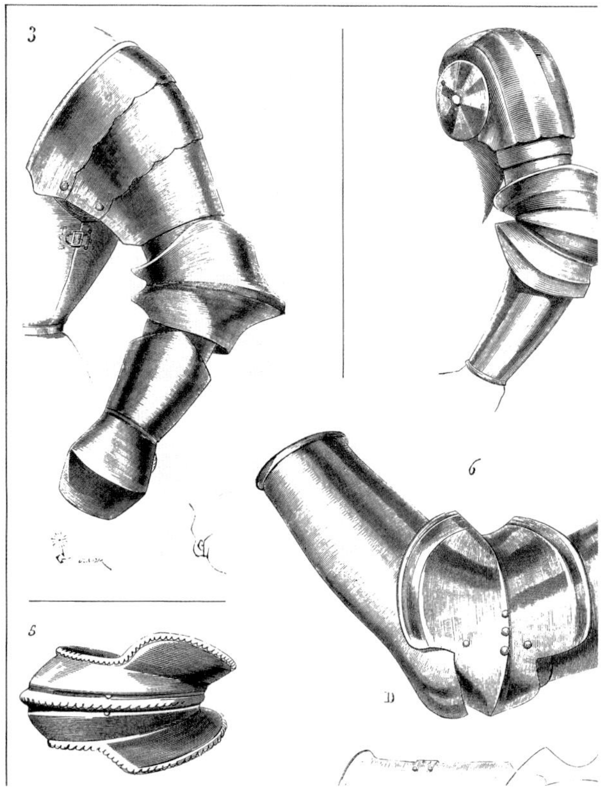

a historical inquiry and sensibility. For Semper and Kapp, however, the interest lay in analogy and representation between human and machine articulations, and it is this perspective that Heuser draws on.

After the publication of *Stilfragen* in 1893, in which Riegl attacked the Darwinist-materialist Semperians, Heuser returned to his topic the very next year and took him on directly.[22] Far from abandoning his Darwinist, materialist, and realist (a new buzzword in the profession at this time) approach to style, he reinforces his battery with additional ammunition: besides Semper, Darwin, Hellwald (folk art scholar/ethnologist), and Adolf Göller (professor of metal structures at Stuttgart polytechnic), now turn up references to archaeologists and historians like Dörpfeld, Bötticher, Lübke, and Viollet-le-Duc, as well as to publications in the various journals of the *Gewerbe* museums (such as the *Westdeutschegewerbeblatt*). In a twist to his argument in which he blends Wölfflin's idea of the Gothic shoe as testimony of the origin of Gothic architecture, and Ernst Kapp's analysis of armor as a piece of technology that surrounds the body without being its extension (as tools might be), Heuser argues that armor work was translated into joinery in medieval times and from there into Gothic architecture (figs. 102, 103). This translation he evidently sees as a decisive argument in support of

FIGURE 101
Armor joints. From Eugène-Emmanuel Viollet-le-Duc, *Dictionnaire raisonné du mobilier français de l'époque carlovingienne à la renaissance* (Paris, 1868–75).

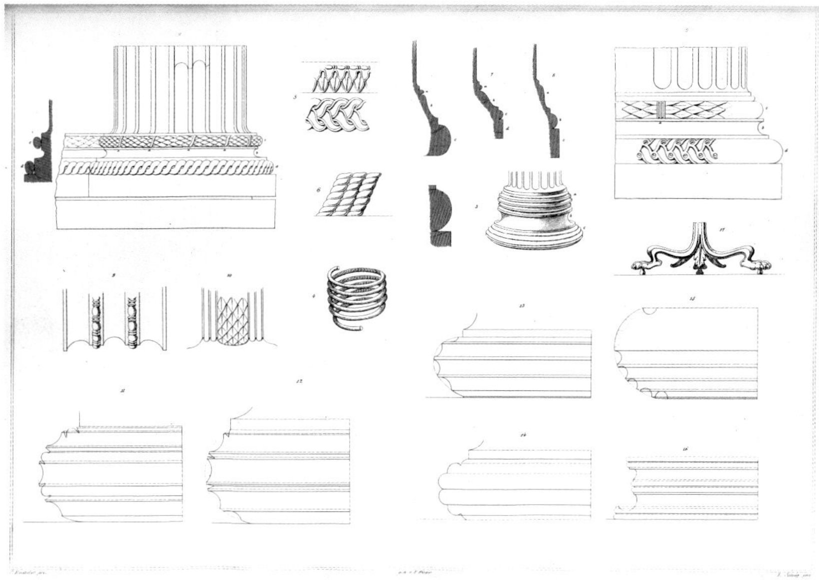

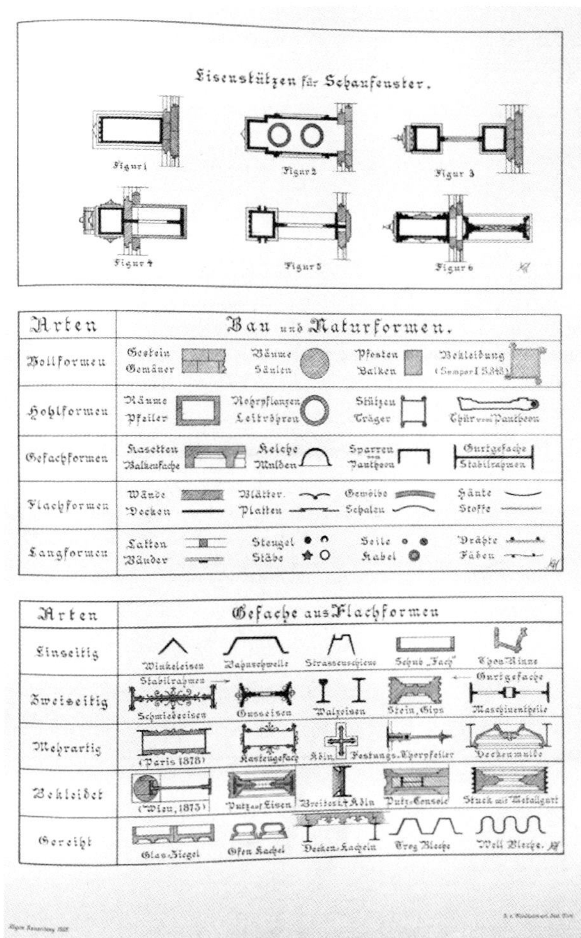

Above **FIGURE 102**
"Junktur." From Karl Gottlieb Wilhelm Bötticher, *Die Tektonik der Hellenen* (Potsdam, 1852).

Right **FIGURE 103**
"Derivation of Fachstyl." From G. Heuser, "Die Stabilrahmen," *Allgemeine Bauzeitung* (1888).

his own derivation of the "articulation style" (*Gelenkstyl*). In addition, his *Fach* or *Gelenkstyl* was also probably indebted to Bötticher's *Junktur,* the term he prominently used to define the connections and connectors between members insistently emphasized by ornament in Greek architecture.[23] Beyond the seepage of discourses into a well-assimilated whole, Heuser's argument shows clearly that for him objects (instruments), ornament, and architecture conversed by way of the assemblage of parts.

Heuser's article had a context, just as Riegl's attack on the materialists and Darwinists was not without its roots in the debates of the Vienna of his own time. The problem of style that Heuser resolves in favor of an iron-based *Gefachstyl* (which he even illustrates and derives from an evolution of column/beam joints from earlier styles) had been forcefully promoted by Bau-Komissar Gruner in the same journal, *Allgemeine Bauzeitung,* in 1888 in his article on "the lie in the art of building."[24] Yet although Gruner argued against historicism and in favor of style arising from a modern material such as steel, he did not forsake ornament. And he proposes an "artistic re-formation" of the "naked functional form"—not as a "mask," as was the case in the Printemps department store in Paris, nor as *Bekleidung,* he adds in an anti-Semper aside, but as a combination of *Kunstform,* material, and construction.[25]

If Gruner stayed close to the rationalist position in emphasizing structure, another architect-contributor, L. Trzeschtik, engaged the same problem from a different angle in the very same journal.[26] He too attacked the mask and the *Scheinarchitektur* (architecture of appearances) and took a realist position, as he claimed. Yet he too was unable to forsake ornament. Building his argument on a host of sources, mostly art historians—besides Semper, who appears to be the reference point for most who engage theory, he uses art historians like Schnaase, Kugler, Schasler, Lübke, Lutzow—he accepts architecture as an art that idealizes the real. However, this cannot be a "little ornamental vestment" (*Prunkmäntelchen*) but must lie somewhere between this and the basic building core (*Baugerippe*). Architecture cannot fully achieve the symbolic level on its own but needs the other arts, he concludes.

It is perhaps to be expected that German-speaking architects should turn to philosophy and aesthetics in particular given that art history (and this included architecture as a matter of course) had been its own offspring, and naturally the interaction between the two fields remained strong. Adamy's article of 1889 on "The Decorative Arts in the System of the Arts" in *Deutsche Bauzeitung* illustrates this connection and the kinds of questions it generated, as well as the permeability of discourses across architects, professional journals, and art history. In what seems essentially a review of philosopher Eduard von Hartmann's chapter on architecture from his history of aesthetics, Adamy defines architecture—in very Semperian terms—as an art of instruments as well as a "space creating art" to which belong all forms of containers large or small. Taking his cue from Hartmann's survey of the definition of architecture in philosophy, he berates philosophers for having ignored the *Kunsthandwerk* from Kant until Vischer (on the basis of the functionality of this artform). However, unlike Wölfflin—whom he does not quote—Adamy separates sculpture from architecture, and, ignoring the whole issue of polychrome and painted architecture (and hence contra Semper), he detaches textiles and painting from both for being two-dimensional arts.[27]

The argument was not lost on art historians. Both the critique of Wölfflin's corporeal reading of architecture and the concept of space as determinant for architecture resonated three years later in Schmarsow's inaugural lecture at Leipzig. Indeed, Adamy's position was probably well known, orally if not otherwise, since, as he himself notes, his article represented the gist of his teaching at the Technische Hochschule in Darmstadt since 1881—that is, long before either Wölfflin or Schmarsow had left the benches of the Gymnasium. This conversation then that started in an architectural journal continued across Schmarsow with Wölfflin, who responded to the argument in an Olympian review of Schmarsow's published lecture, in which he dismissed the work of Hartmann (and the issue of the division of the art as free or not free as proposed by him and Adamy), for being without real consequence for the field and its status vastly overblown.[28] But whether all were in agreement, it is clear that articles like Adamy's were known and read, and penetrated the discourse of architects.

Nevertheless, Adamy's connection of architecture with containers (*Gefässe*) and instruments was neither isolated nor aberrant and drew on a well-known line of argument that went back to Moritz and Schelling.[29] It certainly influenced Schmarsow's concept of contained space as the fundamental style-giver for architecture. The argument also surfaced in Lipps—the other godfather of Schmarsow's aesthetics—who not only used *Gefässe* as virtually the only illustrations in his *Ästhetik,* thus giving them even greater prominence, but, more importantly, used them as examples of forms that elicit empathetic responses alongside (and therefore equivalent to) columns—as corporeal forms rather than containers of space. Perhaps most important, this emphasis on vessels/containers signals the significance of a category of objects that cut across scales: small objects and monumental architecture rubbed shoulders under its umbrella.

AUTHORS AND ACADEMICS

If the press mediated between the academic disciplines and the profession of architecture and thus allowed its theory to absorb a variety of concepts from other fields, those teaching in the schools of architecture contributed even more to the

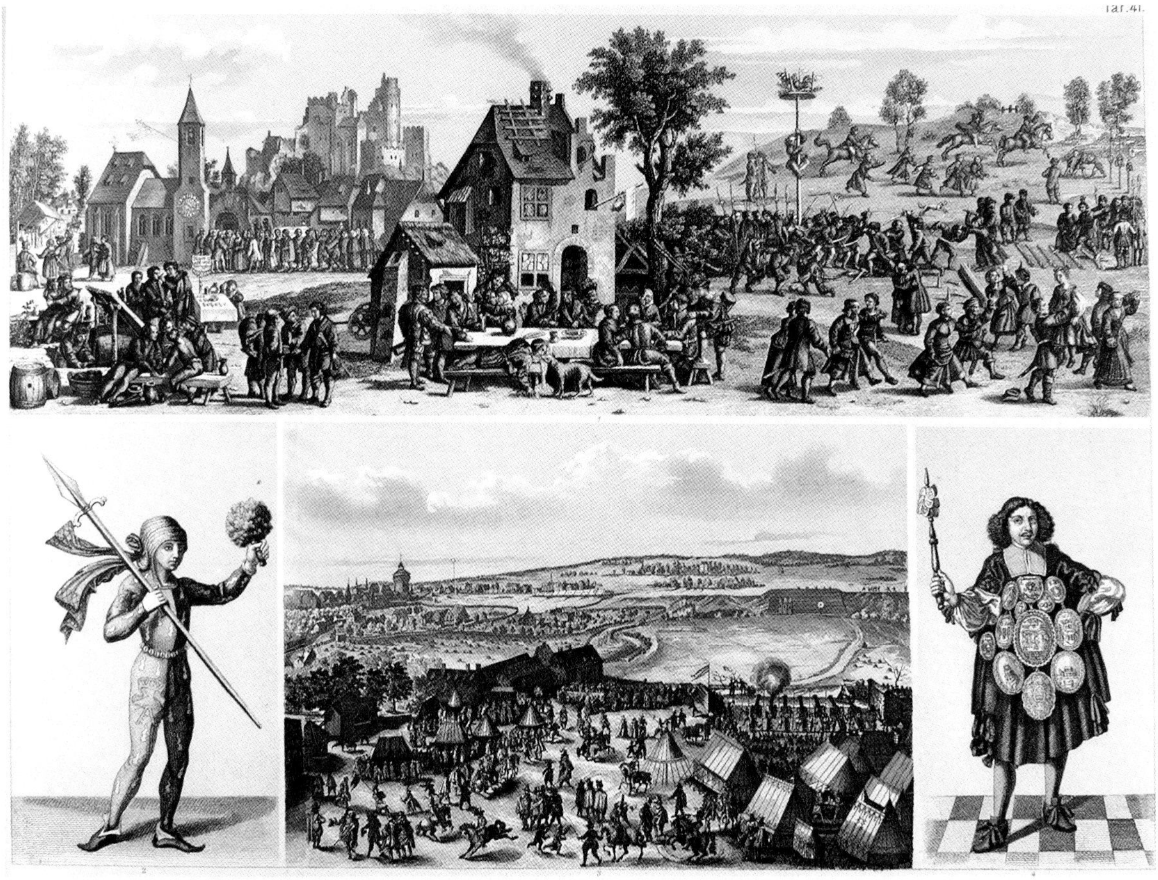

FIGURE 104
"Nürnberg Festival." From von Eye, *Atlas der Culturgeschichte.*

dissemination of these ideas. While the lecture halls of a Wölfflin or a Lipps were filled with students and an interested audience of artists, architects, and critics, it is the exposure to perhaps lesser-known (today) academics like August von Eye, Richard Streiter, Adolf Göller, or Cornelius Gurlitt, who taught in various Technische Hochschulen or even *Gewerbeschulen,* who brought their theories into the classrooms and into their own publications, thus into the architectural debates that stirred the architects themselves. They received and in turn transmitted the various directions available in the field in their own particular ways. Not all issues were covered or even commented upon, depending on the interest of the individuals, but most of them intertwined and developed, becoming of primary relevance for architects.

One such example is August von Eye, art history professor and curator at the Dresdener *Gewerbeschule* and museum. With his background in philosophy, philology, archaeology (from Göttingen), and painting he blended all these interests and entered the terrain of cultural history that had points of contact with anthropology. His travels to Brazil and his extended sojourn on the American continent were not unlike the anthropologist's field trip or Warburg's experience among the Oraibi tribes in Arizona, if with less climactic repercussions. His publications, however (including *Atlas der Kulturgeschichte,* 1875), illustrate precisely the kind of intersection between disciplines in which such polymaths operated and record the attention conferred upon the human body in discussions of evolution, culture, and history. Clothes, tools, housing, and the environment were so many concentric layers surrounding the body, and it is to be assumed that they figured similarly in his teaching (fig. 104). Indeed, this continuous line that connects the bodily core to its surrounding layers is precisely the point he makes when he connects housing (*Behausung*) and clothes (*Bekleidung*) in the 1876 lecture that Ernst Kapp found so relevant to his theory of organ projection.[30] What was latent in von Eye's anthropological history of cultures as a history of bodies and their instruments was teased out by Kapp, if not by von Eye himself. However, the connection with *Kunstgewerbe* issues did not need an intermediary. As co-author of *Kunst und Leben der Vorzeit* (1868) with Jacob von Falke, he came within the orbit of the museum world and the applied arts movement. This connection he himself then embodied within the arts and crafts school at Dresden and the very lively architectural and preservationist milieu there.[31] Moreover, von Eye was one of the first supporters of "ornament preservation" (*Musterschutz*) even as he was active in responding to the needs of German industry.

Like von Eye, Adolf Göller (1846–1902) also straddled several disciplines while teaching at the Polytechnikum in Stuttgart. Perhaps active more laterally than most of his architect colleagues, Göller taught civil engineering (superstructures or *Hochbau*) and railway construction to engineers, and it seems somewhat unexpected that two important works on aesthetics with a discussion of the then popular empathy theory should arise from his pen.[32] Nevertheless, the connection between body and technology had certainly been proposed by Kapp some ten years earlier (and his book had been reviewed in architectural journals), so perhaps such a connection did not need to be considered unusual by Göller's time. If the role of the body in interacting with the environment was more implied than closely analyzed by von Eye, Göller engaged it straight on. Perhaps influenced by Fiedler and Wundt's physiological psychology (which he cites on the first page of his *Zur Äesthetik der Architektur*), he developed an autonomous aesthetics of architectural form.[33] Concerned with the effect of form on the psyche, Göller distanced himself from architectural symbolism in the manner of Bötticher and Semper. Instead, he focused on the subjective reaction provoked by form (construed in the most general terms) and argued that style changes occurred when the effects of form on the collective subjectivity led to the fatigue of the "feeling for form" (*Formgefühl*).[34]

Göller had little to say on objects as such, or on empathy, though like so many he too published an essay (from a lecture) on *Kunstgewerbe* and architecture.[35]

Indeed, he sought to look beyond it. For him, symbol-based anthropomorphic and empathy readings of architecture in the manner of Wölfflin, Bötticher, or Semper, following Hegel's idealist philosophy, were ultimately superficial in that they did not even begin to identify the source of pleasure in forms.[36] However, if his participation in the discourse on objects and architecture does not seem to have been direct, his concept of *Gedächtnisbild* (image memory), which received such wide coverage in the architectural press through readings like Heuser's and Gurlitt's, added a significant piece to the puzzle of the operation of forms (of whatever stripe) on the viewer. Although Wölfflin berated him for proposing the psychological phenomenon of jading or fatigue (*Abstumpfung des Formgefühls* and *Ermüdung*) as causes for changes in style, and focused attention on this argument in particular, there was more to Göller than this.[37] His insistence on pure form and memory invited readings that cut across scales and media, that is, where aesthetic pleasure was understood to arise and grow outside architecture itself—as is the case of instruments and machines—and could migrate there. Formal stimulation could come from anywhere, Göller had implied, thus adding another facet to Semper's translation aesthetic. Although less historically based and hence less concerned with finding step-by-step sequences of such formal migration, Göller nevertheless had reinforced the "open" aspect of architecture, perceiving it to be in a receiving mode to outside stimuli regardless of scale or medium, and in this he insisted on the operation of memory. Thus he proposed a reading of architecture as a succession of experiences of parts, a chain of responses to single and simpler forms.[38] These, according to him, remain embedded in memory, and it is only there that the composite whole can be reassembled. In such a conception, memory emerges as a fundamental instrument that collects forms and connects them; whether they are all architectural is not an issue. The possibility of a continuum of experience across scales and mediums, a form of dialogue between forms across a viewer, is then Göller's ultimate message.

But, perhaps even more interestingly, Göller was championing the new material, iron. If, in Bötticher's terms, wood and stone could be read in the context of an empathy-anthropomorphy, the new material iron/steel—with which he was concerned and of which Kapp's machines were fabricated—could claim its own material-and-mechanical-fastening symbolism with the human body, in which engineering and armor, modernity and history played an equal role (fig. 105). And it is precisely Göller's analysis of metal construction that enabled someone like Heuser to turn to him enthusiastically several years later when he sought to derive his own modern style (*Gefachstyl*) from an evolution of metal construction. Using Göller's memory of forms as the linchpin of his argument, Heuser argued that pleasure in certain features—such as material or the engineer's economy and minimal aesthetic—is gradually absorbed into memory as

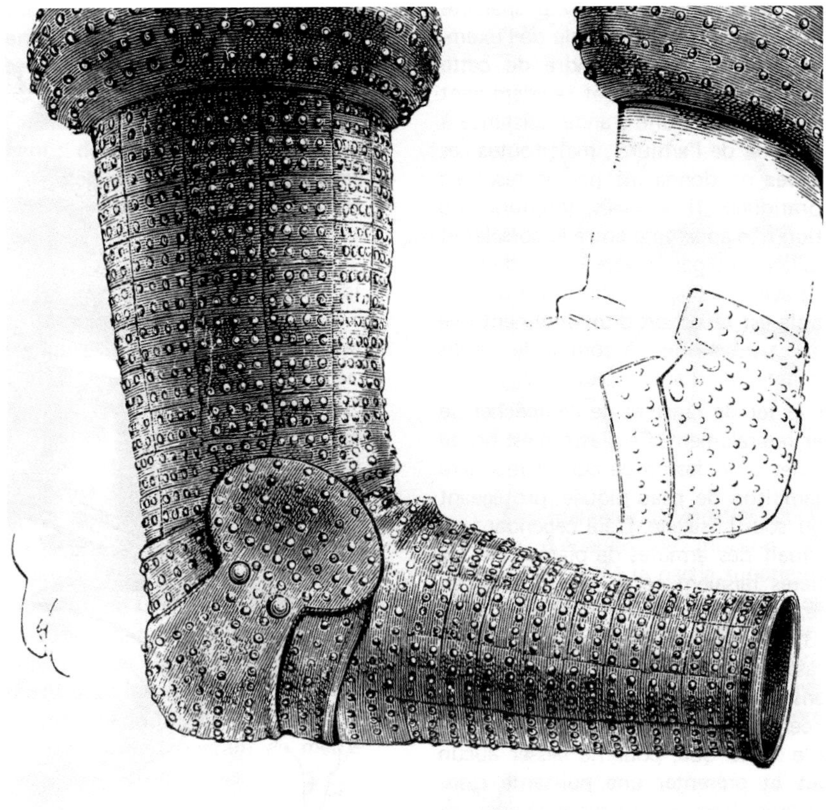

motifs.[39] It is these features, he argued, which had already generated an excitement for the forms of instruments and machines, that contain what can be described as "mechanical beauty."[40]

This process of domestication of forms through habitual use and sight that eventually leads to pleasure Heuser thus ascribed in the first place to objects/instruments, and he suggested this to be the path that eventually led to architectural form.[41] Indeed, the pleasure arising from the plain and smooth surfaces of mechanically produced forms that make up the instruments and machines of modernity, he argued, may lead to the development of an "engineer's aesthetic."[42] His advocacy for metal as origin of a new generation of forms and *Formgefühle* in the sense used by Göller did not preclude him from welcoming an infiltration of forms from other materials too, and he proposed the possibility of enamel infill that hollow metal profiles allowed—on the condition, he warned, that the metal skeleton be visible.[43]

FIGURE 105
Armor joints. From Viollet-le-Duc, *Dictionnaire raisonné du mobilier français de l'époque carlovingienne à la renaissance.*

To be sure, Heuser had taken Göller in a direction into which he had not ventured himself. But it was Göller's concept of pure form, memory, and habit that underpinned Heuser's argument. From such a departure point then Heuser could argue that, once established, pleasure of minimum material, of smoothness, mechanical fastenings, and plain surfaces associated with machine-made objects could generate new forms in architecture. Without footnoting Göller on this issue, Heuser had in fact pulled together Semper, Wölfflin, and Göller: pure form migrates across mediums (Semper), it finds its origins in the smaller objects (Wölfflin), and it gains momentum by the operation of memory (Göller).

Indeed, Göller had also drawn attention—as Gurlitt astutely noted in his enthusiastic review of Göller's book in *Deutsche Bauzeitung*—to the importance of "pure form" as abstract, content-less form and, as such, fundamentally the domain of architecture.[44] This domain was also that of the objects and instruments that Lipps was turning to at much the same time. Scaleless, pure form tied architecture to *(Kunst)Gewerbe* far more than it connected architecture with the other visual arts at this stage, when painting was still deeply tied to representation. It is in the twin domains of architecture and *Gewerbe* that Lipps's swelling (*Wulst*) and contraction (*Einziehung*) manifested themselves. For him the connection between them lay in the human mind, which drew on bodily memory of basic conditions of weight, support, swelling, tension, and so on. Instead, Göller understood the contentless form to act on the mind through the eye muscles (which experience a smoother, hence more pleasurable movement, when scanning beautiful forms). Yet despite this distinction they both focused on elemental forms, thus offering two avenues for the justification of a connection between the objects of daily use (abstract in shape by virtue of their function and component parts) and architecture.

Without accepting Semper's symbolic and empathy-based connections across media, Göller nevertheless saw the beginnings of architectural style to lie in the mobile (*bewegliche*) ornament of textiles and ceramic arts (*Kleinkünste*) that gradually were attached to buildings and became permanent elements of architecture as ornament.[45] What was construction-derived form in the perishable material, so his argument went, became ornament in the permanent one. Certainly Göller did not posit a contemporary path that started in the same way, even if he later pointed to new materials like iron as a possible way out of the decadence of the nineteenth-century "Babylonian mixture of styles." But he offered a context for such thinking that reinforced Semper's and Wölfflin's and could be developed even by those more attracted to the idea of pure, abstract forms than by the proponents and sympathizers of empathy theory. His view had remarkable affinities with Riegl's, who would, some five or six years later, also propose the pleasure of pure form as the driving mechanism behind *Kunstwollen* when he refuted the symbolic argument of Semper and the materialist one of the Semperians.

In a sense, Göller's move toward pure form was not fundamentally different from Adolf von Hildebrandt's or Konrad Fiedler's development of a theory of pure visibility in the 1890s, even if they seem to be dealing with different problems.[46] The connection with the rise of abstraction in the early twentieth century has certainly been posited before. But what is significant for the development of a theory of objects is that Göller posited the concept of a translation across media. In their more or less tributary ways, so did Wölfflin (with direct reference to Hildebrand) and Riegl (without any) and even Schmarsow (following Lipps) when they moved the discussion of the artwork to a nearly abstract reading of form. In this climate that circled around abstraction, the category of objects (*Gewerbe*) was an important middle term. Accessible to all viewers, hence culturally widespread, *Gewerbe* provided a base upon which more sophisticated art forms (such as architecture) could be seen to evolve their own forms. More importantly, these forms could be understood by a viewer/user precisely because they were shared by way of the most intimate gestures of everyday life.

RICHARD STREITER AND HABITUAL FORM

Another direction was offered by Richard Streiter (1861–1912). Like Göller, he was an architect and taught in an architecture school (Technische Hochschule in Munich), and like the far better-known Muthesius—his exact contemporary—he worked for five and a half years (from 1888) in the office of Paul Wallot during the period when he built the Reichstag.[47] However, Streiter straddled art history and the profession as he pursued doctoral studies and obtained his degree in 1896 from Munich with his dissertation on Bötticher's art-historical and aesthetic theories.[48] Lipps was his mentor (and it was he who published Streiter's dissertation in the same series he edited with R. M. Werner on *Beiträge zur Ästhetik*). However, even if Streiter dedicated his book to him, Lipps was not the only influence on his work. A consummate and lively critic, equally at home in the world of architectural publications and aesthetics, Streiter used and argued with and against most of the leading authors in all these domains. Thus not only did he take on Bötticher—a somewhat outdated book by then, yet whose categories *Werkform, Kernform, Junktur,* and material symbolism were still powerfully at work in contemporary discourse—but he entered a debate with Otto Wagner on the issue of contemporary style in which he drew on Heinrich Hübsch, Julius Langbehn, Richard Dohme, Riegl, Heuser, Göller, Semper, Wölfflin, Schmarsow, Walter Crane, and Gurlitt. In other words, in a debate with Vienna's foremost architect he imported the whole edifice of *Gewerbe* and art history literature. Thus, through his work, his public lectures, and his teaching (on which his publications were based) he literally embodied the meeting point between the historical disciplines, the new field of psychology, and the profession of architecture.

Streiter's most significant writings concerned with *Kunstgewerbe* and the achievement of a new style in architecture were his book on Bötticher's *Tektonik der Hellenen* of 1896, the article "Das deutsche Kunstgewerbe und die englisch-amerikanische Bewegung" (of the same year), and his polemical clash with Otto Wagner, which was the thread running through his essay *Architektonische Zeitfragen* of 1898.[49] An active author of articles, Streiter also engaged the issues contained in these essays in smaller reviews and critiques that appeared in the specialized press—in journals such as *Centralblatt der Bauverwaltung* (under Muthesius's editorship between 1896 and 1897, when he left for Britain), *Blätter für Architektur und Kunsthandwerk*, or in *Beilage zur Allgemeinen Zeitung*—and were accessible to the profession more broadly.[50] Thus the reviews he published of Lipps, Schmarsow, Dehio, Strzygowski, and Fritz Schumacher, even Walter Pater, brought their work into the mainstream of architectural discussion and attention and conversely showed that Streiter's own views were fully informed by contemporary directions in art history.

By now it should come as no surprise that, as he was finishing his doctoral dissertation on Bötticher, Streiter should write an extensive article on style, and that it should take *Kunstgewerbe* as its case study. His foray into this topic—an expected territory to explore by now for an art and architecture historian, as well as for an architect—touched on many of the problems that had become virtually commonplace. Thus topics like the absence of a genuine modern style, the crisis in the decorative arts that led to historicism, the dissonance between the historicizing interiors and modern costume—an issue that went back to Falke and Viollet-le-Duc—the unease with revivalism, and the negative outcome of the turn toward historical examples at the beginning of the reform movement recall Riegl.[51] But his most constant reference is Walter Crane, whose works had been enthusiastically translated into German as part of the wave of interest in the English decorative arts following its own successful reform results. Paraphrasing Crane, Streiter called for an art that mirrored contemporary life and, moving beyond him, insisted that this must be even more the case for *Kunstgewerbe*, which is in a much closer relationship with daily life.[52]

The importance, even imperative, of continuity in contemporary life led Streiter, as it had Viollet-le-Duc and Falke, to turn his attention to objects and clothes, but he took the argument much further. The connection he makes in this article is not only based on a desire for visual harmony between them, but it extends to the movements of the body itself. What unites the chair and the clothes is the body wrapped in one and sitting on the other, and, in his view, these two aspects intimately attached to the body must be in harmony with each other so as not to cause a deep crisis, a tear in the body that interacts with both at one and the same time. Indeed, in this essay from 1896, thus two years before Loos's aggressively polemical pieces on similar topics in the *Neue Freie Presse*, clothing became Streiter's focus. Of course this was not coincidental, for Streiter draws here on a well-developed discourse. Even if not all participants felt the tear in the body as acutely as Warburg—who, as we have seen, developed his tragic theory of clothes from this starting point—the issue of the body and its outer layers, such as clothes and tools, with which it came in direct contact, was very topical. It is the body that is the locus of memory and retains the residue of rituals and forms. The fascination with the billowing cloth of dancing maidens in Greek reliefs that Walter Crane noticed, and that probably also drew Aby Warburg's attention to the "bewegtes Beiwerk" of the Renaissance nymph, was part of a contemporary orientation that had placed the body and its dress on its radar screen and that included the English "Faltenrock," the loose coat that allowed women free movement in the outdoors that so much attracted Adolf Loos.[53]

Although Streiter does not seem to make a direct move toward empathy theory or even toward a phenomenology of pure form in the Kantian tradition, he nevertheless focuses on objects manipulated on a daily basis—whether tools or clothes—as the repository of style and style-igniting features. And in so doing he leans directly and explicitly both on Semper and on Wölfflin's *Renaissance und Barock* where he is most concerned with the mechanics of style change. Indeed, the only two quotes he includes are from Semper's 1854 London lecture (published as part of *Kleine Schriften* in 1884) on the origins of architectural style in artifacts, the other, Wölfflin's powerful metaphor of the heartbeat of style ("der Pulschlag der Zeit"), which must be listened to in the minor, decorative arts, not in the ponderous forms of architecture.[54]

Of course Streiter's article is also a paean to Walter Crane and the very recent *The Claims of Decorative Art* of 1892 (translated into German in 1896), particularly as it concerns his social agenda of militancy for an art that would reach the anonymous consumer and be available to the masses. For Streiter this was a call to intervene at the level of the greatest quantitative production, which would also reach the most consumers, or, in other words, the mass market, rather than a thin, exclusive layer of knowledgeable patrons. Thus aimed, such an art would become a true component and representation of the industrial age and of the shift in scale of production this entailed. However, if Crane was moved by his own insights into texts and book illustrations as instruments of education and consequence of mass production, Streiter struck off in a different direction. Like many before him—notably Eitelberger and Wilhelm von Bode—Streiter also looked to Britain and America, which had successfully harnessed industrial production into the manufacture of aesthetically pleasing though not historicizing objects. *Bürgerlichkeit* (middle-class values), *Sachlichkeit* (simplicity), and *Gesundheit* (health) are his cardinal points, and he seeks—once again in the footsteps of Semper and Wölfflin—a way out of the present historicist muddle through the intervention of the decorative arts. It is only when these categories

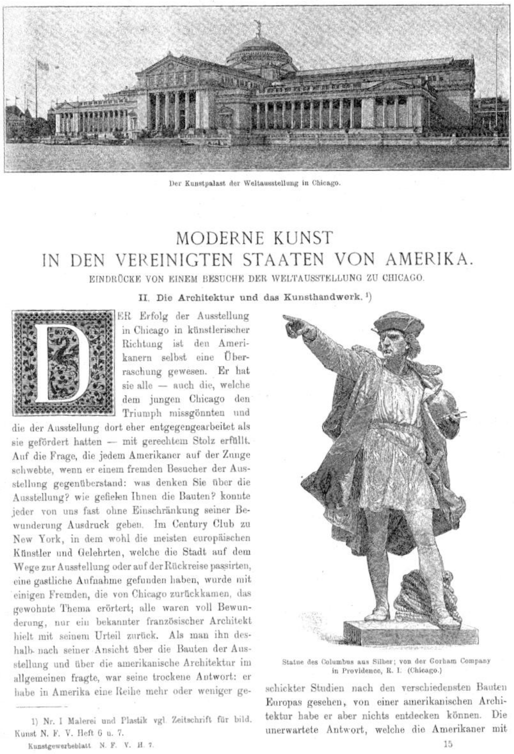

Der Kunstpalast der Weltausstellung in Chicago.

MODERNE KUNST
IN DEN VEREINIGTEN STAATEN VON AMERIKA.

EINDRÜCKE VON EINEM BESUCHE DER WELTAUSSTELLUNG ZU CHICAGO.

II. Die Architektur und das Kunsthandwerk. [1])

DER Erfolg der Ausstellung in Chicago in künstlerischer Richtung ist den Amerikanern selbst eine Überraschung gewesen. Er hat sie alle — auch die, welche dem jungen Chicago den Triumph missgönnten und die der Ausstellung dort eher entgegengearbeitet als sie gefördert hatten — mit gerechtem Stolz erfüllt. Auf die Frage, die jedem Amerikaner auf der Zunge schwebte, wenn er einem fremden Besucher der Ausstellung gegenüberstand: was denken Sie über die Ausstellung? wie gefielen Ihnen die Bauten? konnte jeder von uns fast ohne Einschränkung seiner Bewunderung Ausdruck geben. Im Century Club zu New York, in dem wohl die meisten europäischen Künstler und Gelehrten, welche die Stadt auf dem Wege zur Ausstellung oder auf der Rückreise passirten, eine gastliche Aufnahme gefunden haben, wurde mit einigen Fremden, die von Chicago zurückkamen, das gewohnte Thema erörtert; alle waren voll Bewunderung, nur ein bekannter französischer Architekt hielt mit seinem Urteil zurück. Als man ihn deshalb nach seiner Ansicht über die Bauten der Ausstellung und über die amerikanische Architektur im allgemeinen fragte, war seine trockene Antwort: er habe in Amerika eine Reihe mehr oder weniger geschickter Studien nach den verschiedensten Bauten Europas gesehen, von einer amerikanischen Architektur habe er aber nichts entdecken können. Die unerwartete Antwort, welche die Amerikaner mit

Statue des Columbus aus Silber; von der Gorham Company in Providence, R. I. (Chicago.)

1) Nr. I Malerei und Plastik vgl. Zeitschrift für bild. Kunst N. F. V. Heft 6 u. 7.

Kunstgewerbeblatt N. F. V. H. 7.

15

FIGURE 106
Wilhelm Bode, "Moderne Kunst in den Vereinigten Staaten von Amerika," *Kunstgewerbeblatt* 5 (1894): 115–17.

are truly satisfied that we will achieve a style of our own time, he concludes (fig. 106).[55]

Streiter's proposal is to develop a "machine style" that he describes as consistent with machinery and its products: smooth, precise, simple, crisp, and of an exceptional consistency.[56] And, he insists, these machine-specific features must be exploited rather than manipulated to look like artisanal work. In a throwback to Semper, he notes that ornament added to machine-made objects mimics handmade products and is fundamentally incompatible with the machine. As it is not in the nature of machine cutting, stamping, joining, and polishing, machine-made ornament looks and is awkward and misbegotten, a "surrogate."[57] And he adduces English industrial objects as examples. In terms that recall both Göller and Lipps, Streiter asks that artistic attention be devoted to the "tectonic" form, or what they called "pure form." In his view, it is this basic form (*Grundform*)—a term he borrows from architecture and that underlines the ease with which categories could be transported to a *Kleinarchitektur* of decorative objects—that is not sufficiently attended to in manufacturing. Yet it is here that the intrinsic superiority of machine production, and hence of an original style, could well reside. *Gewerbe* and *Kunstgewerbe* should not be separated—one and

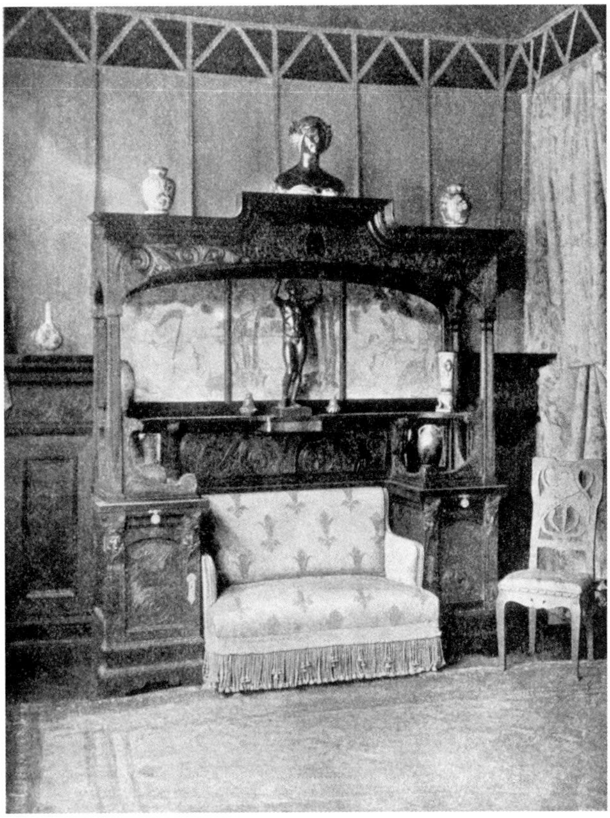

all are *Kunstgewerbe,* regardless of the nature and amount of surface ornament, once the entire object is conceived as both utilitarian and aesthetic. In short, what Streiter looks for is the "simple elegance of the essential form" ("schlichte Eleganz der Grundform").[58] Indeed, he continues, "es wird zu viel dekoriert, zu wenig tektonisch gestaltet" ("too much is decorated, not enough is tectonically conceived").[59]

Perhaps some of Streiter's most radical ideas are based on an entirely novel conception of furniture. Thus Streiter recognizes that the heavy, ponderous (in Wölfflin's terms) furniture associated with interior arrangements that lasted several generations belonged to a lifestyle and forms of ownership that had become anachronistic (fig. 107). Heavy furniture that became permanent fixtures of the house, he argues, must be replaced by light, mobile pieces that respond to the needs of a mobile, metropolitan population: renting and owning generate very different types of furniture requirements, and it is the former that predominates in the industrial age of less stability, developed transportation systems, and apartment buildings. The idea was certainly in the air, though Streiter removes its sting. Michael Haberlandt, for example, compares negatively the snail-like, naturally growing house-container of the peasant with that of the "rootless, houseless

FIGURE 107
L. J. Peter, Built-in sofa. From Theodor Krauth and Franz Sales Meyer, eds., *Die Gesamte Möbelschreinerei* (Leipzig, 1902).

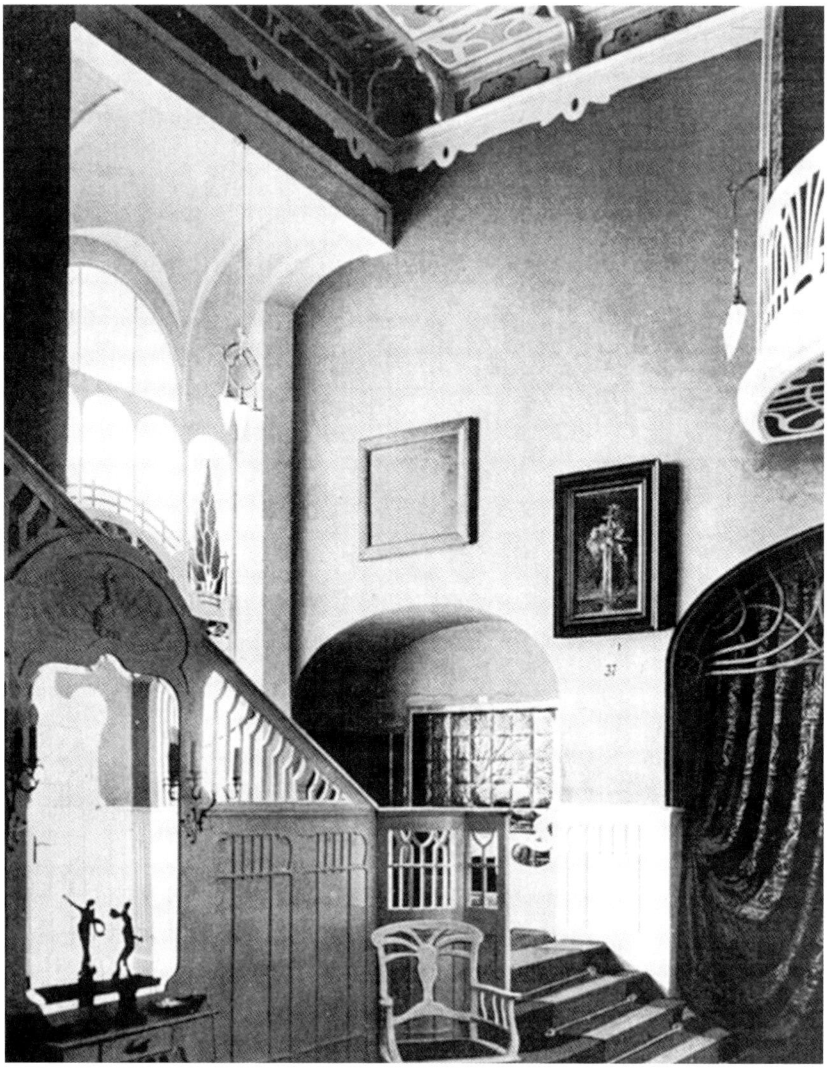

FIGURE 108
Entrance hall. From Krauth and Meyer, *Die Gesamte Möbelschreinerei.*

city dweller," and without using this exact metaphor Georg Simmel had likewise identified a condition of crisis for the metropolitan dweller.[60] Instead, without regrets, sentimentality, or nostalgia, in tones that bring to mind Le Corbusier and Loos, Streiter states that new products must be coherent with modern living conditions and the modern man, and that herein lies the real fountainhead of a new style.[61]

Streiter does not come right out to say that what we now term Art Nouveau interiors contemporary with his writings were anachronistic and futile efforts at generating a new style, and he may well have had in mind the heavy late Victorian furniture suites. But his diagnosis of the condition of a mobility-driven modernity suggests that for him the built-in furniture, the site-specific nature of Art Nouveau objects—from buffets to desks, from tables to floor lamps that

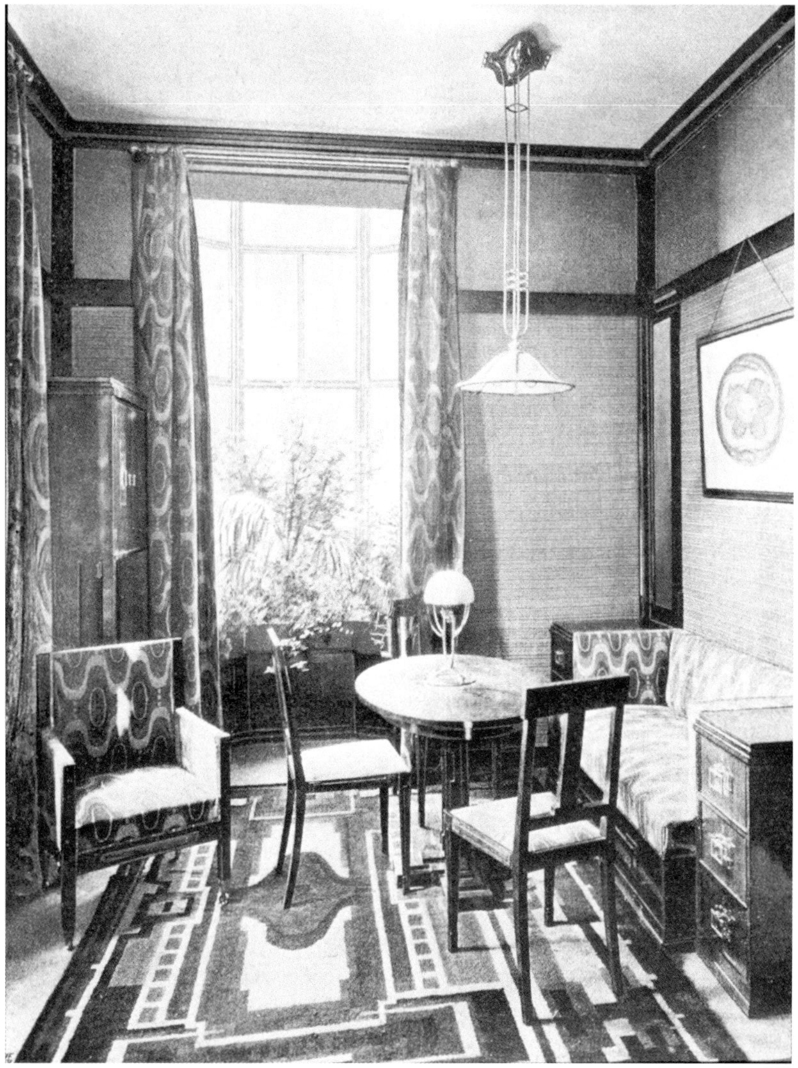

FIGURE 109
Peter Behrens, drawing room, Behrens House, Darmstadt, 1901. From *Dekorative Kunst* 5, no. 1 (October 1901): 26.

flow into the lines of the walls and ceilings and into each other, where upholstery and carpeting, curtains and furniture forms depend upon each other and cannot be separated without compromising the whole—were so many luxury (read: exceptional) items (figs. 108, 109). Indeed, for Streiter such domestic equipment was without a real root in modernity, that is, without a genuine stylistic tie to the industrial, metropolitan, nomadic, lean, decluttered, and economical contemporary *Zeitgeist*. His conclusion is unequivocal: "This development [of a new style]...will take place first in the decorative arts, which can embrace faster and easier the needs of the times than can ponderous architecture."[62] The paraphrase of Wölfflin is striking.

In 1898 Streiter chose to respond to Otto Wagner's *Moderne Architektur* (1896, with many later editions until 1914) with a long essay of his own titled

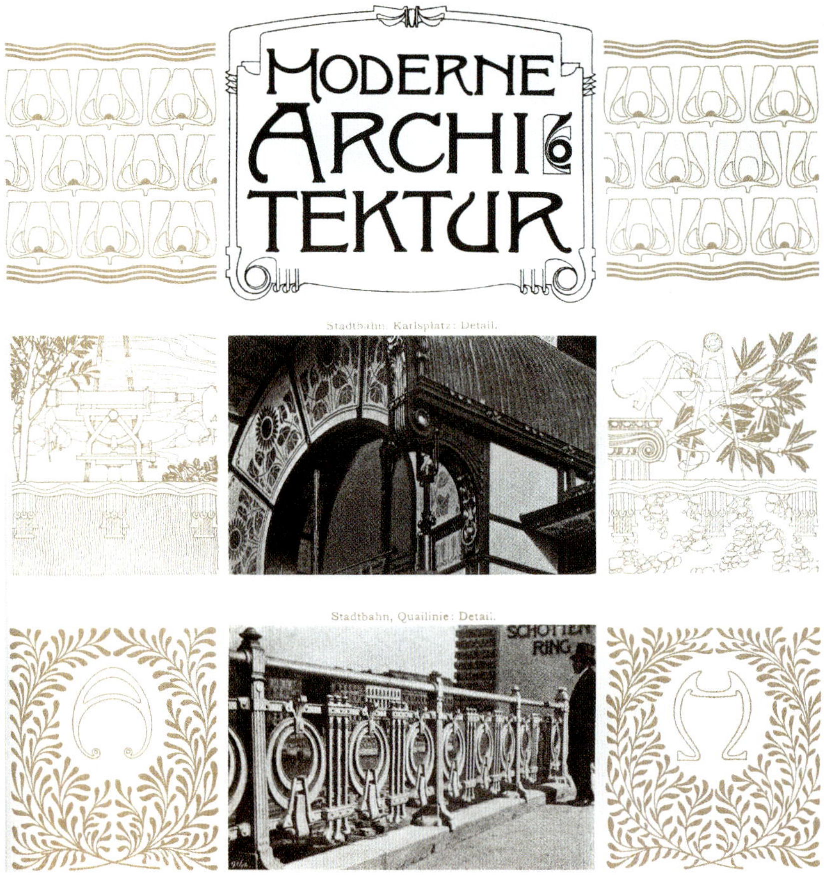

FIGURE 110
Otto Wagner, *Moderne Architektur: Seinen Schülern ein Führer auf diesem Kunstgebiete* (Vienna, 1896).

Architektonische Zeitfragen (Berlin, 1898) (fig. 110). As if echoing Heuser (who had published a good six years before him), Wagner had called for a new architecture in step with new materials: "It is therefore certain that new purposes must give birth to new methods of construction, and by this reasoning also to new forms. Our modern epoch has, like none earlier, produced the greatest number of such new methods of construction (one need only consider the success of iron)." He also called for the "greatest possible convenience and the greatest possible cleanliness," and for a "realist" architecture (once again in the footsteps of Heuser). And like others before him he turned to clothes (at some length) as a clinching argument in favor of a modernity of forms. Yet his own practice did not entirely reflect these ideals, and it is to this apparent contradiction that Streiter turned with much vigor.[63]

Indeed, his response to Wagner is perhaps Streiter's most insightful publication on architecture, and the most representative of his teaching and influence. Not concerned with a historical argument and its consequences, as was his book on Bötticher, nor with what may have seemed a side issue like *Kunstgewerbe* in this book he chose not only to enter a debate with one of the most prominent European architects, but he did so on a topic that was at the epicenter of contemporary architectural discourse: the problem of a style for the modern age. Although he engages Wagner systematically point by point, he nevertheless ranges broadly across the full spectrum of current issues: style and *Zeitgeist*, art versus construction, materials and symbolism. What is particularly noticeable is how the issues he had covered in his essay on *Kunstgewerbe* are absorbed and reappear (sometimes word for word) to inform and provide the material for his polemical engagement with the issues of contemporary architecture.

In chapter 1, "The Question of Style" ("Die Stilfrage," with a clear ricochet to Riegl's *Stilfragen*) Streiter defines the aim of modern style to be "artistic truth, concision, and simplicity" and proposes its origin to lie in architecture and *Kunstgewerbe*.[64] For him, the conduit toward a new style is the physical experience of objects of daily use. And he applies both Wölfflin and Göller with much precision and clarity to modern architecture: through constant exposure (of sight and touch) to the qualities of technology-based objects, he argues, we have become accustomed to them, and therefore our *Formgefühl* has been affected correspondingly. The same is true of our body sense (*Körpergefühl*), which has become sensitized to mobility and speed through the steep rise of transportation means. As result, he concludes, we are impatient with any "ballast" that interferes with this movement, and it is here, in this new sense of self and of objects, that the origins of the new style will be found.[65] This is no passing comment but something Streiter comes back to time and again: seeing and holding objects produced by industry causes habit and familiarity, and it is these two conditions that lie at the root of the *Zeitgeist* as its particular *Formgefühl*. The connection between habitual use, familiarity, and pleasure links Streiter to Göller (his *Gedächtnisbild*) but also to Heuser, and it collects Kapp, Darwin, art history, and iron construction into one argument and promotes the "articulation style."[66] Perhaps most obviously, Streiter also imports empathy theory absorbed from Lipps, Riegl, and Wölfflin into the conversation about modernity.

In chapter 2, Streiter turns to architectural realism as a topic with wider cultural resonance that was recurring in the architectural debates both in books and articles like Heuser's. Streiter argues that construction on its own cannot be art as it causes "artistic impoverishment." Therefore, in chapter 3, "Construction as Artistic Form," he offers a critique of Wagner's concept of *Sachlichkeit* in construction:

> The works of the engineer and of the machine designer both originate in construction as their Ur-cell; but generally they do not belong to tectonic artworks, precisely because they forgo the "symbolism of construction,"

> and because their forms, both as a whole and in their details, do not present themselves with plastic vividness as the unmediated apprehensible expression of an ordered connection to which it is possible to respond directly through empathetic, body-sympathetic behaviour.[67]

Despite the fact that this formulation is so abstract and convoluted—which may go some way in explaining why Streiter's exact contemporary, Muthesius, enjoyed more public popularity—Streiter's description of aesthetic response to machine-based parts is very insightful. Combining Bötticher with Lipps's concepts of *Grundform* and *Kunstform*—even if he does not name them—he develops a critique of pure engineered form. It requires something superfluous, he continues, to turn construction into art, and it is here that Wagner fails, since he does not show how to make artistic form (*Kunstform*) out of construction.[68] Clearly, Streiter argues, the determinant impulse lies in the *Formgefühl* of the artist. But, he asks, what conditions it in the first place? *Zeitgeist* is too vague a term. For support he turns to Wölfflin, who in *Renaissance und Barock* had argued that technique by itself never produces a style. Indeed, argues Streiter, the style of a period is common to all the arts and so cannot possibly be related to the technical features (construction) of only one of them.[69] And he opposes Wagner's view that iron will produce the new style, as he does not believe that this material, both stiff and cold, can arouse empathy in the body of the viewer.[70] In his opinion, this is so because the formal features of iron are fleshless thinness, stiff dryness, static calculation, appearance of sameness of the members, and the confusing mass of intersecting, almost incorporeal lines (fig. 111).[71] It must

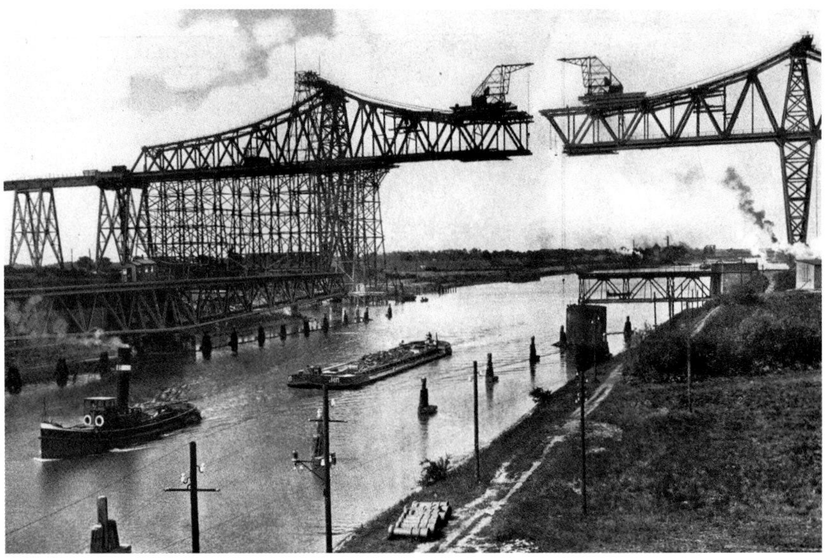

FIGURE 111
"Iron Bridge, Rendsburg." From Gustav Adolf Platz, *Die Baukunst der Neuesten Zeit* (Berlin, 1927).

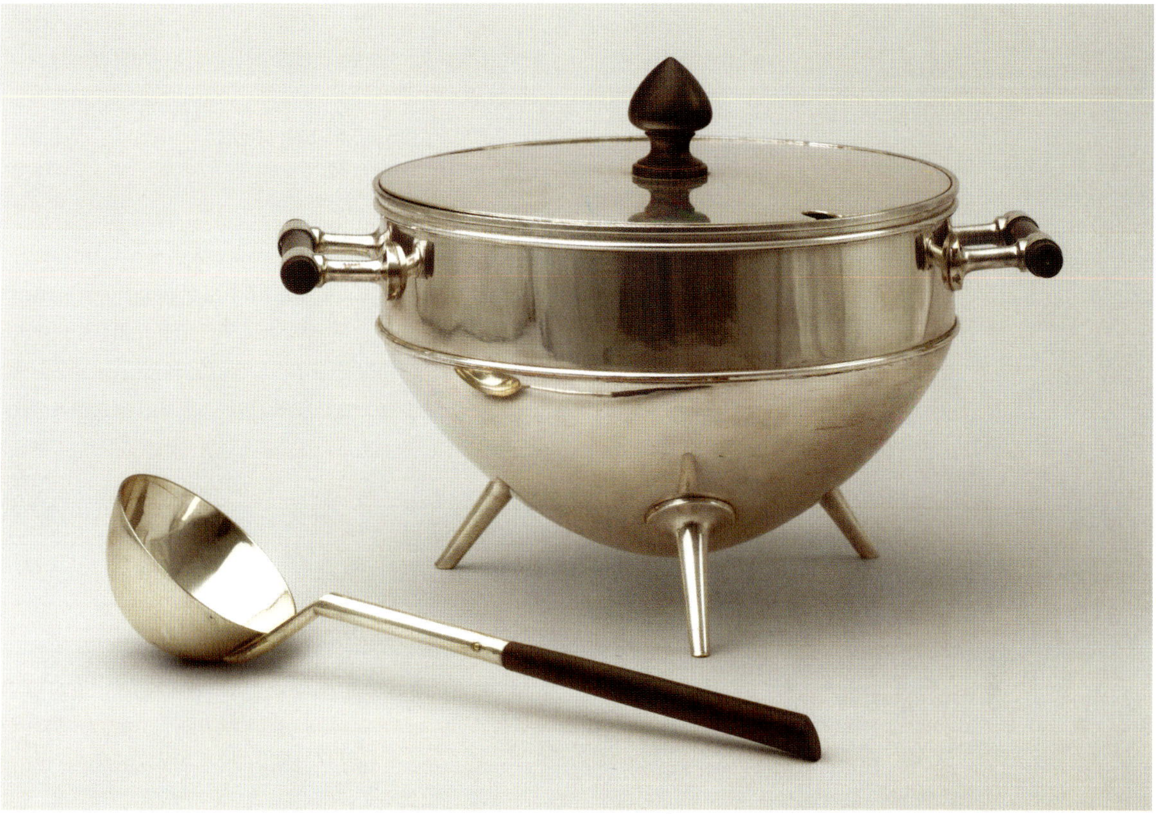

FIGURE 112
Christopher Dresser, soup tureen and ladle. Museum of Modern Art, New York/Scala/ Art Resource, NY.

be stressed that Streiter's term "feeling" (*fühlen*) is meant in the sense of holding and touching, not of emotions, and as such is fundamentally body-oriented.

However, the crisis he intuits is that in the case of new materials the body can no longer be the vehicle of comprehension in the traditional tectonic/symbolic way of monumental members. Therefore for him the body input can assert itself only through the touching (*tasten*) and feeling (*fühlen*) of small objects, that is, not through direct poetic or symbolic representation or even allusion to recognizable body parts or bodily states, but through physical familiarity with forms held by the hand or surrounding the body (fig. 112). And here Streiter introduces a shift in the application of empathy theory. The representational link is a thing of the past for him: the body does not recognize itself through similarity, nor yet through apperception; instead, the layers enveloping it engender a habit and sensual appreciation, and in time even a need for the new forms and surface finishes of modern objects.

Thus, when he turns specifically to the mechanism of achieving a "style of our time," Streiter dismisses material, construction, personal style, and associations with other arts (for example, painterly style) and follows Wölfflin and by extension Semper. For him the origins and manifestations of a new *Formgefühl* are to be found in the decorative arts, it is "prepared" in the small scale.[72] This is also where his debate with Wagner bleeds into his earlier, 1896 essay. For Streiter the everyday is the origin of the "feeling for form" because, despite the dependence on practical demands, it is here that a new form and color sense can develop with greatest freedom.[73] Indeed, he takes sides against the view popular among architects that the manner of containing space lies at the root of architectural style, an idea he traces back to Bötticher though most recently championed by Schmarsow. Surprisingly, he takes Burckhardt as his principal witness against this view and turns to him to argue that unity of spatial styles is produced by the decorative forms that articulate it, not the nature of the void itself.[74] And he goes on to say that the new *Formgefühl* that will produce a unitary style in the future will have to emerge from the individual element and decoration, as Wagner himself acknowledges when he points to the architecture of interiors, of the objects of daily use and the *Kunstindustrie* in general as representative of new tendencies.[75]

In the end, his last chapter, "Zeitgeist and Architecture," takes on the idea of the *Volk* and the nature of a democratic art. Walter Crane reappears, as does a conservative streak in Streiter, who argues that a style that does not produce a significant and characteristic church architecture, the most important building type, in his view, is not a viable style. However, what is particularly interesting in this section is that he does identify a fundamental contradiction in the almost half-century discourse on art and *Volk*. Although he does not have a solution for reengaging the *Volk* with the art of modernity, he recognizes the flaw in Wagner's theory (and Semper's, though he doesn't mention him), as had Riegl about a decade earlier: the culture they promote is that of the capitalist, of the *Grossstadt*—it does not arise in the country, it is not produced by the *Volk* as such, except through the intervention of industry, and no real folk art of the present is envisaged. The *Grossstadt* and the *Grosshandel*—the metropolis and large-scale commerce—produce metropolitan art (*Grossstatdtkunst*). Indeed, he observes, the *Volk* is traditionalist by nature, and the whole notion of a contemporary *Zeitgeist*, complete with its materials, symbols, and construction technique, collapses when folk art is taken into account.[76] Moreover, in his view, modern life—industry and the machine, transportation, the new working relationships that all countries share equally—make the idea of a folk-derived culture, that is, of a nationalist style, seem naïve. All art is therefore similar at its very root rather than distinct by nations. Thus Streiter intuits the internationalism of modern artifacts and architecture a good quarter of a century before it became the battle cry of the modernists.[77] In so doing Streiter takes a position against the contemporary efforts to absorb folk art as a taproot for industrial production. Like Riegl in his "Volkskunst" essay, he feels the incompatible nature of the two worlds and seeks to keep them distinct.

Throughout Streiter's essay turn up terms, concepts, metaphors, and themes that arise from the vast amount of research accumulated in the nineteenth century in various fields and that retain the memory of these publications. These are *Sachlichkeit,* the English and American approach to *Kunstindustrie,* the mask and Potemkintown effect of contemporary architecture, the fundamental importance of a *Formgefühl,* speed, transport, electricity, and consumerism, the devastating effects of the "parvenu taste" on contemporary culture and clothes. Together they constitute a formidable reference grid for what constitutes modernity and the *Grossstadt* and a frame for the desideratum that "particularly with respect to the objects of our daily use, a better taste might penetrate in the wider strata of the *Volk,*" complete with a reference to Langbehn.[78] Phrases such as "simple elegance of the primary form," "economy in the decorative accessories," and "style of machine fabrication," which turned up in his essay of 1896, reappear in 1898 and describe modern objects that respect the machine production and the speed of consumption in modern life.[79]

Shortly thereafter, these themes became mainstays of contemporary architectural criticism and theory in the hands of Muthesius, Loos, and Le Corbusier, even for Giedion and Pevsner, and developed a life of their own, apparently arising from architectural debates and obscuring their complex genealogy. The themes that would seem so radical to the generation coming to maturity at the time of the Great War here reveal their origins. Streiter still footnotes Riegl and Wölfflin, Göller and Lotze, Semper and Bötticher, Schmarsow and Dohme, Heuser and Darwin, and he still draws from the wealth of discussions in the pages of journals such as *Deutsche Bauzeitung* or *Allgemeine Bauzeitung.* Ten years or so later, these references will have disappeared, so much had the discourse become self-evident in architecture. What is then particularly important about Streiter is that he shows the larger context into which Muthesius's and the Werkbund's "strong" discourse about mass production needs to be placed. As his writings indicate, the empathy theory, not traditionally seen as playing a major role in the formulations of mature modernism, provided a supportive background against which those ideas could be developed and received. And discussion about objects and architecture was wider in scope and drew on other strains of reasoning than the apologists of modernism allowed it to have done.

GURLITT AND THE CONTRIBUTION OF THE BAROQUE

Like Streiter, Cornelius Gurlitt (1850–1938) is one of those figures who straddled disciplines and in whose work a lot of threads came together—art history, architecture, *Kunstgewerbe,* and a sustained proselytizing activity both in the press and in the Werkbund (fig. 113). Moreover, his impact on the younger generation, in particular on the architects, was even more substantial than Streiter's: if Wölfflin represents a straight line to Giedion, Gurlitt is a straight line to Muthesius and Walter Kurt Behrendt (both of whose *Doktorvater* he was), as well as to a number of expressionists like Hugo Häring and the artists of Die Brücke. Indeed, he was a particularly active supervisor—overseeing more than seventy dissertations—a fact which suggests how much his approach and ideas about art history, culture, and contemporary issues seeped into the world of the architect.[80] Neither a psychological reading of form nor empathy as a theory preoccupied Gurlitt. Yet, as an important art historian contemporary with Wölfflin, Schmarsow, and Riegl, and working on similar topics—in particular on the Baroque—he brought the issues of his discipline to bear directly on architectural practice, both through publications and teaching.[81] Moreover, like them and like Streiter and Dohme, he was an admirer of Semper (whose built work not coincidentally favored late Renaissance and Baroque forms), and combined architecture and the decorative arts in his own intense and multifaceted activity.[82]

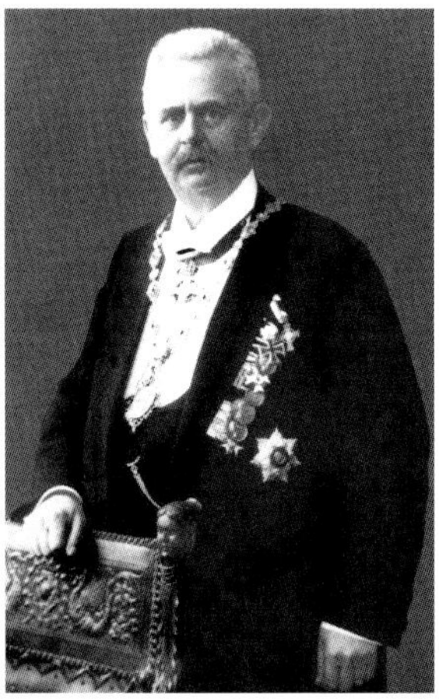

FIGURE 113
Portrait of Cornelius Gurlitt. Nachlass Cornelius Gurlitt http://gurlitt.tu-dresden.de

More than other art historians, Gurlitt was active as journalist and critic, and thus his views reached beyond the classroom to the professional and larger public. Thus his review of Göller in *Deutsche Bauzeitung* (1887), his endorsement of Julius Langbehn's stridently nationalistic *Rembrandt als Erzieher* in *Die Gegenwart* (1890)—for which he had become arts correspondent at Alfred Lichtwark's suggestion—his participation on the editorial board of *Kunstgewerbeblatt* and as author in Joseph August Lux's *Hohe Warte,* ensured that his views reached a broad spectrum of participants in the architecture and *Kunstgewerbe* debates.[83] Even more lasting contributions were his editorship of the series "Kultur" with Marquardt at Berlin, which published Werner Sombart's economics work *Kunstgewerbe und Kultur* (1908), among others, and his own books *Zur Befreiung der Baukunst: Ziele und Taten deutscher Architekten im 19. Jahrhundert* (1900) and *Im Bürgerhause* (1888). Indeed, he has been called "one of Germany's best known critics and exponents of 'modern art' in the last years of the century."[84] Given his interests, it is perhaps no coincidence that, alongside Semper, Gurlitt should also admire Paul Wallot—the architect of the Reichstag and of a sober Baroque style, and since 1894 professor at Dresden, a position obtained through Gurlitt himself. It is also no coincidence that he published significant books on the Baroque and ornament, that he started his career as curator at the Dresden museum for applied arts, that he chose a *Kunstgewerbe* theme focused on armor for his dissertation, and that he was active in the preservation movement, endorsing folk art and architecture in his art historical writings.[85] Perhaps most significant of all is that this activity unfolded predominantly in Dresden—the city of Late German Baroque, of Semper's Opera House (on which he wrote a book), of the Dresdener Kunstgewerbeschule and museum, of the 1906 *Kunstgewerbe*

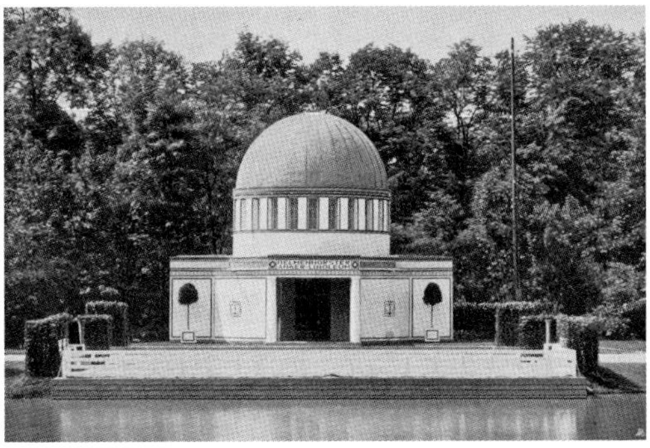

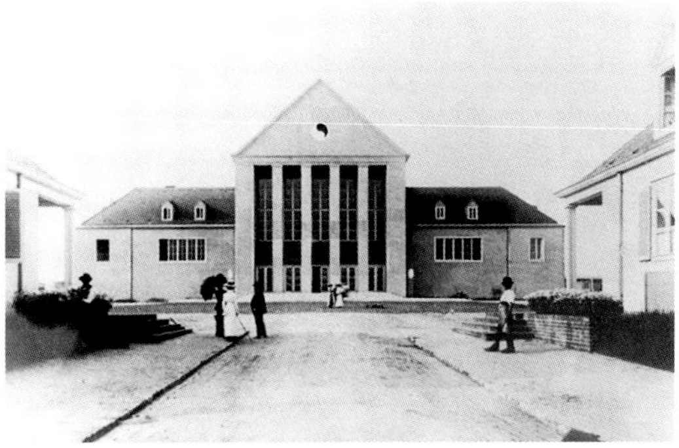

exhibition (which he chronicles in a book alongside Fritz Schumacher, Hans Pölzig, Herrmann Muthesius, and Friedrich Naumann) and eventually of the Deutsche Werkstätte in neighboring Hellerau (figs. 114, 115).[86] Indeed, the mission of the Dresden museum and school (founded in 1876 and 1874, respectively) was "to provide models for industry and the crafts," in particular to encourage the textile and ceramics industries (which were of significance for the economy of Saxony).[87] Moreover, at the school for applied arts Gurlitt succeeded none other than cultural historian-cum-anthropologist August von Eye; and as professor at the Technische Hochschule in Dresden he was colleagues with Fritz Schumacher from 1899 onward. In other words, the Dresden where Gurlitt's activity unfolded was an important junction point between a number of movements, old and new, not least of all that associated with Hellerau, which had such an impact on modernist architecture, from Heinrich Tessenow to Le Corbusier.[88] Moreover, Adolf Loos studied at the Dresden Technische Hochschule from 1890–93 when Gurlitt was starting his career there, and even if there are no records indicating that they crossed paths, at least it can be said that both had their early formation in the same milieu.[89]

Today Gurlitt's fame rests mainly on his having written one of the earliest works on the Baroque, predating Wölfflin's more celebrated *Renaissance und Barock* of 1888.[90] But at the time, his interest in the present was just as strong if not stronger. Gurlitt's take on architecture and the applied arts of the nineteenth century is perhaps most clearly addressed in his *Die deutsche Kunst des XIX Jahrhunderts* of 1899. However, these two directions in his work were not unconnected. Indeed, one of the most noticeable themes he develops is in favor of a neo-Baroque style, and Paul Wallot's in particular.[91] Clearly his time spent on historical work on the Baroque had sharpened his sensitivity to this style, but there is more to his concomitant and imbricated interests in the Baroque, the applied arts, Semper's theory, Göller's pure form, and its reception by the viewer. Indeed, with some variations these were also the paths trodden by Wölfflin, Riegl,

Left **FIGURE 114**
Peter Behrens, Delmenhorster Anker-Linoleum Pavilion, Dresden, 1906.

Right **FIGURE 115**
Heinrich Tessenow, Hellerau, 1906. King's Visualisation Laboratory, King's College London.

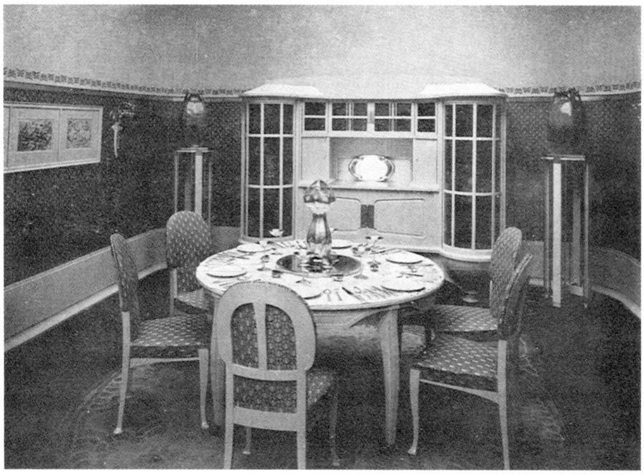

FIGURE 116
Henry Van de Velde, "Esszimmer." From Karl Scheffler, *Moderne Baukunst* (Leipzig, 1908).

and Schmarsow, all concerned with the Baroque and all engaging the discussion on empathy and *Kustgewerbe* at one and the same time.

The rediscovery of the Baroque as a legitimate subject for art historical study and the sympathetic response to its opulent, sculptural aesthetic evident in architectural work of the post-Semper years shows a shift in nineteenth-century taste away from the sober and severe classical sensibility that was championed by Schinkel and his followers. The reasons for this shift are many and range from the desire to represent suitably the political expansiveness and grand ambitions of the colonial empires to the development of materials that could span large spaces, thus allowing monumentality on an unprecedented scale. But at the aesthetic level the ignition mechanism had to do with two interconnected moments: the rise of empathy theory and the arrival of the über-Baroque Pergamon altar in Berlin starting in 1879. Although an architectural ensemble, the Pergamon altar captured viewers' imagination with its highly three-dimensional frieze. The writhing bodies of gods, giants, and snakes reached out into the viewers' space and literally challenged the physical boundaries of both monument and viewers. Historians, artists, and critics from Burckhardt through Adolf von Hildebrand to Wölfflin all responded with enthusiasm and produced nuanced readings of the sculptural architectural ensemble. It led to a reevaluation of the Baroque, until then much vilified vis-à-vis the Renaissance.[92] Given that all these art historians were concerned with an art that had the human body at its center—Italian art of the Renaissance and the Baroque—they were almost programmed to view other domains of visual culture with a similar bias. Thus, in a world already deeply invested in *Sachkultur*, it was almost a natural extension for them to see the objects of daily use—whether luxury items or more modest ones—as a fundamentally mobile layer of miniature sculptural form that acted below the radar of direct observation upon the tactile sense of the viewer. Gurlitt as much as makes the connection when he quotes Henry van de Velde (1897) on this issue and significantly attributes the paternity of the idea to the neo-Baroque architect Wallot. In Gurlitt's telling, for Wallot each room had a center from which its "life" emanated and to which all objects were subordinated. The interior equipment responded to this structure and acted as the "living organs" of spaces.[93] Gurlitt intuits the connection between van de Velde's conception of a room and its components as organs and the neo-Baroque when he describes the work of Otto Rieth—another student of Wallot's—and draws attention to his emphasis on "plastic seeing" and his conception of a dialectic between wall mass and ornament (fig. 116).[94]

Art historical work that Gurlitt knew well provided another reinforcement to this connection between bodies, sculpture, objects, and seeing. Heinrich von Geymüller's and so many other art historians' interest in *Kleinarchitektur*—which encompassed everything from work on the medieval Cosmati to work on Renaissance ciboria, altars, choirs, chancels, lanterns, and such architectural stone "furniture"—was the other pole of this interest in the continuity between architecture and its smaller-scale siblings (fig. 117).[95] Moreover, Gurlitt himself uses the term and concept to describe "architectural furniture." This domain was not theorized as such, but like the many works on ornament it signals an act of attention: art history both fed an existing interest in *Kunstgewerbe* and *Sachkultur* and responded to it at one and the same time. In so doing it turned the spotlight

FIGURE 117
Lanterns, Palazzo Strozzi, Florence. From Heinrich von Geymüller and Carl von Stegmann, *Die Architektur der Renaissance in Toscana* (Munich, 1885–1908).

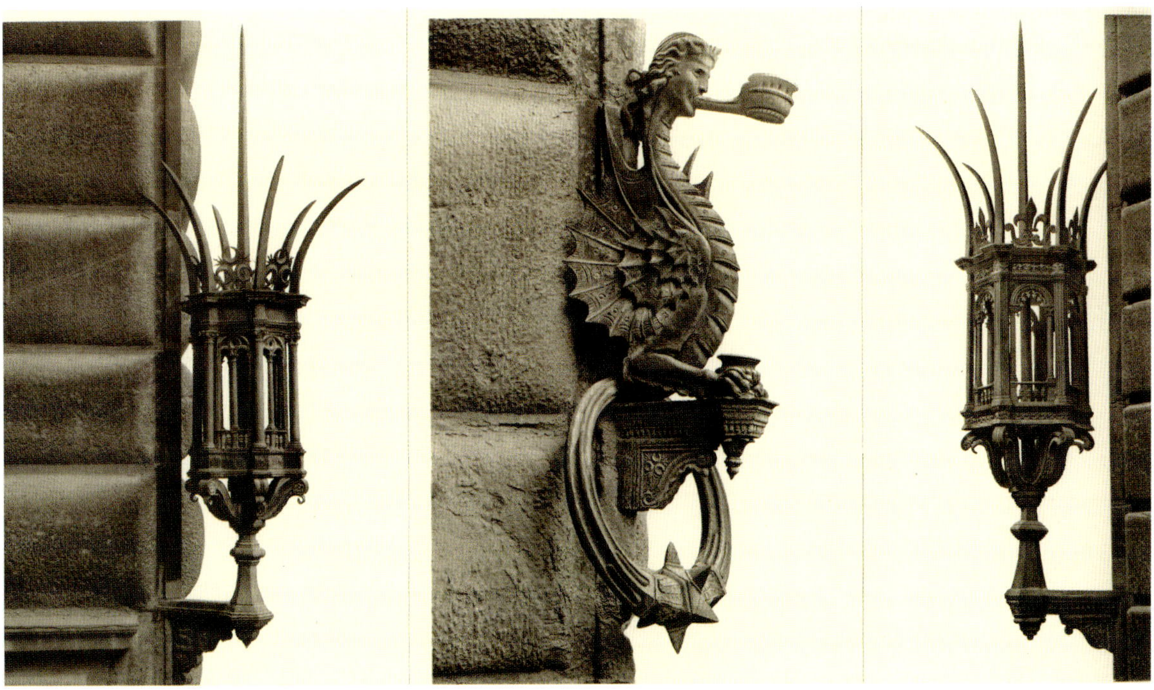

on the extension of architecture into the objects that populated its spaces from yet another angle and encouraged a unitary thinking about forms across all scales.

The other significant contribution that Gurlitt made to the discourse on objects is that as art historian, architect, and critic he brought together the two—apparently very distant poles—in German artistic literature, the aesthetic and the popular, that had operated all along in the background of the *Gewerbe* debates. Thus he became the apologist of Julius Langbehn, the popularizer of a nationalist, folk-based high-art and would-be reformer of German culture, at the same time that he became the apologist of Adolf Göller. The two could not have been further apart, yet through Gurlitt's bridging activity that unfolded on so many fronts he brought both authors into the mix of Baroque studies, Semperiana, and *Kunstgewerbe*.[96]

Langbehn had lived in Gurlitt's house while he was writing *Rembrandt als Erzieher* (1890), and though he had kept this work quiet and published the book anonymously, they did spend significant time together, and this interaction marked Gurlitt strongly.[97] Langbehn's pro-German rant was an exaltation of the artist (influenced by Schopenhauer and Nietzsche), but it was also a very strong pro-artisan position.[98] The combination resonated profoundly with the reading public, and the book went through thirty-nine reprints in the first two years after publication. Gurlitt stated his admiration for Langbehn explicitly in his reviews in *Die Gegenwart*, but more important was that he assimilated those ideas into his definitions of culture and style.[99] Thus his definitions of the craftsman echoed the "peasant artist" and the *Volkstümlichkeit* that Langbehn extrapolated from the iconic Rembrandt figure. In his book on German art of the nineteenth century this mixture of high and low led Gurlitt to arrive at a craft-based definition of the Renaissance: "As in painting, so in the decorative arts *the principal goal was to conquer the crafts*.... Precisely because it was not the great painters but the honest craftsmen who had created something coarse, bulbous, cozy, middle class with a sure fist...that's what provided the greatest joy to the German Renaissance" (my emphasis).[100]

Although Gurlitt describes the Renaissance, his interest was in contemporary issues, especially in view of the current Bavarian revival of its "national" style. These features were precisely what had been acclaimed in Seidel's Bavarian Renaissance style and that allowed it to work with equal success for beer halls and museums. For Gurlitt, the contemporary fascination with folk art and its relevance to *Kunstgewerbe* echoed in his emphasis on an essential Germanic concern with craftsmanship, and its simultaneous high and low roots.[101] Although he did not make the connection in so many words, the language he used to describe the applied arts in an art historical context contained easily recognizable echoes of both Langbehn and the literature on folk objects, and invited the slippage from one into the other.

If Gurlitt's interest in pure form and in Langbehn's folk-based aesthetics needed an axis around which to crystallize a conception of style, Giovanni Morelli provided it. He is the third corner in the triad that marks Gurlitt as he emerges from the influence of Semper and Wallot. How Gurlitt reads Morelli is evident from the enthusiastic 1890 reviews he writes of *Kunstkritische Studien*, which laid out his connoisseurship method. Moved by Morelli's method, Gurlitt arrives at a compelling definition of typical form, which he connects with a profound feeling for style (*Stilgefühl*) in an artist's work.[102] The connection of style and the typical was timely and, indeed, prophetic. Given the connection between the two men, it is an evident source for Muthesius and his later crusade for "Typisierung" at the Werkbund.

The importance of Gurlitt is that as a teacher and popularizer he brought together several strands (Göller, Morelli, Langbehn's bizarre if popular theory of culture, Semper, and art history) and made them available to architects. He also quoted Streiter with reference to iron bridges, thus once again confirming how such texts penetrated in the teaching and writings of the architectural milieu.[103] He did not pull off a new theory of ornament, objects, or architecture—if anything, he was known for an anti-theoretical stance. But he achieved a synthesis of his own and transmitted it throughout his lengthy and successful teaching career. That he did so to architects at two of the most important institutions and cities for the development of the modern movement—Berlin and Dresden—added greatly to his significance.

Through Gurlitt in Dresden, alongside Wölfflin in Berlin, Munich, and Zurich, Schmarsow in Leipzig, Göller in Stuttgart, Lipps and Streiter in Munich, not to mention the less known but equally visible authors of journal articles, the ideas developed in various disciplines and reworked by the art historians reached most of the German-speaking world of architectural students and academe. As the articles in the specialized press amply testify, the designation "German" included Swiss and Austrians, as well as the Germans of Germany, and it is fair to say that before the Great War the German-speakers saw themselves as belonging to a broad unit of language and culture.[104] Thus Vienna with the Museum für Kunst und Industrie, with Riegl, Wickhoff, and Loos, or Zurich with Semper, Burckhardt, and Wölfflin were as much a part of this German mosaic as any German city. Style was the topic around which they all converged, and so it became the breach in the architecture wall that allowed art historical discourse to penetrate, and with it all those other discourses that looked to style and that art history had welded into one. For all the negative associations and reproach heaped on it later by the apologists of modernism—and most famously by Sigfried Giedion—style provided an opportunity for cross-disciplinary conversation that architecture might not have enjoyed otherwise. Objects—artistic, historical, primitive, and quotidian—figured prominently as bridges across which this style-based discourse traveled. Drawn into style's crucible were many profoundly potent ideas: technology's relationship with organic bodies, the history of tools and the manipulation of mobile domestic equipment, the aesthetic value of the typical, and the relationship between habit and taste all blended with empathy theory, with the turn toward the detail and the closeup, and toward the symbolic readings of form. In the process, terms like *Nutzform, Sachform,* or *Formgefühl* acquired an additional resonance for being taken up in aesthetics and psychology and found their way back into the architecture discourse, capable of taking on an even more prominent role in its reformulation. Muthesius, Loos, and Le Corbusier could not have operated the dislocations they caused in the theory of modernism without them.

5 | The Fork in the Road

Muthesius and Loos

> Ornament is the direct expression of feeling and originates in the dynamics of human anatomy because they share the same structural laws of formation.
> —KARL SCHEFFLER (1901)

> Besides, we should not forget that another factor plays an enormous role in our aesthetic perception: the power of habit. Even when pure use-forms are produced, we become quickly accustomed to them; indeed we find them appealing, even if initially our sensibility reacted against them. —HERMANN MUTHESIUS, *Kultur und Kunst* (1904)

> The step from the picture to the crafted ornament, from ornament to furniture, and from here to the whole interior is no greater than from the latter to exterior architecture. It is in this connection to the art of building that the true revolutionary aspect of the decorative art movement rests. —KARL SCHEFFLER, *Moderne Baukunst* (1907)

> The objects are so much in the style of our times that we do not perceive them to be style related. They have grown into our thinking and feeling. Our cars, our glasses, our optical instruments, our umbrellas and sticks, our luggage and saddles, our silver cigarette cases and adornments, our jewelry and clothes are all modern.
> —ADOLF LOOS, "DIE ÜBERFLÜSSIGEN" in *Trotzdem* (1908)

The story that follows is well known. Muthesius, Wagner, the Vienna architects, Mies and Gropius, the Werkbund and the Bauhaus have been the focus of much scholarship. More satellites are constantly being added to these planets—Josef August Lux, Fritz Schumacher, Karl Scheffler, and others—and whole architectural solar systems begin to emerge and gain in clarity and depth. But what preceded them makes the difference. Göller, Gurlitt, and Streiter brought us to the eve of the twentieth century. Like the work of Semper, of the authors of so many types of atlases, of art historians and organizers of Great Exhibitions and specialized museum collections, their work constitutes a context within which the theoretical debates and proselytizing activities of twentieth-century reformers was embedded. Indeed, these connections between the nineteenth-century intellectual framework surrounding ornament and objects and the foundational writings of modernist architecture are hard to miss. The wider context into which Adolf Loos's *Ins Leere gesprochen* or *Ornament and Crime* must be placed, the sources of

Muthesius's *Stilarchitektur und Baukunst* (1902), as well as of his many articles, must be sought here. Muthesius's battlecry "vom Sofakissen zum Städtebau" (from the sofa cushion to city planning) receives a fuller resonance only once we think of the many levels upon which the *Sofakissen* had actually been theorized.[1]

Far more than a break, what can be sensed in Loos's or Muthesius's writings is how profoundly these paradigmatic statements of modernism are part of a century-long discussion that unfolded on many levels and in many disciplines. The projection of the object—be it crafted by the artisan or produced by the machine—into the foreground that occurred simultaneously in so many fields signaled a shift, a dislocation of attention. The object becomes intensely significant. And this significance works its way into architecture. Indeed, what the previous chapters have shown is that this phenomenon cannot be explained only by the interaction with the English Arts and Crafts, or by the rising fascination with technology in Germany or the political-economic context of a capitalist runaway expansion in the face of a global economy, though all of them undoubtedly played a role. It is more profoundly tied to a shift in the theory of architecture that took place on a wider arena and that also embraced the small scale, the hand-held, and portable.

Of course this book cannot follow each thread and explore how the more complicated picture of the nineteenth century drawn here modifies the one we have formed of each and every modernist. But some threads need to be highlighted. Without them neither the fabric's intricacy and connectedness nor the discussion of objects and ornament in the twentieth century would regain their full dimensions. Most importantly, it is significant to see how and where the discussion that transitions from ornament to the objects of daily use folds into the theory of architecture and what it tells us about this shift in architecture's discursive tools. In short, how and at what point does ornament leave off and the object become invested with meaning as the preferred (or more relevant) mediator between building and viewer? Undoubtedly objects and architecture had always been part of a connected visual discourse, and one that accelerates from the eighteenth century onward, embracing architects from Robert Adam to Schinkel and Semper (fig. 118). But when do objects become *the* privileged tool for communicating in architecture?

What is significant to notice then is that the themes associated with objects, their production, and consumption became leading metaphors for the generation of architects and critics of the early decades of the twentieth century. The carpet, clothes, the object as prosthesis, the tattoo, the snail's shell, all recur in connection with architecture like a persistent background noise from which new positions are constructed.[2] Yet the original authors of these metaphors were mostly left out of the discussions, and their names and contributions disappeared

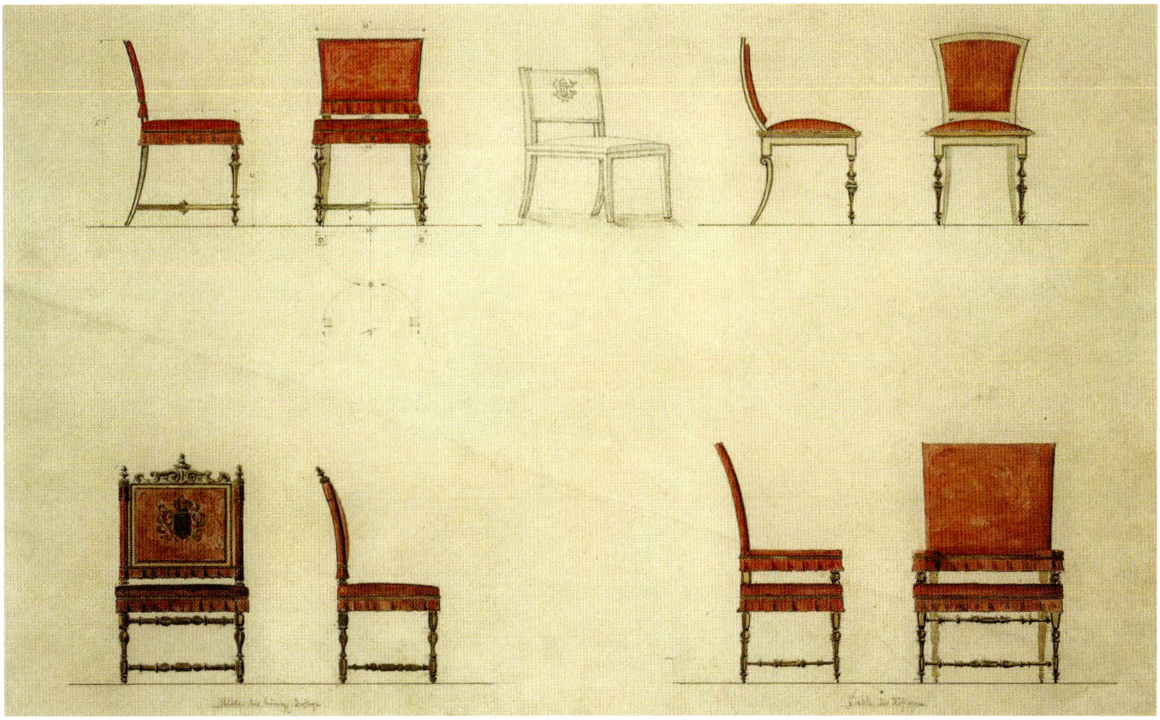

into collective oblivion. Clearly ornament remains a theme, but the sun begins to set on its importance, and a process of vilification follows that of sustained analysis. After an excess of attention for the better part of half a century follows attack and dismissal. The tools of daily life—be they objects of luxury or more humbly conceived, and which for so long accompanied the ornament discussion *de pari pasu*—rise on the horizon of architectural discourse and acquire a status and space of their own. The detail is also taken under the magnifying glass of production if not of theory and acquires a significant dimension on the radar screen of architects. Exposing a detail may owe to the desire to present buildings as real constructs, tooled and assembled with fasteners exposed, and illustrate architecture's participation in the culture of machines and objects. But the key element here remains the object, which signals that participation and literally brings it home to the users, attached as they are to their every gesture, embedded in their daily habits.

The aesthetic categories and instruments developed around them also shift. Empathy (*Einfühlung*) theory recedes from center stage and finds refuge mainly in the work of the Expressionists, only to disappear with their exclusion from the orthodoxy of modernism. Yet despite all protestations to the contrary, the body nevertheless retains its importance as key reference point for architecture. The body is the sine qua non behind the metaphors of clothes, of the soft center of the house/shell that eventually invites the mollusk metaphor from Walter Benjamin,

FIGURE 118
Gottfried Semper, "First Court Theater in Dresden, Upholstered chairs." Deutsches Theatermuseum München.

the wielder of instruments and objects-as-tools that surround it in ever widening though connected circles, increasingly separated from it until they become the exterior walls of the house. Alongside the machine these themes all speak of continuity with the ideas generated in the nineteenth-century literature from Semper to the anthropological atlases and the philosophy of technology-cum-physiology in the manner of Ernst Kapp. The ethnographic and folklore thread wherein body and house exist in a direct physiological/causal relation and that had offered another perspective on objects and bodies, clothes and ornament, architecture and its inhabitants also remained a recurrent reference point even when the forms were as distinct from vernacular nostalgia as they could get. So did the terminology—terms like "type," *Sachform,* or *Formgefühl* echoed through the next decades into the writings of Giedion and Le Corbusier, in English and French. What is Le Corbusier's "emotion type" other than a transformation of *Formgefühl,* as is the far more direct borrowing by Giedion of the same term, from his own *Doktorvater* Wölfflin? When translated into English as "feeling for form" they lose their real intellectual provenance and their rich history of meaning, just as they lose their cultural embeddedness.

HERMANN MUTHESIUS AND THE THEORY OF INTERVENTION

As Muthesius holds a prominent place in all accounts of German modernism, it is perhaps useful to single him out as an example of theoretical continuity across the two centuries. In Germany he repackages all these themes. A publishing dynamo, a man on a mission, a founder of the Werkbund and certainly one of its most important spokesmen, posterity has rightly given him a privileged position in the pantheon of modernism.[3] An exact contemporary of Streiter and speaking to the same issues, he became a hero of the modernist history while the former, perhaps due to his premature death, passed into oblivion. Muthesius's background—studies in art history in Berlin (1881–63) and a continued presence there at the Technische Hochschule Charlottenburg from 1883–87, as well as a Ph.D. in 1902—certainly equipped him to know of and process the full dimension of the literature reviewed here. The art history academy in Berlin in that period was that of Rumohr, Kugler, Schnaase, and Wölfflin, of the debates around the Pergamon altar, of the heritage of Hegel in philosophy and of Dilthey. Even more to the point, Muthesius was the doctoral student of Gurlitt and worked in the office of Wallot (Gurlitt's hero), just like Streiter.[4] The interaction between these two apologists is even more dramatic, as their articles intertwine in the same journals in the 1890s and 1900s.[5] Indeed, their conceptions of modernity intersect and show many similarities that hint at more sources for Muthesius's thinking than those normally adduced in connection with his work. Likewise his opening toward the vernacular both in domestic architecture and its movable objects, normally attributed to the influence of the English Arts and Crafts, surely owed as much to Gurlitt's turn toward German crafts in response to Langbehn, to his pioneering support of the *Heimatschutz* (preservation) movement, as well as to the rising scholarship and museum activity on ethnography.[6]

Muthesius's sojourn in Japan (1887–91) and his collection of Japanese artifacts open another window onto his intellectual makeup and display his interests in the ethnographic enthusiasm and debates of the nineteenth century. These exotic objects colored his focus on the arts and crafts just as much as had Gurlitt or the English Reform Movement. We get a hint of how he may have looked upon them from the debates in these same years around the location of the Japanese collection first exhibited in Vienna at the Great Exhibition of 1873. Originally housed in the Oriental Museum founded by Arthur von Scala, he sought to transfer them to the Museum für Kunst und Industrie (of which he was director) three decades later, but after a period of limbo the bulk finally ended up in the museum of natural history.[7] This snapshot of uncertainty and blurred edges between the museums and collections of decorative arts, ethnography, and natural history illustrates well the multiple chords that such artifacts struck and that included ethnographic curiosity alongside appreciation of exquisite workmanship, exoticism, simplicity, and concern for industry. For someone coming of age in such a museum and collecting-focused ambience, authenticity was equally important, so it is not surprising that Muthesius was very critical of Japonist artifacts produced by the Jugendstil.[8]

If this episode shows Muthesius participating in a larger discourse, so do his early articles, which reflect many of the nineteenth-century publication themes and so reveal his sources: the importance of 1851, the poor quality of the European wares, the rise of museums and schools, the rise of popular publications focused on objects, the interest in the *Kunstgewerbe*.[9] Muthesius's concern with prices, for example, with production, with the "encouragement of quality" and the didactic role of the state resonate in statements such as: "We ourselves are more or less appraised by our wares. The failing effort to produce quality thus has the most prejudicial national results," and ended up being a major issue at the 1911 Werkbund congress and its ensuing 1912 publication.[10] Such a view is neither new nor more urgent to him than it was to Laborde, Semper, Eitelberger, Falke, or many others half a century before; it is neither innovative nor radical but part of a tradition at this point—the climax and most articulated product of that tradition. Even the aims of the Werkbund (its statutes formulated in 1908 and printed in the 1912 *Jahrbuch*) sound strangely familiar, echoing as they do Semper's program of 1852: "The aim of the union is to ennoble industrial work in connection with art, industry, and the crafts through education, propaganda, and a united attitude on relevant issues."[11]

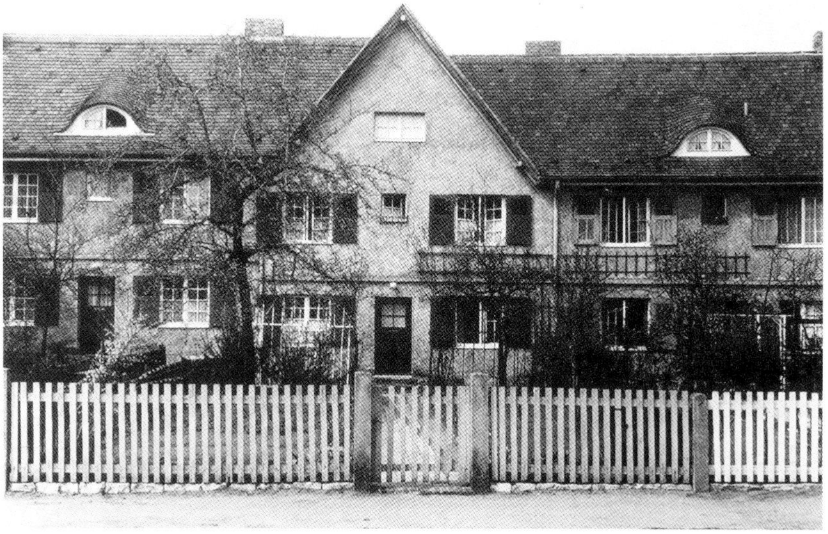

FIGURE 119
Hermann Muthesius, Einfamilienhaus Beim Gräbehen, 1911–12.

Indeed, Muthesius's early articles can be seen as extensions of the mass of publications in German and Austrian journals, such as, for example, the arguments of H. Schatteburg in his "Das Kunstschöne und die Kunstgewerbeschulen" in *Allgemeine Bauzeitung* of 1892.[12] Repackaging Semper for the 1890s, the architect raises his voice against mindless copying ("geistloses Kopistenthum"), praises France, promotes popular education to reach the *Volk* (such as free entry to museums), and argues that the mission of the decorative arts schools is to educate, as is that of illustrated magazines. In a shift of emphasis from Semper, who was concerned with the producers of objects (be they anonymous artisans or artists), he focuses more on the recipient, on the consumer. In his view the target is to produce a knowledgeable public: "The artistic sense is the yardstick for the cultural level a people has reached."[13] There is no real novelty here, only a statement of successful dissemination. Two decades later, in his 1911 opening address at the Werkbund congress, Muthesius would present a very similar argument.[14]

Like almost everybody at this time, Muthesius, through his many activities and his almost obsessive writing, was predominantly focused on the objects of *Gewerbe* and *Kunstgewerbe* (he even argues against a distinction between them), and it is from them that he moves on to write about architecture. The English house, experienced in detail during his English sojourn (1896–1903), had certainly provided a significant case study. But he was well prepared to respond to the English lesson (as was Loos later) by half a century of German literature on the subject.[15] And while the English/German dialogue was a commonplace for the period—witness the almost instant translation of Walter Crane's and William Morris's works—the local German discussion, drawing from a host of other man-based disciplines, which was far less the case in England, had a different physiognomy and also led in different directions.[16] Indeed, the German take on the issue of *Gewerbe, Kunstgewerbe,* and *angewadte Kunst* was far more theoretical than in England (where political and economic issues were foregrounded) or France. As a result it also promoted the aesthetization of the domestic sphere and its inhabitants. Concerned with mass access to quality goods in the mold of Semper, Muthesius railed against one of its offspring—the over-aestheticized and elitist Art Nouveau.[17] Yet he did make *Wohnungskultur* and the house the epicenter of his theory of architecture and the target of his polemic, as he would that of his built work and publications later (fig. 119):

> The German has no proper *house*. . . . In fact a change in our German artistic situation can only take its start in the German house, which essentially is to be created. Art begins, like so much else, at home. Only he who takes an artistic interest in his four walls, who is naturally inclined to shape his personal surroundings artistically, will bring that sensitivity for art from his rooms into the street and the larger environment. And this is imperative if our contemporary world is to have a broader, popular art.[18]

What he is touching on here, very much like his contemporary Streiter, though less radically, is the importance of the unself-conscious education of the body through daily contact with objects. To be sure, at first blush Muthesius does not appear to belong to the *Einfühlung* school of thought. And he promotes the aestheticization of the domestic sphere more outspokenly than habit formation like Streiter. Yet the central role he assigns the intimacy of body contact with architecture suggests that he processed this perspective and channeled it into the "strong" theory of modernist architecture.

Muthesius's is certainly a didactic position, once again much like Semper's. But it is also a confirmation that he too saw architecture arising from the miscellanea of the everyday and that he saw objects and buildings continuous with each other. For him, architecture is the art of daily life.[19] Taking Semper's argument to its logical conclusion, he sees a succession of containers surrounding the body that function like Russian dolls, one leaving its imprint on the next: the body of the dweller wrapped in its clothes, as a first layer, handles objects or *Kunstgewerbe,* which in turn becomes the core around which interior architecture finds its form and then itself generates the architecture of the exterior, as tectonics.[20] This is the progressive route, from inside out, not from outside in, as an imposed "style," that he rejects adamantly.[21] The objects that surround the body and mediate between it and the larger world represent the DNA of culture.

Muthesius's reading of the interior/exterior relation recalls Gurlitt's take on Wallot in his architecture of the nineteenth century. But Muthesius was not alone in reading the revolution of the turn of the century in this way. A few years

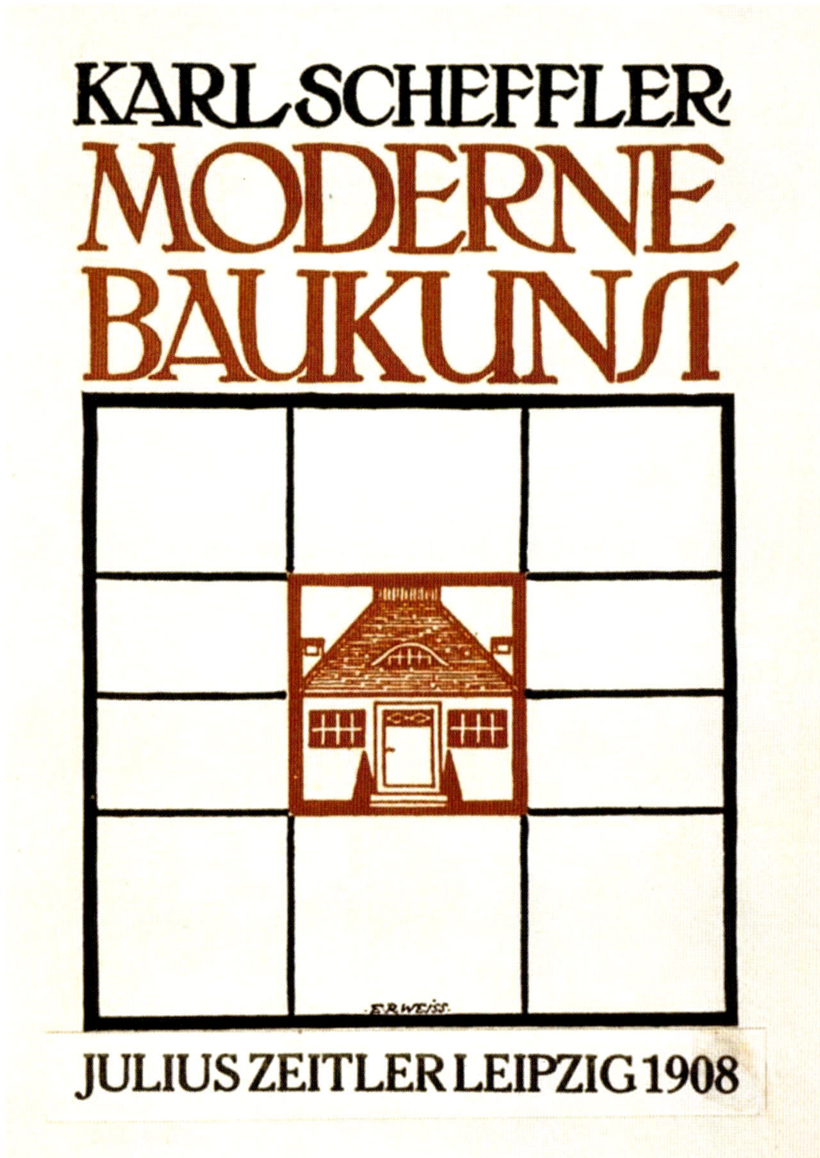

FIGURE 120
Karl Scheffler, *Moderne Baukunst* (Leipzig, 1908).

later (1907) Karl Scheffler would express this idea of continuity between inside and outside even more directly when he reflected upon the contribution of the decorative arts movement to modern architecture (fig. 120). For him the truly revolutionary aspect of the movement resided in the fact that it had connected painting and ornament, furniture and architecture into one seamless sequence that radiated outward from the nucleus of the interior.[22] Here, in 1907, on the eve of Loos's attack, ornament still holds a place as a transitional site for architecture, part of the movement from two-dimensional to three-dimensional object (furniture in this case) that morphs into architecture (fig. 121). And as such, for Scheffler

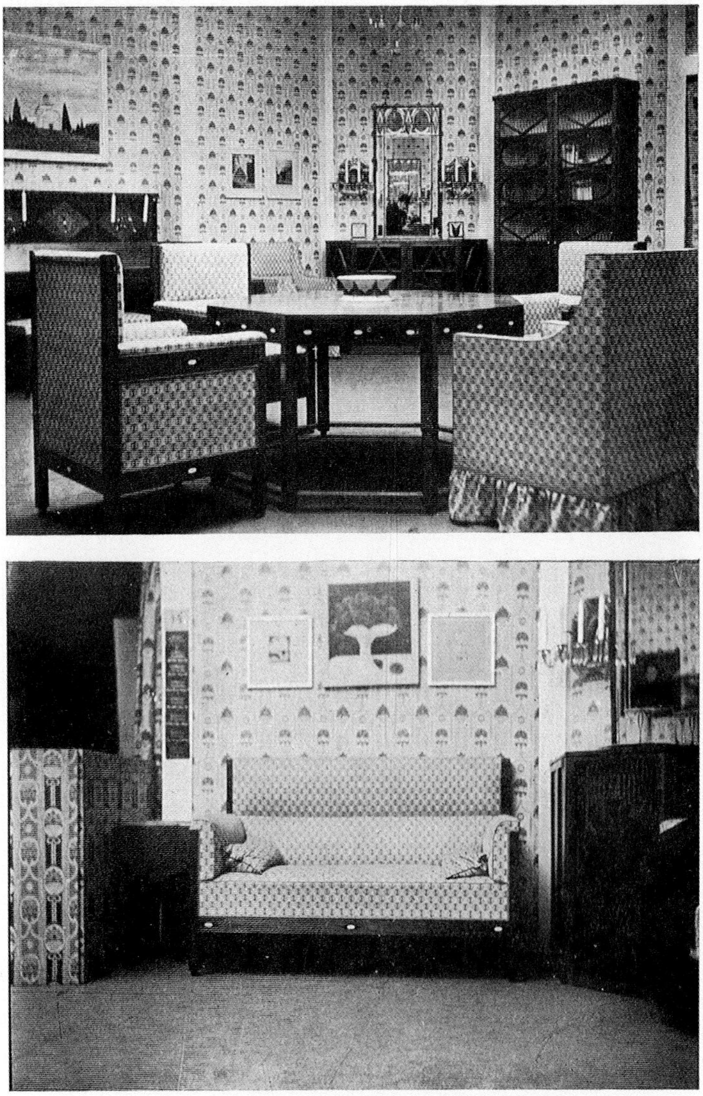

EMIL RUDOLF WEISS ACHTECKIGES WOHNZIMMER (zwei Aufnahmen)

FIGURE 121
Emil Rudolf Weiss, octagonal living room. From Scheffler, *Moderne Baukunst.*

and for his contemporaries, it is the laboratory in which modern architecture was created. For him the renewal of the applied arts (and especially of furniture as experimental site) and architecture cannot be separated.[23]

Not everyone agreed. At precisely the same time, and as if responding to Scheffler, Fritz Schumacher expressed skepticism that the decorative arts had provided leadership for architecture.[24] In his view the abstract mode of expression of architecture did not arise from the *Kunstgewerbe* but operated in the opposite direction: materials, colors, and ornament needed the disciplining agency of architectural thinking. Yet even so, he too saw the two operating together and acknowledged that the experimentation opportunities in the decorative arts far outnumbered those of its monumental sibling and invited innovation more readily. In the end, furniture, architecture, objects of daily use, and the monumental still merged. And he concluded that the whole conception of a *sachlich* piece of furniture is profoundly architectural: "Today's practical house arises from the same thinking as the practical furniture." He even coined the term "furniture-architecture" (*Möbelarchitektur*).[25]

But the idea of objects, as the equipment of daily life, and architecture standing in a symbiotic relationship found support in another quarter that was gaining importance: folk art and ethnography.[26] In time, Muthesius embraced it also, thus reinforcing the idea of a modern vernacular that had been with him for some time.[27] As we have seen, the natural, unself-conscious continuity between the dweller and his abode, as well as all that surrounded him, was one of the arguments that underpinned the decorative arts reform and allied it to the folk movement. At its core was the idea of the natural connection between house and dweller as body, much like the mollusk in its shell. The authenticity of the farmer's life and its products invited this organic analogy and provided a model, as well as a powerful contrast, to the rootless nomadic city dweller. Michael Haberlandt, the father of Austrian folk studies, had adduced the comparison in evaluating folk art and architecture in an ambitious publication on folk architecture sponsored by the Austrian architects' and engineers' union.[28] Semper had penetrated here too—the transference of textile motifs to the wall treatments was one borrowed idea—but also ethnographers, as well as Viollet-le-Duc and Riegl. Riegl's concepts of *Hausindustrie* and *Hausfleiss* found an echo in the "manual dexterity" that, according to the authors, united the construction of the house with its interior furnishings into a single "natural," unself-conscious, unartistic (and hence authentic) activity.[29] At one point Streiter had cut the two loose and promoted a world of objects that were outspokenly modern and mobile like their owners, torn off the house that had been their setting for so long, no longer rooted in the house as if a natural organism. But this did not mean that the object would cease to be in a dialogue with the building. If continuity did not arise from the object to the building, the object not being embedded in it, it nevertheless occurred through the body that touched both. In so arguing, Streiter had pointed in a direction that was different from the set interiors of Art Nouveau.

Muthesius, too, made frequent reference to clothes as the model for architecture and the real index of contemporary culture, as did others who even proposed that the Werkbund introduce and support a reform of men's clothing.[30] Indeed, in his article "Kultur und Kunst" of 1904 when he points to clothes as the only site of *Sachlichkeit* he is almost paraphrasing von Eye: "However, the house is nothing but a further garment that surrounds us."[31] It has been argued that his source was Loos and his articles on clothing from the late 1890s, but both belonged to a far larger and richer context and need not have depended on each other.[32] Both Muthesius and Loos had direct links to Dresden, and a survival of von Eye's thought through Gurlitt is not out of the question. Moreover, echoes of Wölfflin are also noticeable when Muthesius argues that "the level of general taste will always be perceived in the state of the applied arts."[33] His object, as he saw it, was to act upon the generation that was currently furnishing its house so that it would choose "schlichtes Hausgerät von edlem Anstand and echter Vornehmheit" (simple household equipment of noble appearance and genuine dignity), in a turn of phrase that harks back to no less than Winckelmann and his definition of classical Greek art as "edle Einfalt and stille Grösse" (noble simplicity and quiet grandeur).[34] Two years earlier he had made an even stronger connection between clothes and modernity: clothes, he argued, were the signs of the times, just like ships, cars, and machines, all of which had moved toward undecorated form. Adamantly condemning the artificial creation of style within Art Nouveau, he closed with a powerful reminder to look at clothes—especially men's fashion—folk art, and ceramics or textiles as the location of a "naive" or spontaneous impulse toward simplification, elimination of ornament, and a modern *Sachlichkeit*.[35]

Within architecture, Otto Wagner had heaped additional reinforcement on his head, if more was needed, and he did so before Loos had set out to deride Austrian artifacts by way of an analysis of clothes. Indeed, clothes come up frequently in his *Modern Architecture* (1896), and in a significant passage Wagner seems to be reworking Wölfflin's argument about the continuity of style across clothes and architecture. He may well have been the one to draw Loos's attention to this issue, though the connection between clothes and architecture was pretty commonplace by then. To be sure, Wagner does not go on to make the body that is covered by one and contained by the other the link between them, as Wölfflin does, but he does reiterate the connection.

> The pictures of style just evoked logically allow us to perceive the close and hitherto ignored relationship between taste, fashion, and style. Even a slight gift of observation must awaken in us the conviction that outward appearance—man's clothing in its form, color, and accessories—is fully consistent with each period's artistic viewpoints and creations and cannot even be imagined otherwise. No epoch, no style has been an exception to this. This fact is vividly seen in comparing costume designs with contemporary

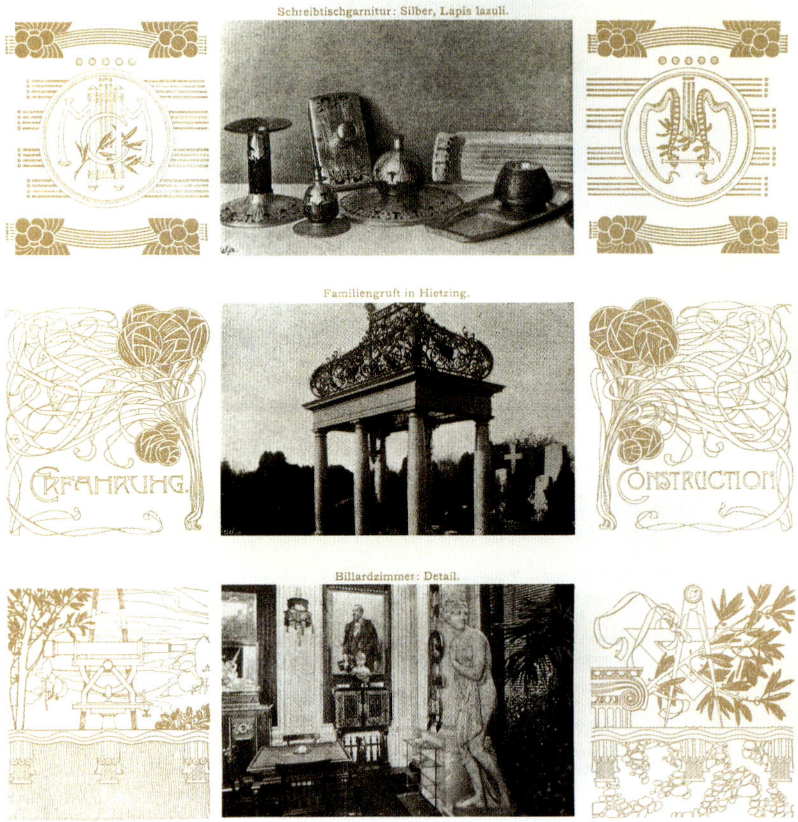

FIGURE 122
Otto Wagner, "Erfahrung. Construction." *Moderne Architektur: Seinen Schülern ein Führer auf diesem Kunstgebiete* (Vienna, 1896).

> works of architecture, or, better still, by inspecting paintings that show both together (Carpaccio, Callot, Bosse, Lepautre, Chodowiecki, Canaletto). [fig. 122][36]

Although the reference to taste and fashion seems to point in another direction—to consumer goods and speed of production and perhaps even to Göller's fatigue (*Ermüdung*)—nevertheless the issue of a homogeneous culture is also present and re-embeds into architecture discourse the anthropological and cultural history argument that connected Wölfflin and von Eye across Falke and Viollet-le-Duc and had been such a prominent feature of nineteenth-century publications.[37]

As the doyen of architects seeking modernity, Wagner was both a target and a beacon: as a great admirer of Semper's he prolonged the afterlife of his treatise, but he also collided with Streiter who in his *Architektonische Zeitfragen* (1890s) had argued against his materialism using Wölfflin.[38] From both points of view Wagner's book (reprinted with four editions between 1896 and 1914) kept these issues alive long after both his interlocutors had left the scene. In fact, it seems likely that all three—Wagner, Muthesius, and Loos—owed to the accumulated literature that blended the body with the instruments it held, the clothes that wrapped it, and the container (or "portable dwelling") that housed it. Viollet-le-Duc, Wölfflin, von Eye, Kapp, and others had made the argument. The literature that focused on culture and had swept from a history of costume to the history of artifacts and architecture across anthropology and archaeology was too significant in quantity and in intellectual novelty to miss.

Much else connected Muthesius to the cultural field outlined here. His terms like *Grundform, Sachform,* and *Formgefühl* were not of his own coining but would have resonated powerfully with his audience, given their references to Semper and Bötticher through Lipps, Schmarsow, and Wölfflin, and provided an intertextual dimension and continuity with the positions that they had taken.[39] One can even imagine that he counted on it, so significant had these terms become in contemporary debates. His famous lecture at the 1911 Werkbund annual meeting was published in 1912 in the *Werkbund Almanach* as "Wo stehen wir?" but was also published immediately in 1911 in *Architektonische Rundschau* with the much more Wölfflinian title: "Die Bedeutung des architektonischen Formgefühls."[40] Likewise when he argues that "the product of the machine can only be an undecorated practical form (*Sachform*), the particular form that the machine produces best," one must also hear Lipps in the background, as he separates thing (*Sache*) from image (*Bild*).[41] Indeed, the term *Sachform* occurred early on in Muthesius's writings, from the 1890s onward, and is a direct link to his later definition of *Sachlichkeit*. This notoriously difficult term has been translated as simplicity or objectivity, but the root of the word is nevertheless "*Sache,*" or "thing." Since as an adjective *sachlich* refers to the appearance of an object and suggests that it stays close to the "Sache" (hence its overlap with "simplicity") both terms "Sachform" and "Sache" are present in its lexical field. Later, in his spirited apology of mass production, Muthesius's *Sachform* became *Grundform,* "essential" or "archetypal" form.[42] Both Streiter and Lipps had used *Grundform,* too: Streiter as tectonic form while Lipps as counterpoint to artistic form, though he insisted that in architecture and applied arts the two overlapped.[43] Muthesius implied this overlap too, and thus also joined into one argument portable objects and architecture, even if he did not turn to empathy in the manner of Lipps or Wölfflin to justify this proximity.[44] Clearly he rejected the separation between thing and image embedded in terms like *Werkform* (Bötticher; Lipps), *Kernform* (Bötticher; Lipps), *Zweckform* (Lipps), *Wurzelform* (Semper) for the one and *Schmuckform* (Lipps) or *Bekleidung* (Semper) for the other. The meaning of this position has been analyzed at great length with respect to its consequences for architecture.[45] But the continuity, even origin, of the idea in the discourse on the mass production of *objects* is what is important here.

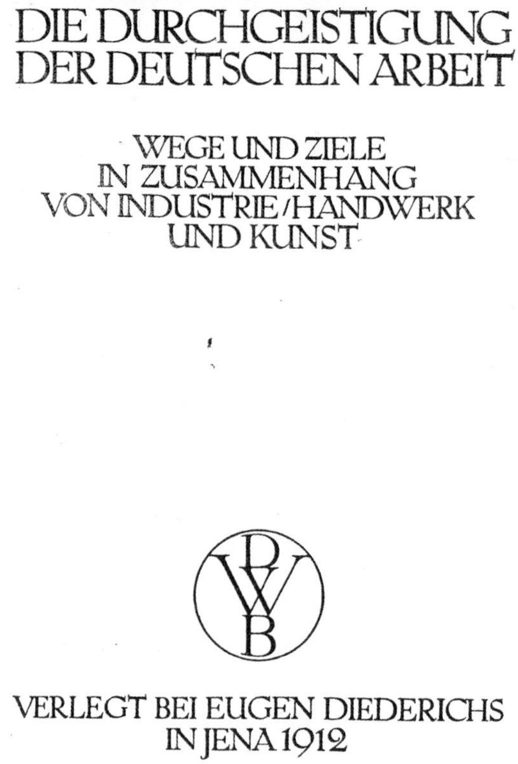

DIE DURCHGEISTIGUNG
DER DEUTSCHEN ARBEIT

WEGE UND ZIELE
IN ZUSAMMENHANG
VON INDUSTRIE / HANDWERK
UND KUNST

VERLEGT BEI EUGEN DIEDERICHS
IN JENA 1912

FIGURE 123
Die Durchgeistigung der Deutschen Arbeit (Jena, 1912).

Perhaps what is most striking about Muthesius is his insistence on the primacy of form *tout-court*. For all—objects of daily use (*Gebrauchsgegenstände*), furniture, architecture, equally, and this is the important point—the goal is to achieve a spiritualized form (*durchgeistigte Form*) to ennoble function.[46] This was his principal message at the 1911 Werkbund congress, but it appears earlier as well (fig. 123). "Culture is unthinkable without the unconditional appreciation of form" is the slogan he proposes.[47] This was not an isolated position, and it suggests a broader push toward formalism within the Werkbund. Witness the contribution "Das Ornament" by Karl Gross at the same Werkbund congress. Uniquely in the literature surveyed here, he separates ornament from decoration (*Schmuck*) and argues that they are not synonymous. The point is polemical, as Gross really means beauty when he talks about decoration (beautiful form does not need ornament), and he berates the previous generation for attempting reform through ornament. But the point he wants to make is that "for all plastic branches of industry the principal task is to ennoble form," and he talks in one breath of architecture, furniture, metalwork, and ceramics.[48] What unites them is sculptural, haptic form.

As we have seen, Streiter made the radical suggestion that repeated handling of objects yields aesthetic appreciation of modern architecture—that objects

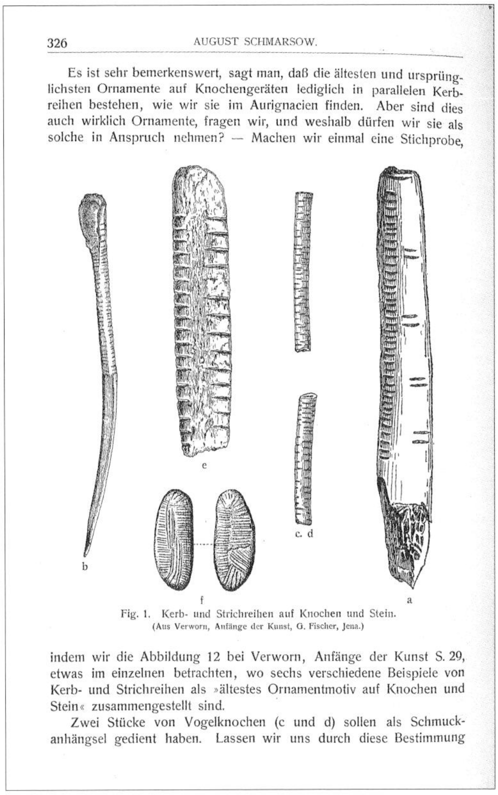

326 AUGUST SCHMARSOW.

Es ist sehr bemerkenswert, sagt man, daß die ältesten und ursprünglichsten Ornamente auf Knochengeräten lediglich in parallelen Kerbreihen bestehen, wie wir sie im Aurignacien finden. Aber sind dies auch wirklich Ornamente, fragen wir, und weshalb dürfen wir sie als solche in Anspruch nehmen? — Machen wir einmal eine Stichprobe,

Fig. 1. Kerb- und Strichreihen auf Knochen und Stein.
(Aus Verworn, Anfänge der Kunst, G. Fischer, Jena.)

indem wir die Abbildung 12 bei Verworn, Anfänge der Kunst S. 29, etwas im einzelnen betrachten, wo sechs verschiedene Beispiele von Kerb- und Strichreihen als »ältestes Ornamentmotiv auf Knochen und Stein« zusammengestellt sind.

Zwei Stücke von Vogelknochen (c und d) sollen als Schmuckanhängsel gedient haben. Lassen wir uns durch diese Bestimmung

FIGURE 124
Ornamented prehistoric tools. From August Schmarsow, "Anfangsgründe jeder Ornamentik," *Zeitschrift für Ästhetik und allgemeine Kunstwissenschaft* 5 (1910).

communicate by way of the unself-conscious haptic experience of the viewer. Muthesius's sense of continuity across media points in the same direction. He too assigns the function of aesthetic education to the experience of objects large and small (clothes, bicycles, bridges, ocean liners). Habit formation (*Gewohnheit*) is his way to understand how objects operate upon aesthetic sensibility. He had already developed this argument in his essay "Die moderne Umbildung unserer ästhetischen Anschauungen" (The Modern Transformation of Our Aesthetic Conceptions) of 1902.[49] And, once again like Streiter, he sees the principal characteristic of machine products to be the smooth form, reduced to its functional essence, from which, he adds, all ornament has been removed.[50] These are also, he continues, the few superfluous yet significant features of simple modern clothing: the shiny top hat, the patent leather shoes, like the silk lapels, "can almost be compared with certain polished and nickel-plated parts of a machine."[51] Thus arguing against Art Nouveau he also argues for a harmonious culture—one where the machines and the automobiles, the bridges and train stations, the *sachlich* products of modernity are compatible with the architecture and the decorative arts, all the way to the clothes worn on the body.[52]

It is here that Muthesius's *Typisierung* concept also comes into play and connects to the concept of habit formation. Although a neologism as a term, as we have seen, the notion of the typical as an aesthetic category had been proposed by Schmarsow in 1910, though the core of his idea was already evident in his lectures of 1903.[53] Schmarsow associated an aesthetic of repetition and the typical with ornament. For him, ornament, being both serial and typical, signaled value through regular and orderly (*regelmässige*) repetition. Tools and objects of "temporary but repeated use" carry the imprint of the body even farther, he argued, and the more the objects move outside the body's direct handling sphere, along a vector that connects the tattoo with architecture, the more analogical they become (fig. 124).[54] Leaning on Lipps and contemporary anthropologists (he used primitive art as his case study), Schmarsow reinforced the view that objects and architecture belonged together by way of the body. In its own way this was another take on the place of objects in an experiential continuum that Streiter intuited and that was also tributary to Lipps.

In the end it was Muthesius who consecrated and brought this idea into the limelight of the Werkbund in much more direct and readable language, without the philosophical baggage of Schmarsow, and reoriented it toward industrial production as process and economic rationale. In his view, not only is the object produced by the machine a step toward acculturating the user to the new aesthetic in Streiter's sense, but it is especially so because it is a *serial object,* a multitude of mass-produced objects that facilitate a new receptivity of the modern aesthetic. Streiter had not coined a term for this mediating function, but Muthesisus did. *Typisierung* ultimately celebrates the positive value of repeated cognition and aesthetic education through handling of simple yet perfect, consistently repeated, and industrially produced objects. For him, architecture responds to the same imperatives as do the objects produced by the machine, and, of all the arts, it is the one most tending toward the typical.[55] What he fears is that the superficial nervousness, mood changes, and disquiet of modern life elsewhere coined "impressionism" would "contaminate" architecture.[56] Though he does not attack it directly, one feels his aversion for the Jugendstil expressed so often over the previous fifteen years. For him architecture is that which is restful, permanent, lasting, and, paraphrasing Semper, the disciplining backbone of all the arts.[57] It is at this point that Muthesius touches on folk art and embraces it within his vision of modernity. Though he backs into it somewhat because a number of speakers at the Werkbund congress—Avenarius and Gurlitt among them, the latter citing Langbehn with enthusiasm—raise the question of a relationship between the Werkbund and the *Heimatschutz* movement (one being industrial-based the other preservationist, nationalist, and folk arts oriented, and therefore potentially at loggerheads), Muthesius is moved to see a rapprochement, and it is precisely on the terrain of the typical that he concedes it.[58] Turning to England as his example, he argues that it was the "heimatliche Bauweise" that produced the new tradition, a tradition of the typical.[59] Of course the Werkbund, both in its German and its Austrian form, manifested strong nationalist leanings, and such a folding of the folk issue into its purposes would have seemed logical in the end.[60] But doing so under the accolade of the typical offered one more opportunity for objects and architecture to be blended into one discourse, as they were among ethnographers.

If the idea of the typical found other formulations as well, it is a testament to its power. Indeed, these other formulations testify to the vectors along which it moved and add nuances to its traditional reading. Friedrich Naumann, for example, coined the term *Normalform* and used it interchangeably with *gewöhnlich* (ordinary), with which he described both architectural types but also everyday goods of any sort (*Normalware*).[61] Multiplication and mechanical reproduction (*mechanische Reproduzierbarkeit*), on which he insists, thus anticipating Benjamin, take his *Normalform* far away from folk objects, but simplification and repetition keep it within the same parameters and show on how many coordinates the type could be laid. Fritz Schumacher used *anspruchlos* (undemanding) in the same breath with *sachlich* and *bürgerlich* to express the same idea.[62] In his response to Muthesius's Werkbund speech, Theodor Fischer came at it from another angle. For him architecture needed to remain in the background, to be almost anonymous, unnoticeable, to recede behind the people it serves.[63] To some degree all were reacting to the extremes of fantasy represented by Art Nouveau, as they were to the overhyped discourse on ornament since the Great Exhibition, and it is interesting that they should reach out to similar low-key foils. What all these sympathetic views seem to be struggling with is the idea of an architecture that disappears, that blends with life to the point of not being noticeable, just like the objects of everyday use that become appropriated as extensions of body wrap or apparel.

The relevance of folk architecture folds into these positions quite logically and may well be their origin. The anonymous quality of the machine-made objects certainly enhanced their perceived effectiveness, as it allied them to the objects of folk art, or at least so went the somewhat utopian view of proselytizers like Muthesius. Like its sibling anthropology, the study of folk art and architecture had provided potentially seminal ideas about the house as universe, and it was a significant reference point for Muthesius. Although he did not embrace the preservation movement as part of the Werkbund goals until the Congress of 1911, he did finally concede precisely on these grounds. Moreover, the folk issue was profoundly embedded in the *Jahrbuch des deutschen Werkbundes* of 1912, which reads like an apology of Langbehn. The vocabulary, the references, the tone, even its overarching title "Die Durchgeistigung der Deutschen Arbeit" echo the nationalistic-artistic and combative prose of *Rembrandt als Erzieher* to

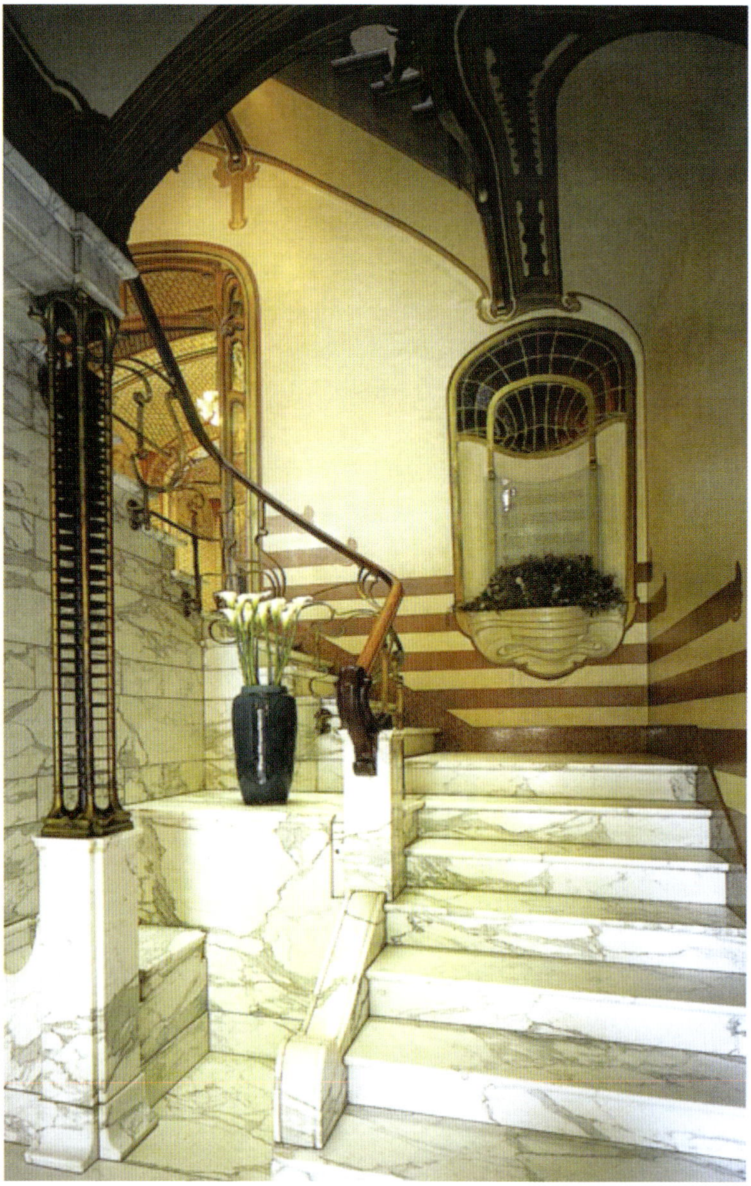

a remarkable degree.[64] In addition, as we have seen, the metaphor of the farm as natural formation, as a "snail house," suggests that here is to be found that profound consistency between the dweller's body and its multiple shells that are its unobtrusive extensions, where there are no breaks, and the continuity across objects is so smooth as not to be noticeable. Schumacher had made the connection explicitly in his 1901 inaugural speech at Dresden for his chair at the Technische Hochschule when he argued that modern *Kunstgewerbe* turns to those forms that folk art had instinctively grasped. Observing that the "traditional yet

FIGURE 125
Victor Horta, Horta House, Brussels. Horta Musée Horta, Bastin & Evrard/ SOFAM.

modern forms" in evidence in the Nordic pavilions at the Paris Exhibition of 1900 had received significant accolades, he declared them a "triumph for folk-art." For him the connecting links are the primitive or root forms that folk art and modern work share.[65]

It is evident how in this context Muthesius could invest the serial object produced by the machine with the significance of prototype, of *Urform*. Indeed, this conception of the artwork may be seen as a reversal of Benjamin's famous later critique of mechanical reproduction that destroys the aura of the art object. Instead, in this view, the machine-made and mass-produced object acquires the aura; the machine is the superior producer (because it is infallibly consistent, unlike the craftsman) and is invested with the attributes of the artist. Instead of mechanical reproduction destroying art by serial repetition, serial repetition is raised to the level of art. The discussions that started with Semper and his turn to the minor arts and culminated in Riegl, who dignified them as the conduit and repository of *Kunstwollen,* led to many shifts in the conception of art, but also to this one. In a reading of art that exalted the unobtrusive and incidental, the objects of daily use produced by the machine could claim the role of cultural catalysts.

THE CRISIS IN THE DECORATIVE ARTS AND THE PROBLEM OF ART NOUVEAU

Perhaps one of the more striking features of the evaluations of modernism and the *Kunstgewerbe* revolution, as it was known, in the first decades of the 1900s was the unveiled contempt for the so-called Art Nouveau. And the attitude set up a precedent that the later apologists and proselytizers reinforced in the 1920s—whether Gustav Adolf Platz, Adolf Behne, Bruno Taut, Le Corbusier, Sigfried Giedion, or Henry-Russell Hitchcock—thus signaling a form of consensus and deliberate distancing (with Platz characteristically remaining more tolerant than others).[66] Earlier theorists such as Muthesius or mavericks such as Loos, on whom these authors depended for their sources, had condemned it in no uncertain terms.[67] So had Fritz Schumacher and others.[68] Some earlier treatments of the period, by Scheffler or van de Velde, were more inclusive and certainly showed bridges from the nineteenth century across what came to be construed as the Art Nouveau hiatus. And it is also true that Muthesius's cry for a harmonious culture was not all that different from the aspirations of the Jugendstil artists who likewise sought a coherent interior. Schumacher himself waxed romantic about the whiplash line and the *Kultus der Linie,* as he called it, only to attack this excessive aestheticism five years later.[69] Moreover, Josef Hoffman was a founding member of the German Werkbund, and for all its aesthetic elitism the Wiener Werkstätte provided many useful ideas for Muthesius and his acolytes.[70] Indeed, despite Muthesius's rejection of Art Nouveau there was much that connected them, and the emphasis on crafting that informed his strictures against the

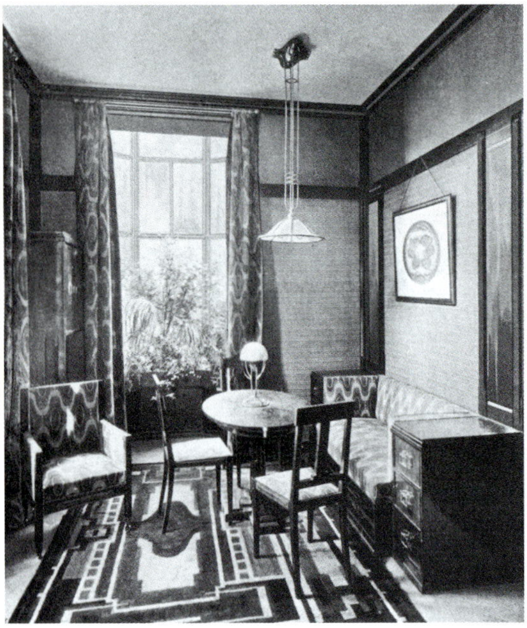

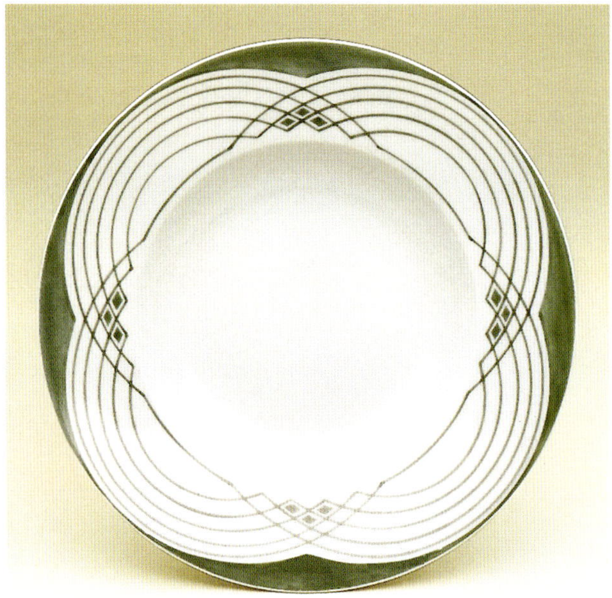

Left **FIGURE 126**
Peter Behrens, Behrens House, Darmstadt, 1901–2. Abb. Damenzimmer im Haus Behrens, 1901.

Right **FIGURE 127**
Peter Behrens, dinner plate, 1900–1901. Hard-pressed porcelain, 10 in. (25.4 cm) diam. The Minneapolis Institute of Arts, Minneapolis, The Modernism Collection, Gift of Northwest Bank Minnesota, L99.318.50.

style craze also united him to the aspirations of a Guimard or a Horta, and certainly to van de Velde.

And so forsaking Art Nouveau may seem surprising, as the intensity of the preoccupation with the house and its continuity into furniture, objects, and clothes was a shared domain with the later modernists, even if the actual forms were not. It was also a connecting link with the English Reform Movement and Arts and Crafts, once again beyond the visual repertory and sources used to derive forms, as Pevsner noted long ago. All embraced enthusiastically the *Sachkultur* that was so much the motor of discourse and manufacturing activity in the nineteenth century. Guimard and Horta may well seem to embody the extreme of that orientation where the "things," the objects that shaped life in the house, became the focus of their attention to a degree that subsumed architecture itself. In Horta's own house, for example, the lamps and furniture become as tectonically rooted as the walls, inseparable and indistinguishable from them (fig. 125). Everything was built in: the furniture, the lamps, even the candelabra on the dining table. In this extreme condition, architecture and objects of daily life merged into each other and became one. It is also fair to note that the conviction that continuity of form was an imperative in the domain of everyday life (be it ever so luxurious or distant from mass production) had defeated eclecticism, whose effect of tearing at the body's link to its historical moment had been so well intuited by Falke and Viollet-le-Duc.[71] The Art Nouveau architects had contributed decisively to promote this view.

Yet for all superficial similarities, the antipathy of a Muthesius or a Loos to the Jugendstil was based on three fundamental differences, whether recognized in so many words or not. For one thing, the Jugendstil architects were perceived to stand for ornament and willful invention rather than a naturally spontaneous evolution of forms that circumscribed daily life. While Endell argued passionately against banality and promoted *Formkunst,* Muthesius, like Lichtwark, Naumburg, Schumacher, and Graul, sought *Sachlichkeit, Bürgerlichkeit,* and "Licht, Luft und Sauberkeit" (light, air, and cleanliness).[72] Light and mobile, the equipment of the house needed to be adapted to metropolitan nomadic life.[73] These imperatives went back to a heterogeneous group of sources: to Semper and his vision of a vigorous art arising from the bottom up, as well as to Gurlitt and Langbehn, who promoted the object of daily use (*Gebrauchgegenstand*) and middle-class values.[74] Though *Formgefühl* was invoked by both camps, they did not seek it in the same location. It is perhaps to be expected then to see Endell illustrating the article in which he promoted a "new" architecture with sculpted effigies and relief art, while Muthesius consistently used the furniture and interiors of Riemerschmid to illustrate his own arguments. Neither made any reference to these images in their texts, but the message was clear: high art versus daily, simple life. As Schumacher insisted: Art Nouveau architecture was exhibition architecture, on display, not meant for living.[75] The Art Nouveau architects had made a case for objects as nerve endings of the buildings they populated, but increasingly a crisis point was felt to have been reached. The enthusiasm for the applied arts that had been broadly shared for more than half a century had moved in divergent directions.

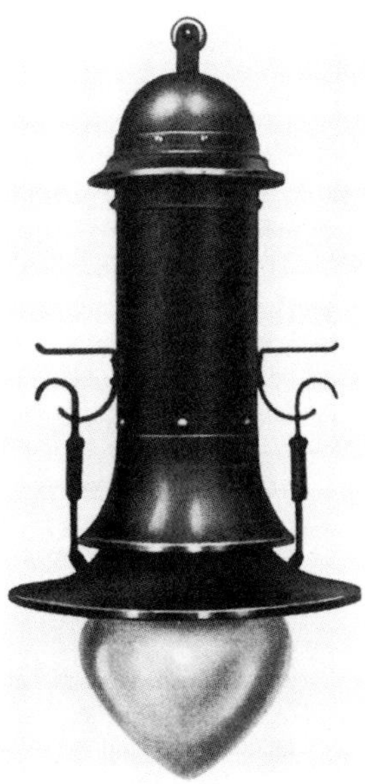

FIGURE 128
Peter Behrens, AEG-Arc Lamp. From *Mitteilungen der Berliner Elektrizitätswerke* 3 (1907): 130.

Second, the Jugendstil objects were not the objects of industry or of the metropolitan nomad. And of this Muthesius was profoundly aware. The visual referents more or less consistently used by the architects loosely gathered under the umbrella of Art Nouveau—be they vegetal or zoomorphic, extensions of the Gothic or of African or Arab formal approaches, structurally rationalist and welcoming modernity in the form of electricity and gas—were not iconically supportive of the industrialization phenomenon that had emerged in the past century, nor was the pared down/vernacular vocabulary of the Arts and Crafts. They did not "look" like industry but were more in tune with an eighteenth-century sensibility and Rococo culture of small-scale sculpture-as-objects. These objects were not produced en masse, nor could they be bought or used as individual pieces.

Indeed, and this was the third point of divergence: the objects populating the Art Nouveau interior belonged together and in no other combination, and as such they escaped the economic structure that had fed the Great Exhibitions and the discourses about industrial production that they had generated. It could be argued that not all work that is nowadays brought under the rubric of Art Nouveau is as profoundly welding objects and architecture, lamps and walls, furniture and floors, candelabra and electrical circuits, which wind their way through floors, walls, and tables to reach an apparently portable object such as a candlestick, as is the case of Horta's house. Peter Behrens's Darmstadt house, for example—all Nietzschean reflections aside—is a harmonious whole in which each object has been conceived with respect to each other and the whole, and where no accidental encounter between objects is anticipated or even permitted (fig. 126). Yet, unlike Horta's house—and it should be noted that architect's houses always exhibit their owner's ideas in their most undiluted and uncompromised form—Behrens's house is not one with its objects. These are not welded to their sites and retain the qualities of mobility and at least the suggestion that they might be arranged and rearranged if necessary. Still, detachable as they may be, these objects—chairs and tables, lamps and carpets—do not engage in the portable life of real objects but remain effectively glued to their preassigned places. They belong here, together, and nowhere else and in no other combination. The lines that define them—in the upholstery, in the curtains, as in the carpet and forms of sofas and armchairs—must extend into each other to get the visual harmony and "vibrations" across. On the other hand, Behrens's simple wood furniture of his Nuremberg and Düsseldorf years point in another direction, toward an interior of not-preordained forms (fig. 127).[76] Compared to Speltz's *Schreinerei* examples, Behrens's lighter, smaller, unassumingly vernacular and self-contained forms, much indebted to the English pro-vernacular, suggest furniture that travels and is not immured, and that accommodates the mobile life of the urban nomad as Streiter envisaged it. As such they are closer to the Behrens of the AEG than of Darmstadt. But what is missing is the leap from artisan to industrial production, the rhetoric of mechanical assemblage.

The same is true of most contemporary evaluations—be they Muthesius's or Giedion's—as Behrens, van de Velde, and others had turned away from their early engagements with the luxury, made-to-measure aesthetic of Art Nouveau toward a rhetoric that embraced, visibly, mass production and mass consumption. This was true at least in appearance, even if the cost of production and of purchasing such objects still kept them within the sphere of luxury.[77] The industrial rhetoric so well described by Streiter as that of smooth, precise, simple, crisp, and consistent forms, to which the unaccustomed public will eventually adjust over repeated encounters, is what had become known as the machine aesthetic, regardless of whether the machine could in fact produce objects in its image, or even regardless of whether they were economically as attractive in practice as they were in theory.

The paradox that the aesthetic itself was well in advance of what industry could supply is well known by now. Both Behrens and later Le Corbusier "doctored" their production-line objects to conform to this aesthetic and produced objects as intensively crafted as any earlier *Kunstgewerbe* object.[78] As Stanford Anderson argued years ago, Behrens's Arc lamp for the AEG was not the result of assembly-line imperatives but of aesthetics (fig. 128).[79] Nor were many of the AEG objects even conceived or marketed for the masses. Making objects both aesthetically superior and widely affordable was as yet in the domain of utopia.[80] Designers like Behrens had learned that simplicity—as Le Corbusier intuited when he used the Parthenon triglyph, that icon of ancient classicism, to illustrate the standardized object—was about effect, not about actual simplicity of production. In fact, then as now, simplicity well executed was far more expensive than its cluttered and belabored "traditional" foil. Simplicity was about appearance, about representation, and existed in the domain of mimesis—a mimesis of what machines were supposed to look like and what they were thought to mean, not about actuality.

ADOLF LOOS AND NIHILIST OBJECT AESTHETICS

If for posterity Muthesius has remained the paradigmatic figure for the alliance between industry and art, it is Adolf Loos who became associated with the crisis of ornament and was seen as its principal voice. Although Loos was younger than Muthesius, their publishing activities overlapped, and to the latter's German perspective at the turn of the century Loos represents, albeit in his own idiosyncratic form, the ambiance of Vienna and its responses to the issues raised here. He trod very similar terrain, yet his approach was more provocative, and to Muthesius's constructive, government-official approach to a national industry he opposed a near-Dada (or pre-Dada) sensibility of provocation, or "épater les bourgeois," the better to raise an issue. Loos's target was ornament, and he administered its death blow with his essay "Ornament and Crime."[81] In his view, ornament was the sexual smear of a degenerate culture, akin to primitive man's tattoo, at odds with modern clothing, food, and objects of daily use. In short, it represented a throwback to a nostalgic past that had been long superseded. Such an attack may seem at odds with Semper, Wölfflin, or Riegl, and the emphasis of two generations of architects and scholars on ornament. Yet even as he struck out on his own he signaled that their object choices had been prophetic: the carpet, the tattoo, the inconspicuous objects of daily use turn up as his principal examples and governing metaphors in much the same way they did for his predecessors. So do clothes, intimate apparel, even food, in a peculiar blend of Riegl's anonymous object as carrier of *Kunstwollen* with Wölfflin's Gothic shoe. With Loos these loci, so tightly connected with the ornament and culture discussions of the nineteenth century, are imported front and center into the architecture debates, as leading images for the architect's imagination. This is a crucial moment: ornament and objects of daily use meet in the same essay, and ornament is cast out.

In 1898 Loos began publishing a series of acerbic articles ridiculing the contemporary Austrian decorative arts scene in the very same newspaper (*Neue Freie Presse*) where Riegl was also publishing at that time.[82] Ostensibly these articles were commentaries on the Austrian performance at the Great Exhibitions and at the Jubilee, and his attention, as architect, to these topics brings full circle the interaction between the world of objects at these great fairs and architecture. Moreover, the views expressed in these articles remained current for Loos, as they constituted the backbone of most of his later publishing, repeated and reused, even recycled time and again throughout his career well into the 1930s; they were the laboratory where he honed his architectural ideas. What is significant is that to get to architecture he felt he had to go through objects. If he did not outright develop a theory of objects as the communicating arm of architecture, he went a long way toward reinforcing their association and herded the discussion away from the academic world of the human sciences and into the realm of the practicing architect.

Like objects, the body also makes a strong showing in Loos's polemical writings. Although he condemned the tattoo as a viable expression for a modern society, his very focus on body covering and the objects pertaining to it revealed it to be an important co-relative for architecture. In "Ornament and Crime," for example, skin, crockery, boots, underclothes, cigarette cases, dresses—all part of the mobile layer that envelops the body and its gestures—are invoked by him as natural correspondents of the built environment, the cues that it must attend to. To be sure, his tone may have been that of one seeking a *succès de scandale,* and resonances from criminal anthropology to Marxist economics have been frequently noted. But beyond this, it is also clear that Loos is drawing on the very same string of nineteenth-century publications on domestic culture and anthropology that had influenced authors from Riegl to Wagner. If Stolpe and Colley-March or Haddon represented one strain in this literature, von Eye represented another, as did the publications on costume and the house by Eitelberger and Falke that sprung up around the Great Exhibitions in Loos's very own Vienna. Loos's essay on Arthur von Scala, director of the Museum für Kunst und Industrie ("Der Fall Scala"), shows him attuned to these debates, as knowledgeable as and siding with Riegl on issues related to *Kunstindustrie,* adamantly against the historical emphasis in the museums and viciously exposing the lack of support for contemporary work.[83]

Yet in the end Loos sets Riegl on his head: whereas Riegl dignified the crafts by lifting them up to the level of the noble arts, Loos levels the field by bringing the architecture of the house down to the level of the tailored suit. For him architecture is not an art, except the monument and the tomb. Instead, the domestic realm, the house, is one more body wrap, one more shell that cradles the body and that he presents in terms that recall forcibly Ernst Kapp as well as

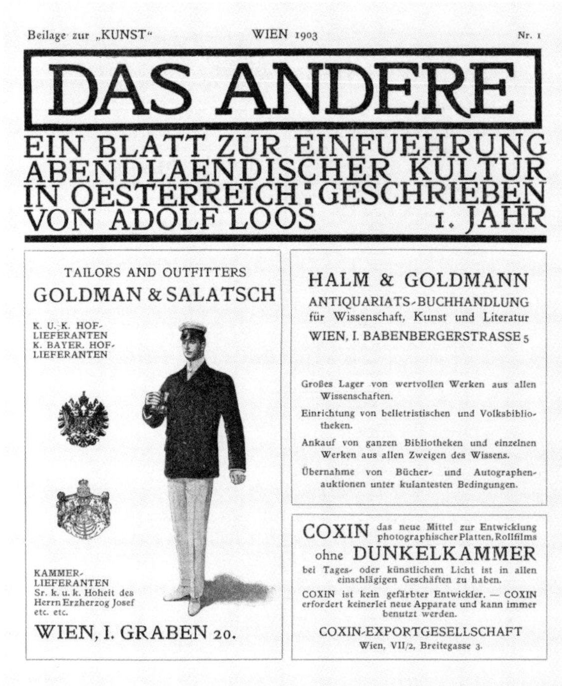

von Eye. The connection is not farfetched: as a student at Dresden, Loos certainly came across resonances of von Eye's work in that milieu, even if he had retired in 1878, some twenty years before Loos arrived there. The covers of his short-lived magazine *Das Andere* (1903), with nearly full-page advertising for a gentleman's black coat and a sailor's uniform, make the point—implicitly, ironically but also unmistakably (fig. 129). The trope remained current for him, and in 1910 he turned to it once more: "The black dress coat is in the style of our time. . . . When I finally received the task of building a house, I said to myself: a house can change externally only as much as a dress coat has changed. . . . I therefore had to replace the gold buttons with black buttons."[84]

Like so many of his generation, Loos began with Semper, a fact not noticed often enough.[85] This dependence is evident across the board, though nowhere more so than in his article "Glass and Clay" of June 26, 1898, in *Neue Freie Presse* (the article appeared after "Men's Clothing" and before "Ladies' Fashion"), in "Das Prinzip der Bekleidung" (also of 1898), in which he ruminates on this most central of all Semperian categories, and in articles such as "Footwear" ("Fussbekleidung"), which invites a deliberate intertextual link to *Bekleidung*. In "Glass and Clay" Loos starts out with a direct reading from Semper's *Der Stil*, particularly the passages on the Nile pitcher from the section on ceramics. His opening quote is Semper's observation that pots (and Loos adds "any implement") indicate the level of civilization of a people. This is perhaps the key to the

FIGURE 129
Adolf Loos, *Das Andere* (Vienna, 1903).

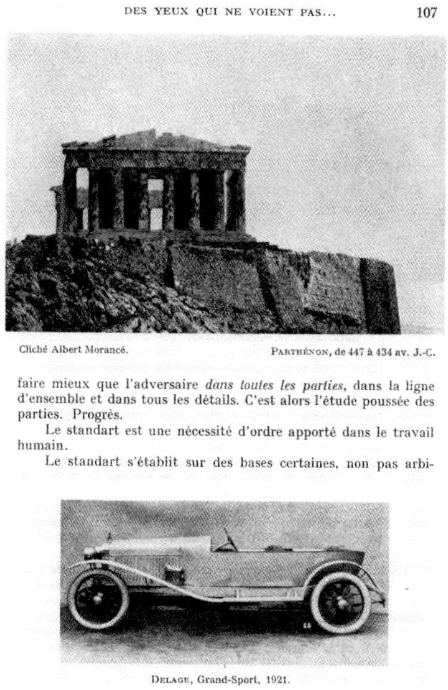
DES YEUX QUI NE VOIENT PAS... 107

Cliché Albert Morancé. PARTHÉNON, de 447 à 434 av. J.-C.

faire mieux que l'adversaire *dans toutes les parties*, dans la ligne d'ensemble et dans tous les détails. C'est alors l'étude poussée des parties. Progrès.

Le standart est une nécessité d'ordre apporté dans le travail humain.

Le standart s'établit sur des bases certaines, non pas arbi-

DELAGE, Grand-Sport, 1921.

FIGURE 130
Parthenon and Delage. From Le Corbusier, *Vers une architecture* (Paris, 1923).

subsequent readings of men's clothes, ladies' fashions, underclothes, references to food, shoes, footwear, hats, and umbrellas in his many essays in *Das Andere*, and in his "Ornament and Crime."

Treading in Semper's footsteps Loos appropriates an anthropological argument, and this allows him to locate architecture (provocatively in his case) among objects of daily use and to work by analogy. In "Glass and Clay" his point is to use the cultural aura associated with ancient Greek art to emphasize its fundamental dependence on practicality and "matter-of-factness." "The Greek vases are beautiful, as beautiful as a machine, as beautiful as a bicycle."[86] And he concludes: "Are there still people today who work as the Greeks worked? Yes, indeed! The English do as a nation, the engineers as a profession. The English and the engineers are our Greeks."[87] Published in Paris in 1921, these collected essays point directly to Le Corbusier: replace the Greek vase with the Parthenon triglyph and the bicycle with the Hispano Souiza and we have the essence of his provocative stance in favor of standardization from the *Esprit Nouveau* articles and *Vers une architecture* (fig. 130). If Le Corbusier's emphasis on standardization owes to Muthesius, the shock of the comparison, complete with its theoretical foundation in Semper, depends on Loos. Indeed, Loos equates issues of great cultural moment in the arts and architecture with elements of everyday life and defines the strategy of "not standing out" as being quintessential for modernity. He makes the point several times: "In order to be dressed correctly one must not stand out at the center of culture" turns up time and again, like a mantra.[88] What had been an application of an object-lesson from anthropology to architecture has become a full-fledged theory of modernity-as-anonymity.

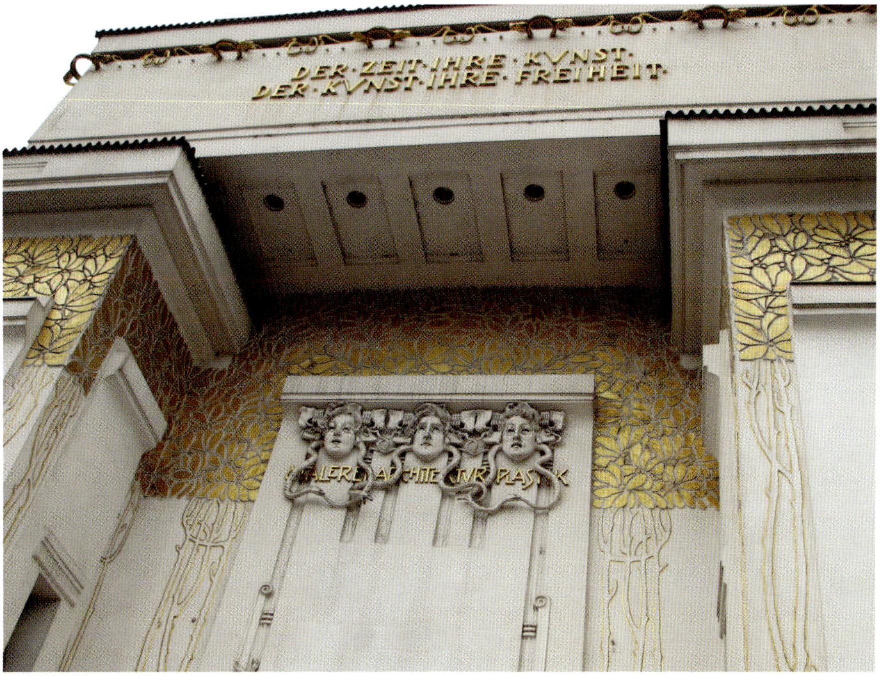

FIGURE 131
Joseph Maria Olbrich, Vienna Secession Building, Vienna, 1898. Artstor.

But this statement can also be understood as arising from his view that the objects permeating a culture (from the bicycle wheel to the clothes on one's back) are coherent with each other and the fundamental drivers of that culture. Delivered with a different rhetorical flourish, this once again rehearses Semper's conception of *Kunstindustrie* as ignition mechanism for high culture. What Loos opposes fiercely, like Muthesius, is the aesthetic of willful novelty of the Jugendstil, in particular the work of his bête-noire, Joseph Maria Olbrich, and the journal *The Studio* (fig. 131). The same thought, though more expansive, appears in *Das Andere* several years later, in the first issue, when once again he turns to clothes. Indeed, the entire issue of *Das Andere* is about "other" (*andere*) things than architecture: objects, behavior, shoes, saddles, clothes. It is a journal about modernity and modern life, and certainly a model for the *L'Esprit Nouveau* of the 1920s.

If in such articles Loos articulates an elliptical theory of harmonious culture that recalls Muthesius, what separates both from the apparently similar formulations of their Jugendstil colleagues, who also called for a coherent relationship between objects, from dress through cutlery and architecture, is their definition of culture itself (fig. 132). For Loos (in the footsteps of Semper), culture means all its manifestations and methods of production, without tearing anachronisms and without unduly privileging the arts, the traditional locus of Hegel's *Zeitgeist*. From this perspective, the Art Nouveau architect worked within a bubble of production and manufacturing that was discontinuous with the rest of culture, in the anthropological sense. For Loos these islands of taste, isolated in the sea of goods produced by society, are mirages somewhat like Potemkintowns, which he adduces as a metaphor nearly ten years later in "Ornament and Crime." To be sure, the term *Jugendstil* was not to be monolithically applied even at the time, as some of its signal architects—such as van de Velde—rejected its umbrella. But certain constants remained even in diversity.[89] And artistic living was one such constant to which even Muthesius subscribed, even if the artistic environment he promoted was eventually produced by the machine. Even more radical than Muthesius, Loos rejects the *Gesamtkunstwerk* concept particularly, since for him most architecture does not qualify as art, and certainly not domestic architecture. In taking this position he unsurprisingly rehearses the century-long debate on whether architecture was a free art that ran from Hegel through Schlegel to Hartmann and beyond.[90] But he also updates it: for him architecture is like clothes, literally, in that it fulfills a public function and must participate appropriately in a common discourse. From this perspective, too, the artistic house of Art Nouveau is not a viable option.[91]

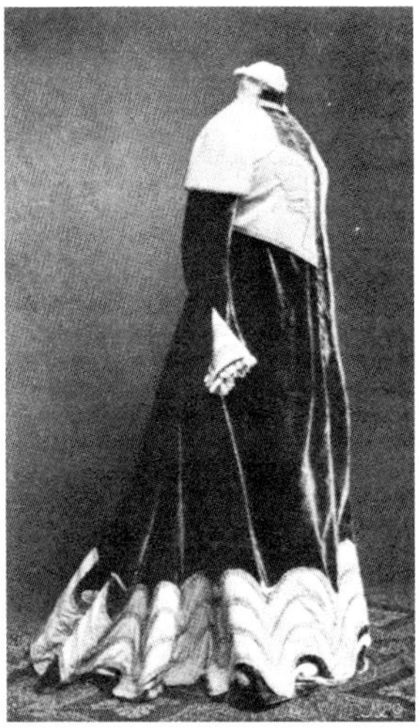

FIGURE 132
Peter Behrens, "Gesellschaftskleid." From *Deutsche Kunst und Dekoration Bd. 10* (1902), photograph S. 368–9.

Gurlitt, Falke, and, later, after the war, Josef Frank expressed much the same form of criticism of the over-aestheticized interior, both directly and couched in biting satire.[92] Indeed, educated in Dresden, where Gurlitt had taught since 1893, Loos may well have developed his own essay "Poor Little Rich Man" from Gurlitt's vignette in *Im Bürgerhause* (1888). In this satire Gurlitt ridiculed the overbearing architect who upbraids his client for introducing an object into his house without his approval. The disconnect between everyday life and the architect's vision of an interior as a work of art was a common thread of criticism. If with greater lucidity Streiter had expressed the quandary of the fin-de-siècle *Wohnungskultur* as that of the nomad vis-à-vis a built-in conception of heavy pieces that anchored family life for generations, others also identified the need to move away from totalizing interiors and abandon the *Garnitur* (matched furniture sets) mentality of the middle class toward single, lighter, simpler, and independent movable pieces.

After Loos proposes them as paradigms, what role do objects play in his vision of a modern architecture? Does he see them as a bridge between the abstraction of the building and the body of the viewer? He accepts, indeed advocates, the scattered, accidental object, but he does not reflect upon its function in a dialogue between architecture and its user. For one, empathy readings in the manner of Streiter are foreign to his deliberately matter-of-fact aesthetic. His architecture is one of restraint, of modest intervention, where the architect does not intrude upon the privacy of the user. He stands aside, content to see good, timeless objects inhabit his spaces, not seeking a stylistic correlation between them. The Chippendale chair, for example—in his view, the perfect chair—had its place in any modern interior; so did wicker and Thonet chairs, even if Le

Corbusier had stolen a march on him, he observes parenthetically, and popularized it with greater success.[93] It is in this tolerance that Tristan Tzara saw the distillation of Loos's architectural message when he contributed to his sixtieth-birthday *Festschrift*.[94] What makes objects modern for Loos is not a style or a historical period. They are modern only when they disappear, become invisible, or blend into their users' limbs and gestures, so closely are they tied to them. An Egyptian stool or a Thonet chair fulfills this requirement equally. Ornament is evidently redundant because it draws attention to itself instead of deflecting it. In a sense, Loos takes an ahistorical position, against the harmonious *Wohnungskultur* of his contemporaries. But in so doing he also takes the object/gesture relationship to its ultimate conclusion: neither is dependent on style.

Instead, for Loos materials have a meaning (once again a throwback to Semper) and take over where ornament leaves off. In a sense, Mies's onyx wall at the Barcelona Pavilion cannot be understood without Loos's Villa Karma or any other of his sumptuous if unornamented interiors. Yet even if he does not conceive of the objects of daily use as a bridge between building and the viewer's experience, he does put much thought on the table that could underpin such a connection. This approach ties him in interesting ways to the groundswell in favor of folk art. That he takes a decidedly anthropological approach to architecture, which he sees as part of material culture, is evident enough. This perspective may also have made him respond to the folk object, just as much as his own experience with the quality of artisanal work in his father's stone-cutting workshop. In this sense the authenticity of the village house by the mountain lake in his "Architecture" (1909) is in line with the impulse that moved Riegl to write *Hausindustrie* so as to defend it, and that made Muthesius finally embrace *Heimatschutz* within the Werkbund, or had moved Haberland to describe the peasant and his house as a snail in its shell. Like Streiter, Loos sees the modern town-dweller cut off from this natural continuity between self and house and its contents. In this world of alienation such a natural order is not possible—neither the user nor the architect have it in their power to create such objects. The best that can be hoped for is anonymity and restraint—the user's in his clothes as in his choice of architecture; the architect's in his resistance to design the full environment.[95] The objects of everyday use cannot be invented; they emerge spontaneously. Likewise in architecture, authenticity stops at the basic level of materials—wood, marble, brass, textiles, the basic units of Semper's *Der Stil,* all unfabricated, presented in their material simplicity. To Streiter's faith in the mediating power of objects, Loos opposes a nihilistic view. The underclothes, coats, saddles, shoes, and bicycles all are relevant to architecture—and he thrusts them into the foreground with a rhetorical power that equals only Semper's. But the architect cannot and should

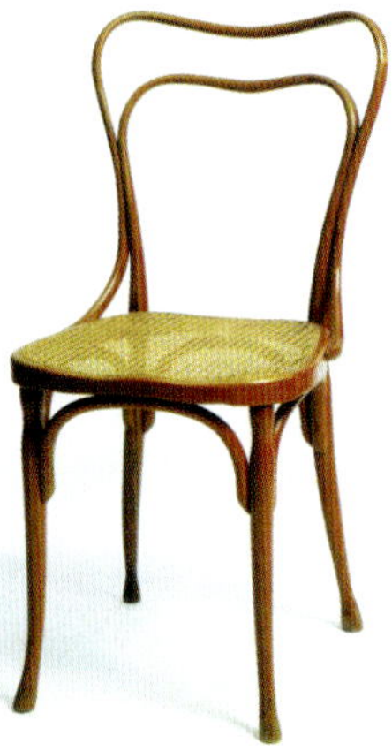

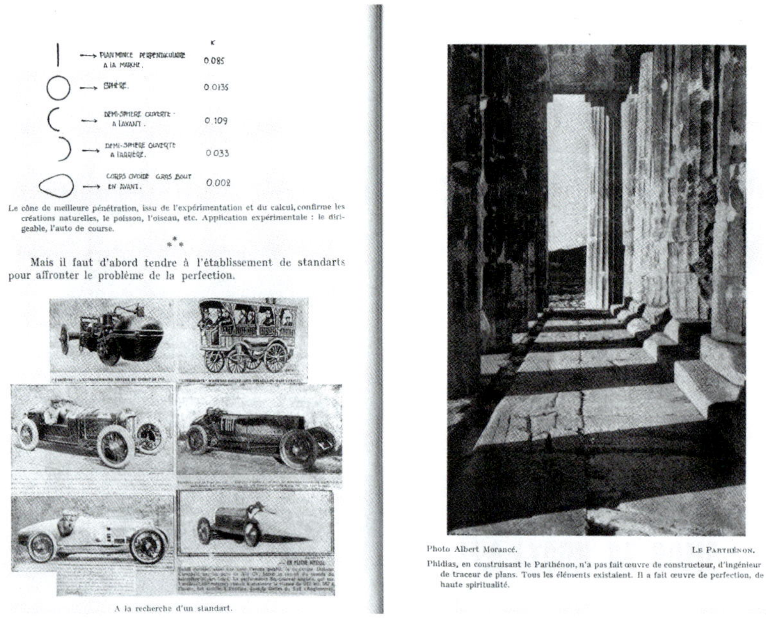

Le cône de meilleure pénétration, issu de l'expérimentation et du calcul, confirme les créations naturelles, le poisson, l'oiseau, etc. Application expérimentale : le dirigeable, l'auto de course.

***

Mais il faut d'abord tendre à l'établissement de standarts pour affronter le problème de la perfection.

A la recherche d'un standart.

Photo Albert Morancé. LE PARTHÉNON.

Phidias, en construisant le Parthénon, n'a pas fait œuvre de constructeur, d'ingénieur de traceur de plans. Tous les éléments existaient. Il a fait œuvre de perfection, de haute spiritualité.

not produce his own. His message is simple as to who gives the cue to whom: the house should be like the underclothes, not the underclothes like the house.

It may seem therefore something of a paradox that Loos designed furniture himself. Given that in his saddlemaker story published in *Das Andere* he ridicules the design culture that seeks to intervene from the top down and improve what artisans have perfected over centuries, this may indeed seem unexpected.[96] Yet his furniture is odd when compared with any produced by his contemporaries. It is openly derivative and recalling well-known pieces—the English Windsor armchair, the Thonet bentwood chair, the Egyptian stool, the Chippendale dining chair. The differences are small, and mostly in the direction of simplification, of reduction, of perfecting an established form without apparent intervention. They move in the direction of the timeless tool, so well adapted to its function that its insertion into a house or a café or a store is practically unnoticeable. In some ways this move recalls Neumann and his concept of the *gewöhnlich* and "normal," as well as Theodor Fischer's plea for interiors that allow the users to be the actors and recede into the background, though one to which he did not give actual shape. The Museum Café chair (1899), the Stossler dining chair (1899), the Café Capua chair (1913), the stool in the Stresser house (1918), the ladder-back chairs in the Brummel residence (1928), and the fan-back Windsor chair for the Vogl residence (1929) show Loos at work making small changes, optimizing what already exists rather than reinventing the wheel (fig. 133).[97] The process is that of refining a standard, an idea that Le Corbusier would illustrate so convincingly with his comparison of the Delage automobile and the details of the Parthenon

Left **FIGURE 133**
Adolf Loos, chair for the Café-Museum, 1899. From Eva Ottillinger, *Adolf Loos Wohnkonzepte und Möbelentwürfe* (Salzburg: Residenz, 1994).

Right **FIGURE 134**
"Standart." From Le Corbusier, *Vers une architecture*.

(fig. 134). Beautifully crafted out of prime quality materials most often by his trusted and irreplaceable carpenter Josef Veillich, the furnishings take their cue from mass-produced wares, reversing the direction that the *Kunstgewerbe* movement had sought to develop.[98] The prototype is not produced by the designer in the hope of providing leadership for industry. Instead, the industrial object becomes the source of models that the designer very lightly adjusts. Like the objects with long traditions, whether of elite or folk origin—be they Chippendale or English farmhouse chairs—the objects of industry (like the Thonet chair) have also undergone natural optimization and editing along the way in a process that for Loos comes close to the Darwinian "survival of the fittest." As such they already embody the modern system of production and its aesthetic sensibility of "matter-of-factness" that requires very little tweaking on a designer's part (fig. 135).

Even more striking, given the contemporary preferences, is that Loos's rooms are decidedly not conceived as coordinated ensembles. Instead they have the comfortable feeling of a casual mixture of objects—all well chosen for representing the best response to a particular need, but certainly not stylistically uniform. Nowhere does Loos embrace the *Garnitur* mentality, furniture pieces designed "to go with" each other and create a coherent group. Therein lies perhaps the most radical stance that Loos took relative to style and objects: all objects

FIGURE 135
Adolf Loos, sitting room, 1902. From Ottillinger, *Adolf Loos Wohnkonzepte und Möbelentwürfe.*

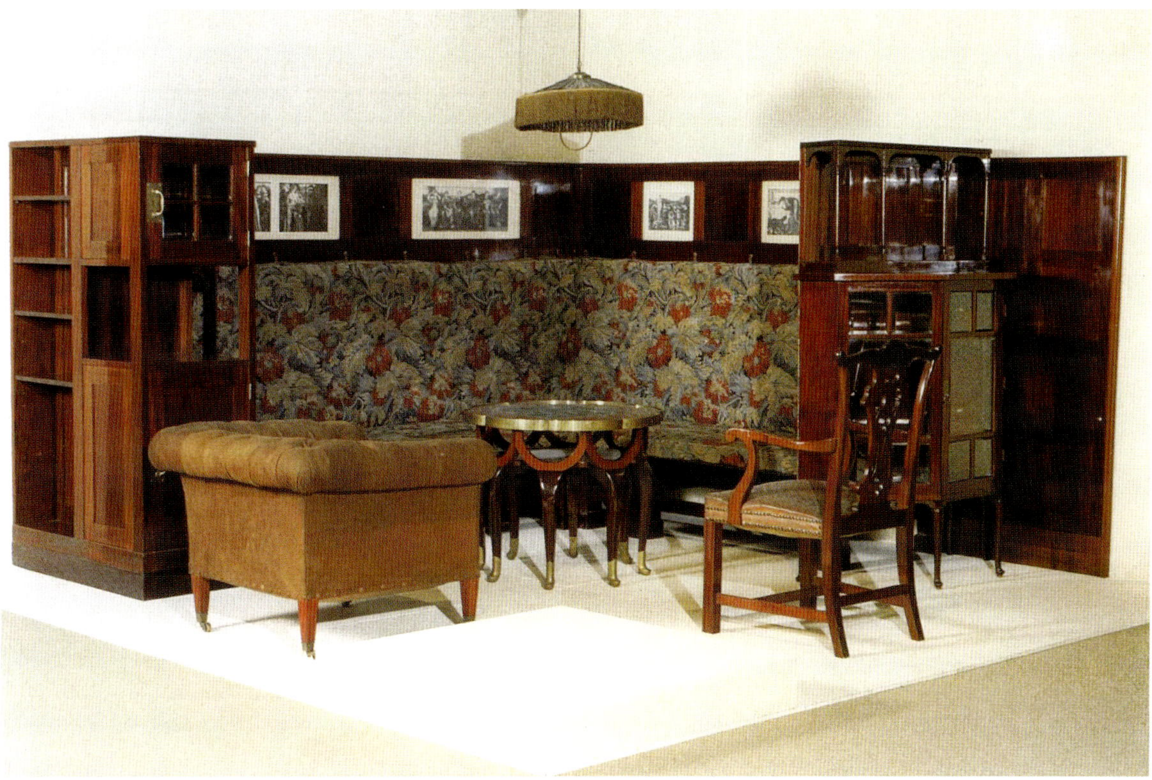

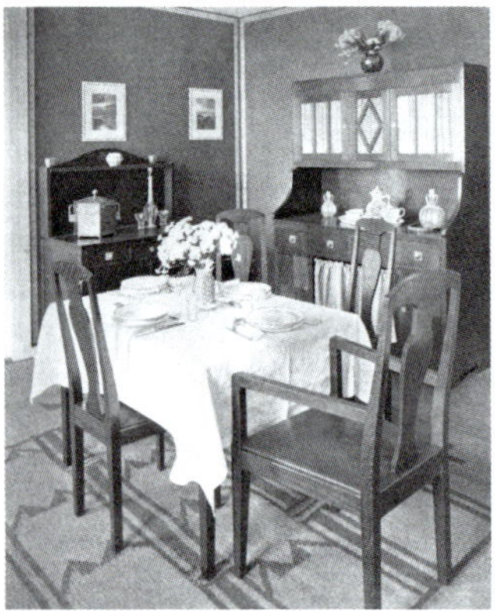

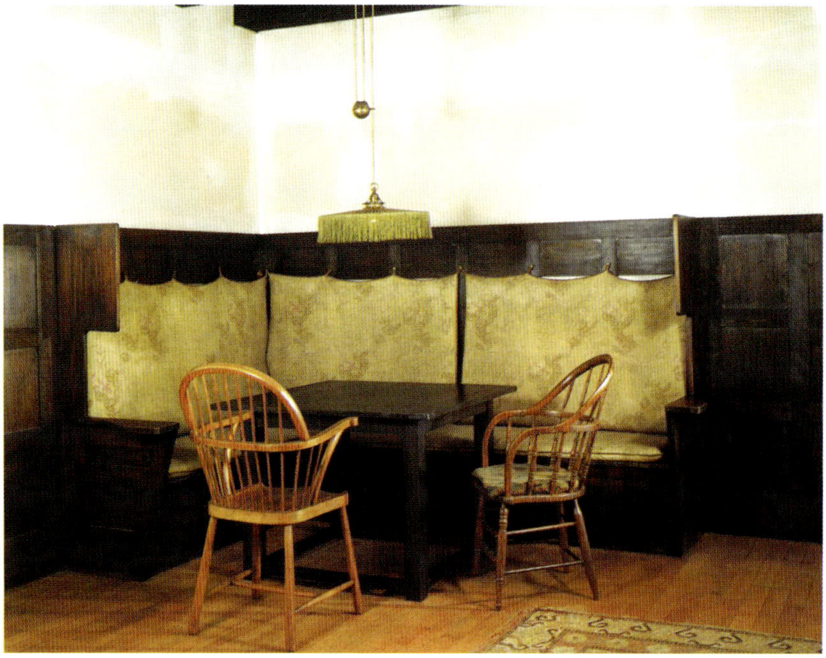

that perform well are modern. This went far beyond what was advocated by Muthesius or other members of the Werkbund, such as Richard Riemerschmid with his *Maschienenmöbel,* or Bruno Paul, who otherwise seemed on the cutting edge of modernist approaches with his standardized and mass-produced *Typenmöbel,* as mobile as any Loos would have conceived himself (fig. 136).[99] If anything, this approach gave actual shape to the concept of the mobile and light urban nomad that Streiter saw as quintessentially modern and that Loos likewise identified. Light pieces that did not look anchored, either to each other or to their locations—occasionally even in Loos's own living spaces—suggested the idea of a lightweight "encampment," of a mobile lifestyle (fig. 137).

In 1930 when he published *Trotzdem* Loos perceived his life's work and greatest contribution to modern architecture to have been his stance, indeed his war, on ornament.[100] In his preface he is both bitter and reflective as he considers his two volumes (*Ins Leere gesprochen* and *Trotzdem*) as the documents of that war, his claim to leadership in the face of latter-day heroes.[101] On this issue his criticism of the Werkbund catalogue *Form ohne Ornament* of 1924 may be unfair—Wolfgang Pfleiderer, who wrote the introduction, may owe much more to Karl Gross's article in the 1912 Werkbund *Jahrbuch* than to Loos himself. From this reflective perspective it is interesting to see what articles Loos chooses to republish in order to substantiate his claim. Read as a whole, they are remarkably consistent, even repetitive and uncompromising, from first to last: shoes, leather goods, clothes, furniture, and objects of daily use (*Gebrauchsgegenstande*) are used as examples of

Left **FIGURE 136**
Bruno Paul, Typenmöbel dining room, 1908. Kat. Typenmöbel, 1908.

Right **FIGURE 137**
Adolf Loos, sitting area of the Loos-Wohnung, 1903. From Ottillinger, *Adolf Loos Wohnkonzepte und Möbelentwürfe.*

modern style and in opposition to all self-consciously style-seeking efforts—be they of the Secession group or of the Werkbund (who found him disturbing in any event and sought to distance him). Unlike the position of many of the twentieth-century "doers" like Le Corbusier, Muthesius, and other proselytizers, Loos's stance remains unique: leave things alone, or, as he puts it in the title of one of his essays: "Hands off."[102] And in an essay written as a response to the Werkbund 1908 congress, he asks provocatively: "Do we need applied artists?"[103] In words that echo Streiter and certainly influenced Le Corbusier he lists those objects that require no input to be modern and to have "grown into" our every day gestures and sensibilities (*verwachsen* is his term): cars, glasses, optical instruments, luggage, saddles, cigarette cases, clothes.[104] Despite apparent similarities, for him Muthesius is only good in theory, when he sets out the goals of the Werkbund, but not in practice (figs. 138, 139). The mission to create a new contemporary culture is at odds with Loos's conception of who or what is the driver: "We didn't sit in such a way because a carpenter made the chair in this way," he argues. "The carpenter made the chair this way because this is how we want to sit."[105] Unobtrusively, unnoticed, the modern culture is all around, particularly in those components of what we now call "material culture" that are on the periphery of attention and as such the most authentic signs of modernity (figs. 140, 141). And once again, Loos lists shoes and boots, luggage and horse buckles, cigarette cases and watches, walking sticks and umbrellas.

On the face of it, Loos looks at odds with the story I'm telling here—taking a position against intervention, he does not insert the object in the place of ornament, as that which carries the elliptical discourse about architecture, as its discursive site. And yet despite this resistance, he too thrusts it into the foreground. For him the objects of daily use are the signs or tropes of modernity. They contain the cue, the essence of what it is to be modern. Undecorated, they signal the direction architecture must travel: toward the elimination of ornament.[106] When it comes to objects of daily use his attitude is hands off; when it

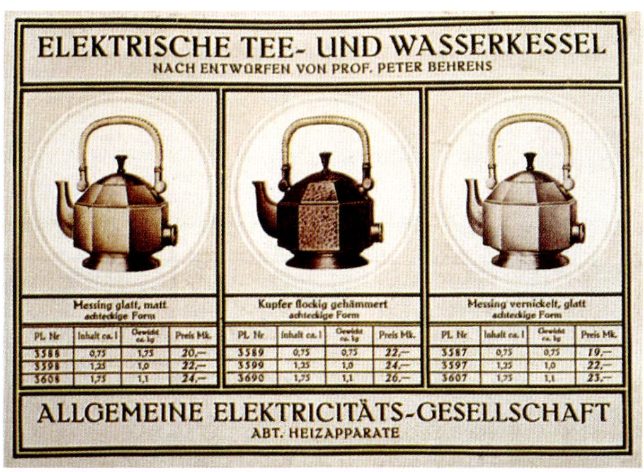

FIGURE 138
Peter Behrens, Electrical tea and water kettles. AEG Price List, "Elektrische Heiz-und Kochapparte," July 1912.

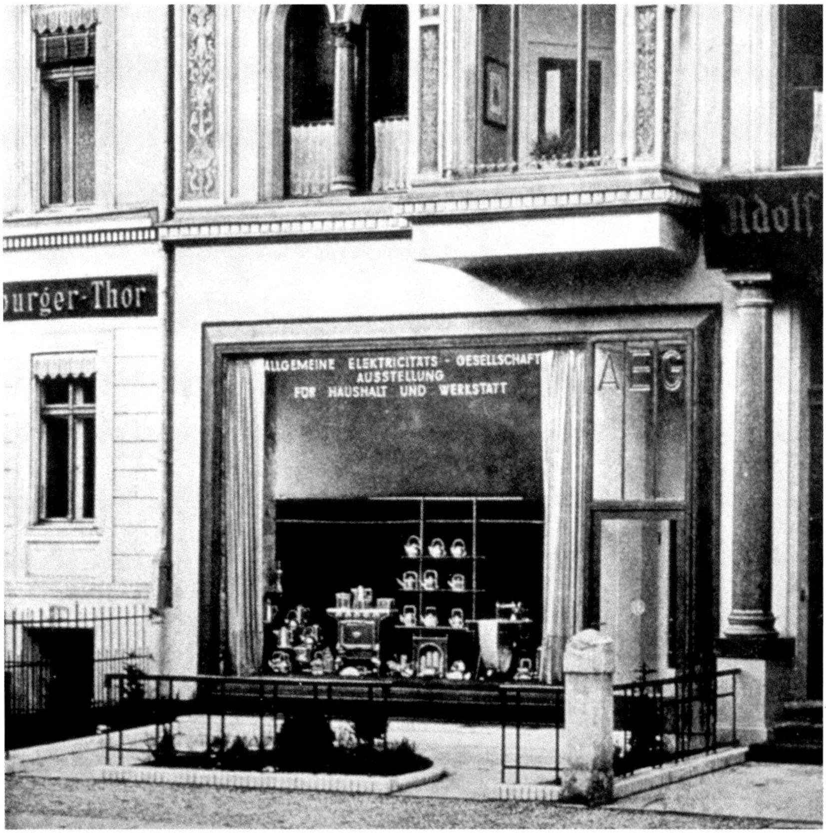

comes to furniture he opposes the Bauhaus as the latest in a string of groups that seek to design all aspects of life, and that he had ridiculed one by one. For him furniture should be left to the carpenter and the upholsterer, as they will naturally, indeed inevitably, produce modern pieces. And he distinguishes a world of mobile pieces that are the domain of the craftsman not the architect. In German, he notes, *mobil* (mobile) and *Möbel* (furniture) have the same root. Several years later, Charlotte Perriand would make the same argument with reference to the French *mobile* and *meubles* and their root in the Latin *mobilis* when defending the furniture of Le Corbusier's team in *The Studio* (1929).[107] For Loos, mobile pieces do not belong to the architect. Like his perennial examples (shoes, luggage, and so forth), they are modern without intervention because they belong to daily life, they serve modern life: "Only furniture that is mobile can be modern. . . . Everything matches everything because they are all modern," he would argue in 1924.[108] Like Streiter, he notices the connection between mobility and modernity and points to the heavy, ponderous storage containers (cupboards, armoires, buffets, vitrines, sideboards) as so many anachronisms. Less categorical than Le Corbusier, who effectively preached for a pared down existence of few belongings, or Streiter, who saw the modern city dweller as a

FIGURE 139
Peter Behrens, Allgemeine Elektricitäts-Gesellschaft shop window. Bildarchiv Foto Marburg.

nomad, traveling light from apartment to apartment, Loos nevertheless puts his finger on the root of modern living.

Despite appearances, Loos and Muthesius did not promote the same definition of modernity. Although both figure in history as modernism's core begetters, there are more differences between them than are generally acknowledged. Loos's critique of the Werkbund was not the reaction of a crotchety lone wolf of architecture but the recognition of a fundamental divide between them. Even if Loos seemed tied to a crafts approach to objects, like many of his Austrian compatriots, what he called for was far more radical than anything Muthesius or the Werkbund envisaged. Despite all his protestations, Muthesius still saw the house as a *Gesamtkunstwerk* within the control of the architect/artist. If he engaged industry in promoting a quality conception of goods, it was still with this ideal in mind: industry was seen as the potential producer of artistic objects under the leadership of architects such as Behrens at the AEG or Karl Schmidt at Hellerau (his longtime friend and inspiration).[109] Although he rejected Art Nouveau's crafts aspect and idiosyncratic design for not being attuned to mass production, he did promote a collaboration between artists and industry. His conception was top-down and profoundly interventionist.

Loos, on the other hand, saw modernity as the status quo—and the manifestations of this modernity did not need to be invented but were already there, since they supported life as it was lived. That is why he turns to clothes and luggage and tries to remove objects from the tyranny of design. His position, if anything, is anti-design: choose what is already there if it is good; don't reinvent the wheel, only adjust it slightly. This is why ancient Egyptian and contemporary Thonet chairs could figure in his interiors with equal success and also why his interiors do not look homogenous. He did not wish to design modern objects—he wanted to place those objects, which were unself-consciously modern, inside his houses and interiors. Matter-of-fact and restrained like his own buildings, they were the natural extensions of modern living. But perhaps more than anything else that Loos put on the table was his war on ornament, which he waged *with* objects. Somewhat like Warburg, he was a most sensitive seismograph who recognized objects' binary and inverse relationship even if he did not articulate it in precisely these terms. It is also Loos who brought architecture, ornament, and objects into one coherent discourse and unequivocally privileged objects as paradigms for and profoundly relevant to architecture. Yet, however different Muthesius and Loos may have been, they shared one thing: the objects of daily use were the principal location of their respective radicalism and the vehicle through which they sought to operate change.

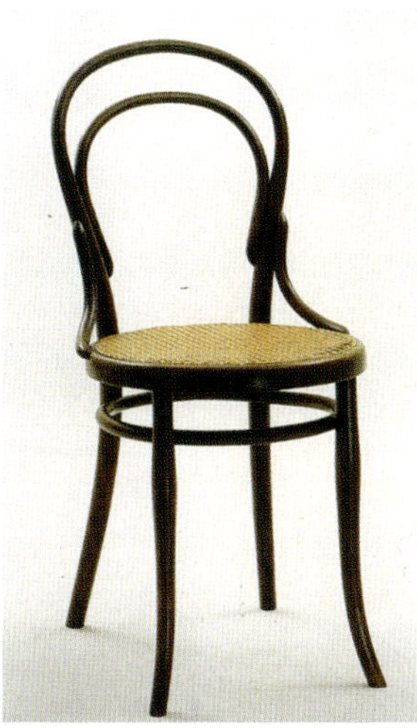

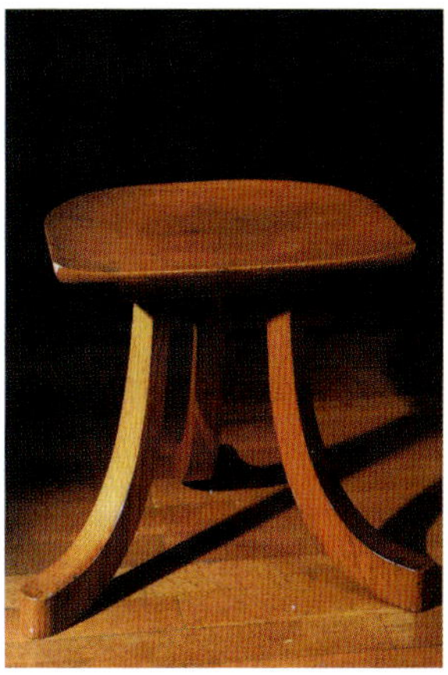

Above, top **FIGURE 140**
Adolf Loos, Thonet chair, 1899. From Ottillinger, *Adolf Loos Wohnkonzepte und Möbelentwürfe.*

Above **FIGURE 141**
Adolf Loos, Egyptian stool, 1903–27. From Ottillinger, *Adolf Loos Wohnkonzepte und Möbelentwürfe.*

6 | The Aftermath

Bauhaus Endgame and Le Corbusier's Poetics of Portability

> Decorative arts = mechanical system that surrounds us, which is no more than the extension of our limbs; its elements in fact artificial limbs. Decorative art becomes orthopedic...a craft analogous to the tailor. —LE CORBUSIER, *The Decorative Art of Today* (1925)

BAUHAUS ENDGAME

The 1910s and 1920s mark the explosion of objects as subjects. This time not in the academic disciplines or museums, or in the popularizing literature of manuals, but as sites of intense artistic exploration, foregrounded in a number of media—in art, architecture and film, by Cubists and Dadaists, in the context of the Bauhaus and Soviet revolutionary art, in magazines such as *Veshch/Objet/Gegenstand* (thing/object) or *G*.[1] From this perspective architecture's relationship to objects may seem to be one more rivulet swelling the vast flow of this stream. Yet each one of the arts arrived here along its own riverbank, which shaped its course as well as its character. In architecture this turn to the object has been most often associated with the Bauhaus in its 1920s glory, the iconic modernist site that picked up the baton from the Deutsches Werkbund, Muthesius's brainchild, and developed its project. Yet the Bauhaus was the endgame of a long history that had started in earnest in 1851.

As the immediate inheritor of a highly developed discourse on the object, the Bauhaus became the site of a collision between two impulses: of the object as economic site, and of architecture's relationship to it. For several decades, collaborations between artists and manufacturers toward artist-designed goods had grown into the main issue surrounding objects. It was the most economically relevant discussion and therefore the most sustained one. With Peter Behrens (an architect, though trained as an artist) very visibly at the helm of the AEG and controlling the designs for all its wares, the architect was given a principal role in the conception of the equipment of modern life. In his persona therefore the two impulses seemed to converge. And it is this convergence that caused the discourse on objects to take a particular flavor at the Bauhaus.

Indeed the Bauhaus, especially under Walter Gropius, sought to produce a generation of designers who could build a society of consumers in step with modernity, which was understood not only as an aesthetic but also a political phenomenon. In so doing it merged a century-long engagement with the object with the new idea of the avant-garde that pressed upon it from the more radicalized sister arts—painting, sculpture, and photography. Yet although it seemed to have opened a new chapter, all the while it was building on the ruins of what was left. For the Bauhaus did not spring fully formed from Gropius's head; rather, the school that he recovered from its ashes after WWI was built upon the foundations of a *Kunstgewerbeschule* conceived in the full sense of the nineteenth-century reforms.

In a way, the Bauhaus was Semper's Museum für Metalltechnik turned into a school. All materials and types of crafting were represented, except architecture: bookbinding, graphic printing, joinery (led by Gropius), woodcarving and sculpture (toys), weaving, metal, and stained glass, mural painting, and textile. Ironically, there was never any systematic architecture teaching at the early Bauhaus in Weimar; the architecture studio was finally introduced in Dessau on April 1, 1927, under the leadership of Swiss architect Hannes Meyer.[2] Yet despite its absence, architecture remained at the center. From the beginning all the workshops were accretive and seen to produce *bauen* (construction).[3]

However, by this stage the original Semperian aims that constituted the foundations of the Weimar Arts and Crafts school founded by Henry van de Velde in 1907 (as the Grand-Ducal Saxon School of Arts and Crafts) were neither straightforward nor uncomplicated.[4] Granted, the view that the object of everyday use was a key ingredient in the individual's participation in modernity, in the large scale of architecture and the city, was still a fundamental and unquestioned premise of the school and its ideals. So was the ambition to intervene at the industrial level by creating the modern standards (or archetypes) of everything that surrounded the body in its domestic environment. But the consequences of such assumptions in the reality of a mature industrial economy became increasingly problematic, revealing profound contradictions at the very heart of the Bauhaus—the problems that were embedded when Muthesius's (rather than Loos's) direction was followed at the fork in the road. The didactic mission that underpinned the Bauhaus from its inception was one such source of contradictions. So was authorship as artistic agency. And so was the relationship between the arts.[5]

The imperative to teach, the didactic mission, came with the nineteenth-century inheritance. The Bauhaus was a school and a school-based philosophy. The original Weimar *Gewerbeschule* under van de Velde belonged to this world, and albeit the war emptied it and denied him reentry, the foundations remained, no matter how strident the differences were made to appear later. *What was made*

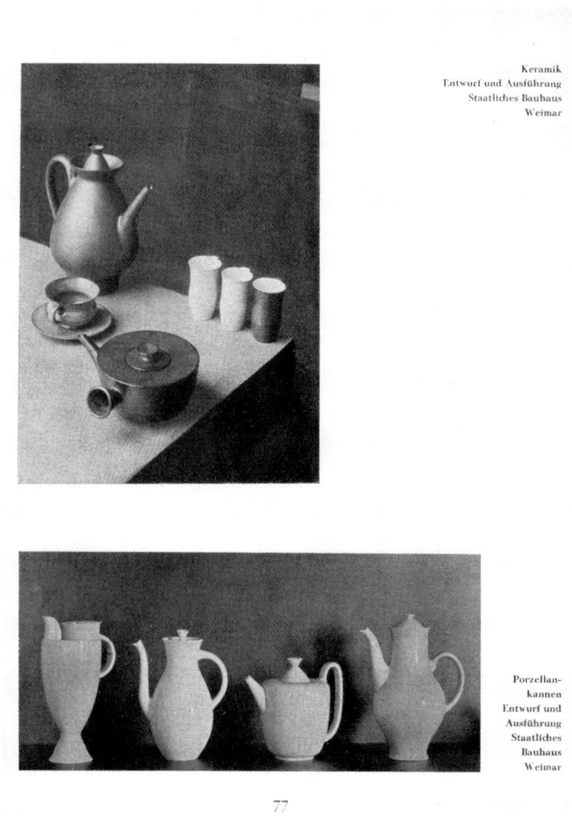

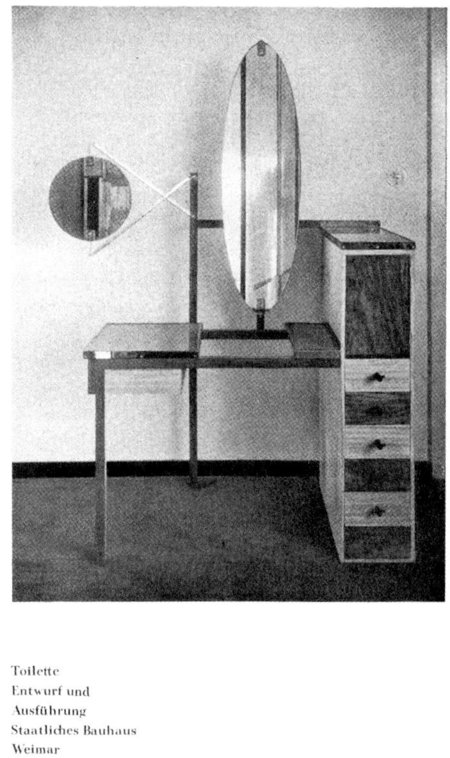

Left **FIGURE 142**
Ceramics and porcelain vessels. Design and execution Bauhaus, Weimar. *Die Form ohne Ornament* (Berlin, 1924).

Right **FIGURE 143**
Toilette. Design and execution Bauhaus, Weimar. *Die Form ohne Ornament.*

had to have been taught. Yet not all art is discursive. Loos did not teach, nor did Le Corbusier; both wrote but did not devise a pedagogical method of conveying their ideas to others. Teaching at the Bauhaus meant that a didactic stance also suffused its physical output. This is not the same as proselytizing for one's ideas—which architects had done since time immemorial. Rather, it meant that when the model house was conceived, so was the model life, and both were presented as "lessons." And this stance was deeply tied to a *Gesamtkunstwerk* mentality, and alongside it to a commitment to crafting all details, to leaving nothing to chance.

True to its didactic mission, therefore, the entire ensemble in which modern life unfolded was pre-thought at the Bauhaus—from cups and spoons to furniture and carpets (figs. 142, 143). The interior of the "Haus am Horn," the exhibition house of 1923, was entirely fitted out with objects manufactured in the school workshops, from the Pyrex dishes (Jena glass) in the kitchen to the light fixtures in the sitting room. Although it looked simpler, less visually cluttered, almost ascetic, it was not substantially different from the earliest architecture projects associated with the Bauhaus, such as the Sommerfeld House of 1921—a commission of Gropius's but executed with the Bauhaus workshops (fig. 144).

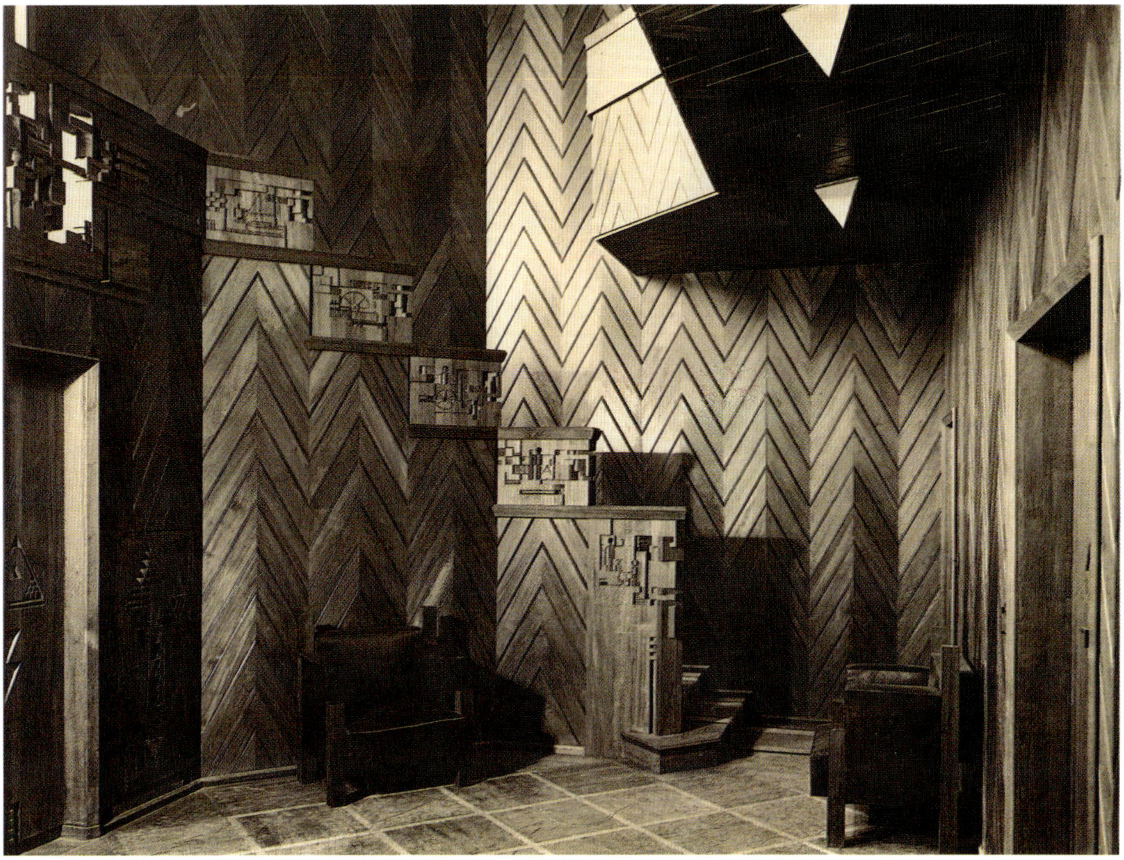

In both nothing was left to chance, nothing penetrated from outside. Clearly this was not an Art Nouveau approach; the objects were proclaiming machine production and submitting to its visual vocabulary. Nor were they site specific, rooted to their spot, built into walls, or fastened to the floor. But the complete environment that they formed and the desire to intervene at the smallest level was reminiscent of Muthesius's "artistic house" and Behrens's Darmstadt one, where the objects belonged together far more tightly than their movable quality suggested. In short, the 1923 Bauhaus prototype was a socially aware version of the aestheticized house of 1900—not spontaneously produced by contemporary forces as envisioned by Loos, but the result of top-down intervention. Ultimately the social mission of the Bauhaus overlapped with its didactic one and contradicted its claim to be a seismograph (rather than inventor) of modernity and mass culture. The object was a means of integration, of locating the user within modernity, a means of access—even if prescriptive and didactically conceived. Architecture was its setting but, more accurately, its support: a cubic house with no trace of ornament, be it sculpted or surface-based, became more discursively modern and persuasive with objects in it.

FIGURE 144
Entrance hall, Sommerfeld House, Berlin, 1920/1. Walter Gropius and the Bauhaus. Bauhaus Archiv.

Of course the *Gesamtkunstwerk* lay hidden behind the appearance of mass-production that the Bauhaus objects proclaimed. And likewise behind the visual rhetoric of the production-line—reinforced by the Bauhaus GmbH limited company founded by Gropius in November 1925, complete with a catalogue of its products—artistic agency was still its driving mechanism.[6] Nothing reveals it better than the arguments about authorship, brought to a head by Marcel Breuer, who rebelled against Gropius and insisted on signing his furniture pieces.[7] Indeed, all objects were carefully designed by artists purposely trained to identify the "essence" of modernity; the "total work of art" was totally controlled. The same was true of the engagement with furniture of Mies van der Rohe, the last Bauhaus director. Although his furniture designing was of short duration (1927–32), it was an important component of his houses. Transparent and seemingly lightweight—floating on air—his furniture communicated the "intentions" of the architecture—of the 1927 Werkbund house, of the Barcelona Pavilion, of the Tugendhat House. Indeed, for all their subsequent (limited) mass production, the various variants of the cantilever tubular chair, the chaise longue, the scissor-shape chair and stool, the Brno chair were conceived and custom made for specific projects; they were part and parcel of a holistic design, its rhetorical arm.[8]

To be sure, in his Coop Zimmer of 1926—one of the images with which this book began—Hannes Meyer came much closer to Loos's understanding of the genuinely anonymous object as diagnostic of modernity than to that of the Gropius Bauhaus. Yet he is not representative of the school's philosophy despite being its director for a short while. Ultimately he rejected the Bauhaus, and more importantly, the Bauhaus rejected him. A testament to and a critique of what the Bauhaus was and could never become, his work spoke to a different definition of modernity.[9] And it is profoundly telling of the will to return to the school's craft-based roots that when he was dismissed in 1930 he was replaced by Mies.

Thus for all the talk about agency at the Bauhaus and its programmatic rejection—the experiments with chance, paper cutting, photography that distanced the hand of the maker, the imperative not to sign work—it remained a top-down system of artistic intervention. Moreover, as Robin Schuldenfrei has argued, many of the objects were luxury items and became part of upper-middle-class chic, while real mass production and mass access, like mass appeal, remained essentially unrealized goals.[10] The key issue was appearance—the appearance of "anonymity," of mass production, the "look" of machine tooling that the objects proclaimed even though they were frequently made by hand and in expensive materials. Craftsman-made, just like other objects exhibited in the Werkbund shows, but "attributed" to the community and to industry/machine, these objects played a game of hide-and-seek with the maker.

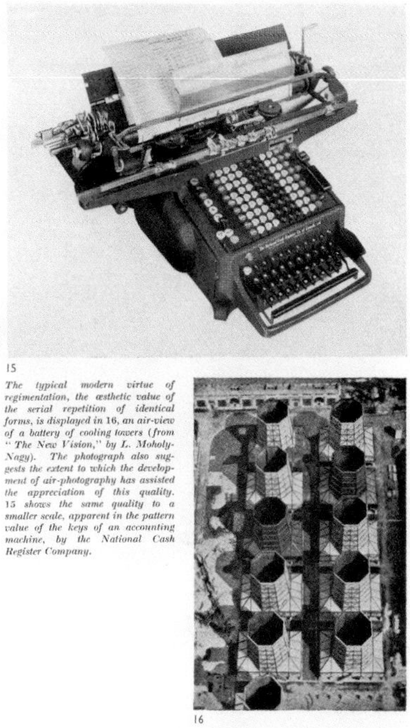
15

The typical modern virtue of regimentation, the æsthetic value of the serial repetition of identical forms, is displayed in 16, an air-view of a battery of cooling towers (from "The New Vision," by L. Moholy-Nagy). The photograph also suggests the extent to which the development of air-photography has assisted the appreciation of this quality. 15 shows the same quality to a smaller scale, apparent in the pattern value of the keys of an accounting machine, by the National Cash Register Company.

16

FIGURE 145
Illustration from J. M. Richards, "Towards a Rational Aesthetic," *Architectural Review* 78 (July–December 1935).

Although the economic/societal role of the object was addressed at length, how the object acted with respect to architecture and the viewer was not articulated in so many words at the Bauhaus. Nevertheless, its place and its importance can be teased out of its relationship with the other arts, with sculpture in particular. Indeed, at the Bauhaus the importance received by the object existed in inverse relationship to that accorded to sculpture, for theirs was a site of collision. The object now claiming the attention of the artist—the toy, the lamp, the teapot, the chair—had taken over as sculpture and moved it to another workshop, gutting the traditional sculpture studio of its significance. In his introduction to the Werkbund catalogue of the 1924 exhibition *Form ohne Ornament,* Wolfgang Pfleiderer approaches the objects of daily use precisely as miniature sculptures.[11] In his view the artists who turn to "technical forms" find them to be the "most powerful and liveliest aesthetic symbols of the times," and it is precisely because these near-abstract forms are "forms without ornament" that they are interchangeable with sculpture. Once the applied ornament on cups and teapots, vases and furniture was removed, these objects could enter the domain of (abstract) sculpture. Devoid of any mimetic charge, they invited the formal exploration of simple, abstract shapes. The idea that sculpture resided in all objects—no matter how small or large, and this included architecture—was not lost on the Bauhaus reception. In his article in the *Architectural Review* of 1935 it is precisely this slippage across scales that J. M. Richards underlines (fig. 145).[12] And in the

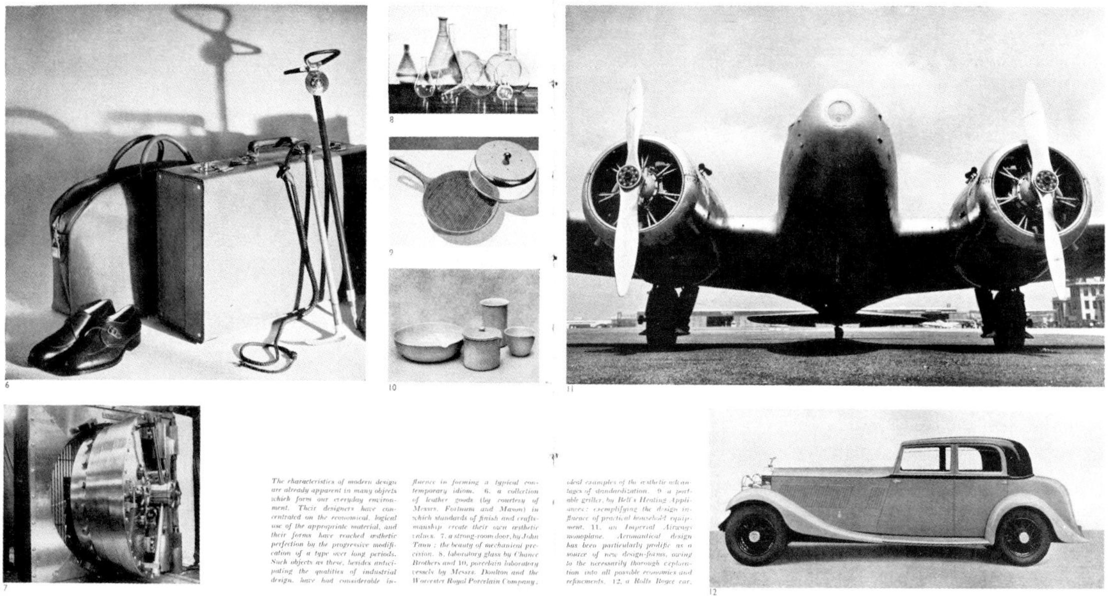

same journal, reviewing Herbert Read's *Art in Industry* (1934), Christian Barman presents objects (large and small) as equivalents to abstract sculpture: typewriters and cooling towers, seaplanes and die-makers' squares—"although very different things, they are beautiful for the same reasons" (fig. 146).[13] The choice of image was not innocent: Gropius's typewriter, photographed by Lucia Moholy, was perceived by both of them as iconic and of great value in publications and lectures.[14] Precisely because the Bauhaus never produced an object such as this, it was also iconic of the aspirations for the anonymous object it had held and never quite attained (fig. 147).

LE CORBUSIER AND *L'ART DÉCORATIF D'AUJOURD'HUI*

Perhaps the best way to reflect on the vicissitudes of the discourse on architecture and objects in the years when the project and forms of modernism were established is to come full circle and return to Le Corbusier. If in the nineteenth century the object/architecture relationship was incubating, with Le Corbusier it came to a head. Much of his intellectual education was tributary to German theory before the Great War, and Muthesius and Loos, Behrens and Berlin left a deep imprint on his views.[15] Paradoxically, he may be seen as the most powerful proselytizer for German architecture theory in the heroic years of modernism. Written in French, his syntheses were not only more accessible to non-German readers, but they also enjoyed the aura associated with Paris as the center of the artistic avant-garde. German architects were more insular in this respect, and their real impact outside of Germany came later, with the exodus of the

FIGURE 146
Illustration from J. M. Richards, "Towards a Rational Aesthetic."

intelligentsia (especially to America) after Hitler's rise to power. Implicitly Giedion highlighted this phenomenon in *Space, Time and Architecture* when he outlined the achievements in the arts that led to the rise of architectural modernism and listed French, Dutch, and Russian artistic movements while passing over the Germans in silence.[16]

To be sure, it may have seemed more natural to end with the Bauhaus, with Gropius, Meyer, and Mies, for after all they represented the legitimate epiphany of the Werkbund generation's travails and would logically extend the thread of the German-speaking argument I have followed. But Le Corbusier provides opportunities for insight that are more useful to examine in closing. For one thing, his is a moment of stock-taking, and he represents a perspective from outside that interprets and makes use of the German-speaking discourse developed over the past seventy years or more. The very fact that he is an interloper in this story demonstrates that the ideas on objects had "arrived," that they had permeated a culture of architectural thinking so thoroughly that an outsider could make use of them and disseminate them as if self-understood truths. For another, Le Corbusier inscribes himself within the literary tradition of architects and treatise writers; he writes and reflects upon this period and this very topic in the 1920s, while his Austrian and German counterparts do not, and certainly not to the same degree. Indeed, one could argue that his *L'art décoratif d'aujourd'hui* (1925) represents a milestone as the last in a century-long tradition of publications on the decorative arts. Most importantly, like Semper's *Der Stil,* it was written by an architect, and it had a similar impact. Finally, his personal and, some would argue, flawed perspective on the state of discourse had a remarkable afterlife, and he remained the most widely read disseminator of these ideas. Even when at odds with him later—as Pevsner, for example, undoubtedly was—scholars and architects could not but engage his polemic.[17] Speaking as someone "who had been there," Le Corbusier remained for many one of the prime witnesses of the advent of modern architecture, his writings the manifestoes of modernism, and his perspective on ornament, objects, and the decorative in modern architecture among the most prominent statements that generations of architects would attend to. In addition, looking at Le Corbusier from the perspective of this discourse on objects that cut across two centuries and two mentalities shows his work in another light and illuminates another of its many important facets.

Born and educated in French Switzerland in a milieu that absorbed Ruskin and Morris into a long tradition of craft-culture, exposed to French but also to German and Austrian theorists and movements in his (and modernism's) formative years before the Great War, Le Corbusier came in contact with a wide array of ideas and directions, many of those recounted here. His syntheses, magisterially delivered at a fast pace in a series of highly readable volumes published between

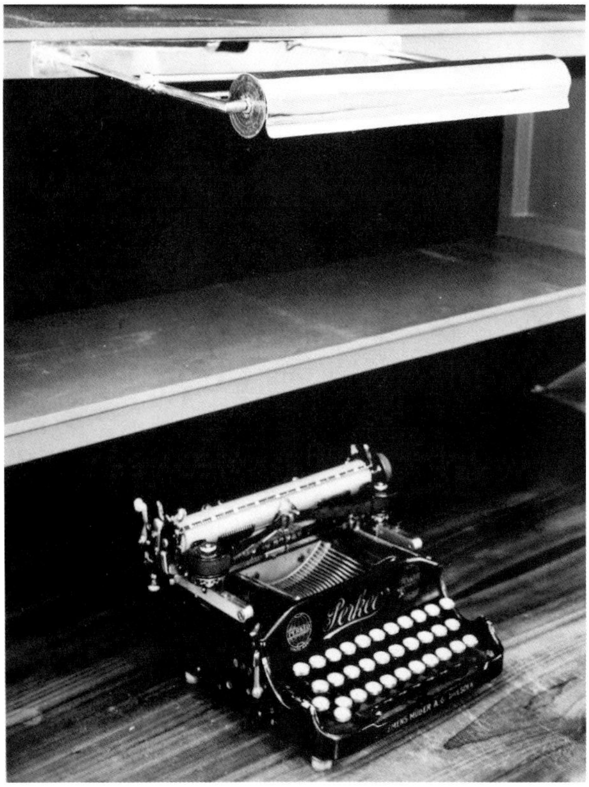

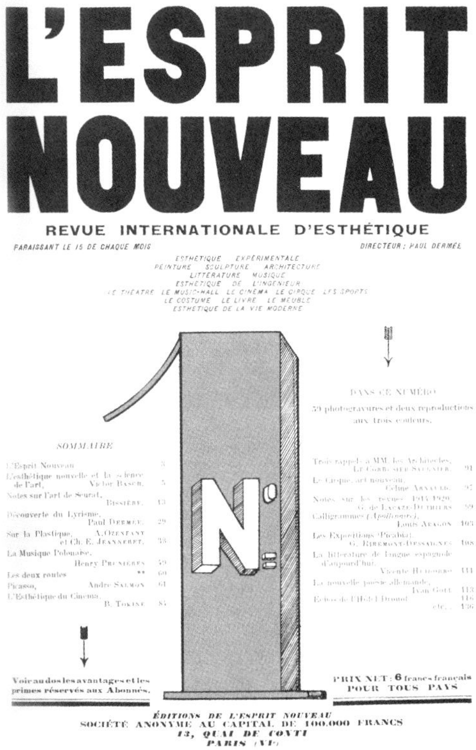

1923 and 1925 (which reworked for a larger audience articles published earlier in his and Amedée Ozenfant's magazine *L'Esprit Nouveau* 1919–25), repackaged much of what he had seen, read, or heard for an audience that was now ready to listen (fig. 148). If not entirely original, his work was so in its synthesis and *factura*, and certainly in its tone and timing. But most importantly it showed how the vast amount of material bequeathed from the nineteenth century had been translated into usable architectural theory—moreover, into a radical position, or at least one that perceived itself to be radical. Le Corbusier's early activity is itself a case of reception and as such it shows upon what vectors the discussion moved, what survived into the mainstream, and how it did so.

Indeed, so continuous was his argumentation with that of his elder mentors that it could be argued that Le Corbusier translated Muthesius and Loos into French. Certainly his focus on the problem of the house and housing in his early work and throughout his career was in line with the preoccupations of both and is a testimony that from his very first steps into architecture he engaged the same domestic environment of house and objects that the fin-de-siècle had propelled to the center of attention. To be sure, such a trajectory was also part of the normal course of a young architect's career. Small commissions such as a villa were easier to obtain than were larger and more complex, not to

Left **FIGURE 147**
Typewriter in Walter Gropius's House, Dessau, 1926. Gelatin silver print, printed c. 1950, Lucia Moholy. Busch Reisinger Museum, Harvard University.

Right **FIGURE 148**
Le Corbusier, *L'Esprit Nouveau* (Paris, 1920).

say more expensive, buildings, where significant professional experience was paramount. His early Swiss work on the houses of the masters of the École d'Art in his hometown of La Chaux des Fonds—the Maisons Fallet, Stotzer, Jacquemet, and others—produced while traveling and with no previous experience, is a case in point. Educated in an Arts and Crafts ambiance by his Swiss teacher Charles l'Eplattenier, converted to recognize the problem of the city early on by Auguste Perret during his apprenticeship in his studio (1908/9), and certainly familiar with Muthesius's battlecry "vom Sofakissen zum Städtebau," Le Corbusier had multiple access points into the problem of habitation.[18] It is no surprise, therefore, that he should make the house—the cell from which the city grows—the focus of his work when presenting his first architecture exhibition. As materialization of a host of discourses, the Pavillon de l'Esprit Nouveau of 1925 was three things at once: ruminations on the city, on the house, and on the nineteenth-century issue of *Kunstgwerbe,* participant as it was in a Great Exhibition of the decorative arts (fig. 149).

Perhaps what was even more important was the fact that Le Corbusier wrote two books to accompany his and Ozenfant's entry in the exhibition: the *Almanach d'architecture moderne* and the *L'art décoratif d'aujourd'hui,* both published in 1925.[19] One traced the building of the pavilion and explained its rationale at length; the other was much broader in scope and attempted to reposition the question of the decorative arts. The *Almanach* was certainly more than a nod at the Werkbund *Jahrbuchs* published in Germany and that recorded the speeches and debates associated with the yearly exhibitions of the union.[20] In fact, Le Corbusier had been quick to note the propaganda instruments of the Werkbund during his stay in Germany, and these observations clearly bore fruit.[21] But he had been equally influenced by other types of publications: the *Deutsche Monatsschrift für das gesamte Leben der Gegenwart* (in which Muthesius published) and Adolf Loos's short-lived journal *Das Andere,* ironically subtitled "A Journal for the Introduction

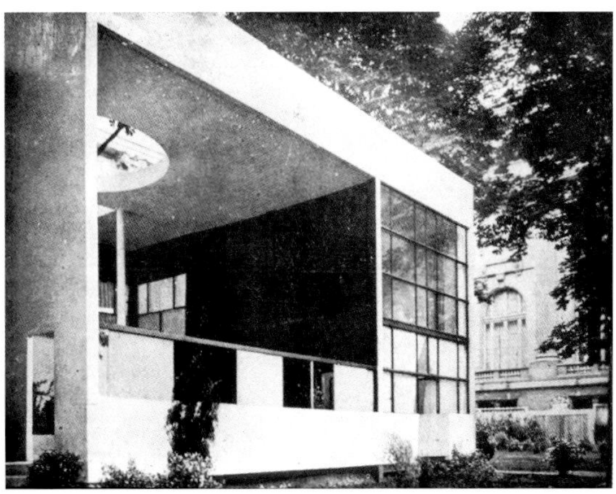

FIGURE 149
"A cell of a building-villa with its hanging garden." From Le Corbusier, *Almanach d'architecture moderne: documents, théorie* (Paris, 1925).

of Western Culture into Austria."[22] Both were undoubtedly among the inspirations for his, Ozenfant's, and Paul Dermée's *L'Esprit Nouveau,* which also aimed at engaging the broad spectrum of contemporary life and included the provocative stance and visual tropes that Loos had introduced into architecture culture.[23] Among the layers of references to the decorative arts debates was also a critique of Sigfried Bing's Art Nouveau store, to which the title alludes though clearly indicating a dynamic, contemporary position with its subtitle *Revue internationale illustrée de l'activité contemporaine.*[24]

But the two books of 1925 were something else again. Accompanying the Pavillon de l'Esprit Nouveau, they described the project and placed it in the context within which its two authors saw it: the decorative arts debates at the Decorative Arts exhibition that they participated in and critiqued at the same time. And the object of everyday use was as much at the core of the pavilion as it was at the core of the books. As Nancy Troy notes, the 1925 Exposition was predicated upon the call for collaboration between art and industry, and Le Corbusier's approach was an extreme case seen against the "genteel" notions of serial manufacturing and the traditional forms that were on display. As she argued, more important was the fact that these differences were masked by a shared history and a "surprisingly" similar rhetoric.[25]

Indeed, Le Corbusier's roots in the *Sachkultur* of the nineteenth century, like those of the exhibition in which he participated, are more than evident. The everyday household object had been Le Corbusier's passport out of Switzerland and into the world of modernity. Armed with l'Eplattenier's charge to report on the decorative arts movement in Austria and Germany, Le Corbusier had begun his fateful voyage to central Europe and the East in 1910. His German notebooks are rich in observations and record his dutiful scouting of people, speeches, events, exhibitions, and sites to visit, as well as sketches of what had caught his eye above and beyond his mandate (fig. 150).[26] The voyage was masterminded by l'Eplattenier, who was intent on creating a decorative arts movement in the Swiss Jura and sought to develop a school for all the arts—painting, architecture, decorative arts—a variation on the model of the many *Kunstgewerbeschulen* in England and Germany.[27] As is well known, this episode centered on reporting on the decorative arts scene, much like Muthesius's trip to England in the 1890s, and it had a profound formative role for the young Jeanneret, reinforcing his early apprenticeship in enamel and metalwork in La Chaux de Fonds and his exposure to the crafts through his artisan family background.[28] Working in Peter Behrens's office in Berlin, but also befriending Thomas Fischer and Muthesius, interacting with Wolf Dorn, Henri Tessenow, and Karl-Ernst Osthaus, visiting educational and exhibition establishments across Germany and Austria, Le Corbusier systematically sampled the German decorative arts environment and

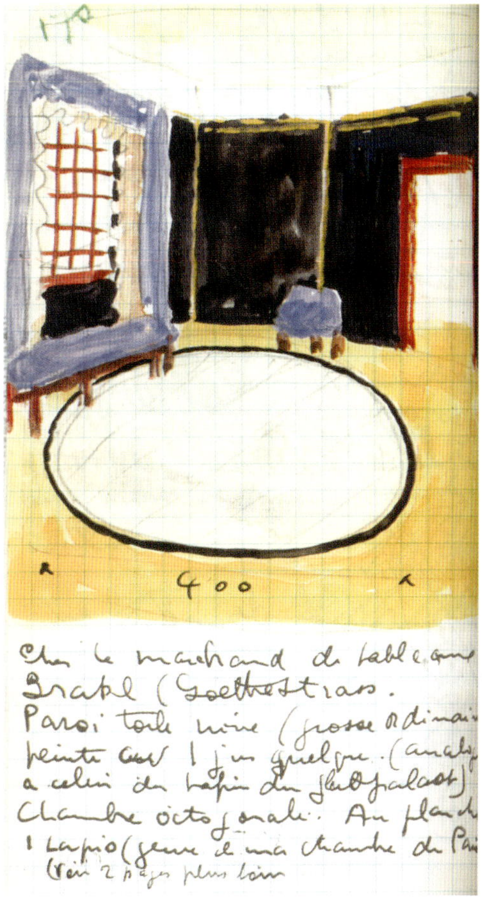

reported knowledgeably about it. In short, the lens through which he looked at architecture from the very beginning was that of the decorative arts, of the objects, and of the nineteenth-century discourse charted here. Never relinquished, this engagement with objects continued into the 1920s, when he designed furniture for his houses, for the Decorative Arts Exhibition of 1925, and from 1927 onward with Charlotte Perriand.[29] And his early notes from his travels, published as *Étude sur le mouvement d'art décoratif en Allemagne* (1912) and initially as reports in the local newspaper *La feuille d'avis,* were the early blueprint for what would become *L'art décoratif d'aujourd'hui.*

But the German perspective was enriched by the arts scene in Paris during the 1920s, and in particular by another personality that he encountered there: Fernand Léger. The object as site of interrogating the artistic act and its author was conspicuous in Paris Dada works, such as Marcel Duchamp's objet trouvé, Francis Picabia's *machiniste* paintings, as well as earlier Cubist collages that re-created the intimate and closed world of the artist's studio/interior by way of real and fictive objects. Ozenfant and Jeanneret critiqued this work but at

FIGURE 150
Le Corbusier, *Les Voyage d'Allemagne: Carnets* (Paris, 1925). Sketch FLC/ADAGP.

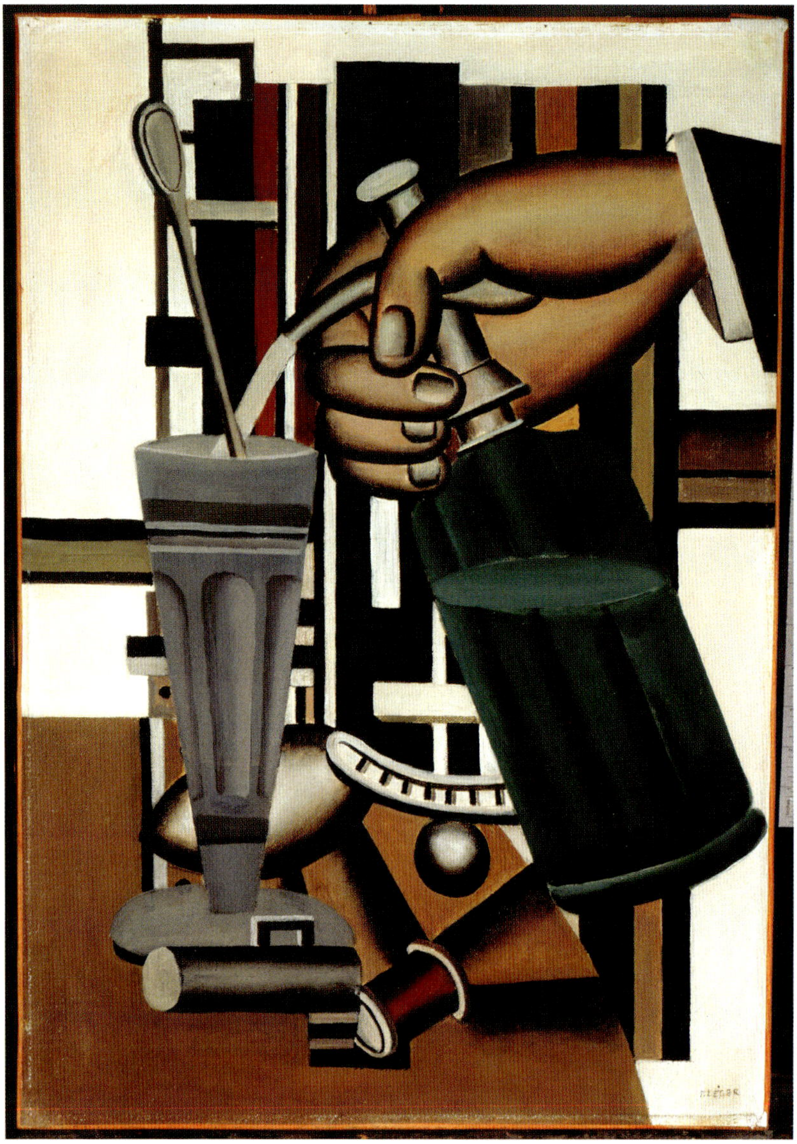

FIGURE 151
Fernand Léger. *Le Siphon*, 1924. Oil on canvas, 35¾ × 28⅛ in. (90.8 × 71.4 cm). Albright-Knox Art Gallery/Art Resource, NY.

the same time used its devices for their own "movement": Purism. The friendship with Léger, Le Corbusier's mentor in the world of speed and engines, of planes and cars—sharpened this interest further. It is Léger who made conspicuous use of random modern objects (such as the siphon or the baluster) in his paintings and insisted on their relevance (figs. 151, 152). It is clear that when Le Corbusier selected his painting *Le Balustre* to occupy the principal position opposite the entrance of his 1925 pavilion, he was acknowledging that they spoke the same language.

Reflecting on their collaboration after the fact in his article "Actualités," written in Berlin in 1928 and dedicated to Le Corbusier, Léger insisted that the

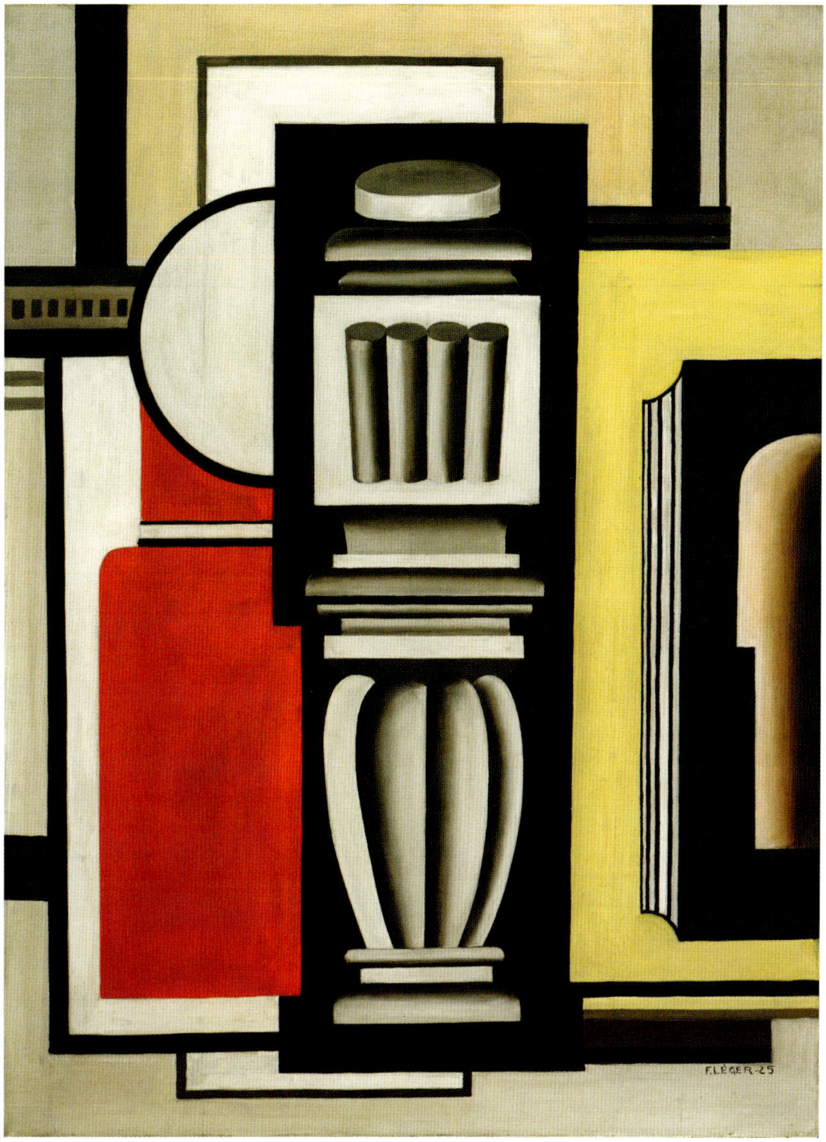

FIGURE 152
Fernand Léger, *The Baluster*, 1925. Oil on canvas, 51 × 38¼ in. (129 × 97.2 cm). Museum of Modern Art, New York/SCALA/Art Resource, NY.

"most significant event of our times is the rise in importance of the object."[30] And he sees this turn running deeper even than Le Corbusier presented it. The new mentality, he argues, is to explore all recesses, to understand mechanisms, functions, and motors in the smallest detail. "The ensembles do not suffice anymore—we want to feel and catch the details of these ensembles—and we notice that these details, these fragments, if isolated, have a complete and peculiar life of their own."[31] Although his illustrations turn to cinema—and in particular to the closeup (*gros plan*), which he explored in films such as *Ballet mécanique* (1923–24)—his focus is on architecture and objects of daily life (as "closeup" of modern life).

According to Léger, in this new aesthetic of the detail and of the fragment, objects become interchangeable: isolated, personified they enhance the spectacle of the street. A shoe is as beautiful as a painting, a painting is as beautiful as an X-ray. Simplicity, precision, clarity—the features noted long ago by Streiter and later repeatedly by Le Corbusier—are the ones he identifies as well, and he proceeds to point to the "northern spirit" as the driver behind this trend for a "new taste for the object." Architecture is his leading example. His conclusion is once again reminiscent of Streiter: "If architecture is willful—and it is—it doesn't bear anything other in its interiors but objects in the same spirit—and this architecture, these objects, are either accepted by the initiated or borne by the majority of people who in time become accustomed to them and accept them in their turn."[32] In a parallel issue of *Selection: Chronique de la vie artistique* published in Antwerp 1929 and dedicated to Fernand Léger, a number of authors, among them Le Corbusier and Waldemar George, returned the compliment. George attributes to Léger the discovery of the object that "becomes not only a plastic entity but a microcosm of the world," while Le Corbusier sees Léger's work literally requiring a new architecture and thus indirectly explains why he chose one of his works as icon for his pavilion.[33] Indeed, the fact that he replaced the painting by Léger initially hung there with *Le Balustre* shows that the subject matter of the painting mattered profoundly and that the baluster "demanded" a particular architecture in a way that the more abstract composition that he had first selected did not.[34]

Much of Le Corbusier's position on objects and their relationship to architecture is contained in his 1925 manifesto *The Decorative Art of Today*. His mantra is spelled out in a few punchy one-liners: "Modern decorative art is not decorated"; "The machine is all geometry"; "When [the objects of utility are] used up, we replace them."[35] The tone is in turns Loosian in its anti-museum iconoclasm and its provocative anthropological reading of ornament, Wölfflinian when he invokes "the new sense of feeling," and Muthesius-like when he connects "type needs" and "type furniture."[36] A new and key factor was his interest in travel culture and its objects—in suitcases, trunks, bags, *étuis,* and containers.

But perhaps the most striking aspect is his association of tools with the body that radicalizes anything Streiter might have said about habit formation and uncannily harks back to Ernst Kapp. For Le Corbusier the objects of daily use are "human limb objects," which "supplement our natural capabilities."[37] "Tools [are] organisms performing functions similar to those of the natural world. . . . A perfect object is a living organism, animated by the sense of truth."[38] Once he embraces such an anthropomorphic conception of instruments, the definition of the decorative arts as a "mechanical system that surrounds us, which is no more than the extension of our limbs; its elements in fact *artificial limbs*. Decorative art becomes *orthopedic*...a craft analogous to the *tailor*" is a natural extension.[39] There is no possible connection between Le Corbusier and Warburg's Kreuzlingen seminar (with which his book is nevertheless contemporary), but the tropes and the conclusions are the same, even if he looks confidently into the future while Warburg characteristically sensed a tragic dimension. What both point to, in their different contexts, is a common root, a common discourse that invited such conclusions and such connections.

Such a view then allows Le Corbusier to develop a theory of *outils* (tools) that covers the full range from clothes to the house in a centrifugal movement that starts with the body as its core. "Decorative art is an inexact and wordy phrase by which we denote the totality of limb-objects."[40] Such a view of tools and the house tool (*maison-outil*) goes some way toward explaining the analogy house/snail (a metaphor that occurs frequently and centrally in his 1925 *Almanach*), as well as his most famous analogy, the house as "machine à habiter." A container of "limb-objects," the house is their aggregate, itself an object, a machine.

Another thread that Le Corbusier clearly picked up from the object-focused discourse he encountered in Germany was that of folk art and architecture. Once again following in the footsteps of Loos (rather than following Muthesius's or Tessenow's more literal-minded references), he too absorbed it into a theory of modernity, as the preeminent example of "matter-of-factness." He had turned to folk architecture—the Jura farmhouse—since his early days at the School of Art at La Chaux de Fond, and this was certainly a direction he pursued when he took the Mediterranean/Balkan whitewashed village house as his model for his houses of the 1920s. The presence of folk art in the foreground of German theory and consumption struck him during his German stay. In the reports drafted for l'Eplattenier for publication in the local journal *La feuille d'avis,* he observes with much interest the permanent ethnographic exhibition at the Wertheim stores in Berlin and describes it as a sales counter for the folk objects of Europe, but also of Asian and African wares. He found the significant success of the exhibition particularly worthy of note, and the memory stuck.[41]

But there are also traces of Muthesius's *Typisierung* here in this interest in folk—read: primitive—cultures. In *Almanach d'architecture moderne* Le Corbusier made it quite clear that folk art and architecture were about "types" just as much as the machinist objects, and he concludes with one of his typical pithy slogans: "Besoin types, maison types. Style Breton."[42] The emphasis on types ("type-needs, type-furniture") is certainly not missing from *L'art décoratif,* though the Breton reference has been discarded. Instead he articulates the concept of an industrial vernacular—the factories, grain elevators, and so on—that he was famously exposed to in Germany and blends the concepts associated with an anonymous craft-based culture with those of anonymous industrial mass production. Once again he leaned on but went further than both Loos and Muthesius. In so doing he articulated what lay implicit in Loos's apparently paradoxical posture to create aggressively modernist spaces only to furnish them with handcrafted items that often took their cue from farmers' objects: the classic Austrian farmhouse *Stube* with its wood paneled walls and built-in bench and table, the inglenook fireplace, or the simple wooden chairs. Le Corbusier tolerates no such contrasts. For him, the banal objects of everyday use mass-produced by industry reveal the unself-conscious thumbprint of culture, and it is for this reason that he identifies and exhibits them as cues and signs of modernity: "We will become certain that the folk culture of today is in process of formation, indeed already exists, born of unanimous collaboration."[43] The virtues of the folk object read like the list of features Streiter identified for the industrial object: it is "clean, concise, brief, economical, intense, essential."[44] This sleight of hand that blends industry and folk art allows him to keep the essential and useful ingredients of folk culture theory but to eschew the inherent sentimentality in the preservation of folk objects and patterns.[45] For him modernity is folk culture. "Work has begun. The unanimity of the new sense of feeling, which reflects an epoch of precision dominated by the machine, is tending to establish standards which will be our own folk culture."[46] Wölfflin's *Zeitgefühl* combined with Muthesius's folk object and Léger's fascination for machines have produced a powerful new rhetoric.

Of course this was not the only reason some ("primitive") folk objects such as pots and carpets entered his sparsely furnished interiors. Another source was Riegl and the German art historiographic tradition. Such a connection need not seem surprising. Le Corbusier's companion during his voyage to the East in 1910/11 was August Klipstein, a doctoral candidate in art history at Munich. Though their comradeship is well known, not much has been made of the fact that Le Corbusier undertakes the voyage that will mark him most with an art historian. Klipstein's dissertation was on El Greco; his advisors included Wilhelm Worringer, and his education certainly included Wölfflin (who had taught at Munich and would return in 1912) and Lipps (who also taught at Munich during Klipstein's stay there). That Klipstein was writing a thesis on El Greco in 1910 deserves comment, for El Greco was only a very recently accepted figure in the Pantheon of Renaissance artists. In fact Klipstein was on the crest of the wave that established El Greco studies, which started only two years earlier, in 1908, with the publication of a first catalogue of his œuvre by the Spanish art historian Manuel Cossio.[47] Absorbed into his critical evaluation of Expressionism in 1912 by Julius Meier-Graefe, it is clear why an El Greco dissertation should have appealed to Worringer, and it goes some way to flesh out Klipstein's intellectual personality.[48] Moreover, the voyage to the East that was to change Le Corbusier's life (and modern architecture, for that matter), was conceived so

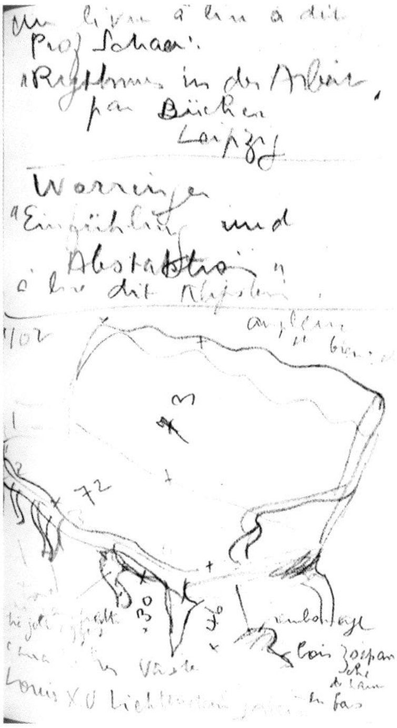

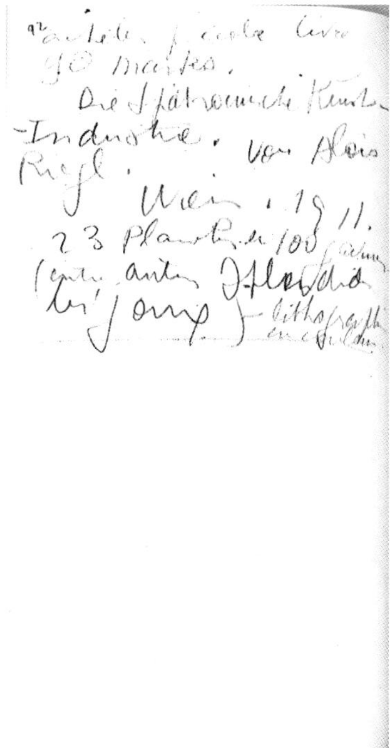

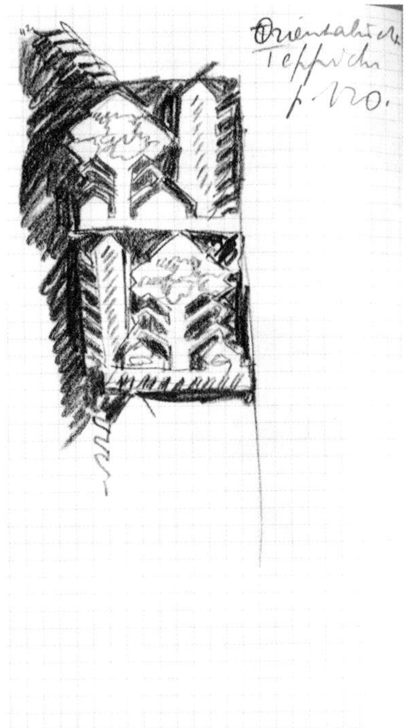

Left **FIGURE 153**
Le Corbusier, *Voyage d'Orient. Carnets* (Milan, 1925).

Center **FIGURE 154**
Le Corbusier, *Voyage d'Orient.* FLC/Art Resource.

Right **FIGURE 155**
Le Corbusier, *Voyage d'Orient.* FLC/Art Resource.

that Klipstein could see the El Grecos held in Vienna and in the famous collection of Queen Carmen Sylva of Romania. In short, Klipstein can be seen as very much au courant with the latest art history trends, and sympathetic to the latest ideas and theories.

It is therefore evident even from the pithy notes in the *carnets* that Klipstein passed on much to Le Corbusier. In his notebooks—both from his German sojourn and his trip to the East—Le Corbusier underlines that he must read Worringer's *Abstraction and Empathy* ("must read says Klipstein") and that he must buy *Römische Kunstindustrie* for the School of Art at La Chaux de Fonds, and he copies illustrations of carpets from Riegl's *Altorientalische Teppiche* (figs. 153–55).[49] These are not inconsequential comments but gain their full significance once they are seen in the context of the object/ornament discourse. While the reference to Worringer has been read in conjunction with his interest in geometry and abstraction,[50] the combination with Riegl's work on carpets and on the central role of small, anonymous artifacts in displaying the *Kunstwollen* suggests ways in which his later take on objects and the place of folk objects (the Berber geometric rugs and the pots he uses in the Pavillon de l'Esprit Nouveau) drew on a broader theory base. Indeed, the carpet and the ceramic vase were the classic sites in the discourse on objects from Semper through Riegl and Bode, Schmarsow and Lipps, or Grasset in France, and it was precisely to these that Le Corbusier turned to populate his sparsely furnished interiors.[51]

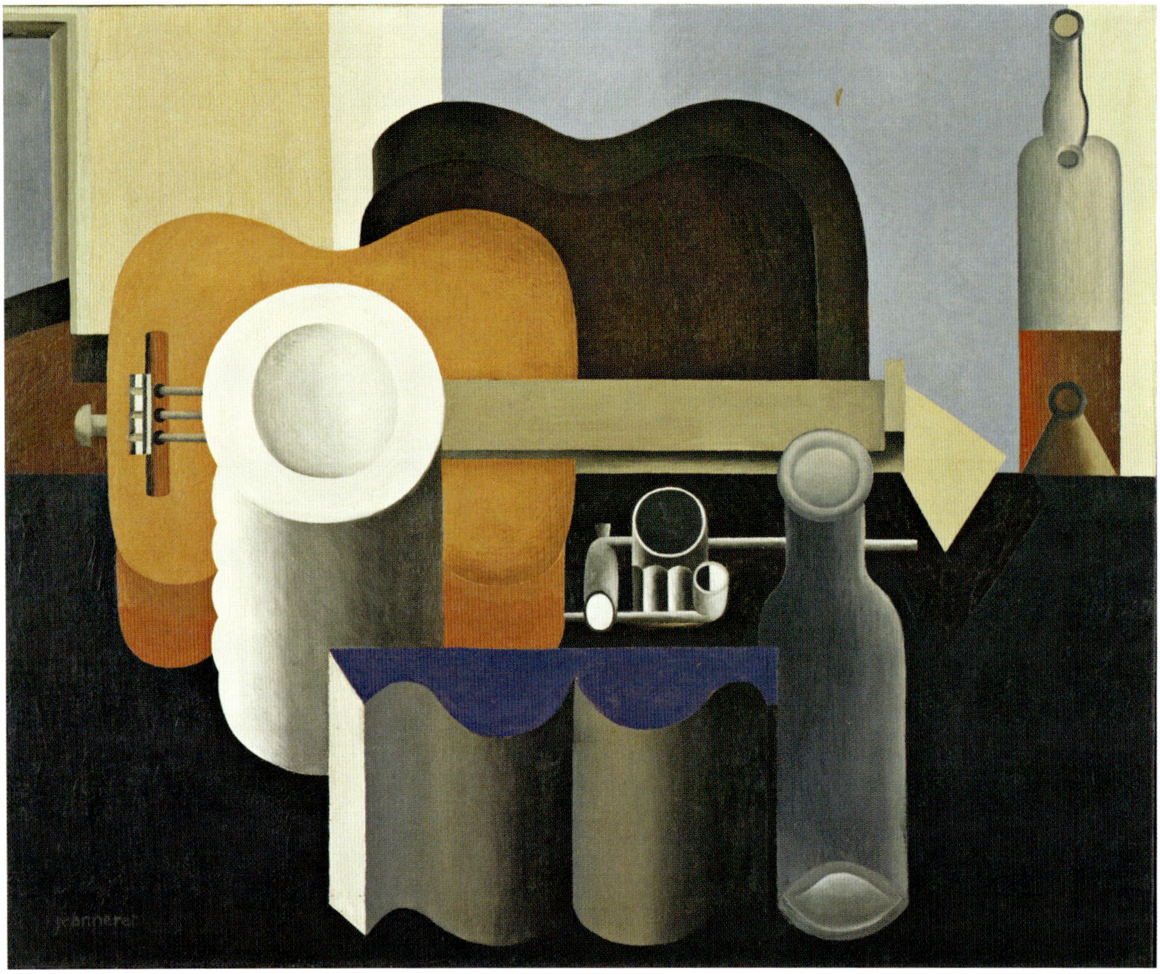

FIGURE 156
Charles-Edouard Jeanneret, *Still Life*, 1920. Oil on canvas, 31⅞ × 39¼ in. (80.9 × 99.7 cm). Museum of Modern Art, New York/SCALA/ Art Resource, NY.

Le Corbusier's purist painting explored similar issues. Indeed, this work is another engagement with the world of everyday objects, a directly visual one that predated the literary, reflective work. Although he and Ozenfant conceived of Purism as a response to Cubism—it was, after all, their way to gain entry into the hothouse of the Parisian arts scene in the late teens and early 1920s—Le Corbusier's purist work must be seen in the context of his longtime decorative arts interests. As is well known, there was much transference between his painting and architecture—indeed, he famously would have preferred painting as his principal occupation had it not been for l'Eplattenier's singleminded mentorship and pressure. From Le Corbusier's earliest efforts, his paintings show an intense craftsmanly quality (precision, evident construction, and careful application of paint) and a profound concern for the haptic qualities of the objects depicted, for their integrity as 3D sculptural entities even as they oscillate between disintegration and reconstitution within their architectural environment.[52] His tables groaning with objects are reminiscent of Baroque Dutch still lifes, though unlike them, and unlike the Cubist work, they are organized on strict grids and display a fascination with ordinary objects of everyday use that are mostly mass-produced. Distancing himself deliberately from Cubism, even from Léger, who still included bodies and larger landscapes in his work, Le Corbusier singlehandedly focused on *Kunstgewerbe* (fig. 156). No other forms, such as texts, bodies, flowers, or collages, interfere with the parade of machine-made objects (and only occasionally musical instruments)—of cups and saucers, siphons and plates, pipes and beakers, architectural moldings and automobile parts—all evidently ordinary, anonymous, and mass-produced, conveying neither nostalgia nor narrative but a profound matter-of-factness.[53]

The images more powerful, the language more decisive and crisp than any of the earlier books on the object, Le Corbusier's *L'art décoratif d'aujourd'hui* was written for the *vie contemporaine:* with its short sentences, fast pace, and pithiness it literally represented as well as addressed the modern urban dweller. The images—almost exclusively of storage units, luggage, shoes, hats, typewriters, cars, Thonet chairs, fuselages, scientific illustrations, and mechanical devices—represented a visual counterpart to the text, a powerful and even aggressive parallel visual discourse that enhanced the message. In this 1925 book on the decorative arts the images finally worked with the text and provided a genuine visual rhetorical dimension; with Muthesius and his Werkbund colleagues, not to mention Streiter and even Loos, the visual discourse was more hit and miss, and most often entirely absent. The objects were not there yet to support it.

THE OBJECT AS SYNECDOCHE

If the book was a statement, so was the 1925 pavilion. Unlike houses built for clients, this structure was built for display, as a statement that embodied the book. In his treatment of objects, Le Corbusier took an approach that was fundamentally different from that of the generation preceding him or of his German colleagues: his starting point was modern culture as it was lived, not the desire to invent it or turn it into art.[54] He had already made the selection in his Purist painting and had identified what was the essence of that culture. Bare lightbulbs, cups, glasses, and siphons were his staples, as was his Voisin car, the visual emblem and fulcrum of his houses, invariably photographed beside them (fig. 157).[55] "Harmony lies in the work that comes out of the workshops, or the factory. This is not Art, not the Sistine Chapel, nor the Erechtheum; they are the quotidian works of a whole universe working with awareness, intelligence, precision, with imagination, daring, and rigor," he had stated in *Vers une architecture*.[56] Indeed, he went as far as to describe these objects—especially the vase, that most paradigmatic of all objects singled out by so many authors, from Semper

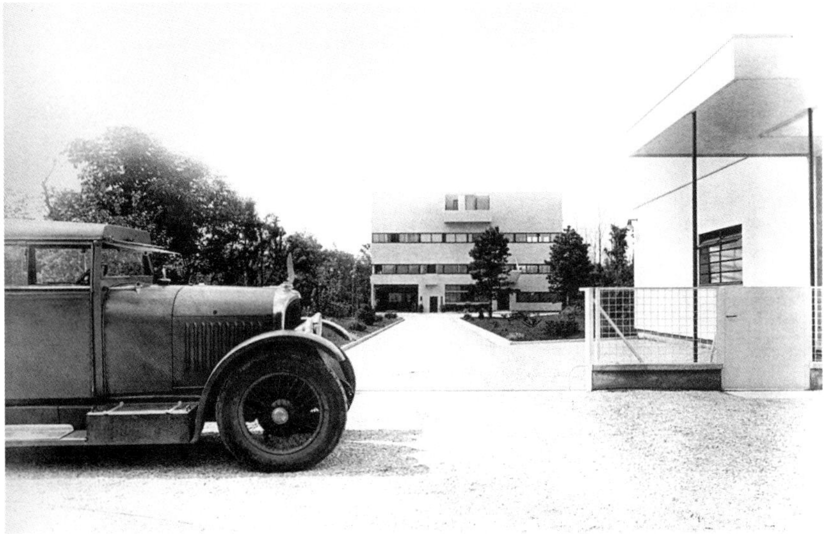

FIGURE 157
Le Corbusier, Villa Stein, 1926, Garches. Photograph FLC/ADAGP.

through Lipps to Schmarsow—as "architectural elements," recalling the contours of bottles and cups, which morph into blown-up, isolated architectural details and moldings in his paintings.[57] Thus when he comes to furnishing his houses, Le Corbusier uses the *Gebrauchsgegenstände* as he finds them, banal, invisible, below the radar of attention, a natural extension of life as lived and for that reason *d'un modernisme aigu* ("a sharp modernism"), he underlines. The objects are emphatically *not* art, which is kept quite distinct from them. This strategy is very different from that of his contemporaries.[58] Unlike the Bauhaus interiors of bare walls, Le Corbusier's are covered with paintings. But objects and art exist in different realms even if they create fields of energy between them, and even if the art is using the objects as its subject matter.

For Le Corbusier, modern life is encapsulated in its objects. Like the illustrations in his books they function like so many synecdoches of his architecture: he combines tools and clothes to create the image of the prototypical modern man, "intelligent, cold, and calm," and he might have added "organized, unsentimental, and focused," for that is what is implied. His tools are "the suit, the fountain pen, the Eversharp pencil, the typewriter, the telephone, the admirable office furniture,... the Gillette razor and English pipe, the bowler hat and the limousine, the ocean liner and the plane."[59] The objects are the material traces of the body of the owner: it is the furniture, the equipment that suggest how life is lived, not the four (or more) walls of a room, no matter how exciting the space; it is the objects which facilitate and define the "vie contemporaine." The chair suggests how one sits—for how long, how upright or how slouched, how relaxed or how formal. Indeed, the body and its positions were the starting point for his furniture. His sketches in the *Oeuvre complète,* titled "Studies on the different manners of sitting to which our chairs ought to be adapted," bear witness to this thinking process.[60] His furniture is about posture, clothes, about the way the body moves: "The evolution of women's dress in particular, and the rules of polite behavior, authorize entirely new attitudes. The salon of yesterday is out of step; a new age of furniture begins."[61] André Wogenscky, Le Corbusier's chief architect of public buildings for twenty years, recalled:

> More important, however, is the fact that the architecture of Le Corbusier evolved out of and for people and the surroundings they live in. When he thought of a house, he first thought of a man, woman, a child, their movements, and their behavior. And that's also the way he thought in furniture: the basic needs in terms of the movements possible in a chair, a table, in a bed were to be catered to. So that's why he first put someone in an armchair or a chair, and then positioned him in a landscape. Then he thought about the architecture surrounding this person, like a sensitive passe-partout defining the space around this person and his furnishings. First the person, in other words, then his table, his chair, his bed. . . . Many think that Le Corbusier developed furniture to go with his architecture. I prefer to take the view that he designed architecture to go with his furniture. Thinking on the scale of the furniture means thinking about the body, about hands and eyes—this is the origin of Le Corbusier's architecture.[62]

Whatever the path to the design of the chair *grand confort* or the chaise longue and the collaboration with Charlotte Perriand, the starting point, the message, and the function of these objects as emotional and sensation triggers in dialogue with his architecture was Le Corbusier's own, clearly present from his earliest Paris houses.[63] The objects are the gestures of modern man made visible: "Are not our gestures entirely transformed?" he asks in *Almanach d'architecture moderne*.[64]

And, as an echo of a metaphor that went back to the nineteenth century and forward to Walter Benjamin, Le Corbusier equates the house and its inhabitant with the snail in its shell: "The snail is in a snail's shell; it is true. . . . *Machinisme* must return the snail to its shell."[65] And he explains the analogy of house-machine, house-tool, house-useful object in terms of the mollusk: "The house is attached to our gestures: it is the snail's shell. Therefore it must be made to our measure."[66] His illustration of a hand cradling an object (the Mikiphone) for the section on the products by Innovation in the *Almanach* is telling in this respect: a miniature phonograph, it is both "attached to our gestures" and completely portable.[67] Ultimately his city dweller is a nomad like Streiter's: the scenario he describes in *Almanach* leaves no doubt.[68] The interior is reduced to chairs, tables, and *casiers*—these he defines as boxes (*caisses*). Indeed, the *casiers* were the key to

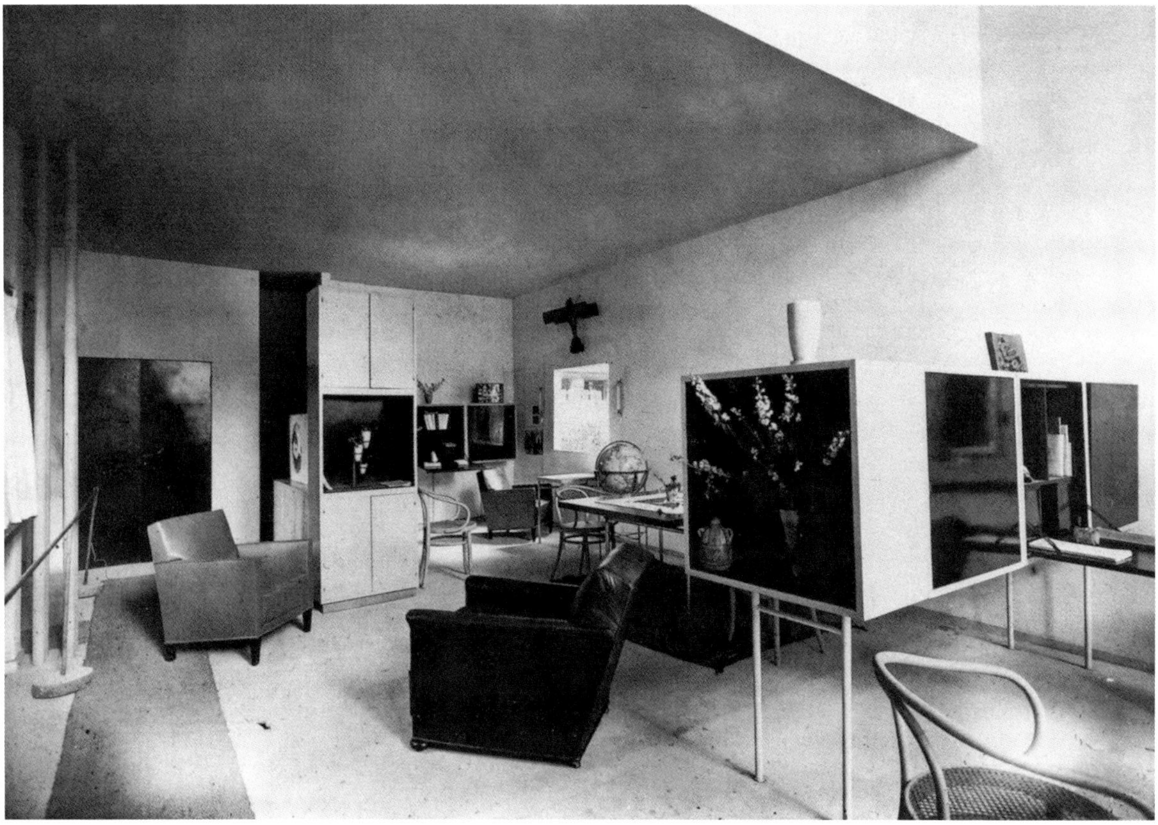

FIGURE 158
"View under loft (dining room)." From Le Corbusier, *Oeuvre complète*, vol. 1, 1910–29 (Paris, 1929). French text reads "*Vue sous le soupente (salle à manger)*." Photograph FLC/ADAGP.

his notion of architecture and objects. As his notes clearly show, for Le Corbusier they were the principal message of the *vie contemporaine* and of his pavilion: "pure little machines" ("des pure petites machines"), they were "the armature of the right wing of the pavilion. Without them the demonstration failed" (fig. 158).[69] His typical interior, made up of storage boxes, a few chairs and a table, a metal bed like the ones he uses in the Salvation Army's building, can be easily packed, and in fact are already packed and ready to go. Unlike Loos's storage, which is built into walls, disappearing from view, to be sure, but still custom made and permanently embedded in the architecture, Le Corbusier's *casiers* can be lifted and stacked and reinstalled somewhere else where they will be equally at home and detached, ready for the next relocation. These floating storage walls were the quintessential sign of the metropolitan nomad and traversed from object-status to architecture, functioning as both at the same time.[70]

It is no coincidence that Le Corbusier should have been so fascinated with the Innovation trunks and armoires-as-trunks: the paradigm for his *casiers* was about travel, about mobility. Like the snail, the modern house dweller travels with his objects, which become one with his house. (figs. 159, 160).[71] Vuitton, Hermes, and the Innovation trunks he illustrates were phenomena of the period to which

98 1925

jour tout bonnement *pesée* dans l'atelier de dessin d'une entreprise de lustrerie d'art, pèsera lourd de ses seuls 50 grammes dans la balance qui jugera de la destinée de ces industries vouées à la disparition; la firme technique remplacera la firme d'art : c'est écrit.

Ainsi, à mesure que des matières nouvelles et des formes neuves étaient impérativement introduites dans les industries

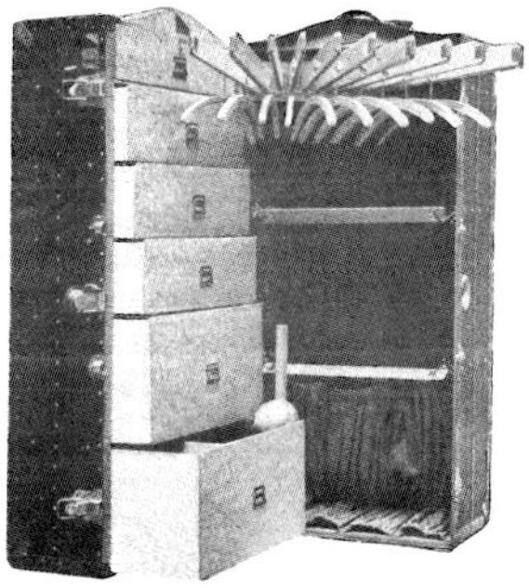

Malle « Innovation ».

d'art décoratif par le dieu tout-puissant du prix de revient et de l'efficacité, des esprits alertes et curieux notaient au passage les lois de constance qui dictaient la formation de ces objets neufs. Ces lois de constance affectaient toutes choses d'un indice commun et la sécurité qu'elles apportaient à l'esprit constituait les bases d'un sentiment neuf de l'harmonie.

Nous arrêtant pour réfléchir sur le cas, nous sommes conduits à admettre que point n'est besoin d'attendre davantage d'objets utiles.

Sans révolution de barricades, sans coups de feu, mais par une simple évolution accélérée par le rythme rapide de l'époque, nous voyons l'art décoratif à son déclin et notons que la presque hystérique ruée de ces dernières années vers le décor quasi orgiaque n'est que le dernier spasme d'une mort déjà prévisible.

L'ART DÉCORATIF 91

des tables à fumer turques, des parapluies japonais, des vases de nuit ou bidets en Lunéville ou en Rouen, des parfums façon Bichara, des abat-jour façon lupanar, des coussins forme potiron, des divans où s'étalent les lamés d'or et d'argent, les velours noirs avec flocs de Grand-Turc, des carpettes avec corbeilles de fleurs et colombes entre-baisées, des linoléums imprimés de rubans Louis XVI. La belle petite bergère midinette en cretonne fleurie, fraîche comme un printemps, semble, dans ce bazar, quelque

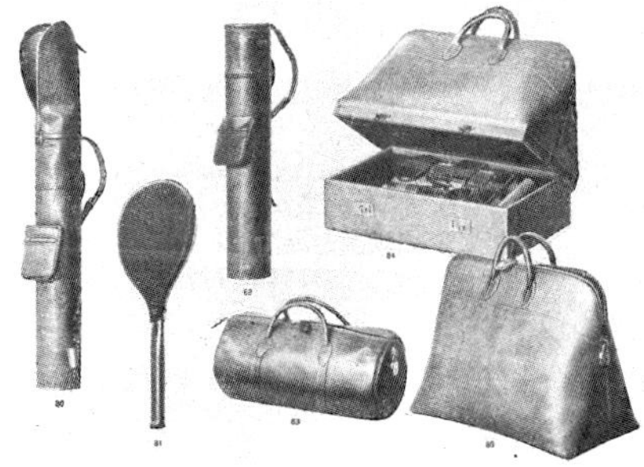

Ad. Hermès, Paris.

apparition écœurante de ces vitrines à costumes historiques des musées ethnographiques.

Non seulement cet afflux de fausse richesse est malpropre, mais surtout et avant tout cet esprit de décorer tout autour de soi est un esprit faux, une abominable petite perversion. Je retourne le tableau; la bergère midinette est dans une gentille chambre claire et limpide, mur blanc, bonne chaise de paille ou de Thonet; table de bazar de l'Hôtel-de-Ville (tradition Louis XIII, très belle table) peinte au ripolin. Une bonne lampe bien astiquée, de la vaisselle de porcelaine blanche; et sur la table on s'aperçoit que trois tulipes dans un vase sont une présence princière. C'est sain, net, décent. Et pour faire gentil, il suffit de si peu.

he responds like a seismograph: participants in the Great Exhibitions, suppliers of the portable lifestyle of the increasingly mobile European, they entered the world of the machine, the plane, and the ocean liner with great creativity. Portable beds as suitcases for the likes of Savrognan de Brazza during his expeditions in Congo, portable libraries and boudoirs as well as studies, these trunks may have been luxury goods, but they were also signals of a shift in culture. The *valise* that Le Corbusier picks out as a symbol of modernity shows him responding with great sensitivity to popular culture, a culture of travel and greater mobility increasingly evident in developing consumer goods.

When Le Corbusier came to deploying the objects of daily life in his houses, beyond the obvious references to the forms of industry his conception was that of loose, scattered, small-scale sculptural elements that articulated an experience of space and movement through it. Whatever else the differences may have been from the interiors of his Art Nouveau predecessors and colleagues, or even from those of his contemporaries who exhibited in 1925 and showed built-in, site-specific furnishings, in the Pavillon de l'Esprit Nouveau, as in his Maison la Roche and other contemporary houses, objects floated against colorful walls, set up individually, isolated, like three-dimensional abstract paintings in a gallery

Left **FIGURE 159**
"Innovation" trunk. From Le Corbusier, *L'art décoratif d'aujourd'hui* (Paris, 1925).

Right **FIGURE 160**
Hermès luggage, Paris. From Le Corbusier, *L'art décoratif d'aujourd'hui.*

(fig. 161). Sometimes they seemed to penetrate each other through transparency (as do the objects in his Purist paintings) seen in compressed perspective along the visual corridors he created in his houses; or their forms merged, fleetingly connected in the memory of the viewer moving through his ethereal spaces, as an enactment of the "marriage des contours" in real space and real time.

Le Corbusier hints at this dynamic conception in his own work when he reflects on the relationship between spaces, shapes, and colors in a tribute to Fernand Léger: "The rooms are no longer square; they interpenetrate, they flow into each other; some walls extend, others roll into cylinders, into spirals."[72] His fat *grand confort* armchairs seem to levitate on their *pilotis* like his boxy houses on their thin stilts (figs. 162, 163). Reworking his architecture in miniature and at the scale of the body—which is literally cocooned inside this enveloping chair, where the leather molds itself on the body, touching it at every point—Le Corbusier produces a haptic simulacrum of his houses.[73] If not exactly light, the chair suggests lightness as it hovers over the plane of the floor, which runs uninterrupted across the full expanse of the plan. Like the armchair, the chairs, chaise longues, coffee tables, or bookcases (*casiers*) exist in a state of elastic self-sufficiency, where the

FIGURE 161
Lofted library in the pavilion's grande salle. From Le Corbusier, *Oeuvre complète*, vol. 1, 1910–29.

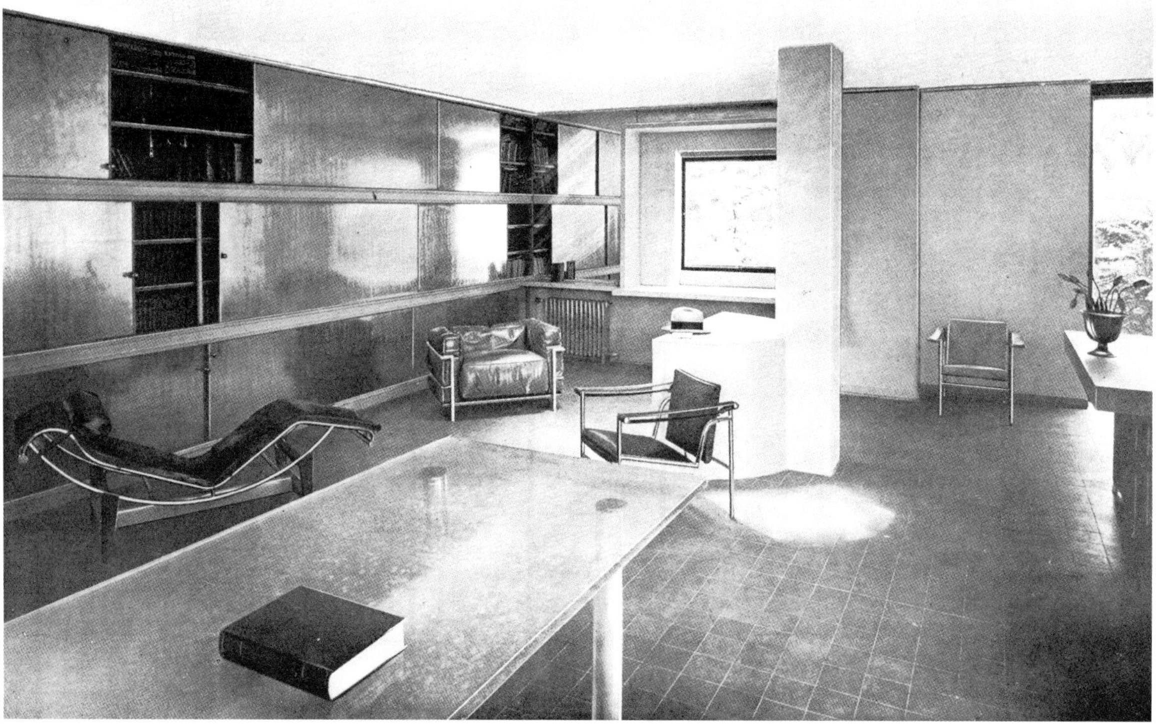

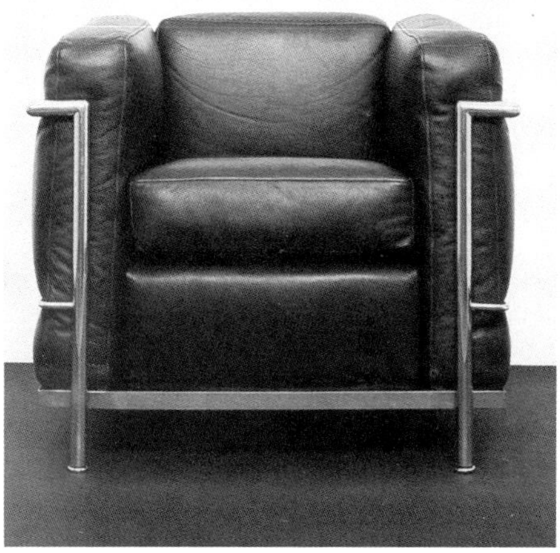

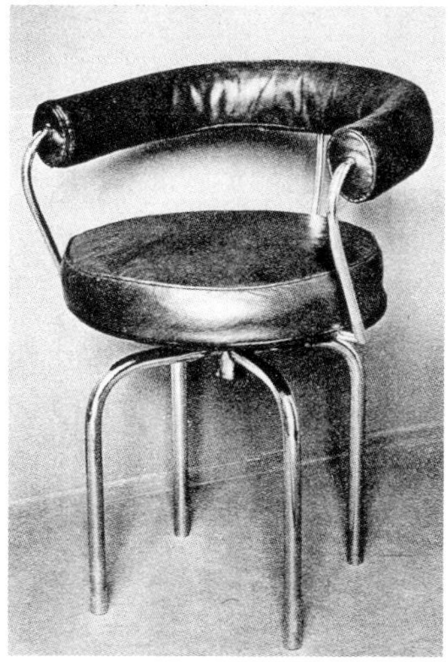

Left **FIGURE 162**
Le Corbusier and Charlotte Perriand, Fauteuil Grand Confort, 1927–28. FLC/Art Resource.

Right **FIGURE 163**
Le Corbusier, Pierre Jeanneret, and Charlotte Perriand, "Pivotant" Chair (Siège C1), 1927–28. Archives Charlotte Perriand.

cumulative experience of moving and encountering them as a series of detached suspended objects distills the experience of the house and dramatizes modern living in a rootless world of little baggage, where neither attics nor cellars tie a building to its soil or to its past (fig. 164).[74] The house as a box is itself a *casier.*

Detachment and portability are essential categories of being for Le Corbusier that connect all his production in this period. His houses, like his furniture, are suspended on *pilotis,* that is, they participate in the same lightness of being, they are detached and detachable. Whether self-contained or suspended cells in a concrete beehive, they float like planes and suggest mobility, like cars and ocean liners. The objects in them, few and matter-of-fact, explain the philosophy of this refreshing take on living. Reduced in number to a minimum and isolated in the spaces he creates for them, the objects acquire an added pathos, an extra eloquence quotient. They attract attention to themselves like display objects in an exhibition. Even the staircases—the prefabricated steel stair in the pavilion or the "ladder" in Ozenfant's studio—anchored in two points, disconnected from walls, and completely transparent, support this message of mobility and impermanence (fig. 165). The anchors are lifted, nothing weighs heavy: neither walls, nor attics, nor cellars, and certainly not possessions. The houses as "tabernacles" give way to mobility and lightness.[75] The ballast is thrown overboard. It is a fiction, of course, a rhetorical trope, but the point is unmistakable: the house is an object, just like the miniature objects inside it. Like them it is a tool, a "machine."

The photography for Le Corbusier's 1920s houses in the *Oeuvre complète* makes the argument most forcibly. Read in a sequence and individually, the images bring together the modern objects—especially those associated with speed—with those used most intimately by the body, such as glasses, and connect them across the architecture of the house. To be sure, the glasses carelessly left

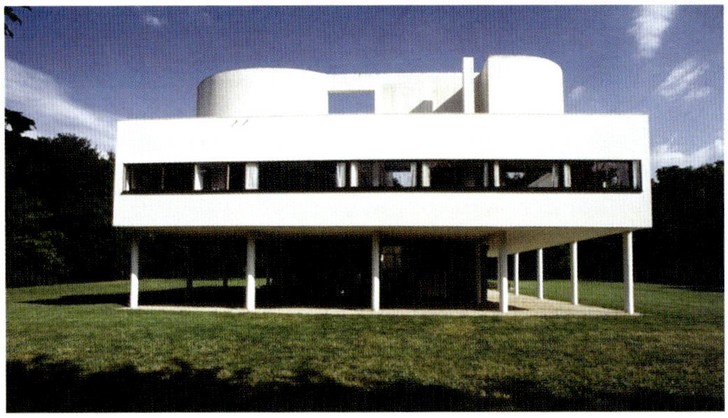

FIGURE 164
Le Corbusier, Villa Savoye, Poissy, 1928. Photograph Paul Koslowski, FLC/ADAGP.

on the table, or the garden chair left casually out of place, imply the speed of modern life, the informality of the new way of living, the new interactions within a simplified interior. But they also collapse the far and the near view and bring them into dialogue, cross-referencing the wheel of the automobile with the frame of the glasses. As in *Vers une architecture,* the car and the object (whether glasses, pipe, or triglyph) create an elliptical link to the architecture—whether the modernist house or the Parthenon.

Significantly, Le Corbusier gives a name and builds a theory around the seemingly random arrangement of these objects, thus tying them into a larger conception of architecture rather than add-ons: he calls it *désordre apparent* (apparent disorder). In his bare, decluttered interiors the objects gain huge visibility and emerge as "soloists," visual and sensual counterpoints to the architecture (walls, volumes, cutouts). The objects function as cues and visual recalls between the different parts of the interior. They too constitute a *désordre apparent,* just like the architectural components scattered across the horizontal plane reenacting the experience of the Parthenon platform, with its randomly sited temples, that so impressed him on his first voyage to Athens. The objects in the Studio Ozenfant—the stair placed like a random ladder leaning against the wall (just like his spiral staircases later, which look like the lemon peel in a Dutch still-life)—are architectural features treated as discrete objects, inhabiting his spaces just like his Maple armchairs and Thonet chairs, in tension with them and with the shell that contains them. In this sense the Maison la Roche with its modern art gallery and the Pavillon de l'Esprit Nouveau are perhaps Le Corbusier's most perfect interiors of the 1920s: the house is an object exhibited, and the objects within are also conceived as if in a modern museum setting.

Finally, a significant amount of art (paintings by himself, Ozenfant, and Léger, sculptures by Lipschitz, even when introduced only for the photo shoot) reminds the viewer what the decluttered life makes room for: aesthetic contemplation. In this respect his text in the *Oeuvre complète* (as in the earlier *Almanach* and *L'art décoratif*) is unambiguous. Le Corbusier does not want "decorative arts," he does not want decoration, "faire du decorum."[76] Instead, "l'œuvre d'art va se concentrant," that is, aesthetic experience, is obtained by reduction and concentration, by elimination and focus. The paintings, with their compressed shapes and colors that recall the architecture and the objects placed within them, like the sculptures, are meant to intervene in the interior and create fields of interaction between all the carefully orchestrated ingredients.[77] The rhetorical apparatus, the mediator is no longer the ornament attached to architecture (and to which the exquisite detail still clings). In Le Corbusier's work, the radical move initiated decades ago that passed through Wölfflin and Riegl, Warburg and Streiter, Muthesius and Loos reaches it ultimate conclusion: the mobile pieces of "equipment" are materializations of discourse, moments of reflection upon the architecture; they "explain" the building, they are its eloquence. And Le Corbusier is quite clear about this function: his example of standardization in *Vers une architecture* is the triglyph, an architectural ornament belonging to the Doric style. And it is this ornament that he confronts with the utilitarian, mass-produced object, the Voisin car. "Ceci tuera cela," in Victor Hugo's words.

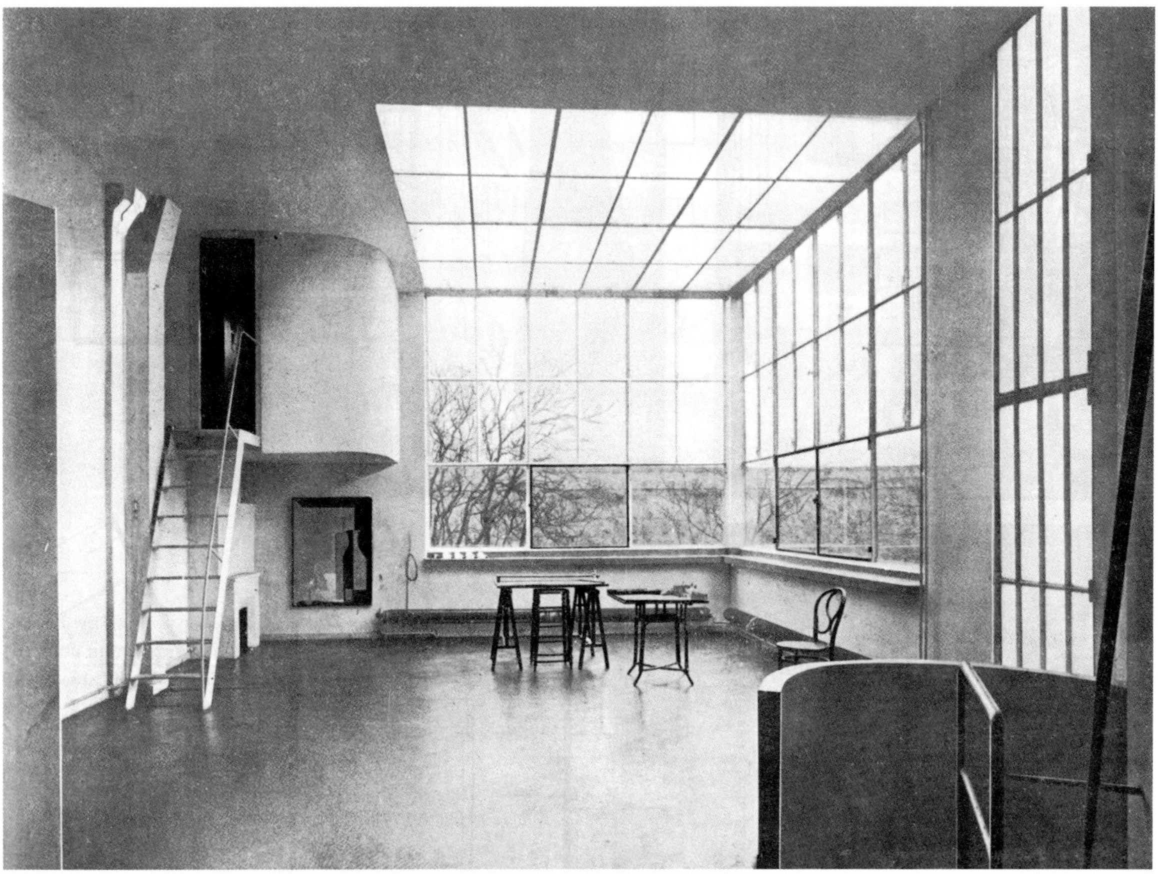

FIGURE 165
"Atelier of a painter." From Le Corbusier, *Oeuvre complète*, vol. 1, 1910–29.

BEYOND LOOS AND MUTHESIUS

Summarizing one last time the discourse on the object in modern architecture, Le Corbusier moves into the foreground here also because in appropriating this essentially German-speaking theory of objects he dislocated it and wrenched it into another and final direction. Ultimately following neither Muthesius nor Loos, Le Corbusier strikes out on a path of his own, while the Bauhaus and its associates follow more closely the Muthesius/Behrens model. In Le Corbusier's interiors, as architecture envelops the viewer in an experience that extends in time and is never graspable as a whole but only as an accumulation of individually experienced parts, the object behaves like its surrogate—small, contained, graspable, part useful object, part abstract sculpture, part sign—it conveys subliminally the aesthetic message of the building; it allows bodily, intimate, direct "knowledge" of architecture. His objects behave like intense concentrations of architectural meaning and deliver the rhetorical punch line. They are not conceived as "garniture," or sets, like the furniture of the Deutsche Werkstätte, of Josef Frank, Bruno Paul, and even of the Bauhaus, for all their insistence on "Typenmöbel." Le Corbusier zeroed in very early on the characteristic features of German modernism as regards the objects (fig. 166):

> The AEG case: Since then... they have taken on a modest, sober, almost impersonal aspect. They are quiet witnesses, where before they contributed to ugliness. That is because Peter Behrens has designed all their forms, and nothing comes out of the AEG be it building or industrial object which has not been seen by him. The good fortune of this authoritarian intervention of art could easily have been a sorry result had the right man for the occasion not been found.[78]

But for all his admiration, this was not his approach. Le Corbusier makes no attempt to provide a "line" of objects and furniture that would equip the house in one coherent language controlled by his design. Even the Salon of 1929, where he shows his furniture designed with Charlotte Perriand and where he may seem closest to offering a "line" of furniture, is one more gesture in the mold of the 1925 exhibition—an effort to suggest *la vie contemporaine* through a few pieces of furniture, not to design every aspect of it.

Instead, his objects in the pavilion, like his 1920s houses, come across as pieces randomly collected from the surrounding modern life that now (at last, he implies) fit into an interior rather than collide with it. His objects are heterogeneous and almost deliberately don't "go" together, unlike those created by the Bauhaus artists who were working on the full environment: carpets and wall-hangings, cups and saucers, lamps and chairs, tables and cutlery still reminiscent of the *Gesamtkunstwerk* of Art Nouveau.[79] What Le Corbusier can, he buys off

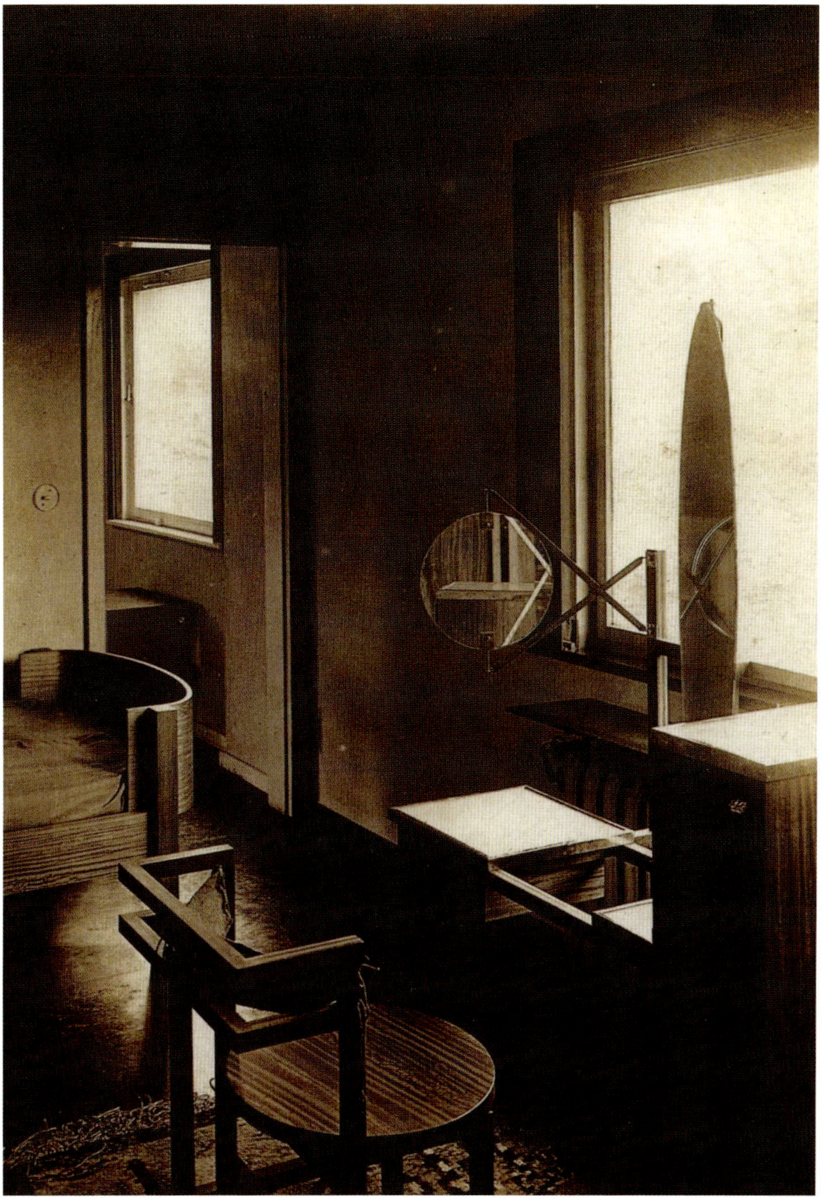

FIGURE 166
Marcel Breuer, *Room for a Woman, Haus-am-Horn*, 1923. Bauhaus Archiv. Photograph V. Parker.

the shelf. In the *Almanach d'architecture* he makes it quite clear: "The pots in the pavilion, of glass and clay, were all quite simply bought from a laboratory supplier: beakers, mortars, pestles. For many visitors they seemed intensely modern. Ahead of the work of art as such, they were the products of mechanical selection."[80] Fewer and unobtrusive, his objects syncopate the interiors—they are more rhetorically active for being more economically deployed.

Such a position was critical for Le Corbusier. He clearly *did not want* to invent the whole universe of modern objects, as Behrens and Gropius wished

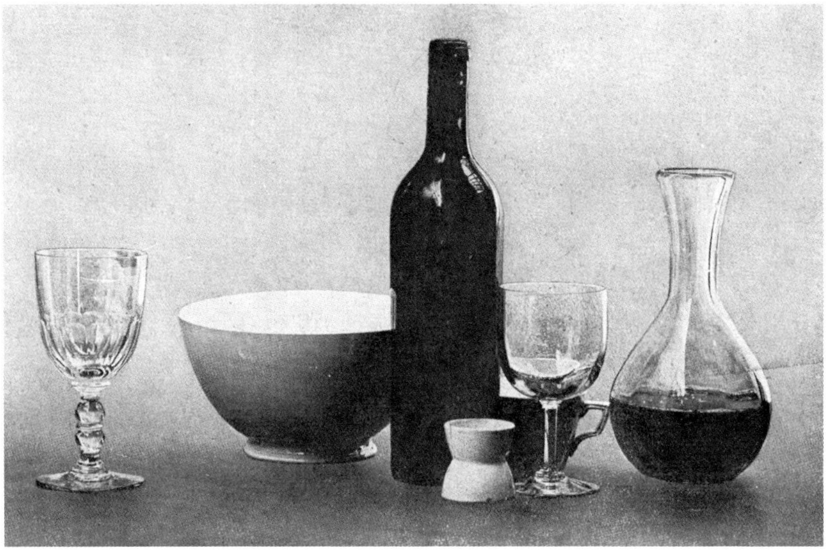

to do on the shoulders of Semper and the nineteenth-century *Gewerbe* debates. And in so doing he was closer to Loos; like him he wanted to make a selection from what was already there, "functional objects born of a new style... the office installations (yes, indeed), those of banks, of automobile bodies, clothes, dishes, glassware... a multitude of objects well proportioned, easily handled, pleasant, conditioned to suit our gestures" (fig. 167).[81] Production by the machine and availability in the marketplace is the covenant that all these objects participate in its logic. Fresh from his experience of Berlin, and in the midst of his turn to machine-made objects in his Purist phase, Le Corbusier was already stating clearly his position in *Après le cubisme* (1918):

> One cannot remain untouched by the intelligence that controls certain machines, by the proportion of their organs rigorously conditioned by mathematical calculations, by the precision with which their elements are executed, by the honest beauty of their materials, by the assurance of their movements; we have here almost a projection of natural laws. The halls that harbor them are vessels of a purity that cannot be expressed in words.[82]

Novelty and conspicuous design is not what drives him. For him the "useful objects will be the active and tranquil milieu of our existence."[83] Efficient action and tranquility are for Le Corbusier the poles between which modern life operates, and the interior must be an oasis of calm. Objects are either tools and nothing else, or art and nothing else. For Le Corbusier the object must simply be there, a neutral setting for the *vie contemporaine*.[84]

To be sure, commercial production necessarily meant a "line" of objects rather than disparate pieces, and in this sense the German groups were perhaps

FIGURE 167
Commercial glassware and crockery. From Le Corbusier, *L'art décoratif d'aujourd'hui*.

nearer the economically viable mass-production ambition of the reformers. And certainly Le Corbusier, working as a single individual, had limitations as to how much and how far he could influence industry. He did try to have his *casiers* produced by a Brno manufacturer who reneged on their deal although in the end produced them with very small changes for a different company and showed them at the Art Deco Exhibition, much to Le Corbusier's indignation.[85] The crux of Le Corbusier's demonstration, they were a new invention to replace a host of storage furniture ("hybride et mal adaptée") and *had* to be designed to order so as to deliver the punch line.[86] And yet—and this is the critical point—his choices in the end are not about total control of production, even if he seeks total control of the interiors he creates and the image they present. There is a significant distinction here, which is not only about what he could have manufactured and what he could not.

Thus Le Corbusier brings the Werkbund's industry lesson together with Loos's definition of modernity: he identified the simplest and most efficacious mass-produced objects/tools he could find and used them with minimum intervention. But whereas Loos remained attached to the craft of making—witness his sentimental adieu to Veillich, his master carpenter—Le Corbusier embraced "machinism," as he called it.[87] The object remained the critical starting point for architectural thinking, but this time it embraced the industrial anonymity of its modern manufacture.

For all his novelty and tabula-rasa stance, without his Arts and Crafts education that drew its life juices from the nineteenth-century engagement with objects, and without the German experience which had taken that engagement into the world of modern industry, both Le Corbusier's work and his message in *Vers une architecture* would have been fundamentally different. Even if he leaves wood, craftsmanship, representation, and historical (or vernacular) referents far behind, he keeps the most important lessons from the nineteenth-century theorists and architects we have followed: the site of architectural eloquence is the object of everyday use. Neither columns nor framing devices, neither carvings nor sculpture—no ornament—describe the architecture he builds. It is the object-as-clue that synoptically carries the message: of industry, of mass production, of redirecting attention to the essential, to what matters. And for him what matters are not possessions or the things that surround us, which must exist below the radar of conscious daily operations; what matters is contemplation and reflection in the company of music and art.

Le Corbusier's synthesis, like all convincing syntheses, had buried its traces. Like so many issues that he blends into a unitary vision, the empathy theory developed by several generations of philosophers and artists in Germany had also left no obvious traces in his work. And yet the body and its translation into the objects it handles occupy a central place in his aesthetic. To be sure, in close contact with the art historian Klipstein and evidently aware of Riegl and Worringer, he must have been acquainted with the principal lines of the argument at the very least. After all, had he not defined Purism as being based on the "physiology of sensations, that is, on the constancy of the primary reactions, on the universality of reactions of the senses in front of forms and lines"?[88] The limb-objects, the snail house, the prosthetic tools, the conception of objects as tactile nerve endings of architecture, its sensate haptic elements, are all so many instances of an assimilated discourse that has generated a wholly original architectural *parti*.[89]

But although Le Corbusier had erased the traces, he nevertheless transmitted the discourse. And in so doing he "cleansed" it of its nineteenth-century associations with the decorative arts movement and its Art Nouveau and Art Deco offspring. He also lifted it out of the German milieu—architectural and intellectual—and made it not only accessible but connected it to Paris, capital of the artistic avant-garde, thus legitimizing it as the official position of modernism, springing out of and beyond Cubism. But more than anything else Le Corbusier formulated outright what had been building up in nearly a century of intense focus on the object.

> The house is made up of objects responding to our functions. This is where architectural composition manifests itself: these objects constitute an organism that carries a particular intention, precise. . . . There is nothing to add, everything is inside it. Architecture is not added. It is situated in the particular quality of order that has been impressed upon a group of objects belonging to the house.[90]

His modern man is restless, constantly on the move—packing his clothes in suitcases, his belongings in *casiers,* moving by car, by plane. Impermanently housed, the objects are the only permanence he is granted. In his chapter "La maison outil," Le Corbusier can take that discussion to its radical and ultimate conclusion: architecture has become its objects.

Conclusion

Sculpture and Scale

In this *longue durée* story of architecture's travails into modernity from 1851 to 1925, we have witnessed a gradual transference of the explicating and rhetorical function traditionally shouldered by ornament to the objects of daily use. Several factors contributed to this shift. In the face of runaway industrialization the expansive discourse of the nineteenth century focused on *Sachkultur,* and in so doing equalized ornament and objects, positing them as principal signifiers of aesthetic impulses; once established as cultural quotients and acquiring equal status, the objects could take on a leading role in the relationship between viewer and architecture. What allowed them to do so beyond their newly acquired aesthetic dignity was the rise of a theory of objects as haptic devices. Handled and used on a daily basis, they were seen to pass below the radar of consciousness and create a physical awareness of forms and materials that could communicate productively with the forms and materials of architecture. Small abstract shapes dictated by their use—so the argument went—the objects allowed an aesthetic of abstraction and mass production to be domesticated and ultimately accepted. At first the discourse that generated this view was pervasive and broad-based, ranging across many disciplines, all of which contributed to this reevaluation. Eventually, however, art historians in particular gathered the many threads available and developed a theory of culture in which objects and ornament played a significant and foundational role. Because art history reached widely, touching the museum and its educational arm and ultimately also finding its way into popular culture, the theories of style and object/viewer relationships it formulated informed how architects, critics, historians, and educators addressed the issue of architecture's tools and its mediators. Gradually seeping into architectural discourse—affecting personalities as different as Gropius and Le Corbusier—this perspective on culture and its agents marked architectural modernism profoundly.

Of course this conclusion cannot be posited for all those involved with the modernist project. America, Britain, Scandinavia, and Russia, among others, had their own paths into its territory. But the German-language discourse—in history, architecture, education, philosophy, and the museum, in art history, archaeology, and anthropology—with all its cultural peculiarities was significant, and once it crossed the language barrier it affected profoundly the larger intellectual orientation as well. In short, it was a provider of theory. The diaspora during WWII contributed to this phenomenon. Not only was the departure of German architects of great significance, but also that of the art historians and critics, and the turn to the English language of Giedion and Pevsner was no less significant than that of Panofsky and the Warburgians. For all their rejection of German politics, they promoted their native discourse and did much to make it the underpinning of what followed.

Likewise, the rise of the object as a site of concentrated attention for architecture was not only a factor of the demise of ornament and of the emergence of theories of viewer reception. But examining this neglected reciprocal relationship offers insights into how architects thought of architecture no matter what political, social, or economic reasons they may have otherwise invoked. Certain unexpected themes emerge. For example, among architects and critics the discussion tended to focus mostly on the house, its inhabitant and its format. Although the attention of the modernists for the domestic realm is well known, the genealogy of this problematic and the reasons it became so pervasive are far less so. The house had been an early focus for the decorative arts and ornament discussion in the nineteenth century and carried over into the first decades of the twentieth century. It was argued with increasingly sophisticated analytical tools that in order to embrace modern industry and its consequences for every aspect of life—from private to public—a modern man must also emerge, one who could respond positively (rather than nostalgically) to the new forms and formats that the machine generated. In order to achieve this adaptation to a new reality of relationships and materials, a physical acculturation was deemed necessary, and it is precisely the objects of daily use that were seen as its most effective agents.

Naturally, once the house was perceived as the site of interaction between man and tools/objects, as well as the organic extension of its owner, and this owner as the unit of the modern polis, it became *the* location where intervention was seen to be most critical and urgent because it was most foundational. This was ultimately a didactic mission, but it was one built upon a foundation laid long since, in the early days of Semper in Britain, and it remained its backbone. Still, the nature of this didactic intervention varied and morphed among the various players. For all they had in common, Gropius and Le Corbusier did not conceive of the house and its equipment in the same way.

Much has been made of the turn to function as driving parameter of modernist architecture and design. Yet the rhetorical function—a function just the same—has been less if at all articulated. To be sure, in a world of few possessions and maximum mobility, each object had to be fully effective. And naturally this

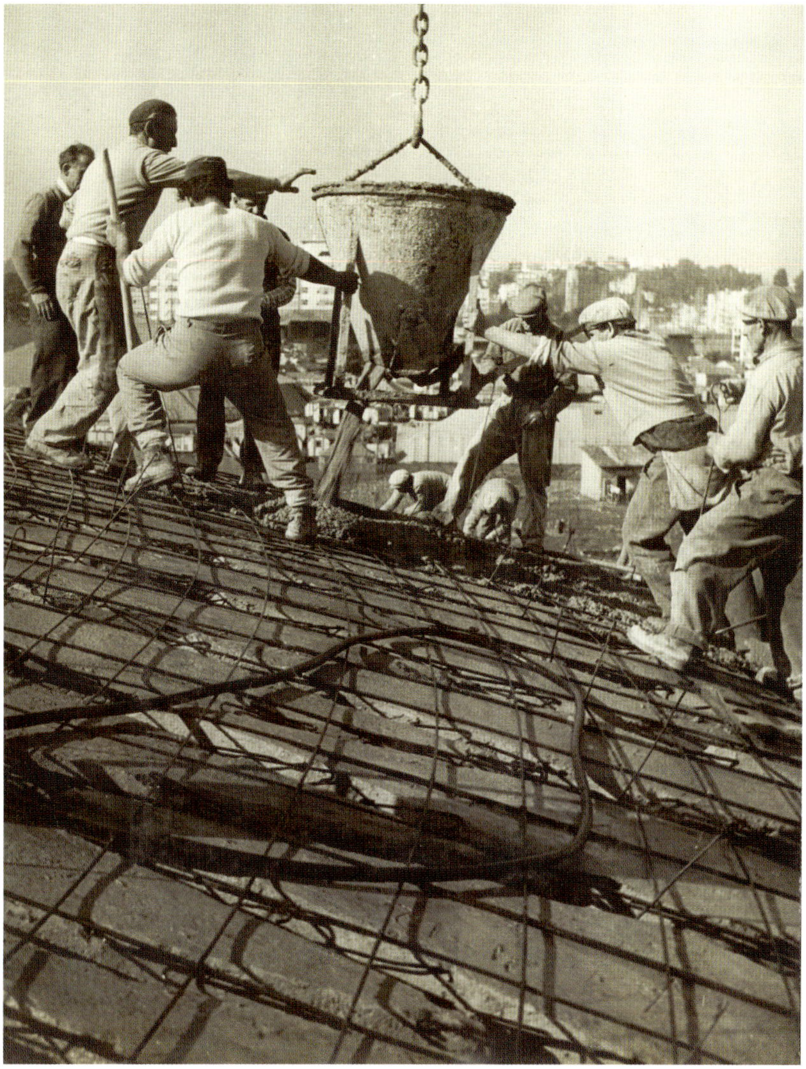

FIGURE 168
Building site of Palazetto dello sport, Pier Luigi Nervi and Annibale Vitellozzi, Rome, 1954–57. MAXXI Museo Nazionale Delle Arti del XXI Secolo, Rome.

issue captured much attention. Yet the object's less overt function as mediator or bridge between viewer and house-machine and house-metropolis was equally if not more significant. For one thing, it allowed scale to be comprehended and overcome, facilitating a direct and physical interaction with the products of industry that resembled those of architecture. The reason the object acquired significance for architecture was that it was made of the materials and according to the methods of industry, and as such allowed the users to become familiar with these novel forms through intimate handling. A steel frame chair, like a glass coffee or dining table, suggested elliptically that the house was made from the same materials as the object, and in the same way, as a mechanical, production-line assemblage. By extension the house becomes not only an object but is understood to be the result of the same industrial, mass-production process.

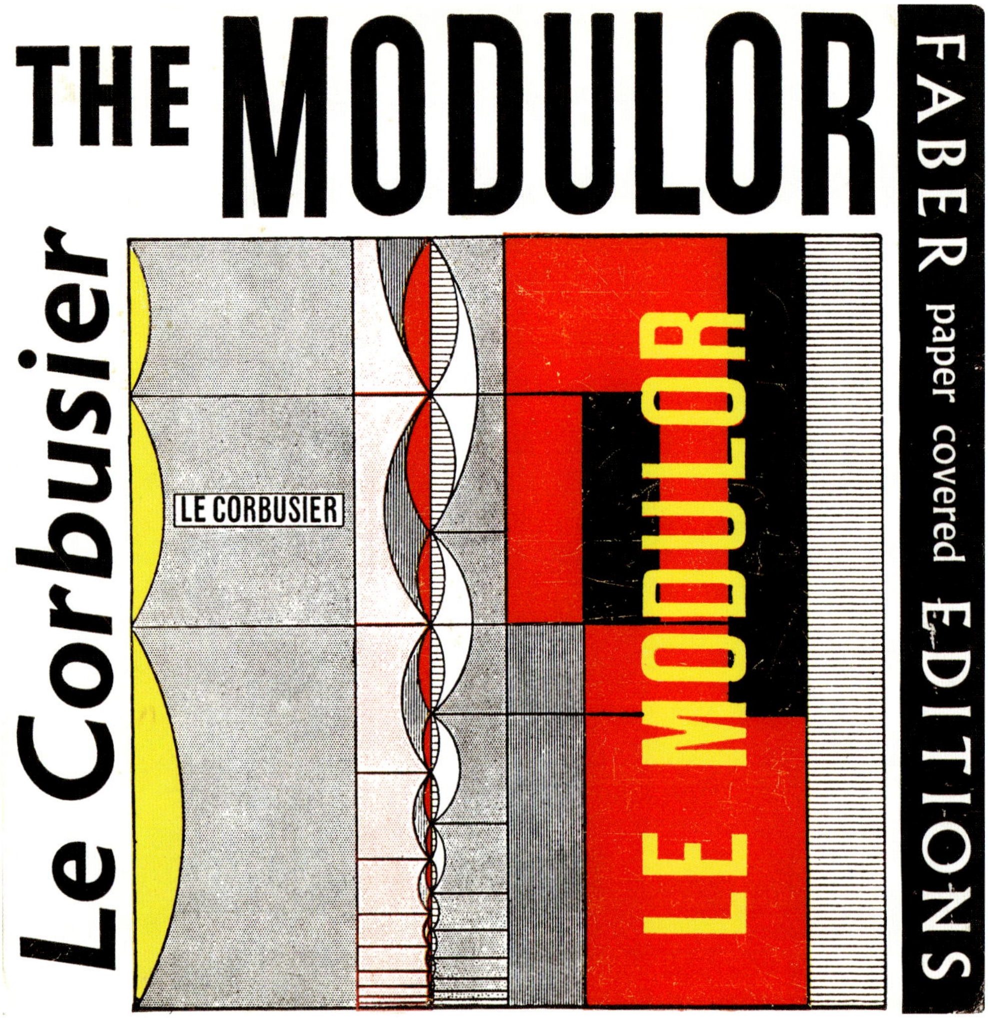

FIGURE 169
Le Corbusier, *The Modulor* (London, 1961).

Yet this was a fiction more often than not. A piece of rhetoric, an eloquent gesture. Indeed, one other but essential factor recommended the object to the attention of modernist architects. It is primarily through the object that the house and with it all other architecture participated in the visual rhetoric of standardization and mass production, since at the time both the building site and the construction technology were far behind the aesthetic imagination. Naturally steel and its by-products were perceived as the more industrial material—its thinness, its fastenings, the purity of the sharp lines participated in the aesthetic of the machine itself, which was made of iron or steel and had thin members, mechanical fasteners, and sharp edges. Concrete did not participate in the same rhetoric of the machine; nor did brick or stone. Theirs was a messy site, and somewhat artisanal: concrete mixes are not calculated to the same precision as steel standards, which tolerate very small variations (fig. 168). Likewise the products of concrete did not achieve the same sense of lightness and appearance of mobility to reflect the lightness and mobility of metropolitan living. Nor were objects made from concrete. Steel, however, and metals more generally—nickel, brass, and other alloys—were the materials of machines, of objects, and of large-scale precisely engineered structures. This may be why Le Corbusier, working in masonry and concrete in the 1920s, invented and was so keen on the *pilotis,* which were then recalled in the tubular steel and leather vocabulary of his armchairs. Through their agency his concrete and stucco houses were transformed and took on an industrial language of thinness. This also explains why for the modernists it was imperative to throw out the forms/objects associated with a different aesthetic and to seek control inside the house precisely because they recognized that *the new buildings could not be comprehended without the appropriate tools,* since the buildings themselves did not participate in the new systems of production and consumption as visibly as they could have wished.

Finally, what also becomes clear from the architecture/object relationship is that for a nonrepresentational art the communication tools had to be nonrepresentational as well. Moreover, the transition from the abstraction and monumental scale of the building—be it an apartment house (and no longer an individual house) or an office tower or office slab—had to be performed by a device. The tooled detail, like the tooled object with which it existed in a state of reciprocity—of scale, material, assemblage—provided access to the whole, to the overscale. Le Corbusier's Modulor scale, which connects the monumental with the smallest object into one device and one system, was a way to bring home that connection (fig. 169). Nearly thirty years after the early Paris houses he still conceives of architecture and its "equipment" as one single, continuous problem:

> The word "Architecture" here covers: The art of building houses, palaces, and temples; ships, cars, railway trucks, and aeroplanes. Domestic and industrial equipment and the equipment of trade. The art of typography as it is used in the making of newspapers, periodicals, and books. The word "Mechanics" covers the construction of machines that owe their being directly to the hand of man, and the spaces which surround them.[1]

Embedding within their forms the materials and processes of modern industry and mass production far better than the architecture itself, the objects became essential. Handled and surrounding the body, they created a layer of forms that entered in dialogue with the architectural whole by recalling or suggesting its fastenings and its materials, its precision and calculation, and presenting them for physical touch. The intermediary was not ocular—an ornament to be read off an architectural surface—but a haptic one, an object held by the hand (fig. 170). Ultimately, what this history has shown is how much and for how long the body

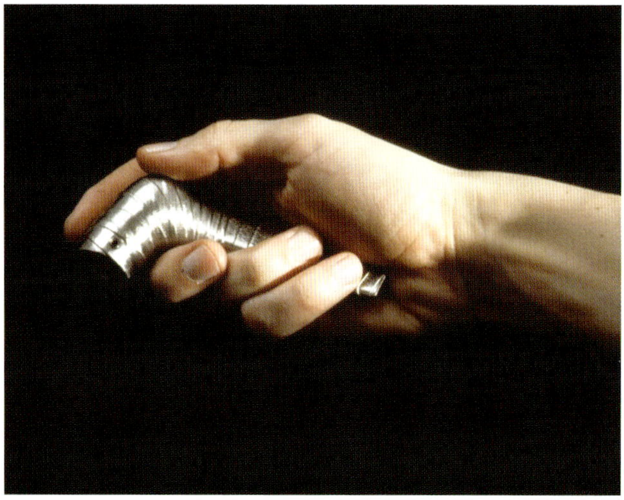

FIGURE 170
Adam Yarinksi, mock-up for door handle. Architecture Research Office, New York.

remained at the center of architecture's signifiers, even when its forms ceased to be representational. Body and technology surprisingly blended, and it is not coincidental that armor captured the imagination of so many in the period of enchantment with steel and iron, fastenings and articulations, sharp edges and gleaming sheaths.

This is another way of saying that what emerges with some force from this story is the significant role of sculpture for architecture. Not of the building as sculpture, not of sculpture as an art form, but of the *small object as sculpture*. A close relative of *Kleinarchitektur* and micro-architecture—those sculptural ventures of architects in the early modern period that mitigated between the viewer's scale and that of the building—sculpture as object of daily use steals upon the viewer instead of meeting him head-on. Always an issue for architecture, sculpture reemerges as a critical partner even if it does so as a subverted medium, taking refuge in cups and saucers, vases and chairs, lamps and tables.

Perhaps most important, the story told here draws attention to the genealogy of modernism—to the absence of a tabula rasa, of categorical caesuras, of radical breaks; to the importance of biography of people and of their ideas. And it points to where the continuities were located. Not in forms but in discourse. There was a lot more traffic across disciplines than we have so far acknowledged. The accumulated discourse in aesthetics, history, and so forth (on the body, reception mechanisms, memory, habit formation, abstraction, on the origins of style, on the everyday, on high and low) did not make architecture as such. But it made architects attentive to a class of objects and a class of forms; and, as discourse often does, it mobilized the creative and intellectual energy of those who make art. From the written word to the drafting table.

NOTES

INTRODUCTION

Epigraph: Léger quoted in "Actualités," *Variétés*, February 15, 1929.

1 Adolf Loos's "Ornament and Crime" is traditionally dated to 1908. The dating of Loos's writings is difficult to establish, as he was not particularly careful to record it. The essay was presented as a lecture on January 21, 1910 (for the Akademischer Verband für Literatur und Musik), and in 1913 (for the Akademischer Architekten Verband) in Vienna. Reports of the lectures were printed in Munich and Berlin, where they caused consternation (in Munich) and excitement (in Berlin). The essay was printed for the first time in German in *Frankfurter Zeitung* on October 24, 1929, but it was first published in *Cahiers d'aujourd'hui* in June 1913. See Adolf Opel, "Introduction," in *Adolf Loos: Trotzdem*, ed. A. Opel (Vienna: Prachner, 1997), 7–17. For a different dating, see Burckhardt Rukschcio, "Ornament und Mythos," in *Ornament und Askese im Zeitgeist des Wien der Jahrhundertwende* (Vienna, 1985), 57–68. The essay was published in *Der Sturm* in 1912 and in *L'Esprit Nouveau* in 1920.

2 Rayner Banham describes the instantaneous appropriation of Loos's argument as a self-evident truth that essentially erased his authorship. In "Ornament and Crime: The Decisive Contribution of Adolf Loos," *Architectural Review*, December 1957.

3 Le Corbusier, *The Decorative Art of Today* (Cambridge, Mass.: MIT Press, 1987), xxiii.

4 Wolfgang Pfleiderer, "Introduction," in W. Riezler, ed., *Die Form ohne Ornament: Werkbundausstellung 1924* (Berlin: Deutsche Verlags-Anstalt, 1924), 3–22.

5 Fondation le Corbusier, Le Corbusier correspondence.

6 Le Corbusier, *Vers une architecture* (Paris: Cres, 1923), iv.

7 Mary McLeod, "Architecture or Revolution," *Art Journal* 43 (Summer 1983): 132–47; Nancy Troy, *Modernism and the Decorative Arts in France* (New Haven: Yale University Press, 1991).

8 J. M. Richards, "Towards a Rational Aesthetic," *Architectural Review*, July–December 1935, 211–18.

9 On the concept in Giedion and its place in radical definitions of modernism that sought a recovery of monumentality, see Irving Wohlfarth, "'Construction Has the Role of the Subconscious': Phantasmagorias of the Master Builder (with Constant Reference to Giedion, Weber, Nietzsche, Ibsen and Benjamin)," in A. Kostka and I. Wohlfarth, eds., *Nietzsche and "An Architecture of Our Minds"* (Santa Monica: Getty Issues and Debates, 1990), 141–98.

10 Walter Benjamin, "Der destruktive Charakter," in *Gesammelte Schriften*, Bd. IV.1. (Frankfurt am Main: Tillman Rexroth, 1980), 397.

11 The statement appears in "Experience and Poverty" and is used by Wohlfarth to argue for a crisis of the dwelling. See ibid., 148. For a developed argument, see Francesco dal Co, *Figures of Architecture and Thought* (New York: Rizzoli, 1990).

12 On the Pergamon altar and its effects, see Alina Payne, "Portable Ruins: The Pergamon Altar, Heinrich Wölfflin, and German Art History at the *fin de siècle*." *RES: Journal of Aesthetics and Anthropology* 54/55 (Spring–Autumn 2008): 168–89.

13 Among the first to raise the issue from the perspective of sociology and semiotics was Jean Baudrillard; see his *Le système des objets* (Paris: Gallimard, 1968). For the current rise and accelerating buildup of the issue among a broad range of disciplines, see, for example, Arjun Appadurai, ed., *The Social Life of Things: Commodities in Cultural Perspective* (Cambridge, Mass.: MIT Press, 1986); Alfred Gell, *Art and Agency* (Oxford: Clarendon, 1998); Frederic Nef, *L'objet quelconque: Recherches sur l'ontologie de l'objet* (Pari: J. Vrin, 1998); Lorraine Daston, ed., *Things That Talk: Object Lessons from Art and Science* (New York: Zone, 2004); Bruno Latour, *Reassembling the Social: An Introduction to Actor-Network Theory* (New York: Oxford University Press, 2005); Bill Brown, "Reification, Reanimation, and the American Uncanny," *Critical Inquiry* 32, no. 2 (Winter 2006): 175–207, and Brown, "Objects, Others, and Us (The Refabrication of Things)," *Critical Inquiry* 32, no. 2 (Winter 2010): 183–217. More lateral though no less insightful is Miguel Tamen, *Friends of Interpretable Objects* (Cambridge, Mass.: Harvard University Press, 2001). Falling into this category, though more by accident than by design, according to the editor's introduction, is Stephen Melville, ed., *The Lure of the Object* (New Haven: Yale University Press, 2005). For the topic as an issue for art history, see the

theme for the 2012 CIHA conference in Nürnberg: "The Challenge of the Object."

14 Peter Stallybrass, "Marx's Coat," in P. Speyer, ed., *Border Fetishisms: Material Objects in Unstable Spaces* (New York: Routledge, 1998), 203.

15 Alina Payne, "L'Ornament architectural: Du langage classique des temps modernes à l'aube du XXe siècle," *Perspective: Revue de l'INHA* 1 (2010): 77–96.

16 For the state of the literature on ornament (which covers both monographic treatments and movement-oriented work), see n. 13. On the whole, when objects have been attended to, it has been for their well-documented presence in the activity of many architects; for example, see Susan Soros, ed., *E. W. Goodwin: Aesthetic Movement Architect, Designer* (New York: Bard Graduate Center, 1999). The study of the decorative arts has been a parallel trend in the scholarly concern with objects. For exemplary treatments of the topic, see Troy, *Modernism and the Decorative Arts in France;* Stefan Muthesius, *Das englische Vorbild* (Munich: Prestel, 1974); Christopher Long, "*Wiener Wohnkultur:* Interior Design in Vienna, 1910–1938," *Studies in the Decorative Arts* (1997–98), 29–51.

17 Manfredo Tafuri, *Architecture and Utopia: Design and Capitalist Development* (Cambridge, Mass.: MIT Press, 1976).

18 On the *longue durée* history of the relationship between high art and minor arts, see the fundamental contribution by Ferdinando Bologna, *Dalle arti minori all'industrial design: Storia di una ideologia* (1972; Naples: Paparo Edizioni, 2009).

19 Alina Payne, "Materiality, Crafting, and Scale in Renaissance Architecture," *Oxford Art Journal,* December 2009, 365–86.

20 For example, Marco Frascari, "The Tell-the-Tale Detail," in Paula Behrens and Anthony Fisher, eds., *The Building of Architecture, Via* 7 (1984); Francesco Dal Co, "Excellence: The Culture of Mies as Seen in His Notes and Books," in John Zukowsky, ed., *Mies Reconsidered: His Career, Legacy, and Disciples* (New York: Art Institute of Chicago and Rizzoli, 1986), 72–85; Kenneth Frampton, *Studies in Tectonic Culture* (Cambridge, Mass.: MIT Press, 1995).

21 Rudolf Wittkower, *Architectural Principles in the Age of Humanism* (London: Warburg Institute, 1949); Alina Payne, "Rudolf Wittkower and Architectural Principles in the Age of Modernism," *Journal of the Society of Architectural Historians* 53 (September 1994): 322–42.

22 Herbert Read, *Art in Industry* (London: Faber, 1934); Richards, "Towards a Rational Aesthetic"; Nikolaus Pevsner, *Pioneers of the Modern Movement* (London: Faber and Faber, 1936); Pevsner, *An Enquiry into Industrial Art in England* (Cambridge: Cambridge University Press, 1937).

23 This theme is pervasive in Giedion's work but is most lyrically expressed in the "subconscious of architecture" passage: "Apart from a certain *haut-goût* charm, the artistic drapery of the last century has gone musty. What remain fresh in the architecture of this period are above all the rare breakthroughs of the constructive principle. . . . In the nineteenth century, construction has the role of subconscious. Outwardly, it maintains the old grandiloquence [pathos]; underground, hidden behind facades, it constitutes the basis of our whole present-day existence." Sigfried Giedion, *Bauen in Frankreich, Bauen in Eisen, Bauen in Eisenbeton* (Leipzig: Klinkhardt and Biermann, 1928). He returns to this idea in *Space, Time and Architecture* (Cambridge, Mass.: Harvard University Press, 1941).

24 For his early conception of modernism, see Nikolaus Pevsner, "Review of Le Corbusier and Jeanneret, Pierre, *Ihr gesamtes Werk von 1910 bis 1929,*" *Göttingische gelehrte Anzeigen* 8 (August 1931): 303–12.

25 On Pevsner locating the sources of architectural modernism in the decorative arts, unlike Henry-Russell Hitchcock and Sigfried Giedion, see Alina Payne, "Architecture and Objects: The Power of Pevsner," *Harvard Design Magazine,* Spring 2002, 66–70. Pevsner's argument (especially the role of the English Arts and Crafts movement) maintained a presence in the major surveys of the period, and was developed and refined by one of his students. See Stefan Muthesius, *Das englische Vorbild* (Munich: Prestel, 1974). The topic was not ignored by Giedion (though he turned to it only in the late 1940s), but was framed in a more Wölfflinian way as he concentrated on the "anonymous" equipment of daily life (from baths and tractors to trains and locks), especially as it had been modified by mechanization. The change in posture is a recurrent argument for the changes in furniture and harks back to Wölfflin's key argument behind style change, which he developed in his early work. However, Giedion does not address the relationship to architecture. He also essentially ignores the "heroes" of Pevsner (Art Nouveau and Arts and Crafts). Giedion, *Mechanization Takes Command: A Contribution to Anonymous History* (New York: Oxford University Press, 1948) and "Furniture Design and the Common Object," in S. Papadaki, ed., *Le Corbusier: Architect, Painter, Writer* (New York: Macmillan, 1948), 39–40. On Giedion's take on objects and his debt to Le Corbusier's Pavillon de l'Esprit Nouveau and associated writings, see Stanislaus von Moos, "Giedion e il suo tempo," *Rassegna* 25 (1979): 6–17.

26 Trailblazing works include Tilmann Buddensieg, *Industriekultur: Peter Behrens and the AEG, 1907–1914* (Cambridge, Mass.: MIT Press, 1984); Stanford Anderson, "Modern Architecture and Industry: Peter Behrens and the Cultural Policy of Historical Determinism," *Oppositions* 11 (Winter 1977); Anderson, "Peter Behrens and the AEG Industrial Design," *Oppositions* 21 (Summer 1980): 78–97. Representative of more recent trends in scholarship on this topic are Klaus-Peter Arnold, *Geschichte der deutschen Werkstätten und der Gartenstadt Hellerau* (Dresden, 1993); Mark Jarzombek, "The *Kunstgewerbe,* the *Werkbund,* and the Aesthetics of Culture in the Wilhelmine Period," *JSAH* 53, no. 1 (March 1994): 7–19; Frederic Schwartz, "Cathedrals and Shoes: Concepts of Style in Wölfflin and Adorno," *New German Critique* 76 (Winter 1999): 3–48;

Christopher Long, "*Wiener Wohnkultur:* Interior Design in Vienna, 1910–1938," *Studies in the Decorative Arts* (1997–98): 29–51.

27 Henry-Russell Hitchcock, *Modern Architecture: Romanticism and Reintegration* (New York: Payson and Clarke, 1929); Read, *Art in Industry;* Frampton also notes this bias in *Studies in Tectonic Culture.*

28 Payne, "L'Ornament architectural."

29 On the crisis of representation in modern architecture, see Neil Levine, *Modern Architecture: Representation and Reality* (New Haven: Yale University Press, 2009).

30 On the mass-produced ornament, see Valerie Nègre, *L'ornement en serie: Architecture, terre cuite et carton-pierre* (Sprimont: Madraga, 2006).

31 "Technizismus und Klassizismus sind einander keine Feinde, im Gegenteil, sie sind zusammengehörig. Der Technizismus ist die geistige Verfassung, der Klassizismus ist sein künstlerischer Ausdruck. Sie hat uns das Vorbild aller modernen Reissbrettarchitektur beschert und uns verleitet, alle Architektur als glatt unmöglich zu verdächtigen, die kreuz und quer, quellend, bunt, dithyrambisch ist." Adolf Behne, *Die Wiederkehr der Kunst* (1919; Nendeln: Kraus, 1973), 73–74.

32 Pfleiderer, "Introduction," 3–22.

33 Harry Francis Mallgrave, ed. and trans., *Empathy, Form, and Space: Problems in German Aesthetics, 1873–1893* (Santa Monica: Getty Center, 1994); Juliet Koss, *Modernism after Wagner* (Minneapolis: University of Minnesota Press, 2010) and "Bauhaus Theatre of Human Dolls," Art Bulletin 85, no. 4 (December 2003): 724–45. Koss looks in particular at the Weimar Bauhaus experiments with dolls and automata so as to create a theatrical experience straddling empathy/familiarity and uncanniness/estrangement. More lateral in that he focused on ancient architecture yet nevertheless a major impetus toward the reevaluation of empathy theory has been Joseph Rykwert, *The Dancing Column* (Cambridge, Mass.: MIT Press, 1998). Finally, related though framed from the perspective of organicism as an issue for nineteenth-century theory, is Caroline van Eck, *Organicism in Nineteenth-Century Architecture: An Inquiry into its Theoretical and Philosophical Background* (Amsterdam: Architectura and Natura, 1994).

34 See Alina Payne, "Notes from the Field: Anthropomorphism," *Art Bulletin* (March 2012): 29–31.

35 For example, see Susan Stewart, *On Longing: Narratives of the Miniature, the Gigantic, the Souvenir, the Collection* (Durham, N.C.: Duke University Press, 1993); Naomi Schor, *Reading in Detail: Aesthetics and the Feminine* (New York: Methuen, 1987); Patricia Fumerton, *Cultural Aesthetics: Renaissance Literature and the Practice of Social Ornament* (Chicago: University of Chicago Press, 1991); Gaston Bachelard, *La poétique de l'espace* (Paris: Presses Universitaires de France, 1958); Andreas Grote, ed., *Macrocosmos in Microcosmo: Die Welt in der Stube* (Opladen, 1994); Bridget Elliott and Janice Helland, *Women Artists and the Decorative Art, 1880–1935: The Gender of Ornament* (London: Ashgate, 2002). For an assessment of this literature and its effects on ornament studies, see Payne, "L'Ornament architectural."

36 Daston, *Things That Talk: Object Lessons from Art and Science*; Brown, "Thing Theory," 1–22.

37 See, most recently, G. Davies and K. Kennedy, eds., *Medieval and Renaissance Art: People and Possessions* (London: V&A, 2009).

38 This is particularly the case in Islamic scholarship. See Eva Hoffman, "Pathways of Portability: Islamic and Christian Interchange from the Tenth to Twelfth Century," *Art History* 24, no. 1 (February 2001): 17–50; Avinoam Shalem, "Objects as Carriers of Real or Contrived Memories in a Cross-Cultural Context," *Mitteilungen zur Spätantike Archäologie und Byzantinischen Kunstgeschichte* 4 (2005): 101–19.

39 Martina Droth, ed., *Taking Shape: Finding Sculpture in the Decorative Arts*, exh. cat. (Los Angeles: J. Paul Getty Museum, 2009).

40 For a proposal to reevaluate the small scale in Renaissance architecture, see Payne, "Materiality, Crafting, and Scale."

41 It is in the context of a discussion of minimalism that the term "objecthood" was coined to address precisely this vexed relationship between artistic object and miniature architecture (which Fried unpacks and ultimately opposes as a critical category). Michael Fried, "Art and Objecthood," *Artforum* 5 (June 1967): 12–23.

42 Winfried Menninghaus, *Das Versprechen der Schönheit* (Frankfurt am Main: Suhrkamp, 2003).

43 Bruno Latour, *The Pasteurization of France* (Cambridge, Mass.: Harvard University Press, 1988).

44 Hans Heinz Holz, *Vom Kunstwerk zur Ware* (Neuwied: Hermann Luchterhand, 1972).

45 Julius Langbehn, *Rembrandt als Erzieher* (Leipzig: C. L. Hirschfield, 1890); Oswald Spengler, *Der Untergang des Abendlandes, Gestalt und Wircklichkeit* (Munich: Beck, 1918).

46 For example, see Dal Co, *Figures of Architecture and Thought;* Frederic Schwartz, *The Werkbund: Design Theory and Mass Culture Before the First World War* (New Haven: Yale University Press, 1996).

47 A compelling account of one such instance—whiteness as fashion item and ornament in modern architecture—is offered by Mark Wigley, *White Walls, Designer Dresses* (Cambridge, Mass.: MIT Press, 1995). See also William W. Braham, *Modern Color/Modern Architecture* (London: Ashgate, 2002).

CHAPTER 1 | SEMPER'S HERITAGE

1 See especially Sigfried Giedion, *Space, Time and Architecture* (1941); Nikolaus Pevsner, *Pioneers of the Modern Movement* (1936); Pierre Francastel, *Art and Technology in the Nineteenth and the Twentieth Centuries* (1956).

2 See, for example, Jakob von Falke, *Geschichte des modernen Geschmacks* (1866; Leipzig: T. O. Weigel, 1880). For a history of the educational movement in Vienna, see Gottfried Fliedl, *Kunst und Lehre am Beginn der Moderne: Die*

Wiener Kunstgewerbeschule, 1867–1918 (Salzburg: Residenz, 1986).

3 Henry Cole (writing as Felix Summerly) provides a history of the initiative that led to the Great Exhibition and started with competitions organized at the Society of Arts to award prizes to high-quality mass-produced objects and attributes much of the vision to Prince Albert. He specifically mentions the impulse to industrial education as one of the important "fruits" of the exhibition, although of course it had been present in the conception of the School of Arts, a program that he had been very critical of and did his utmost to reform. Henry Cole, "Extracts from the Preface to the Catalogue of the Exhibition of 1851," in Summerly's Art Manufactures, *Fifty Years of Public Work* (London: George Bell and Sons, 1884), 2: 252. On the debates in England following the Great Exhibition, see Kurt Reising, "Kunst, Industrie und die Gesellschaft in England," in Peter Noever, ed., *Kunst und Industrie: Die Anfänge des Museums für Angewandte Kunst in Wien* (Vienna: Hatje Cantz Verlag, 2000), 49–66. More recently on the Victorian debate on industrialization and the associated move toward the aestheticization of manufacture, see Joseph Bizup, *Manufacturing Culture: Vindications of Early Victorian Industry* (Charlottesville: University of Virginia Press, 2003).

4 Owen Jones, "Gleanings from the Great Exhibition of 1851," *Journal of Design and Manufactures* 5 (June 1851); Richard Redgrave, "Supplementary Report on Design," in *Reports by the Juries* (London: William Clowes and Sons, 1852); Ralph Wornum, "The Exhibition as a Lesson in Taste," in *The Crystal Palace Exhibition Illustrated Catalogue* (London, 1851).

5 For a review of such publications, see Dietrich Schneider Henn, *Ornament und Dekoration* (Munich: Prestel, 1997).

6 Awareness of this two-pronged readership is evident in the almost innumerable journals that appeared. See, for example, *Kunst und Gewerbe: Wochenschrift zur Förderung deutscher Kunst-Industrie* (started 1867); *Bayerisches Industrie und Gewerbeblatt* (started 1869); *Blätter für Kunstgewerbe* (1871); *Allgemeine illustrierte Industrie und Kunstzeitung* (started 1874); *Kunstgewerbeblatt* (started 1885); *Dekorative Kunst* (started 1897); *Deutsche Kunst und Dekoration* (started 1897). Quite often such journals were the organs of newly created museums. For example, *Mitteilungen des k.k. Oesterreichischen Museums für Industrie und Kunst; Mitteilungen des Mährischen Gewerbemuseums; Kunst und Kunsthandwerk* (from 1898 as journal of the Museum für Kunst und Industrie).

7 Bizup, *Manufacturing Culture*, 127.

8 Augustus W. N. Pugin, *Designs for Gold and Silversmiths* (London: Ackerman, 1836); Pugin, *Floriated Ornament* (London: Bohn, 1849).

9 For an analysis of Victorian approaches to aesthetic education, social welfare, and economics as result of the Industrial Revolution, see Bizup, *Manufacturing Culture*.

10 This perspective was already present in Ruskin's first great publication success, *The Seven Lamps of Architecture*: "XIX. The Lamp of Truth. The last form of fallacy which it will be remembered we had to deprecate, was the substitution of cast or machine work for that of the hand, generally expressible as Operative Deceit. There are two reasons, both weighty, against this practice: one, that all cast and machine work is bad; the other, that it is dishonest... Ornament, as I have often before observed, has two entirely distinct sources of agreeableness: One, that of the abstract beauty of its forms... the other, the sense of human labour and care spent upon it." He continues: "XXI. The Lamp of Life.... I said, early in this essay, that hand-work might always be known from machine-work;... but so long as men work as men, putting their heart into what they do, and doing their best, it matters not how bad workmen they may be, there will be that in the handling which is above all price." And: "XXIV. The Lamp of Life. I believe the right question to ask, respecting all ornament, is simply this: was it done with enjoyment—was the carver happy while he was about it?" John Ruskin, *The Seven Lamps of Architecture* (London: Smith, Elder, 1849), 53, 169, 173.

11 For example, in 1848 William Dyce, head of the London School of Design (the system of Schools of Design was founded in 1837 to raise the standard of British manufactures) felt the need to argue that the level of art education (and masters) in the School of Design should be as high as that in the Academy of Fine Art, and used the careers and education of famous Renaissance artists/craftsmen such as Benvenuto Cellini to make his point. William Dyce, "Lecture of Ornament Delivered to the Students of the London School of Design," *Journal of Design* (1849): 28–29.

12 Women's magazines played an important role for the *Hausindustrie* from the 1880s. See *Illustrierte Frauen-Zeitung*. Bernward Deneke, "Die Entdeckung der Volkskunst für das Kunstgewerbe," *Zeitschrift für Volkskunde* 60 (1964): 196. Semper himself had deferred to the ladies in the audience at his conference "Über die formelle Gesetzmässigkeit des Schmuckes und dessen Bedeutung als Kunstsymbol," subsequently published in 1856 in Zurich in *Monatsheft des wissenschaftlichen Vereins*.

13 Jakob von Falke, *Die Kunst im Hause: Geschichtliche und kritischaesthetische Studien uber die Dekoration und Ausstattung der Wohnung* (Art in the House: Historical, Critical, and Aesthetical Studies on the Decorating and Furnishing of the Dwelling) (Vienna: Gerold, 1871; English ed., Boston: Prang, 1879); Charles Blanc, *Grammaire des arts décoratifs: Décoration intérieure de la maison*, 2nd ed. (Paris: Renouard, 1882); Lewis F. Day, *Every-Day Art: Short Essays on the Arts Not Fine* (London: B. T. Batsford, 1882). Falke was particularly active on this arena of popularization. See also his *Aesthetik des Kunsthandwerks: Ein Handbuch für Haus, Schule und Werkstätte* (Stuttgart: W. Spemann, 1883).

14 William Dyce, "Instruction in Practical Art in Foreign Schools of Design, Made in 1839," in *A Catalogue of the Articles of Ornamental Art Selected for the Exhibition of the Works of Industry of*

All Nations in 1851, and Purchased by the Government (London: Chapman and Hall, for the Department of Practical Art); Dyce, *The Drawing Book of the Government School of Design* (1842); Richard Redgrave, *Report on Design: A Supplement to the Report of the Jury of Class XXX of the Exhibition of 1851* (London: William Clowes, 1852).

15 Henry Cole was among the first to note this fact: "I freely admit, that in the execution of art applied to industry, the French are, upon an average, better educated and better workmen than ourselves." Cole, *Fifty Years*, 2: 251.

16 For this term and the Austrian response, see Kathrin Pokorny-Nagel, "Zur Gründungsgeschichte des k.k. Österreichischen Museums für Kunst und Industrie," in Noever, *Kunst und Industrie*, 52–89; for the German response, see Barbara Mundt, *Die deutschen Kunstgewerbemuseen im 19. Jahrhundert* (Munich: Prestel, 1974), chapters 2 and 3.

17 For example, see William Dyce and Charles Wilson, *A Letter to Lord Meadowbank and the Committee of the Honourable Board of Trustees for the Encouragement of Arts and Manufactures: On the Best Means of Ameliorating the Arts and Manufactures of Scotland in Point of Taste* (Edinburgh: Thomas Constable, May 30, 1837); Werner Sombart, *Die gewerbliche Arbeiterfrage* (Leipzig: G. J. Göschen, 1904).

18 Owen Jones, *The Grammar of Ornament* (London: Day and Son, 1856); Ralph Wornum, *Analysis of Ornament: The Characteristics of Styles. An Introduction to the Study of the History of Ornamental Art* (London: Chapman and Hall, 1855; original lectures given 1848–50); W. and G. Audsley, *Outlines of Ornament in the Leading Styles: Selected from Executed Ancient and Modern Works, a Book of Reference for the Architect, Sculptor, Decorative Artist and Practical Painter* (London: Sampson, Low, Marston, Searle and Rivington, 1881); Jules Bourgoin, *Theorie de l'ornement* (Paris: Ducher, 1883); Heinrich Dolmetsch, *Ornamentschatz: Ein Musterbuch stilvoller Ornamente aus allen Kunstepochen* (Stuttgart: Julius Hoffmann, 1889); Richard Glazier, *A Manual of Historic Ornament* (London: B. T. Batsford, 1899); F. Edward Hulme, *Birth and Development of Ornament* (London: Swan Sonnenschein, New York: Macmillan, 1893).

19 Rudolf von Eitelberger, *Die Kunstbewegung in Oesterreich seit der Pariser Weltausstellung im Jahre 1867: Im Auftrage des KK. Unterrichts Ministerium* (Vienna: K. K. Schulbucher, 1878); Cornelius Gurlitt, *Die internationale Kunstausstellung zu Berlin, 1891* (Munich: F. Hanfstaengl, 1891).

20 Falke, *Geschichte des modernen Geschmacks.*

21 Jakob von Falke and Johann A. von Eye, *Kunst und Leben der Vorzeit vom Beginn des Mittelalters bis zu Anfang des 19. Jahrhunderts* (Nürnberg: Bauer and Raspe, 1868).

22 Charles Blanc, *Art in Ornament and Dress* (New York: Scribner, Welford and Armstrong, 1877; trans. of *L'art de la parure*); Jakob von Falke, *Costümegeschichte der Culturvölker* (Stuttgart: W. Spemann, 1880); Jakob von Falke, *Die deutschen Trachten und Modenwelt, ein Beitrag zur deutschen Culturgeschichte* (Leipzig: Meyer, 1858).

23 Falke, *Die Kunst im Hause;* Blanc, *Grammaire des arts décoratifs;* Christopher Dresser, *The Art of Decorative Design* (London: Day and Son, 1862); Dresser, *Principles of Decorative Design* (1873); Dresser, *Studies in Design* (1876).

24 Leon Battista Alberti, *On the Art of Building in Ten Books*, trans. J. Rykwert, R. Tavernor, and N. Leach (Cambridge Mass.: MIT Press, 1988); Lucian, *The Hall*, trans. A.M. Harmon, Loeb Classical Library (Cambridge, Mass.: Harvard University Press, 1913); Sebastiano Serlio, *Tutte l'opere d'architettura et prospettiva*, Book VII, (Ridgewood, N.J.: Gregg, 1964; facs. ed. Venice, 1619), f.126.

25 On this topic, see Alina Payne, "Architects and Academies: Architectural Theories of *imitatio* and the Debates on Language and Style," in G. Clarke and P. Crossley, eds., *Architecture and Language* (Cambridge: Cambridge University Press, 2000), 118–133, 195–202; contra Ursula Franke, who sees the "Autonomisierung" of ornament as starting with Philip Moritz in the later eighteenth century. Franke, "Bausteine für eine Theorie ornamentaler Kunst: Zur Autonomisierung des Ornaments bei Karl Philip Moritz," in U. Franke and H. Paetzold, eds., *Ornament und Geschichte* (Bonn: Bouvier, 1996), 89–106.

26 Alina Payne, *The Architectural Treatise in the Italian Renaissance* (New York: Cambridge University Press, 1999).

27 Benedetto Varchi and Vincenzo Borghini, *Pittura e scultura nel Cinquecento*, ed. P. Barocchi (Livorno: Sillabe, 1998).

28 Hans-Lothar Kroll, *Das Ornament in der Kunsttheorie des 19. Jahrhunderts* (Hildesheim, 1987). For a vertical study through essays by several scholars, see Isabelle Frank and Freia Hartung eds., *Die Rhetorik des Ornaments* (Berlin: Wilhelm Fink, 2001).

29 On Moritz and Kant as anticipating abstraction in their definitions of beauty, see David Morgan, "The Idea of Abstraction in German Theories of Ornament from Kant to Kandinsky," *Journal of Aesthetics and Art Criticism* 50 (Summer 1992): 231–42. On Moritz and his œuvre, see Ruth Ghisler, "Vorbegriffe zu einer Theorie der Ornamente von Karl Philip Moritz. Fragmente einer Architekturlehre aus Goethes römischen Freundenkreis," *Jahrbuch des Freien Deutsche Hochstifts* (1970), 32–58; and Franke, "Bausteine für eine Theorie ornamentaler Kunst."

30 In the chapter on arabesques he states: "Es ist das Wesen der Zierde selbst, die sich an kein Gesetz bindet, weil sie keinen Zweck hat, als den zu vergnügen." Karl Philipp Moritz, *Vorbegriffe einer Theorie der Ornamente von K. P. Moritz* (Nördlingen: Dr. Alfons Uhl, 1986; facs. ed. Berlin, 1793), 28. His description of the column contains throwbacks to Alberti, who defines ornament as complement and light of beauty ("lux pulchritudinis") (Leon Battista Alberti, *De re aedificatoria. Index verborum*, ed. H.-K. Lücke [Munich: Prestel, 1976], 4: 93v, 28): "Durch die angebrachte Zierrath soll unsere Aufmerksamkeit mehr auf die Sache selbst hingeheftet werden, so dass wir bei ihrem blossen Anblick

gern verweilen. Die *Zierrath* muss also nichts fremdartiges enthalten, sie muss nichts enthalten, wodurch unsre Aufmerksamkeit von der Sache abgezogen wird, sondern sie muss vielmehr das Wesen der Sache, woran sie befindlich ist, auf alle Weise andeuten, und bezeichnen, damit wir in der Zierrath die Sache gleichsam wieder erkennen und wieder finden." Ibid., 18.

31 For Moritz, the shape of the vase symbolizes (and represents) dynamically (*thätig*) "the live concept of holding" (*den lebendigen Begriff des Fassens*) as well as that of preserving (*Aufbewahren*). It is derived from nature, from the flower's bloom, which widens at the top to allow the dew to be captured, but also "die Form der Vase ergiebt sich von selbst aus der natürlichen Idee des Fassens." Ibid., 39.

32 For example, see his speach of 1792 at the academy, "Über den Einfluss des Studiums der schönen Künste auf Manufakturen und Gewerbe."

33 Kroll notes the terminological expansiveness that complicated definitions. Kroll, *Das Ornament in der Kunsttheorie,* 12. For the ancient rhetoric category "ornament," see Richard Volkmann, *Die Rhetorik der Griechen und Römer in systematischer Übersicht* (Leipzig: B. G. Teubner, 1885).

34 Schelling's *Philosophie der Kunst* was published posthumously in 1859, but he had taught at Berlin since 1841, and his differences from Hegel were the subject of open discussions right away. On the philosophical tradition on this point, see Eduard von Hartmann, *Die deutsche Ästhetik seit Kant* (Leipzig: Friedrich, 1887), 2: 461–62. For an extensive discussion of these implications for the discourse of the arts, see Maria Ocon-Fernandez, *Ornament und Moderne: Theoriebildung und Ornamentdebatte im deutschen Architekturdiskurs (1850–1930)* (Berlin: Reimer, 2004).

35 The literature on Semper is vast. For the most recent contributions and bibliography, see Harry Francis Mallgrave, *Gottfried Semper, Architect of the Nineteenth Century* (New Haven: Yale University Press, 1996); Mallgrave, "Introduction," in Gottfried Semper, *Style* (Los Angeles: Getty Center, 2004); Mari Hvattum, *Gottfried Semper and the Problem of Historicism* (New York: Cambridge University Press, 2004); Winfried Nerdinger and Werner Oechslin, eds., *Gottfried Semper, 1803–1897: Architektur und Wissenschaft,* exh. cat. (Zurich: GTA, and Berlin: Prestel Verlag, 2004); Sokratis Georgiadis, *Gottfried Semper (1803–1879): Griechenland und die lebendige Architektur* (Stuttgart: Staatliche Akademie der bildenden Künste and University Studio Press, 2005); for an earlier groundbreaking publication, see Eva Börsch-Soupan, *Berliner Baukunst nach Schinkel* (Munich: Prestel, 1977).

36 Jones, *Grammar of Ornament;* Cole, *Fifty Years;* Leon de Laborde, *De l'union des arts et de l'industrie,* 2 vols. (Paris: Imprimerie imperiale, 1856).

37 A fundamental account of Semper's activities and engagement with various milieus in Dresden and London remains Mallgrave, *Semper,* 149–64, 189–205.

38 The essay was published as a book by his faithful publisher Vieweg, who supported him in his years of exile in France and England. Gottfried Semper, *Wissenschaft, Industrie und Kunst: Vorschläge zur Anregung des nationalen Kunstgefühls* (Brunswick: Vieweg, 1852; ed. H. Wingler, Mainz: Florian Kupferberg, 1966). Hereafter *WIK.* English translation H. Mallgrave and W. Herrmann, "Science, Industry and Art," in Gottfried Semper, *The Four Elements of Architecture* (Cambridge: Cambridge University Press, 1989).

39 Scholarship on Semper's role in the creation of the V&A is divided, some seeing him as a significant force in its creation, others seeing him more as a receiver of ideas. On Semper's role in the circle of Prince Albert and his influential though unsuccessful proposal for a museum building and an entire cultural center (what later became the V&A and the Royal Albert Hall) in London in 1855, see Rainald Franz, "Das System Gottfried Semper's. Reform des Kunstgewerbes und Grundlagen für ein Museum für Kunst und Industrie in ihren Auswirkungen auf das Österreichische Museum," in Noever, *Kunst und Industrie,* 41–51; and Gert Reising, "Kunst, Industrie und Gesellschaft: Gottfried Semper in England," in E. Börsch-Soupan, ed., *Gottfried Semper und die Mitte des 19. Jahrhunderts* (Basel: Birkhauser, 1976), 49–66. On Semper's relationship to Henry Cole and the latter's help in finding work for Semper within the exhibition, see Sonja Hildebrand, "'. . . grossartigere Umgebungen': Gottfried Semper in London," and Heidrunn Laudel, "Werkverzeichniss," both in Nerdinger and Oechslin, *Gottfried Semper,* 260–68, 275–78. For a view of Semper more as an interpreter of the English movement for the Continent and less as an influence on the English scene, see Michael Conforti, "The Ideal Enterprise and the Applied Arts," in M. Baker and B. Richardson, eds., *A Grand Design: The Victoria and Albert Museum* (London: V&A, 1997), 23. One contemporary voice—that of Cornelius Gurlitt—argues that the developments in London were the work of two Germans: Prince Albert and Semper. It was their idea to "erzieherisch durch Museen und Schulen auf das Gerwerbe zu wirken." Gurlitt refers to confidential information from one J. W. Appell, librarian at V&A, on how the English keenly covered up the German origin of their museum and tried to hide the poverty of the *Kunstgewerbe* in their country. Cornelius Gurlitt, *Die deutsche Kunst des XIX Jahrhunderts* (Berlin: Georg Bondi, 1899), 73.

40 Gottfried Semper, *Der Stil,* 2 vols. (1860–63; Munich: Fr. Bruckmann Verlag, 1878). On Semper's planned but never finished third volume, see Michael Gnehm, "'Kritik gegenwärtiger Zustände'—als Ursprungskritik zum dritten Band des *Stil,*" in Nerdinger and Oechslin, *Gottfried Semper,* 314–20. Gottfried Semper, *Die vier Elemente der Baukunst* (Braunschweig: Vieweg und Sohn, 1851); Semper, *Kleine Schriften* (1856), ed. M. and H. Semper (Berlin: W. Spemann, 1884).

41 Semper's essay "Ideales Museum für Metalltechnik" of 1852 (translated

from "Practical Art in Metal and Hard Materials and Its Technology and History," 1852 ms. in the Victoria and Albert Museum) was dedicated in 1867 to Rudolf von Eitelberger, the first director of the Vienna museum; it was first published years later in Julius Leisching, "Gottfried Semper und die Museen," *Mitteilungen des Mährischen Gewerbemuseums* (Brünn, 1903). G. Semper, "Über die formelle Gesetzmässigkeit des Schmuckes und dessen Bedeutung als Kunstsymbol," *Monatsheft des wissenschaftlichen Vereins* (Zurich: Meyer and Zeller, 1856); reprinted in *Kleine Schriften* (1884).

42 Among anthropologists influenced by Semper were the German Franz Boas, the English H. Colley March, the Swede Hjalmar Stolpe, and the Irish Alfred Haddon, thus testifying to a broad international reception of his ideas over the span of fifty years. On a more in-depth discussion of this phenomenon, see chapters 2 and 3. Reception among English- or French-speaking architects was limited to those with a good knowledge of German, since the book was not translated until very recently. For example, Lawrence Harvey lectured in London at the RIBA in 1884–85, describing Semper's theory so as to popularize it. "This exceptional esteem is principally due to Semper's writings, of which his book, *Der Stil*, is the most important, containing as it does the substance of his former works.... As Semper was convinced that the beginnings of art are to be found in the humble crafts that supply the necessaries of every-day life, and that even now they have the greatest influence in forming our taste, he was one of the first to maintain the importance of founding museums of art work." Lawrence Harvey, "Semper's Theory of Evolution in Architectural Ornament," in *Transactions of the RIBA*, n.s., vol. 1 (1884–85): 1, 32.

43 Leon Battista Alberti, *De pictura* (1435).

44 Georg Wilhelm Hegel, *Introductory Lectures on Aesthetics*, ed. M. Inwood (London: Penguin, 1993), 76. Semper himself deplores the distinction. *Der Stil*, 1: ix.

45 Wolfgang Herrmann, *Gottfried Semper: In Search of Architecture* (Cambridge, Mass.: MIT Press, 1984), 223. On Semper's revisions of the system of the arts, see Joseph Rykwert, "Semper and the Conception of Style," in Börsch-Soupan, *Gottfried Semper und die Mitte des 19. Jahrhunderts*, 70–78.

46 Semper, *Der Stil*, 1: vii. His terms are *Kunsttrieb*, *Verfall der Künste*, and *Zukunftskunst*, all of which will echo through many subsequent publications.

47 "Aber jene höheren Regionen der Kunst bezeichnen nur die äusserste Grenze des zu behandelnden Gebietes, bei dessen Eintritt wir jenen einfacheren Werken der Kunst begegnen, an welchen diese sich am frühesten bethätigte, ich meine den Schmuck, die Waffen, die Gewebe, die Töpferwerke, den Hausrath, mit einem Wort die *Kunstindustrie*, oder das, was man auch die *technischen Künste* nennt. Auch diese sind in unserer Aufgabe, und zwar in erster Linie enthalten;— zunächst weil die aesthetische Notwendigkeit, um die es sich handelt, gerade an diesen ältesten und einfachsten Erfindungen des *Kunsttriebes* am klarsten und fasslichsten hervortritt; zweitens weil sich an ihnen bereits ein gewisser Gesetzcodex der praktischen Aesthetik typisch festgestellt und formuliert hatte, *vor* der Erfindung der monumentalen Kunst, die von ihnen, wie gezeigt werden wird, eine bereits fertige Formensprache entlehnte, und auch in anderer ganz unmittlebarer Weise ihrem Einflusse gehorcht; drittens aber und vornehmlichst, weil jene von der Kunstgelehrtheit so qualificirten *Kleinkünste* der Einfluss unserer gegenwärtigen Volkserziehung und die Tendenz des Jahrhunderts am empfindlichsten trifft, und zur beabsichtigten Hebung des Kunstsinnes im Allgemeinen, und mit ihr die Kunst, nichts mehr noththut als gerade auf dem Gebiete der technischen Künste diesen Gewalten entgegen zu wirken. Denn es ist nicht zu bezweifeln, dass die Kunst, inmitten eines grossartigen Strudels von Verhältnissen, ihr Steuer, ihren Kurs, und zugleich, was das Schlimmste ist, ihre Triebkraft verloren hat." Ibid., 1: ix.

48 "wie die Natur—ebenso liegen auch der Kunst nur wenige Normalformen und Typen unter, die aus urälteste Tradition stammen in stetem Wiederhervortreten dennoch eine unendliche Mannigfaltigkeit darbieten, und gleich jene Naturtypen ihre Geschichte haben." Ibid., 1: viii."Diese Typen sind den verschiedenen technischen Künsten entlehnt, wie sie in primitivster Handhabung oder selbst in vogerückter Entwicklung als die ursprünglichsten Beschützerinnen der heiligen Herdflamme gedacht worden. Sie erhielten sehr frühzeitig symbolische Bedeutung, wurden aber zugleich in ihrer ursprünglichsten technisch-räumlichen Benützung niemals abgeschafft, sondern führen auch in diesem Sinne fort, bei den späteren Umbildungen der architektonischen Formen als wichtige Agentien nachzuwirken." Ibid., 1: 6.

49 Johann August Schlettwein, *Grundfeste der Staaten oder die politische Oekonomie* (Giessen: Krieger, 1779), 265, 311.

50 Hartmut Meyer, 12; Franz Jacob Schmitt, "Nekolog Karl Bötticher," *Deutschen Nekolog*, 1889, 80; Schmitt, "Nekrolog Karl Bötticher"; Wolfgang Herrmann, "Introduction," *In What Style Should We Build?* (Santa Monica: Getty Center, 1992).

51 Semper could have seen a copy of Bötticher's book in 1842 Leipzig, where it was displayed at the first congress of German architects shortly before its official launch. Since no traces of a reaction to it surfaced in his manuscripts in this period, Herrmann has argued that he did not actually read it until December 13, 1852, at the British Library in London and that the many similarities between their views (on textile as Ur-wall, symbol, core vs. artistic form) were in fact coincidental. See Wolfgang Herrmann, *Gottfried Semper: Theoretischer Nachlass* (Basel: Birkhauser, 1981), 26–27. However, Bötticher had also published an article on his theories in 1840 ("Entwicklung der hellenischen Tektonik") in *Allgemeine Bauzeitung* 5 (1840): 316–30, and Semper may well have

been aware of them long before his English exile. On Bötticher's article, see Eva Börsch-Soupan, *Berliner Baukunst nach Schinkel* (Munich: Prestel, 1977), 20, 205.

52 See Christian Beuth, *Vorbilder für Fabrikanten und Handwerker* (1821–36), to which Bötticher contributed most to the last of three volumes.

53 Karl Bötticher, *Die Tektonik der Hellenen*, 2 vols. (Berlin: Ernst and Korn, 1874), 1: 26.

54 The great archaeologist Ernst Curtius, excavator of Olympia, owed much to Bötticher and was also a participant at the Schinkelfests, celebrations of Schinkel's birthday by the Berlin Architects' Union. At the Fest on March 13, 1853, he delivered the lecture "Über die Kunst der Hellenen." Adolf Michaelis, "Ernst Curtius," *Biographische Jahrbuch und Deutscher Nekrolog*, ed. A. Bettelheim (Berlin: Georg Reimer, 1897), 65. Cornelius Gurlitt, among many, noted with something resembling contempt this failing in Bötticher's preparation.

55 "Das griechische Wort für Bauen bedeutet daher auch Schmücken, in ganz ähnlichem Doppelsinne wie der früher hervorgehobene des Wortes Kosmos. Das Gehänge, der Kranz, und jener namelose Schmuck der die Richtung markiert, sind die wichtigsten Symbole, deren sich die hellenische Baukunst bedient, um das Angedeutete zu erreichen. Sie haben ihre Analogien nicht unmittelbar in der Natur, sondern fast auschliesslich im Schmuck, der den menschlichen Körper ziert." *Gottfried Semper: Über die formelle Gesetzmässigkeit des Schmuckes und dessen Bedeutung als Kunstsymbolik* (Zurich: Meyer and Zeller, 1856), 2, 6.

56 Herrmann, *Gottfried Semper*, 219, 223. "wo der Mensch schmückt, hebt er nur mit mehr oder weniger bewusstem Tun eine Naturgesetzlichkeit an dem Gegenstand, den er ziert, deutlicher hervor."

57 "allein es ist nicht absolut notwendig, dass der Stoff als solcher zu der Kunsterscheinung als Faktor hinzutrete." *Der Stil*, 1: xvi. What he rejects is the position that "die architektonische Formenwelt ausschliesslich aus stöfflichen konstruktiven Bedingungen hervorgegangen und liesse sich nur aus diesen weiter entwickeln; da doch vielmehr der Stoff der Idee dienstbar, und keinsewegs für das sinnliche Hervortreten der letzteren in der Erscheinungswelt alleinig massgebend ist." (xv–xvi).

58 Ibid., 1: 88.

59 Ibid., 1: 8.

60 "biegsam, zäh" (textile); "weich, plastisch" (ceramics); "stabformig, elastisch" (wood); "fest, dicht" (stone). Ibid., 1: 9.

61 "Jeder Stoff bedingt seine besondere Art des bildnerischen Darstellens durch die Eigenschaften, die ihn von anderen Stoffen unterscheiden und eine ihm angehörige Technik der Behandlung erheischen. Ist nun ein Kunstmotiv durch irgend eine stoffliche Behandlung hidurchgeführt worden, so wird sein ursprünglicher Typus durch sie modificiert worden sein, gleichsam eine bestimmte Färbung erhalten haben; der Typus steht nicht mehr auf seiner primären Entwicklungstufe, sondern eine mehr oder minder ausgesprochene Metamorphose ist mit ihm vorgegangen." Ibid., 1: 218, 219.

62 For the fundamental presentation of Laugier's interpretation of the trope, see Wolfgang Herrmann, *Laugier and Eighteenth-Century French Theory* (London: A. Zwemmer, 1962). On the primitive hut as a central paradigm for Western architecture, see Joseph Rykwert, *On Adam's House in Paradise: The Idea of the Primitive Hut in Architectural History* (New York: Museum of Modern Art, 1972), and Rykwert, *The Dancing Column* (Cambridge, Mass.: MIT Press, 1998). On Laugier and Quatremère de Quincy nearing Semper's definition, see Hvattum, *Gottfried Semper and the Problem of Historicism*. Reassessing the interpretation of this architectural trope with specific reference to its rejection by Viollet-le-Duc, see Neil Levine, *Modern Architecture: Representation and Reality* (New Haven: Yale University Press, 2009), chap. 2 and 153–57.

63 "eine grob materialistische Anschauung, wonach das eigene Wesen der Baukunst nichts sein soll als durchgebildete Konstruktion, gleichsam illustrierte und illuminierte Statik und Mechanik, reine Stoffkundgebung. Dieses Prinzip hat sich in der Römerzeit, wie es scheint, zuerst erhoben, konsequenter im sogennanten gothischen Baustile entfaltet und erst in der neuesten Zeit offen bekannt." Semper, *Der Stil*, 1: 6–7. In vol. 2 Semper reiterates his contempt for the materialistic translation theory of wood supports into stone, and attacks the Vitruvian model again and ridicules Viollet-le-Duc (2: 200). Yet he accepts the Vitruvian model of the primitive hut at the symbolic level (2: 262–63). Viollet-le-Duc's vol. 1 of his *Entretiens* had come out in 1863, and it is in the second volume, titled "Des constructions primitives," where he develops an antirepresentational stance that Semper refers to in his own second volume of *Der Stil*, published likewise in 1863. Eugène-Emmanuel Viollet-le-Duc, *Entretiens sur l'Architecture* (Paris: A. Morel, 1863), 33–68.

64 "Als früheste von Händen producirte Scheidewand . . . den der Mensch erfand möchten wir den verbundenen und verflochtenen Zaun erkennen . . . Flechten der Zweige . . . ; von da kam man auf die Erfindung des Webens . . ." Semper, *Der Stil*, 1: 213.

65 "Unmöglichkeit des unvermittelten Übergangs des Bedürfnissbaues in die lapidarische Säulenarchitektur," Ibid., 1: 403. On his critique of the Vitruvian model, see 2: 200.

66 Semper develops the concept of *Bekleidung* halfway into his first volume in the chapter "Textile Kunst: Das Prinzip der Bekleidung in der Baukunst," *Der Stil*, 1: 213–17.

67 "Die Gerüste, welche dienen diese Raumabschlüsse zu halten, zu befestigen und zu tragen, sind Erfördernisse, die mit Raum und Raumesabtheilung unmittelbar nichts zu thun haben. Sie sind der ursprünglichen architektonischen Idee fremd und zunächst keine formenbestimmenden Elemente." Ibid., 1: 214. On the structure/ornament debate in the nineteenth century, particularly in France, and its

repercussions on art historical evaluations; see the seminal Anne-Marie Sankovitch, "Structure/Ornament and the Modern Figuration of Architecture," *Art Bulletin* 80 (1998): 687–717. On architectural representation and its corollary in ornament theories, see Neil Levine, "The Romantic Idea of Architectural Legibility: Henri Labrouste and the Neo-Grec," in A. Drexler, ed., *The Architecture of the École des Beaux-Arts* (New York: MoMA, 1977), 324–416, and, more recently as the main theme in Levine, *Modern Architecture*.

68 Semper, *Der Stil*, 1: 200.

69 "das älteste und berühmteste Prachtzelt"; "eine neue Anwendung des Prinzips der Bekleidung in der Architektur der frühesten Zeiten, nämlich die Umhüllung der konstruktiven Theile eines Baues." As a result, tent structures and baldachins are important connecting elements for Semper. Ibid., 1: 287–78. This idea had come up in Quatremère de Quincy's history of architecture, a book that Semper greatly admired. However, Quatremère did not make it the linchpin of his theory of architecture but simply presented it as one of the origins of architecture (of the nomadic peoples). For a discussion of Semper's use of Quatremère, see Hvattum, *Gottfried Semper and the Problem of Historicism*, 35–42.

70 "uraltversteinerten Verhüllung." Semper, *Der Stil*, 1: 282.

71 "und [waren] bereits in vormonumentaler Zeit an dem beweglichen Hausrath zu vollster und sehr ausgesprochener Entwicklung und Ausbildung gelangt." Ibid., 1: 200.

72 Ibid., 1: 214.

73 Ibid., 1: 247.

74 Semper identifies in Indian architecture the precedence of stucco over other materials ("dieses ältesten struktiven Bekleidungsstoffs der aus Erde und Ziegeln konstruirten Wände") and argues that it predated the terracotta applications. Ibid., 1: 247, 421.

75 Ibid., 1: 259.

76 "architektonische Einrichtung." Ibid., 1: 283

77 "zur Bekleidung [der Decke] des alten Hekatompedon gedient hatten" [predecessor to the Parthenon]. "Hier bleibt die Frage offen, wie das mit Terrakotten bekleidete Holzwerk des Epistyls und der Decke mit dem gleichfalls in alter Zeit holzernen Stützwerke (den Säulen) in Harmonie gebraucht wurde? Ich meinerseits zweifle nicht, dass die archäischen Holzsäulen eine dem Deckenwerke entsprechende Bekleidung gehabt haben." Ibid., 1: 418.

78 Ibid., 1: 224, 213. "die Anfänge des Bauens mit den Anfängen der Textrin zusammenfallen."

79 "Wo immer eine Mauer überhaupt Façade bilden und zu einer architektonischen Wirkung beitragen sollte, war sie polychromiert, und zum Theil mit historischen oder scenischen Malereien geziert." Ibid., 1: 34.

80 Ibid., 1: 247.

81 "Das Prinzip ihrer Verzierung [der Tempel] ist noch das plastisch polychrome, ein laxeres, reicheres, üppigeres als dasjenige der späteren dorischen Kunst." Ibid., 1: 421. Whether or not one accepts Semper's theory of *Bekleidung*, his historical ordering of the Doric developments is in fact correct. Modern scholarship has confirmed the dating of such buildings as the Basilica at Paestum vis-à-vis the "classic" Doric. See Frederick Winter, *Studies in Hellenistic Architecture* (Toronto: University of Toronto Press, 2006).

82 For the paradigmatic power of this metaphor in later architecture, see Werner Oechslin, "The Evolutionary Way to Modern Architecture: The Paradigm of *Stilhulse und Kern*," in Harry Francis Mallgrave, ed., *Otto Wagner: Reflections on the Raiment of Modernity* (Santa Monica: Getty Center for Art History and Humanities, 1993), 363–410.

83 Semper, *Der Stil*, 1: 419–20.

84 "Jedes Band gibt sich als textiles Produkt." Ibid., 1: 18; "Ein noch kräftigerer Ausdruck des Grundbegriffes *binden* wird durch Geflecht erreicht" (19).

85 "und verraten ihren stilistischen Ursprung in dieser Technik die wie bekannt in Korinth sehr früher Zeit in grosser Blüthe stand. Ich möchte die korintische Ordnung als die vorzugsweise keramische bezeichnen." Ibid., 2: 418–19.

86 Vitruvius is the origin of the sequence of orders, with Corinthian the last to be invented. Vitruvius, *De architectura*, 4, 1, 8.

87 "die Grundgesätze der gesamten ägyptischen Architektur scheinen in dem Nileimer gleich wie im Embryo enthalten zu sein, und nicht minder auffallend ist die Verwandschaft der Form der Hydria mit gewissen Typen des dorischen Baustils! Beide Formen sind Verkünderinnen dessen, was die Baukunst erfand, indem sie danach rang, das Wesen beider Völker monumental auszudrücken." Semper, *Der Stil*, 2: 5.

88 Ibid., 2: 88ff.

89 "der Formenkreis der sich in ihr [Gefässkunst] eben so sehr aus utilitarischen wie technischen Grundbedingungen herausbildete hatte eine hohe Bedeutung... für die traditionelle Formensprache aller Künste, und ganz besonders der Baukunst. Nicht nur sind die allgemeinen Grundsätze formaler Gliederung, und die Gegensätze zwischen den Theilen, die diese Gliederung ausmachen, in der Baukunst ganz die gleichen mit denen so eben entwickelten, auch einen grossen Theil der herkömmlichen Zeichen und Termen ihrer formalen Kunstsprache hat die genannte Kunst offenbar von der ursprünglicheren Gafässkunst entlehnt." Ibid., 2: 113.

90 See David van Zanten, *The Architectural Polychromy of the 1830s* (New York, 1977).

91 Franz Christian Gau, *Neu entdeckte Denkmäler von Nubien an den Ufern des Nils/ Antiquités de la Nubie, ou monuments inédits des bords du Nil* (Stuttgart: Cotta, 1822). In this book Gau had presented his findings of polychromy in Egypt and speculated that all ancient architecture would have been painted. Jakob Ignaz Hittorff, "De l'architecture polychrôme chez les Grecs, ou restitution complète du temple d'Empédocles, dans l'acropole de Sélinunte," in *Annali dell'Instituto di corrispondenza archaeologica* (1830), 2: 263–84, and

Jakob Ignaz Hittorff and L. Zanth, *Architecture antique de la Sicile* (Paris: P. Renouard, 1835). Semper himself started publishing on this topic in 1834. He had met Hittorff in Paris and seen his plates for the 1850 book on the temple of Selinunte. Both later lectured at the RIBA in London on polychromy, in January and February 1851. The London event included an exhibition of Semper's drawings of a polychrome Parthenon. The British interest in polychromy had started in 1836, when a commission was established to decide whether the Elgin marbles had been originally painted; in 1842 they published the report revealing that they had been. Gottfried Semper, *Vorläufige Bemerkungen über bemalte Architectur und Plastik bei den Alten* (Altona, 1834) and reprinted in *Kleine Schriften* (1884). For a detailed account of this period in Semper's career, see Mallgrave, *Semper*, 177–83. On Semper's early archaeological work, see Salvatore Pisani, "'Die Monumente sind durch Barbarei monochrom geworden': Zu den theoretischen Leitmaximen in Semper's *Vorläufige Bemerkungen über bemalte Architectur und Plastik bei den Alten*," in Nerdinger and Oechslin, *Gottfried Semper*, 101–8.

92 Semper, *Der Stil*, 2: 242, with a long explanatory footnote.

93 In a footnote Semper points to this genealogy of his thought. The publications he lists are "On the Study of Polychromy and Its Revival," *Museum of Classical Antiquities* 3 (July 1851); *Die vier Elemente der Baukunst* (Braunschweig, 1851); and "On the Origin of Polychromy in Architecture," in Owen Jones, *An Apology for the Colouring of the Greek Court* (London, 1854), 1: 212.

94 Wolfgang Herrmann, ed., *In What Style Should We Build?* (Santa Monica: Getty Center, 1992).

95 For example, J. Mordaunt Crook, *The Dilemma of Style: Architectural Ideas from the Picturesque to the Post-Modern* (London: J. Murray, 1987).

96 Indeed, he was as impatient with the materialists, who sought a new style in new materials alone, as with the "historians" who looked at past forms to establish a thesaurus of alternatives. Semper, *Der Stil*, 1: xv–xviii.

97 "die Stillehre dagegen fasst das Schöne einheitlich als Produkt oder Resultat, nicht als Summe oder Reihe." In his view this leads to "einem Ergebnisse voll von Lücken." Ibid., 1: viii.

98 Ibid., 1: 6.

99 "die Grundgesätze des Stiles in den technischen Künsten identisch sind mit denjenigen, die in der Architektur walten, dass diese Grundsätze dort in ihren enifachsten und klarsten Ausdrucken hervortreten, dass sie an ihnen zuerst sich feststellen und entwickelten." Ibid., 1: 7.

100 Semper, *WIK*. Semper reiterates this definition in slightly different words in his "Über die formelle Gesetzmäßigkeit," 42–43. Harry Francis Mallgrave has noted an evolution in Semper's definition of style across his many manuscripts and publications. However, the determinant role of the *Kunstindustrie* remained a constant. Mallgrave, "The Idea of Style: Gottfried Semper in London," Ph.D. diss., University of Pennsylvania, 1983, and Mallgrave, "A Commentary on the November Lecture," *RES: Journal of Anthropology and Aesthetics* 6 (Autumn 1983): 23–31.

101 Semper, *Der Stil*, 7–8. Here he adds the function/purpose (*Zweck*) as well.

102 On Semper's two exiles (one after a duel and the other after the 1849 revolution in Germany), see Herrmann, *Gottfried Semper: In Search of Architecture*, 12ff.

103 Indeed, he stated as much quite clearly in one of his preparatory texts toward *Der Stil* from c. 1856–59 (ms. 179, fols. 1–46). When he justifies his plan for the book ("to start with prearchitectural industrial art and to consider house furniture before the house") it is to the experience of the London exhibition that he points. "Another significant reason causes me to adopt this plan—the importance that industrial art and the crafts have always had but that the general public has only recently been made aware of through the great industrial exhibitions; these have also made it evident that a book on the theory of art must devote an important section to this artistic activity, which is much neglected by our aestheticians who, feeling superior, look down on it from the point of view of fine art." Herrmann, *Gottfried Semper: In Search of Architecture*, 57.

104 Ibid., 137.

105 See, for example, "Die hier niedergelegte Theorie über den Einfluss des Stucks auf die Weiterbildung monumentaler Typen und Stile... ist umwälzend... für die gesamte Kunstlehre..." Semper, *Der Stil*, 1: 247.

106 Semper, *WIK*, 138.

107 "Für die Maschiene soll erst ein besonderer Stil geschaffen werden, wobei vor allem das Zweckliche, als von der Maschiene unabhängig, die Entscheidung zu geben hat." Semper, *Der Stil*, 2: 244.

108 Semper, *Der Stil*, 2: 105–12.

109 Ibid., 2: xiii.

110 Ibid., 2: 138.

111 Riegl's famous attack on Semper is not about his "materialist view," which he rightly attributes to the "Semperians," but about the dubious historical chronology and geography of inventions that he constructs. "In the case of the Geometric Style, it is especially necessary to dispel once and for all the misconceptions surrounding its purely technical, material origin and the allegedly ahistorical nature of its development." Alois Riegl, *Problems of Style: Foundations for a History of Ornament* (1893; Princeton: Princeton University Press, 1993), 6, 304–5.

112 Semper, *WIK*, 136.

113 See especially Mallgrave on this topic. Harry Francis Mallgrave, "Gustav Klemm and Gottfried Semper," *RES: Journal of Anthropology and Aesthetics* 9 (Spring 1985): 69–80.

114 Semper, "Über die formelle Gesetzmäßigkeit," 42.

115 For a discussion of this discourse in Italy, see Philip Sohm, *Style in the Art Theory of Early Modern Italy* (New York: Cambridge University Press, 2002).

116 Semper was not alone in moving in this direction. Schinkel had been influenced by Humboldt; likewise, Goethe's forays into plant morphology

exerted an influence on German-speaking theorists. However, Semper developed these latent tendencies into a comprehensive theory.

117 Semper, *Der Stil,* 1: xv–xvi. Semper used Rumohr's *Italienische Forschungen* in particular.

118 Ibid., 1: 8ff. "Classification of the Technical Arts."

119 Semper, *Der Stil,* 2: 459.

120 "Vom Flechten der Zweige ist der Übergang zu dem Flechten des Bastes zu ähnlichen Zwecken leicht und natürlich. Von da kam man auf die Erfindung des Webens, zuerst mit Grashalmen oder natürliche Pflanzenfasern, hernach mit gesponnenen Faden aus vegetabilischen oder thierischen Stoffen." Semper, *Der Stil,* 1: 213.

121 On the gradual emergence of anthropology out of natural sciences, anatomy, and philology before it broke up into prehistoric archaeology, human biology, and ethnology, see Christian F. Feest, "The Origins of Professional Anthropology in Vienna," in B. Rupp-Eisenreich and J. Stagl, eds., *Kulturwissenschaften im Vielvölkerstaat* (Vienna: Bohlau, 1995), 113–31.

122 On the impact of Cuvier and Darwin on Semper's definition of style, see Joseph Rykwert, "Semper and the Conception of Style," and Adolf Max Vogt, "Gottfried Semper und Joseph Paxton," both in Börsch-Soupan, *Gottfried Semper und die Mitte des 19. Jahrhunderts,* 75–77, 193–95. Harry Mallgrave argues against placing too much weight on the impact of Cuvier and Darwin on Semper's thinking. Mallgrave, "Commentary on the November Lecture," 26.

123 On the sources for Dresser, Redgrave, and Jones, see Michael Snodin and Maurice Howard, *Ornament: A Social History Since 1450* (London: V&A and Yale University Press, 1996); Isabelle Frank, ed., "Introduction," in *The Theory of Decorative Art* (New Haven: Yale University Press, 2000), 1–29; Michael Whiteway, ed., *Christopher Dresser: A Design Revolution* (London: V&A, 2004); also the literature cited in Barry Bergdoll, *European Architecture, 1750–1890 (Oxford: Oxford University Press, 2000),* 218–20.

124 Vogt, "Gottfried Semper und Joseph Paxton," 193–95. He refers to Cuvier's *Das Thierreich* (trans. Leipzig, 1831).

125 Semper, *Der Stil,* 1: 1–2, 6.

126 "So kommt es, dass die fossilen Töpfe für die Geschichte der Kunst (sowie der Menschheit im Allgemeinen) das gleiche Interesse haben, welches der Naturforscher and den vorweltlichen Überresten der Pflanzen und der animalischen Welt findet. Sie sind die ältesten und beredtesten Dokumente der Geschichte. Man zeige Töpfe, die ein Volk hervorbrachte und es lässt sich im Allgemeinen sagen, welcher Art er war und auf welcher Stufe der Bildung es sich befand!" Semper refers to these studies in the text. Semper, *Der Stil,* 2: 212. See also Wolfgang Herrmann, "Gottfried Semper und Viehweg," in Börsch-Soupan, *Gottfried Semper und die Mitte des 19. Jahrhumderts,* 199–237, and Mallgrave, "Commentary on the November Lecture," 24–25.

127 On Semper's archaeological experiences, see Werner Oechslin, "Gottfried Semper und die Archaeologie in ihren neuerlichen Anfängen um 1830," in Nerdinger and Oechslin, *Gottfried Semper,* 92–100.

128 Adolphe-Théodore Brongniart, *Tableau des genres de végétaux fossiles considéré sous le point de vue de leur classification botanique et de leur distribution géologique* (Paris: L. Martinet, 1849), 2: 3.

129 "allgemeines Bedürfniss des Menschen" or "Verziehrungtrieb." Semper, *Der Stil,* 1: 7.

130 Gustav Klemm's *Kulturgeschichte der Menschheit* (Leipzig, 1843–1852) may have been a source for Semper, and their paths seem to have crossed in Dresden. Joseph Rykwert, "Semper and the Conception of Style," in Börsch-Soupan, *Gottfried Semper und die Mitte des 19. Jahrhunderts,* 67–82, and Mallgrave, "Gustav Klemm and Gottfried Semper."

131 For a crisp and pithy delineation of this argument, see Semper, "Über die Gesetzmässigkeit," 7–10.

132 For a discussion of the hearth in the context of the primitive hut, see Herrmann, *Gottfried Semper,* 171.

133 "Die grosse Londoner Industrieaustellung im Jahre 1851 gab über die uns beschäftigende Frage gar manchen Stoff zu Betrachtungen. Dazu gehörten besonders die textilen Produkte der wilden und zahmen Völker nicht-europäischer Kulturen und ihr naher Zusammenhang mit den häuslichen und baulichen Einrichtungen dieser Völker." Semper, *Der Stil,* 1: 223.

134 "Let me be allowed to give one example of the far-reaching influence of primitive form . . . on the development of the arts. The mat and the woven carpet derived from it . . . were the earliest spatial dividers and thus became the basic motif for all later wall decorations and for many other related branches of industry and architecture." Semper, *WIK,* 136–37.

135 "Unter den Erscheinungen, die darauf hindeuten [Abhängigkeit aller bildenen Künste von der Textrin], war mir keine so auffallend wie das Bauwesen der Neuseeländer, das sich wirklich zu einer Art von monumentaler Kunst erhoben hat, dessen Basis und materieller Hintergrund das ursprüngliche Zaungeflecht in seinem reinsten und ungemischtesten Wesen ist. Die Baukunst übernahm dieses Motiv hier so unmittelbar aus den Händen der Natur, wie dieses bei keinem andern Volke sich nachweisen lässt." Semper, *Der Stil,* 1: 224.

136 Semper, *WIK,* 137.

137 Semper, *Der Stil,* 2: 242.

138 "Proben dieser Kunst [chinesische Stickerei] sah ich im Jahre 1851 in der Ausstellung zu London, die mich in Stil und Behandlung so lebhaft an die bekannten ninivitischen Flachreliefs erinnerten, dass ich seit in diesen nichts anderes mehr erkennen konnte als eben in den Alabaster übersetzte Teppichstickerei der alten Assyrier, und zwar Reliefstickerei gleich jenen dem Datum nach modernen, dem Stile nach fast antediluvianischen chinesischen Tapeten." Semper, *Der Stil,* 1: 233.

139 The spoon is "eine Gefässform die schon bei den wilden und halbwilden Völkern die sorgfältigste und studierteste Ausbidlung hatte. Ich habe in der ethnographischen Sammlung des brit. Museums von derartigen Proben der Industrie der Eskimos, Uralasker

etc. . . . sowie der civilisirten aber der Natur festhaltenden Inder Skizzen gemacht, wovon ich hier Exempel beifüge." Semper, *Der Stil*, 2: 40.

140 Giorgio Vasari, *Le vite de' piu eccelenti pittori, scultori ed architettori* (1550).

141 Alina Payne, "Architecture, Style, and the Origins of Historicizing Art," *RES: Journal of Anthropology and Aesthetics* 40 (Fall 2001): 51–76.

142 Oswald Spengler, *The Decline of the West* (1918; Oxford: Oxford University Press, 1991), 110, 115.

143 For a synthesis and comprehensive statement on the symbol, see Ernst Cassirer, *Wesen und Wirkung des Symbolbegriffs* (1922–23; Darmstadt: Wissenschaftliche Buchgesellschaft, 1994).

144 See Leopold Schmidt, *Das österreichische Museum für Volkskunde* (Vienna, 1960). The term was actually not coined by Riegl but by Rudolf von Eitelberger in his essay "Die Volkskunst und die Hausindustrie," *Kunstgewerbliche Zeitfragen*, 1876. On the development of a discourse on folk art, see Bernward Deneke, "Die Entdeckung der Volkskunst für das Kunstgewerbe," *Zeitschrift für Volkskunde* 60 (1964): 168–201.

145 Semper, *Der Stil*, 2: 262–95.

146 Marco Frascari, "The Tell-the-Tale Detail," in Paula Behrens and Anthony Fisher, eds., *The Building of Architecture, Via* 7 (1984).

147 "Band, Decke, Naht, Saum und Bordüre gelten auch für das tektonische umrahmte Füllwerk" though taking into account the rigidity of the material which involves some formal changes. Semper, *Der Stil*, 2: 201.

148 Semper describes his interest in "das Werk als Resultat des Stoffes, der bei der Produktion benützt wird, sowie der Werkzeuge und Proceduren die dabei in Anwendung kommen."

149 Carlo Ginzburg, "Clues: Roots of an Evidential Paradigm," in *Clues, Myths, and the Historical Method* (1986 [Italian]; Baltimore: Johns Hopkins University Press, 1992).

150 Early on in *Der Stil*, Semper states his basic premise: "Wo der Mensch schmückt, hebt er nur mit mehr oder weniger bewussten Tun eine Naturgesetzlichkeit an dem Gegenstand, den er ziert, deutlicher hervor." Semper, *Der Stil*, 1: 6.

151 The statement occurred in one of the last lectures he delivered in Dresden (1849). Herrmann, *Gottfried Semper: In Search of Architecture*, 168.

152 Semper, *Der Stil*, 2: 88–89, 113.

153 Ibid., 2: 89, 231, 420.

154 Semper, "Über die Gesetzmässigkeit," 19.

155 Ibid., 18–25.

156 "Das Streben nach Massengleichgewicht und Symmetrie; der Mensch entwickelt sich vertical aufwärts und ist horizontal gerichtet." Ibid., 34, 30.

157 "Der in dem umrahmten Füllwerke enthaltene energische Gegensatz zwischen dessen beiden Bestandtheilen, dem Rahmen und der Füllung, führte sehr bald den künstlerischen Sinn zu seiner idealen Verwerthung und Verbildlichung, indem man ihn symbolisch ausdruckte. Man schmückt das in struktive Beziehung unthätige, in diesem Sinne leere, Feld mit Symbolen, die zunächst der Nichtbeteiligung des Füllwerkes an der Struktur entsprechen. . . . Dieser Gegensatz, der sich noch entschiedener und wohl ursprünglicher im eingefassten Kleinod zu erkennen gibt," Semper, *Der Stil*, 2: 202. See Semper, *Der Stil*, 1: xxxiv on statics, equilibrium, inertia, resistance of mass, symmetry, and connection to movement and equilibrium, and on the natural tendency to intensification of parts—*Verdichtung*—toward the center. Ibid., 1: xxxvii.

158 "Das Ornament sei der Repräsentant der erhaltenden Kräfte, denen das Pegma seine Festigkeit verdankt." Semper, *Der Stil*, 2: 207.

159 Semper, "Über die Gesetzmässigkeit," 9–10.

160 "Sicherlich steht die Sitte des Hautbemalens und Tätowierens mit dem Prinzip der Polychromie in den Künsten des Altertums und überhaupt mit den Anfängen der Kunst im innigsten Zusammenhange." Semper, "Über die Gesetzmässigkeit," 10.

161 "Die Kunst des Bekleidens der Nackheit es Leibes (wenn man die Bemalung der eigenen Haut nicht dazu rechnet, wovon oben die Rede war) ist vermutlich eine jüngere Erfindung als die Benützung deckender Oberflächen zu lagern und zu räumlichen Abschlüssen." Semper, *Der Stil*, 1: 213.

162 *Behang, Ring*, and *Richtungsschmuck* are his terms. Semper, "Über die Gesetzmässigkeit," 26. See also pp. 11 and 30 for the development of the anthropomorphic argument.

163 Hermann Lotze, *Geschichte der Ästhetik in Deutschland* (Munich: Cotta, 1868); Lotz, *Mikrokosmus: Ideen zur Naturgeschichte und Geschichte der Menschheit. Versuch einer Anthropologie* (Leipzig: Hirzel, 1856–64); Robert Vischer, *Über das optische Formgefühl* (Leipzig: Hermann Credner, 1873); Johannes Volkelt, *Der Symbolbegriff in der neuesten Ästhetik* (Jena: H. Dufft, 1876). In his review of the literature Wölfflin points out the contributions they made to the concept of "das Miterleben der fremden Form." Heinrich Wölfflin, "Prologomena zu einer Psychologie der Architektur," in *Kleine Schriften*, ed. J. Gantner (1886; Basel: Schwabe, 1946), 16–17. For a compendium of sources for empathy theory, see Harry Francis Mallgrave and Eleftherios Ikonomou, eds. and trans., *Empathy, Form, and Space: Problems in German Aesthetics, 1873–1893* (Santa Monica: Getty Center, 1994). For art-historical sources in archaeology, see, for example, Heinrich von Brunn, one of Wölfflin's teachers. On this issue, see Alina Payne, "Portable Ruins: The Pergamon Altar, Heinrich Wölfflin, and German Art History at the *fin de siècle*." *RES: Journal of Anthropology and Aesthetics* 54/55 (Spring–Autumn 2008): 168–89.

164 Eva Börsch-Soupan, "Der Renaissance Begriff der Berliner Schule im Vergleich zu Semper," in Börsch-Soupan, *Gottfried Semper und die Mitte des 19. Jahrhunderts*. Caroline van Eck, *Organicism in Nineteenth-Century Architecture: An Inquiry into Its Theoretical and Philosophical Background* (Amsterdam: Architectura and Natura, 1994).

165 On Moritz, see Nègre, *L'ornement en serie;* Bötticher, *Die Tektonik*.

166 On Semper's relationship with Vischer, see Kaegi who lays out the intellectual milieu surrounding Semper and Burckhardt in the 1850s in Zurich. Werner Kaegi, *Jacob Burckhardt: Eine Biographie* (Basel: Schwabe).

167 This argument is put forward by Mallgrave, *Semper.*

168 On Semper and the London exhibition, see Klaus Lankheit, "Gottfried Semper und die Weltausstellung London 1851," in Börsch-Soupan, *Gottfried Semper und die Mitte des 19. Jahrhunderts*, 23–47.

169 Semper, *WIK*, 132.

170 Ibid.

171 Ibid., 133.

172 Ibid., 161.

173 Leisching, "Gottfried Semper und die Museen."

174 Semper, *WIK*, 118, 24.

175 Leisching, "Gottfried Semper und die Museen," 185.

176 Semper knew and quoted with evident approval Karl Friedrich Rumohr's *Italienische Forschungen* (1827–31). Rumohr had introduced a well-balanced approach between idealism and materialism in scholarship on art, a middle way between Winckelmann and Burckhardt. Mallgrave, *Semper*, 151–54.

CHAPTER 2 | THE UBIQUITY OF OBJECTS

Epigraph: Ernst Kapp, *Grundlinien einer Philosophie der Technik:* "Die Andeutung wird genügen, dass die Begriffe Costüm und Architektur aus den ursprünglich auf den Schutz des Körpers berechneten Vorrichtungen, aus Bekleidung und Behausung, hervorgegangen sind, mit deren primitivster Beschaffenheit die mehr als bildweise Bezeichnung der Körperbedeckung als eine 'portative Wohnung' sehr wohl sich verträgt."

1 For the list of sources Semper cites in his treatise, see Gottfried Semper, *Style: Style in the Technical and Tectonic Arts* (Los Angeles: Getty Research Institute, 2004), 921–46.

2 See Henry Cole's account of the events leading up to the Great Exhibition of 1851, such as the creation of prizes by the Society of Arts for design of objects. Henry Cole, *Fifty Years of Public Work* (London: George Bell and Sons, 1884), 2: 178–79, 208–32.

3 Henry Shaw, *The Encyclopaedia of Ornament* (London, 1842), v.

4 A sampling of such titles would include A. Pugin, *Gothic Ornaments, Selected from Various Ancient Buildings, Both in England and France* (London: H. G. Bohn, 1831; repr. 1854); A. W. N. Pugin, *Floriated Ornament* (London: Bohn, 1849); Owen Jones, *The Grammar of Ornament* (London: Day and Son, 1856); W. and G. Audsley, *Outlines of Ornament in the Leading Styles: Selected from Executed Ancient and Modern Works. A Book of Reference for the Architect, Sculptor, Decorative Artist and Practical Painter* (London: Sampson, Low, Marston, Searle and Rivington, 1881).

5 Du Sommerard's collection became the foundation for the Musée Cluny. For a history, see Alain Erlande-Brandenburg, "Le Musée des Monuments francais et les origines du Musée de Cluny," in B. Deneke and R. Kahsnitz, eds., *Das Kunst und Kulturgeschichtliche Museum im 19. Jahrhundert* (Munich: Prestel, 1977), 49–58.

6 Anthony Burton, *Vision and Accident: The Story of the Victoria and Albert Museum* (London: V&A, 1999), 59.

7 Lenoir's museum came from a "dépôt d'objets" confiscated during the Revolution and made up of architectural fragments, sculpture, furniture, metal objects, etc., and was made famous by his catalogue, which went through twelve editions in French and was translated into English. The museum was characterized by his display strategy, which was to create an "ambience" with a series of objects in context rather than display them individually. See Erlande-Brandenburg, "Le Musée des monuments français."

8 Burton, *Vision and Accident.*

9 For a critical analysis of this transition, see Hans Heinz Holz, *Vom Kunstwerk zur Ware: Studien zur Funktion des ästhetischen Gegenstands im Spätkapitalismus* (Neuwied: Hermann Luchterhand, 1972). Werner Sombart's many books on the economic significance of objects and their mass production constitute a high-density point for this discourse. Werner Sombart, *Technik und Wirtschaft* (Dresden: Vortag and Zahn & Jaensch, 1901); Sombart, *Gewerbewesen* (Leipzig: G. J. Göschen, 1904); Sombart, *Die gewerbliche Arbeiterfrage* (Leipzig: G. J. Göschen, 1904); Sombart, *Kunstgewerbe und Kultur* (1906; Berlin: Marquardt, 1908); Heinrich Waentig, *Wirtschaft und Kunst: Eine Untersuchung über die Geschichte und Theorie der modernen Kunstgewerbebewegung* (Jena: Gustav Fischer, 1909).

10 On the European opinion of the American contributions, see Semper, *WIK*, as well as the most complimentary article in *Kunstgewerbeblatt* following the Columbian Exhibition of 1889. "Moderne Kunst in the Vereinigten Staaten von Amerika. Eindrücke von einem Besuche der Weltausstellung zu Chicago. Architektur und Kunsthandwerk," *Kunsgewerbeblatt* 5 (1894): 110–21. See also S. Bing, *La culture artistique en Amerique* (Paris, 1896). On the history of the status of French artisans, their education and membership in the Academie de S. Luc, and *bâtiments du roi* from the early eighteenth century, see Bruno Pons, *De Paris a Versailles, 1699–1736: Les sculpteurs ornemantistes parisiens et l'art decoratif des Bâtiments du roi* (Strasbourg: Universités de Strasbourg, 1986).

11 The director of the Vienna Museum für Kunst und Industrie, Jakob von Falke, expressed it crisply in his introduction to one such educational publication: "Dieses Museum hat die Aufgabe zur Besserung des gegenwärtig so tief gesunkenen Geschmacks beizutragen." Jakob von Falke, *Geschichte des modernen Geschmacks* (1866; Leipzig: T. O. Weigel, 1880), vii.

12 "Comment lutter pour maintenir notre suprématie incontestable encore sur tous les points? Par une régénération de l'enseignement des arts, par le maintien du gout public, par des garanties qui viennent se substituer a celles qu'offrait l'ancienne organisation des corps de métiers." Léon de Laborde, *De l'union des arts et de*

l'industrie, (Paris: Imprimerie impériale, 1856), 2: 515–16. Henry Cole, like Semper, acknowledged the French supremacy: "I freely admit, that in the execution of art applied to industry, the French are, upon an average, better educated and better workmen than ourselves." Cole, *Fifty Years of Public Work,* 2: 251.

13 For a contemporary testimony on the fragmented display opportunities for the decorative arts in Paris and the lack of systematic organization, see the article by the director of the Musée Cluny, Alfred Darcel, "Les arts décoratifs au musée de Cluny," *Revue des arts décoratifs,* October 1886, 97–111. On the arts and crafts in France, see Léonce Benedite, "Frankreich," in Richard Graul, ed., *Die Krisis im Kunstgewerbe: Studien über die Wege und Ziele der modernen Richtung* (Leipzig: S. Herzel, 1901), 21–38. "L'union centrale des beaux-arts appliqués a l'industrie" was set up in 1864 as an answer to the South Kensington Museum, but it was small and its locale relatively makeshift, a real museum eluding its proponents until the Musée des arts décoratifs was established in 1905 (although it had been in the works since 1877). The *Revue des arts décoratifs* started in 1879/80, while the École des arts décoratifs had been founded in 1766 under a different name, like the Berlin academies of *Kunstgewerbe,* and went through a series of changes in the nineteenth century—most notably when Viollet-le-Duc was its director from 1843–50—and ultimately morphed into the Société des Artistes Décorateurs (1901) under Hector Guimard. On the history of the institution, see Sylvie Martin, "The École Nationale des Arts Décoratifs in Paris: Architecture and the Applied Arts Between the World Wars," *Studies in the Decorative Arts* 8, no. 1 (Spring–Summer 2001): 77–104; see also Yvonne Brunhammer, *Le beau dans l'utile: Un musée pour les arts décoratifs* (Paris: Gallimard, 1992). On earlier examples of interest in developing the arts and crafts in France, see the state-sponsored applied arts exhibitions in the eighteenth century (a vehicle to generate patronage after the Revolution wiped out the traditional patron class, the aristocracy), and the Société d'encouragement pour l'industrie nationale in Paris, founded in 1801 following the English model. Hubert Locher, *Kunstgeschichte als historische Theorie der Kunst, 1750–1950* (Berlin: Wilhelm Fink, 2001).

14 Rudolf von Eitelberger, *Österreichische Kunst-Institute und Gewerbliche Zeitfragen* (Vienna: Wilhelm Braumuller, 1879), 280. This particular essay was written in 1876.

15 "Aujourd'hui, tout le monde veut être meublé avec le luxe qui convient à un financier; . . . les fabricants s'évertuent à donner l'apparence du luxe et de la richesse aux objets les plus vulgaires comme façon et matière." Eugène Emmanuel Viollet-le-Duc, *Dictionnaire raisonné du mobilier français de l'époque carlovingienne a la renaissance* (Paris: Librairie centrale d'architecture, 1873–4), 427.

16 "Parmi ces splendeurs à bon marché, ce faux goût et ce faux luxe, nous sommes ravi quand nous trouvons un banc bien fait, une bonne table de chêne portant d'aplomb sur ses pieds, des rideaux de laine qui paraissent être de laine, une chaise commode et solide, une armoire qui s'ouvre et se ferme bien." Ibid, 431.

17 "Je crois plus que personne à la vertu des principes; s'il ne font pas concevoir des belles choses, ils empêchent d'en produire de mauvaises: c'est déjà beaucoup." Charles Blanc, *Grammaire des arts décoratifs: Décoration intérieure de la maison,* 2nd ed. (Paris: Renouard, 1882), 69.

18 For this insider account, see Falke, *Geschichte des Geschmacks,* 359. On the broader phenomenon of decorative arts education in Austria, see Gottfried Fliedl, *Kunst und Lehre am Beginn der Moderne: Die Wiener Kunstgewerbeschule, 1867–1918* (Salzburg: Residenz Verlag, 1986). The topic of the decorative arts education and impulse in the aftermath of the Great Exhibition has been much discussed in modern scholarship. The tendency has been to look at the situation in individual countries or at individual institutions. See, for example, Nancy Troy, *Modernism and the Decorative Arts in France* (New Haven: Yale University Press, 1991); Stefan Muthesius, *Das englische Vorbild* (Munich: Prestel, 1974); Klaus-Peter Arnold, *Geschichte der deutschen Werkstätten und der Gartenstadt Hellerau* (Dresden, 1993).

19 Falke, *Geschichte des Geschmacks,* 357. On the related goal to educate craftsmen and on the intersection between museum, crafts, and industry in Vienna, see Jakob von Falke, "Das Kunstgewerbe," in *Wien, 1848–1888* (Vienna: C. Konegen, 1888), 261.

20 According to advertising by the publisher Hermann Seemann in Leipzig, by 1902 four books by Walter Crane had received authorized translations in German (and one was already in its second German edition) and no fewer than seven titles by William Morris. Rudolf von Eitelberger noted the importance of these English texts and cited, as early as 1876, Owen Jones, Racinet, Gruner, Dupont-Auberville, Bourgoin, and Prisse d'Avennes. Rudolf von Eitelberger, "Kunstgewerbliche Zeitfragen," in *Gesammelte kunsthistorische Schriften und Kunstgewerbliche Zeitfragen* (Vienna: Wilhelm Braumüller, 1879), 280.

21 Fritz Schumacher, "Ruskin Apostle der modernen englischen Kunstbewegung," *Kunst und Handwerk,* 1897/8 and 1898/9, and Hermann Muthesius, *Der kunstgewerbliche Dilettantismus in England* (Berlin, 1900). For an in-depth look at the relationship between England and Germany, see especially Muthesius, *Das englische Vorbild,* who refined and enlarged on Pevsner's 1936 thesis of a continuous thread tying together Morris and Gropius. See Nikolaus Pevsner, *Pioneers of Modern Design: From William Morris to Walter Gropius* (London, 1936).

22 See, for example, as it reached his German readers, Walter Crane, *Die Förderung der decorativen Kunst,* trans. O. Wittich (Berlin: G. Siemens, 1896), in particular his chapter "Die Aussichten der Kunst unter dem Sozialismus," 30–40.

23 "Sodann ist die ornamentale Kunst so gut wie die hohe Kunst, wie die Literatur, die Tracht, die Sitte eine Äusserung des gleichzeitigen Culturlebens, eine charakteristische Erscheinung des Zeitgeises . . ." Falke, *Geschichte des Geschmacks*, viii.

24 Ruskin's views were unambiguous: "All cast and machine work is bad, as work," and "it is dishonest" (53); "All good work must be free hand-work" (169) and "I believe the right question to ask, respecting all ornament, is simply this: Was it done with enjoyment—was the carver happy while he was about it?" (73). Moreover, he attributed the pleasure derived from ornament to the "sense of human labour and care spent on it" (53). John Ruskin, *The Seven Lamps of Architecture* (London: Dover, 1889; repr. of 1880, G. Allen, ed.). On Morris's change of heart, see Klaus-Peter Arnold, *Geschichte der deutschen Werkstatten und der Gartenstadt Hellerau* (Dresden, 1993).

25 "eine Frage der Cultur . . . eine Frage des Staates wie des Hauses." Falke, *Geschichte des Geschmacks*, 360.

26 "Vorbilder zur Wiedererneuerung eines guten und richtigen Geschmacks." Jakob von Falke, *Aesthetik des Kunstgewerbes: Ein Handbuch* (Stuttgart: W. Spemann, 1883), 5.

27 See, for example, the extremely popular series of the 1870s "Art in the Home," edited by W. J. Loftie; Mrs. Haweis, *The Art of Decoration* (1881); and Rhoda and Agnes Garrett, *Suggestions for House Decoration* (1879). On this topic, see especially Adrian Forty, *Objects of Desire: Design and Society, 1750–1980* (London: Thames and Hudson, 1986), 94–119. See also Lewis F. Day, *Every-Day Art : Short Essays on the Arts Not Fine* (London: B. T. Batsford, 1882); Day, *Some Principles of Every Day Art: Introductory Chapters on the Arts Not Fine* (London: B. T. Batsford, 1890).

28 On art journals and magazines as a new genre, see Maria Rennhofer, *Kunstzeitschriften der Jahrhundertwende in Deutschland und Österreich, 1895–1914* (Vienna: Christian Brandstaetter, 1987), esp. 36–168.

29 Semper's work was reissued and was available in various forms after his death. See, for example, Gottfried Semper, *Kleine Schriften von Gottfried Semper*, ed. Manfred and Hans Semper (Berlin: W. Spemann, 1884); Semper, *Der Stil*, 2 vols., ed. Hans Semper (Munich: Fr. Bruckmann, 1878); see also the important circulation of the ms. "Museum for Metalltechnik," which was not published until 1903.

30 Cornelius Gurlitt, "Göller's ästhetische Lehre," *Deutsche Bauzeitung* 21 (17 December 1887): 602–4, 606–7.

31 "l'homme du peuple ou des classes moyennes . . . ; donner une idée de la civilisation générale que la masse de cette nation avait atteinte." A. Hoffmann, review of Charles Garnier's *Histoire de l'habitation humaine* in *Deutsche Bauzeitung* 23 (August 1889).

32 Ibid., 415.

33 "das intime Leben im Hause, das Gehen und Treiben, die Auststattung, die Vertheilung der Räume, die Tracht der Bewohner und ihre Haltung, ihre Art zu gehen und stehen, zu arbeiten und zu ruhen." Ibid.

34 Eugène Emmanuel Viollet-le-Duc, *Habitations modernes*, 2 vols. (Paris: Morel, 1875–77).

35 Years later Muthesius emphasized the connection between the house and *Kunstgewerbe*: "In England ist die neue Kunstbewegung von der Entwicklung des Hauses nicht zu trennen." Hermann Muthesius, "England," in Graul, *Die Krisis*, 1.

36 Gustav Klemm, *Allgemeine Cultur-Geschichte der Menschheit: Nach den bessten Quellen bearbeitet und mit xylographischen Abbildungen der verschiedenen Nationalphysiognomien, Geräthe, Waffen, Trachten, Kunstproducte u.s.w. versehen* (Leipzig: B. G. Teubner, 1843–52).

37 Jakob von Falke, *Costümegeschichte der Culturvölker* (Stuttgart: W. Spemann, 1880); Falke, *Die deutschen Trachten und Modenwelt, ein Beitrag zur deutschen Culturgeschichte* (Leipzig: Meyer, 1858); Falke, *Geschichte des Geschmacks im Mittelalter, und andere Studien auf dem Gebiete von Kunst und Kultur* (Berlin: Allgemeiner Verlag für deutsche Literatur, 1892).

38 For example, in *Innen-Dekoration* and *Deutsche Monatsschrift für das gesamte Leben der Gegenwart*.

39 Alexandre Lenoir, *Musée des monuments français; ou, Description historique et chronologique des statues en marbre et en bronze, bas-reliefs et tombeaux des hommes et des femmes célèbres pour servir à l'histoire de France et à celle de l'art: Ornée des gravures; et augm. d'une dissertation sur les costumes de chaque siècle*, 8 vols. (Paris: Musée des monuments français, 1800–21).

40 Charles Blanc, *L'art de la parure* (translated as *Art in Ornament and Dress*) (New York: Scribner, Welford, and Armstrong, 1877); Auguste Racinet, *Le costume historique*, 6 vols. (Paris: Firmin-Didot, 1876–88).

41 "il parait ridicule aujourd'hui de voir une femme en robe bouffante assise sur un fauteuil imité d'un siège grec . . . des hommes habillés comme nous le sommes assis dans des fauteuils du temps de Louis XV." Viollet-le-Duc, *Dictionnaire raisonnée du mobilier*, 1: 427–28.

42 "Ce que nous voudrions trouver dans nos habitations, c'est une harmonie parfaite entre l'architecture, le mobilier, les vêtements et les usages." Ibid.

43 "Le signe le plus certain d'une civilisation avancée c'est l'harmonie entres les mœurs, les diverses expressions de l'art et les produits de l'industrie. Montre-moi ton mobilier, et je te dirai qui tu es." Ibid.

44 Jakob von Falke, *Die Kunst im Hause; geschichtliche und kritischaesthetische Studien über die Dekoration und Ausstattung der Wohnung* (Vienna: Gerold, 1871). (English trans. 1879 from 3rd German ed.: *Art in the House: Historical, Critical, and Aesthetical Studies on the Decorating and Furnishing of the Dwelling* [Boston: Prang, 1879], 168.)

45 "es ist ein wertvolles Hilfsmittel beim Studium der hohen Kunst, der Architektur wie der Malerei. In *kulturhistorischer* Richtung bietet es den Einblick in das häusliche Leben der Völker; das Mobiliär hat man daher nicht mit Unrecht "die Seele des Hauses" genannt. Von hervorragender Bedeutung its es für das Kentniss des Stils in seiner Entwicklung zu

den verschiedenen Zeiten und bei den verschiedenen Völkern." Wilhelm von Bode, *Italienische Hausmöbel der Renaissance* (1902), 2.

46 Bode's cultural history approach to the layout of his so-called Renaissance museum in Berlin (now Bode Museum) was influenced by his relationship with Jacob Burckhardt himself. On this "master/student" relationship, see Max Seidel, "Das Renaissance Museum: Wilhelm Bode als 'Schüler' Jacob Burckhardt's," in Max Seidel, ed., *Storia dell'arte e politica culturale intorno al 1900* (Venice: Marsilio, 1999), 55–108. On Bode's attempts to encourage patronage, see a contemporary review by Peter Jenssen, "Ausstellung von Kunstwerken des Mittelalters aus Berliner Privatbesitz (Berlin, 1899)," *Kunstgewerbeblatt* 11, no. 9 (1899): 158–60.

47 Werner Sombart, *Kunstgewerbe und Kultur* (1906; Berlin: Marquardt, 1908).

48 "Sodann ist die ornamentale Kunst so gut wie die hohe Kunst, wie die Literatur, die Tracht, die Sitte eine Äusserung des gleichzeitigen Culturlebens, eine charakteristische Erscheinung des Zeitgeistes." Falke, *Geschichte des modernen Geschmacks*, viii–ix.

49 Hanna Egger, "Die Anfänge des K.K. Österreichischen Museums für Kunst und Industrie und der Wiener Schule der Kunstgeschichte," in Peter Noever, ed., *Kunst und Industrie: Die Anfänge des Museums für angewandte Kunst in Wien* (Vienna: MAK and Hatje Cantz, 2000), 271–83.

50 "mächtige Aufschwung des Kunstgewerbes."

51 Wilhelm von Bode, *Vorderasiatische Knüpfteppiche aus älterer Zeit* (Leipzig: H. Seemann Nachfolger, 1902).

52 Wilhelm von Bode, *Bilderrahmen in alter und neuer Zeit* and *Florentiner Majoliken des 15. Jahrhunderts.*

53 The essays were "Von der Weltausstellung in Chicago" (1893) and "Die Aufgaben unserer Kunstgewerbemuseen" (1896). See Wilhelm von Bode, *Kunst und Kunstgewerbe am Ende des 19. Jahrhunderts* (Berlin: Cassirer, 1901). On Bode, see Udo Kultermann, *Geschichte der Kunstgeschichte: Der Weg einer Wissenschaft* (Frankfurt: Ullstein, 1981), 247, and, more recently, Manfred Ohlsen, *Wilhelm von Bode: Zwischen Kaisermacht und Kunsttempel* (Berlin: Gebr. Mann, 2007).

54 Bode, *Kunst und Kunstgewerbe.*

55 A. W. N. Pugin, *Glossary of Ecclesiastical Ornament and Costume* (London: Bohn, 1844); F. W. Fairholt, *Costume in England: A History of Dress* (London: Chapman and Hall, 1846); J. R. Planché, *An Encyclopaedia of Costume or Dictionary of Dress* (London: Chatto and Windus, 1876); Auguste Racinet, *Le costume historique* 6 vols. (Paris: Firmin-Didot, 1876–1888); Charles Blanc, *Art in Ornament and Dress* (New York: Scribner, Welford and Armstrong, 1877); Jakob von Falke, *Costumegeschichte der Culturvölker* (Stuttgart: W. Spemann, 1880); Falke, *Die deutschen Trachten und Modenwelt, ein Beitrag zur deutschen Culturgeschichte* (Leipzig: Meyer, 1858).

56 Ernst Kapp, *Grundlinien einer Philosophie der Technik: Zur Entstehungsgeschichte der Cultur aus neuen Gesichtspunkten* (Braunschweig: George Westermann, 1877). Kapp includes a chapter on "die Maschinentechnik" in which he gives credit to Franz Reuleaux for creating a new science. See Reuleaux, *Theoretische Kinematik: Grundzüge einer Theorie des Maschinenwesens, von F. Reuleaux . . . Mit einem Atlas und Zahlreichen in den Text Eingedruckten Holzstichen* (Braunschweig: F. Vieweg und Sohn, 1875).

57 "Der Begriff der Arbeit für Maschinen aus dem Vergleich mit dem Menschen hergenommen sei, schliesst die unmittelbare Folgerung in sich, dass auch die Maschine selbst, wenn sie soll Menschen-arbeit ersetzen können, entsprechend—d.h. entsprechend dem Organismus, dessen Artbeit sie ersetzen soll—construiert sein wird." Kapp, *Grundlinien*, 132.

58 Ibid., 133.

59 "Die Bewegung des Handwerkzeuges ist die Fortsetzung der Hand- und Armbewegung durch Ueberleitung derselben auf die technische Verlängerung, die in Form eines Gliedansatzes an das Organ stattfindet." Ibid., 61.

60 Ibid., 139–42.

61 Ibid., 101–3.

62 "Die Architektur der Spongiosa." Ibid., 107ff.

63 Ibid., 133.

64 "Gefässe, Geräthe, Möbel, Waffen, Kleider, Teppiche, Schmucksachen u drgl. bis in die allerdings auch höhere ideellen Bezuge nicht ermangelnde Architektur hinein, endlich in der Ornamentik." Ibid., 256.

65 Ibid., 208.

66 Ibid., 267.

67 "Alles, was der Körper tragt, hinaus auf die nächste von der Menschenhand geschaffene Einrichtung des Wohnraumes und von da auf die angrenzende Umgebung." Ibid., 268.

68 Hermann Klencke, *Kosmetik oder menschliche Verschönerungs-kunst auf Grundlage rationeller Gesundheitslehre* (Leipzig: Kummer, 1869).

69 "Zimmer, Kammer, Haus und Garten eine Fortsetzung, eine Erweiterung unserer Kleidung bilden." Kapp, *Grundlinien*, 267.

70 For example, see the catalogue of the Vincent frères factory (whose business had started at the turn of the eighteenth/nineteenth century). Valerie Nègre, *L'ornement en serie: Architecture, terre cuite et carton-pierre* (Sprimont: Madraga, 2006).

71 Vitruvius, *De architectura*, 3: 1.

72 On this topic, see, for example, Alina Payne, "Reclining Bodies: Figural Ornament in Renaissance Architecture," in R. Tavernor and G. Dodds, eds., *Body and Building* (Cambridge, Mass.: MIT Press, 2001), 94–113, 375–78.

73 Alina Payne, "Creativity and *bricolage* in Architectural Literature of the Renaissance," *RES: Journal of Anthropology and Aesthetics* 34 (Fall 1998).

74 Alina Payne, "Architects and Academies: Architectural Theories of *imitatio* and the Debates on Language and Style," in G. Clarke and P. Crossley, eds., *Architecture and Language* (Cambridge: Cambridge University Press, 2000), 118–33, 195–202. Ursula Franke locates this moment in the eighteenth century. See Franke, "Bausteine für eine Theorie ornamentaler Kunst: Zur Autonomisierung des Ornaments bei Karl Philip Moritz," in

U. Franke and H. Paetzold, eds., *Ornament und Geschichte* (Bonn: Bouvier, 1996), 89–106.

75 "in nearly all the [Greek] carved ornament we may trace the imitation and elaboration of painted ornament derived primarily from pottery-decoration." A. D. F. Hamlin, *A History of Ornament, Ancient and Medieval* (London: B. T. Batsford, 1916), 116. Richard Glazier's purpose in writing his book is made evident in his subtitle: *A Manual of Historic Ornament Treating upon the Evolution, Tradition, and Development of Architecture and the Applied Arts Prepared for the Use of Students and Craftsmen* (London: B. T. Batsford, 1899). Among the plethora of books on ornament, see also W. and G. Audsley, *Outlines of Ornament in the Leading Styles, Selected from Executed Ancient and Modern Works: A Book of Reference for the Architect, Sculptor, Decorative Artist, and Practical Painter* (London: Sampson, Low, Marston, Searle, and Rivington, 1881); F. Edward Hulme, *Birth and Development of Ornament* (London: Swan Sonnenschein; New York: Macmillan, 1893); James Ward, *Historic Ornament: Treatise on Decorative and Architectural Ornament* (London: Chapman and Hall, 1897); Frank G. Jackson, *Lessons on Decorative Design* (London: Chapman and Hall, 1913); text is based on lectures given at the Birmingham Municipal School of Art.

76 Alfredo Melani, *Manuale d'arte decorativa antica e moderna* (1888; Milan: U. Hoepli, 1907); Auguste Racinet, *Ornement polychrome* (Paris, 1875); E. Collinot and A. de Beaumont, *Ornements turcs: Recueil des dessins pour l'art et l'industrie* (Paris: Canson 1883)—Collinot and Beaumont also published *Ornements de la Perse* and *Ornements du Japon* in the same series. In German scholarship, Franz Sales Meyer, *Ornamentale Formenlehre* (Leipzig, 1886); Heinrich Dolmetsch, *Ornamentschatz: Ein Musterbuch stilvoller Ornamente aus allen Kunstepochen* (Stuttgart: Julius Hoffmann, 1889).

77 Cornelius Gurlitt, *Das Barock-und Rococo-Ornament Deutschlands: Architektur und Kunstgewerbe des XVII und XVIII Jahrhunderts* (Berlin: Wasmuth, 1883–89).

78 Jackson's book was also the result of lectures given at the Birmingham Municipal School of Art. On this aspect of the English publications on ornament, see Locher, *Kunstgeschichte als historische Theorie der Kunst*, 329–59.

79 "I believe the right question to ask, respecting all ornament, is simply this: Was it done with enjoyment—was the carver happy while he was about it?" Ruskin, *Seven Lamps of Architecture*, 173.

80 This was the case with the so-called Cosmati work, which was signed, as was other work by contemporary *marmorarii*. See Gustave Clausse, *Les marbriers romains et le mobilier presbytéral* (Paris: E. Leroux, 1897).

81 Fritz Schumacher, "Architektur und Kunstgewerbe (1906)," in Schumacher, *Streifzüge eines Architekten: Gesammelte Aufsätze* (Jena: Eugen Diederichs, 1907).

82 "Allen Kunstindustriellen, welche stylistische Ornamente benötigen, sei es für Teppiche, Tapeten, Kirchen- und Möbelstoffe, Spitzen, Stickereien bedruckte Zeuge, Glas-, Porzellan-, Holz-, und Metalldecoration etc. etc. empfiehlt sein Atelier Friedrich Fischbach, Zeichner des k.k. Museum für Kunst und Industrie in Wien. Theresianumgasse 13, Wien." *Kunst und Gewerbe, Wochenschrift zur Forderung deutscher Kunst-Industrie* 9 (February 1868).

83 As Gerda Breuer argues, *Kunstgewerbe* was a very broad term that encompassed all *Gewerbe* that had the slightest artistic content. Gerda Breuer, "Geschmacksveredlung am Ort-Auswirkungen einer restaurativen Kulturutopie," in *Der westdeuschte Impuls 1900–1914: Kunst und Umweltgestaltung im Industriegebiet. Das Museum zwischen Jugendstil und Werkbund* (Krefeld: Kaiser Wilhelm Museum, 1984), 23–51.

84 Rudolf von Eitelberger, *Die Kunstbewegung in Österreich seit der Pariser Weltausstellung im Jahre 1867: Im Auftrage des KK. Unterrichts Ministerium* (Vienna: K. K. Schulbucher, 1878); Jakob von Falke, *Die Kunstindustrie der Gegenwart* (Leipzig, 1868); Bruno Bucher, *Geschichte der technischen Künste, 2 vols.* (Stuttgart, 1875); Jakob von Falke, *Aesthetik des Kunstgewerbes: Ein Handbuch* (Stuttgart: W. Spemann, 1883); Jakob von Falke, *Geschichte des deutschen Kunstgewerbes* (1888); Cornelius Gurlitt, *Die internationale Kunstausstellung zu Berlin, 1891* (Munich: F. Hanfstaengl, 1891); Graul, *Die Krisis*. Finally, Bode wrote a series of essays on the topic: "Von der Weltausstellung in Chicago (1893): Die Aufgaben unserer Kunstgewer bemuseen (1896).—Künstler im Kunsthandwerk. Die Ausstellungen in München und Dresden (1897).—Zur Illustration moderner deutscher Kunstbücher (1899).—Beim Eintritt in das neue Jahrhundert (1900)." Bode, *Kunst und Kunstgewerbe*.

85 See n. 9 above.

86 As a sample, see Eitelberger's and Falke's sustained publication activities while directors of the Vienna museum, and academics; see also Jean Louis Sponsel (editor of the *Kunstgewerbe* series), who was director of the Kupferstichkabinett, Münzkabinett, and the Historisches Museum in Dresden.

87 Martin Wörner, *Vergnügung und Belehrung: Volkskultur auf den Weltausstellungen, 1851–1900* (New York: Waxmann, 1999), 97ff.

88 Cole, *Fifty Years*, 2: 258.

89 Eitelberger makes the point forcibly in his article for *Zeitschrift der bildenden Kunst* of 1877: "Eine Neuerung, die für die Industriellen von der grössten Wichtigkeit ist, war die in dem kaiserlichen Handschreiben vom 7. März getroffene Verfügung, dass im Österreichischen Museum industrielle Erzeugnisse der Gegenwart ausgestellt werden sollen, mit andered Worten, dass das Museum für die Industriellen sei, was für die Künstler der Kunstverein ist." Rudolf von Eitelberger, "Die Wiener Akademie im Jahre 1872 und die österreichischen Staats-Pensionare in Rom 1873," in *Gesammelte kunsthistorische Schriften*, 115. For a broad look at the nationalist subtext evident in much European nineteenth-century architecture and culture more

generally, see the proceedings arising from the 2003 CIHA conference in Jacek Purchla and Wolf Tegethoff, eds., *Nation, Style, Modernism* (Cracow: International Cultural Center and Zentralinstitut für Kunstgeschichte, 2006).

90 Burton, *Vision and Accident*, 110ff.

91 The first public exhibition of folk objects at the Museum für Kunst und Industrie in Vienna, with a thousand exhibits, was held in 1895. Leopold Schmidt, *Das österreichische Museum für Volkskunde* (Vienna, 1960), 41. In Germany, one such example was the Hamburg Museum für Kunst und Gewerbe, where Justus Brinckmann worked on the revival of German folk art in the 1890s. Breuer, "Geschmacksveredlung am Ort- Auswirkungen einer restaurativen Kulturutopie," 24.

92 Eitelberger was among the first to write on the subject and, as such, anticipated Riegl's longer but essentially very similar essay on *Hausindustrie* of 1894. Eitelberger, "Die Volkskunst und Hausindustrie," in *Gesammelte kunsthistorische Schriften und Kunstgewerbliche Zeitfragen* (Vienna: Wilhelm Braumüller, 1879), 267–75.

93 Osthaus had acquired his collection during 1897–98 in Asia and Africa.

94 "Es wird die Zeit kommen, wo man einsehen muss, dass eine Förderung der künstlerischen Kultur gleichbedeutend its mit einer Steigerung der werbenden Kräfte der Nation." Breuer, "Geschmacksveredlung am Ort- Auswirkungen einer restaurativen Kulturutopie," 31 (citing Georg Fuchs).

95 In Austria, some such journals were *Mitteilungen des k.k. Oesterreichischen Museums für Industrie und Kunst* and *Mitteilungen des Mährischen Gewerbemuseums (Zeitschrift des Verbandes Oesterreichischer Kunstgewerbemuseen)*. In Germany one such example was the *Kunstgewerbeblatt: Monatsheft für Geschichte und Literatur der Kleinkunst, Organ für die Bestrebungen der Kunstgewerbe Vereine*, which started in 1885–9 and whose editorial board for the Neue Folge of 1889–1917 included Cornelius Gurlitt, Jakob von Falke, Bruno Bucher, Julius Lessing under the editorship of Arthur Pabst, director of the Kunstgewerbemuseum in Köln.

96 Wörner, *Vergnügung und Belehrung*, 49–113.

97 "Eine Sammlung von Industrie- und Kunstgegenständen wurde möglicherweise am besten erreicht werden, wenn man sie in fünf Klassen teilte, nämlich eine für jedes grundliegende Motiv und eine fünfte Klasse für die Verbindung der vier Elemente: für die hohe Kunst und Architektur." Julius Leisching, "Gottfried Semper und die Museen," *Mitteilungen des Mährischen Gewerbemuseums* (Brünn, 1903), 191.

98 For example, the first chair of anthropology was established at a university in Austria only in 1913.

99 On the early development of anthropology and especially its relations to philology (language being perceived as "die äussere Erscheinung des Geistes der Völker" and its most authentic and immediate representation), see Matti Bunzl, "Franz Boas and the Humboldtian Tradition: From *Volksgeist* and *Nationalcharakter* to an Anthropological Concept of Culture," in G. W. Stocking, Jr., *Volksgeist as Method and Ethic: Essays on Boasian Ethnography and the German Anthropological Tradition* (Madison: University of Wisconsin Press, 1996), 17–78.

100 Christian F. Feest, "The Origins of Professional Anthropology in Vienna," in B. Rupp-Eisenreich and J. Stagl, eds., *Kulturwissenschaften im Vielvölkerstaat* (Vienna: Bohlau, 1995), 113–31.

101 On Germany as the *Kulturnation*, see Suzanne Marchand, *Down from Olympus: Archaeology and Philhellenism in Germany, 1750–1970* (Princeton, N.J.: Princeton University Press, 1996). On the commodification of the nation, see M. Umbach, "The Vernacular International: *Heimat*, Modernism, and the Global Market in Early Twentieth-Century Germany," *National Identities* 4, no. 1 (2002): 45–68.

102 Feest, "Origins of Professional Anthropology."

103 Ibid., 113.

104 Ibid., 120.

105 The *Kronprinzwerk* was published 1886–1902 in twenty-four volumes in German and twenty-one volumes in Hungarian. See Ch. Zintzen, "Enzyklopädische Utopie: Ethnographie als Stiftung von Einheit im Diversen," in A. Moravansky, ed., *Das entfernte Dorf* (Vienna: Bohlau, 2002), 183–205.

106 See, for example, Franz Boas. Bunzl, "Franz Boas," 55.

107 Hjalmar Stolpe, "Entwicklungerscheinungen in der Ornamentik der Naturvölker," *Mittheilungen der Anthropologischen Gesellschaft in Wien* 22 (1890); H. Colley March, "The Meaning of Ornament, or Its Archaeology and Its Psychology," *Transactions of the Cheshire and Lancashire Anthropological Society*, 1889.

108 Henry Balfour, *The Evolution of Decorative Art: An Essay Upon Its Origins and Development as Illustrated by the Art of Modern Races of Mankind* (London: Rivington, Percival, 1893), vi.

109 Ibid., vii. Pitt Rivers published some of his findings on "Principles of Classification" and "Evolution of Culture" in 1872 and 1884, respectively.

110 Balfour, *Evolution of Decorative Art*.

111 "bei jedem Volke das Eigenartige und Charakteristische im Stil zu finden." Stolpe, "Entwicklungerscheinungen in der Ornamentik der Naturvölker," 20.

112 Colley March, "Meaning of Ornament," 75.

113 Franz Boas, "The Decorative Art of the Indians of the North Pacific Coast," *Bulletin of the American Museum of Natural History* 9 (1897): 123–76.

114 Ira Jacknis, "The Ethnographic Object and the Object of Ethnology in the Early Career of Franz Boas," in Stocking, *Volksgeist*, 185–87.

115 Deneke argues that the museum of culture and *Kulturgeschichte* did not overlap much. Evidently, the boundaries between anthropology and history were beginning to be drawn more sharply, and the museum exhibit of one and the historical/philosophical ambitions of the other did not overlap. Bernward Deneke, "Die Museen und die Entwicklung der Kulturgeschichte," in *Das Kunst und Kulturgeschichtliche Museum im 19. Jahrhundert*, 49–58.

116 Philippe-Alain Michaud, *Aby Warburg et l'image en mouvement* (Paris: Mac-

ula, 1998), 175. Michaud cites Boas's 1896 letter to Ward Putnam regarding the installations for the American Natural History Museum in New York.

117 Alfred Haddon, *The Decorative Art of British New Guinea: A Study in Papuan Ethnography* (Dublin, 1894); Haddon, *Illustrated Archaeologist* 1 (1893).

118 Alfred Haddon, *Evolution in Art: As Illustrated by the Life-Histories of Design* (London: Walter Scott, 1902). Haddon (75, 85) draws on Stolpe and cites Colley March (who invented the term skeuomorph) as well as G. Perrot and C. Chipiez's *A History of Art in Ancient Egypt* (1883).

119 Haddon, *Evolution in Art*, 108.

120 Ibid., 10. Quoted from his own article in *Illustrated Archaeologist*.

121 See Marchand, *Down from Olympus*.

122 Ibid.; see especially Anke Bohne, "Rezeption des Pergamonaltars im deutschen Bürgertum," in M. Baumbach, ed., *Tradita et inventa: Beiträge zur Rezeption der Antike* (Heidelberg: C. Winter, 2000), 441–58.

123 Marchand, *Down from Olympus*, 112.

124 Maria Luigia Pagliani, "L'archaeologia italiana nella seconda metàdell '800 e la formazione del metodo Morelliano," in G. Agosti et al., eds., *Giovanni Morelli e la cultura dei conoscitori*, (Bergamo: Pierluigi Lubrina, 1993), 399–407.

125 Ibid.

126 Marchand, *Down from Olympus*, 104–15.

127 Pagliani, "L'archaeologia italiana nella seconda meta'dell '800 e la formazione del metodo Morelliano." Marchand argues that archaeologists based their stylistic analysis on "objective" comparison of details (the new technology of photography helped in this process), while art historians tended to look to style's philosophical principles. Archaeologists tended to defer interpretation and, due to the pressures of scholarship and state politics, they expedited the excavations and left (cultural) analysis for the future. As a result, they were much more concerned with classification than with "reconceptualizing the European past." Marchand, *Down from Olympus*, 104–14.

128 Adolf Michaelis, "Ernst Curtius," *Biographische Jahrbuch und Deutscher Nekrolog*, ed. A. Bettelheim (Berlin: Georg Reimer, 1897), 79.

129 See Alina Payne, "Portable Ruins: The Pergamon Altar, Heinrich Wölfflin, and German Art History at the *fin de siècle*." *RES: Journal of Anthropology and Aesthetics* 53/54 (Spring–Autumn 2008): 166–87.

130 Bunzl, "Franz Boas," 28ff.

131 I. Bauer, "Das Beyerisches Nationalmuseum und die 'Heimatkunst,'" in I. Bauer, ed., *Das Beyerisches Nationalmuseum* (Munich: Hirmer, 2000), 240.

132 Ibid., 243.

133 Ibid. Reinhard Falter and Gerti Fluhr-Meyer, "Anwalt für die Isar," in V. Hofer, *Gabriel von Seidl: Architekt und Naturschützer* (Kreuzlingen: Hugendubel, 2002), 175–90.

134 Deneke, "Die Entdeckung der Volkskunst,"196.

135 See, for example, Alois Riegl, "Die Ausstellung weiblicher Handarbeitten im Österr. Museum," *Mittheilungen des k.k. Oesterreichischen Museums für Kunst und Industrie* 6 (June 1886): 115–20, 135–40. Riegl, "Spätantike Stickereien," *Kunstgewerbeblatt* 2 (1891): 127–31.

136 On Warburg's work in this area, see Ernst Gombrich, *Aby Warburg: An Intellectual Biography* (London: Warburg Institute, 1970). Lessing, Bucher, and Falke were on the editorial board of the *Kunstgewerbeblatt*. On their other collaborations, see above n. 84.

137 See Jakob von Falke, "Die nationale Hausindustrie," *Gewerbehalle* 10 (1872): 1–3, 17–19, 33–36, 49–51, and Falke, *Cultur und Kunst* (Vienna, 1878). Apparently Falke concluded that in Vienna the artistic-industrial viewpoint receded behind the ethnographic one, hence it was not the success he had expected (179). Bernward Deneke, "Die Entdeckung der Volkskunst für das Kunstgewerbe," *Zeitschrift für Volkskunde* 60 (1964): 174–77, 245. For an overview of the effects on architects of the rising interest in folk architecture started with the Great Exhibitions, see Akos Moravansky, "Die Entdeckung des Nahen," in Moravansky, ed., *Das entfernte Dorf* (Vienna: Böhlau, 2002), 95–123.

138 Bauer, "Das Beyerisches Nationalmuseum," 243. Maiken Umbach, "The Vernacular International: *Heimat*, Modernism, and the Global Market in Early Twentieth-Century Germany," *National Identities* 4, no. 1 (2002): 45–68.

139 Leopold Schmidt, *Das österreichische Museum für Volkskunde* (Vienna, 1960), 15.

140 Albrecht Kurzwelly, "Lage und Zukunft der Volkskunst," in Graul, *Die Krisis*, 90, 93. Kurzwelly expresses his concern with extinction (*Aussterben*) of folk art as seen in recent Great Exhibitions (not only in Germany but also in France).

141 W. H. Riehl et al., eds., *Bavaria, Landes-und Volkskunde des Königreichs Bayern* (Munich: Literarisch-artistische Anstalt, 1860).

142 See August Thiersch, *Bauernhäuser und volkstümliche Hausmalereien im bayerischen Hochlande* (1900); see also his publication in *Süddeutsche Bauzeitung; Das Bauernhaus im deutschen Reiche und seine Grenzgebieten* (1906); *Das Bauernhaus in der Schweiz* (1906); *Das Bauernhaus in Österreich-Ungarn und in seine Grenzgebieten* (1906), 2 vols.

143 "ein treffliches Muster sachgemässer Bauweise und gesunder, baustoffgerechter Zierformen. . . . ein Schatz von nachahmungswerter Bauweise und angemessene Schmuckformen, der auf die Baukunst erfrischend und befruchtend einwirken konnte." *Das Bauernhaus in Österreich-Ungarn und in seine Grenzgebieten* (Vienna: Verlag des Österr. Ingenieur- und Architekten-Vereins, 1906), 1: xiii. Although now better known for his study of proportions, August Thiersch had written on folk art, in *Bauernhäuser und volkstümliche Hausmalereien im bayerischen Hochlande* (1900), as well as in journals like *Süddeutsche Bauzeitung*. A parallel movement to the one in the German-speaking countries, and imbricated with it, was taking place in northern Europe, where nationalism, romanticism, and the study of folk art converged and generated a vernacularizing architecture— especially in the domestic sphere—that tied into Scandinavian modernism. A splendid and definitive work on this topic is Barbara Miller Lane, *National Romanticism*

and Modern Architecture in Germany and the Scandinavian Countries (New York: Cambridge University Press, 2000).

144 Michael Haberlandt, "Einführung," *Das Bauernhaus in Österreich-Ungarn*, 4. On Benjamin's metaphor, see Irving Wohlfarth, "'Construction Has the Role of the Subconscious': Phantasmagorias of the Master Builder (with Constant Reference to Giedion, Weber, Nietzsche, Ibsen, and Benjamin)," in A. Kostka and I. Wohlfarth, eds., *Nietzsche and "An Architecture of Our Minds"* (Santa Monica: Getty Issues and Debates, 1999), 147.

145 *Das Bauernhaus in Österreich-Ungarn*, 181.

146 "eine in geübte Handfertigkeit." Ibid., 183.

147 Stephen Bann, "Historical Text and Historical Object: The Poetics of the Musée Cluny," *History and Theory* 17, no. 3 (1978): 251–66.

CHAPTER 3 | ART HISTORIANS, OBJECTS, AND EMPATHY

Epigraphs: Heinrich Wölfflin, *Klassische Kunst: Eine Einführung in die italienische Renaissance* (Munich: F. Bruckmann, 1899), 227: "Auch sie [Architektur] . . . ist ja wie die Kleidung eine Projektion des Menschen und seines Körpergefühls nach aussen." Philippe-Alain Michaud, *Aby Warburg et l'image en mouvement* (Paris: Macula, 1998). My translations.

1 Moritz Thausing, "Die Stellung der Kunstgeschichte als Wissenschaft," in *Wiener Kunstbriefe* (Leipzig: E. A. Seemann, 1884), 1–20; first published in *Österreichischer Rundschau*, May 1883.

2 The connection of aesthetics, anthropology, and natural science was particularly important, as it affected art history from two sides: the positivistic and philosophical. As these fields also communicated, they invited additional overlap. See Winfried Menninghaus, *Das Versprechen der Schönheit* (Berlin: Suhrkamp, 2003).

3 For example, see Riegl, Thausing, and Wölfflin, publishing articles as well as book and exhibition reviews in the leading papers in Munich, Berlin, Vienna, and other cities.

4 Anke Bohne, "Rezepzion des Pergamonaltars im deutschen Bürgertum," in M. Baumbach, ed., *Tradita et inventa: Beiträge zur Rezepzion der Antike* (Heidelberg: C. Winter, 2000), 441–58. For political exploitation of the find, see Lionel Gossman, "Imperial Icon: The Pergamon Altar in Wilhelmine Germany," *Journal of Modern History* 78 (September 2006): 551–87.

5 Harry Francis Mallgrave, ed., *Empathy, Form, and Space: Problems in German Aesthetics, 1873–1893* (Santa Monica: Getty Center, 1994).

6 The classic argument for the rise of the "clue" mentality is Carlo Ginzburg, *Clues, Myths, and the Historical Method* (Baltimore: Johns Hopkins University Press, 1992). Nevertheless, the turn toward the clue is even broader than he argues and embraces the whole *Sachkultur* of the nineteenth century.

7 G. M. Urbani de Gheltof, *Les arts industriels à Venise au moyen-age et à la renaissance* (Venice: Usiglio and Diena, 1885) (translated from Italian). Alfredo Melani, *Manuale d'arte decorativa antica e moderna* (1888; Milan: U. Hoepli, 1907).

8 On Hübsch, see Wolfgang Herrmann, ed., *In What Style Should We Build?* (Santa Monica: Getty Center, 1992).

9 Philip Sohm, *Style in the Art Theory of Early Modern Italy* (New York: Cambridge University Press, 2002).

10 Wolfgang Kemp, "Alois Riegl," in H. Dilly, ed., *Altmeister moderner Kunstgeschichte* (Berlin: Dietrich Reimer, 1990), 37.

11 The argument has been made most frequently in connection with the work of Erwin Panofsky and his reading of northern art. For the broader phenomenon, see Michael Ann Holly, *Past Looking: Historical Imgination and the Rhetoric of the Image* (Ithaca: Cornell University Press, 1996).

12 Adolf Göller was an architect and a teacher at the Polytechnikum in Stuttgart and the author of *Zur Aesthetik der Architektur* (1887; collection of speeches) and *Entstehung der architektonischen Stilformen: eine Geschichte der Baukunst nach dem Werden und Wandern der Formgedanken* (1888). See Mallgrave, *Empathy*, 51–56; Cornelius Gurlitt was both architect and art historian, as well as, most importantly, teacher at the school of applied arts (*Kunstgewerbeschule*) in Dresden. Among many others he was the author of *Das Barock-und Rococo-Ornament Deutschlands* (Berlin: Wasmuth, 1883–89) in the series *Architektur und Kunstgewerbe des XVII und XVIII Jahrhunderts*. On Gurlitt, see Jürgen Paul, *Cornelius Gurlitt* (Dresden: Hellerau, 2003), 98–99. On both these figures, see chapter 4 below.

13 On Wölfflin and abstract art, see Martin Warnke,"L'emprise de son époque," in J. Hart, R. Recht, and M. Warnke, eds., *Relire Wölfflin* (Paris: Musée du Louvre, 1995), 107. For his essays on Böcklin, Marees, and Hildebrand, see H. Wölfflin, *Kleine Schriften*, ed. J. Gantner (Basel: Benno Schwabe, 1946).

14 On Hildebrand's, Fiedler's, and Morelli's influence on Wölfflin in this period, see Hart, Recht, and Warnke, *Relire Wölfflin*, 79ff. On von Brunn's Raphael work and his impact on Wölfflin, see Joseph Gantner, *Schönheit und Grenzen der klassischen Form* (Vienna: Anton Schroll, 1949), 104–5.

15 On the influences upon the young Wölfflin, see especially Joan Goldhammer Hart, "Heinrich Wölfflin: A Biography," Ph.D. diss., University of California, Berkeley, 1980.

16 The fact that he was aware of these issues is evident in his essay "Die Architektur der deutschen Renaissance" of 1914. See Wölfflin, *Gedanken zur Kunstgeschichte*, 110.

17 Hubert Locher, *Kunstgeschichte als historische Theorie der Kunst, 1750–1950* (Berlin: Wilhelm Fink, 2001), 378–79. For a detailed description of the German aesthetic formalism, see Mallgrave, *Empathy*, 5–85. On Wölfflin's engagement with this literature, see his constant references to these representatives of psychological aesthetics, and to Volkelt, Lotze, and R. Vischer in particular. For Wölfflin's engagement with Lipps, see his review of Lipps,

Raumästhetik und geometrisch-optische Täuschungen (Leipzig: J. A. Barth, 1897) in *Kunstchronik*, 1898, 292–93.

18 Adolf Michaelis, "Ernst Curtius," *Biographische Jahrbuch und Deutscher Nekrolog*, ed. A. Bettelheim (Berlin: Georg Reimer, 1897), 78; Alina Payne, "Portable Ruins: The Pergamon Altar, Heinrich Wölfflin, and German Art History at the fin de siècle," *RES: Journal of Anthropology and Aesthetics* 54/55 (Spring–Autumn 2008): 168–89.

19 Alina Payne, "Materiality, Crafting, and Scale in Renaissance Architecture," *Oxford Art Journal* 32, no. 3 (December 2009): 365–86.

20 Locher, *Kunstgeschichte*.

21 "der Gegensatz von Stoff und Formkraft," 22, contra Schopenhauer's *Schwere* and *Starrheit*, a dynamic argument set against a static one.

22 "Körperliche Formen können charakteristisch sein nur dadurch, dass wir selbst einen Körper haben. Wären wir bloss optisch auffassende Wesen, so müsste uns eine ästhetische Beurteilung der Körperwelt stets versagt bleiben." Wölfflin, *Prolegomena zu einer Psychologie der Architektur* (Diss., 1886), in J. Gantner, ed., *Heinrich Wölfflin Kleine Schriften* (Basel: Benno Schwabe, 1946), 15. "Ein architektonischer Stil gibt die Haltung und Bewegung der Menschen seiner Zeit wieder" (44).

23 "Das Ornament ist Ausdruck überschüssiger Formkraft." Wölfflin, *Prolegomena*, 41. "Nur mit Mühe hat bisher die Erörterung des Ornaments zurückgeschoben werden können" (40).

24 Ibid., 43, n. 1.

25 "die Schwere ist überwunden, der Überschuss der strebenden Kraft . . . feiert den höchsten Triumph in den plastischen Figuren, die, dem Druck enthoben, hier frei sich entfalten können." Ibid., 41. Heinrich von Brunn, "Über die kunstgeschichtliche Stellung der Pergamenischen Gigantomachie," *Jahrbuch der königlichen preussischen Kunstsammlungen* 5 (1884). On Wölfflin and the Pergamon altar, see Payne, "Portable Ruins."

26 "gegenseitige Durchdringung von Bauwerk und Bildwerk." Von Brunn, "Über die kunstgeschichtliche Stellung der Pergamenischen Gigantomachie," 283, 286.

27 For the currency of the term *Kleinarchitektur*, see the subject covered in the curriculum of the Polytechnische Schule in Hanover. Carl Kořistka, *Der höhere polytechnische Unterricht* (Gotha, 1863), 71.

28 "Und nun ist klar dass sie *[Architektur] als Kunst körperlichen Massen* nur auf den Menschen als körperliches Wesen Bezug nehmen kann." Wölfflin, *Renaissance und Barock* (1888), 56.

29 Ibid.

30 "Den Pulsschlag des Volksgemüts muss man dann anderswo beobachten: nicht in den grossen, schwerbeweglichen Formen der Baukunst, sondern in den kleineren dekorativen Künsten. Hier befriedigt sich das Formgefühl ungehemmt und unmittelbar und von hier wird man dann auch die Spuren einer Erneuerung des Stils vermutlich immer zuerst entdecken." Ibid., 58.

31 "der Mensch selbst nach seiner Körperlichkeit ist ein anderer geworden und eben in der neuen Empfindung seines Körpers und in der neuen Art ihn zu tragen und zu bewegen, steckt der eigentliche Kern eines Stiles." Wölfflin, *Klassische Kunst*, 216.

32 Adolf Göller, *Zur Ästhetik der Architektur* (K. Wittwor, 1887); Göller, *Entstehung der Stilformen* (K. Wittwor, 1888).

33 Cornelius Gurlitt, "Göller's ästhetische Lehre," *Deutsche Bauzeitung*, December 17, 1887, 602–4, 606–7 and G. Heuser, "Das Werden von Stylformen: Fortsetzung Darwinistischer Studien," *Allgemeine Bauzeitung* (1894).

34 See, for example, his interest in *Formpsychologie* in Heinrich Wölfflin, *Kunstgeschichtliche Grundbegriffe: Das Problem der Stilentwicklung in der neueren Kunst* (1915; Munich: Hugo Bruckmann, 1920), 8.

35 See, for example, essays in Hart, Recht, and Warnke, *Relire Wölfflin*.

36 "Im Kostüm kommt zuerst die Art zum Ausdruck, wie man sich halten und bewegen will, und es ist nicht schwer zu zeigen, dass die Architektur mit dem Zeikostüm übereinstimmt. . . . Der menschliche Fuss hat eine Richtung nach vorn; aber tritt das in der stumpfen Linie, in der er aufhört, hervor? Nein. Es war der Gotik unleidlich, hier nicht den exakten Ausdruck des Willens zu finden, und so liess sie den Schuh in spitzem Schnabel auslaufen. (die Schnabelshuhe erscheinen im 12. Jahrhundert)." Wölfflin, *Prolegomena*, 44–45. Mallgrave, *Empathy*, 182–83.

37 Hermann Weiss, *Kostümkunde: Geschichte der Tracht und des Geräths* (Stuttgart: Ebner and Seubert, 1881–83).

38 Fechner (*Vorschule der Ästhetik* 1: 239) "errinert daran wie der ganze kunstgeschichtliche Stil und Geschmack einer Epoche durch Gewandung und Haartracht treffend charakterisiert werden kann (griechische Gewandung, römische Toga, Zopf-und Perückengeschmack), obwohl doch Kleidungsstücke und Modesachen nur niedere Gegenstände des Geschmackes sind." Eduard von Hartmann, *Die deutsche Ästhetik seit Kant* (Leipzig: Friedrich, 1887), 482. Gustav Fechner, *Vorschule der Ästhetik* (Leipzig: Breitkopf and Härtel, 1876), 1: 239. On Hartmann, see especially Maria Ocon-Fernandez, *Ornament und Moderne: Theoriebildung und Ornamentdebatte im deutschen Architekturdiskurs (1850–1930)* (Berlin: Reimer, 2004).

39 Hartmann also drew attention to Schelling in his article. Ibid., 462–68.

40 For "Grundstimmung der Zeit" as source of style, see ibid., 56. He footnotes Semper, *Der Stil*, 2: 5.

41 Meinhold Lurz, *Heinrich Wölfflin: Biographie einer Kunstheorie* (Darmstadt: Wernersche Buchgesellschaft, 1981), 316.

42 "Die Natur des Materials, die Art seiner Bearbeitung, die Konstruktion werden nie ohne Einfluss sein. Was ich aber aufrechthalten möchte—namentlich gegenüber einigen neueren Bestrebungen [no footnote]—ist das, *dass die Technik niemals einen Stil schafft*, sondern wo man von Kunst spricht, ein bestimmtes Formgefühl immer das Primäre ist." Wölfflin, *Renaissance und Barock*, 57.

43 Ibid.

44 Ibid., 56.

45 Wilhelm von Bode, *Die italienischen Hausmöbel der Renaissance* (1902), 2. See chpt. 2, n. 45.

46 "Wenn man sagt, es sei ein neuer Stil emporgekommen, so denkt man immer zuerst an eine Umformung der tektonischen Dinge. Sieht man aber naher zu, so ist es nicht nur die Umgebung des Menschen, die grosse und kleine Architektur, nicht nur sein Gerät und seine Kleidung, die eine Wandlung durchgemacht haben, der Mensch selbst nach seiner Körperlichkeit ist ein anderer geworden und eben in der neuen Empfindung seines Körpers und in der neuen Art ihn zu tragen und zu bewegen, steckt der eigentliche Kern eines Stiles." Wölfflin, *Klassische Kunst*, 216. "Jede Generation sieht in der Welt das, was ihr gleichartig ist" (229). "es liegt auf der Hand, dass die neue Körper-und Bewegungsgefühle . . . auch in der Bildgestaltung sich geltend machen müssen."

47 "Auch sie [Architektur] ist ja wie die Kleidung eine Projektion des Menschen und seines Körpergefühls nach aussen." Wölfflin, *Klassische Kunst*, 227.

48 "Man weiss, wie es auf diesen Gebieten jetzt noch um die Kunstwissenschaft bestellt ist. So übel, dass dieselbe für die wichtigsten Formenunterschiede nicht einmal Namen besitzt, dass sie in den wenigen Begriffen des Rundstabes oder der Hohlkehle, der steigenden oder fallended Welle, der Volute, der Eiform etc. beliebige äusserlich einander ähnliche, aber ihrem ästhetischen Charakter nach ausserordentlich mannigfaltige und gelegentlich durchaus heterogene Formen unterbringt. Es ist nicht ungerecht, wenn ich meine, es sei der Weg von solcher 'Kunstwissenschaft' zur wircklichen Kunstwissenschaft nicht viel weniger weit, als der Weg von der Botanik der Küche zur Botanik der Pflanzenphysiologie." Wölfflin, "Lipps's *Raumästhetik*," *Kunstchronik*, 1898, 293.

49 "Jede künstlerische Auffassung ist schon nach bestimmten Gesichtspunkten des Gefallens organisiert . . . Jede Art der Naturwiedergabe bewegt sich schon innerhalb eines bestimmten dekorativen Schemas . . . Erst wo das dekorative Gefühl ein anderes geworden ist, hat man eine Wandlung in der Art der Darstellung zu erwarten." Wölfflin, *Grundbegriffe*, 17–18. For *Zeitstil*, see p. 9; for *Zeitausdruck/Lebensideal*, see p. 10.

50 Both Fiedler and Hildebrand had influenced Wölfflin in this respect. Fiedler's ideas had been published as early as 1878. See Konrad Fiedler, "Bemerkungen über das Wesen und Geschichte der Baukunst," *Deutsche Rundschau* 15 (1878): 361–83. This article had been republished in 1913/14 as part of Fiedler's *Schriften zur Kunst*.

51 "Natürlich ist es nicht nur die grosse Architektur, sondern auch die Kleinwelt der Möbel und Geräte, aus der Beispiele geholt warden konnen . . . die Umwandlung lag in der allgemeinen Richtung des Geschmacks und hatte sich gewiss auf jeden Fall durchgesetzt" (with reference to choir stalls, armoire, table, and Rococo interior). *Grundbegriffe*, 206. He also still refers to Göller's "Reizabstumpfung," 248—but now he responds to it with the "Wirkung von Bild auf Bild" (the effect of image upon image).

52 For Wölfflin's take on Morelli, see his comparison of Botticelli and Lorenzo di Credi: "In der Zeichnugn eines blossen Nasenflügels müsste man schon das Wesentliche des Stilcharakters erkennen." *Grundbegriffe*, 3, and "Eine ganz besonders reiche Ausbeute bietet dem Formpsychologen das stilisierte Gefält in diesem Zeitalter." Ibid., 3. On Morelli's "system," see Gabriele Bickendorf, "Die Tradition der Kennerschaft: Von Lanzi über Rumohr und Waagen zu Morelli," in G. Agosti et al., eds., *Giovanni Morelli e la cultura dei conoscitori* (Bergamo: Pierluigi Lubrina, 1993), 25–47.

53 Richard Pau, "Le origini scientifiche del metodo Morelliano," in Agosti et al., *Giovanni Morelli*, 301–19.

54 "alles Wesentliche der Formempfindung schon im kleinsten Bruchteil vorhanden ist." Ibid., 6.

55 Ibid., 34.

56 "jeder Maler . . . minder wichtige Körpertheile sich eine typische Form wählt, die er unwillkürlich überall dort wiederholt, wo seine Aufmerksamkeit nicht gerade auf jene Theile gelenkt wird." Cornelius Gurlitt, "Lermolieff's kunstkritische Studien," *Die Gegenwart* 27 (1890): 103–5. By then Morelli was well known. He had published in German his first article, "Die Galerien Roms," in *Zeitschrift für bildende Kunst*, in 1875; Moritz Thausing, one of the fathers of the Vienna School of art history, had reviewed and praised his system highly in his "Ivan Lermoliew" in *Neue Freie Presse*, December 22, 1880. See M. Thausing, "Ivan Lermoliew," in Thausing, *Wiener Kunstbriefe* (Leipzig: E. A. Seemann, 1884), 183–90.

57 "das Typische durchzufühlen im Individuellen." The reference appears in notes to a Marees lecture from September 1909. See Wölfflin, *Kleine Schriften*, 252.

58 "nationale Formpsychologie," Wölfflin, *Grundbegriffe*, 8; also "Historisches und Nationales" as chapter headings, 33. *Volksgemüt* is one of his recurrent terms.

59 W. Riehl, "Kunstarchitektur und Volksbauart," in Riehl et al., eds., *Bavaria: Landes-und Volkskunde des Königreichs Bayern* (Munich: Literarisch-artistische Anstalt, 1860), 251. See also his detailed definition of architectural styles: "Der monumentalen Kunst eines Landes entspricht das Wohnhaus des Volkes in ähhnlicher Weise, wie das Volkslied der Kunstmusik. Ja, die rohen, massiven, schweren aber kräftigen, romanischen und gothischen Dorfkirchen Altbayerns sind selbst schon entschiedener Zeugnisse des Volksgeschmackes als einer bestimmten Kunstrichtung" (278–79).

60 See in particular his enthusiastic review of August von Thiersch's concept of the Golden Section in *Deutsche Bauzeitung*, 1889.

61 Wölfflin returns to his conviction in the recurrence of styles as ways of seeing and their cyclical nature in *Renaissance und Barock*, *Klassische Kunst* (276), and *Grundbegriffe*.

62 Giedion's often recurrent term "feeling" is an avatar of Wölfflin's *Formgefühl*, sometimes blended with

Schmarsow's *Raumgefühl*—an example of intertextuality that is lost in translation. For example: "[Mathematical physicists and cubists gave architects] the objective means of organizing space in ways that gave form to contemporary feelings"; or, "Their technical aspects [engineering construction] will not concern us so much as the general methods that appear in them and their *content of feeling*—prophetic of architectonic expressions which come later"; and, "Up to 1910, architects tried many ways of arriving at a new feeling for space [*Raumgefühl*]—the basis and the strongest impulse for original architectonic creation. Around 1910 an event of decisive importance occurred: the discovery of a new space conception in the arts. Working in their studios as though in laboratories, painters and sculptors investigated the ways in which space, volumes, and materials existed for feeling"; also, "There is an astonishing unity subsisting between methods of thought and of feeling: more precisely, there is a direct connection between artistic and mathematical knowledge." Sigfried Giedion, *Space, Time and Architecture* (Cambridge, Mass.: Harvard University Press, 1941), 26, 24, 26, and 56, respectively. On Giedion's debt to a range of sources and people, see Sokratis Georgiadis, *Sigfried Giedion: Eine intellektuelle Biographie* (Zurich: GTA/Ammann, 1989).

63 Immensely popular, his books went through many editions even during the war, and his public lectures were famously well attended. One such testimony of the public attendance at his lectures is by Walter Benjamin, though he is mercilessly critical and has praise only for Riegl. See Thomas Y. Levin, "Walter Benjamin and the Theory of Art History," *October* 47 (Winter 1988): 84–90.

64 Fritz Schumacher, "Die künstlerische Bewältigung des Raums: Randbemerkungen zu Heinrich Wölfflins Buch *Kunstgweschichtliche Grundbegriffe*," *Zeitschrift für Ästhetik und allgemeine Kunstwissenschaft* 13 (1918): 397–402. Julius Baum, *Baukunst und dekorative Plastik der früheren Renaissance in Italien* (Stuttgart: J. Hoffman, 1926), v. For his membership in the Werkbund, see *Jahrbuch des deutschen Werkbunbdes*, 1911.

65 On Riegl and formalism, see Herni Zerner, "Alois Riegl: Art, Value, and Historicism," *Daedalus* 105 (1976): 177–88; Richard Woodfield, *Framing Formalism: Riegl and the History of Art* (Amsterdam: G+B Arts International, 1999), and in the context of the Vienna School (with most recent bibliography), see Christopher Wood, "Introduction," in Wood, ed., *The Vienna School Reader* (New York: Zone, 2000), 26–29.

66 In its early days as an academic discipline, art history was taught within the department of history, the Institut für österreichische Geschichtsforschung. Max Dvorak, "Alois Riegl," in *Gesammelte Aufsätze zur Kunstgeschichte* (published as "Nachruf," 1905; Munich: R. Piper, 1929), 279–98. Von Sickel, Riegl's professor in history, was a former student of the École des Chartes and singlehandedly put on the historical studies map in Vienna both paleography and diplomatic studies, raising them from their erstwhile "serving" status. Julius von Schlosser, "Die Wiener Schule der Kunstgeschichte," *Mitteilungen des Österreichischen Instituts für Geschichtsschreibung* 13, no. 2 (1954): 181–93. See also Margaret Olin, *Forms of Representation in Alois Riegl's Theory of Art* (University Park, 1992), 6, 193.

67 On the medievalist Moriz Thausing, see Schlosser, "Die Wiener Schule," and Olin, *Forms of Representation*. On Thausing's relationship to Morelli, see Moritz Thausing, *Wiener Kunstbriefe* (Leipzig: Seemann, 1884), which was dedicated to Morelli. On the place of paleography in the methodology of the early Vienna School, see Artur Rosenauer, "L'École de Vienne: L'autonomie de l'histoire de l'art?" in *Histoire de l'histoire de l'art*, vol. 2, ed. E. Pommier (Paris: Louvre and Klincksieck, 1997), 419.

68 "das formende Handwerk bei der Verfertigung der *Gegenstände des täglichen Gebrauchs* sich mit der formended Kunst berührt und . . . indem es dieselbe theils als Naturformen gestaltet, theils mit solchen schmückt, oder mehr streng geometrisch 'stilisiert,' auf das Gebiet der Sculptur oder *der baukünstlerischen Ornamentik* hinüberstreift, wo Kunst und Kunsthandwerk zusammentreffen" (my emphasis). Robert Zimmermann, *Allgemeine Ästhetik als Formwissenschaft* (Vienna, 1865), 486, quoted by Dieter Bogner, "Das constructive Ornament—der Beitrag Wiens zur Abstraktion," in M. Bruderlin, ed., *Ornament und Abstraktion: Kunst der Kulturen, Moderne und Gegenwart im Dialog*, exh. cat. Fondation Bayeler, Basel, June–September 2001, 39.

69 Hans Belting. *Bild und Kult: Eine Geschichte des Bildes vor dem Zeitalter der Kunst* (Munich: C. H. Beck, 1990), 9.

70 For example, in John Ruskin, *The Seven Lamps of Architecture* (New York: Dover, 1989; 1880 ed.), 53–4 and John Ruskin, *The Stones of Venice* (New York: Thomas Crowell, n.d.), 2: 207–8.

71 Alois Riegl, *Die mittelalterliche Kalenderillustration, ihr Ursprung und Entwicklung bis zur vollständigen Ausbildung der Typen im 11. Jahrhundert* (Innsbruck: Wagner'sche Universität-Buchdruckerei, 1889), 43.

72 Riegl's term for these calendars was *Bauernkalender.* Alois Riegl, "Die Holzkalender des Mittelalters und der Renaissance," *Mittheilungen des Instituts für österreichischen Geschichtsforschung*, 1888. He returned to this topic when he wrote "Ein kärtnersicher Bauernkalender," *Carinthia* 1 (1891).

73 See especially his articles in *Mitteilungen des kk Österreichischen Museums für Kunst und Industrie* in the 1880s. Stefan Muthesius has interpreted this essay as a statement against *Volkskunst.* However, he is much closer to his erstwhile teacher Eitelberger, who had first broached this topic and promoted folk art. See Eitelberger, "Die Volkskunst und Hausindustrie," *Gesammelte kunsthistorische Schriften*, 267–75.

74 For an exhaustive list, see the bibliography of his writings in A. Rosenauer, ed., *Gesammelte Aufsätze;* 1st ed. H. Sedlmayr (Vienna: WUV, 1996).

75 Alois Riegl, *Stilfragen: Grundlegungen zu einer Geschichte der Ornamentik* (Berlin: Richard Carl Schmidt, 1926), xii.

76 Ibid.

77 Riegl acknowledges as much. Ibid., 11–12.

78 "um so zwingender werden wir hingewiesen auf die Annahme vom ursprünglichen Vorhandensein einer dem Menschen immanenten Fähigkeit zur Hervorbringung gewisser elementarer Verziehrungsformen." Alois Riegl, "Neuseeländische Ornamentik," *Mittheilungen der anthropologischen Gesellschaft in Wien* 20 (1890): 86. Riegl also published on folk art in the same journal. Alois Riegl, "Die Volkskunst vom wirtschaftlichen Standpunkte," *Mittheilungen der anthropologischen Gesellschaft in Wien* 24 (1894): 2–3.

79 "die in Rede stehende materialistische Strömung in der Auffassung der Kunstanfänge nichts Anderes ist, als so zu sagen die Uebertragung des Darwinismus auf ein Gebiet des Geisteslebens." Riegl, *Stilfragen*, vii.

80 Alois Riegl, *Problems of Style: Foundations for a History of Ornament* (1893; Princeton: Princeton University Press, 1993), 6; and Riegl, *Stilfragen*, vi–vii.

81 Ibid., 78.

82 Alois Riegl, *Spätrömische Kunstindustrie* (1901; Darmstadt: Wissenschaftliche Buchgesellschaft, 1964), 9.

83 Riegl, *Stilfragen*, vi–vii.

84 This turn of phrase occurs in Riegl, *Spätrömische Kunstindustrie*, 9, where he refers to *Stilfragen*.

85 On Riegl's awareness of the *Vielvölkerstaat* issues through his having lived in many parts of the empire (Bukovina, Banat, etc.), see Olin, *Forms of Representation*, 19–20. Stefan Muthesius has argued that this experience also determined Riegl's view of folk art. Stefan Muthesius, *Das englische Vorbild* (Munich: Prestel, 1974). See in this context the major Austrian enterprise *Die österreichisch-ungarische Monarchie in Wort und Bild* (1886–1902; 24 vols. German, 21 vols. Hungarian) known as *Kronprinzwerk*. See Ch. Zintzen, "Enzyklopädische Utopie: Ethnographie als Stiftung von Einheit im Diversen," in A. Moravansky, ed., *Das entfernte Dorf* (Vienna: Böhlau, 2002), 183–205. On art history and anthropology, see Johannes Fabian, who distinguishes between ethnic and anthropological object (and hence discourses—the former being historical- or remembrance-based, the latter ahistorical). Fabian, "Ethnische Artefakte und ethnographische Objekte: Über das Erkennen von Dingen," in A. Moravansky, *Das entfernte Dorf*, 21–40.

86 On Riegl's resistance to the concept of "Barbarisierung" and pejorative references such as "Völkerwanderungselemente," used to discredit late antique art, see Riegl, *Spätrömische Kunstindustrie*, 20; Christopher Wood, "Riegl's "Mache," *RES: Anthropology and Aesthetics* 46 (Autumn 2004): 164–66.

87 "Architektur und Kunstgewerbe offenbaren die leitenden Gesetze des Kunstwollens oftmals in nahezu mathematischer Reinheit." Riegl, *Spätrömische Kunstindustrie*, 19.

88 "[in den kleinen dekorativen Künsten] befriedigt sich das Formgefühl in reinster Weise." Wölfflin, "Prolegomena," 46.

89 Wolfgang Kemp notes the origin of this interest in *Historische Grammatik*, Riegl's 1890/91 lectures notes at the University of Vienna. Kemp, "Alois Riegl," 37–60.

90 Sheldon Nodelman, "Structural Analysis in Art and Anthropology," in J. Ehrmann, *Structuralism* (Garden City, N.Y.: Doubleday, 1966), 79–94.

91 Riegl, *Spätrömische Kunstindustrie*, 9. On this issue as a problem with a long history, see Ferdinando Bologna, *Dalle arti minori all'industrial design. Storia di una ideologia* (1972; Naples: Paparo Edizioni, 2009).

92 Kemp has argued that Riegl used this publication to make a larger claim and move out of the museum and textile department to which he had been reduced for so long. I hope to have shown that the internal coherence of Riegl's work points in another direction. Riegl himself recognized that the work went beyond its title and defended his approach by arguing that since the laws at work in *Kunstindustrie* are also at work in the other arts he needed to examine them too, so as to validate his results. To do so he had to write the history of these arts as no one else had done it, given the anti-antique prejudices of art historians. Kemp, "Nachwort," in A. Riegl, *Spätrömische Kunstindustrie*, 1–2.

93 Originally the terms Riegl used were *optisch/taktisch*, but he changed them to *optisch/haptisch* when responding to criticism in an article of 1902 for *Allgemeine Zeitung Beilage*. Wölfflin drew attention to the similarity himself. Heinrich Wölfflin, review of A. Riegl, *Entstehung der Barockkunst in Rom* in *Repertorium für Kunstwissenschaft* 31 (1908): 356–57.

94 Kaschnitz von Weinberg observed this fact: "Riegl [machte] die Kentniss des Objekts von einem rein sinnlichen Akt des Sehens und des auf das Sehen reduzierte Tastens abhängig." Guido Kaschnitz von Weinberg, Review of *Spätrömische Kunstindustrie*, *Gnomon* 5 (1929): 199.

95 Wolfgang Kemp, "Nachwort," in Riegl, *Spätrömische Kunstindustrie*.

96 Alois Riegl, "Der moderne Denkmalkultus, sein Wesen, seine Entstehung," in Alois Riegl, *Gesammelte Aufsätze* (Vienna: WUV, 1996). The essay was written in 1903 as the introduction to the Denkmalschutzgesetz; it was published with the law in February 27, 1905, in the *Neue Freie Presse*. Kemp has argued that Benjamin was influenced by Riegl. Kemp, *Nachwort*.

97 Hans Sedlmayr, "Introduction," in Riegl, *Gesammelte Aufsätze*, xxxi.

98 "Die Eigenschaften der Dinge verraten sich in Reizen, die sie auf die Sinne des wahrnehmenden Subjektes ausüben. Diese Reize sind von zweierlei Art: 1. rein optische, das sind die farbigen Eigenschaften, die ausschliesslich auf die Augen einen Reiz ausüben; 2. sogenannte taktische, das sind die körperlichen Eigenschaften der Dinge, ihre Ausdehnung und ihre Begrenzung im Raume, die den Tastsinn des beanschauendes Subjektes reizen, aber auf Distanz auch durch die Augen vermittelt werden." "Über antike und moderne Kunstfreunde," lecture given at the Gesellschaft der Wiener Kunstfreunde, 1904, in Riegl,

Gesammelte Aufsätze, 185–96.

99 Hans Sedlmayr, "Introduction," Riegl, *Gesammelte Aufsätze*, xxix.

100 Tilmann Buddensieg, *Industriekultur: Peter Behrens and the* AEG, *1907–1914* (1979; Cambridge, Mass.: MIT Press, 1984).

101 On Schmarsow and Semper, see Mallgrave, *Empathy*.

102 Michaud, *Aby Warburg;* Georges Didi-Huberman, *L'image survivante* (Paris: Minuit, 2002).

103 Wilhelm Worringer, *Abstraktion und Einfühlung* (Neuwied: Heuser, 1907).

104 Mitchell W. Schwarzer, "The Emergence of Architectural Space: August Schmarsow's Theory of *Raumgestaltung*," *Assemblage* 15 (1991): 50–61.

105 "auf der anderen Seite kann die einseitige Bevorzugung der Malerei... oder die ebenso einseitige Beachtung der Kunstgewerbe, der Dekoration oder Ornamentik... nur jeden Weg zum innersten Verständnis des geschichtlichen Prozesses verschliessen. Die gemeinsame Voraussetzung für unser Urteil muss sich überall in der Kunstgeschichte auf das Verhältnis der drei Hauptkünste zu einander grunden." In August Schmarsow, *Barock und Rokoko, eine Auseinandersetzung über das Malerische in der Architektur* (Leipzig, 1897), 2.

106 August Schmarsow, *Zur Frage nach dem Malerischen* (Leipzig, 1896); Schmarsow, *Barock und Rokoko;* and Schmarsow, "Kunstwissenschaft und Kulturphilosophie mit gemeinsamen Grundbegriffen," *Zeitschrift für Ästhetik und allgemeine Kunstwissenschaft* 13 (1919): 165–90, 225–58. Alina Payne, "Architecture, Ornament and Pictorialism: Notes on the Relationship Between the Arts from Wölfflin to Le Corbusier," in *The Built Surface* (London: Ashgate, 2002), 54–72.

107 "Es ist also eine Verirrung der aesthetischen Lehre, wenn sie, den Grad von Belebung übertreibend, die Analogien unserer Körpergefühle überall sucht und dieses objektiven Widerhaltes vergisst. Für die Anhänger dieser Auffassung geht ein grosser wichtiger Bestandteil der Architektur als Kunst verloren." Schmarsow, *Über das Malerische in der Architektur*, 22.

108 "Der Begriff des Malerischen gehört zu den wichtigsten, aber zugleich auch vieldeutigsten und unklarsten, mit denen die Kunstgeschichte arbeitet." Schmarsow, *Zur Frage*, 1.

109 "Ich sehe in dieser Einseitigkeit, wie gesagt, nur das Weiterwirken des plastischen Ideales, das in der Antike herkommend ihren Masstab für alle Baukunst nur vom hellenistischen Tempel entlehnt." Ibid., 23.

110 Franz Wickhoff, "Review of A. Schmarsow, *Grundbegriffe des Kunstwissenschaft"* (Leipzig, 1905), in *Abhandlungen, Vorträge und Anzeigen*, vol. 2 (Berlin: Meyer and Jessen, 1913), 365–70; H. Wölfflin, "Review of A. Schmarsow, *Das Wesen der architektonischen Schöpfung,"* in *Repertorium für Kunstwissenschaft* 17 (1894): 141–42.

111 Riegl disagrees with Schmarsow's notion that architecture starts with space in his class lectures published as *Historische Grammatik* (Graz: Bölan, 1966), 301.

112 One noteworthy exception is Mallgrave, *Empathy*, although here too the emphasis is on Schmarsow's impact on the space/time discourse.

113 August Schmarsow, *Das Wesen der architektonischen Schöpfung* (Leipzig: Karl Hiersemann, 1894).

114 For Hartmann, Schmarsow quotes his "Gehört die Baukunst zu den freien Künsten?" *Gegenwart* (1887), 391ff, and his *Ästhetik* (Berlin, 1887); for Semper he quotes *Kleine Schriften* (Berlin, 1884). Finally he states that he has been teaching this material for ten years (since 1883/84 at Breslau and then Göttingen).

115 "jede Auseinandersetzung des Menschen mit einem Gegenstande... vom Leibe aus beginnt." *Unser Verhältnis zu den bildenden Künsten* (1903), 89. "Der menschliche Körper bleibt immer der Mittelpunkt aller ausstrahlenden Wirkungen in die Weite, und ebenso der Zielpunkt aller Einstrahlungen von den Grenzen unsrer Sinnessphären her" (109). "alle Erfahrungen der eigenen Köperlichkeit spiegeln sich auch in dem Ergebnis wieder" (83).

116 "das Gefühl für den eigenen Leib als Körper im allgemeinen Raum ist auch die Grundlage für die Tektonik , und nicht nur für sie allein, sondern auch für das weitere Schaffen der Architektur... hier wieder der Schlüssel der ästhetischen Ausbildung und Genussfähigkeit... zu suchen ist." Ibid, 97.

117 "Wertbezeichnung des eigenen Leibes." Ibid., 82

118 "lebendige Werkzeuge." Ibid., 83. "dem Dienste des lebenswarmen Organes anschmiegt" (97). "Dieser bereitwillige Anschluss an die Körperbewegung des Menschen und die Arbeitsleistung, die von ihm verlangt wird, gibt dem Werkzeug eine bleibende Gebärde" (98).

119 Ibid., 97.

120 Ibid., 98, 100.

121 As summary: "Der menschliche Körper bleibt immer der Mittelpunkt aller ausstrahlenden Wirkungen in die Weite." Ibid., 108.

122 "jede Auseinandersetzung des Menschen mit einem Gegenstände, auf den er 'stösst'... eigentlich unmittelbar vom eigenen Leibe aus beginnt....] Vergleichungen zwischen unserm eigenen leiblichen Bestande und den Dingen um uns her." Ibid., 89.

123 His earlier work had been *Ästhetische Faktoren der Raumanschauung* (Hamburg: L. Voss, 1891) and *Raumästhetik und Geometrisch-Optische Täuschungen*, 8 vols. (Leipzig: A. Barth, 1893–97). Lipps wrote on ornament in *Die ästhetische Betrachtung und die bildende Kunst*, vol. 2 of *Ästhetik: Psychologie des Schönen und der Kunst* (1903–6). On Lipps, see Frank-Lothar Kroll, *Das Ornament in der Kunsttheorie des 19. Jahrhunderts* (Hildesheim, 1987), 83–86.

124 Lipps published in the newspaper *Die Zukunft*.

125 "gewerbliche und industrielle Künste oder des Kunsthandwerkes:... Bauwerke, Sitzmöbel, Gitter, Gefässe, Teppiche." Lipps, *Die ästhetische Betrachtung*, 483.

126 "[d]as Ziel der ästhetischen Betrachtung sind im keinen Falle... die materiellen Leistungen oder Funktion des Materials... Sondern... das Physische eingefühlte Leben." Ibid.

127 His categories are *Kunstform, Grundform, Werkform* (or *Kernform*), and *Schmuckform* (to which belongs also

ornament). Ibid., 490–98.

128 Ibid., 491.

129 "Die Schmuckformen des technischen Kunstwerkes sind für diese genau das, was die Metapher für die Rede ist . . . in die Raumkunst übertragene Bildersprache." Ibid., 513.

130 Ibid., 588–90.

131 August Schmarsow, "Anfangsgründe jeder Ornamentik." *Zeitschrift für Aesthetik und allgemeine Kunstwissenschaft* 5 (1910): 191–215, 321–55. Schmarsow will return to the topic in later articles but not with significant changes to the questions at issue here. "Die reine Form in der Ornamentik aller Künste." *Zeitschrift für Aesthetik* 16 (1922): 491–500; 17 (1923): 1–17, 129–45, 209–34, 305–29; 18 (1924): 83–107.

132 Schmarsow, "Anfangsgründe," 198.

133 Ibid., 192.

134 Ibid., 201.

135 "durch regelmässige Wiederholung eines relativen Wertes, der einen höheren Wert auszeichnen, hervorheben und begleitend vermitteln; . . . überall tritt die typische Bildung an die Stelle der individuellen Verschiedenheit. Das Wort *Typus* bedeutet . . . Grundform." Ibid., 209–11. This argument is revisited in "Zur Lehre vom Ornament," *Zeitschrift für Aesthetik und allgemeine Kunstwissenschaft* 16 (1922): 511–26.

136 Gustavus George Zerffi, *A Manual of the Historical Development of Art, with Special Reference to Architecture, Sculpture, Painting, and Ornamentation* (London, 1876).

137 "vorhandene Werte zu begleiten, auszuzeichnen und hervorzuheben." Ibid., 327. "Während die eigentliche Kunst den Wert, den sie verherrlichen will, selber erschafft und ausgestaltet, will und kann die Ornamentik diesen Wert nicht selber darstellen und hervorbringen, sondern vermittelt nur den vorhandenen." Schmarsow, "Anfangsgründe jeder Ornamentik," 214. The concept that ornament is a mediator between life and art had been proposed by Vischer.

138 "selbstständigen Gegenstände des Hausrats zu *vorübergehenden* aber *wiederkehrenden* Gebräuche." Ibid., 349.

139 Ibid., 348. Schmarsow's source for this observation was probably the 1908 edition of Lübke's history of ancient art that included prehistory and illustrated such carved tools. Wilhelm Lübke, *Die Kunst des Alterums*, new ed. by Max Semrau (Esslingen: Paul Neff, 1908), 1–3.

140 "Je unabhängiger solche Erzeugnisse auch ausserhalb der Handhabung durch den Menschen noch für sich bestehen, desto deutlicher nähert sich bald ihre Behandlung durch die Ornamentik dem Vorbild des Menschenkörpers und prägt in der struktiven Plastik der Form schon die Analogie mit der Haltung des aufrechten oder sitzenden oder liegenden Lebewesens aus . . . ganz ohne die Absicht auf Nachahmung." Schmarsow, "Anfangsgründe jeder Ornamentik," 349.

141 Ibid., 355. Among anthropologists he attacks Max Verworn, *Anfänge der Kunst* (1909).

142 Melani, *Manuale d'arte decorativa*; G. M. Urbani de Gheltof, *Les arts industriels a Venise au moyen âge et a la renaissance* (Venice: Usiglio and Diena, 1885; trans. from Italian).

143 Riegl, for example, uses it to describe fountain architecture, which he additionally identifies as *kunstgewerblich*. Alois Riegl, *Die Entstehung der Barockkunst in Rom* (1907; Munich: Mäander, 1977), 129.

144 One such course (identified as a *Baukurs*) was Hase and Luer's "Ornamentik des Details. Kleinarchitektur (Meubles)" at the Hannover Polytechnikum, one of the best known and attended. Carl Koristka, *Der höhere polytechnische Unterricht in Deutschland, in der Schweiz, in Frankreich und England: Ein Bericht* (Gotha: Besser, 1863), 71.

145 See, for example, Hermann Lotze, *Geschichte der Aesthetik in Deutschland* (1868), p.535; Cornelius Gurlitt, *Geschichte des Barockstiles in Italien* (1887), 381; Georg Dehio, *Die kirchliche Baukunst des Abendlandes* (1892), 457; August Thiersch, *Architektonische Composition* (1893), 68; Alois Riegl, *Entstehung der Barockkunst in Rom* (1908), 129; Hermann Muthesius, *Das Englische Haus* (1908), 101.

146 Fritz Hoeber, *Orientierende Vorstudien zur Systematik der Architekturproportionen* (Frankfurt a. M.: Kunz und Gabel, 1906), 52.

147 For a discussion of *Kleinarchitektur* and its reception in the nineteenth-century scholarship, see Payne, "Materiality, Crafting, and Scale."

148 [Die Laternen und Fackelhalter des Palazzo Strozzis] "Erstere sind als achteckige Tempietti mit vorgestellten Säulchen an den Ecken, wie in der Kanzel von S. Croce, ganz architektonisch gedacht und von Caparra nach dem Modelle B. da Majanos ausgeführt. Dekorativ wirken der Konsolenfuss und die strahlenartige Bekrönung verzüglich." Carl von Stegmann, and Heinrich von Geymüller, *Die Architektur der Renaissance in Toscana* (Munich: F. Bruckmann, 1885–1908), 4: 9.

149 "ein Juwel der dekorativen Kunst . . . Der Tempietto ist das Modell für einen Kuppelbau und zeigt den feinen Architekten." Ibid., 4: 2.

150 "On était venu en France, a cette époque [xv & xv ieme] à faire de l'architecture en petit lorsqu'on voulait une armoire, un dressoir." Viollet-le-Duc, *Dictionnaire raisonnée du mobilier français* (1873–74), 424. His term for objects of daily use: "les objets necessaires a la vie journaliaire" (422).

151 "on ne transporte pas un edifice, et l'on transporte facilement un meuble." Ibid., 420.

152 Burckhardt, *Geschichte der Baukunst*, 211.

153 Zucker states in the introduction his methodological underpinning: "dass sich in zwitterartigen Gebilden eine neue kommende Gesinnung schon ausspricht—dass dabei die Übergänge zwischen den einzelnen Kunstzweigen verwischt werden und die gleichsam 'beweglichste' Kunst als erste die neuen Stilmerkmale ausprägt. Am konservativsten werden sich immer die schweren Steinmassen der Architekturen zeigen." Zucker footnotes both Wölfflin's *Klassische Kunst* and *Renaissance und Barock*. Paul Zucker, *Raumdarstellung und Bildarchitekturen im Florentiner Quattrocento* (Leipzig: Klinkhardt and Biermann, 1913), 1.

154 "Eine Zeit, deren Stil mehr war als eine bestimmte Manier bestimmte Kunstwerke zu schaffen, deren Stil intensiv einwirkte auch auf das Leben der Bürger, die dem Kunstschaffen sehr fern standen—denn jedes Hausgerät, jeder Gebrauchsgegenstand, jedes Fest, das gefeiert wurde, war von diesem Stil geprägt—, eine solche Zeit, sich selbst getreu bis ins kleinste Detail hinein, musste auch im Nebensächlichsten ihre Ausdrucksformen aufweisen." Ibid., 2.

155 See, e.g., Alois Riegl, *Die Entstehung der Barockkunst in Rom* (1907), in which he uses the term *taktisch* for an essential feature of Baroque art. Alina Payne, "Beyond *Kunstwollen:* Alois Riegl and the Theoretization the Baroque," in Alois Riegl, *The Origin of Baroque Art in Rome* (Los Angeles: Getty Institute, 2010), 1–33.

156 Heinrich Wölfflin, "Review of A. Riegl, *Entstehung der Barockkunst in Rom,*" *Repertorium für Kunstwissenschaft* 31 (1908): 356–57.

157 Payne, "Portable Ruins."

158 Between 1886–88 he studies art history and psychology in Bonn with Carl Justi, Hermann Usener (historian of religions), and Karl Lamprecht (psychological reading of history). See Kurt Forster, "Introduction," in Aby Warburg, *The Renewal of Pagan Antiquity* (Santa Monica: Getty Research Institute, 1999), 9–10. 1888–89: a student in Schmarsow's seminar in Florence; he contributes his Sasseti chapel article to the 1907 Schmarsow Festschrift (*Kunstwissenschaftliche Beiträge August Schmarsow gewidmet zum fünfzigsten Semester seiner akademischen Lehrtätigkeit,* by H. Weizsäcker Leigzig, K. W. Hiersemann, et al., 1907. He was also profoundly influenced by Wilhelm Wundt's *Völkerpsychologie,* especially the issue of gesture as language. Didi-Huberman, *L'image survivante,* 218–19.

159 Didi-Huberman argues that the fact that Wölfflin worked on similar body-related issues was only a coincidence. It seems unlikely. As a student, Warburg (working in Florence in Schmarsow's seminar in 1889–90) had to have read him, especially as he was interested in Vischer. Didi-Huberman, *L'image survivante,* 406. Warburg's essay on the Laocoon and *malerisch* reliefs for Schmarsow's seminar in Florence indicates that he had absorbed the literature on the altar as well as the debates on the *malerisch* surrounding it. See Aby Warburg, "Die Entwicklung des Malerischen in den Reliefs des Ghiberti: Entwurf einer Kritik des Laokoon an der Kunst des Quattrocento in Florenz," in Warburg, *Opere I,* ed. Maurizio Ghelardi (London: Warburg Institute, and Turin: Nino Aragno, 2004), 53–75.

160 On Darwin's aesthetics, see Winfried Menninghaus, *Das Versprechen der Schönheit* (Berlin: Suhrkamp, 2003).

161 "La ténacité des survivances, leurs 'puissance' même, comme dit Tylor, vient au jour dans la ténuité de choses minuscules, superflues, dérisoires ou anormales. C'est dans le symptôme récurrent et dans le jeu, c'est dans la pathologie de la langue et dans l'inconscient des formes que gît la survivance en tant que telle." Didi-Huberman, *L'image survivante,* 57, 241. Didi-Huberman makes much of the anthropological turn in Warburg's art history and of the influence of Edward B. Taylor's *Primitive Culture* (London, 1871). With this book Taylor established a "science of culture" and influenced Warburg's concept of *Nachleben* "in trivial details" (51–60).

162 Ibid., 391, 414–17.

163 Gertrude Bing, "A. M. Warburg," *Journal of the Warburg and Courtauld Institute* 28 (1965): 307. Spyros Papetros, "World Ornament: The Legacy of Gottfried Semper's 1856 Lecture on Ornament," *RES* 57/58 (Spring–Autumn 2010).

164 Bing, *Warburg,* 305.

165 Ibid.

166 "Warburg a compris avant Walter Benjamin, que l'historien n'avait une chance d'accéder aux longues durées de la survivance que dans le regard déplacé du 'chiffonnier,' qui ose faire de l'histoire avec les haillons de l'histoire: l'ex-voto pourrissant d'une église de Florence en face d'un chef d'œuvre du musée des Offices, les *ricordanze* d'un banquier en face de la *Divine Comédie,* les *chap-books* américains en face de toute la grande littérature, les feuillets de propagandes, horoscopes, réclames et autres timbres-poste en face des gravures de Rembrandt." Didi-Huberman, *L'image survivante,* 419. On Benjamin and Riegl and his decisive influence in this direction, see Levin, "Walter Benjamin and the Theory of Art History," 84–90.

167 Kurt Forster also notes the coincidence of interest in detail evident in the work of Riegl and Warburg (with Semper as a forerunner), with Riegl working on nomads and rug making, migration of individual motifs (volute of Ionic capital), and the disintegration of art forms in the Austrian empire, while Warburg looked at waxworks and votive sculptures in the Renaissance, rituals among North American Indians and suchlike. Forster, "Introduction," in Warburg, *Renewal of Pagan Antiquity,* 9–10.

168 Warburg, *Renewal of Pagan Antiquity,* 319.

169 On the *Volkskundekongress,* see Ernst Gombrich, *Aby Warburg: Eine intellektuelle Biographie* (Frankfurt am Main: Suhrkamp 1984), 179. On Schumacher as the architect of Heilwigstrasse, see Michaud, *Aby Warburg,* 22.

170 See Franz Boas, "The Decorative Art of the Indians of the North Pacific Coast," *Bulletin of the American Museum of Natural History* 9 (1897): 123–76; Boas, "Facial Painting of the Indians of Northern British Columbia," *Memoirs of the American Museum of Natural History* 2 (1898): 13–24, on adapting animal form to the decorative field. On Warburg's conferences, see Michaud, *Aby Warburg,* 175, 183.

171 Warburg, *Renewal of Pagan Antiquity,* 157–68, 185–221.

172 Translated from Michaud, *Aby Warburg,* 264–65. Although these ideas were certainly present in Warburg's notes, the text as we know it now was significantly smoothed by Fritz Saxl. I thank Maurizio Ghelardi for sharing with me these insights from his deep knowledge of Warburg's *Nachlass.*

173 Thomas Carlyle, *Sartor Resartus: On Heroes and Hero Worship* (London: Everyman's Library, 1967), 26.

174 Didi-Huberman, *L'image survivante,* 411.

CHAPTER 4 | THE ARCHITECT'S WORLD BETWEEN CULTURE AND STYLE

1 See, for example, Wolfgang Herrmann, ed., *In What Style Should We Build?* (Santa Monica: Getty Center, 1992).

2 Didi-Huberman draws attention to this perspective in Warburg's work. Didi-Huberman, *L'image survivante.*

3 The impact of empathy theory in architecture has been studied far more than the impact upon art history as a whole. In art history, most work has focused either on Wölfflin and Worringer (as well as his impact on the Expressionists) or on the advent of abstraction with which it has been associated, but its impact on the broader reading of art of all historical periods and geographic origin has not received much attention. See, for example, David Morgan, "The Idea of Abstraction in German Theories of Ornament from Kant to Kandinsky," *Journal of Aesthetics and Art Criticism* 50 (Summer 1992): 231–42; Meinhold Lurz, *Heinrich Wölfflin: Biographie einer Kunstheorie* (Darmstadt: Wernersche Buchgesellschaft, 1981); Joan Hart et al., eds., *Relire Wölfflin* (Paris: École Nationale Supérieure des Beaux-Arts, 1995). For architecture, see especially Harry Francis Mallgrave, ed. and trans., *Empathy, Form, and Space: Problems in German Aesthetics, 1873–1893* (Santa Monica: Getty Center, 1994).

4 L. Trzeschtik, "Die Prinzipien der Baukunst," *Allgemeine Bauzeitung* (1891), 4.

5 See, for example, one Emerich A. Werner, a Chicago engineer. Harvard's copy of the issue is stamped "1891," thus indicating that it was available at the time of publication. Werner, "Träger auf zwei Stützen," *Allgemeine Bauzeitung* (1890), 41. M. Scherwinski from Riga (Georgia) also published in the same issue, thus indicating its spread in the Euro-Middle East region as well. Scherwinski, "Die Baukunst in Georgien," *Allgemeine Bauzeitung* (1890), 29.

6 Wölfflin, "Review of August Thiersch," *Deutsche Bauzeitung* (1889). Jay Hambidge, *Dynamic Symmetry: The Greek Vase* (New Haven: Yale University Press, 1920).

7 R. Adamy, "Kunsthandwerk und Architektur im System der Künste," *Deutsche Bauzeitung* (1889), 545–50; Bodo Ebhardt, "Das Kunstgewerbe auf der nordischen Ausstellung zu Kopenhagen 1888," *Deutsche Bauzeitung* (1889).

8 H. Schatteburg, "Das Kunstschöne und die Kunstgewerbeschulen," *Allgemeine Bauzeitung* (1892); Schatteburg, "Der Einfluss der Maschiene auf das Gewerbe," *Allgemeine Bauzeitung* (1893).

9 "der Kunstsinn ist der Gradmesser für die Kulturstufe die ein Volk erklommen hat." Ibid., 17. On the resistance to historicizing the education arm of the museum under Scala and also championed by Riegl, see Kathrin Pokorny-Nagel,"Zur Gründungsgeschichte des k.k. Österreichischen Museums fur Kunst und Industrie," in P. Noever, ed., *Kunst und Industrie: Die Anfänge des Museums für Angewandte Kunst in Wien* (Vienna: Hatje Cantz Verlag, 2000): 86–87.

10 Hermann Muthesius, *Kultur und Kunst: Gesammelte Aufsätze* (1904; Nendeln: Kraus, 1976).

11 H. Schatteburg, "Eine Skizze zur kulturgeschichtlichen Entwicklung der Stylarten," *Allgemeine Bauzeitung* (1894), 16; Schatteburg, "Einiges über die Farbe in der Architektur," *Allgemeine Bauzeitung* (1895), 19.

12 For an extensive analysis of Adamy's article, see Maria Ocon-Fernandez, *Ornament und Moderne: Theoriebildung und Ornamentdebatte im deutschen Architekturdiskurs (1850–1930),* (Berlin: Reimer, 2004).

13 "das intime Leben im Hause, das Gehen und Treiben, die Ausstattung, die Vertheilung der Räume, die *Tracht der Bewohner und ihre Haltung, ihre Art zu gehen und stehen,* zu arbeiten und zu ruhen." Hoffmann, *Deutsche Bauzeitung* (August 1889), 417 (my emphasis).

14 Friedrich von Hellwald, *Kulturgeschichte in ihrer natürlichen Entwicklung bis zur Gegenwart,* 3rd ed. (Augsburg: Lampart, 1883–84); Von Hellwald, *Haus und Hof ihrer Entwickelung mit Bezug auf die Wohnsitten der Völker* (Leipzig: H. Schmidt and C. Günther, 1888); Julius Langbehn, *Rembrandt als Erzieher* (Leipzig: C. L. Hirschfield, 1890).

15 It is interesting to note that Gurlitt makes the same argument about German Renaissance crafts in his 1899 *Die deutsche Kunst des XIX Jahrhunderts.*

16 "neue Kunstformen sich ohne unsere Vorsehung bilden, sie werden uns durch die Eigenschaften der Rohstoffe und die Lebenszwecke aufgedrängt." G. Heuser, "Darwinistisches über Kunst und Technik," *Allgemeine Bauzeitung* (1890), 26. See also his "Zur Entstehung des Gefachstyles, insbesondere der Gelenklager," *Allgemeine Bauzeitung* (1892), 19. Heuser developed his ideas in some dozen articles. On his theory of architectural realism and its relationship to French developments, as well as its concomitance with Otto Wagner's similar theory, see J. Duncan Berry, "From Historicism to Architectural Realism: On Some of Wagner's Sources, " in Harry Francis Mallgrave, ed., *Otto Wagner: Reflections on the Raiment of Modernity* (Santa Monica: Getty Center, 1993), 255–56.

17 Ernst Kapp, *Grundlinien einer Philosophie der Technik: Zur Entstehungsgeschichte der Cultur aus neuen Gesichtspunkten* (Braunschweig: George Westermann, 1877).

18 On Kapp's position on philosophical issues and his debt to Hegel, see Benoit Timmermans, "L'influence hegelienne sur la *Philosophie de la Technique* de Ernst Kapp," in P. Chabot and G. Hottois, eds., *Les philosophes et la technique,* 95–108.

19 Ibid., 139–42.

20 Heuser's term is *Gebrauchsorgane.* Heuser, "Darwinistisches über Kunst und Technik," 26.

21 Ibid., 64. Heuser cites Viollet-le-Duc among his sources.

22 G. Heuser, "Das Werden von Stylformen: Fortsetzung Darwinistischer Studien," *Allgemeine Bauzeitung* (1894), 54, 68.

23 Bötticher, *Die Tektonik der Hellenen.*

24 Gruner, "Die Lüge in der Baukunst," *Allgemeine Bauzeitung* (1888), 85, 90.

25 "künstlerische Durchbildung," "nackte Nutzform," "maskiert," "Maskeraden." Ibid.

26 L. Trzeschtik, "Die Architektur und ihr Verhältniss zur Malerei, Plastik und Gartenkunst," *Allgemeine Bauzeitung* (1888), 12, 20. His concern with style continued, and he also published "Die Prinzipien der Baukunst," *Allgemeine Bauzeitung* (1891), 4, 13, 20, 27.

27 His terms are "Raumbildende Kunst," "Geräthekunst," "Gefässbildungen," "Körperbildende Kunst," "Kunst der Fläche." Ibid., 450. Eduard von Hartmann, *Die deutsche Ästhetik seit Kant* (Leipzig: Friedrich, 1887). On this topic, see especially Ocon-Fernandez, *Ornament und Moderne,* who uses Adamy in conjunction with philosopher Eduard von Hartmann as the primary evidence of her argument about the debate on the location of the individual arts in the pantheon of art more generally. The issue of ornament as a transitional category between artistic media was first raised with reference to early modern art by Alina Payne, "Von *ornatus* zu *figura:* Das figürliche Ornament in der italienischen Architektur des 16. Jahrhunderts," in I. Frank and F. Hartung, eds., *Die Rhetorik des Ornaments* (Berlin: Fink Verlag, 2001), 205–39.

28 Heinrich Wölfflin, review of A. Schmarsow, *Das Wesen der architektonischen Schöpfung* in *Repertorium für Kunstwissenschaft* 17 (1894): 141–42.

29 See chapter 1.

30 Kapp, *Grundlinien einer Philosophie der Technik.*

31 Klaus-Peter Arnold, *Geschichte der deutschen Werkstätten und der Gartenstadt Hellerau* (Dresden, 1993).

32 See the chapter "Adolf Göller" in Harry Francis Mallgrave, ed., *Empathy, Form, and Space: Problems in German Aesthetics, 1873–1893* (Santa Monica: Getty Center, 1994).

33 Adolf Göller, *Zur Äesthetik der Architektur* (Stuttgart: K. Wittwor, 1887). This publication was a collection of speeches. Of particular importance are "Was ist die Ursache der immerwahrenden Stilveränderung in der Architektur? 1–48, and "Was ist die Wahrheit in der Architektur?" 89–120. Adolf Göller, *Entstehung der architektonischen Stilformen: Eine Geschichte der Baukunst nach dem Werden und Wandern der Formgedanken* (Stuttgart: K. Wittwor, 1888).

34 Göller, *Entstehung der architektonischen Stilformen.*

35 His lecture was titled "Was ist die Wahrheit in der Architektur?"

36 Göller, *Entstehung der architektonischen Stilformen,* 7–11. "Die Architektur [ist] die wahre schmückende Kunst, die wahre Kunst der sichtbaren reinen Formen."

37 Wölfflin, *Renaissance und Barock.*

38 "Von jeder grösseren Form, ja *von allen Formen* ist das Gedächtnissbild kein einzelnes Residuum, sondern eine Association, eine Kette von einfacheren Gedächtnissbildern, die einander nothwendig ins Bewusstsein rufen. Denn eine jede grössere Form erfassen wir nach und nach; es ist uns unmöglich, an einem Bauwerk gleichzeitig etwa das Ornament an einer Konsole und einige Meter davon den Fuss einer Säule aufmerksam zu betrachten. Das Bild einer grösseren Form zieht also als eine Kette von Vorstellungen in das Gedächtniss ein, und ebenso wird es auch reproduziert." Göller, *Entstehung der architektonischen Stilformen,* 18.

39 Heuser cites an article by du Bois-Raymond in *Deutsche Bauzeitung* (1893).

40 Ibid., 68.

41 Ibid. On the connection between *Formgefühl* and *Gedächtnissinhalt/bild,* see Göller, *Entstehung der architektonischen Stilformen,* 16: "Die Erfahrung lehrt uns, dass unser Gefühl für das Schöne eine Art Erziehung durchmacht, dass es abhängig ist von dem, was wir früher gesehen und im Gedächtniss behalten hatten."

42 "So mag in der That eine Schönheit in der Baukunst an Geltung gewinnen, welche in natürlicher Züchtung durch die Ingenieure entstand ohne die Mitarbeit der Architekten, welche die plastische Schönheit hierbei zu sehr vermissen." Heuser, "Das Werden von Stylformen," 68. Indeed, he compares the increasing aesthetic acceptance of iron with the shift in aesthetic caused by the invention of photography. See also earlier "neue Kunstformen sich ohne unsere Vorsehung bilden, sie werden uns durch die Eigenschaften der Rohstoffe und die Lebenszwecke aufgedrängt." Heuser, "Darwinistisches über Kunst und Technik," 26.

43 Heuser, "Das Werden von Stylformen," 68.

44 "Nach allem ist die Architektur die wahre schmückende Kunst, die wahre Kunst der sichtbaren reinen Formen." Göller, "Was ist die Ursache der immerwahrenden Stilveränderung in der Architektur?" in *Zur Asthetik der Architektur,* 7, 11.

45 "Durch lange Zeiträume hindurch scheint das Schaffen aller alten Völker ohne merklichen Fortschritt sich hingezogen zu haben und allen Schmuck der Bauwerke nur ein beweglicher, bei der textilen und keramischen Kunst entlehnter gewesen zu sein. Später erst, wenn eine höhere Kulturstufe erreicht wird, gehen die Schmuckformen auf den Bau selber über." Göller, *Entstehung der architektonischen Stilformen,* 33.

46 Adolf von Hildebrand, *Das Problem der Form* (1893); Konrad Fiedler, *Schriften zur Kunst,* ed. G. Boehm (1913/14; Munich: Wilhelm Fink, 1971).

47 For Streiter's biography see the introduction in Richard Streiter, *Ausgewählte Schriften zur Ästhetik und Kunstgeschichte,* ed. Franz von Reber and Emil Sulger-Gebing (Munich: Delphin, 1913). On the many overlaps with Muthesius (although no interaction between the two is posited or explored), see Fedor Roth, *Hermann Muthesius und die Idee der harmonischen Kultur* (Berlin: Gebrüder Mann, 2001).

48 Richard Streiter, *Karl Bötticher's Tektonik der Hellenen als Ästhetische und Kunstgeschichtliche Theorie: Eine Kritik* (Hamburg: Leopold Voss, 1896). Streiter has not been much attended by modern scholarship. Among the very few instances when he is drawn into a discussion of architectural modernity, see Harry Francis Mallgrave, "From Realism to *Sachlichkeit:* The Polemics of Architectural Modernity in the 1890s," in Mallgrave, ed., *Otto Wagner: Reflections on the Raiment of Modernity* (Santa Monica: Getty Center, 1993), 281–321.

49 This view was proposed by his editors when his collected works appeared posthumously in Streiter, *Ausgewählte Schriften* (1913). The essay on *Kunstgewerbe* had appeared in *Beilage zur Allgemeinen Zeitung* of 1896, in issues 121 and 122.

50 The essays in *Ausgewäahlte Schriften* were published first in these two journals as shorter articles.

51 Streiter, *Ausgewählte Schriften*, 2–3.

52 Streiter pays particular attention to the following passage in Crane: [Art must be] "dem Frisch pulsierenden Leben entspringen.... Ein Spiegelbild muss sie sein des Lebens das sie umgibt." Ibid., 5.

53 On Warburg's *nympha*, see his essay "The Art of Portraiture and the Florentine Bourgeoisie" on the fresco cycle in the Sassetti chapel, Florence, in Warburg, *The Renewal of Pagan Antiquity* (Santa Monica: Getty Research Institute, 1999).

54 Streiter, *Ausgewählte Schriften*, 29.

55 "Dann wird sich am sichersten und gesundesten aus der Stilmischung etwas Selbstständiges herausentwickeln, was wir als Stil unserer Zeit sehnlich erhoffen." Ibid., 28.

56 "glatt, exact, einfach, scharfe Formen, regelmässig." Ibid.

57 Ibid., 15.

58 It is precisely the quality of machine-produced luxury items from the United States and Britain that suggests the possibility of achieving beauty through mass production. Ibid., 14.

59 Ibid., 16.

60 "Entwurzelte, hauslose Städter." Ibid. On Haberlandt, see also chapter 2. Georg Simmel, "The Metropolis and Mental Life," in *Georg Simmel on Individuality and Social Forms: Selected Writings*, ed. D. Levine (Chicago, 1971).

61 "Namentlich mit Rücksicht auf häufige Umzüge von einem Ort zum anderen oder nur innerhalb der Stadt ist eine grössere Leichtigkeit unseres Mobiliärs entschieden wunschenswert. Wir moderne Menschen sind infolge der riesig gesteigerten Verkehrsverhältnisse viel beweglicher als die Mehrzahl der Menschen in früheren Jahrhunderten es war; demnach muss auch unser Hausrat leichter beweglich sein." "die neuen Erzeugnisse den neuen Lebensverhältnissen, unserem modernen Menschen anzupassen" requires "Berücksichtigung der Zweckmässigkeit und Bequemlichkeit, zugleich mit grösster Sachlichkeit und Solidität." Streiter, *Ausgewählte Schriften*, 19, 20.

62 "diese Entwicklung wird zunächst im Kunstgewerbe vor sich gehen, das sich leichter und rascher den Bedürfnissen der Zeit anschmiegen kann, als die schweren beweglichen Architektur." Ibid., 28.

63 Otto Wagner, *Modern Architecture*, intr. and trans. Harry Francis Mallgrave (Santa Monica: Getty Center, 1988), 93, 76–77. On this contradiction and its causes, see essays in the volume on Wagner edited by Mallgrave, *Otto Wagner: Reflections on the Raiment of Modernity*.

64 "künstlerische Wahrhaftigkeit, Knappheit and Sachlichkeit." Streiter, *Ausgewählte Schriften*, 28.

65 "Haben sich durch *das beständige Sehen und Benutzen* jener Erzeugnisse [der modernene Technik] unsere Augen und unsere *Tastgefühl* mehr und mehr an die struktiv-technische Sachlichkeit *gewohnt* und unser tektonisches *Formgefühl* dementsprechend beeinflusst, so ist zudem noch unser *Korpergefühl* durch die ausserordentliche Steigerung der Verkehrsmittel für eine grössere Bewegungsfähigkeit sehr empfänglich und demnach für allen hemmenden und beschwereden Ballast sehr empfindlich geworden. Diese psychologische Tatsache, die Beeinflussung also unseres Körpergefühls, damit auch unseres statischen Gefühls, unseres Formengefühls überhaupt durch unsere ganzen von der modernen Technik umgestalteten Lebensverhältnisse kann allein den Schlüssel bieten zur Erkenntnis der spezifischen modernen Auffassungsweise tektonischer Aufgaben." Ibid., 81–82.

66 The German term Heuser uses is *Gelenkstyl*. "Mit der Zeit aber wird das Zweckerfüllende Minimum von Material Wohlgefallen erwecken, der Klageruf der Styllosigkeit wird aufhören, wenn erst durch allmalige Auslese gereifte Motive im Gedächtniss der Menschen leben und berreits ist in Geräthen und Maschienen ein Formenreiz entstanden, welchen du Bois-Raymond als 'mechanische Schönheit' bezeichnet" (see *Deutsche Bauzeitung* [1893], 149). G. Heuser, "Das Werden von Stylformen: Fortsetzung Darwinistischer Studien," *Allgemeine Bauzeitung* (1894), 68.

67 "Die Werke der Ingenieurs, des Maschinentechnikers gehen gleichfalls auf die Konstruktion als Urzelle zurück; aber sie gelten im allgemeinen nicht als tektonische Kunstwerke, eben weil sie jener 'Symbolik der Konstruktion' entbehren, weil ihre Formen im ganzen und in den einzelnen Teilen nicht in *plastischer* Anschaulichkeit als *der unmittelbar fühlbare Ausdruck* einer von uns gewissermassen *miterlebbaren*, uns sympathischen körperlichen Verhaltgungsweise in einem leicht aufassbaren, ordnungsmässigen Zusammenhang sich darstellen." Streiter, *Ausgewählte Schriften*, 99.

68 Ibid., 100.

69 Ibid., 103–4.

70 "denn die Möglichkeit, eine Eisenkonstruktion durch struktur-symbolische Formung des Ganzen, wie namentlich der Teile zu einem nicht mehr *abstract-starren*, sondern konkretlebendingen statischen Organismus auszubilden, dessen Glieder durch den Ausdruck ihrer Körperlichkeit uns ihr Zusammenwirken zu einem Zustand 'glücklichen Gleichgewichts' *unmittelbar fühlen lassen*, diese einzige Möglichkeit tektonischer 'Idealisierung' der Werkform ist durch die Natur des Materials und durch die Art seiner Zusammenfügung ausgeschlossen." Ibid., 110.

71 "fleischlose Dünnheit; steife Trockenheit; statische Berechnung; äussere Gleichartigkeit der Glieder; verwirrende Menge sich durchkreuzender fast körperloser Linien." Ibid.

72 "im Kleinen vorbereitet." Ibid., 119.

73 *Lebensgefühl* and *Formgefühl* are his terms. "denn hier kann sich trotz starker Abhängigkeit von den

praktischen Aufforderungen des täglichen Lebens am freiesten und leichtesten ein neuer Formen- und Farbensinn ausleben, hier berührt und verschlingt sich am *unmittelbarsten* und mannigfaltigsten die zwecklich bedingte *Körperlichkeit* tektonischer Gebilde mit der Gestaltenwelt der malerischen, plastischen und dichterischen Phantasie." He quotes *Renaissance und Barock* and Semper's 1854 lecture in London and his *Der Stil*. Ibid., 115.

74 Ibid., 117–18.

75 Ibid., 119.

76 Ibid., 138–39.

77 Ibid., 137.

78 Ibid., 29.

79 Ibid., 15, 86.

80 On Gurlitt as Doktorvater of Muthesius, see Roth, *Hermann Muthesius*, 28, n. 34. Of the over seventy of these he surpervised, most were by architects not art historians. Jürgen Paul, *Cornelius Gurlitt* (Dresden: Hellerau, 2003), 122–23. As Paul introduces him, Gurlitt "gehörte zu den bedeutendsten geistigen Persönlichkeiten des Übergangs vom 19. zum 20. Jahrhundert in Deutschland. Architekt und Kunsthistoriker, war Gurlitt einer der Hauptverträter der Reformbewegung um 1900, der modernen Kunstkritik, der wissenschaftlichen Architekturgeschichte, der sächsischen Landes- und Kunstgeschichte, Theoretiker und Pionier der modernen Denkmalpflege wie der Reform des Städtebaus. Durch sein vielfältiges Wirken in und für Dresden wurde er zu einer der geistigen Vaterfiguren dieser Stadt."

81 Cornelius Gurlitt, ed., *Das Barock-und Rococo-Ornament Deutschlands* (Berlin: Wasmuth, 1883–89) in the series *Architektur und Kunstgewerbe des XVII und XVIII Jahrhunderts*. He also wrote monographs on Andreas Schlüter (1891) and Palladio (1914).

82 Werner Sombart, *Kunstgewerbe und Kultur* (Berlin: Marquardt, 1908).

83 *Die Gegenwart, Wochenschrift für Literatur, Kunst und öffentliches Leben*, started in 1872 by Paul Lindau, was a central intersection point for debates on arts and politics. Lux turned to Gurlitt in his enthusiasm for his *Im Bürgerhause* (Dresden, 1888), which drew on Semper, outlined a cultural history of interiors, and promoted a contemporary style. On Gurlitt's proto-*Sachlichkeit* and its influence on Muthesius, see Harry Francis Mallgrave, *Otto Wagner: Reflections on the Raiment of Modernity* (Santa Monica: Getty Center, 1993).

84 Mallgrave, *Semper*, 339.

85 His closing chapter in *Deutsche Kunst des 19 Jahrhunderts* addresses "das Bauernhaus." On Gurtlitt's life and activity, see Paul, *Cornelius Gurlitt*, 31. Gurlitt's dissertation (at Leipzig for Anton Springer) was very Warburgian: "Deutsche Tourniere, Rüstungen und Plattner des 16. Jahrhunderts" (1889). Paul, *Cornelius Gurlitt*, 135, n. 141. For Gurlitt's activity at the Dresden museum for applied arts, see Ulrike Kalteich, "Die Geschichte des Gewerbewuseum zu Dresden zwischen 1876 und 1907," in *Das Kunstgewerbemuseum Dresden*, Staatliche Kunstsammlung Dresden, exh. cat. (Dresden: Minerva, 1998). Gurlitt's publications included Cornelius Gurlitt, *Die internationale Kunstausstellung zu Berlin, 1891* (Munich: F. Hanfstaengl, 1891).

86 Cornelius Gurlitt, "Die kirchliche Kunst," in *Das deutsche Kunstgewerbe 1906: III Deutsche Kunstgewerbeaustellung Dresden 1906* (Munich: F. Bruckmann, 1906); Gurlitt, *Das neue königliche Hoftheater zu Dresden* (Dresden, 1878)

87 "Den speziellen Zweck verfolgen, Industrie und Gewerbe Vorbilder zu bieten." The mission was to collect models; collect materials for teaching; develop taste, particularly "beim kaufkräftigen Besucher." Kalteich, "Die Geschichte des Gewerbewuseum zu Dresden," 9, 255.

88 On Le Corbusier at Hellerau, see H. Allen Brooks, *Le Corbusier: The Formative Years* (Chicago: University of Chicago Press, 1997), 235, 346–47; on Tessenow and Hellerau, see Michele De Michelis, *Heinrich Tessenow, 1876–1950* (Milan: Electa, 1991).

89 On Dresden's place in the *Kunstgewerbe* movement, see Klaus-Peter Arnold, *Geschichte der deutschen Werkstätten und der Gartenstadt Hellerau* (Dresden, 1993). On Gurlitt and Schumacher, see Paul, *Cornelius Gurlitt*, 33–34.

90 Cornelius Gurlitt, *Geschichte des Barockstils in Italien* (Stuttgart: Ebner and Seubert, 1887).

91 Follows the Renaissance revival with the revival of the Baroque (as if one naturally followed from the other) in which he names such art historians as Dohme (who, he claims, borrowed much from Gurlitt's own work) and Friedrich Adler, Springer, Zahn, and Gustav Ebe as agents, but Albert Ilg (from Vienna, in his *Die Zukunft des Barockstils*, 1880) and himself as promoters of the "tatsächliche Wiederaufnahme des Stils" in the active profession. He also associates the revival with Dresden and Semper's earliest work there. Gurlitt, *Deutsche Kunst*, 431.

92 On the significance of the Pergamon altar for the reevaluation of the Baroque and for Wölfflin in particular, Alina Payne, "Portable Ruins: The Pergamon Altar, Heinrich Wölfflin, and German Art History at the *fin de siècle*," *RES: Journal of Aesthetics and Anthropology* 54/55 (Spring–Autumn 2008).

93 "Jedes Zimmer ein Haupt-und Knotenpunkt hat, von dem sein Leben ausstrahlt und dem sich alle anderen Gegenstände darinnen angliedern und unterordnen mussen. Diesem neuentdeckten Skelett des Zimmers gemäss, fährt er fort, wird man die Einrichtungsgegenstände anordnen, die man fortan als lebende Organe des Zimmers und der Wohnung empfinden wird." C. Gurlitt, *Die deutsche Kunst des XIX Jahrhunderts* (Berlin: Georg Bondi, 1899), 645.

94 Ibid., 640–42.

95 For example, Geymüller compares the torchéres on the Palazzo Strozzi with a *tempietto:* "Erstere [Laternen und Fackelhalter des Palazzo Strozzi] sind als achteckige Tempietti mit vorgestellten Säulchen an den Ecken, wie in der Kanzel von S. Croce, ganz architektonisch gedacht und von Caparra nach dem Modelle B. da Majanos ausgeführt. Dekorativen wirken der Konsolenfuss und die strahlenartige Bekrönung vorzüglich." Carl von Stegmann and

Heinrich von Geymüller, *Architektur der Renaissance in Toscana* (Munich: F. Bruckmann, 1885–1908), 4: 9.

96 Langbehn, *Rembrandt*. The book had been reprinted twenty-three times in the year of its publication, and thirty-nine times in the first two years.

97 Paul, *Gurlitt*, 66–69.

98 By his own admission, "a historian has to be nationalist, racist, engaged, patriotic and must use his work to revive the national self-consciousness." Quoted in Paul, *Gurlitt*, 67.

99 For Gurlitt's views on Langbehn, see Cornelius Gurlitt, "Neue Weltanschauungen eines Deutschen," *Die Gegenwart* 37 (1890): 149–53, and Gurlitt, "Nochmals 'Rembrandt als Erzieher,'" *Die Gegenwart* 38 (1890): 212–16.

100 "Wie in der Malerei, so gilt im Kunstgewerbe als erstes Ziel die Eroberrung des *Handwerklichen*.... Gerade dass es nicht grosse Meister waren... sondern dass biedere Handwerkmeister *etwas Derbes, Knölliges, Gemutliches, Bürgerliches mit sicherer Faust geschaffen hatten*... das schuf der Deutsch-Renaissance die eifrigsten Freude.... [Die Meister von Nürnberg, und Augsburg, von Dresden und Prag] hatten einfach etwas Schönes aus dem Stoff machen wollen und gewusst, wie man den Stoff bearbeitet" (my emphasis). Gurlitt, *Deutsche Kunst*, 430–31. Langbehn's proposition found a clear echo here: "Bisher hat man vielfach in Deutschland die Kunst von oben herab betrieben; versuche man es einmal von unten herauf; die Ergebnisse werden besser sein." Langbehn, *Rembrandt*, 191.

101 "die (Pilotyschule) in ihren Bestrebungen die Gesamtheit des Volkes umfasste... brachte die Möglichkeit ein *Volksgewerbe* zu schaffen, uns im Geschmack von Frankreich zu sondern und so uns selbst zu finden." Gurlitt, *Deutsche Kunst*, 76.

102 "Je stärker das Stilgefühl im Künstler ist, desto stärker wird sich die typische Form äussern." Cornelius Gurlitt, "Lermolieff's kunstkritische Studien," *Die Gegenwart* 37 (1890): 103–5.

103 Gurlitt, *Deutsche Kunst*, 464–65.

104 For example, Hoffmann argues that the search for stylistic identity and the movement that established the Renaissance style as the national style since unification also draws in the Austrian-Germans. His article appears in the Austrian journal of architecture. Albert Hoffmann, "Im welchen Style sollen wir bauen?" *Allgemeine Bauzeitung* (1890). An example of the self-definition of the German-speaking public symptomatic is the subtitle of the German arts journal *Deutsche Kunst und Dekoration*, published in Darmstadt: "Illustrierte Monatshefte zur Förderung deutscher Kunst und Formensprache in neuzeitl. Auffassung aus Deutschland, Schweiz und den deutsch-sprechenden Kronländern Österreich-Ungarns."

CHAPTER 5 | THE FORK IN THE ROAD: MUTHESIUS AND LOOS

Epigraphs: Hermann Muthesius, *Kultur und Kunst* (1904): "Im übrigen ist nicht zu vergessen, dass in unserem aesthetischen Empfinden noch ein besonderer Umstand eine ganz ungeheure Rolle spielt: die Macht der Gewohnheit. Selbst wo reine Nutzformen hervorgebracht werden, gewöhnen wir uns in kurzer Zeit an sie, ja finden wir sie gefällig, auch dann wenn sich unser Empfinden zunächst dagegen sträubte." Karl Scheffler, *Moderne Baukunst* (1907): "Nicht weiter wie der Schritt vom Bild zum gewerblichen Ornament, vom Ornament zum Möbel und von diesem zum Gesamtinterieur ist der Schritt von dort zur Außenarchitektur. In dieser Beziehung zur Baukunst liegt das wahrhaft Revolutionäre der kunstgewerblichen Bewegung." Adolf Loos, "Die Überflüssigen" in *Trotzdem* (1908): "Sie [Gewerbe] sind so im Stile unserer Zeit, dass wir sie–und das ist das einzige Kriterium—gar nicht als stilvoll empfinden. Sie sind mit unserem Denken und Empfinden verwachsen. Unser Wagenbau, unsere Gläser, unsere optischen Instrumente, unsere Schirme und Stöcke, unsere Koffer und Sattelwaren, unsere silberne Zigarettentaschen und Schmuckstücke, unsere Juwelenarbeiten und Kleider sind modern."

1 Hermann Muthesius, "Wo stehen wir?" in *Jahrbuch des Deutschen Werkbundes 1912: Die Drchgeistigung der deutschen Arbeit: Wege und Ziele in Zusammenhang von Industrie/Handwerk und Kunst* (Jena: Diedrichs, 1912), 16. Mallgrave has argued similarly for a more inclusive approach to nineteenth-century sources in assessing the "established" modernists in his work on Otto Wagner. See Harry Francis Mallgrave, ed., *Otto Wagner: Reflections on the Raiment of Modernity* (Santa Monica: Getty Center, 1993), 1–17.

2 Masheck identified the carpet as a recurrent theme in modern aesthetics but focused mostly on its implications for painting and the rise of abstraction. Joseph Masheck, "The Carpet Paradigm: Critical Prolegomena to a Theory of Flatness," *Arts Magazine* 51 (September 1976): 82–109.

3 Starting with Nikolaus Pevsner, *Pioneers of the Modern Movement: From William Morris to Walter Gropius* (London: Faber and Faber, 1936); Stefan Muthesius, *Das englische Vorbild* (Munich: Prestel, 1974); Stanford Anderson, "Introduction," in Hermann Muthesius, *Style-Architecture and Building-Art* (1902; Santa Monica: Getty Center, 1996), 1–43; more recently, Fedor Roth, *Hermann Muthesius und die Idee der harmonischen Kultur* (Berlin: Gebrüder Mann, 2001); John Maciuika, *Before the Bauhaus: Architecture, Politics, and the German State* (New York: Cambridge University Press, 2005). Muthesius also figures large in the vast literature on the Werkbund that ranges from Tilmann Buddensieg's *Industriekultur: Peter Behrens and the AEG* of 1979 to Frederic Schwartz's *Werkbund* of 1996.

4 Muthesius was a student of Gurlitt's in 1902 at the Technische Hochschule in Dresden, indeed, his first architect/Ph.D. there (although he came from another university). His Dr.-Ing. dissertation was on the church design of English religious sects. See Jürgen Paul, *Cornelius Gurlitt* (Dresden: Hellerau-Verlag, 2003), 33, 122. Roth raises the parallelism between Streiter and Muthesius, though he stops short

of documenting whether they knew each other. Roth, *Hermann Muthesius,* 28.

5 For example, Streiter published in *Blätter für Architektur und Kunsthandwerk* (from 1889 to 1896), *Centralblatt der Bauverwaltung* (every year from 1894 to 1900), in *Pan* (1896), in *Beilage zur Allgemeinen Zeitung* (from 1896 to 1907). See Richard Streiter, *Ausgewählte Scriften* (Munich: Delphin, 1913), 320–24. Muthesius also published in *Centralblatt der Bauverwaltung* continuously from 1891 to 1905. See Muthesius, *Style-Architecture,* 107–15.

6 For the emphasis on the English reform movement, see Muthesius, *Das englische Vorbild,* which follows and develops Pevsner's argument.

7 Johannes Wieninger, "'Er brachte viel Eigenatrtiges und Notwendiges mit.' Arthur von Scala als Mittler zwischen Ost und West und die Grundlegung der Asiensammlung des heutigen Museums der angewandten Kunst," in *Kunst und Industrie: Die Anfänge des Museums für Angewandte Kunst in Wien* (Vienna: Hatje Cantz, 2000), 164–74, and Christian F. Feest, "The Origins of Professional Anthropology in Vienna," in B. Rupp-Eisenreich and J. Stagl, eds., *Kulturwissenschaften im Vielvölkerstaat* (Vienna: Böhlau, 1995), 120.

8 On Japonisme and Jugendstil, see Gerda Breuer, "Japanische Kunst als Vorbild," *Der westdeuschte Impuls 1900–1914: Kunst und Umweltgestaltung im Industriegebiet. Das Museum zwischen Jugendstil und Werkbund* (Krefeld: Kaiser Wilhelm Museum, 1984), 121–32.

9 For example, see his collected articles. Hermann Muthesius, *Kultur und Kunst: Gesammelte Aufsätze* (1904; Nendeln: Kraus, 1976), and *Kunstgewerbe und Architektur* (1907; Nendeln: Kraus, 1976). For a full list of his articles, see Anderson, "Introduction," in Muthesius, *Style-Architecture and Building-Art.*

10 For example, see the opening article of the 1912 *Jahrbuch.* Peter Jessen, "Der Werkbund und die Grossmächte der deutschen Arbeit," in *Jahrbuch des Deutschen Werkbundes,* 2–10.

11 "Der Zweck des Bundes ist die Veredlung der gewerblichen Arbeit im Zusammenhang von Kunst, Industrie und Handwerk durch Erziehung, Propaganda und geschlossene Stellungnahme zu einschlägigen Fragen." *Jahrbuch des Deutschen Werkbundes,* article #2.

12 H. Schatteburg, "Das Kunstschöne und die Kunstgewerbeschulen," *Allgemeine Bauzeitung* (1892).

13 "Der Kunstsinn ist der Gradmesser für die Kulturstufe, die ein Volk erklommen hat." Ibid., 17.

14 "Denn die architektonische Kultur ist und bleibt der eigentliche Gradmesser für die Kultur eines Volkes überhaupt." Muthesius, "Wo stehen wir?" 19.

15 "In England ist die neue Kunstbewegung von der Entwicklung des Hauses nicht zu trennen." Richard Graul, ed., *Die Krisis im Kunstgewerbe* (Leipzig: S. Hirsel, 1901), 1. Robert Dohme's *Das Englische Haus* (1888) was the first to correlate the design of modern vehicles and ships with domestic design. Anderson notes Muthesius's dependence on this book. Anderson, "Introduction," 7. Muthesius himself acknowledges it and praises Dohme. Hermann Muthesius, "Neues Ornament und neue Kunst," *Die Kunst* 4, no. 9 (1901): 364.

16 The translations of Walter Crane were *Dekorative Illustration des Buches in alter und neuer Zeit; Linie und Form; Grundlagen der Zeichnung.* From Morris's publications, most notable translations were *Kunsthoffnungen und Kunstsorgen* (Hopes and Fears for Art); *Zeichen der Zeit* (Signs of Change); and the collective volume *Kunst und Handwerk* (Arts and Crafts Essays). The characteristics of the English "Ruskinian" perspective were clear to the generation working in the 1900s. Scheffler, for example, notes the direction toward religion, socialism, and morality it contributed. Karl Scheffler, *Moderne Baukunst* (1907; Leipzig: Julius Zeitler, 1908), 159.

17 Muthesius is severely outspoken against the Jugendstil already in *Style-Architecture,* 87. In "Kultur und Kunst" of 1904 he is even more withering: "Der Jugendstil ist eine Kunst, die nicht von Künstlern, sondern von kleinen Musterzeichnern aus der Taufe gehoben wurde" (11).

18 Muthesius, *Style-Architecture,* 95. For the problem of *Wohnungskultur,* see Muthesius, "Kultur und Kunst," 34. On Muthesius's built work and especially his later publications on houses, see Laurent Stalder, *Herrmann Muthesius, 1861–1927: Das Landhaus als kulturgeschichtliches Entwurf* (Zurich: GTA Verlag, 2008).

19 Muthesius, *Style-Architecture,* 95–97.

20 Hermann Muthesius, "Die Bedeutung des Kunstgewerbes," *Die Kunst* 10, no. 5 (1907): 170–80. Earlier he had articulated the concept of house as clothes with even greater recall to Ernst Kapp and von Eye: "Die Wohnung ist aber das weitere Kleid, das uns umgibt." "Kultur und Kunst" (1904), in *Kultur und Kunst,* 35.

21 The argument is quite similar to that of Scheffler, who likewise sees the new architecture evolving outward from elements of the interior and who may well be indebted to Muthesius, who published his thoughts on the topic early and continuously in *Centralblatt für Bauverwaltung.* The relationship between clothes and architecture in Muthesius has been attributed to the influence of Loos by Anderson and Schwartz. However, as earlier chapters have shown, the connection was a constant theme in Semper, Wölfflin, Wagner, August von Eye, and Ernst Kapp that could easily have been conveyed to him through Gurlitt in Dresden if not through his own readings.

22 "Von den einzelnen Gegenständen sind sie Schritt vor Schritt zum Ganzen gelangt und wenn auch in ihren Interieurbildungen die 'Idee' oft noch starker ist als der *Sachgedanke,* so müssen sie allein auch hier als Anreger für Die gelten, deren Sinn mehr auf das nützliche Zweckhafte gerichtet ist. Für den so vom Dekorativen zur Architektur, zur Raumbildnerei Gelangten ist es aber nur ein Schritt, um vollständig Architekt zu sein. *Nicht weiter wie der Schritt vom Bild zum gewerblichen Ornament, vom Ornament zum Möbel und von diesem zum Gesamtinterieur ist*

der Schritt von dort zur Außenarchitektur: In dieser Beziehung zur Baukunst liegt das wahrhaft Revolutionäre der kunstgewerblichen Bewegung." Scheffler, *Moderne Baukunst*, 1907; 1908, p. 165 (my emphasis).

23 Ibid., 157–68.

24 Fritz Schumacher, "Architektur und Kunstgewerbe," in Fritz Schumacher, *Streifzüge eines Architekten: Gesammelte Aufsätze* (1907; Nendeln: Kraus, 1976), 68. The essay was written in 1906. In this essay, as in his inaugural speech at the Technische Hochschule in Dresden in 1901, Schumacher is antagonistic to Art Nouveau and van de Velde in particular and ridicules the infatuation with line and surface ornament that he associated with the style. See "Das Bauschaffen der Jetztzeit und historische Überlieferung," in Schumacher, *Streifzüge*, 5–31.

25 Schumacher, "Architektur und Kunstgewerbe," 65–66.

26 Fritz Schumacher recognizes it and makes the argument forcefully in "Das Bauschaffen der Jetztzeit und historischer Überlieferung," 28–29; the Heimatschutz movement contributed much to this connection being made. On the importance of the vernacular in central Europe especially, see A. Morvansky, ed., *Das Entfernte Dorf* (Vienna: Böhlau, 2002), and Akos Moravansky, *Die Erneuerung der Baukunst: Wege zur Moderne in Mittel-Europa* (Salzburg: Residenz, 1988).

27 Muthesius, *Style-Architecture*, 96. His alliance with the Heimatschutz movement occurs at the 1911 Werkbund congress.

28 Haberlandt describes the folk house as "die inhaltsreichste Verkörperung des Volksgeistes" and "nationales Zeugnis" and compares it (as the *Schneckenhaus*) with the nomadic metropolitan dweller ("entwurzelte und hauslose Stadter") whose house is the equivalent of the beehive constructed by the industry lords. Michael Haberlandt, "Geschichtlicher Teil," *Das Bauernhaus in Österreich-Ungarn und in seine Grenzgebieten*, 2 vols. (Vienna: Osterreichischer Architektverein and Gerhard Kühtmann, 1906), 2: 4–5.

29 Anton Dachler, "Anlage, Herstellung und Zierformen des Bauernhauses," *Das Bauernhaus*, 181.

30 See his section "Dress and Dwelling," where he argues that the signs of aesthetic progress toward *Sachlichkeit* are confirmed by "our clothing," and he identifies the bourgeois ideal of simplicity in the development of nineteenth-century clothing. Muthesius, *Modern Architecture*, 79–80. As ever, Muthesius repeated the argument in several venues. The idea returns in his 1911 speech at the Werkbund annual meeting: "Die Kleidung, bei der von Anbeginn die Schönheit über die Nützlichkeit steht, folgt künstlerisch-architektonischen Grundsätzen und fügt sich dem Wohllaut des menschlichen Äusserungskreises harmonisch ein." Muthesius, "Wo stehen wir?" 13. On the reform of men's fashions, see Max Schmid's response to Muthesius at the Werkbund congress of 1911. *Jahrbuch des Deutschen Werkbundes*, 31.

31 Muthesius, "Kultur und Kunst," in *Kultur und Kunst*, 35.

32 Schwartz argues that Muthesius is influenced by Loos; so does Anderson.

33 Muthesius, "Kultur und Kunst," in *Kultur und Kunst*, 36.

34 Johann Joachim Winckelmann, *Gedanken über die Nachahmung der griechischen Werke in der Malerei und Bildhauerkunst* (1755; LaSalle, Ill.: Open Court, 1987).

35 "nur eins unverfälscht auf unsere Zeit herüber gerettet worden: unser moderner Anzug"; "Unsere Maschienen und Fahrzeuge, unsere Brücken und Bahnhofshallen werden der Sachlichkeit treu bleiben, ebenso wie sie in unserer Kleidung die Oberhand behalten." Hermann Muthesius, "Die moderne Umbildungen unserer aesthetischen Anschauungen," *Deutsche Monatsschrift für das gesamte Leben der Gegenwart* 1 (1902): 686–702 (republished in *Kultur und Kunst*, 61, 75).

36 Otto Wagner, *Modern Architecture* (Santa Monica: Getty Center, 1988), 76.

37 On the parallel concern with fashion and its effects on architecture within the culture of capitalism, see especially Frederic Schwartz, *The Werkbund: Design Theory and Mass Culture Before the First World War* (New Haven: Yale University Press, 1996), 26–43.

38 On Wagner and Semper, see J. Duncan Berry, "From Historicism to Architectural Realism: On Some of Wagner's Sources," in Harry Francis Mallgrave, ed., *Otto Wagner: Reflections on the Raiment of Modernity* (Santa Monica: Getty Center, 1993): 243–80.

39 For example, see Hermann Muthesius, "Die Bedeutung des architektonischen *Formgefühls* für die Kultur unserer Zeit: Vortrag, gehalten auf der Jahressammlung des Deutschen Werkbundes in Dresden 1911." *Architektonishe Rundschau* 11 (1911): 121–125, 133–139.

40 Muthesius, "Die Bedeutung des architektonischen Formgefühls." This article is followed by a similarly Wölfflinian one dedicated to engineering and published both in Germany and Switzerland.

41 Hermann Muthesius, *Handarbeit und Massenerzeugnis* (Berlin: Zentralinstitut für Erziehung und Unterricht, 1917), as cited in Schwartz, *Werkbund*, 100. Muthesius also refers to *Sachkunst* much earlier (and praises the beauty of the machine) in articles such as "Der Weg und das Endziel des Kunstgewerbes," *Die Kunst* 12, no. 8: 189.

42 "The goal of all techniques is the multiplication of a model (*Grundform*), [and] everything is dependent on the nature of this model; it is the mother of the hundreds and thousands of offspring hurled out by the machine." Schwartz, *Werkbund*, 100.

43 "schlichte Eleganz der Grundform." Richard Streiter, "Das deutsche Kunstgewerbe und die englisch-amerikanische Bewegung (1896)," in Streiter, *Ausgewählte Schriften* (Munich: Delphin, 1913), 15.

44 Hermann Muthesius, *Das deutsche Kunstgewerbe, 1906* (Munich: F. Bruckmann, 1906), 42.

45 In particular, though without referencing Muthesius, see Werner Oechslin, "The Evolutionary Way to Modern Architecture: The Paradigm of *Stilhülse und Kern*," in Mallgrave, *Otto Wagner*, 363–410.

46 Muthesius, "Wo stehen wir?" 26.

47 "Kultur ist ohne eine bedingungslose Schätzung der Form nicht denkbar." Ibid., 19. Schwartz notes a shift in Muthesius's argumentation here and a softening of the mass-production argument in favor of form.

48 Gross talks of "Veredlung der Form." Karl Gross, "Das Ornament," in *Jahrbuch des Deutschen Werkbundes,* 60–64.

49 "Wir haben also, wenn wir von aesthetischen Anschauungen reden, durchaus das Recht, das menschliche Bilden in seiner Gesamtheit zu betrachten. Und wir können Veränderungen in der Art dieses Bildens ebensogut an Brücken, an Maschienen, an der Kleidung, an Fahrzeugen, wie an den unter 'Kunst' rangierenden Werken menschlicher Tätigkeit studieren. Im übrigen ist nicht zu vergessen, dass in unserem asthetischen Empfinden noch ein besonderer Umstand eine ganz ungeheure Rolle spielt: *die Macht der Gewohnheit.* Selbst wo reine Nutzformen hervorgebracht werden, gewöhnen wir uns in kurzer Zeit an sie, ja finden wir sie gefällig, auch dann wenn sich unser Empfinden zunächst dagegen sträubte." In Muthesius, *Kultur und Kunst,* 56. "Wir entdecken die schmucklose Gebrauchsform ohne Ornament, ohne irgend eine Spur der Betätigung der alten schmückenden Ästhetik. *Und wieder finden wir, dass wir uns bereits an diese Formen gewöhnt haben,* ja sie zum Teil schön finden. Ist nicht ein schmuckloser Ozeandampfer ein Werk, das sich künstlerisch betrachten lässt? . . . Vielleicht gibt es viele, die hier noch nicht ganz mitfühlen können . . . Es bleibt uns angesichts der sich täglich mehrenden Werke des Ingenieurs und der Erzeugnisse der Maschiene gar nichts anderes übrig, als sie beide ästhetisch einzureihen" (64–65, my emphasis).

50 "Die glatte, auf das Nützliche reduzierte Form ist das, was wir von dem Maschienenerzeugnis erwarten." Ibid., 67.

51 Muthesius, *Style-Architecture,* 80.

52 Ibid., 74–75.

53 On the new term and its use by the Werkbund before it became a concept in economics, see Schwartz, *Werkbund,* 124–25.

54 August Schmarsow, *Unser Verhältnis zu den bildenden Künsten* (Leipzig: Teubner, 1903), 108.

55 "Wenn irgendeine Kunst so strebt die Architektur nach dem Typischen." Muthesius, "Wo stehen wir?" 24.

56 Among architects, Hendrik Berlage had argued for an impressionist architecture in response to the speed of city life. In his telling this would be an architecture devoid of ornament and with reduced details that would deal only in the "impression-forming" broad gesture. This position was published in Dutch in *Architectura* 2, no. 22 (June 1894). Hendrik Berlage, *Thoughts on Style, 1886–1909,* ed. Harry Francis Mallgrave (Santa Monica: Getty Center, 1996), 113–17. On ornament and Berlage's argument, see Alina Payne, "Architecture, Ornament and Pictorialism: Notes on the Relationship Between the Arts, from Wölfflin to Le Corbusier," in K. Koehler, ed., *The Built Surface* (London: Ashgate, 2002), 65–66.

57 Muthesius, "Wo stehen wir?" 25. In the subsequent discussion Karl Ernst Osthaus reinforced the call for an aesthetic of the type. He argued that the type can and should be crafted artistically, and gave Rennes as a paradigmatic example (28).

58 For Gurlitt's response picking up the praise of Langbehn, see *Jahrbuch des Deutschen Werkbundes,* 27. For the earlier antagonism between the two movements (Werkbund and Heimatschutz), which finally find a way to come together at the congress, see Schwartz, *Werkbund,* 155–56.

59 "Diese Hervorhebung des Typischen in der Architektur halte ich für ausserordentlich wichtig für die Zukunft unserer Baukunst. Eine Parallele mit England gibt uns darüber Belehrung. . . . Es ist ein modernes Ausdrucksmittel aus den Bestrebungen der heimatlichen Bauweise enstanden." Muthesius, "Wo stehen wir?" 35. The debate following Muthesius's speech is well known. Some speakers, for example, Karl Ernst Osthaus, expressed worry about too close an alignment with the Heimatschutz, as in his view the issue of materials (new versus traditional) could be affected (28–29).

60 Christopher Long notes the nationalist chords in the Werkbund rhetoric and cites Austrian Werkbund president Baron Bachhofen von Echt, who insisted that "the Werkbund ideas can and should further enhance and deepen the folkish national efforts." Christopher Long, "'A Symptom of the Werkbund': The Spring 1912 Exhibition at the Austrian Museum for Art and Industry, Vienna," *Studies in the Decorative Arts* (2000), 109.

61 The term occurs in Semper's writings, though not in the sense of "average" that Naumann uses. Friedrich Naumann, "Kunst und Industrie," in *Das deutsche Kunstgewerbe, 1906* (Munich: F. Bruckmann, 1906), 32–35. Naumann identifies the "Normalschule," the "normale Arbeiterhaus," the "normale Gerichtssaal." He also talks about the "gewöhnliche" (ordinary) bed, cupboard, and "normal" livingroom (the Berliner Normalsalon) and office furniture, which are all industrialized.

62 Schumacher, "Architektur und Kunstgewerbe," 66.

63 "Wechselrede über ästhetische Fragen der Gegenwart," in *Jahrbuch des deutschen Werkbundes 1912,* 32–33.

64 "Das erste deutlich hervortredende literarische Anzeichen der beginnenden neuen Geistesrichtung war jenes krauses Buch 'Rembrandt als Erzieher' das den Deutschen die Wichtigkeit der künstlerischen im Gegensatz zu der wissenschaftlichen Kultur ins Gedächtnis rief. . . . Was der Rembrandtdeutsche seinen Zeitgenossen predigte, fing wenige Jahre darauf an, sich einzustellen." Muthesius, "Wo stehen wir?" 14–16. Germans were not the only ones to feel the pull of Langbehn. Austrian painter and writer Joseph August Lux, editor of *Hohe Warte* and in close contact with the Werkbund members, wrote "Die Durchgeistigung der Deutschen

Arbeit" (1915), similarly indebted to Langbehn. On Lux, see Mark Jarzombek, "Joseph August Lux: Werkbund Promoter, Historian of a Lost Modernity," *JSAH* 63, no. 2 (June 2004): 202–19. On the unproblematic blending of Langbehn and Nietzsche in Germany in Muthesius's milieu, see Anderson, "Introduction," 6.

65 Fritz Schumacher, "Das Bauschaffen der Jetztzeit und der historische Überlieferung," in *Streifzüge*, 28–29. The paths of Behne and others were not that different. See Friedrich Naumann's lecture "Kunst und Volk" (1902) (cited in Ingolf Bauer, "Das Beyerisches Nationalmuseum und die 'Heimatkunst,'" in I. Bauer, ed. *Das Beyerisches Nationalmuseum* [Munich: Hirmer, 2000], 249), and Naumann, "Kunst und Industrie," in *Das deutsche Kunstgewerbe, 1906*, 32–35. Recently, Maiken Umbach has argued against labeling such folk-centered theories as conservative and antagonistic to modernism, leading directly to the Heimatkunst of National Socialism. Instead, she rightly identifies a "universalism" or "internationalism" in the attempt that was just as much at the root of the turn to folk art as was nationalism. Maiken Umbach, "The Vernacular International: *Heimat*, Modernism and the Global Market in Early Twentieth-Century Germany," *National Identities* 4, no. 1 (2002): 45–68.

66 Walter Gropius, *Internationale Architektur* (1925); Adolf Behne, *Der moderne Zweckbau* (1926); Ludwig Hilbereimer, *Internationale neue Baukunst* (1927); Bruno Taut, *Bauen: Der neue Werkbau* (1927); W. G. Behrendt, *Der Sieg des neuen Baustils* (1927); Gustav Adolf Platz, *Die Baukunst der neuesten Zeit* (1927); Bruno Taut, *Die neue Baukunst in Europa und Amerika* (1929); Henry-Russell Hitchcock, *Modern Architecture: Romanticism and Reintegration* (1929); Sigfried Giedion, *Space, Time and Architecture* (1941).

67 Muthesius, for example, describes the Art Nouveau productions exhibited by the Belgians and French at the 1900 Paris Fair as *höheres Blödsinn* ("high imbecility"): not practical, invented by painters, infatuated with line-work, fashion oriented. Instead, here and in subsequent articles he promotes Richard Riemerschmidt and Bruno Paul, both active at the Deutsche Werkstätte. Muthesius, "Neues Ornament und neue Kunst," 352. Muthesius's antipathy toward Jugendstil gets rehearsed in many of his articles, which often repeat each other, though as a group this repetition allows him to proselytize a very consistent position.

68 See especially Schumacher, "Das Bauschaffen der Jetztzeit." This was his inaugural speech, given May 10, 1901, at the Technische Hochschule Dresden.

69 Ibid.

70 Long, "'Symptom of the Werkbund'", 91–121.

71 See chapter 2.

72 August Endell, "Möglichkeit und Ziele einer neuen Architektur," *Deutsche Kunst und Dekoration* 1 (October 1897–March 1898): 141–53; Alfred Lichtwark, *Palastfenster und Flügeltür* (1899; Berlin: Gebr. Mann, 2000), where his chapters are earlier articles such as "Bürgerliche Baukunst," "Sachliche Baukunst," and "Unsere Möbel"; Paul Schultze-Naumburg, *Kulturarbeiten* (Munich: G. D. W. Callwey, 1902); Fritz Schumacher, "Die Architektur und die Decoration auf der Pariser Weltaustellung," in Graul, *Die Krisis*, 215–37; Graul, "Deutschland," in *Die Krisis*, 39–51.

73 "Wir brauchen helle und saubere Räume ohne Staubecken und Staugfänge, glatte und einfache Möbel, die sich ebenso leicht abstauben wie verschieben lassen, eine luftige und durchsichtige Disposition des ganzen Raumes, die uns das selbstverständliche Bewusstsein gibt, dass hier Licht, Luft und Sauberkeit . . . zu Hause sind." Muthesius, "Neues Ornament und neue Kunst," 365. Muthesius notes the nomadic life of the city dweller. Muthesius, *Style-Architecture*, 95.

74 See Cornelius Gurlitt, *Im Bürgerhause* (Dresden: Gilbers'sche Königl., 1888). It is noteworthy that Gurlitt wrote the book in England; Langbehn, *Rembrandt*, 191.

75 Schumacher, "Die Architektur," 233.

76 See Germanisches Nationalmuseum Nürnberg, *Peter Behrens und Nürnberg*, exhibition catalogue, September 20–November 9, 1980 (Munich: Prestel, 1980).

77 Robin Schuldenfrei, "The Irreproducibility of the Bauhaus Object," in J. Saletnik and R. Schuldenfrei, eds., *Bauhaus Construct* (London: Routledge, 2009), 37–60.

78 Mary McLeod, "'Architecture or Revolution': Taylorism, Technocracy, and Social Change," *Art Journal* 43 (Summer 1983): 141; Stanford Anderson, "Peter Behrens and the AEG Industrial Design," *Oppositions* 21 (Summer 1980): 78–97.

79 Anderson, "Peter Behrens and the AEG Industrial Design."

80 Schuldenfrei, "Irreproducibility of the Bauhaus Object."

81 The essay was probably written as a lecture in 1908. See Adolf Opel, "Introduction," in *Adolf Loos: Trotzdem*, ed. A. Opel (Vienna: Prachner, 1997), 7–17 and Introduction n.1.

82 Among these articles were "The Luxury Vehicle" (*Neue Freie Press*, July 3, 1898); "Ladies' Fashion" (*NFP*, August 31, 1898, in Dokumente *der Frau*, March 1, 1902); "Poor Little Rich Man" (*Neues Wiener Tagblatt*, April 26, 1900); "Potemkin City" (*Ver sacrum*, July 1898); "Men's Hats" (*NFP*, July 22, 1898); "Men's Footwear" (*NFP*, August 7, 1898); "Men's Fashion" (*NFP*, May 22, 1898); "Underclothes" (*NFP*, September 25, 1898); "The Principle of Cladding" (*NFP*, September 4, 1898).

83 Loos wrote two essays on Scala (who became the champion of modern objects and against the traditional and historical bias of the Austrian guild establishment): "Der Fall Scala" in *Die Potemkinsche Stadt: Verschollene Schriften, 1897–1933* (Vienna, 1983), and the satire "Das Scala-Theater in Wien" in *Sämtliche Schriften*, vol. 1 (Vienna, 1962), originally published in *Wage*, November 5, 1898. On Scala's directorship and ultimate success, see Kathrin Pokorny-Nagel, "Zur Gründungsgeschichte des k.k. Österreichischen Museums für Kunst und Industrie," in P. Noever, ed., *Kunst und Industrie: Die Anfänge des Museums für Angewandte Kunst in Wien* (Vienna: Hatje Cantz Verlag, 2000), 81–89.

84 "Architecture," 1910.

85 For an exception, see John Archer, "The Architect and the Mountain Lake: Adolf Loos and the Crisis of Culture," *Midgard* 1, 63–77, and Harry Francis Mallgrave, "Adolf Loos and the Ornament of Sentiment," *Midgard* 1, 79–87.

86 Loos, "Spoken into the Void" (MIT, 1982), 35–36.

87 Ibid.

88 Ibid., 12.

89 Sibylle Wilhelm notes that the negative reaction to the Jugendstil already at the turn of the century prompted some artists to dissociate themselves from it and adopt labels such as "neue Kunstgewerbe" or "der neue Stil." Wilhelm, *"Kunstgewerbebewegung" Ästhetische Welt oder Macht durch Kunst?* (Frankfurt-am-Main: Peter Lang, 1991), 9–11.

90 Maria Ocon-Fernandez, *Ornament und Moderne: Theoriebildung und Ornamentdebatte im deutschen Architekturdiskurs (1850–1930)* (Berlin: Reimer, 2004).

91 "Ich bin ein Gegner jener Richtung, die etwas besonderes vozügliches darin erblickt, dass ein Gebäude bis zur Kohlenschaufel aus der Hand eines Architekten hervorgehe... Weder der Archäologe, noch der Dekorateur, noch der Architekt... soll uns die Wohnung einrichten. Ja, wer soll es denn dann tun? Nun ganz einfach: Jeder sei sein eigener Dekorateur." Quoted in Eva B. Ottilinger, *Adolf Loos: Wohnungskonzepte und Möbelentwurfe* (Salzburg: Residenz, 1994), 23.

92 Falke, *Kunst im Hause* (1878); Gurlitt, *Im Bürgerhause* (1888). The point is also made in Ottillinger, *Adolf Loos*, 23–24. For Josef Frank, see Christopher Long, "*Wiener Wohnkultur:* Interior Design in Vienna, 1910–1938," *Studies in the Decorative Arts* (1997–1998): 29–51.

93 The passage occurs in Loos's moving tribute to his furniture maker Veilich. "Josef Veillich" (1929), in *Trotzdem*, 248.

94 On Loos's acceptance of life as it is lived rather than prescribed by the architect, see Tristan Tzara's moving tribute in Loos's sixtieth-birthday *Festschrift:* "Le seul ajourd'hui dont les realisations ne sont pas photogeniques. [Je m'associe a l'hommage que vous addressez ajourd'hui á Adolf Loos] pour une perfection qui n'exclut ni les microbes ni les scories ni les impuretés dans la vie." Festschrift 1930, in Massimo Cacciari, *Loos e il suo angelo* (Milan: Electa, 2002), 135.

95 In "Man's Fashion" (first published in *Neue Freie Presse* in May 22, 1898, and republished in *Ins Leere gesprochen* [Innsbruck, 1931]), he makes the point forcibly: "In order to be dressed correctly, one must not stand out at the center of culture." Loos, "Spoken into the Void," 12. The quote is recycled in *Das Andere* (1903), 1: 8: "Modern gekleidet ist man wenn man im Mittelpunkt der abendländischen Kultur nicht auffällt."

96 Adolf Loos, "Der Sattlermeister," in *Das Andere* 1 (1903): 24–25.

97 Ottillinger, *Adolf Loos: Wohnkonzepre und Möbelentwürfe*.

98 Loos, "Josef Veillich" (from 1929), in *Trotzdem*, 248–55.

99 W. Owen Harrod, "Bruno Paul's *Typenmöbel*, the German Werkbund and Pragmatic Modernism, 1908–1918," *Studies in the Decorative Arts* 9, no. 2: (Spring–Summer 2002): 33–57. For Loos's influence on a younger generation of designers, such as Josef Frankl, who took his positions even further and produced what is now known as the *Wiener Wohnkultur* as an alternative to the total environments of Marcel Breuer or Mies van der Rohe, see Christopher Long, "*Wiener Wohnkultur:* Interior Design in Vienna, 1910–1938," *Studies in the Decorative Arts* (Fall–Winter 1997–98): 29–51. Elsewhere Long also notes that Austria was far less industrialized than Germany and as a result its designers—be they members of the Austrian Werkbund or Loos and his followers—moved in a different direction, toward craftsmanship and luxury goods, even if they offered early examples to their German colleagues. Long, "'Symptom of the Werkbund,'" 91–121.

100 Loos, *Trotzdem*, Preface.

101 Loos, *Ins Leere gesprochen*.

102 Loos, "Hands Off" (May 1917), in *Trotzdem*, 145.

103 Loos, "Die Überflüssigen," in *Trotzdem*, 71.

104 "Sie [Gewerbe] sind so im Stile unserer Zeit, dass wir sie–und das ist das einzige Kriterium—gar nicht als stilvoll empfinden. Sie sind mit unserem Denken und Empfinden verwachsen. Unser Wagenbau, unsere Gläser, unsere optischen Instrumente, unsere Schirme und Stöcke, unsere Koffer und Sattelwaren, unsere silberne Zigarettentaschen und Schmuckstücke, unsere Juwelenarbeiten und Kleider sind modern." Loos, "Die Überflüssigen" (1908), in *Trotzdem*, 71.

105 Loos, "Kulturentartung" (1908), *Trotzdem*, 74.

106 "Dem Menschen, der die heutige Kultur besitzt gefallen Gebrauchsgegenstände aus Glas, Porzellan, Majolika und Steingut am besten, wenn sie undekoriert sind." Loos, "Keramika" (1904), *Trotzdem*, 50.

107 Charlotte Perriand, "Wood or Metal?" *The Studio* 97, no. 433 (April 1929): 278–79.

108 "nur Möbel die mobil sind können modern sein... alles passt zu allem, weil alles modern ist." Adolf Loos, "Die Abschaffung der Möbel" (1924), in *Trotzdem*, 196–98.

109 Karl Schmidt was a longtime friend of and inspiration for Muthesius, and his Deutsche Werkstätte at Hellerau became a model for the Werkbund. Klaus-Peter Arnold, *Vom Sofakissen zum Städtebau: Geschichte der deutschen Werkstätten und der Gartenstadt Hellerau* (Dresden, 1993), 69.

CHAPTER 6 | THE AFTERMATH: BAUHAUS ENDGAME AND LE CORBUSIER'S POETICS OF PORTABILITY

1 The Dadaist magazine *G. Material zur elementaren Gestaltung* appeared intermittently between 1923 and 1926 (only six issues) and was produced and edited by Hans Richter in Berlin (the journal was founded with filmmaker Viking Eggeling). Articles dealt with emergent culture and covered car engines, men's clothing, poems, film, etc. *Veshch/Objet/Gegenstand* appeared in 1922 (only three issues) and was conceived and edited by Ilya Ehrenburg and El Lissitzky, also in Berlin.

On the Soviet revolutionary objects, see Christina Kiaer, *Imagine No Possessions: The Socialist Objects of Russian Constructivism* (Cambridge, Mass.: MIT, 2005) and Maria Gough, *The Artist as Producer: Russian Constructivism in Revolution* (Berkeley: University of California Press, 2005). See also Detlef Mertins, "Architecture of Becoming: Mies and the Avant-Garde," in B. Bergdoll and T. Riley, eds., *Mies in Berlin*, exh. cat. (New York: MoMA, 2001), 106–33.

2 Magdalena Droste, *Bauhaus, 1919–1933* (Berlin: Bauhaus Archiv and Benedikt Taschen Verlag, 1990), 42, 111–13.

3 "*Das Endziel aller bildnerischen Tätigkeit ist der Bau!*... Wollen, erdenken, erschaffen wir gemeinsam den neuen Bau der Zukunft, der alles *in einer Gestalt* sein wird: Architektur und Plastik und Malerei, der aus Millionen Händen der Handwerker einst gen Himmel steigen wird als kritallenes Sinnbild eines neuen kommenden Glaubens." The same ideal is reiterated in the teaching program: "Das Bauhaus erstrebt die Sammlung aller künstlerischen Schaffens zur Einheit, die Wiedervereinigung aller werkkünstlicherischen Disziplinen—Bildhauerei, Malerei, Kunstgewerbe und Handwerk—zu einer neuen Baukunst als deren unablösliche Bestandteile." Walter Gropius, *Bauhaus Manifesto and Program*, 1919. This core position was reiterated in Gropius's 1923 publication on the Bauhaus and translated and modified for the 1938 retrospective exhibition on the Bauhaus at MoMA organized by Alfred Barr, Jr., and Herbert Beyer. In this guise it reached a wide English-speaking readership. See Walter Gropius, *Idee und Aufbau des staatlichen Bauhauses Weimar* (Weimar-Munich: Bauhausverlag, 1923). Compare with H. Beyer, W. Gropius, and I. Gropius, eds., *Bauhaus, 1919–1928* (New York: Museum of Modern Art, 1938).

4 Kathleen James-Chakraborty, "Henry van de Velde and Walter Gropius: Between Avoidance and Imitation," in James-Chakraborty, ed., *Bauhaus Culture: From Weimar to the Cold War* (Minneapolis: University of Minnesota Press, 2002), 26–42.

5 On the embedded problems surfacing at the Bauhaus in more or less explicit form, and their roots in its nineteenth-century heritage, see Alina Payne, "Bauhaus Endgame: Ambiguity, Anxiety and Discomfort," in J. Saletnik and R. Schuldenfrei, eds., *Bauhaus Construct: Fashioning Identity, Discourse and Modernism* (London: Routledge, 2009), 247–66.

6 There was a growing interest at the Bauhaus to commercialize the objects produced in the workshops—those from the furniture workshop since 1922, those from the ceramics workshop from November 1923 onward. Droste, *Bauhaus*, 134.

7 See, for example, most recently the discussion of Marcel Breuer's and Mies van der Rohe's efforts to sign their chairs against Walter Gropius's directives. See Magadalena Droste, "The Bauhaus Object Between Authorship and Anonymity," in Saletnik and Schuldenfrei, *Bauhaus Construct*, 205–25.

8 On Mies's furniture, see Otakar Mácel, "From Mass Production to Design Classic: Mies van der Rohe's Metal Furniture," Vitra Design Museum, *Mies van der Rohe: Architecture and Design in Stuttgart, Barcelona, Brno* (Geneva: Skira, 1998), 18–64.

9 On Hannes Meyer's work and its political dimension, see K. Michael Hays, *Modernism and the Post-Humanist Subject: The Architecture of Hannes Meyer and Ludwig Hilberseimer* (Cambridge, Mass.: MIT Press, 1992).

10 Robin Schuldenfrei, "The Irreproducibility of the Bauhaus Object," in Saletnik and Schuldenfrei, *Bauhaus Construct*, 37–60.

11 Wolfgang Pfleiderer, "Introduction," in *Die Form ohne Ornament: Werkbundausstellung, 1924* (Berlin: Deutsches Verlags-Anstalt Stuttgart, 1924), 3–22.

12 See J. M. Richards, "Towards a Rational Aesthetic," *Architectural Review* 78 (July–December 1935): 211–18.

13 Christian Barman, "Review of Herbert Read," *Art in Industry, Architectural Review* 77 (January–June 1935): 3–8.

14 On the accusations and disagreements between Walter Gropius and Lucia Moholy on the use and property rights of this and other negatives, see Jeffrey Saletnik and Robin Schuldenfrei, "Introduction," in Saletnik and Schuldenfrei, *Bauhaus Construct*, 6–8.

15 For a detailed examination of Le Corbusier's exposure to central European thought before WWI, see H. Alan Brooks, *Le Corbusier's Formative Years* (Chicago: University of Chicago Press, 1997), chpt. 2.

16 Sigfried Giedion, *Space, Time and Architecture* (Cambridge, Mass.: Harvard University Press, 1941), 355–70.

17 Pevsner's rejection of Le Corbusier's claims came early, in his 1931 review of the first volume of the *Oeuvre complète*. Nikolaus Pevsner, Review of Le Corbusier and Pierre Jeanneret, *Ihr gesamtes Werk von 1910 bis 1929* in *Göttingische gelehrte Anzeigen* 8 (August 1931): 303–12. On this and Pevsner's continued resistance to Le Corbusier's claims, see Alina Payne, "Architecture and Objects: The Power of Pevsner," *Harvard Design Magazine* (Spring 2002): 66–70.

18 For Le Corbusier's relationship with Perret, see especially their correspondence, see Le Corbusier, *Lettres à Auguste Perret*, ed. Marie-Jeanne Dumont (Paris: Editions Linteau, 2002). For his relationship with l'Eplattenier, see Le Corbusier, *Lettres à Charles L'Eplattenier*, ed. Marie-Jeanne Dumont (Paris: Edition Linteau, 2006).

19 Le Corbusier, *L'art décoratif d'aujourd'hui* (Paris: Crès, 1925) (English translation: James Dunnett, *The Decorative Art of Today*, 1987). Charles-Edouard Jeanneret Gris (Le Corbusier), *Almanach d'architecture moderne* (1925; Turin: Bottega d'Erasmo, 1975). In the Preface of the *Almanach* Le Corbusier describes the book as the *livre d'or* of the pavilion.

20 Jeanneret had attended the 1910 Werkbund congress in Berlin and (on June 12) heard Muthesius debate the relative merits of archaeological reconstruction of old buildings versus the use of new materials (which he favors and seeks the Heimatschutz movement's support to this end). Le Corbusier (Ch.-E. Jeanneret), *Les voyages*

d'Allemagne. Carnets. Voyage d'Orient. Carnets (Milan: Electa and Fondation Le Corbusier, 2000), 32–33.

21 Charles-Edouard Jeanneret (Le Corbusier), *Étude sur le mouvement d'art décoratif en Allemagne* (1912; New York: Da Capo, 1968), 22–24. On the impact of the German milieu on Le Corbusier, see Brooks, *Le Corbusier's Formative Years*, 252.

22 *Das Andere: Ein Blatt zur Einführung Abendländischer Kultur in Oesterreich* had only two issues (entirely written by Loos), in October 1903.

23 Le Corbusier's encounter with Loos's writings happened in 1913 through the agency of Auguste Perret. On this, see Francesco Passanti, "Architecture: Proportion, Classicism, and Other Issues," in Stanislaus von Moos and Arthur Rüegg, eds., *Le Corbusier Before Le Corbusier* (New Haven: Yale University Press, 2002), 88–89. Loos published "Ornament and Crime" in *L'Esprit Nouveau* 2 (1920): 159–69, and his *Ins Leere gesprochen* was published in Paris by Crès in 1921. They were evidently on friendly terms, as in 1925 Loos alerted Le Corbusier that the Brno manufacturer who contracted to build the *casiers* for his pavilion would default. Le Corbusier, "Exposé bref de nos tribulations." Ms notes, B2–16, Fondation Le Corbusier (hereafter FLC), 17.

24 The subtitle changes in 1921 with issue no. 4. Prior to this, when Paul Dermée was sole director, the subtitle was "Revue internationale d'esthétique." The label "Pavillon de l'Esprit Nouveau" itself was probably a direct reference to and a signal of difference from Bing's "Pavillon de l'Art Nouveau" at the 1900 Paris Exposition. On the latter, see Nancy Troy, *Modernism and the Decorative Arts in France* (New Haven: Yale University Press, 1991), 35.

25 Ibid., 196.

26 Jeanneret, *Les voyages d'Allemagne*.

27 Among the many publications on this topic, see Brooks, *Le Corbusier's Formative Years*, and Le Corbusier, *Lettres à Charles L'Eplattenier*; Paul Venable Turner, *The Education of Le Corbusier* (New York: Garland, 1977); and Von Moos and Rüegg, *Le Corbusier Before Le Corbusier*. On the correspondence between Le Corbusier and his first master ("mon cher maître"), see Le Corbusier, *Lettres à Charles L'Eplattenier*.

28 Le Corbusier's early reading—such as Ruskin, a favorite at the school of La Chaux de Fonds—also testifies to the influence of l'Eplattenier's teaching and the interest in nature and the decorative arts that he was seeking to develop in his students. Brooks, *Le Corbusier's Formative Years*, 68–69; for Le Corbusier's library, see Venable Turner, *Education of Le Corbusier*.

29 On Perriand, see Joan Ockman, "Lessons from Objects: Perriand from the Pioneer Years to the 'Epoch of Realities,'" in M. McLeod, ed., *Charlotte Perriand: An Art of Living* (New York: Harry Abrams), 154–81. See also Charlotte Perriand, *Io, Charlotte: Tra Le Corbusier, Léger e Jeanneret* (Bari: Laterza, 2006).

30 "L'événement le plus significatif de notre époque est la mise en valeur de l'objet, des objets." Fernand Léger, "Actualités," *Variétés*, February 15, 1929, 522, X 1–08, FLC. Léger had written about objects and fabrication since 1924 and, according to von Moos, influenced Le Corbusier's own writings. See Fernand Léger, "L'esthétique de la machine: L'objet fabriqué—l'artisan et l'artiste," in *Bulletin de l'effort moderne* 1 (January 1924); on Léger and Le Corbusier, who shared much even if Léger rarely published in *L'Esprit Nouveau*, see Stanislaus von Moos, "Le Corbusier und Loos," in *L'Esprit Nouveau: Le Corbusier und die Industrie, 1920–1925* (Zurich: Museum für Gestaltung, 1987), 215; on Purism and Léger, see Carol Eliel, "Purism in Paris, 1918–1925," in Eliel, *L'Esprit Nouveau: Purism in Paris, 1918–1925* (Los Angeles: Los Angeles Museum of Art, 2001), 11–70; Christopher Green, "Léger, Purism and the Paris Avant-Garde," *Art News* 69 (December 1970): 54–56; and Green, *Léger and the Avant-Garde* (New Haven: Yale University Press, 1976).

31 Léger, "Actualités," 522.

32 Ibid., 524.

33 Waldemar George, "Léger et les objets dans l'espace," and Le Corbusier, "L'architecture et Fernand Léger," *Selection: Chronique de la vie artistique* 5 (February 1929): 5–6, 24.

34 Christopher Green first noted the exchange of paintings. Green, "Painting for the Le Corbusian Home," *Studio International*, September–October 1975, 103–7.

35 Le Corbusier, *Decorative Art*, xxiii, xxiv, xxi.

36 "The unanimity of the new sense of feeling, which reflects an epoch of precision dominated by the machine." Ibid., 36. "The more educated a people becomes, the more decoration disappears" (85, xxiii).

37 Ibid., xxii.

38 Ibid., xxvi.

39 Ibid., 73. Romy Golan has argued that the body comes into Le Corbusier's furniture in the 1930s with a more general rise of interest in rusticity and vernacular in French culture. However, though Le Corbusier was certainly moving into a more nature-friendly direction and away from the machinist aesthetic, the body had always been a key coordinate for his theory and designs. Romy Golan, *Modernity and Nostalgia: Art and Politics in France Between the Wars* (New Haven: Yale University Press, 1995), 95–97.

40 Ibid., 77.

41 Jeanneret, *Étude sur le mouvement d'art décoratif en Allemagne*, 38.

42 Jeanneret Gris, *Almanach*, 85.

43 Le Corbusier, *Decorative Art*, 32.

44 Ibid.

45 "Folk culture is a magnificent creation. An achievement purified by time and number . . . [it] is so powerful that we all immediately respond to it." Le Corbusier, *L'art décoratif d'aujourd'hui*, 36.

46 Ibid., 36.

47 Udo Kultermann, *Geschichte der Kunstgeschichte: Der Weg einer Wissenschaft* (Frankfurt: Ullstein, 1981), 352–53.

48 This relevance to modern tastes—even Purist tastes—as well as echoes of the importance of this youthful friendship, probably account for the fact that much later Le Corbusier included images of El Greco in *L'Esprit Nouveau*. See catalogue in *L'Esprit Nouveau: Le Corbusier und die Industrie, 1920–1925*. Museum für Gestaltung, Zurich, 1987, 207.

49 Jeanneret, *Les voyages d'Allemagne.* In *Voyage d'orient,* carnet i, 43; *Voyage d'orient,* carnet iii, 92;*Voyage d'orient,* carnet vi, 42. By now Le Corbusier's German (to improve which he had sought out help from Klipstein early on during his stay in Berlin) had reached a level to allow him to read Goethe's *Aus meinem Leben Dichtung und Wahrheit* (as he indicates in his *carnet*), and thus reading texts such as Riegl's or Worringer's would have been well within his power.

50 Brooks, *Le Corbusier's Formative Years,* 256.

51 "Les tapis berbères sont du haut folklore. . . . Sa couleur et sa géométrie font comme une moyenne proportionnelle entre les matières et les surface des murs et des meubles." See his chapter "Des pots" and "Des tapis décoratifs" in Jeanneret Gris, *Almanach,* 167–71.

52 In his definition of Purism and architecture, from his notes for the no. 4 of *L'Esprit Nouveau* on "Architecture et Purisme" and reused in *Almanach d'architecture moderne,* Le Corbusier notes: "Le Purisme se manifeste: Par la recherche de l'essentiel, l'éloignement de l'accidentel; Par l'emploi des standards, c'est a dire des éléments épurés, mis au point . . . en se basant sur la physiologie des sensations, c'est a dire sur la constance des réactions primaires, l'universalité des réactions des sens à la vue des formes et des lignes." Signed Le Corbusier Saugnier (FLC, C3–16), 83.

53 On Le Corbusier's Purist work, see Troy, *Modernism,* and the essays in Eliel, *L'Esprit Nouveau: Purism in Paris, 1918–1925.*

54 "Nous voulions aménager notre pavillon avec des produits industriels ou la loi d'économie, la sélection commerciale, avaient pu agir et conférer à ces objets ce qu'on peut appeler un style." Jeanneret Gris, *Almanach,* 145. On Le Corbusier's persistent effort to keep apart objects and art (especially decorative art), unlike the members of the decorative arts movement in France (or elsewhere for that matter), see Troy, *Modernism,* 193–96.

55 Jean-Louis Cohen, "Erhaben, zweifellos erhaben: Vom fesselnden Wesen der technischen Objekte," in Vitra Design Museum, *Le Corbusier: The Art of Architecture* (Weil-am-Rhein: Vitra Museum, 2007), 209–33.

56 "L'harmonie est dans les ouvrages qui sortent de l'atelier, ou de l'usine. Ce n'est pas de l'Art, ce n'est pas la Sixtine, ni l'Érechthéion; ce sont les œuvres quotidiennes de tout un univers qui travaille avec conscience, intelligence, précision, avec imagination, hardiesse, et rigueur." Le Corbusier, *Vers une architecture* (1923; Paris: Edition Arthaud, 1977), 80.

57 Jeanneret Gris, *Almanach,* 145, 168.

58 A significant distinction from Art Nouveau. See also Troy, *Modernism,* 192–96.

59 "son costume, son stylo, son Eversharp, sa machine a écrire, son appareil téléphonique, ses meubles de bureau admirables, . . . le rasoir Gillette et la pipe anglaise, le chapeau melon et la limousine, le paquebot et l'avion." Le Corbusier, *Vers une architecture,* 73.

60 "Études sur les différentes manières de s'asseoir, auxquelles nos sièges devraient s'adapter." Le Corbusier, *Oeuvre complète,* 1: 157.

61 "l'évolution de la toilette féminine en particulier, et des règles de la politesse, autorisent des attitudes absolument nouvelles. Le salon d'autrefois est débordé; c'est un nouvel âge du meuble qui commence." Ibid., 1: 157. In his notes for the article in L'Esprit Nouveau on Purism Le Corbusier had already articulated his view on tools as the origin of style and therefore of architecture (a passage he would return to in *Almanach d'architecture*): "LE STYLE. Notre époque se caractérise par un outillage nouveau et merveilleux; tous les outils sont là pour les grandes entreprises: chimie et mécanique . . . L'ingénieur a tout préparé; une production industrielle immense a occupe notre vie et a attaché nos regards. Un aspect unitaire spécifique a animé toutes les choses; il s'est répété assez et avec assez d'unité pour nous donner les certitudes d'un style." C3–16, p. 82, FLC.

62 André Wogenscky in "Movement, Furniture and Le Corbusier" (Paris, 1978) (typed manuscript).

63 For example, in his *Almanach* of 1925, Le Corbusier describes the Thonet armchair as carrying "de la noblesse, tant sa pauvreté est un concentré des formes susceptibles de s'harmoniser au corps" (145). In *Vers une architecture* he described forms (Greek temple ornaments) to provoke "des sensations catégoriques." Le Corbusier, *Vers une architecture,* 173. On the furniture in his early work and his presentation of three sitting "machines" in the pavilion that lie at the origin of his later chairs, see Arthur Rüegg, "Der Pavillon de l'Esprit Nouveau als *musée imaginaire,*" in *L'Esprit Nouveau: Le Corbusier und die Industrie, 1920–1925,* 134–51. On the constant engagement of Le Corbusier with "la question du mobilier," furniture, and its continuation in Paris with the work for Marcel Lavaillant, see Arthur Rüegg, "Marcel Lavaillant and 'la question du moblier,'" in Von Moos and Rüegg, *Le Corbusier Before Le Corbusier,* 109–31.

64 "nos gestes ne sont-ils pas totalement transformés?" Jeanneret Gris, *Almanach,* 81.

65 "la coquille de l'escargot. L'escargot est dans une coquille d'escargot; c'est vrai. . . . Le machinisme doit reconduire l'escargot à sa coquille." Ibid., 5. His other analogy is with Diogenes in his barrel—a similar case of a tightly fitting wrap surrounding a naked body which it protects, like clothes and house in one. Le Corbusier, *Decorative Art of Today* (trans. Dunnett).

66 "la maison s'attache a nos gestes: c'est la coquille de l'escargot. Il faut donc qu'elle soit faite a notre mesure." Jeanneret Gris, *Almanach,* 29. The statement had occurred before, in *Vers une architecture* when he described the house/object as having to "satisfy the exigencies of the body" (29).

67 Jeanneret Gris, *Almanach,* 197.

68 Ibid., 111–12.

69 "l'armature de l'aile droite du pavillon. Sans eux toutes démonstration échouait." "Exposé bref de nos tribulations," Ms notes on the Pavillon, B2–16, FLC, 31.

70 Indeed, Le Corbusier is adamant about this function: "Le meuble ici ne vient pas ajouter son architecture possible à une architecture déjà arrêtée. Il fait architecture." Le Corbusier, *Almanach,*

145. The Innovation trunks were manufactured by an American company, and Le Corbusier had so enthusiastically endorsed their product line (which included an armoire modeled on the trunks) that he had become their "marketing" arm in Paris, choosing illustrations for their ads and writing the copy from 1923. See Troy, *Modernism*, 213–17.

71 "Le meuble ici ne vient pas ajouter son architecture possible a une architecture déjà arrêtée. Il fait architecture." Jeanneret Gris, *Almanach*, 145.

72 "Les pièces ne sont plus carrées; elles se pénètrent, se continuent; certains de leurs murs s'étendent, d'autres se roulent en cylindres, en spirales." Le Corbusier, "L'architecture et Fernand Léger," *Variétés*, February 15, 1929, 522, X 1- 08, FLC, 24.

73 Not coincidentally, the name "Purism" suggests cleansing and reduction at all levels—"the period of Vacuum-cleaning" that Ozenfant recalls in his *Memoirs* as an essential part of the Purist years. See Eliel, "Purism in Paris," 22.

74 Le Corbusier expresses this thought in his evaluation of the Thonet armchairs he used to furnish the pavilion: "Et nous croyons que ce fauteuil, dont les millions d'exemplaires meublent notre continent et les deux Amériques, porte de la noblesse, tant sa pauvreté est un concentré des formes susceptibles de s'harmoniser au corps." Jeanneret Gris, *Almanach*, 145.

75 "des maisons comme des tabernacles." Le Corbusier, *Vers une architecture*, 72. The red thread through his furniture design in the pavilion is likewise portability: "Nous les avons admises [les tables] comme pouvant se transporter aisément d'une pièce à l'autre." And he describes how he designed an armchair for the space so that it could fit through seventy-centimeter doors, which his favorite Maple armchair could not. Jeanneret Gris, *Almanach*, 145.

76 Le Corbusier, *Oeuvre complète*, 106.

77 "Nous détachons du mur la sculpture et la peinture et les laissons seules agir avec le radium qu'elles peuvent contenir." Jeanneret Gris, *Almanach*, 146. Ozenfant's *Doric Vases* (1925), Leger's *Le Balustre* (1925), and Jeanneret's *Still Life from the Pavillon de l'Esprit Nouveau* (1924) all carried architectural references (references to smokestacks, silos, Doric columns, pistons, etc.), even the latter, which recalled a cityscape even if it did not constitute the most rigorously Purist of his constructions. The relationship between painting and architecture was so critical that the hanging of the collection in Raoul La Roche's house (in April 1925) led to strain between Ozenfant and Le Corbusier that ultimately led to their break-up (in July 1925). Tim Benton, "Raoul La Roche—Sammlung und Haus," in *L'Esprit Nouveau: Le Corbusier und die Industrie, 1920–1925*, 87.

78 "Le Cas de AEG: Depuis lors . . . ont revêtu un aspect modeste, sobre, presque impersonnel. Ils sont des témoins discrets, alors qu'autrefois ils enlaidissaient. Car Peter Behrens a dessiné toutes leurs formes, et il ne sort pas de AEG une pièce visible de la battisse ou de l'industrie qui n'ait été revue par lui. Le bonheur de cette intervention autoritaire de l'art eut pu se changer en lamentable résultat s'il ne s'était précisément trouvé l'homme de le circonstance." Jeanneret, *Étude sur le mouvement d'art décoratif en Allemagne*, 43.

79 Rüegg also notes this feature of Le Corbusier's interiors but attributes it to his effort to create a Purist *Gesamtkunstwerk* where the composition of a Purist still-life affords the unity. Rüegg, "Der Pavillon," 139.

80 "Les pots du pavillon, verre et terre cuite, furent tout simplement achetés chez l'appariteur de laboratoire: éprouvettes, mortiers, creusets. A beaucoup de visiteurs, ils apparurent d'un modernisme aigu. En attendant l'œuvre d'art en soi, c'était la des produits de sélection mécanique." Jeanneret Gris, *Almanach*, 168–69.

81 "sont nés des objets d'usage d'un style nouveau . . . : les installations de bureaux (mais oui!), de banque, la carrosserie d'automobile, le vêtement, la vaisselle, la verrerie . . . une multitude d'objets bien proportionnés, maniables, agréables, conditionnés pour l'agrément de nos gestes." Ibid., 82.

82 "On ne reste pas insensible devant l'intelligence qui régit certaines machines, devant la proportion de leurs organes rigoureusement conditionnés par les calculs, devant la précision d'exécution de leurs éléments, devant la beauté probe de leurs matières, devant la sécurité de leurs mouvements; il y'a là comme une projection des lois naturelles. Les halls qui les abritent sont des vaisseaux d'une limpidité sans phrases." Le Corbusier (Charles-Edouard Jeanneret) and Ozenfant Amédée, *Après le cubisme* (Paris, 1918), 24.

83 "l'objet utile constituera le milieu actif et tranquille de notre existence." Jeanneret Gris, *Almanach*, 75.

84 "The human limb-object is a docile servant. A good servant is discreet and self-effacing, in order to leave his master free." Le Corbusier, *Decorative Art*, 79.

85 "Exposé bref de nos tribulations," Ms notes on the Pavillon, B2–16, FLC, 30. For a detailed account of the production problems of the *casiers* and Le Corbusier's changing materials specifications from polished wood, to combination polished/painted to metal, see Arthur Rüegg, "Der Pavillon de l'Esprit Nouveau als *musée imaginaire*," in *L'Esprit Nouveau: Le Corbusier und die Industrie, 1920–1925*, 134–51.

86 He wanted to eliminate buffets, armoires, vitrines, commodes, desks, linen boxes, etc. Jeanneret Gris, *Almanach*, 145, and "Expose," 8.

87 Adolf Loos, "Josef Veillich," in *Trotzdem*, 213–18.

88 "la physiologie des sensations, c'est à dire sur la constance des réactions primaires, l'universalité des réactions des sens à la vue des formes et des lignes?" See above n. 37.

89 Romy Golan sees the return to man as a later phenomenon, of the 1930s, most clearly evident in his contribution to the French exhibition "Le Foyer de Famille" at the Brussels International Fair of 1935. Golan, *Modernity and Nostalgia*. Yet Le Corbusier was profoundly focused on the body all along. Here I also disagree with Tag Gronberg, who describes Le Corbusier's limb-objects as "grotesque" and

generally reads his take on objects as male fetishism. Tag Gronberg, "Speaking Volumes: The Pavillon de l'Esprit Nouveau," *Oxford Art Journal* 15, no. 2 (1992): 58–69. See also n. 39 above.

90 "La maison est faite d'objets répondant à nos fonctions. C'est là que se manifeste la composition architecturale: ces objets constituent un organisme porteur d'une intention particulière, précise. . . . Il n'y a plus rien à ajouter, tout est dedans. L'architecture ne s'ajoute pas. Elle est située dans la qualité particulière d'ordre qu'on a imprimé au groupement des objets de la maison." Jeanneret Gris, *Almanach*, 138.

CONCLUSION | SCULPTURE AND SCALE

1 Le Corbusier, *The Modulor: A Harmonious Measure to the Human Scale Universally Applicable to Architecture and Mechanics* (1951; London: Faber and Faber, 1961), 9.

BIBLIOGRAPHY

ADAMY, R. "Kunsthandwerk und Architektur im System der Künste." *Deutsche Bauzeitung* 23 (1889): 545–50.

ADORNO, THEODOR. "Functionalism Today." In *Rethinking Architecture*. Ed. N. Leach. New York, 1997, 6–19.

ALBERTI, LEON BATTISTA. *On the Art of Building in Ten Books*. Trans. Joseph Rykwert et al. Cambridge, Mass.: MIT Press, 1988.

ANDERSON, STANFORD. "Modern Architecture and Industry: Peter Behrens and the Cultural Policy of Historical Determinism." *Oppositions* 11 (Winter 1977).

———. "Peter Behrens and the AEG Industrial Design." *Oppositions* 21 (Summer 1980): 78–97.

———. "Introduction." In H. Muthesius, *Style-Architecture and Building-Art*. 1902 (in German); Santa Monica: Getty Center, 1996, 1–43.

APPADURAI, ARJUN, ED. *The Social Life of Things: Commodities in Cultural Perspective*. Cambridge, Mass.: MIT Press, 1986.

ARCHER, JOHN. "The Architect and the Mountain Lake: Adolf Loos and the Crisis of Culture." *Midgard* 1 (1987): 63–77.

ARNOLD, KLAUS-PETER. *Geschichte der deutschen Werkstätten und der Gartenstadt Hellerau*. Dresden, 1993.

AUDSLEY, W., and G. AUDSLEY. *Outlines of Ornament in the Leading Styles: Selected from Executed Ancient and Modern Works, a Book of Reference for the Architect, Sculptor, Decorative Artist and Practical Painter*. London: Sampson, Low, Marston, Searle and Rivington, 1881.

BACHELARD, GASTON. *La poétique de l'espace*. Paris: Presses Universitaires de France, 1958.

BANHAM, RAYNER. *Architectural Review*, 1955.

BANN, STEPHEN. "Historical Text and Historical Object: The Poetics of the Musée Cluny." *History and Theory* 17, no. 3 (1978): 251–66.

BARMAN, CHRISTIAN. "Review of Herbert Read." *Art in Industry, Architectural Review* 77 (January–June 1935): 3–8.

BAUDRILLARD, JEAN. *Le système des objets*. Paris: Gallimard, 1968.

BAUER, INGOLF. "Das Beyerisches Nationalmuseum und die 'Heimatkunst.'" In I. Bauer, ed., *Das Beyerisches Nationalmuseum*. Munich: Hirmer, 2000, 233–50.

BAUM, JULIUS. *Baukunst und dekorative Plastik der früheren Renaissance in Italien*. Stuttgart: J. Hoffman, 1926.

BEEBY, THOMAS. "Grammar as Ornament/Ornament as Grammar." *Via* 3 (1977): 11–28.

BEHNE, ADOLF. *Die Wiederkehr der Kunst*. 1919; Nendeln: Kraus, 1973.

———. "Art, Craft, Technology." In Francesco Dal Co, ed., *Figures of Architecture and Thought*. New York, 1990.

———. *The Modern Functional Building*. 1923; Santa Monica: Getty Center, 1996.

BELTING, HANS. *Bild und Kult: Eine Geschichte des Bildes vor dem Zeitalter der Kunst*. Munich: C. H. Beck, 1990.

BENJAMIN, WALTER. "Der destruktive Charakter." In *Gesammelte Schriften*, Bd. IV.1. Frankfurt am Main: Tillman Rexroth, 1980.

BENTON, TIM. "Raoul La Roche—Sammlung und Haus." In *L'Esprit Nouveau: Le Corbusier und die Industrie, 1920–1925*. Zurich: Museum für Gestaltung, 1987, 80–93.

BENTON, TIM, AND CHARLOTTE BENTON ET AL., EDS. *Form and Function: A Source Book for the History of Architecture and Design: 1890–1939*. London: Crosby Lockwood Staples, 1975.

BERGDOLL, BARRY. *European Architecture, 1750–1890*. New York: Oxford University Press, 2000.

BERLAGE, HENDRIK PETRUS. *Thoughts on Style, 1886–1909*. Ed. Harry Francis Mallgrave. Santa Monica: Getty Center, 1996.

BERRY, DUNCAN J. "From Historicism to Architectural Realism: On Some of Wagner's Sources." In Harry F. Mallgrave, ed., *Otto Wagner: Reflections on the Raiment of Modernity*. Santa Monica: Getty Center, 1993, 243–80.

BEUTH, CHRISTIAN PETER WILHELM, AND KARL FRIEDRICH SCHINKEL. *Vorbilder für Fabrikanten und Handwerker*. Berlin: Königliche Technische Deputation für Gewerbe, 1821–36.

BEYER, HERBERT, WALTER GROPIUS, AND ISE GROPIUS, EDS. *Bauhaus, 1919–1928*. New York: Museum of Modern Art, 1938.

BICKENDORF, GABRIELE. "Die Tradition der Kennerschaft: Von Lanzi über Rumohr und Waagen zu Morelli." In G. Agosti et al., eds., *Giovanni Morelli e la cultura dei conoscitori*. Bergamo: Pierluigi Lubrina, 1993, 25–47.

BING, GERTRUDE. "A. M. Warburg." *Journal of the Warburg and Courtauld Institute* 28 (1965): 299–313.

BIZUP, JOSEPH. *Manufacturing Culture: Vindications of Early Victorian Industry*. Charlottesville: University of Virginia Press, 2003.

BLANC, CHARLES. *Art in Ornament and Dress*. New York: Scribner, Welford and Armstrong, 1877.

———. *Grammaire des arts décoratifs: Décoration intérieure de la maison*. 2nd ed. Paris: Renouard, 1882.

BLOCH, ERNST. "Formative Education, Engineering Form, Ornament." In *Rethinking Architecture*. Ed. N. Leach. New York, 1997, 43–50.

BOAS, FRANZ. "The Decorative Art of the Indians of the North Pacific Coast." *Bulletin of the American Museum of Natural History* 9 (1897): 123–76.

———. "Facial Painting of the Indians of Northern British Columbia." *Memoirs of the American Museum of Natural History* 2 (1898): 13–24.

BODE, WILHELM VON. *Kunst und Kunstgewerbe am Ende des 19 Jahrhunderts.* Berlin: Cassirer 1901.

———. *Die italienischen Hausmöbel der Renaissance.* Leipzig: Hermann Seemann, 1902.

BOGNER, DIETER. "Das constructive Ornament—der Beitrag Wiens zur Abstraktion." In M. Bruderlin, ed., *Ornament und Abstraktion: Kunst der Kulturen, Moderne und Gegenwart im Dialog.* Exh. cat. Basel: Fondation Bayeler, June–September, 2001.

BOHNE, ANKE. "Rezepzion des Pergamonaltars im deutschen Bürgertum." In M. Baumbach, ed., *Tradita et inventa: Beitrage zur Rezepzion der Antike.* Heidelberg: C. Winter, 2000, 441–58.

BOLOGNA, FERDINANDO. *Dalle arti minori all'industrial design: Storia di una ideologia.* 1972; Naples: Paparo, 2009.

BÖRSCH-SOUPAN, EVA. "Der Renaissance Begriff der Berliner Schule im Vergleich zu Semper." In E. Börsch-Soupan, ed., *Gottfried Semper und die Mitte des 19. Jahrhunderts.* Basel: Birkhauser, 1976.

———. *Berliner Baukunst nach Schinkel.* Munich: Prestel, 1977.

BÖTTICHER, KARL G. W. "The Hellenic and Germanic Ways of Building." In *In What Style Should We Build?* Ed. Wolfgang Herrmann. Santa Monica: Getty Center, 1992.

———. "Entwicklung der Formen der hellenischen Tektonik." *Allgemeine Bauzeitung,* 1840, 316–30.

———. *Die Tektonik der Hellenen.* 2 vols. Potsdam: Ferdinand Riegel, 1844–52.

———. "Das Prinzip der hellenischen und germanischen Bauweise." *Allgemeine Bauzeitung,* 1846, 111–25.

———. "Rede am Schinkelfest zu Berlin 13. Marz 1848." *Allgemeine Bauzeitung,* 1848, 143–48.

———. *Die Tektonik der Hellenen.* 2 vols. Berlin: Ernst and Korn, 1874.

BOURGOIN, JULES. *Théorie de l'ornement.* Paris: Ducher, 1883.

BRAHAM, WILLIAM W. *Modern Color/Modern Architecture.* London: Ashgate, 2002.

BREUER, GERDA. "Geschmacksveredlung am Ort- Auswirkungen einer restaurativen Kulturutopie." In *Der westdeuschte Impuls 1900–1914: Kunst und Umweltgestaltung im Industriegebiet. Das Museum zwischen Jugendstil und Werkbund.* Krefeld: Kaiser Wilhelm Museum, 1984, 23–51.

BROOKS, H. ALAN. *Le Corbusier's Formative Years.* Chicago: University of Chicago Press, 1997.

BROWN, BILL. "Reification, Reanimation, and the American Uncanny." *Critical Inquiry* 32, no. 2 (Winter 2006): 175–207.

———. "Objects, Others, and Us (The Refabrication of Things)." *Critical Inquiry* 36, no. 2 (Winter 2010): 183–217.

BRUNN, HEINRICH VON. "Über die kunstgeschichtliche Stellung der Pergamenischen Gigantomachie." *Jahrbuch der königlichen preussischen Kunstsammlungen* 5 (1884): 231–92.

BUCHER, BRUNO (WITH J. BRINCKMANN). *Geschichte der technischen Künste.* 2 vols. Stuttgart, 1875.

BUCK, AUGUST. *Berliner Baukunst nach Schinkel.* Munich, 1977.

———, ED. *Renaissance und Renaissancismus von Jakob Burckhardt bis Thomas Mann.* Tübingen: Max Niemeyer, 1990.

BUDDENSIEG, TILMANN. *Industriekultur: Peter Behrens and the AEG, 1907–1914.* 1979; Cambridge, Mass.: MIT Press, 1984.

BÜCHER, KARL. *Die Entstehung der Volkswirtschaft.* Tübingen, 1893.

BUNZL, MATTI. "Franz Boas and the Humboldtian Tradition: From *Volksgeist* and *Nationalcharakter* to an Anthropological Concept of Culture." In G. W. Stocking, Jr., *Volksgeist as Method and Ethic: Essays on Boasian Ethnography and the German Anthropological Tradition.* Madison: University of Wisconsin Press, 1996, 17–78.

BURCKHARDT, JACOB. *Kultur der Renaissance in Italien.* 1860.

———. *Geschichte der Renaissance in Italien.* Stuttgart, 1868.

BURCKHARDT, LUCIUS. *The Werkbund: Studies in the History and Ideology of the Deutscher Werkbund, 1907–1933.* London: Design Council, 1980.

BURTON, ANTHONY. *Vision and Accident: The Story of the Victoria and Albert Museum.* London: V&A, 1999.

CACCIARI, MASSIMO. *Loos e il suo angelo.* Milan: Electa, 2002.

CAMPBELL, JOAN. *The German Werkbund: The Politics of Reform in the Applied Arts.* Princeton, 1978.

CASSIRER, ERNST. *Wesen und Wirkung des Symbolbegriffs.* 1922–23; Darmstadt: Wissenschaftliche Buchgesellschaft, 1994.

CHAPPLE, GERALD, AND HANS SCHULTE, EDS. *The Turn of the Century: German Literature and Art, 1890–1915.* Bonn: Bouvier, 1981.

CICERO. *Orator.* London: Loeb Classical Library, 1971.

CLAUSSE, GUSTAVE. *Les marbriers romains et le mobilier presbytéral.* Paris: E. Leroux, 1897.

COHEN, JEAN-LOUIS. "Erhaben, zweifellos erhaben: Vom fesselnden Wesen der technischen Objekte." In Vitra Design Museum, *Le Corbusier: The Art of Architecture.* Weil-am-Rhein: Vitra Museum, 2007, 209–33.

COLE, HENRY. *Fifty Years of Public Work.* 2 vols. London: George Bell and Sons, 1884.

COLLINOT, E., and A. BEAUMONT. *Ornements turcs: Recueil des dessins pour l'art et l'industrie.* Paris, 1883.

CONZE, ALEXANDER. *Melische Thongefässe.* Leipzig: Breitkopf and Härtel, 1862.

———. *Frammenti di vaso di bronzo trovati nel tirolo meridionale.* 1874.

———. "Über das Relief der Griechen." *Sitzungsberichte der königlichen preussischen Akademie der Wissenschaften zu Berlin* 26 (1882): 563–77.

CRANE, WALTER. *Linie und Form.* Berlin: Hermann Seemann, n.d.

CROOK, MORDAUNT J. *The Dilemma of Style: Architectural Ideas from the Picturesque to the Post-Modern.* London: J. Murray, 1987.

CROWLEY, DAVID. "The Uses of Peasant Design in Austria-Hungary in the Late Nineteenth and Early Twentieth Centuries." *Studies in the Decorative Arts* (1995): 2–28.

CUVIER, GEORGES. *Das Thierreich geordnet nach seiner Organisation.* 6 vols. Leipzig: Brockhaus, 1831–43.

DAL CO, FRANCESCO. "Excellence: The Culture of Mies as Seen in his Notes and Books." In John Zukowsky, ed., *Mies Reconsidered: His Career, Legacy, and Disciples.* New York: Art Institute of Chicago and Rizzoli, 1986, 72–85.

———. *Figures of Architecture and Thought.* New York: Rizzoli, 1990.

DARCEL, ALFRED. "Les arts décoratifs au musée de Cluny." *Revue des Arts Décoratifs*, October 1886, 97–111.

DASTON, LORRAINE, ED. *Things That Talk: Object Lessons from Art and Science*. New York: Zone, 2004.

DAVIES, G., AND K. KENNEDY, EDS. *Medieval and Renaissance Art: People and Possessions*. London: V&A, 2009.

DAY, LEWIS F. *Every-Day Art: Short Essays on the Arts Not Fine*. London: B. T. Batsford, 1882.

———. *Some Principles of Every Day Art: Introductory Chapters on the Arts Not Fine*. London: B. T. Batsford, 1890.

DE MICHELIS, MICHELE. *Heinrich Tessenow, 1876–1950*. Milan: Electa, 1991.

DENEKE, BERNWARD. "Die Entdeckung der Volkskunst für das Kunstgewerbe." *Zeitschrift für Volkskunde* 60 (1964): 168–201.

———. "Die Museen und die Entwicklung der Kulturgeschichte." In B. Deneke and R. Kahsnitz, eds., *Das Kunst und Kulturgeschichtliche Museum im 19. Jahrhundert*. Munich: Prestel, 1977, 49–58.

DENEKE, BERNWARD, AND RAINER KAHSNITZ, EDS. *Das germanische Nationalmuseum Nürnberg, 1852–1977*. Munich: Deutscher Kunstverlag, 1978.

DERRIDA, JACQUES. *Parergon: The Truth in Painting*. Chicago: University of Chicago Press, 1987. (1st. ed.: *La verité en peinture*. Paris: Flammarion, 1978.)

DIDI-HUBERMAN, GEORGES. *L'image survivante*. Paris: Minuit, 2002.

DOHME, ROBERT. *Geschichte der deutschen Baukunst*. Berlin, 1886.

———. *Das Englische Haus*. 1888.

———. *Barock und Rokoko Architektur*. Berlin, 1892.

DOLMETSCH, HEINRICH. *Ornamentschatz: Ein Musterbuch stilvoller Ornamente aus allen Kunstepochen*. Stuttgart: Julius Hoffmann, 1889.

DRESSER, CHRISTOPHER. *Unity in Variety, as Deduced from the Vegetable Kingdom*. London, 1860.

———. *The Art of Decorative Design*. London: Day and Son, 1862.

———. *Principles of Decorative Design*. 1873.

———. *Studies in Design*. 1876.

DROSTE, MAGDALENA. *Bauhaus, 1919–1933*. Berlin: Bauhaus Archiv and Benedikt Taschen Verlag, 1990.

———. "The Bauhaus Object Between Authorship and Anonimity." In J. Saletnik and R. Schuldenfrei, eds., *Bauhaus Construct: Fashioning Identity, Discourse, and Modernism*. London: Routledge, 2009, 205–25.

DVORAK, MAX. "Alois Riegl. " In *Gesammelte Aufsätze zur Kunstgeschichte*. Munich: R. Piper, 1929, 279–98.

DYCE, WILLIAM. "Instruction in Practical Art in Foreign Schools of Design, Made in 1839." In *A Catalogue of the Articles of Ornamental Art Selected for the Exhibition of the Works of Industry of All Nations in 1851, and Purchased by the Government*. London: Chapman and Hall, for the Department of Practical Art.

———. *The Drawing Book of the Government School of Design*. 1842.

DYCE, WILLIAM, AND CHARLES WILSON. *A Letter to Lord Meadowbank and the Committee of the Honourable Board of Trustees for the Encouragement of Arts and Manufactures: On the Best Means of Ameliorating the Arts and Manufactures of Scotland in Point of Taste*. Edinburgh: Thomas Constable, May 30, 1837.

ECK, CAROLINE VAN. *Organicism in Nineteenth-Century Architecture: An Inquiry into Its Theoretical and Philosophical Background*. Amsterdam: Architectura and Natura, 1994.

EGGER, HANNA. "Die Anfänge des K.K. Österreichischen Museums für Kunst und Industrie und der Wiener Schule der Kunstgeschichte. " In Peter Noever, ed., *Kunst und Industrie, die Anfänge des Museums für Angewandte Kunst in Wien*. Vienna: MAK and Hatje Cantz, 2000, 271–83.

EITELBERGER, RUDOLF VON. *Die Kunstbewegung in Öesterreich seit der Pariser Weltausstellung im Jahre 1867: Im Auftrage des K.K. Unterrichts Ministerium*. Vienna: K. K. Schulbucher, 1878.

———. *Gesammelte kunsthistorische Schriften und Kunstgewerbliche Zeitfragen*. Vienna: Wilhelm Braumüller, 1879.

ELIEL, CAROL. *L'Esprit Nouveau: Purism in Paris, 1918–1925*. Los Angeles: Los Angeles Museum of Art, 2001.

ERLANDE-BRANDENBURG, ALAIN. "Le Musée des Monuments français et les origines du Musée de Cluny." In B. Deneke and R. Kahsnitz, eds., *Das Kunst und Kulturgeschichtliche Museum im 19. Jahrhundert*. Munich: Prestel, 1977, 49–58.

EYE, AUGUST VON. *Atlas der Culturgeschichte*. 1875.

FABIAN, JOHANNES. "Ethnische Artefakte und ethnographische Objekte: Über das Erkennen von Dingen." In A. Moravansky, ed., *Das entfernte Dorf*. Vienna: Böhlau, 2002, 21–40.

FALKE, JAKOB VON. *Die deutschen Trachten und Modenwelt, ein Beitrag zur deutschen Culturgeschichte*. Leipzig: Meyer, 1858.

———. *Die Kunstindustrie der Gegenwart*. Leipzig, 1868.

———. *Die Kunst im Hause: Geschichtliche und kritischäesthetische Studien über die Dekoration und Ausstattung der Wohnung*. Vienna: Gerold, 1871. English trans. from 3rd German ed.: *Art in the House: Historical, Critical, and Aesthetical Studies on the Decorating and Furnishing of the Dwelling*. Boston: Prang, 1879.

———. *Costümegeschichte der Culturvölker*. Stuttgart: W. Spemann, 1880.

———. *Geschichte des modernen Geschmacks*. 1866; Leipzig: T. O. Weigel, 1880.

———. *Äesthetik des Kunstgewerbes: Ein Handbuch*. Stuttgart: W. Spemann, 1883.

———. *Geschichte des deutschen Kunstgewerbes*. 1888.

———. *Geschichte des Geschmacks im Mittelalter, und andere Studien auf dem Gebiete von Kunst und Kultur*. Berlin: Allgemeiner Verlag für deutsche Literatur, 1892.

FALKE, JAKOB VON, AND JOHANN A. VON EYE. *Kunst und Leben der Vorzeit vom Beginn des Mittelalters bis zu Anfang des 19. Jahrhunderts*. Nürnberg: Bauer and Raspe, 1868.

FAIRHOLT, F. W. *Costume in England: A History of Dress*. London: Chapman and Hall, 1846.

FALTER, REINHARD, AND GERTI FLUHRMEYER. "Anwalt für die Isar." In V. Hofer, ed., *Gabriel von Seidl: Architekt und Naturschützer*. Kreuzlingen: Hugendubel, 2002, 175–90.

FECHNER, THEODOR GUSTAV. *Vorschule der Ästhetik*. Leipzig: Breitkopf and Härtel, 1878.

FEEST, CHRISTIAN F. "The Origins of Professional Anthropology in Vienna." In B. Rupp-Eisenreich and J. Stagl, eds., *Kulturwissenschaften im Vielvölkerstaat*. Vienna: Bohlau, 1995, 113–31.

FERNÁNDEZ, MARÍA OCÓN. *Ornament und Moderne: Theoriebildung und Ornamentdebatte im deutschen Architekturdiskurs (1850–1930)*. Berlin: Dietrich Reimer, 2004.

FIEDLER, KONRAD. "Bemerkungen über das Wesen und Geschichte der Baukunst." *Deutsche Rundschau* 15 (1878): 361–83.

———. *Schriften zur Kunst*. Ed. G. Boehm. 1913/14; Munich: Wilhelm Fink, 1971.

FLIEDL, GOTTFRIED. *Kunst und Lehre am Beginn der Moderne: Die Wiener Kunstgewerbeschule 1867–1918*. Salzburg: Residenz, 1986.

FOCILLON, HENRI. *The Life of Forms in Art*. Cambridge, Mass.: MIT Press, 1989. 1st ed.: *La vie des formes*. Paris, 1934.

FORTY, ADRIAN. *Objects of Desire: Design and Society, 1750–1980*. London: Thames and Hudson, 1986.

FRAMPTON, KENNETH. *Studies in Tectonic Culture*. Cambridge, Mass.: MIT Press, 1995.

FRANCASTEL, PIERRE. *Art and Technology in the Nineteenth and the Twentieth Centuries*. New York: Zone; 1956.

FRANK, ISABELLE, AND URSULA HARTUNG, EDS. *Die Rhetorik des Ornaments*. Berlin: Wilhelm Fink, 2001.

FRANKE, URSULA. "Bausteine für eine Theorie ornamentaler Kunst: Zur Autonomisierung des Ornaments bei Karl Philip Moritz." In U. Franke and H. Paetzold, eds., *Ornament und Geschichte*. Bonn: Bouvier, 1996, 89–106.

FRANZ, RAINALD. "Das System Gottfried Semper's. Reform des Kunstgewerbes und Grundlagen für ein Museum für Kunst und Industrie in ihren Auswirkungen auf das Österreichische Museum." In *Kunst und Industrie: Die Anfänge des Museums für Angewandte Kunst in Wien*. Ed. Peter Noever. Vienna: Hatje Cantz, 2000, 41–51.

FRASCARI, MARCO. "The Tell-the-Tale Detail." In Paula Behrens and Anthony Fisher, eds., *The Building of Architecture*, *Via* 7 (1984).

FUMERTON, PATRICIA. *Cultural Aesthetics: Renaissance Literature and the Practice of Social Ornament*. Chicago: University of Chicago Press, 1991.

GANTNER, JOSEPH. *Schönheit und Grenzen der klassischen Form*. Vienna: Anton Schroll, 1949.

GELL, ALFRED. *Art and Agency*. Oxford: Clarendon, 1998.

GEORGE, WALDEMAR. "Léger et les objets dans l'espace." *Selection: Chronique de la vie artistique* 5 (February 1929): 5–6.

GEORGIADIS, SOKRATIS. *Sigfried Giedion: Eine intellektuelle Biographie*. Zurich: GTA/Ammann, 1989.

———. "Semper, die Griechen und die Anderen." In Sokratis, ed., *Gottfried Semper (1803–1879): Griechenland und die lebendige Architektur*. Cologne: Romiosini, 2005, and Thessaloniki: University Studio Press, 2005, 91–121.

GERMANISCHES NATIONALMUSEUM NÜRNBERG. *Peter Behrens und Nürnberg*. Exh. cat. 20 Sept.–9 Nov. 1980. Munich: Prestel, 1980.

GEYMÜLLER, HEINRICH VON, AND CARL VON STEGMANN. *Die Architektur der Renaissance in Toscana*. 11 vols. Munich: F. Bruckmann, 1885–1908.

GHISLER, RUTH. "Vorbegriffe zu einer Theorie der Ornamente von Karl Philip Moritz. Fragmente einer Architekturlehre aus Goethes römischen Freundenkreis." *Jahrbuch des Freien Deutsche Hochstifts* (1970): 32–58.

GIEDION, SIGFRIED. *Bauen in Frankreich, Bauen in Eisen, Bauen in Eisenbeton*. Leipzig: Klinkhardt and Biermann, 1928.

———. "Situation de l'architecture contemporaine en Italie." *Cahiers d'Art* (1931): 442–49.

———. *Space, Time and Architecture*. 1st ed. Cambridge, Mass: Harvard University Press, 1941.

———. *Mechanization Takes Command: A Contribution to Anonymous History*. New York: Oxford University Press, 1948.

———. "Furniture Design and the Common Object." In S. Papadaki, ed., *Le Corbusier: Architect, Painter, Writer*. New York: Macmillan, 1948, 39–40.

GINZBURG, CARLO. "Clues: Roots of an Evidential Paradigm." In *Clues, Myths, and the Historical Method*. 1986 (Italian); Baltimore: Johns Hopkins University Press, 1992.

GLAZIER, RICHARD. *A Manual of Historic Ornament*. London: B. T. Batsford, 1899.

GNEHM, MICHAEL. "'Kritik gegenwärtiger Zustände'—als Ursprungskritik zum dritten Band des '*Stil*'." In N. Winfried and W. Oechslin, eds., *Gottfried Semper, 1803–1897: Architektur und Wissenschaft*. Zurich: GTA, and Berlin: Prestel Verlag, 2004, 314–20.

GOLAN, ROMY. *Modernity and Nostalgia: Art and Politics in France Between the Wars*. New Haven: Yale University Press, 1995.

GÖLLER, ADOLF. *Zur Äesthetik der Architektur*. Stuttgart: K. Wittwor, 1887.

———. *Die Entstehung der architektonischen Stilformen*. Stuttgart: K. Wittwor, 1888.

GOMBRICH, ERNST. *Aby Warburg: An Intellectual Biography*. London: Warburg Institute, 1970.

———. *The Sense of Order*. London: Phaidon, 1979.

GOODYEAR, W. G. *The Grammar of the Lotus*. London, 1891.

GOUGH, MARIA. *The Artist as Producer: Russian Constructivism in Revolution*. Berkeley: University of California Press, 2005.

GRABAR, OLEG. *The Mediation of Ornament*. Princeton, N.J.: Princeton University Press, 1992.

GRAUL, RICHARD. "Deutschland." In R. Graul, ed., *Die Krisis im Kunstgewerbe*. Leipzig: S. Hirsel, 1901, 39–51.

GREEN, CHRISTOPHER. "Léger, Purism ad the Paris Avant-Garde." *Art News* 69 (December 1970): 54–56.

———. "Painting for the Corbusian Home." *Studio International*, no. 190 (September–October 1975): 103–7.

———. *Léger and the Avant-Garde*. New Haven: Yale University Press, 1976.

GRONBERG, TAG. "Speaking Volumes: The Pavillon de l'Esprit Nouveau." *Oxford Art Journal* 15, no. 2 (1992): 58–69.

GROPIUS, WALTER. *Idee und Aufbau des staatlichen Bauhauses Weimar*. Weimar-Munich: Bauhausverlag, 1923.

GROSS, KARL. "Das Ornament." In *Jahrbuch des Deutschen Werkbundes: Die Durchgeistigung der deutschen Arbeit. Wege und Ziele in Zusammenhang von Industrie/Handwerk und Kunst*. Jena: Diederichs, 1912, 60–65.

GROTE, ANDREAS, ED. *Macrocosmos in Microcosmo: Die Welt in der Stube*. Opladen, 1994.

GURLITT, CORNELIUS, ED. *Das neue königliche Hoftheater zu Dresden*. Dresden, 1878.

———. *Das Barock-und Rococo-Oranament Deutschlands*. In series *Architektur und Kunstgewerbe des XVII und XVIII Jahrhunderts*. Berlin: Wasmuth, 1883–89.

———. *Geschichte des Barockstiles in Italien*. Stuttgart: Ebner and Seubert, 1887.

———. "Göller's ästhetische Lehre." *Deutsche Bauzeitung* 21 (December 17, 1887): 602–4, 606–7.

———. *Im Bürgerhause*. Dresden: Gilbers'sche Königl. Hof-Verlagsbuchhanddlung, 1888.

———. "Lermolieff's kunstkritische Studien." *Die Gegenwart* 27 (1890): 103–5.

———. *Die internationale Kunstausstellung zu Berlin, 1891*. Munich: F. Hanfstaengl, 1891.

———. *Die deutsche Kunst des XIX Jahrdhunderts*. Berlin: Georg Bondi, 1899.

HABERLANDT, MICHAEL. "Einführung." *Das Bauernhaus in Österreich-Ungarn und in seine Grenzgebieten*, 2 vols. Vienna: Verlag des Österr. Ingenieur- und Architekten-Veriens, 1906.

HADDON, ALFRED C. *The Decorative Art of British New Guinea: A Study in Papuan Ethnography*. Dublin, 1894.

———. *Evolution in Art: As Illustrated by the Life-Histories of Design*. London: Walter Scott, 1902.

HAMBIDGE, JAY. *Dynamic Symmetry: The Greek Vase*. New Haven: Yale University Press, 1920.

HAMLIN, A. D. F. *A History of Ornament: Ancient and Medieval*. London: B. T. Batsford, 1916.

HARROD, OWEN W. "Bruno Pauls's Typenmöbel, the German Werkbund, and Pragmatic Modernism, 1908–1918." *Studies in the Decorative Arts* 9, no. 2 (Spring–Summer 2002): 33–58.

HART, JOAN GOLDHAMMER. "Heinrich Wölfflin: A Biography." Ph.D. diss., University of California, Berkeley, 1980.

HART, J., R. RECHT, AND M. WARNKE, EDS. *Relire Wölfflin*. Paris: Musée du Louvre, 1995.

HARTMANN, EDUARD VON. "Gehört die Baukunst zu den freien Künsten?" *Gegenwart*, 1887.

———. *Die deutsche Ästhetik seit Kant*. Leipzig: Friedrich, 1887.

HARVEY, LAWRENCE. *Semper's Theory of Evolution in Architectural Ornament, Extracted from the Transactions of the Royal Institute of British Architects*. London: RIBA, 1885.

HAUCK, GUIDO. "Die Grenzen zwischen Malerei und Plastik und die Gesätze des Reliefs." *Jahrbuch der königlichen preussischen Sammlungen*, 1885, 3–20.

HAYS, K. Michael. *Modernism and the Post-Humanist Subject: The Architecture of Hannes Meyer and Ludwig Hilberseimer*. Cambridge, Mass.: MIT Press, 1992.

HEGEL, GEORG WILHELM. *Introductory Lectures on Aesthetics*. Ed. M. Inwood. London: Penguin, 1993.

HERRMANN, WOLFGANG. "Gottfried Semper und Viehweg." In E. Börsch-Soupan, ed., *Gottfried Semper und die Mitte des 19 Jahrhunderts*. Basel: Birkhauser, 1976, 199–237.

———. *Gottfried Semper: Theoretischer Nachlass*. Basel: Birkhauser, 1981.

———. *Gottfried Semper: In Search of Architecture*. Cambridge, Mass., 1984.

HERRMANN, WOLFGANG, ED. *In What Style Should We Build?* Santa Monica: Getty Center, 1992.

HEUSER, G. "Darwinistisches über Kunst und Technik." *Allgemeine Bauzeitung*, 1890, 17–19, 25–27.

———. "Zur Entstehung des Gefachstyles, insbesondere der Gelenklager." *Allgemeine Bauzeitung*, 1892, 19.

———. "Das Werden von Stylformen. Fortsetzung Darwinistischer Studien." *Allgemeine Bauzeitung*, 1894, 53–69.

HILDEBRAND, ADOLF VON. "The Problem of Form in Painting and Sculpture." In Harry Malgrave, ed., *Empathy, Form and Space*. Santa Monica: Getty Center, 1994.

HILDEBRAND, SONJA. "'. . . grossartigere Umgebungen': Gottfried Semper in London." In Winfried Nerdinger and Werner Oechslin, eds., *Gottfried Semper 1803–1897: Architektur und Wissenschaft*. Zurich: GTA, and Berlin: Prestel Verlag, 2004, 260–68.

HITCHCOCK, HENRY-RUSSELL. *Modern Architecture: Romanticism and Reintegration*. New York: Payson and Clarke, 1929.

HOFFMAN, EVA. "Pathways of Portability: Islamic and Christian Interchange from the Tenth to Twelfth Century." *Art History* 24, no. 1 (February 2001): 17–50.

HOLLY, MICHAEL ANN. *Past Looking: Historical Imgination and the Rhetoric of the Image*. Ithaca: Cornell University Press, 1996.

HOLME, CHARLES, ED. *Peasant Art in Austria and Hungary*. London: Studio, 1911.

———. *Peasant Art in Russia*. London: Studio, 1912.

———. *Peasant Art in Italy*. London: Studio, 1913.

HOLZ, HANS HEINZ. *Vom Kunstwerk zur Ware: Studien zur Funktion des ästhetischen Gegenstands im Spätkapitalismus*. Neuwied: Hermann Luchterhand, 1972.

HULME, F. EDWARD. *Birth and Development of Ornament*. London: Swan Sonnenschein, New York: Macmillan, 1893.

HVATTUM, MARI. "Gottfried Semper: Between Poetics and Practical Aesthetics." *Zeitschrift für Kunstgeschichte* 64 (2001): 537–46.

———. *Gottfried Semper and the Problem of Historicism*. New York: Cambridge University Press, 2004.

JACKNIS, IRA. "The Ethnographic Object and the Object of Ethnology in the Early Career of Franz Boas." In G. W. Stocking Jr., *Volksgeist as Method and Ethic: Essays on Boasian Ethnography and the German Anthropological Tradition*. Madison: University of Wisconsin Press, 1996, 185–214.

JACKSON, FRANK G. *Lessons on Decorative Design*. London: Chapman and Hall, 1913.

JAMES-CHAKRABORTY, KATHLEEN. "Henry van de Velde and Walter Gropius: Between Avoidance and Imitation." In K. James-Chakraborty, ed., *Bauhaus Culture: From Weimar to the Cold War*. Minneapolis: University of Minnesota Press, 2002, 26–42.

JANIK, ALLAN. *Wittgenstein's Vienna*. New York, 1973.

JARZOMBEK, MARK. "The *Kunstgewerbe*, the *Werkbund*, and the Aesthetics of Culture in the Wilhelmine Period." *JSAH* 53, no. 1 (March 1994): 7–19.

JOMBERT, CHARLES-ANTOINE. *Repertoire d'artistes, ou recueil de compositions d'architecture et d'ornement antiques et modernes, de toutes espèces: Par divers auteurs, dont Marot, Loire, Le Pautre, Cottart, Pierretz, Cotelle, Le Roux, Berain*. 1764; Paris, 1913.

JONES, OWEN. *An Apology for the Colouring of the Greek Court*. London, 1854.

———. *The Grammar of Ornament*. London: Day and Son, 1856.

KAEGI, WERNER. *Jacob Burckhardt: Eine Biographie*. Basel: Benno Schwabe, 1947.

KAISER WILHELM MUSEUM, KREFELD. *Der Westdeustche Impuls, 1900–1914: Kunst und Umweltgestaltung im Industriegebiet*. Krefeld, 1984.

KALTEICH, ULRIKE." Die Geschichte des Gewerbemuseum zu Dresden zwischen 1876 und 1907." In *Das Kunstgewerbemuseum Dresden*, Staatliche Kunstsammlung Dresden. Exh. cat. Dresden: Minerva, 1998.

KANT, IMMANUEL. *Critique of Judgement*. Intro. and trans. W. S. Pluhar. Indianapolis, Ind.: Hackett, 1987.

KAPP, ERNST. *Grundlinien einer Philosophie der Technik: Zur Entstehungsgeschichte der Cultur aus neuen Gesichtspunkten*. Braunschweig: George Westermann, 1877.

KEMP, WOLFGANG. "Alois Riegl." In H. Dilly, ed., *Altmeister moderner Kunstgeschichte*. Berlin: Dietrich Reimer, 1990, 37–60.

———. "Nachwort." In A. Riegl, *Spätrömische Kunstindustrie*.

KIAER, CHRISTINA. *Imagine No Possessions: The Socialist Objects of Russian Constructivism*. Cambridge, Mass.: MIT Press, 2005.

KLEMM, GUSTAV. *Allgemeine Cultur-Geschichte der Menschheit: Nach den bessten Quellen bearbeitet und mit xylographischen Abbildungen der verschiedenen Nationalphysiognomien, Geräthe, Waffen, Trachten, Kunstproducte u.s.w. versehen*. Leipzig: B. G. Teubner, 1843–52.

KLENCKE, HERMANN. *Kosmetik oder menschliche Verschönerungs-kunst auf Grundlage rationeller Gesundheitslehre*. Leipzig: Kummer, 1869.

KOSS, JULIET. *Modernism After Wagner*. Minneapolis: University of Minnesota Press, 2010.

———. "Bauhaus Theatre of Human Dolls." *Art Bulletin* 85, no. 4 (December 2003): 724–45.

KROLL, FRANK-LOTHAR. *Das Ornament in der Kunsttheorie des 19. Jahrhunderts*. Hildesheim, 1987.

———. "Zur Problematik des Ornaments im 18. Jhd." In U. Franke and H. Paetzold, eds., *Ornament und Geschichte*, 63–88. Bonn: Bouvier, 1996.

KULTERMANN, UDO. *Geschichte der Kunstgeschichte: Der Weg einer Wissenschaft*. Frankfurt: Ullstein, 1981.

KURZWELLY, ALBRECHT. "Lage und Zukunft der Volkskunst." In Richard Graul, ed., *Die Krisis im Kunstgewerbe: Studien über die Wege und Ziele der modernen Richtung*. Leipzig: S. Herzel, 1901, 88–108.

LABORDE, LEON DE. *De l'union des arts et de l'industrie*. 2 vols. Paris: Imprimerie imperiale, 1856.

LANGBEHN, JULIUS. *Rembrandt als Erzieher*. Leipzig: C. L. Hirschfield, 1890.

LANKHEIT, KLAUS. "Gottfried Semper und die Weltausstellung London 1851." In E. Börsch-Soupan, ed., *Gottfried Semper und die Mitte des 19. Jahrhunderts*. Basel: Birkhauser, 1976, 23–47.

LATOUR, BRUNO. *Reassembling the Social: An Introduction to Actor-Network Theory*. New York: Oxford University Press, 2005.

———. *The Pasteurization of France*. Cambridge, Mass.: Harvard University Press, 1988.

LE CORBUSIER. *L'art décoratif d'aujourd'hui*. Paris: Crès, 1925. (English trans.: James Dunnett, *The Decorative Art of Today*, 1987.)

———. *Vers une architecture*. 1923; Paris: Arthaud, 1977.

——— (CH-E. JEANNERET). *Les voyages d'Allemagne. Carnets. Voyage d'Orient. Carnets*. Milan and Paris: Electa and Fondation Le Corbusier, 2000.

——— (CH-E. JEANNERET). *Étude sur le mouvement d'art décoratif en Allemagne*. 1912; New York: Da Capo, 1968.

———(CH-E. JEANNERET GRIS). *Almanach d'architecture moderne*. 1925; Turin: Bottega d'Erasmo, 1975.

———. "Exposé bref de nos tribulations." Ms notes, B2–16, FLC.

———. "L'architecture et Fernand Léger. " *Variétés*, February 15, 1929, p. 522, X 1-08, FLC, pp. 21–24.

———. *Lettres à Auguste Perret*. Ed. Marie-Jeanne Dumont. Paris: Linteau, 2002.

———. *Lettres à Charles L'Eplattenier*. Ed. Marie-Jeanne Dumont. Paris: Linteau, 2006.

———. *Œuvre complète*, vol. 1. Paris, 1929.

LE CORBUSIER (CH-E. JEANNERET) AND OZENFANT AMÉDÉE. *Après le cubisme*. Paris, 1918.

LE CORBUSIER (CH-E. JEANNERET) AND OZENFANT, AMÉDÉE. *La peinture moderne*. Paris: G. Crès, 1925.

LÉGER, FERNAND. "Actualités." *Variétés*, February 15, 1929, p. 522, X 1- 08, FLC.

LEISCHING, JULIUS. "Gottfried Semper und die Museen." In *Mitteilungen des Mährischen Gewerbemuseums*. Brünn, 1903.

LEVIN, THOMAS Y. "Walter Benjamin and the Theory of Art History." *October* 47 (Winter 1988): 84–90.

LEVINE, D., ED. *Georg Simmel on Individuality and Social Forms: Selected Writings*. Chicago, 1971.

LEVINE, NEIL. *Modern Architecture: Representation and Reality*. New York: Yale University Press, 2009.

———. "The Romantic Idea of Architectural Legibility: Henri Labrouste and the Neo-Grec." In A. Drexler, ed., *The Architecture of the École des Beaux-Arts*. New York: MoMA, 1977, 324–416.

LEWIS, MICHAEL J. *The Politics of the German Gothic Revival*. New York, 1993.

LICHTWARK, ALFRED. *Palastfenster und Flügeltür*. 1899; Berlin: Gebr. Mann, 2000.

LIPPS, THEODOR. *Ästhetische Faktoren der Raumanschauung*. Hamburg: L. Voss, 1891.

———. *Ästhetik: Psychologie des Schönen und der Kunst*. 2 vols. Hamburg, 1903–6.

———. *Bewusstsein und Gegenstände*. Leipzig: W. Engelmann, 1905.

———. *Raumästhetik und Geometrisch-Optische Täuschungen*. 8 vols. Leipzig: A. Barth, 1893–97.

LOCHER, HUBERT. *Kunstgeschichte als historische Theorie der Kunst 1750–1950*. Berlin: Wilhelm Fink, 2001.

LONG, CHRISTOPHER. "'A Symptom of the Werkbund': The Spring 1912 Exhibition at the Austrian Museum for Art and Industry, Vienna." *Studies in the Decorative Arts* (2000): 91–121.

———. "*Wiener Wohnkultur*: Interior Design in Vienna, 1910–1938." *Studies in the Decorative Arts* (1997–98): 29–51.

LOOS, ADOLF. *Das Andere*. Vienna, 1903.

———. *Ins Leere gesprochen*. Paris: G. Crès, 1921.

———. *Spoken Into the Void: Collected Essays 1897–1900*. Trans and ed. Jane O. Newman and John H. Smith. Cambridge, Mass., 1982.

———. *Trotzdem*. Innsbruck: Brenner, 1931.

LOTZE, HERMANN. *Geschichte der Ästhetik in Deutschland*. Munich: Cotta, 1868.

———. *Mikrokosmus; Ideen zur Naturgeschichte und Geschichte der Menschheit; Versuch einer Anthropologie*. Leipzig: Hirzel, 1856–64.

LURZ, MEINHOLD. *Heinrich Wölfflin: Biographie einer Kunstheorie*. Darmstadt: Wernersche Buchgesellschaft, 1981.

MÁCEL, OTAKAR. "From Mass Production to Design Classic: Mies van der Rohe's Metal Furniture." Vitra Design Museum, *Mies van der Rohe: Architecture and Design in Suttgart, Barcelona, Brno.* Geneva: Skira, 1998, 18–64.

MACHT, HANS. "Das constructive Prinzip in der Ornamentik." *Mitteilungen des k.k. österreichischen Museums für Kunst und Industrie* 144 (1897).

MACIUIKA, JOHN. *Before the Bauhaus: Architecture, Politics, and the German State.* New York: Cambridge University Press, 2005.

MALLGRAVE, HARRY FRANCIS. "A Commentary on the November Lecture." *RES* 6 (Autumn 1983): 23–31.

———. "The Idea of Style: Gottfried Semper in London." Ph.D. diss., University of Pennsylvania, 1983.

———. "Gustav Klemm and Gottfried Semper." *RES* 9 (Spring 1985): 69–80.

———. "Adolf Loos and the Ornament of Sentiment." *Midgard* 1 (1987): 79–87.

———. "From Realism to *Sachlichkeit*: The Polemics of Architectural Modernity in the 1890s." In Harry Francis Mallgrave, ed., *Otto Wagner: Reflections on the Raiment of Modernity.* Santa Monica: Getty Center, 1993, 281–321.

———. ED. AND TRANS. *Empathy, Form, and Space: Problems in German Aesthetics, 1873–1893.* Santa Monica: Getty Center, 1994.

———. *Gottfried Semper, Architect of the Nineteenth Century.* New Haven: Yale University Press, 1996.

MARCH, H. COLLEY. "The Meaning of Ornament, or Its Archaeology and Its Psychology." *Transactions of the Cheshire and Lancashire Anthropological Society*, 1889.

MARCHAND, SUZANNE L. *Down from Olympus: Archaeology and Philhellenism in Germany, 1750–1970.* Princeton, N.J.: Princeton University Press, 1996.

MARTIN, SYLVIE. "The École Nationale des Arts Décoratifs in Paris: Architecture and the Applied Arts Between the World Wars." *Studies in the Decorative Arts* 8, no. 1 (Spring–Summer 2001): 77–104.

MASHEK, JOSEPH. "The Carpet Paradigm: Critical Prolegomena to a Theory of Flatness." *Arts Magazine* 51 (September 1976): 82–109.

MAYER, HARTMUT. *Die Tektonik der Hellenen: Kontext und Wirkung der Architekturtheorie von Karl Bötticher.* Suttgart: Axel Menges, 2004.

MCLEOD, MARY. "Architecture or Revolution." *Art Journal* 43 (Summer 1983): 132–47.

MEAD, CHRISTOPHER CURTIS. *Charles Garnier's Paris Opéra: Architectural Empathy and the Renaissance of French Classicism.* Cambridge, Mass.: The Architectural History Foundation, 1991.

MELVILLE, STEPHEN, ED. *The Lure of the Object.* New Haven: Yale University Press, 2005.

MENNINGHAUS, WINFRIED. *Das Versprechen der Schönheit.* Berlin: Suhrkamp, 2003.

MERTINS, DETLEF. "Architecture of Becoming: Mies and the Avant-Garde." In B. Bergdoll and T. Riley, eds., *Mies in Berlin.* Exh. cat. New York: MoMA, 2001, 106–33.

MEYER, FRANZ SALES. *Ornamentale Formenlehre.* Leipzig, 1886.

MICHAELIS, ADOLF. "Ernst Curtius." *Biographische Jahrbuch und Deutscher Nekrolog.* Ed. A. Bettelheim. Berlin: Georg Reimer, 1897, 56–88.

MICHAUD, PHILIPPE-ALAIN. *Aby Warburg et l'image en mouvement.* Paris: Macula, 1998.

MILLER LANE, BARBARA. *National Romanticism and Modern Architecture in Germany and the Scandinavian Countries*, New York: Cambridge University Press, 2000.

MOOS, STANISLAUS VON. "Le Corbusier und Loos." In *L'Esprit Nouveau: Le Corbusier und die Industrie, 1920–1925.* Zurich: Museum für Gestaltung, 1987, 122–133.

———. "Giedion e il suo tempo." *Rassegna* 25 (1979): 6–17.

MORAVANSKY, AKOS. "Die Entdeckung des Nahen." In A. Moravansky, ed., *Das entfernte Dorf.* Vienna: Böhlau, 2002, 95–123.

MORGAN, DAVID. "The Idea of Abstraction in German Theories of Ornament from Kant to Kandinsky." *Journal of Aesthetics and Art Criticism* 50 (Summer 1992): 231–42.

MORITZ, KARL PHILIPP. *Vorbegriffe einer Theorie der Ornamente von K. P. Moritz.* 1793, facs. ed.; Nördlingen: Dr. Alfons Uhl, 1986.

MÜLLER, SEBASTIAN. "Ästhetische Erlösermystik an der Quelle der funktionalistischen Kulturrevolution. Zur Stellung des Deutschen Museums für Kunst im Handel und Gewerbe in der Kunstgeschichte." *Der westdeuschte Impuls, 1900–1914: Kunst und Umweltgestaltung im Industriegebiet. Das Museum zwischen Jugendstil und Werkbund.* Krefeld: Kaiser Wilhelm Museum, 1984, 23–52.

MUNDT, BARBARA. *Die deutschen Kunstgewerbemuseen im 19. Jahrhundert.* Munich: Prestel, 1974.

MUTHESIUS, HERMANN. "Künstlerischer Unterricht für Handwerker in England." *Dekorative Kunst* 1 (1898): 15–20.

———. "Italiensiche Reise-eindrücke." *Centralblatt der Bauverwaltung* 18 (1898): 378, 386, 393, 423, 433.

———. "England." In Richard Graul, ed., *Die Krisis im Kunstgewerbe: Studien über die Wege und Ziele der modernen Richtung.* Leipzig: S. Herzel, 1901, 1–20.

———. *Style-Architecture and Building-Art (Stilarchitektur und Baukunst).* Intro. and trans. S. Anderson. 1902; Santa Monica: Getty Center, 1996.

———. *Kultur und Kunst: Gesammelte Aufsätze.* 1904; Nendeln: Kraus, 1976.

———. *Kunstgewerbe und Architektur.* 1907; Nendeln: Kraus, 1976.

———. "Neues Ornament und neue Kunst." *Die Kunst* 4, no. 9 (1901): 349–66.

———. "Kunst und Maschiene." *Die Kunst* 5, no. 1 (1902): 141–47.

———. "Die moderne Umbildungen unserer äesthetischen Anschauungen." *Deutsche Monatsschrift für das gesamte Leben der Gegenwart* 1 (1902): 686–702.

———. "Der Weg und das Endziel des Kunstgewerbes." *Die Kunst* 9, nos. 5–6 (1905): 181–238.

———. "Die Bedeutung des Kunstgewerbes." *Die Kunst* 10, no. 5 (1907): 177–92.

———. "Wo stehen wir?" In *Jahrbuch des Deutschen Werkbundes: Die Durchgeistigung der deutschen Arbeit. Wege und Ziele in Zusammenhang von Industrie/Handwerk und Kunst.* Jena: Diederichs, 1912, 11–26.

———."DAS *Formproblem* IM INGENIEURBAU." In *Jahrbuch des Deutschen Werkbundes* (1913).

MUTHESIUS, STEFAN. *Das englische Vorbild.* Munich: Prestel, 1974.

NAUMANN, FRIEDRICH. "Kunst und Industrie." In *Das deutsche Kunstgewerbe, 1906.* Munich: F. Bruckmann, 1906, 32–35.

NEF, FREDERIC. *L'objet quelconque: Recherches sur l'ontologie de l'objet*. Paris: J. Vrin, 1998

NÈGRE, VALERIE. *L'ornement en serie: Architecture, terre cuite et carton-pierre*. Sprimont: Madraga, 2006.

NERDINGER, WINFRIED, AND WERNER OECHSLIN, EDS. *Gottfried Semper, 1803–1897: Architektur und Wissenschaft*, Museum für Gestaltung Zurich 01.11, 2003–25.01, 2004. Exh. cat. Zurich: GTA, and Berlin: Prestel Verlag, 2004.

NODELMAN, SHELDON. "Structural Analysis in Art and Anthropology." In J. Ehrmann, *Structuralism*. Garden City, N.Y.: Doubleday, 1966, 79–94.

NOEVER, PETER, ED. *Kunst und Industrie: Die Anfänge des Museums für Angewandte Kunst in Wien*. Vienna: Hatje Cantz, 2000.

OCKMAN, JOAN. "Lessons from Objects: Perriand from the Pioneer Years to the 'Epoch of Realities.'" In M. McLeod, ed., *Charlotte Perriand: An Art of Living*. New York: Harry Abrams, 154–81.

OCÓN-FERNÁNDEZ, MARIA. *Ornament und Moderne: Theoriebildung und Ornamentdebatte im deutschen Architekturdiskurs (1850–1930)*. Berlin: Reimer, 2004.

OECHSLIN, WERNER. "The Evolutionary Way to Modern Architecture: The Paradigm of *Stilhülse und Kern*." In *Otto Wagner: Reflections on the Raiment of Modernity*, edited by Harry F. Malgrave, 363–410. Santa Monica: Getty Center, 1993.

———. "In Search of 'True Style.' The Rigorists' Distinction between 'Right' and 'Wrong.'" *Daidalos* 8 (June 1983): 21–37.

OLIN, MARGARET. *Forms of Representation in Alois Riegl's Theory of Art*. University Park, Pa., 1992.

———. "Self-Representation: Resemblance and Convention in Two Nineteenth-Century Theories of Architecture and the Decorative Arts." *Zeitschrift für Kunstgeschichte* 1 (1986): 376–97.

OTTILLINGER, EVA. *Adolf Loos: Wohnungskonzepte und Möbelentwürfe*. Salzburg: Residenz, 1994.

PAGLIANI, MARIA LUIGIA. "L'archaeologia italiana nella seconda meta'dell '800 e la formazione del metodo Morelliano." In G. Agosti et al., eds., *Giovanni Morelli e la cultura dei conoscitori*. Bergamo: Pierluigi Lubrina, 1993, 399–407.

PASSANTI, FRANCESCO. "Architecture: Proportion, Classicism, and Other Issues." In Stanislaus von Moos and Arthur Rüegg, eds., *Le Corbusier Before Le Corbusier*. New Haven: Yale University Press, 2002, 69–98.

PAUL, JÜRGEN. *Cornelius Gurlitt*. Dresden: Hellerau-Verlag, 2003.

PAYNE, ALINA. "Rudolf Wittkower and Architectural Principles in the Age of Modernism." *Journal of the Society of Architectural Historians* 54 (September 1994).

———. "Creativity and *Bricolage* in Architectural Literature of the Renaissance." *RES* 34 (Fall 1998).

———. "Architectural History and the History of Art: A Suspended Dialogue." *Journal of the Society of Architectural Historians*, Special Millennium Issue, 59–60 (September–December 1999): 292–99.

———. *The Architectural Treatise in the Italian Renaissance: Architectural Invention, Ornament and Literary Culture*. Cambridge: Cambridge University Press, 1999.

———. "Architects and Academies: Architectural Theories of *imitatio* and the Debates on Language and Style." In G. Clarke and P. Crossley, eds., *Architecture and Language*. New York: Cambridge University Press, 2000, 118–33 and 195–202.

———. "Reclining Bodies: Figural Ornament in Renaissance Architecture." In R. Tavernor and G. Dodds, eds., *Body and Building*. Cambridge, Mass.: MIT Press, 2001, 94–113, 375–78.

———. "Von *ornatus* zu *figura*: Das figürliche Ornament in der italienischen Architektur des 16. Jahrhunderts." In I. Frank and F. Hartung, eds., *Die Rhetorik des Ornaments*. Berlin: Fink Verlag, 2001, 205–239.

———. "Vasari, Architecture, and the Origins of Historicizing Art." *RES* 40 (Fall 2001): 51–76.

———. "Architecture and Objects: The Power of Pevsner." *Harvard Design Magazine* (Spring 2002): 66–70.

———. "Architecture, Ornament and Pictorialism: Notes on the Relationship between the Arts from Wölfflin to Le Corbusier." In K. Koehler, ed., *The Built Surface*. London: Ashgate, 2002, 54–72.

———. "Portable Ruins: The Pergamon Altar, Heinrich Wölfflin, and German Art History at the *fin de siècle*." *RES* 54/55 (Spring–Autumn 2008): 168–89.

———. "Bauhaus Endgame: Ambiguity, Anxiety, and Discomfort." In J. Saletnik and R. Schuldenfrei, eds., *Bauhaus Construct*. London: Routledge, 2009.

———. "Materiality, Crafting and Scale in Renaissance Architecture." *Oxford Art Journal* 32, no. 3 (December 2009): 365–86.

———. "Beyond *Kunstwollen*: Alois Riegl and the Theoretization the Baroque." In Alois Riegl, *The Origin of Baroque Art in Rome*. Los Angeles: Getty Institute, 2010, 1–33.

———. "L'Ornament architectural: du langage classique des temps modernes à l'aube du XXe siècle." *Perspective. Revue de l'INHA*, 2010, 1: 77–96.

———. "Notes from the Field: Anthropomorphism," *Art Bulletin*, March 2012, 29–31.

PAUL, JÜRGEN. *Cornelius Gurlitt*. Dresden: Hellerau, 2003.

PERRIAND, CHARLOTTE. "Wood or Metal?" *Studio* 97, no. 433 (April 1929): 278–79.

———. *Io, Charlotte: Tra Le Corbusier, Léger e Jeanneret*. Bari: Laterza, 2006.

PEVSNER, NIKOLAUS. Review of Le Corbusier and Jeanneret, Pierre, *Ihr gesamtes Werk von 1910 bis 1929*. In *Göttingische gelehrte Anzeigen* 8 (August 1931): 303–12.

———. *Pioneers of the Modern Movement: From William Morris to Walter Gropius*. London: Faber and Faber, 1936.

———. *An Enquiry into Industrial Art in England*. Cambridge: Cambridge University Press, 1937.

PFLEIDERER, WOLFGANG. "Introduction." In W. Riezler, ed., *Die Form ohne Ornament. Werkbundausstellung 1924*. Berlin: Deutsche Verlags-Anstalt, Stuttgart, 1924, 3–22.

PISANI, SALVATORE. "'Die Monumente sind durch Barbarei monochrom geworden.' Zu den theoretischen Leitmaximen in Sempers *Vorläufige Bemerkungen über bemalte Architektur und Plastik bei den Alten*." In *Gottfried Semper, 1803–1879*. Ed. W. Nerdinger and W. Oechslin. Zurich: GTA Verlag, 2003, 109–23.

PLANCHÉ, J R. *An Encyclopaedia of Costume or Dictionary of Dress*. London: Chatto and Windus, 1876.

PLATZ, GUSTAV ADOLF. *Die Baukunst der neuesten Zeit*. Berlin: Propyläen-Verlag and Bauwelt, 1927.

PODRO, MICHAEL. *The Critical Historians of Art*. New Haven: Yale University Press, 1982.

———. *Manifold in Perception: Theories of Art from Kant to Hildebrand*. Oxford: Clarendon Press, 1972.

POKORNY-NAGEL, KATHRIN. "Zur Gründungsgeschichte des k.k. Österreichischen Museums für Kunst und Industrie." In P. Noever, ed., *Kunst und Industrie: Die Anfänge des Museums für Angewandte Kunst in Wien*. Vienna: Hatje Cantz, 2000, 52–89.

PONS, BRUNO. *De Paris a Versailles, 1699–1736: Les sculpteurs ornemantistes parisiens et l'art décoratif des Bâtiments du roi*. Strasbourg: Universités de Strasbourg, 1986.

PUGIN, AUGUSTUS W. N. *Designs for Gold and Silversmiths*. London: Ackerman, 1836.

———. *Floriated Ornament*. London: Bohn, 1849.

———. *Glossary of Ecclesiastical Ornament and Costume*. London: Bohn, 1844.

———. *Gothic Furniture in the Style of the 15th Century*. London: Ackerman, 1835.

———. *Gothic Ornaments, Selected from Various Ancient Buildings, Both in England and France*. London: Bohn, 1831.

———. *Ornaments of the XVth and XVIth Centuries*. London: M. A. Nattali, 1837.

PURCHLA, JACEK, AND WOLF TEGETHOFF, EDS. *Nation, Style, Modernism*. Cracow: International Cultural Center and Zentralinstitut für Kunstgeschichte, 2006.

RACINET, AUGUSTE. *Le costume historique*. 6 vols. Paris: Firmin-Didot, 1876–88.

———. *Ornement polychrome*. Paris: 1875.

READ, HERBERT. *Art in Industry*. London: Faber, 1934.

REDGRAVE, RICHARD. *Manual of Design: Compiled from the Writings and Addresses of Richard Redgrave*. London: Chapman and Hall, 1876.

———. *Report on Design: A Supplement to the Report of the Jury of Class XXX of the Exhibition of 1851*. London: William Clowes and Sons, 1852.

REISING, KURT. "Kunst, Industrie und die Gesellschaft in England." In Peter Noever, ed., *Kunst und Industrie: Die Anfänge des Museums für Angewandte Kunst in Wien*. Vienna: Hatje Cantz, 2000, 49–66.

RENNHOFER, MARIA. *Kunstzeitschriften der Jahrhundertwende in Deutschland und Österreich, 1895–1914*. Vienna: Christian Brandstaetter, 1987.

REULEAUX, FRANZ. *Technology and Civilization*. Washington, D.C.: Government Printing Office, 1891.

———. *Theoretische Kinematik: Grundzüge einer Theorie des Maschienenwesens*. Braunschweig: Friedrich Vieweg, 1875.

RICHARDS, J. M. "Towards a Rational Aesthetics." *Architectural Review* 78 (July–December 1935).

RIEGL, ALOIS. *Die mittelalterliche Kalenderillustration, ihr Ursprung und Entwicklung bis zur vollständigen Ausbildung der Typen im 11. Jahrhundert*. Innsbruck: Wagner'sche Universität-Buchdruckerei, 1889.

———. "Neuseeländische Ornamentik." *Mittheilungen der anthropologischen Gesellschaft in Wien* 20 (1890): 84–87.

———. *Altorientalische Teppiche*. Leipzig, 1891.

———. *Stilfragen: Grundlegungen zu einer Geschichte der Ornamentik*. Berlin: Georg Siemens, 1893.

———. *Problems of Style: Foundations for a History of Ornament*. Trans. Evelyn Kain (*Stilfragen*, 1893). Princeton, N.J.: Princeton University Press, 1992.

———. *Die Entstehung der Barockkunst in Rom*. Vienna, 1908.

———. *Historische Grammatik der bildenden Künste*. Graz, 1966.

———. "Der moderne Denkmalkultus, sein Wesen, seine Entstehung." *Gesammelte Aufsätze*. Ed. A. Rosenauer. 1905; Vienna: WUV, 1996.

———. *Spätrömische Kunstindustrie*. 1901; Darmstadt: Wissenschaftliche Buchgesellschaft, 1964.

———. *Volkskunst, Haussfleiss und Hausindustrie*. Berlin, 1894.

———. "Pferdeschmuck aus Westungarn." *K.K. Zentral-Kommission für Kunst-und historische Denkmäle* 1 (1903).

———. *Gesammelte Schriften*. Intro. by Hans Sedlmayr. 1927; Vienna: WUV-Universitätsverlag, 1996.

RIEHL, WILHELM H. von. "Kunstarchitektur und Volksbauart." In Riehl et al., eds., *Bavaria, Landes-und Volkskunde des Königreichs Bayern*. Munich: Literarisch- artistische Anstalt, Cotta'schen Buchhandlung, 1860.

ROSENAUER, ARTUR. "L'école de Vienne. L'autonomie de l'histoire de l'art?" In *Histoire de l'histoire de l'art*, vol. 2. Ed. E. Pommier. Paris: Louvre and Klincksieck, 1997, 415–41.

ROTH, FEDOR. *Hermann Muthesius und die Idee der harmonischen Kultur*. Berlin: Gebrüder Mann, 2001.

RÜEGG, ARTHUR. "Der Pavillon de L'Esprit Nouveau als musée imaginaire." In *L'Esprit Nouveau: Le Corbusier und die Industrie, 1920–1925*. Zurich: Museum für Gestaltung, 1987, 134–51.

———. "Marcel Lavaillant and 'la question du mobilier.'" In Stanislaus von Moos and Arthur Rüegg, eds., *Le Corbusier Before Le Corbusier*. New Haven: Yale University Press, 2002, 109–31.

———. "Autobiografische Interieurs: Die Wohnungen Le Corbusiers." In Vitra Museum, *Le Corbusier: The Art of Architecture*. Weil-am-Rhein: Vitra Museum, 2007.

RUPP-EISENREICH, B., AND J. STAGL, EDS. *Kulturwissenschaften im Vielvölkerstaat*. Vienna: Böhlau, 1995.

RUSKIN, JOHN. *The Stones of Venice*. Orpington, Kent, 1881.

———. *The Seven Lamps of Architecture*. 1880; London: Dover, 1889.

RYKWERT, JOSEPH. "Semper and the Conception of Style." In E. Börsch-Soupan, ed., *Gottfried Semper und die Mitte des 19 Jahrhunderts*. Basel: Birkhauser, 1976.

———. *On Adam's House in Paradise*. Cambridge, Mass.: MIT Press, 1981.

———. *The Dancing Column*. Cambridge, Mass.: MIT Press, 1998.

SALIN, BERNHARD. *Ur Djur-och Vaxtmotivens Ut vecklingshistoria*. Stockholm: Haeggstrom, 1890.

SALETNIK, JEFFREY. "Pedagogic Objects: Josef Albers, Greenbergian Modernism and the Bauhaus in America." In J. Saletnik and R. Schuldenfrei, eds., *Bauhaus Construct*. London: Routledge, 2009, 83–102.

SANKOVITCH, ANNE-MARIE. "Structure/Ornament and the Modern Figuration of Architecture." *Art Bulletin* 80, no. 4 (1998): 687–717.

SCHASLER, M. "Die Kunstindustrie vom kulturpolitischen Gesichtspunkt: Ein Beitrag zur Philosophie des Luxus." *Kunst und Gewerbe* 1. Leipzig, 1867, 66–67.

SCHATTEBURG, H. "Das Kunstschöne und die Kunstgewerbeschulen." *Allgemeine Bauzeitung*, 1892.

———. "Der Einfluss der Maschiene auf das Gewerbe. " *Allgemeine Bauzeitung*, 1893.

———. "Eine Skizze zur kulturgeschichtlichen Entwicklung der Stylarten." *Allgemeine Bauzeitung*, 1894.

———. "Einiges über die Farbe in der Architektur." *Allgemeine Bauzeitung*, 1895.

SCHEFFLER, KARL. *Der Geist der Gotik.* Leipzig: Insel, 1922.

———. *Italien. Tagebuch einer Reise.* Leipzig: Insel, 1916.

———. *Moderne Baukunst.* 1907; Leipzig: Julius Zeitler, 1908.

SCHINKEL, KARL FRIEDRICH. *Aus Schinkel's Nachlass*, edited by A. Freiherr v Wolzogen. 4 vols. Berlin, 1862–64.

SCHLOSSER, JULIUS VON. "Die Wiener Schule der Kunstgeschichte." *Mitteilungen des österreichischen Instituts für Geschichtsschreibung* 13, no. 2 (1954).

SCHMARSOW, AUGUST. "Anfangsgründe jeder Ornamentik." *Zeitschrift für Ästhetik und allgemeine Kunstwissenschaft* (1910): 191–215, 321–55.

———. *Zur Frage nach dem Malerischen.* Leipzig: S. Hirzel, 1896.

———. *Barock und Rokoko oder Über das Malerische in der Architektur.* Leipzig: S. Hirzel, 1897.

———. "Die reine Form in der Ornamentik aller Künste." *Zeitschrift für Ästhetik* 16 (1922): 491–500; 17 (1923): 1–17, 129–45, 209–34, 305–29; 18 (1924): 83–107.

———. *Unser Verhältnis zu den bildenden Künsten.* Leipzig: Teubner, 1903.

———. "Vom Wesen des Ornamentes." *Innendekoration* 36 (1925).

———. "Kunstwissenschaft und Kulturphilosophie mit gemeinsamen Grundbegriffen." *Zeitschrift für Ästhetik und allgemeine Kunstwissenschaft* 13 (1919): 165–90, 225–58.

———. "Ein Entwurf Michelangelo's zum Grabmal Julius II." *Jahrbuch der königlichen preussischen Kunstsammlungen* 5 (1884): 63–231.

———. *Das Wesen der architektonischen Schöpfung.* Leipzig, 1894.

———. "Zur Lehre vom Ornament." *Zeitschrift für Ästhetik und allgemeine Kunstwissenschaft* 16 (1922): 511–26.

SCHMIDT, LEOPOLD. *Das österreichische Museum für Volkskunde.* Vienna, 1960.

SCHMITT, FRANZ JACOB. "Nekrolog Karl Bötticher." *Deutscher Nekrolog*, 1889, 80.

SCHNEIDER-HENN, DIETRICH. *Ornament und Dekoration.* Munich: Prestel, 1997.

SCHOR, NAOMI. *Reading in Detail: Ästhetics and the Feminine.* New York: Methuen, 1987.

SCHULDENFREI, ROBIN. "The Irreproducibility of the Bauhaus Object." In J. Saletnik and R. Schuldenfrei, eds., *Bauhaus Construct.* London: Routledge, 2009, 37–60.

SCHUMACHER, FRITZ. *Das Bauschaffen der Jetzzeit in historische Überlieferung.* Leipzig: Diederichs, 1901.

———. "Die Architektur und die Decoration auf der Pariser Weltaustellung." In R. Graul, ed., *Die Krisis im Kunstgewerbe.* Leipzig: S. Hirsel, 1901, 215–37.

———. *Streifzüge eines Architekten: Gesammelte Aufsätze.* Jena: Diederichs, 1907.

SCHWARTZ, FREDERIC. *The Werkbund: Design Theory and Mass Culture Before the First World War.* New Haven: Yale University Press, 1996.

———. "Cathedrals and Shoes: Concepts of Style in Wölfflin and Adorno." *New German Critique* 76 (Winter 1999): 3–48.

SCHWARZER, MITCHELL W. *German Architecture Theory and the Search for Modern Identity.* New York, 1995.

———. "Ontology and Representation in Karl Bötticher's Theory of Tectonics." *JSAH* 52 (September 1993): 267–80.

———. "Ethnologies of the Primitive in Adolf Loos's Writings on Ornament." *Nineteenth-Century Contexts* 18 (1994): 225–47.

———. "The Emergence of Architectural Space: August Schmarsow's Theory of *Raumgestaltung*." *Assemblage* 15 (1991): 50–61.

SEIDEL, MAX. "Das Renaissance Museum. Wilhelm Bode als "Schüler" Jacob Burckhardt's." In Max Seidel, ed., *Storia dell'arte e politica culturale intorno al 1900.* Venice: Marsilio, 1999, 55–108.

SEMPER, GOTTFRIED. *Die vier Elemente der Baukunst.* Braunschweig: Vieweg und Sohn, 1851.

———. *The Four Elements of Architecture (1851) and Other Writings.* Ed. W. Herrmann. Cambridge, 1989.

———. "On the Study of Polychromy and Its Revival." *Museum of Classical Antiquities* 3 (July 1851).

———. "On the Origin of Polychromy in Architecture." Appendix to Owen Jones, *An Apology for the Colouring of the Greek Court.* London, 1854, 1: 212.

———. *Kleine Schriften.* Zurich: Meyer and Zeller, 1856. Ed. Manfred and Hans Semper.

———. "Über die formelle Gesetzmässigkeit des Schmuckes und dessen Bedeutung als Kunstsymbol." *Monatsheft des wissenschaftlichen Vereins.* Zurich: Meyer and Zeller, 1856.

———. *Der Stil in den technischen und tektonischen Künsten oder Praktische Äesthetik.* 2 vols. 1860–63; Munich: F. Bruckmann, 1878.

———. *Style: Style in the Technical and Tectonic Arts.* Los Angeles: Getty Research Institute, 2004.

———. *Wissenschaft, Industrie und Kunst und andere Schriften.* Ed. Hans Wingler. Mainz: Florian Kupferberg, 1966.

———. "Theorie des Formell-Schönen." In Wolfgang Hermann, *Gottfried Semper in Search of Architecture.* Cambridge, Mass.: MIT Press, 1984, 219.

———. "Science, Industry and Art." In *The Four Elements of Architecture.* Cambridge: Cambridge University Press, 1989.

SHALEM, AVINOAM. "Objects as Carriers of Real or Contrived Memories in a Cross-Cultural Context." *Mitteilungen zur Spätantike Archäologie und Byzantinischen Kunstgeschichte* 4 (2005): 101–19.

SHAND, MORTON P. "The Architecture of Wine." *Architectural Review* 66 (1929): 101–87.

———. "Underground." *Architectural Review* 66 (1929): 217–25.

SHAW, HENRY. *The Encyclopedia of Ornament.* London: William Pickering, 1842.

SIMMEL, GEORG. "Fashion." In *Georg Simmel on Individuality and Social Forms: Selected Writings.* Ed. D. Levine. Chicago, 1971.

SNODIN, MICHAEL. *Karl Friedrich Schinkel: A Universal Man.* New Haven: Yale University Press, 1991.

SNODIN, MICHAEL, AND MAURICE HOWARD. *Ornament: A Social History Since 1450.* London, 1996.

SOHM, PHILIP. *Style in the Art Theory of Early Modern Italy*. New York: Cambridge University Press, 2002.

SOMBART, WERNER. *Technik und Wirtschaft*. Dresden: Vortag and Zahn and Jaensch, 1901.

———. *Die gewerbliche Arbeiterfrage*. Leipzig: G. J. Göschen, 1904.

———. *Gewerbewesen*. Leipzig: G. J. Göschen, 1904.

———. *Kunstgewerbe und Kultur*. Berlin: Marquardt, 1908.

SPELTZ, ALEXANDER. *Styles of Ornament*. Berlin: Hessling, 1906 (trans. of 2nd German ed.).

SPENGLER, OSWALD. *The Decline of the West*. New York: Knopf, 1934.

STALLYBRASS, PETER. "Marx's Coat." In P. Speyer, ed., *Border Fetishisms: Material Objects in Unstable Spaces*. New York: Routledge, 1998, 183–207.

STEWART, SUSAN. *On Longing: Narratives of the Miniature, the Gigantic, the Souvenir, the Collection*. Durham, N.C.: Duke University Press, 1993.

STOCKING, GEORGE W. JR. *Victorian Anthropology*. New York: Free Press, 1987.

STOLPE, HJALMAR. "Entwicklungerscheinungen in der Ornamentik der Naturvölker." *Mittheilungen der Anthropologischen Gesellschaft in Wien* 22 (1890): 19–62.

STREITER, RICHARD. *Karl Bötticher's Tektonik der Hellenen als ästhetische und kunstgeschichtliche Theorie: Eine Kritik*. Hamburg: Leopold Voss, 1896.

———. *Ausgewählte Schriften*. Munich: Delphin, 1913.

SULLIVAN, LOUIS H. *A System of Architectural Ornament, According with a Philosophy of Man's Powers*. New York, 1920.

TAFURI, MANFREDO. *Architecture and Utopia: Design and Capitalist Development*. Cambridge, Mass.: MIT Press, 1976. (First published in *Contropiano* 1 [1969].)

TAMEN, MIGUEL. *Friends of Interpretable Objects*. Cambridge, Mass.: Harvard University Press, 2001.

THAUSING, MORITZ. "Die Stellung der Kunstgeschichte als Wissenschaft." In M. Thausing, *Wiener Kunstbriefe*. Leipzig: E. A. Seemann, 1884, 1–20.

———. "Ivan Lermoliew." In Thausing, *Wiener Kunstbriefe*. Leipzig: E. A. Seemann, 1884, 183–90.

TROY, NANCY. *Modernism and the Decorative Arts in France*. New Haven: Yale University Press, 1991.

TRZESCHTIK, L. "Die Architektur und ihr Verhältniss zur Malerei, Plastik und Gartenkunst." *Allgemeine Bauzeitung*, 1888, 12, 20.

———. "Die Prinzipien der Baukunst. "*Allgemeine Bauzeitung*, 1891, 4, 13, 20, 27.

TURNER, PAUL VENABLE. *The Education of Le Corbusier*. New York: Garland, 1977.

UMBACH, MAIKEN. "The Vernacular International: *Heimat*, Modernism and the Global Market in Early Twentieth-Century Germany." *National Identities* 4, no. 1 (2002): 45–68.

VAN DE VELDE, HENRY. *Kunstgewerbliche Laienpredigten*. Leipzig: Hermann Seemann, 1902.

———. *Formules de la beauté architectonique moderne*. 1917; Brussels, 1978.

VIOLLET-LE-DUC, EUGÈNE EMMANUEL. *The Architectural Theory of Viollet-le-Duc*. Ed. M. F. Hearn. Cambridge, Mass., 1995.

———. *Dictionnaire raisonnée du mobilier français de l'époque carlovinginenne à la Renaissance*. Paris: Librairie centrale d'architecture, 1873–74.

VITRA MUSEUM. *Le Corbusier: The Art of Architecture*. Weil-am-Rhein: Vitra Museum, 2007.

VITRUVIUS, MARCUS POLLIO. *De architectura: On Architecture*. London: Loeb Classical Library, 1983.

VOGT, ADOLF MAX. "Gottfried Semper und Joseph Paxton." In E. Börsch-Soupan, ed., *Gottfried Semper und die Mitte des 19. Jahrhunderts*. Basel: Birkhäuser, 1977, 193–95.

VOLKELT, JOHANNES. *Der Symbolbegriff in der neuesten Ästhetik*. Jena: H. Dufft, 1876.

WAENTIG, HEINRICH. *Wirtschaft und Kunst: Eine Untersuchung über die Geschichte und Theorie der modernen Kunstgewerbebewegung*. Jena: Gustav Fischer, 1909.

WAGNER, OTTO. *Modern Architecture*. Intro. and trans. Harry Francis Mallgrave. Santa Monica: Getty Center, 1988.

WARBURG, ABY. *The Renewal of Pagan Antiquity*. Intro. K. Forster. Texts and Documents. Santa` Monica: Getty Research Institute, 1999.

WARD, JAMES. *Historic Ornament: Treatise on Decorative and Architectural Ornament*. London: Chapman and Hall, 1897.

WARNKE, MARTIN. "L'emprise de son époque." In J. Hart, R. Recht, and M. Warnke, eds., *Relire Wölfflin*. Paris: Musée du Louvre, 1995.

WEINGARDEN, LAUREN. "Sullivan's Ornament and the Poetics of Architecture." In *Chicago Architecture, 1872–1922: Birth of a Metropolis*. Chicago: Art Institute of Chicago, 1987.

WIENINGER, JOHANNES. "'Er brachte viel Eigenatrtiges und Notwendiges mit.' Arthur von Scala als Mittler zwischen Ost und West und die Grundlegung der Asiensammlung des heutigen Museums der angewandten Kunst." In *Kunst und Industrie: Die Anfange des M useums für Angewandte Kunst in Wien*. Vienna: Hatje Cantz, 2000, 164–74.

WIGLEY, MARK. *White Walls, Designer Dresses*. Cambridge, Mass.: MIT Press, 1995.

WILHELM, SIBYLLE. *"Kunstgewerbebewegung": Ästhetische Welt oder Macht durch Kunst?* Frankfurt am Main: Peter Lang, 1991.

WIND, E. "Warburg's Concept of Kulturwissenschaft and Its Meaning for Aesthetics." In E. Wind, *The Eloquence of Symbols*. Oxford: Clarendon, 1983.

WINTER, FREDERICK. *Studies in Hellenistic Architecture*. Toronto: University of Toronto Press, 2006.

WOGENSCKY, ANDRÉ. "Movement, Furniture and Le Corbusier." Paris, 1978 (Typed Manuscript) in *The LC4 Chaise Longue by Le Corbusier, Pierre Jeanneret and Charlotte Perriand, Volker Fischer*. Frankfurt am Main: Form, 1997.

WOHLFARTH, IRVING. "'Construction Has the Role of the Subconscious': Phantasmagorias of the Master Builder (with Constant Reference to Giedion, Weber, Nietzsche, Ibsen and Benjamin)." In A. Kostka and I. Wohlfarth, eds., *Nietzsche and "An Architecture of Our Minds."* Santa Monica: Getty Issues and Debates, 1999.

WOLFF, JOHANN HEINRICH. *Beiträge zur Ästhetik der Baukunst oder die Grundgesätze der plastischen Form, nachgewiesen an den Haupttheilen der griechischen Architektur*. Leipzig, 1834.

WÖLFFLIN, HEINRICH. "Prolegomena zu einer Psychologie der Architektur." In *Kleine Schriften*. Ed. J. Gantner. 1886; Basel: Benno Schwabe, 1946, 13–47.

———. *Renaissance und Barock: Eine Untersuchung über Wesen und Entstehung des Barockstils in Italien*. 1888; Munich: F. Bruckmann, 1907.

———. Review of August Thiersch. *Deutsche Bauzeitung*, 1889.

———. Review of A. Schmarsow. *Das Wesen der architektonischen Schöpfung*. In *Repertorium für Kunstwissenschaft* 17 (1894): 141–42.

———. *Die Klassiche Kunst: Eine Einführung in die italienische Renaissance*. Munich: F. Bruckmann, 1899.

———. *Die Kunst Albrecht Dürer's*. Munich: F. Bruckmann, 1905.

———. Review of A. Riegl, *Entstehung der Barockkunst in Rom*. In *Repertorium für Kunstwissenschaft* 31 (1908): 356–57.

———. *Kunstgeschichtliche Grundbegriffe: Das Problem der Stilentwicklung in der neueren Kunst*. 1915; Munich: Hugo Bruckmann, 1920.

———. *Gedanken zur Kunstgeschichte: Gedrucktes und Ungedrucktes*. 1940; Basel: Benno Schwabe, 1941.

———. *Kleine Schriften*. Ed. J. Gantner. Basel: Benno Schwabe, 1946.

WOOD, CHRISTOPHER. "Introduction." In C. Wood, *The Vienna School Reader*. New York: Zone, 2000.

———. "Riegl's 'Mache.'" *RES* 46 (Autumn 2004): 154–72.

WOODFIELD, RICHARD. *Framing Formalism: Riegl and the History of Art*. Amsterdam: G+B Arts, 1999.

WOODWARD, W., AND M. ASH, EDS. *The Problematic Science: Psychology in Nineteenth-Century Thought*. New York, 1982.

WÖRNER, MARTIN. *Vergnügung und Belehrung: Volkskultur auf de n Weltausstellungen, 1851–1900*. New York: Waxmann, 1999.

———. *Die Welt an einem Ort*. Berlin: Dietrich Reimer, 2000.

WORNUM, RALPH. *Analysis of Ornament: The Characteristics of Styles. An Introduction to the Study of the History of Ornamental Art*. Lectures given 1848–50. 6th ed. London: Chapman and Hall, 1855.

WORRINGER, WILHELM. *Abstraction and Empathy: A Contribution to the Psychology of Style*. 1908; New York, 1967.

———. *Abstraktion und Einfühlung*. Neuwied: Heuser, 1907.

———. *Form in Gothic*. Ed. Herbert Read. 1910; London: G. P. Putnam, 1927.

———. *Formprobleme der Gotik*. 1910.

WYATT, MATTHEW DIGBY. *An Attempt to Define the Principles Which Should Determine Form in the Decorative Arts*. London: G. Barclay, 1852.

ZAHN, WILHELM J. K. *Ornamente aller klassischen Kunstepochen nach den Originalen in ihren eigentümlichen Farben*. Berlin: Reimer, 1843.

VAN ZANTEN, DAVID. *The Architectural Polychromy of the 1830s*. New York, 1977.

ZEISING, A. *Äesthetische Forschungen*. Frankfurt am Main, 1855.

ZIMMERMANN, ROBERT. *Allgemeine Äesthetik als Formwissenschaft*. Vienna, 1865.

ZINTZEN, CH. "Enzyklopädische Utopie: Ethnographie als Stiftung von Einheit im Diversen." In A. Moravansky, ed., *Das entfernte Dorf*. Vienna: Böhlau, 2002, 183–205.

ZUCKER, PAUL. *Raumdarstellung und Bildarchitekturen im Florentiner Quattrocento*. Leipzig: Klinkhardt and Biermann, 1913.

INDEX

Page numbers in *italics* refer to illustrations.